D1832785

TERRORISM IN NORTHERN INDIA

TERRORISM IN NORTHERN INDIA

JAMMU AND KASHMIR AND THE PUNJAB

(In Two Volumes)

(Volume 1)

COL. VED PRAKASH

PUBLICATIONS

KALPAZ PUBLICATIONS

DELHI-110052

Terrorism in Northern India

Rs. 1800 (Set)

© Col. Ved Prakash

ISBN: 978-81-7835-703-4 (Set)
ISBN: 978-81-7835-734-8 (Vol. 1)

All rights reserved. No Part of this book may be reproduced in any manner without written permission.

Published in 2008 in India by
Kalpaz Publications
C-30, Satyawati Nagar,
Delhi-110052
E-mail: kalpaz@hotmail.com
Phone : 9212729499

Laser Type Setting by: Quick Media, Delhi
Printed at : **G. Print Process, Delhi**

DEDICATION

*The book is dedicated to the hapless Kashmiri Pandits rendered homeless in their own country by the mindless violence unleashed by the Islamist **Jehadis**.*

Contents

Preface

It is a truism that the terrorism is a conflict against a nation itself. To terrorise and kill innocent people has always been a way of putting pressure on their leaders to change policy, or at least to make major concessions to the perpetrators.

Even if the issue of terrorism is engaging the best brains of the international community, each nation is fighting it in its own way. As to the nations fighting it collectively, it is a distant dream as the UN has failed to even find definiton of the term acceptable to all its constituent member states.

Coming to individual countries, India has suffered the ravages of terrorism since its very Independence in 1947 when some tribes in the North-East raised the banner of revolt and resorted to violence to achieve their revanchist goals. It was followed by Islamist terrorism in Jammu and Kashmir aimed at tearing the State from India and making it a part of Pakistan. It took virulent form in 1979 and has continued since with varying degree of stridence.

The violence in Jammu and Kashmir was abetted by Pakistan. When the time was opportune, that country also added to India's woes and travails by helping Punjab's separatists with arms, manpower, material resources and training in the late 1970s. Anti-Indianism has been an important plank of Pakistan's national policy since its very birth. It became an obsession after 1971 break-up of its Eastern Wing as Bangladesh. Disintegration of India is high on the agenda of its establishment, particularly its Army eversince its humiliating defeat in December, 1971. Export of terrorism has been an important instrumentality of Pakistan's foreign policy. It does not seem to have given up that policy even when its home-bred terrorists—Taliban, and to an extent, Al Qaeda—posed a serious threat to its security and integrity in 2007 and continue to do so in the new year. In addition, as and when an opening was seen by it, the Pakistani polity took resort to adventurous course. The latest example of it was the Kargil misadventure.

As to what stance the civilian government would take which should come into power consequent to the February 2008 elections is something in the womb of future.

It is only after the 9/11 and the underground bombings in London that the terrorism because an "international" threat. The West, especially the United States, never took seriously the atrocities and sufferings inflicted on India by the terrorists. Ironically, India was advised to negotiate with Pakistan to resolve the Kashmir issue. A greater travesty of situation is unlikely to be seen. Interestingly, no nation or an individual is known to have advised the United States to seek "peaceful" negotiations with the Al Qaeda!

What is the seriousness of threat to India's security and integrity posed by the Jihadis? It is self-obvious from the quantities of arms and ammunition seized by the Indian security forces in Jammu and Kashmir since the beginning of the organised militancy in 1989 till mid-2002:

- AK series rifles — over 21,000
- Machine guns — Over 2,000
- Pistols and revolvers — 8,456
- Rockets — 3,307
- Mines — 5,03
- Small arms ammunition — Over 3 million rounds

Records show that 40,493 people—including terrorists, security forces and civilians—have been killed in the State between 'January 1990 and 30 April, 2006. Of these civilians number 16,010. The Kashmiri separatists put the fatalities at more than 100,000.

The fatalities climbed to 42,147 till mid-February 2007.

Under the continuous threat and attacks from the Jihadis, some 524,000 Pandits left the valley. These luckless people are living as refugees in their own land, in camps at places like Jammu, Delhi, Bangalore etc. The silent migration continues, which has left only 7,000 Pandits in the valley as of March, 2007 against 13,000 in 2002.

Here is summary of violent incidents in Jammu and Kashmir since 1990. 66,590 such incidents took place in the 18 years of militancy from 1990 to 2007. The highest number of violent incidents—gunfights, blasts and killings—was recorded in 1995 when 5,946 incidents took place. 926 incidents occurred in 2007, the lowest in these 18 years.

Statistics say 6,045 incidents of hurling of grenades on security forces occurred. The figure rose to maximum in 1994 with 821 such attacks. But after 2001, there was downward trend, as shown below:

- 242 in 1990
- 402 in 1991
- 509 in 1992
- 678 in 1993
- 821 in 1994
- 579 in 1995
- 444 in 1996
- 168 in 1997
- 187 in 1998
- 201 in 1999
- 243 in 2000
- 373 in 2001
- 283 in 2002
- 199 in 2003
- 243 in 2004
- 152 in 2005
- 226 in 2006
- 98 in 2007

5,615 IED explosions occured in the State during these 18 years. Of these highest number, 1280, was in 1990 and the lowest, 47 in 2007. Year-wise numbers follow:

- 1280 in 1990
- 275 in 1991
- 248 in 1992
- 327 in 1993
- 347 in 1994
- 366 in 1995
- 358 in 1996
- 255 in 1997
- 264 in 1998
- 293 in 1999
- 294 in 2000
- 402 in 2001
- 255 in 2002
- 228 in 2003
- 157 in 2004
- 136 in 2005
- 83 in 2006
- 47 in 2007

These 18 years saw 21,309 incidents of cross firing between the ultras and the security forces which claimed large number of civilians. The highest number of such incidents, 1891, occurred in 1995—the lowest 346, coming in 2007.

Security forces have come under frequent attacks from the Islamist militants during these 18 years. Highest number of such attacks, 2,675, took place in 1994, which tapered down to 189 in 2007. The year-wise break-down of such attacks is given below:

- 732 in 1990
- 1358 in 1991
- 1934 in 1992
- 2288 in 1993
- 2675 in 1994
- 2570 in 1995
- 1473 in 1996
- 1149 in 1997
- 1181 in 1998
- 1209 in 1999
- 1498 in 2000
- 1109 in 2001
- 870 in 2002
- 683 in 2003
- 481 in 2004
- 327 in 2005
- 330 in 2006
- 189 in 2007

Undoubtedly, there is decline in all kinds of terrorist violence in 2007, and there could be any number of reasons for this trend—chiefly, the domestic turbulence within Pakistan and the Jihadis and Islamist militants turning on the Pakistani Army. But India has no cause for smugness to be written all over its face. It must wait and watch for the stance of the civilian government that ascends to power past 18 February, 2008 elections.

Having viewed the scenario in Jammu and Kashmir, it should be profitable to have a look into Punjab situation, even though the active insurgency, (1978-93), might have been over a decade and a half ago.

The 15-year-long terrorist violence had consumed 21,469 lives, before the movement for Khalistan was comprehensively defeated by KPS Gill and his Punjab Police in 1993. The State seemed to be on an even keel till the end of the 1990s, but some disturbing incidents have been coming to the surface since the beginning of the 21st century.

It deserves to be noted that some Khalistani activists and their secessionist outfits are still active in foreign countries like

Pakistan, Canada, USA etc. Such elements may be dormant in India of their own free will for tactical reasons, but they are certainly not extinct. They are simply lying low, just below the surface—waiting for any opportune occasion. More dangerous are their overground counterparts and sympathisers. Both are ever-willing and even eager to light the fires of religious bigotry and secessionist passions at the slightest provocation and seeing half a chance. They are in the forefront to fan the conflagration.

We are all aware how the April, 1978 confrontation between Bhindranwalle-led extremists and the Nirankari congregation at Amritsar provided the spark for the 15-year long Khalistani terrorism. The analysts and observers apprehended the repeat of the April, 1978 scenario when the Sikh and the SGPC leadership took up cudgels against the Dera Sacha Sauda Chief and his follower for his alleged act of dressing up like the 10th Sikh Guru and administaring *amrit* to the new entrants into his faith. There were many instances of confrontations—including some violent ones—between the Dera followers and the Sikhs. Leadership of the anti-Dera movement, normally with the SGPC, had been wrested by the extremist elements of the Sikh community who were generally known to be pro-Khalistan and sympathetic towards the extremist ideology. All this has been detailed in the book.

The basic problem is competitive politics of the Congress Party and the Akali Party to win and vie for the Sikh votes to come to power in Punjab. Both parties have displayed unhealthy hunger for power through means fair and foul. Some recent disturbing actions taken by these parties are noted here. Congress Chief Minister Amrinder Singh appointed a known Khalistani activist to a government post in Punjab. Even worse, he paid a visit to a pro-Khalistan Gurudwara in Canade, with large board on one of its walls displaying pro-Khalistani inscription emblazoned on it. Luckily, he and his Congress Party lost the elections, yielding power to the Parkash Singh Badal-led Akali Party. What does the latter do? The Badal Government, bowing to extremist sentiments, instituted several court cases against the Dera Chief. Even worse, in the late 2007, it installed the photo of the Chief Khalistan secessionist leader, the late Bhindranwalle, in the holiest of the Sikh holies, the Golden

Temple at Amritsar. So, there may be calm in Punjab, but the situation can be described as far from comforting.

From the preceding, it is obvious that Indian polity must be on the alert for the situation in both the states cannot be seen as normal. If in Jammu and Kashmir, Pakistan can simply open the tap and flood the state with Jihadis and human bombs if its domestic situation so demands in an uncertain future, in Punjab, Khalistan militants and their over ground sympathisers can re-ignite the conflagration given half a chance by the fractious politicians and their inane and venal politics. Simply put, there is no place for any smugness and complacency on the part of the ruling parties and chair security establishments in the two states.

This is a comprehensive book dealing with all aspects of terrorism in the two states of Jammu and Kashmir and Punjab, situated in India's North-West. The Author will feel amply rewarded if the book is found useful by the common readers and the students of terrorism.

The data cited in the book is from published sources. The Author owes special thanks to the Institute for Conflict Management and the South Asia Terrorism Portal for download of considerable information and statistical data from the Institute's Web site.

Ved Prakash

March, 2008

JAMMU AND KASHMIR

1

Terrorist Outfits in Jammu and Kashmir

(AAC, ABQ, AFF, AJF, AMF, APHC, AUM, DEM AND HUA)

Jammu and Kashmir has a plethora of militant/terrorist/ secessionist organisations operating within its boundaries. While some of these outfits are indigenous, majority of them are Pakistan (ISI) sponsored from across the border. These outfits belonging to either category are, with few exceptions, sponsored and maintained by the ISI, including the coordination of their terrorist activities.

Interestingly, the terror leaders seem to have no problems in finding new names for their outfits, including their acronyms – all different, never the same. Most of the outfits are named after the Islamic, historic heroes, famed for their combat records. Some of these are even named after the Prophet.

The terrorist outfits, popularly called *tanzeems* in Pakistani parlance, are discussed in alphabetic order, preceded by a brief 'overview'.

Terrorist Outfits : An Overview

A sustained campaign of insurgency in the Indian State of Jammu and Kashmir (J & K) for over a decade and a half has been made possible by the presence of a dynamic Islamist terrorist Infrastructure, largely controlled by Pakistan's Inter-Services Intelligence (ISl). In the aftermath of the September 11, 2001 terrorist attacks on US targets, Islamist terrorism has come under global condemnation and Pakistan has faced pressure to withdraw its support. In response, some cosmetic measures have been taken by Pakistan in curbing the overt activities of terrorist organisations based on its soil. However, the support these organisations receive from official sources - to further the insurgency in J&K has shown no signs of receeding.

The ISI has gradually built up its control over the terrorist violence in the State. When insurgency first broke out in 1989, this agency, which was pre-occupied with supervising the Afghan jihad, was caught completely unawares by the anti-State sentiments that built up in J&K following the 1986 elections to the State Legislative Assembly that were allegedly rigged. As a result, it took a few years before a network of loyal terrorist outfits operating under its command could be established.

The Jammu and Kashmir Liberation Front (JKLF), and the People's League were two notable terrorist fronts that were in existence before insurgency began in 1989. Of these, the JKLF (originally established in 1964) was more active and took the initiative to propel militancy in the State. With the benefit of hindsight, it can be said that the JKLF merely ignited the insurgency in the State over which the ISl assumed total control in the subsequent years.

It was after 1986 that some youth from J&K crossed the Line of Control (LoC) in search of weapons and training. Pakistan coordinated with the JKLF, the only active terrorist outfit at that point of time, in training and equipping these youth. Simultaneously, a network was established to indoctrinate more youth in J&K and encourage them to cross the LoC for arms and training. The JKLF's importance during the initial phase of the insurgency was demonstrated by the concentration of militancy in Srinagar, the chief base of operations of the outfit.

Problems between JKLF (which made no secret of its preference for an Independent J&K) and Pakistan (which has repeatedly stressed its claim on the State) prompted efforts by the ISl to sideline the JKLF and promote other outfits, particularly the Hizb-ul-Mujahideen (HM) that would further Pakistani interests. Another objective, following the age-old prescription of 'divide and rule', was to create numerous outfits which could be manıpulated through the provision of resources such as arms and money. Each outfit was, thus, made dependent on the ISl.

The ISI had gained expertise in effectively supporting and coordinating the Jihadi elements in Afghanistan. This expertise was put to use in J&K in marginalising the pro-autonomy and nationalist elements and promoting radical elements within and outside the JKLF. The initial strategy of Pakistan was to create outfits largely manned by Kashmiris and dedicated to Islamisation of the nascent insurgency in J&K. The easy targets were disgruntled JKLF cadres. These cadres parted ways with the JKLF owing to differences with the leadership and formed smaller outfits such as the Jammu and Kashmir Students Liberation Front and the Al Badr (established in 1989 and different from the present Al Badr formed in late 1998 by foreign terrorists). The latter was chosen by the ISl for intensive promotion and it was renamed as Hizb-ul Mujahideen. Other notable outfits targeted by the ISl included the Ikhwan-ul Muslimeen (the Islamised nomenclature adopted in April 1991 by the terrorist faction of Jammu and Kashmir Students' League) and Al Umar (established in early 1990).

The Islamisation drive also implied replacing the predominantly Sufi culture of the local population with an orthodox and fundamentalist version of Islam corresponding to the variety practised in Pakistan. This movement preceded the insurgency with the setting up in 1987 of a woman's quasi-military front Dukhtaraan-e-Millat (DeM, Daughters of the Nation). This outfit has since then been 'persuading' Muslim women in the State to conform to orthodox Islamic life-style in matters of dress and values. Other outfits involved in the 'persuasion' process are the Allah Tigers and the Hizb-ul Nisa.

By 1991, the ISl appears to have assumed control over the State's militancy, having successfully sidelined the JKLF. It then sought to ensure co-ordination among the numerous outfits it had helped create. Two organizations, Tehrik-e-Hurriyat-e-Kashmir and Mutahida Jehad Council, were reportedly mandated with this responsibility (the organisations were formed in 1990 but assumed their co-ordinating roles only in April 1991).

The nature of the insurgency in J&K witnessed a major shift in the post-1992 phase when the involvement of foreign terrorists increased rapidly. Several factors contributed to this change. Pakistani Intelligence agencies and the army harboured a deep mistrust of the Kashmiris after the 1965 episode. On that occasion, information provided by locals in the Valley helped the Indian army to neutralize and capture some of the top, covert subversive units of the Pakistan Army that were sent as a part of Operation Gibraltar. The ability of Kashmiri terrorists in effectively spreading terror and attacking Indian security forces, too, was doubted by their Pakistani sponsors. As the counter-insurgency response from India began to gain effectiveness, the terrorist-potential of Kashmiri outfits declined. These outfits' activities were largely restricted to some hit-and-run attacks on security forces and abductions to secure the release of jailed terrorists.

Since 1992, the ISI has aimed at escalating militancy in J&K by imparting a more violent and brutal face to it (the militancy). This was sought to be achieved through creating outfits manned by Afghans, Pakistanis and mercenaries from other countries.

With a view to create an Islamic hard-line terrorist outfit, the ISI helped to create the Harkat-ul Ansar (HuA) (established in October 1993). Two outfits that actively waged *jihad* in Afghanistan, the Harkat ul-Jihad al-lslami and Harkat-ul Mujahideen (the latter was a splinter organisation of the former) were to be merged into this front. While the merger of these outfits' cadre in Pakistan was accomplished, Maulana Masood Azhar (who was released from an Indian prison in the wake of the hijacking of the Indian Airlines Flight IC 814 in December 1999), was appointed general secretary of the Harkat-ul Ansar and sent to J&K to ensure a smooth merger of the local units of the two outfits. However, he was arrested in February 1994, immediately after his arrival, and the merger remained incomplete. Occasional actions have been reported by the Harkat ul-Jihad al-lslami.

The average active life span of a Kashmiri terrorist has been variously estimated to be between 6 and 12 months. Though a comparable average is yet to be calculated for the outfits, they, too, grow and dwindle as a result of sustained anti-insurgency operations by security forces. The Harkat-ul Ansar has been a victim of this process. After most of its leaders were arrested the organisation's role in J&K gradually declined. To remedy this, a last ditch attempt was made by some elements within the outfit to obtain the release of some of the jailed leaders. The Al-

Faran was formed to further this objective. The precaution of using a front organisation to abduct foreigners did not pay, when some of the hostages were killed and the US banned the Harkat-ul Ansar. Consequently, the Harkat-ul Ansar adopted the nomenclature of Harkat-ul Mujahideen (HuM) (1997), one of its original factions.

With the decline of the Harkat-ul Ansar, the ISI promoted the growth of a new front, Lashkar-e Toiba (LeT) (began operations in Kashmir in 1993), which has emerged as a major actor in insurgency in J&K. Another outfit that is jostling for a space in the State's militancy is a new organisation launched by Maulana Masood Azhar, the Jaish-e-Mohammad (JeM) (established in February 2000). Some recent reports had hinted at a merger of the Harkat-ul Mujahideen and the Jaish-e-Mohammad, but these were denied by the former.

Besides these major groups, numerous smaller outfits, created at different points of time, operate in the State's insurgency. Locally known as *tanzeems*, these are more in the nature of small militia outfits, normally associated with the larger outfits. For instance, when the People's League declined after the arrest of its chief, Shabbir Shah, his colleague Firdaus Ahmad Baba alias Babar Badr started the Muslim Janbaz Force (established in May 1990) which largely comprised of People's League cadre who were trained in Pakistan. It later merged with the Kashmir Jehad Force to form the Al Jehad Force.

There are also several lesser known terrorist groups operating in J & K.

In the later years, say 1990s, APHC came on the centre stage as political face of the violent separatist outfit. Today it stands split in two faction, led respective by Mirwaiz Farooq and Ali Shah Geelani. The latter is the hard-line outfit, while the Mirwaiz is dubbed a moderate.

The peace process in the state is creating new dynamics in its political landscape. If APHC (Mirwaiz) is losing ground to its counterpart, APHC (Geelani), the one-time dreaded HM is yielding ground to the LET. No wonder the analysts are advising these two outfits on the decline – APHC (Mirwaiz) and HM—to reinvent themselves if they are to remain relevant in the coming days of changes in the political dynamics of Jammu and Kashmir. One way out for them is to join the Round Table Conference discussions which Prime Minister Manmohan Singh is holding periodically. Its third round was held on 24 April 2007.

Presently, there is some inter-party churning and intra-party dissensions. If PDP seems to be brownie browny points with its demilitarisation demand, the NC is reverting back to its autonomy plank.

The table below mentions the terrorist organisations discussed in this chapter.

AAC

ABQ
AFF
AJF
AMF
APHC (KJHC)
AUM

DEM
HuA

Awami Action Committee (AAC)

Formation	1964
Headquarters	Srinagar
Strength	12000 sympathisers (analysts)
	100,000 sympathisers
Objectives	Self-determination by Kashmiris
Sponsors	ISI influence

Organisational Structure

- Chairman, Vice-Chairman, General Secretary, and a Working Committee.
- Pattern repeated in districts.

Leadership

- Mirwaiz Maulvi Mohammad Farooq, Chairman (Assassinated May 1990 by HUM).
- Mirwaiz Umar Farooq – Chairman (Current incumbent, and son of the predecessor).

- Syed Ahmad Shah, Vice Chairman.
- Advocate Mohd Yaqoob, General Secretary.

Areas of Influence

Kashmir Valley.

Links with Political Parties/Groups

ISI, POK, JKJEI, PC, MC, JKLF, KJHC/APHC, Anjuman-e-Nusrat-ul-Islam (Social Work Wing of AAC), and People's League which runs a number of religious schools (*madrasas*) through the *Anjuman*.

Finances

Pakistan, POK, ISI, APHC, collections in congregations at the Jamia Mosque, Srinagar.

Origins, Links with NC and Veering to Militancy

The AAC was formed in 1964 by Maulvi Mohd Farooq, and subsequently he wanted it to help resolve the Kashmir issue politically. It lent full support to Pak infiltrators in 1965.

It opposed the 1975 Sheikh Abdullah-Indira Gandhi Accord. Barring the interregnum 1977-80 when the Maulvi supported the Janata Party government at the Centre, the AAC has maintained an anti-India stance. After the Sheikh's death, the Maulvi extended support to his son Farooq and his government. In the 1983 J & K Assembly polls, the AAC supported Farooq Abdullah's NC candidate. It also supported him when he lost power in 1984 due to GM Shah-led defections. During the 1987 Assembly polls, the Maulvi got two party activists – Mohd Shafi Khan and Peer Mohd Shafi – elected on the NC tickets. But subsequently, the relations between the AAC and the NC went downhill.

Some of Maulvi Farooq's supporters, including Mushtaq Zargar popularly known as *bakras* as they sported goatees, crossed over to Pakistan to receive arms training.

AAC – dominated areas in Srinagar came to be the nerve centres of militancy and proved safe havens for the Mujahideens/terrorists in the initial stages of insurgency. Subsequently, young men loyal to the Maulvi formed the militant outfit, Al Umar Mujahideen (AUM) around 1989.

Links with APHC, and Subsequent Splits

Once he and his loyalists burched towards militancy and practically embraced it through creation of the AUM, the Maulvi's image of being a leading cleric of the valley did suffer certain diminishing. And terrorist outfits are no respectors of religion, or its leading lights. Maulvi Farooq was assassinated on 21 May 1990, falling a victim to inter-terrorist outfits' animosities and personal feuds. His son, Umar, succeeded him not only in the position of Mirwaiz of Kashmir but also as Chairman, AAC. The young Umar continued maintaining an anti-India orientation he had inherited from his father.

It was the period when an effort was mounted to bring all the secessionist outfits/forces operating in J and K on one political platform, taking advantage of Mirwaiz Umar Farooq's oppeal as widely respected cleric. Because of too many claimants with personal ambitions to seek political leadership, political unity was bound to be a mirage but what indeed was achieved was the creation of an overarching structure that took all the secessionist outfits, at least most of them, under its wings. A meeting of prominent Muslim political and socio-religious leaders was convened on 27 December 1992. Another one took place on 7 March 1993. It was attended by representatives of AAC, JKJEI, JKPC, MC, JKLF, and JKPL. On 3 September 1993, the endeavour resulted in the formation of KJHC (= APHC), on amalgam of 36 organisations.

Despite opposition from JKJEI/HUM, Umar Farooq was appointed Chairman, APHC. Thence on, AAC's activities got projected from a much larger platform of APHC. Umar started opposing strongly any electoral process in J & K and formally launched an anti-election compaign.

AAC/AUM was considerably weakened after the killing/ arrest of its top leaders, including Mushtaq Zargar's on 14 May 1992. Consequently, the influence of Umar Farooq and his AAC was on the wane in his strong hold of Srinagar. He also became susceptible to threats from the HUM, which was also responsible for the assassination of his father.

Seeking International Platform

Between 13 December 1994 and 9 February 1995, Maulvi Umar Farooq and Maulvi Abbas Ansari (Executive Council Member, APHC) visited Morocco, Saudi Arabia, Kuwait and the UK to drum up support for separatist cause of Kashmiris. They attended during their sojourn the OIC meeting in Casablanca as representatives of the APHC, which has an observer status at the OIC. SAS Gillani, Yasin Malik and other veteran Hurriyat leaders never expected New Delhi permitting the two Maulvis to leave the country. They resented the two hogging the limelight at the Muslim forum.

Maulvi Farooq yet again was to attend the meeting of the OIC Contact Group on Kashmir in New York during 28-29 September 1995. He made use of the opportunity to hold confabulations with the leaders of all hues ready to lend their ears : Pakistan/POK-based secessionist leaders; Sardar Asaf Ali, then Pak Foreign Minister; Sardar Abdul Qayoom Khan, then Prime Minister of POK; Robin Raphel, Assistant Secretary of State for South Asian Affairs; and several US senators. Helped by GNFai, he projected APHC as the sole representative body of Kashmiris. He also went over to Colombia during 16-17 October 1995 but failed to make it to the Non-Aligned Movement (NAM) Summit.

Decline and Ascent, Again

ISI, perhaps, did not find the 'maverick Maulvi' strident enough in his anti-India stance, so the staunch Pro-Pak SAS Gillani replaced Umar as Chairman of the APHC on 24 April 1998. Even if the AAC leadership tried to distance itself from the APHC, it used its platform to project the AAC agenda.

In the coming 6-7 years, the situation completed a full circle yet again. During 2004-05, Gillani became too hot even for Pakistani leaders, as he blamed them for making a u-turn in their Kashmir Policy and abandoning the interests of the Kashmiris. Consequently, he became persona nona grata for Islamabad and a pliant Maulvi Farooq once again became its blue-eyed boy and Chairman of the APHC.

Presently there are two outfits bearing the imprimatur APHC, respectively headed by Maulvi Farooq and Gillani.

Al Barq (ABQ)

Formed	1990
Headquarters	Srinagar
Strength	350, including 20 foreigners.
Arms Held	Over 150 weapons, including 100 AK rifles
Objectives	Liberation of Kashmir through armed struggle and establishment of Islamic Rule. Recently, opposed acts of random terrorism, favoured dialogue.
Sponsors	ISI, JKPC.

Organisational Structure

- Supreme Council : Patron, C-in-C, three Deputy Chiefs, *Amir*, *Naib Amir*.
- Valley divided into three divisions, with each Divisional Commander looking after two districts.

Leadership

- Abdul Ghani Lone, Patron. Former Chairman. JKPC; assassinated 21 May 2002.
- Bilal Lodhi, Founder Member.
- Mohammed Yousuf Shah, *Amir-e-Ala*.
- Advocate Zahid Iqbal, *Amir*.
- Nazim-ul-din Afghani, C-in-C.
- Bilal Rahi, C-in-C (POK).
- Abidi Hussain, Supreme Commander.

Areas of Operations

- Bandipur, Handwara (Kupwara), Beeru (Badgam), Pulwama, Srinagar, Muzaffarabad.
- Office, transit camps in Muzaffarabad; training camps in Mansheera.

Links with Political Parties and Groups

Pakistan, POK government, SEJ; member of UJC (POK).

Foreign Links

Pakistan; POK government; ISI, HEI and JEI (Pakistan/Afghanistan).

Finances

ISI and other foreign sources, including about Rs. 7 lakh per month through *hawala transactions*

- Other Equipment.

Advanced communication system.

Major Acts of Terrorism

- 15 Nov 90. Bridge at Beeru, Badgam, set ablaze.
- 23 Nov 90. Attacked a Security Forces (SF) convoy, Lor, Ganderbal, Srinagar.
- 16 Oct 93. 5 militants, including ABQ Chief Commander, killed in an encounter at Kupwara.
- 4 May 96. Attacked SF, Srinagar; 2 militants killed in ensuing encounter.
- 3 Oct 97. Attacked a police patrol at Beeru, Badgam.
- 31 Aug 98. Police vehicles destroyed through a remote-controlled IED at Kare; Karen 3 killed 7 injured.

Origins

The JKPC, a Kashmiri political party headed by Abdul Ghani Lone, fought elections in 1987 and 1988. Its cadres came from the Gujjar belt of Baramulla and Kupwara.

In 1990, Lone sent his Working Committee member Bilal Lodhi to POK due to threats from HUM. Following the upsurge of militancy in the valley, the two floated ABQ. It was sponsored by the ISI with the blessings of POK Prime Minister Sardar Abdul Qayoom Khan. Abdul Rashid Qureshi and Mushtaq Khan were nominated as representatives of the ABQ in POK; both were in Muzaffarabad after leaving the JKLF.

Lone made several trips to Pakistan on Indian passport to seek financial and political support for the outfit. Directly controlled and financed by the ISI, it had ground level support from the MDI.

Recruitment and Training

The ABQ had a transit camp at Chelapindi, near Muzaffaradad and recruited youth from among the exfiltrants under training in/around Muzaffarabad. Later it concentrated on Gujjars for their importance in infiltration and exfiltration, and on sympathisers of the JKPC. The Gujjar factor drew attention of the ISI.

Clashes with Other Outfits

During 1991, Lodi and ABQ came under heavy attack from the HUM which wanted to disarm ABQ cadres. Lodi sought protection from the Muslim Janbaaz Force (MJF), but failed to merge ABQ with it.

After his release in April 1992, Lone exhorted JKPC cadres to join ABQ operations. He tried to win over the Shias and Hanifias of HUM with the twin aims of infiltrating the HUM cadres and neutralise its leadership. That led to armed clashes between the two as well as heavy losses of men and material on both sides.

In early 1993, Lone visited the UK and the US and developed rapport with the leaders of World Kashmir Freedom Movement (WKFM) and Kashmir American Council (KAC). This also led to reduction of hostilities between HUM and ABQ.

Induction of Foreign Mercenaries : A First

In 1991, the ABQ was the first Kashmiri group to mull over the induction of foreign mercenaries in the Kashmir valley. In 1992, its leaders in Pakistan developed linkages with Afghan Mujahideen group like the HEI and JEI. The first batch of foreign mercenaries joined ABQ operations in May 1992 on six-month assignment, as a result of bilateral agreement with the MDI which also agreed to arm these mercenaries. In September 1992, four Afghan mercenaries were killed in an exchange of fire in Kupwara district.

In October 1992, an ISI-organised meeting between the ABQ (AG Lone, Tajmul Islam, and Farooq Qureshi, ABQ representative in Pakistan) and the MDI (Hafiz Mohammed Yahya, *Amir*) in Tehran led to further induction of MDI Afghan War veterans to work with ABQ cadres (About 300 by 1994).

The ISI financed the expenditure incurred on these Afghan mercenaries.

Since 1992 to 2002, 25 ABQ foreign mercenaries (from Afghanistan and Pakistan) have been killed in encounters with the Indian SF.

Al Fateh Force (AFF)

Formation	February 1991 (1994)
Strength	35
Arms	Over 30 weapons including 15 AK rifles, MG, rockets.
Headquarters	Bandipur, Baramulla district
Objectives	Merger of J & K with Pakistan
Sponsor	ISI, JKPL-R.

Organisational Structure

- Apex : Chief Patron, a Chief Commander, two Deputy Chief Commanders, Military Adviser.
- Field : District Commanders, Area Commanders.

Leadership

- Mohd Farooq Ahmad Shah Rehmani (Chairman, JKPL-R) Patron.
- GM Khan Sopori, Patron.
- Mohd Yousuf Chopan, C-in-C.
- Bilal Ahmad Wani, Chief Commander (J & K).
- Abdul Rashid Hakim, Chief Commander (POK).

Areas of Operations

- Baramulla, Pulwama, Bandipur, Kupwara, Pampur, Khanyar, Nowhatia.
- Offices in Chattar and Muzaffarabad; transit camp in Sinkyari.

Links with Political Parties/Groups

Pakistan; POK; ISI : Islamic Resistance Force (IRF); ideologically of JK JEI and HUM.

Foreign Links

Pakistan, POK, ISI.

Finances

Liberal financial and military help from Pakistan – e.g., grant of Rs. 3 Lakh per month as member of the IRF.

Major Acts of Terrorism

- 15 Feb 91. Rocket attack on house of Handoo, JKPL member and ex-Minister, NC Government.
- 4 Apr 91. Killed Mohd Subhan Butt, ex-MLA, NC, at Tral, Pulwama.

Origins

Farooq Rehmani visited Pakistan in September 1990 to firm up his links with the ISI. In October 1990, he floated a militant outfit – Tehrik Mazahmat Kashmir (TMK). Due to his differences with Muzaffar Ahmad Shah, it was re-christened Kashmir Jihad Force (KJF). Shah floated his own oufit – Tehrik-e-Jihad Islami (TEJI). He also claimed the patronage of JKPL.

Under orders from Pakistan in December 1991, two factions of the JKPL – JKPL (R) of Rehmani and JKPL-S of Shabir Shah – were merged to form a 'united' outfit, JKUPL, along with their armed wings, viz KJF and MJF respectively. The united military wing was named AJF – Al Jihad Force. Naturally, the past of AJF was bound to dog its future, and it did.

Again, this merger was bound to head for a failure since most key posts were cornered by JKPL-R/KJF. The JKUPL was becoming anathema for Rehmani as the Pak Authorities started projecting Shabir Shah as its undisputed leader. Early 1992, Rehmani directed his loyalists to force the Shabir followers out of the JKUPL. Later, Rehmani created – rather revived – JKPL (R), even if it was opposed by his senior colleagues. Finally, Javed Ahmad Shah revived the JKPL (R)/KJF in the Valley, with the blessings of Rehmani. Rehmani, also Chairman of Tehrik-e-Hurryat Kashmir (TEHK) and confidente of top ISI officers, managed to recruit youth from across the border into the KJF.

After arrest of Abdul Aziz Sheikh, Chief Commander of AJF and former General Secretary of JKPL (R), S Hamid took over

AJF. The Sheikh loyalists broke away from the JKUPL to set up a parallel outfit with the same name. On 30 March 1994, S Hamid expelled GM Khan Sopori and some senior AJF Commanders.

Sopori later floated a rival faction of the AJF with the cadres loyal to Sheikh. This faction later merged with the KJF to form AFF.

Splits, Mergers, and Decline

In July 1995, the AFF suffered a serious setback when some top Commanders (including Javed Ahmad Shah and Mir Niazi) defected to the counter-insurgency group, Ikhwan-ul-Musalmeen (IUM) led by Kuka Parey. The ISI also discontinued funding the AFF since it had no affiliation with any secessionist outfit – a pre-requisite for assistance. Its Patron, Rehmani, too fell from grace due to his open criticism of Pak policies on Kashmir.

In June 1996, the ISI combined the AFF, HIZB, and HMM to form the IRF. This resulted in the renewal of ISI funding. The IRF used AFF/KJF offices and training camps in Muzaffarabad.

Aijzaz Rehmani, Chief Commander, AFF, participated in the July 1998 meeting of UJC where Salahuddin of the HUM was nominated its President. In early July 1996, a Coordination Committee involving the leaders of the LET/HUM, HUA, and AFF was formed to intensify terrorist activities aimed at disrupting the polls in J & K for the Lower House (Lok Sabha) of the Indian Parliament.

Current Status

With the departure of its leadership to POK, it is nearly defunct since mid-1990s.

Al Jihad Force (AJF)/Al Jihad

Formation	December 1991
Strength	125, including 25 foreign mercenaries
Headquarters	Srinagar
Objectives	Liberation of Kashmir through armed struggle.
Sponsors	Pakistan, POK, ISI, JKPL (S).

Operational Structure

- Apex : War Council.
- Chief Commander, a Deputy Chief, three Divisional Commanders (one each for two districts of the Valley and one for Jammu); Districts have Commanding Officers.

Leadership

- Shabir Shah, Patron.
- S. Hamid, Chairman (late).
- Mohd Ashraf Guru, *Amir-e-Ala*.
- Munir Ahmad Kumhar, Chief Commander.
- Gen Haider Ali, Chief Commander.
- Nazir Ahmad Sofi, Chief Commander (POK).

Areas of Operation

Kashmir Valley, Doda, Pulwama, Anantnag, Baramulla, Srinagar, Badgam, Handwara, Kupwara.

Foreign Links

Pakistan, POK, ISI.

Links with Political Parties/Groups

ISI, IRF, SEJ; has clashed with HUM.

Finances

Pakistan, POK, ISI, Local Collections.

Major Acts of Terrorism

- Dec 91. Kidnapped French engineer Antonio Silva, working on the Dulhasti Power Project in Kishtwar (Doda).
- 26 Jan 92. Rocket attack in Lal Chowk, Srinagar.
- 5 May 92. One woman killed when it attacked motor code of Rajesh Pilot, then MOS Home Affairs, at Nowpora, SGR.
- 15 Aug 92. Rocket attack on Bakshi Stadium, SGR, venue for Independence Day celebrations.
- 2 Jun 93. Kidnapped two police officials from SGR.
- 16 Sep 94. Firing on the house of Mufti Mohd Syed.

- 6 Jan 96. Abducted 7 civilians of Moti Marwat village, Doda; released on 9 Jan 96 after being tortured.
- 2 Apr 96. Raided, looted Hindu households in SGR locality; torched 2 houses and a shop.

Origins

In December 1991, there was Pak-ordered merger of two factions of JKPL to create JKUPL (See details under AFF). Their respected armed wings (KJF and MJF) united to form AJF and emerged as a heavily equipped and highly trained force with advanced communications systems.

Abdul Aziz Sheikh (earlier, Chief Commander of KJF) was nominated C-in-C of the AJF and Altaf Alamgir (then acting chief of MJF) his Deputy. Even after the merger, MJF cadres, constituting 80 per cent of the AJF, continued to maintain their stockpile of arms – not a happy angury for the future of the AJF.

The AJF maintained an office in Muzaffarabad. Even if it was not included in the UJC, it was made member of the IRF.

Clashes with Other Outfits

Several smaller outfits like the Islami Jung (IJ) later merged with the AJF. That caused concern to the leaders of HUM/JKJEI, since it would threaten the predominance of the latter in the secessionist movement. Consequently, the HUM engaged AJF cadres in armed clashes in the Valley, especially Baramulla and it also encouraged defection from the AJF to its own fold. Among the prominent defecters was Ghulam Qadir, former MJF District Commander, who had been involved in the kidnapping of Swedish engineers from Uri.

Splits and Setbacks

In a move which was opposed by his own confidante, Abdul Aziz Sheikh who wanted to keep AJF united, the Pak-based JKUPL leader Farooq Rehamni revived his own faction – the JKPL (R)/KJF, in May 1992. In 1993, the AJF suffered seriously with the arrest of its top 3 leaders: Sheikh, Mod Altaf Khan (Deputy Chief), and Bilal Ahmad Gagloo (Acting Chief). Death of Ghulam Mohiudden, Chief Commander, in an encounter with the SF was another serious blow.

The internicine conflicts between various constituents of the AJF subsequently led to splits in 1994, seriously affecting its operational capabilities. The main split was caused by pro-Rehmani faction of the JKUPL/AJF. The ISI discontinued financial aid to the AJF in 1995 in the face of complaints of misappropriation of funds by its leaders, including S. Hamid.

Revival and Networking

AJF become a constituent of the Shora-e-Jihad (SEJ), formed in July 1996 to revitalise the militancy under a unified command. The SEJ, now composed of AJF, HUA, HUM, AUM, and TUM, was mandated to neutralise Indian counter-insurgency groups as also to coordinate terrorist activities to disrupt the 1996 poll process in the State. S. Hamid was appointed its first Chairman.

The AJF forged a working relationship with the HUM in the valley. S. Hamid developed close personal understanding with Fardous Kirmani, Finance Chief of HUM, who assured arms supply and financial aid to the AJF, provided it helped the HUM in intensifying militancy (Firdous was killed in March 1997).

Mohammed Ashraf Guru, No. 2 in the AJF, managed the outfit's network in Kathmandu. It was the Kathmandu base which arranged the movement of terrorists – also benignly called 'cadres', 'activists', and more accurately, 'militants' – from Pakistan to India via Nepal.

The AJF operations in POK were handled by Nazir Ahmad Sofi, Sheikh Shah Nawaz, and Raja Gowhar.

Present Status

After mid – 1990s, its situation may only be slightly better than that of the AFF. In 1998, the AJF suffered due to a split in the JKUPL as did AFF. The analysts were unable to draw any viable or logical conclusions from August 1998 press statement of Nayeem Khan, General Secretary, JKUPL : "JKUPL will not have any truck with the AJF."

All Mujahid Force (AMF)

Formation	August 1992
Headquarters	Muzaffarabad
Strength	125

Objectives — Meger of Kashmir with Pakistan through armed action.

Sponsors — Pakistan, POK, ISI.

Organisational Structure

Chief of the Command Council, Supreme Commander, Deputy Chief Commanders for Kashmir and Jammu regions.

Leadership

- Sardar Abdul Qayoom Khan (Former Prime Minister POK, later President), Founder.
- Zahid Iqbal (Ex-*Naib Amir*, POK), Chief Patron.
- Iqbal Shah, Chief of the Command Council (operates from the office of *Srinagar News*, Srinagar).
- Sardar Atiq Khan, Supreme Commander.
- Rashid Shah, Chief Commander.

Areas of Operations

Kashmir Valley, Poonch/Rajour Muzaffarabad.

Links with Political Parties/Groups

Muslim Conference, POK; Kashmir Army Force (KAF); J & K Muslim Liberation Army (JKMLA); Pir Panjal Tigers (PPT), HKMN; MM; AUC, Al Mustafa (AMUS); JKLT.

Foreign Links

Pakistan, POK, ISI.

Finances

Pakistan, POK, ISI.

Major Acts of Terrorism

- 14 Oct 94. Major encounter in Ilaichibagh, Srinagar; most of the 10 foreign mercenaries killed belonged to AMF.

Origins

Sardar Qayoom (President POK 2001-05) floated AMF on 25 August 1992 as an armed wing of the Muslim Conference (POK). Its creation was the result of amalgamation of several militant outfits including KAF, JKMLA, PPT, and HKMN. Col Farooq, Military Secretary to the POK Prime Minister was the guardian angel – less loftily, a mid-wife – to the merger. In public utterances, Sardar Qayoom claimed that "AMF has been working for the liberation of Kashmir and its merger with Pakistan since 1947" – some terminological inexactitude' this, to borrow from Sir Winston Churchill.

A politician's ploy. Qayoom did not command much of support among the Kashmiri Muslims. He publicly invited non-Kashmiri Muslims (particularly Gujjars, Soodans, and Pahadis) who were politically opposed to the Kashmiri Muslim domination in his fiefdom, to join his outfit, AMF, to participate and add their mite in the liberation of Kashmir. He was consciously creating his 'sphere of influence' in J & K through this specific constituency. To Qayoom's political objective, the ISI saw another angle : To inject a dose of militancy in the Poonch-Rajouri areas.

Master Ahsan Dar, who had gone to POK in May 1992 after splitting away from the HUM, was persuaded by Qayoom to take over the AMF to invest it with a creditable leadership. Dar had made a name for himself as a competent organiser and capable commander as Supreme Commander of HUM till November 1991, and rightly earned the title 'Master', before he was edged out by Salahuddin. Understandably, Qayoom assured him of liberal military, financial and logistic support by the POK government and the ISI to successfully carry out his new responsibility.

Linkages, Operations and Splits/Mergers

Master Ahsan Dar took over as *Amir* of the AMF in October 1992. Returning to the Kashmir Valley on 18 January 1993, he used his proverbial organisational skills and negotiating acumen to create the Muslim Mujahideen (MM), an amalgam, through merger of his AMF with AUC, AMUS, KLT (Kashmir Liberation Tigers), JKMLA, and AMFI (Al Mujahideen Fil Islam). But, the POK-based non-Kashmiri leaders of the AMF retained the identity of their outfit.

The AMF provided the link between Prof Abdul Ghani, President, MC, and Sardar Qayoom.

Sardar Atiq Khan and his protege, Sher Khan, engaged the leadership in an internicine warfare over mis-appropriation of AMF funds. The Pakistan Muslim League had persistently demanded the removal of these leaders. Consequently through an understanding between the ISI and Sardar Qayoom in 1997 most AMF cadres joined the TEJ.

Current Status

Consequent to the 1997shift of its cadres to the TEJ, it went into long hibernation barring periodic statements. But there were some reports of increasing presence of AMF terrorists during the late 1990s.

Kul Jamaat Hurriyat Conference (KJHC)

Or

Al-Party Hurriyat Conference (APHC)

Formed	3 September 1993
Headquarters	Srinagar
Objectives	The creation of APHC in 1993 was aimed at mounting a 'new' thrust for the liberation of J and K, riding on the terrorist campaign by the existing militant outfits, in synch with the old concept of tripartite talks involving India, Pakistan and the APHC as the sole representative body of the Kashmiris. The other equally important objectives were the protection and preservation of the Islamic identity of J & K and its Muslim majority character.
Sponsors	Pakistan, POK, ISI

Organisational Structure

- General Body : Representatives from all its 26 constituents – major/minor political/militant organisations.
- Executive Council : Mainly six major constituents.
- Coordination Committee : For inter-face management functions.

Leadership

General Body

- Abdul Ghani Bhatt, Muslim Conference (MC), Chairman.

- Maulvi Umar Farooq, AAC/AAJM.
- SAS Geelani, JKJEI.
- Abdul Aziz Sheikh, JKPL.
- Bilal Lone, JKPC.
- Yasin Mailk, JKLF.
- Maulvi Abbas Ansari, AUM (AIM?).
- Ishtiaq Qadir, AJKEC.
- Representative of EWC.
- Maulana Tahiri, JAEH.
- Maulana Mohd Mubarak, KBT.
- Maulana Yasin Hamdani, JEH.
- Mian Abdul Qayoom, KAB.
- Abdul Samad, POC.
- Maulana Mohd Tari, TEHK.
- Abdul Ghani Azhari, JUI.
- Ms. Zamrooda Habib, MKM.
- Noorul Hasan, JKHRC.
- Justice Mufti Bahauddin Farooqi, JKPBRPC.
- Shakeel Bakshi, ISL.
- Dr. Mohd Yusuf Khan, ISC.
- Ghulan Mohd Bhatt, AJM.

Executive Council.

- Abdul Ghani Bhatt, MC.
- SAS Geelani, JKJEI.
- Maulvi Umar Farooq, AAC.
- Maulvi Abbas Ansari, AIM (AUM?).
- Bilal Lone, JKPC.
- Yasin Malik, JKLM.

Coordination Committee.

- SAS Geelani, JKJEI.
- Maulvi Umar Farooq, AAC.
- Dr. Mohd Yusuf Khan, ISC.

- Yasin Malik, JKLF.
- Maulana Mohd Mubarak, KBT.
- Pir Hafizullah Maqdoomi, JKPC.

Areas of Operations

J & K, POK.

Links with Political Parties/Groups

Pakistan, POK, ISI, MC, AAC, AAJM, JKJEI/HUM JKPC, JKLF, AIM, KLC, AJKEC, EWC, JAEH, KBT, JEH, KBA, POC, TEHK, JUI, MKM, JKHRC, JKPBRPC, EWCA, ISL, ISC, KAB, KAC, AIPRF, JKSF, AJM.

Foreign Links

Pakistan, ISI, POK, OIC, Chairman, Pakistan Parliamentary Commitee on Kashmir, Sardar Abdul Qayoom.

Finances

ISI to constituents; diverse foreign sources.

Origins

To have a united and an active, visible political face as the 'front end' for several militant/secessionist organisations spawned by the ISI to serve its purpose in Jammu and Kashmir, it had forged the TEHK in early 1990. However, the conglomerate seemed to have been losing its coherence, partly because of arrest of its prominent leaders, and partly because of ego clashes among some senior leaders. More relevantly, JKJEI's domination of the TEHK was seen as oppressive, and hence, deeply resented by others. Yet again, the absence of JKLF and JKPL in the councils of the TEHK had been a question mark about its representative character for the Kashmir people in totality. Hence the decline and progressive decay of the TEHK was inbuilt in its structure because that significant absence. So the need and talk about the new umbrella organisation to replace the TEHK had been in the air for sometime.

In the given circumstance, the release of five prominent separatist leaders (including Geelani, AG Bhatt, AG Lone, and Abbas Ansari) provided an impetus to forge a new conglomerate.

Three meetings were convened for the purpose on 17 December 1992, 7 March 1993, and 3 September 1993 — with promoters from 26 organisations trying their hands at midwifery. The last meeting succeded in creating a hydra-headed combine, appropriately christened All Party (initially, Kul Jamaat) Hurriyat (= Freedom) conference. As an analyst put it tersely, the APHC was a "sort of 'holding company' with a cause, but no shares in the affiliated 'militancy companies'." The APHC units were later flaunted in Pakistan and some other countries in West Asia, Europe, and America.

The APHC appeared to be a strange puppet show, dominated by the quarrelling Chiefs and squabbling tribes, with the puppeteer nowhere on the stage — rather ensconced in the safe haven of Pakistan.

The analysts saw the colour and character of the APHC as pre-determined by its genes : explicit hostility towards India; boycotting and violent disruption of elections—as if they were afraid of people's democratic verdict; refusal to engage in constructive dialogue with New Delhi; condoning, even rationalising, the terrorist violence against the innocent and highly exaggerative concern for the human rights violations by the SF, while in reality they and their constituents were themselves fully responsible for these so-called violations; and demand for compliance with the UN resolutions, even when fully aware that the 'conditions precedent' have not been allowed to set in. It did not need any extraordinary prescience to see the influence of the hardliners like Geelani behind this anti-India orientation of the newly-created APHC.

The Charar-e-Sharif Incident

The shrine was occupied during March-May 1995 by the terrorists led by Mast Gul, an Afghan mercenary. Indian SF besieged the ultras holed inside the shrine to flush them out. They burnt the shrine and a major portion of the town on 11 May 1995 in an escape bid.

The role played by the APHC was expectedly clever, self-serving and even devious. It exploited the incident to whip up anti-India and anti-SF sentiment—hoping to garner the support of local Muslim population for itself. While it provided food to the besieged ultras, it simultaneously arganised protest marches to seek withdrawal of the SF. When the terrorists fled leaving a burnt down shrine behind, the APHC rejected the State's offer to rebuild it. Whatever its calculations, the APHC suffered certain erosion in its credibility for it inability or unwillingness to prevent the destruction of the much revered, Centuries — old shrine and public property/people's houses. It seemed its action boomranged on the APHC — its image taking certain beating consequent to this blatant act of blasphemy. Some people even perceived the couglomerate to have abetted the terrorist act in its eagerness to garner brownie points against the State and its SF.

Soon after shrine stood torched , the APHC despatched a team to Saudi Arabia to discuss the issue and future course of action. This mecting in Mecca created the Charar-i-Sharif fund committee with Geelani as Chairman. There was large inflow of funds for reconstruction of the shrine as also for relief of sufferers whose property was destroyed in the fire lit by the terrorists in their escape bid. The utilisation — or misutilisation or misappropriation—of these funds became the cause of dispute among the APHC leaders. Naturally there were raised eye-brows all around. The mutual distrust and recriminations among the APHC leaders should be a proof enough to make the point that *Jihadi* leaders should not be entrusted with responsibilities like reconstruction or relief and rehabalitation of people, victims of tragedies-natural or man-made. The farce was repeated when the LET was given similar responsibility vis-a-vis the heople ruined in 2006 earthquake in the POK. As it was disclosed subsequently, most of the money found their way to sweel the jihadi swell coffers and was used to buy weapons and IEDs for terrorist activities.

The Al Faran Incident

In July 1995, six foreign tourists were abducted, and a Norwegian national was beheaded. A little-known terror group, Al Faran, claimed responsibility, but later it turned out that the HUA were the real culprits. APHC leadership failed to effectively step in and secure the release of the captives, because the incident was bound to adversely affect the in-flow of the foring tourists that would eventually cause hardship to the common

Kashmiris who depended so much on the tourist trade for their livelihood. Beheading of an innocent foreigners and inability of the APHC to secure the release of the remaining five hostages did cause popular swell of resentment. It was a loss of face again for the APHC, as was the case in the Charar-e-Sharif burning of the shrine and the town. This time around, the unease and consternation that spread among the international community was an additional cause of serious worry for the APHC leaders.

Long last, on 13 Angust 1995, the APHC awoke to the need of stemming any further damage to its image. It publicly announced its dissociation from the kidnapping of the six foreigners and condemned the beheading of the Norwegian national.

APHC opposes Ladakh Autonomy .

Respecting the democratically-expressed desire of the Ladakhis for greater autonomy to their region and as a result of prolonged negotiations on the issue, Srinagar and New Delhi had agreed to the demand.

The APHC, claiming to be the sole representative of the people of the State, and thus feeling ignored if not slighted, announced its opposition to the proposal and ironically, organised a *bandh* against the constitution of the Leh Autonomous Hill Development Council (LAHDC) on 28 August 1995 in the Kashmir Valley. The LAHDC was the instrumentality, devised by the three parties to the agreement, to ensure faster development of the region, enabled by the greater autonomy bestowed on it.

APHC disrupts electoral democracy

The APHC called for a *bandh* on 8 November 1995 to protest the visit of Chief Election Commissioner (CEC) to the valley to oversee the preparations for the 1996 parliamentary polls, a routine for the CEC. Later, at the joint meeting of the General Body and the Council, it summarily rejected dialogue with New Delhi on the issue. It ran a door-to-door campaign against the elections and called for *bandhs* on the polling days. Not giving up even after the completion of the polling, in a statement it alleged that the people had been coerced into casting their votes, and therefore, the elction results were irrelavent. The outfit could hardly conceal its chagrin and frustration at the fact that the people had exercised their franchise even in the face of the threats issued at the gun point. In this war, the ballot had won against the bullet — and the APHC could not digest the bitter truth.

An APHC delegation had earlier net the US Ambassador Frank Wisner during his 25 June 1995 visit to Srinagar. He was believed to have underscored the desirability of holding elections J & K, not as an end in itself but as a means to involve the people in the decision-making process and to restore much-desired peace in the State. The leaders, expectedly, rejected Wisner's wise advice.

On 11 July, 1996, it described the econom package announced by the Prime Minister as a 'hoaxxx', simultaneously asserting that the elections are not a solution to the problem. It also dismissed the after of unconditional talks by the Minister of State concerned as 'futile' and 'meaningless'.

Its leaders also tried to drum up support beyond the confines of the State, attending seminars organised by All India People's Resistance Forum (AIPRF) in Guwahati on 10-11 October 1996, Hyderabad on 27-28 October 1996 and Patna on 21 November 1996; and by the Students Islamic Movement of India (SIMI) in Delhi on 1 December 1996. To add own mite to the cause, the APHC organised a demonstration in New Delhi on 10 December 1996 to coincide with the International Human Rights Day.

Despite its inability to emerge as a unifying political force to espouse secessionism in J and K as its sole representative even in the limited area of the Kashmir Valley, the APHC did succeed in attracting the attention of some governments, essentially in the Islamic world. Projecting itself as the *sole representative* of the Kashmiri people, as is its wont, it has sought to highlight the human rights issues in J and K, and suggested/proposed 'situation monitoring' by the International Red Cross, Amnesty International, and others.

APHC Registers Presence in the OIC

Pakistan successfully campaigned for securing for the APHC an Observer status in the OIC, and Hamid Al Gabid, Secretary

General, OIC, invited it to attend its 7-9 September 1994 Foreign Ministers' Conference. But it could not honour the invitation as India chose to refuse the necessary travel documents to its delegation. But Maulvis Umar Farooq and Abbas Ansari did attend the next such meet as Observers at Casablance in December 1995.

At the 9-11 December 1994 OIC Conference in Tehran, Pakistan succeeded in persuading the member countries to create the "OIC Contact Group on Kashmir — a major victory for Pakistan and a constant headache for India.

Maulvi Farooq attended a meeting of the OIC Contact Group on Kashmir in New York during 28-29 September 1995. Besides meeting Pakistan /Pok-based secessionist leaders there, Farooq also interacted with Pak Foreign Minister Sardar Asif Ali, Sardar Abdul Qayoom Khan, Prime Minister, POK, Robin Raphael, US Assistant Secretary of State, and several US senators.

Farooq, enlisting the help of GN Fai of the KAC, tried to project the APHC as the sole representative of the Kashmiri people during these interactions.

An APHC delegation, headed by Abbas Ansari, attended the OIC Contact Group on Kashmir meeting in August 1996 at Islamabad. Very next month, Farooq briefed this Group in New York (on 30 September 1996). All concerned were obviously overactive to keep Kashmir in the international headlines, and possibly help a fraternal Muslim nation to wrest Kashmir from India, *dar-ul-Harb*.

After briefing the Contact Group on 30 September 1996, Farooq continued the good work at the UN General Assembly, then in its annual session — meeting with several delegates attending the session from different countries, with the help of the Pak UN Mission and Fai's KAC.

Pleading at SAARC Summit 1995.

Before his exertious in 1996 session of the General Assembly, Farooq and his Cohorts had made a pitch for their cause at the 8th SAARC Summit at New Delhi from 2 to 4 May 1995. They (Shabir Shah, GM Bhatt, Forooq, Abbas Ansari) submitted a memorandum to the heads of the SAARC governments. The delegation had a 45-minute meeting with the Pakistan

President, Farooq Leghari, who is believed to have advised a peaceful solution of the issue. They also met with Bangladesh Prime Minister, Begum Khalida Zia.

Knocking at the UNHRC Door.

A 3-Member APHC delegation—GM Bhatt, Noorul Hassan and Jalil Andrabi—attended the UNHRC meeting in Geneva in August 1995. Several diplomatic missions based at Geneva met the delegation and sought its intevention for release of the five western hostages still in the custody of terrorist group, Al Faran.

Thereafter, the APHC focussed it gaze on the Non-Aligned Movement Summit, then in session, 16-17 October 1995, in Colombia. Despatched to Colombia for the purpose, Farooq failed to get permission to attend the Summit. Then he flew to London and met Lord Avebury, British Parliamentarian and Human Rights activists in Novermber 1995. To his chagrin, Farooq was advised by the good Lord to find and seek solution through democrative means.

Scaring the World with the "nuclear flash point " Chimera

India's Shakti -98 series of nuclear tests in May 1998 and the Pak response in kind handed an excellent opportunity to the APHC, helped and encouraged by Islam abad, to internationalise the Kashmir issue by assiduously spreading the canard about over-wrought theory of a 'nuclear flashpoint' in the 'volatile' subcontinent, that could blow it up over the long-festering but still unresolved Kashmir issue! The Corollary: The world must help the two nations to resolve the Kashmir issue. Earlier the danger was of the two nations hurtling into a clash, equipped with conventional weapons. Now the situation is qualilatively different and exponentially more lethal as post - 1998, the two adversary nations are nuclear powers. So went the scary scenario and so went the argument for urgency in solving the festering flash-point—the Kashmir issue.

For certain western countries, and 'committed' analysts there, any reason is good enough to go along with Pakistan concerns about 'Kashmir' degenerating into lethal war between the two 'distant' neighbours, even when they are sharing common physical international borders. Any number of 'occasions' were painted by the western, especially the US, scholars when the two countries were supposed to have come close to nuclear blows. These scare-mongering events were dismissed by India, and others who understand the causes behind India becoming a 'reluctant' nuclear weapons State, as imaginative outpourings of some fertile, perhaps febrile, brains.

Yes, there is indeed some discomfort in certain sections of western strategic analysis community about the mismatch between India's 'No First Use' (NFU) policy and Pakistan's enthusiastic adoption of the defunct NATO doctrine of 'first use' in the face of 'Conventional asymmetry' with respect to Warsaw Pact nations. Certain 'confidence building measures' have already been discussed by two nations to address this discomnfort. The 'situation of concern' should further under- go a change for the better during the ongoing 'peace process' negotiations between India and Pakistan. In any case, if the US and the Soviet Union could live with the thousands of nuclear weapons in fully armed status, for 45 years when one of it disappeared, there is no reason to believe that some madman in uniform or civvies would blow up the Sub-continent in a fit of anger.

The Inevitable Dissonance Within

The domination of the JKJEI and pro-Pakistan hardline was an ever - present hurdle that came in the way of establishing and maintaining harmonious relations among the leaders of the APHC. In hypothetical terms even if the APHC succeeded in its secessionist objective of snipping Kashmir from India in a quick surgery, the leadership will be vertically divided between the pro-Pakistan hard liners led by Geelani and pro-independence advocates headed by Yasin Malik. This ideological differences have been the cause of continuous friction within the APHC leadership, seldom capable of forging a united stand on any important issues. The mutual recriminations and distrust have been the bane of the APHC.

The assassination of Dr. Qazi Nissar by the HUM militants on 20 June 1994 increased the hiatus and suspicion among the

APHC leaders. The non-JKJEI leaders pressed for identification of the culprits but the JKJEI supporters stalled all moves in this direction. The committee appointed by the APHC to investigate the assassination could not proceed ahead because of the pressure mounted by the JKJEI/HUM directly, and indirectly through the ISI. This led to the boycott of the APHC meetings by leaders like AG Bhatt and Abbas Ansari.

The assassination created public ire against the APHC leadership. At a public function held at Anantnag to commemorate first death anniversary of Qazi's murder, the APHC was openly criticised for its inability to discipline the JKJEI/HUM. Even its role and relevance were challenged. When AG lone tried to defend the APHC, he was hackled. He quit the stage in a huff and departed for Srinagar. *Enroute,* he was Kidnapped by the IUM cadres. Ironically, he was later released on the intervention of Shabir Shah.

There was internal criticism against the APHC for its having no coherent agenda. Its image and credibility suffered during the Hazratbal and Charar-e-Sharif episodes. When the SF bunkers were finally dismantled in the Hazratlbal area on 6 August 1994 as a result of agitation, including the hunger strike, launched by Yasin Malik, the APHC occupied the shrine lest Yasin and his JKLF garner credit for this victory. His hunger-strike had been declared an un-Islamic act and his explanation was sought for acting in a manner prejudicial to APHC unity. Consequent to all this, Yasin boycotted the APHC, but Geelani and Lone succeeded in persuading him to rejoin it in August 1995.

When Shabir Shah came out of detention on 14 October 2004, there was enthusiastic public response to it in the valley and Jammu region. Concerned at his expanding his popular base among the people, APHC leaders made strong efforts to convince him to join them. But Shabir set out three pre-conditions:

- merger of all the constituents of the APHC into a single organisation.
- election of as single leader.

- representation for Jammu and Ladakh regions in the APHC.

In addition, he also demanded that the misguided militants be identified lest the sanctity of the liberation movement is violated. These conditions were not acceptable to pro-Pakistan hardliners of the APHC, especially the JKJEI. But after some persuation by Kashmiri leaders and Pak officials, Shabir joined the APHC.

Sabir Shah getting special attention in Delhi was not to the liking of others in the APHC. His meetings with former Prime Minister VP Singh on 5 May 1996 and the US Ambassador Frank Wisner on 1 August 1996 were frowned upon by the APHC leaders. Consequently, he was suspended from its membership on 8 August 1996.

In 1998, all factions of the JKPL, including JKPL -(Nayeem Khan) and JKPL-(Abdul Aziz Sheikh), were merged to create the new united JKPL, and it was made an executive member of the APHC. Since the Chairman of the new JKPL, Abdul Aziz Sheikh was still under detention, its Deputy Chairman Bashir Ahmad Tota was invited to attend the APHC meetings. The move, it seemed, was essentially meant to marginalise factions led by Shabir Shah. The inter-group polities/jealousies were all there for any one to see, the APHC seldom being able to rise above them all.

The foreign visits of Maulvis Umar Farooq and Abbas Ansari as the representatives of the APHC were resented by Geelani and Yasin who themselves were keen to participate in such foreign tours. The expatriates and Pakistan/Pok-based JKJEI leaders were upset that these two Mulvis had side-lined the JKJEI agenda and exposed the firsure between the JKJEI and non-JKJEI leaders. Due to these simmering differences, personal and ideological, the APHC was unable to send a delegation to Brussels to brief the European MPs at a meeting organised by the TEHK for the purpose on 20 November 1995.

However , on the initiative of Shabir Shah, the APHC opened a liaison office in New Delhi under the name of Kashmir Awareness Bureau (KAB) in October 1995 for interaction with the diplomatic community based there.

ISI creates J & K Solidarity Forum (JKSF)

Unhappy with the lacklustre functioning of the APHC and its inability to sink mutual differences among its top leaders, the ISI floated intearly 1997 yet another umbrella organisation, JKSF, to bring together on one platform all those political parties and their armed wings in J & K/PoK which have an anti-India secessionist agenda. The creation of the parallel organisation was resented by the APHC as it was perceived as a threat to its primacy in the field of Kashmir struggle. To prove that primacy and to regain its somewhat tattered credibility, the APHC planned a human chain from the UNMOGIP, Muzaffarabad to the UNMOGIP, Srinagar on 24 October 1997. But to its great chagrin and deeptsense of mortification, the much-vaunted APHC human chain plan turned out to be a damp squib.

The dissensions within the APHC, continued after Geelani took over as Chairman from Umar Farooq on 24 April 1998. Neither did they disappear when AG Bhatt replaced Geelani and made a statement on the need for the JKJEI to delink from the militancy.

Status around turn of the Millennium

In the changed international situation, post 9-11, the APHC leaders embarked upon an action programme to highlight the day-to-day problems faced by the Kashmiris. It continued to work for unity among the terrorist outfits for achieving their ultimate desideratum and going all out to ensure the return of the leaders like Shabir Shah.

It continued to maintain its usual anti-India stance and oppose the elections due to be held in September 2002. This opposition remained unabated despite the international opinion generated in favour of Kashmir elections, especially after the July 2002 visits by US Secretary of State and the British Foreign Secratary.

Its policy towards the negotiations with New Delhi and subsequent split into two parallel bodies will be discussed later.

Al Umar Mujahideen (AUM) Al Umar

Formation	December 1989
Headquarters	Srinagar

Strength	700
Objectives	Liberation of Kashmir through armed struggle and merger with Pakistan.
Sponsors	Awami Action Committee (AAC); ISI.

Organisational Structure

- Supreme Command: Chief Commander; two Deputy Chief Commanders.
- Field Formations: District Commanders and Regimental Commanders.

Leadership

- Mushtaq Ahmad Zargar, Chairman and Supreme Commander.
- Manzoor Ahmad Ganai, Chief Commander and organiser of Training.
- Latif-ul-Haq, Acting Chief Commander (Pakistan-based)
- Jamshed Khan, Deputy Chief Commander (Former Chief of the Madar Yalgar Group)
- Aamir Jameel, Deputy Chief (POK-based).
- Bilal Haider, Intelligence Chief (Pakistan-based)
- Jasbir Singh (SIKH Member)

Arean of Operations

- Srinagar Baramulla, Kupwara, Pulwama, Muzaffarabad.
- office in Muzaffarabad, Transit camp in Duli – 2, Manshera

Links with Political Parties / Group

Pakistan, PoK , ISI, AAC, UJC (PoK), SEJ.

Foreign Links

Pakistan, PoK, ISI, Kashmir Action Committee, Tehrik Alia ka Sipahi (Pakistan).

Finances

Receives Rs. 3 to 4 lakh per month from ISI / Pakistan, local collections (Extortion / Protection money).

Arms Holding

Over 25 weapons including 20 AK rifles, 5 pistols.

Major Acts of Terrorism

- 17 Jun 90. Raided house of JL Ganjoo, Srinagar; killed 4 member of family including 2 women and injured 4 others; incident caused a split in the AUM.
- 18 Jun 90. Kidnapped, decapitated Mohd Amin Chantgar of Nowhatta, Srinagar.
- 13 Jul 90. Killed a Hindu youth, Nanaji, Batmaloo, SGR.
- 27 Jul 90. Kidnapped Tasleen Bilal and blew up, with explosives around waist, a Muslim youth; Nalamar Chowk, SGR.
- 4 Sep 90. Kidnapped Bashir Ahmad Sheikh from home and blew him up with explosives; Rambagh, SGR.
- 14 Oct 90. Raided house of Shyam Lal Kaul in Rehman Sahib, SGR; shot dead four member of the family, including 2 women; in the same area, 2 more Hindus shot dead.
- 15 Oct 90. Killed Pir Mohd Shafi, ex-MLA, NC (Farooq) at Lal bazar, SGR.
- 27 Oct 1990. Kidnapped, killed a businessman, Syed Kauroosa, SGR.
- 1 Mar 91. JKLF, HIZB, AVM terrorists jointly opened fire on a police party in Batmaloo, Srinagar.
- 11 Mar 91. Attacked a police party in Lar, Ganderbal, SGR.
- 11 Apr 91. Fired on senior civil officers at Jamia Mosque, SGR; Killed one officer and a woman.
- 3 May 91. Killed Ghulam Mohd Bandey, NC (Farooq) worker; Nawakadal, SGR.
- 6 May 91. killed Sheikh Sadiq, cousin of former Chief Minister Farooq Abdullah, in Nagin, SGR.
- 4 Jun 91. Killed Hisamuddin Bandey, ex-Minister, Hazratbal, SGR.

- 20 Jun 91. J.K Police constables, Saifuddin and Mohd Akbar Lone, kidnapped from Bandipur area on 6 Jun 91; Blown up with explosives.
- 1 Aug. 91. Riaz Ahmad Zargar of Al Barq, abducted and killed.
- 22 Sep 91. Kidnapped Tassadug Hussain Devbrother-in-law of Ghulam Nabi Azad, Union Minister from Haiderpora, Badgam; released along with Mohd Shafi Khan on 17 Jan 92 in exchange for 8 militants, including Bashir Ahmad Jan, Attar Hussain Bakshi and Muzaffar Ahmad Sofi.
- 7 Nov 91. Kidnapped Mohd Shafi Khan, brother of Hamidullah Khan, Adviser to Governor, for the release of Muzaffar, Area Commander AUM, arrested Nov 90.
- Nov 91. Dispute between Ashfaq, AUM cadre, and an HMM cadre, over the marriage of the former with A Srinagar (SGR) girl; led to clashes in Badgam and adjoining area in Nov 91; HMM seized around 40 weapons from the AUM and raided its bases in Saidpura and Alisteng; the AUM was chastened.
- 12 Fab 92. Kidnapped Dr. Ghulam Nabi Butt, Director, Forensic Laboratory, J & K from his SGR office.
- 9 Mar 92. Kidnapped Dr. R K Sharma, Head, Physics Department, and RS Sharma, Head, Chemistry Department, Kashmir University, SGR.
- 18 Jan 96. Missile attack on Hotel Shangrila, SGR.

Origins

In a manner of speaking, it was kidnapping of Rubaiya Syed, daughter of the then Union Home Minister Mufti Mohammed Syed by the JKLF in 1998 that led to the birth and subsequent rising aspirations of the Al Umar Mujahideen (AUM). By February 1989, Chairman Zargar aka Latrum had developed some differences with his top JKLF colleagues, especially Ishfaq Majidwani, then the Chief Commander and Javed Naik, over the release of 5 JKLF detenues (including Irfan, a close associate of Zargar) in exchange of Rubaiya's.

Zargar floated the new outfit, AUM, on 13 December 1989 with the approval of Maulvi Mohd Farooq, Chairman, AAC.

Soon its cadres numbered 55. Subsequently, AUM created ten regiments which were allotted specific operational areas in SGR. At its peak, it had over 700 militants/terrorists.

Training, Operations, and Splits/Mergers.

The AuM built up its cadres, initially, recruiting musclemen and hoobgans police records. From 1990, its cadres have been trained in Pakistan, arranged by Majid Tariq of ISI. It earned notoriety in J & K for employing brutality in killing its victims.

Perhaps exactly a year after its birth, it had first split in December 1990, when Shabir Ahmad Bangaroo, then its Deputy Chief, walked out with 30 loyalists and formed Al Umar Commandos (AUC).

1991 saw several clashes between the AUM and HUM, with the latter diarming many AUM cadres. It was the kidnapping of Ghulam Nabi Nowsheri of the JKJEI by AUM in March 1991 in Ganderbal area that compelled a face-to-face meeting between Zargar and Master Ahsan Dar, then Chief of Operations, HUM to reach a settlement lest the situation spins out of control.

In March 1991 itself, Jamshed Khan, Supreme Commander of Al Madad Yalgar-e-Ali (AMYA), joined the AUM with his 60 followers. He was anointed the Deputy Chief. The very next month, he was arrestead.

In March 1992 Khalid Javed, Military Adviser of IUM joined the AUM in the same capacity. AUM's Military Adviser Shabir Hussain got demoted as its Deputy Intelligence Chief. It caused another split in AUM. Its District Commander, SGR, Nazir Podari, went over to JKLF with his men. Later, Javed himself was expelled from the AUM.

The defection of AUM cadres to the JKLF with their weapons, a much-prised asset, led to periodic armed clashes between them in downtown Srinagar. In these clashes, the AUM was backed by HUM and JUM cadres. Finally, Javed Ahmad Shalla, IUM leader, intervened to restore peace but these splits and blood-lettings had left the AUM weakened.

The AUM suffered a serious blow when Mushtaq Zargar was arrested on 14 May 1992, and then came the death of Iqbal

Zargar. Manzoor Ahmad Ghanai returned to the Valley as its Chief Commander and started reorganising its cadres.

By mid-1994, it was an ineffective entity, unfit to be of any use to its ISI paymasters. Expectedly, in July 1994 it cut out all aid to the AUM.

AUM's Links with Sikh Terrorists

The AUM forged links with Sikh terror groups, especially the Khalistan Liberation Force (KLF), promising them arms if they could try and spread terrorism to other parts of India beyond Panjab, and especially to Delhi. Jasbir Singh, an important AUM member, was the link between the two. Arms were supplied to the Sikhs through Sukhwinder Singh of Ludhiana and Avtar Singh of Patiala.

Latif Zafar, Acting Chief of AUM had planned in 1994 the abduction of the cricket icon Kapil Dev and of son of the J & K Legislative Assembly speaker to secure the release of his detained Chief, Zargar. It proved abortive even when the assistance from the Sikh groups had been sought.

Collaborative nexus and current status

Besides joining the UJC (PoK) , the AUM is also a constituent of the SEJ. Its PoK Chief, Bilal Haider, participated in the UJC meet at Muzaffarabad in July 1998 where Salahuddin, HUM Chairman, was anointed President of the UJC.

Manzoor Ghanai visited PoK in July 1994 to plead with the ISI to restore supply of life-saving oxygen to AUM. Notwithstanding all that, AUM activities have been at a low ebb ever since 1996. It was no surprise as its C-in-C, Nayeem-ul-Haq, was arrested in Delhi in July 1996 while returning to Kashmir.

Dukhtaran-e- Millat (DEM)

Formation	March 1987
Headquarters	Srinagar
Strength	1000

Objectives	Merger of Kashmir with Pakistan; Islamic tenets for Muslim women; support to Nizam-e-Mustafa.
Sponsors	Pakistan, Mahaz-e-Islami, ISI, JEI.

Organisational Structure

8 – Member Majlis-e-Shora with a President, General Secretary, and District President.

Leadership

- Ashiya Anadrabi, President
- Nahida Nasreen, Gen Secretary
- Rubaiya Firdous, District President, SGR.
- Nasreen Sheikh nee Dar, District President, Baramulla.
- Fahmeeda Shah, District Pereisdent, Badgam.
- Jameela, District President, Pulwama
- Zuneira Yasmin, District President, Anantnag

Areas of Operatious

Kashmir Valley

Foreign Links

Pakistan, ISI

Links with Political Parties / Groups

JUM (through Ashiq Hussain, Finance Chief and husband of Andrabi) , JKJEI.

Finances

Pakistan; ISI through TEHK

Origins and Activities

Andrabi organised demonstrations in 1982 against the sale of liquor/ narcotics and display of obscence posters. In March 1987, she floated Dukhtran-e-Fatima, with herself as President and Nahida Nasreen as General Seretary. The outfit exhorted Muslim women to observe *purdah,* desist from watching TV, video' and movies. Subsequently, her zeal attraeted the attention of JKJEI, and she was invited to join it.

In the later years, Dukhtran-e-Fatima was renamed Dukhtran-e-Millat.

The DEM sees J & K as part of Pakistan, and has led many anti–India demonstrations. In 1990, DEM joined the TEHK and extended support to secessionists/terrorists.

Interestingly and it being a women's outfit, DEM was vociferous in supporting LEJ (Lashkar-e-Jabbar), an outfit that grabbed headlines after its cadres threw acid on two Srinagar women for not complying with the 'Islamic' dress code. This says something about place of women in the Islamic society.

DEM suffered a setback when Andrabi was arrested on 5 February 1993 at Srinagar airport on her return from Delhi. Released on 21 February 1994, she resumed the mobilisation of Muslim women against the security forces.

Channel for Illegal ISI Money

Interestingly, perhaps surprisingly, the ISI has chosen DEM to transfer large sums of hawala money to J & K for disburrement among different secessionist/terrorist outfits, including the HUM. The money trail involves Ayub Thakur (London), Imtiaz Bazaz (Srinagar), and Andrabi. APHC leader SAS Gillani has also received funds through the DEM.

Harkat-ul-Ansar (HUA)

Formation	October-November 1993
Headquaters	Rawalpindi
Strength	800 Pak/Afghan trained militants, including 300 – 350 foreigners; 10,000 followers.
Arms/Equipment	50 LMG/UMG ; 50 RL; 400 AK 56/47, 10 sniper rifles; 100 pistols/revolvers and sizeable quantities of explosives.
	Advanced Communication network
Objectives	Establishment of the supremacy of Islam the world over; liberation of Muslims not following *Shariat;* protection of minority Muslims in non-Muslim areas.
Sponsors	Pakistan, PoK, ISI, JUI (PoK), Tabligh-ul-Islam (TUI) (Pak), HEI (Yunus Khalis/ Yunus Hakkani)

Organisational Structure

- Policy leval: 8-member Majlis-e-Amla and 13-member majlis-e-Shora.
- Executive Level: *Amir,* Chief Commander, Deputy Chief Commander.

Leadership

- Jalaluddin Haqqani, Patron.
- Maulvi Abdul Rashid, Patron (in Pakistan).
- Maulvi Mohd Amin, *Amir-e-Ala.*
- Maulana Fazal-ul-Rahman Khalili, *Amir* (in Pakistan).
- Farooq Kashmiri, *Naib Amir* in PoK, *Amir* for J & K and Tajikistan.
- Maulana Kalimullah, Head, Bangladesh Chapter.
- Hataf Bhai, Chief Commander.
- Nissar Ahmad, District Chief, Srinagar.
- Ustad Ahmad Ali, District Chief, Doda.

(There are posts on similar lines for Finance, Training, Publicity, Kupwara, Anantnag, Badgam, etc. not detailed here).

Majlis-e-Amla

- Maulvi Mohd Yunus, *Amir.*
- Mohd Manzoor Ahmad, *Naib Amir,* SGR.
- Khadim Hussain, Finance Chief, SGR.
- Parvez Ahmad Baba, Jammu.
- Aijaz Ahmad Ahangar, Srinagar (Later Joined TUM).
- Abdul Fazal, Chief Commander, Srinagar.
- Mohd Muzahar Lankar, Publicity Chief.

Majlis-e-Shora

- All Members of Majlis-e-Amla.
- District Commanders of Srinagar, Badgam, Kupwara, Anantnag, and Doda.

Areas of Operations

- Darah (Srinagar), Anantnag, Doda, Badgam, Pulwama, Baramulla, Kupwara, Poonch and Rajouri areas along the LOC.
- Active in Myanmar, Bangladesh, Tajikistan, and Pakistan (Islamabad, Karachi, Gujranwala, Nourang Serai, Lahore, Peshawar, Rahimyar Khan, Dera Ismael Khan, Sarghoda, Dera Ghazi Khan, Quetta, Multan and Hyderabad).

Links with Political Parties and Groups

Pakistan, PoK; ISI; UJC; APHC; founder member, SEJ.

Foreign Links

JUI (Pakistan), TUJ (Pakistan), Ittehad-e-Islami (Afghanistan), HEI (Afghanistan, Pakistan).

Finances

Pakistan; Islamic countries; UK; US.

Major Acts of Terrorism

- 14 Aug 93. Hijacked a passenger bus and killed 16 Hindu passengers at Kishtwar, Doda.
- 30 May 94. Killed local BJP leader, Swami Rajkatal at Doda and another Hindu; 8 injured.
- 6 Jun, 94. Abducted two British nationals, Anantnag.
- 7 Jun 94. (1) Looted four foreigners, Aroo, Anantnag. (2) Shottdead BPJ *tehsil* President, Ruchar Kumar at Bhaderwah, Doda; Communal clashes ensued.
- 17 Sep 94. Killed two villagers during raid at Badalkot.
- 2-4 Mar 95. Seven HUA militants, including a Sudanese and an Afghanese, killed in an encounter with SF
- 17 Mar 95. 12 killed, including three foreign nationals, in an encounter with SF; Kupwara.
- 10 Apr 95. Five killed, including three foreign nationals; Kupwara.
- 11 May 95. Charar-e-Sharif shrine torched and SF attacked; 29 HUA terrorists killed in the encounter.

- 14 May 95. Shot dead six members of a Hindu family in village Dhulli, Doda.
- 4 Jul 95. A bdyucted seven American and British tourists, Aroo, Anantanag. Three released next day; one US tourist escaped 9 Jul 95.
- 8 Jul 95. Abducted a Germantourist on pahalgam-Amarnath route at Zozibal, Anantnag.
- 10 Jul 95. Abducted Norwegian tourist Hans Christian on Pahalgam-Amarnath route at Zozibal, Anantnag; tortured to death, decapitated body left in village Hapatnag, Anantnag district.
- 20 July 95. Killed 17 Hindus, 36 injured; in a powerful blast in Mandi, Jammu.
- 26 Jul 95. Killed one civilian, injured 36, in poweful blast in Shalimar Chowk, Jammu.
- 15 Aug 95. Injured ten Anarnath Yatra pilgrims in a powerful blast in a hostel on BC Road, Jammu.
- 7 Sep 95. Explosion in the BBC correspondent's office on Pratap Park, SGR.
- 5 Jan 96. 6 terrorists killed in a closh with HUM; Zainakot, Badgam.
- 6 Jun 96. 15 Hindus hacked to death; six houses looted; Barsala, Doda.
- 30 Jan 96. Three militants, including two Afghans, killed in encounter at Qazigund, Anantnag.
- 30 Jun 96. Shot dead 8 members of a Hindu family; one women injured; Kamlari, Doda.
- 1 Jul 96. 5 militants, including a Pak national, killed in encounter at Zachaldar and Loduvsnag, Kupwara.
- 2 Sep 96. Abducted, killed a prominent business-man in Pasharla, Doda.
- 3 Dec 96. Shot dead seven at Barshalla, Doda.
- 13 Nov 97. 25 militants attacked a police patrol party in Poonch; three Afghans killed.

(SGR is used for Srinagar)

Origins and Difficult Birth : Longwinding Process

The Harkat-ul-Ansar (HUA) is successor to the Pan-Islamic terrorist outfit, Harkal-ul-Jihad-e-Islami International (HUJI), floated in 1980 by Muslim youth affiliated to the Jamaat-ul-Ulemah-e-Islam (JUUI) and Tabligh Jammat of Pakistan. The HUA was created in 1993 through the merger of a number of groups like HUJI, HKUM and JUM.

Initially, the HUJI, alongwith Afghan Mujahideen took part in the armed resistance against the regime of Babrak Karmal. After Maulvi Irshad Ahmad took over as its Chief Commander, the outfit set Jihad in Afghanistan as its objective, and famously received support from the ISI, and hold your breath, the CIA! (This was the strategic decision. America and the world are still paying for. In a manner of speaking, this was also the decision that gifted Osama to the international Community).

At very early stage, HUJI cadres – mostly from West Punjab, (Pakistan) had offered volunteer relief work in Afghan Mujahideen refugee camps in the NWFP, Pakistan. Subsequently, having received arms training from Pak Army, they fought the government troops in Afghanistan along with Ittehad-e-Islami (Afghanistan). The HUJI also forged an operational relationship with HEI (Yunus Khalis faction) of Afghanistan.

When Maulvi Irshad Ahmad died early 1985 in Afghanistan, Qazi Saifullah took over as *Amir* of HUJI. Due to personality clashes, its C-in-C Fazal-ul-Rehman quit and established a separate group named Harkat-ul-Mujahideen, HKUM.

The split of HEI (Afghanistan) into Hikmatyar and Yunus Khalis factions also had implications for the HUJI. While the HUJI continued its links with the Ittehad-e-Islami, the JKHUM hitched itself to the HEI (Khalis) group. In Afghanistan, this (Latter) group functioned under the banner of Harkat-e-Islami (HKEI), with Maulana Aslam Khan Rehamani as Chief.

Early 1990, Maulana Masood Kashmiri split with Khalili to form his own outfit, JUMA (Jamaat-ul-Mujahideen Almi).

Now the final act in the creation of HUA. Maulana Sadaatullah took over HUJI as *Amir* in 1991 and encouraged Deobandi ulemah to unify HUJI and JKUM. Three clerics who joined hands to achieve the desired unification were : (1) Maulana Kalimullah, Chancellor, Dar-ul-Uloom, Jamia Farooqia, Karachi, (2) Mufti Rashid Ahmad, Chancellor, Dar-ul-Iftawal Irshad, Karachi; and (3) Mufti Rafi Usmani, Chancellor, Dar-ul-Uloom, Karachi. Crowning their exertions, HUJI and HKUM merged in October-November 1993 to form Harkat-ul-Ansar (HUA), with its Headquarters at Rawalpindi. Mohammed Masood Azhar was appointed General Secretary of the HUA.

HUA : Jihad is Sine Qua non to Purify Islam

HUA is widely believed to enjoy the sponsorship—and consequent confidence – of the JUUI and Tabligh Jamaat of Pakistan, a well-known fanatical Sunni entity following the Deobandi school of Islamic thought. It sees itself as a true network of genuine Muslim holy *warriors* – a community of the faithful. As a well-accepted and well-known Islamic tenet, its own Pan-Islamic view does not believe in geographical and political frontiers and considers all Muslims as one *nation, ummat*. As a natural corollary to this overaching ideology the HUA leadership enjoins upon its cadres to participate in *jihad* in any part of the world to protect Islam and Muslims in distress, not only where they are in minority but also in the Muslim-majority and Muslim-ruled states not following the *Shariat*. In fact, they are duty-bound to do so, if they are true Muslims.[1]

The outfit considers the USA and Israel as the worst enemies of Islam.[2] Its manifesto, United Muslim Power, is rather explicit on the issue.

HUA cadres are sworn to a pledge to regain to restore the lost prestige and power of Islam[3] and to revitalise its purity through the instrumentality of Jihad.

HUA is Exported to Jammu and Kashmir

The HKUM had indeed inducted its first group of 30-40 into Jammu and Kashmir under Sajjad Afghani, a Pak national and Chief Commander HKUM, in June 1990 to set up an HKUM unit in in the state. Sajjad, in turn, set up a training centre at Darah in Srinagar to train and prepare the Kashmiri Youth for the holy task. The HUJI inducted its own militants into J & K a little later, in early 1992. The HUJI then inducted Nasarullah

Manzoor Langaryal (*Naib Salar*) in November 1992 to plan and execute operations in the valley. He set up a training camp at Kapran, Anantnag district. He was arrested on 19 November 1993.

The formation of the HUA can be traced to the visit of Maulana Masood Azhar, who travelled on a fake Portuguese passport to oversee the merger of the HUJI and HKUM units in J &K. Complicating the fruition of the idea, JUMA (J & K) chose to continue as a distinct entity even if it had already merged with HUA in Pakistan. But before anything concrete could be achieved, both Azhar and Sajjad were arrested by Indian SF on 11 February 1994.

Due to frequent allegations of misappropriations of funds and personality clashes between faction leaders the merger of HKUM and HUJI did not run smooth in J & K. HUJI alleged that the HKUM had received Rs. 2 crore from the ISI in 1992-93 through Prof. Mohammad Ashraf of Jamia Milia Islamia, Delhi.[4] On the other hand, foreign mercenaries complained of discrimination by the local militants in the distribution of funds.

In January 1994, Aijaz Ahmad Ahangar, Chief of HKUM took over as Chief Commander of HUA after the return of Amjad Balal to Pakistan. But Ahangar and HUJI Chief Mehrajuddin Sheikh developed serious differences over matters organisational. First week of May 1994, Nasir Ahmad Sodozey, a Pakistani national, took over as Finance Chief in Kashmir valley to resolve the problems of foreign mercenaries.

On 17 December 1994, at a *Majlis-e-Shora* (meeting) of the HUA, Qazi Zarar, a Pakistani national was appointed Chief Commander of the HUA to replace Ahangar, who later joined the TUM after marrying the daughter of Abdullah Ghazali, *Amir-e-Ala* of TUM. Early 1997, Zarar shifted to Dhaka.

HUA Spreads its Tentacles in the Islamic World

The HUA established its units in Bangladesh, Myanmar, Pakistan, India, UK, Bosnia, Tajikistan, and Chechnya. Its recruits come from Saudi Arabia, Burma, Bosnia, Tajikistan, Bangladesh, Pakistan, Afghanistan, and of course, Kashmir.

The Mayanmar unit, located in the Arakans, trains its local Muslims in handling arms/explosives and in guerrilla warfare.

In Tajikistan and Chechnya its cadres have operated with local separatist elements. The initial group of HUA then HUJI militants entered Bosnia in 1992.

In Bangladesh, he HUA established a network to facilitate Pakistan ISI's trans-border operations directed against India.

The outfit has links with the Ittehad-e-Islami of Somalia which fought against the US Peace Keeping Force, alongwith the insurgents led by Gen Aididi.

Maulana Ismail of Clapton Morque, London, was nominated as HUA leader in the UK. He successfully motivated local Muslim Youth to undergo arms training in Pakistan/ Afghanistan. One of his recruits, Ahmad Omar Syed Sheikh, received his training at Peshawar. He was later arrested in Delhi in connection with the kidnapping of four foreign tourists from Delhi in October 1994.

In October 1992, Maulana Masood Azhar, General Secretary, HUA, was invited to London by Maulana Ismail. During the visit, Azhar raised Rs. 15 lakh for the *tanzeem*. Hafiz, a cloth merchant in Dunbury, UK, secured a Portuguese passport for Azhar in the name of *vali Adam* Issa.

The HUA has a network of sympathisers in the Gulf Countries, Saudi Arabia, Zambia, South Africa and Kenya. In 1994, a group of Pakistani nationals with the HUA affiliation were arrested in Mainila, charged with a conspiracy to attack the Pope during his visit to the Philippines.

Foreign alumni who had studied at the JUUI-run *madaris* in Karachi and elsewhere spread the HUA's ideology in their countries on their return.

The radical Palestinian group *Hamas* expressed support to the HUA and sent a delegation to attend its annual conference at Lahore in 1994.

HUA Garners Support from Militant *Tanzeems* and ISI

The JUUI, a HUA sponsor in Pakistan, was a coalition partner in the Benazir Bhutto government. Maulana Fazalur Rehman, chief of JUUI. Pakistan, was Chairman of the Senate Foreign Relations Committee. Tabligh Jamaat, another sponsoring organisation, has a large following in Pakistan. Its one million-strong annual *ijtemahs* (= gatherings, literally; conferences) held at Lahore are often attended by that country's Presidents.

The JUUI runs a chain of well funded Deobandi *madrassas* (= religious schools) all over Pakistan. These are the ready and enthusiastic recruiting grounds for the ever-increasing militant *tanzeems*. Both, the JUUI and Tabligh Jamaat, are supplementing each other's endeavours in spreading extremism and fundamentalism in Pakistan and have been associated with causing and nurturing sectarian strife in that nation.

The ISI started funding the operations of HKUM and HUJI (HUA constituents) in Kashmir from September 1991. Earlier, the ISI had extended preferential funding to the JEI/HUM.

Inter-political parties' interests and their ambitions and aspirations also helped the militant organisations. The appointment of Lt Gen Javed Nasir, a member of Tabligh Jamaat, as Director General, ISI early 1992, coupled with Banazir Bhutto's return to power was a god send for the HKUM/HUJI combine and later, the HUA, because that pushed the combine on a rapid growth trajectory. Benazir Bhutto's support to the HUA can be directly ascribed to her rivalry with Nawaz Sharif's Islamic Democatic Alliance (= Islami Jamhoori Ittehad) which had patronised the JEI/HUM combine in the Kashmir Valley. So, politics touches all aspects of life : political, social, economic, and more importantly, religious.

It is important to note that the HUA emerged as the second largest militia in Pakistan, next only to JEI. Its projected strength stood at 10,000. Interestingly, though initially patronised by Ms. Bhutto, the HUA continued to receive full ISI support even after the change of guard when her bete noire Nawaz Sharif took over the reins of power in February 1997.

The HKUM commenced its militant operations in the Kashmir Valley in 1990. The ISI acknowleged its significance by including it in the UJC when the amalgam was created in January 1991, which had 10 other pro-Pakistan outfits like the HUM, ABQ, TUM, JEI and MJF. Within the UJC, the responsibility of transport and logistics was assigned to the HKUM.

It is an accepted fact by now that most, if not all the terrorist outfits in J & K are funded by the ISI, and consequently, also controlled by it. In the case of the HUA, ISI funding rose from Rs. 1.5 lakh in 1991 to Rs. 27 lakh per month in 1996. In addition, it also equipped HUA with better and heavier weaponry through a dedicated Detachment located along the LOC in POK and controlled from Muzaffarabad. Public claims by the HUA notwithstanding, the ISI had assigned different areas in Rajouri district to the HUA, LET and HUM.

During 1995, five foreign tourists were abducted by a new, and till then unknown outfit, Al Faran. One Norwegian national was beheaded and his body handed over to his relatives. The HUA was known to be supporting All Faran operations. A meeting of the Refugee Management Cell, Chaired by Lt Gen Shah Fahad of the ISI, was convened at Hamaza Camp, Islamabad, to discuss the kidnapping. It was atteded by a HUA representative, Farooq Kashmiri. When the General expressed anguish at the abduction by Al Faran in J & K as it caused a great deal of embarrassment to Pakistan, Farooq simply disowned Al Faran.

The ISI sent large quantities of arms, ammunition and IEDs for the terrorists operating in the Surankot and Thanamandi areas of Poonch and Rajouri districts, respectively.

HUA helps raising Taliban in Pakistan

In 1994, the ISI-HUA twin recruited and trained a large number of Afghans and Pushto-speaking Pakistanis from JUUI-run *madrassas* in Pakistani provinces of NWFP and Baluchistan. These were the building blocks of the new militant outfit – Taliban, who subsequently overthrew the Rabbani Government and took over Afghanistan.

In Pakistan, HUA had a sister terrorist outfit, Anjuman-e-Sipah-e-Sahiba (AESS), engaged in anti-Shia campaign in Pakistan. The AESS was formed by Maulana Haq Nawaz Jangi in the mid – 1980s. The HUA provided training facilities to the AESS cadres at Yawar. It was Masood Azhar who mativated the AESS cadres to join the Jihad in J & K. Some of them were inducted into J & K in 1993.

Recruitment, Training Camps, and Training Curriculum.

The HUJI recruited most of its cadres from Pakistan's Panjab and Baluchistan provinces while the HKUM did so from the Sindh and NWFP provinces. Deobandi *madrassas* were the hatcheries for the two outfits.

The HUA had a training camp at Yawar in the Khost province of Afghanistan. It was originally run by the HEI (Yunus Khalis group) but later handed over to the HKUM/HUA in 1986. It was a major camp, having under ground bunkers used as air raid shelters. The Yawar training centre had a capacity to train 1,500 – 6,000 recruits at a time. Nasir Ahmad Sodozey (Finance Chief of HUA, arrested on 25 April 1996) disclosed that the youth from Pakistan, Afghanistan, Kashmir, Fiji, South Africa, China, Bangladesh, Myanmar, Indonesia, Malayasia, France, the UK, the US (blacks only) received training at this camp.

On the other hand, the HUJI faction conducted its training at Liza camp near village Maidakak in Afghanistan. The training capacity was 500-600 recruits at a time. It was reportedly closed after the merger of HUJI and HKUM into HUA.

HKUM/HUJI cadres also received their training at some centres like the Salaman Farsi Camp (also called the 139 Khilid bin Walid camp) near Khost, Bari Camp and Markaz Abu Badar Camp. HUA cadres had special courses planned for them at the ISI-run camps in Kotli and Kahuta.

In the latter half of 1996, the Taliban handed over the Al Badar I and II training camps in Khost to the HUJI after wresting them from the JEI/HUM/JEI (Pakistan).

In building its cadres, the HUA based its curriculum on three cardinal principles : Haj Habi Tabligh (= religious indoctrination); Tarbiyat (= training); and Jihad (= crusade).

The HUA attached no condition to its arms training. On completion of training, the trainees could join any *tanzeem*. They were also free to choose the area/country of operations.

The training programmes were categorised as :

- *Tehsisiya.* A basic one month course which includes exposure to AK 47/56 rifles, anti-aircraft guns, mortars, LMGs, pistols, RCLs, and guerrilla warfare tactics.
- *Jundullah.* A specialised three month course which includes fabrication and detonation of IEDs, mines, WT communications, Sniper rifles, MMGs/HMGs, missiles, anti-tank guns, RLs, advanced guerrilla warfare, mountain warfare, map reading, secure communications.

Documents seized by the SF on 9 September 1993 from the HUA training camp in Kapran, Anantnag, confirm the activities of this 'Polytechnic School for Terrorists'.[5]

Operations in Jammu and Kashmir

Before their merger, HKUM and HUJI operated in Anantnag and Doda districts independently.

To loudly register their presence, HUJI resorted to 'spectacular acts' like the attack on police party on 26 June 1993, killing 10 policemen, and selective killing of 16 Hindus male bus passengers near Kishtwar on 14 August 1993.

After their merger, the area of operations was extended to include Badgam, Pulwama, Baramulla, Rajouri and Poonch districts. The HAU succeeded in attracting large number of 'free lance' militants by offering attractive pecuniary benefits. It also established a network of harbourers in infiltration areas.

The arrest of their leaders like Nasarullah Langariyal (19 November 1993), Sajjad Afghani (11 February 1994) and Masood Azhar (11 February 1994) forced the HUA to undertake abduction to secure their release. In May 1995, the HUA abducted foreign tourists, prominent politicians and intelligence officials in J & K – Qazi Zarar personally supervising these operations. He also deputed a group of Pakistani nationals led by a Turkish national, Hamid Turkey, to Pahalgam for the abduction of foreign tourists.

The spate of abductions commenced with Maj Bhupinder Singh's Border Road Organisation, from Anantnag on 17 January 1994. His body was recovered on 23 January 1994. It was followed by the abduction of two British nationals on 6 June

1994 from Pahalgam and three Britishers and one US national in Delhi, 29 September – 20 October 1994. The HUA also sprang attacks/ambushes against SF in the Pir Panjal ranges.

Al Faran Kidnappings : 4-9 July 1995

6 Foreign tourists were abducted from Pahalgam. While the Norwegian, Hans Christian Ostro, was killed, an American, John Childs, escaped. The abduction was claimed by Al Faran and Al Hadid.

The prolonged captivity caused international consternation, and that resulted in a rift in the Majlis-e-Amla. While Qazi Zarar was keen to take credit for the release of detained HUA leaders against freeing of the hostages, Hamid Turki, leader of the kidnappers, started acting independently. When reprimanded by the Qazi for killing the Norwegian, Turki ascribed it to Nimaz-e-Ishtekhara (= message from God after *namaaz*).

Negotiations for release of the hostages with the State Government were aborted by an uncompromising stance adopted by the HUA. On 26 October 1995, Qazi Zarar resigned as Chief Commander, coming under severe criticism from all members at the meeting of Majlis-e-Amla. Javed Ahmad replaced him. Nadeem Zuber was nominated Finance Chief in place of Sodozey.

The new leaders continued the hardline stance in negotiations. More significantly, they also continued to receive instructions from Masood Azhar, Sajjad Afghani, and Manzoor Longriyal who were in custody in Delhi's Tihar Jail.

The killing of Hamid Turki along with his four Pakistani associates — Abu Khalifa, Nabil Gaznair, Sikander Mohd, and Mohd Haroon – in an encounter with SF at Dabron, Anantnag on 4 December 1995 put paid to the negotiations.

On 10 December 1995, HUA leader Nadeem Zuber issued a statement for Al Faran, asserting that four hostages were rescued by Indian SF, which was denied by the latter. Sodozey disclosed that the hostages were executed on the orders of Javed Ahmad Butt.

The HUA attempted the ultimate ploy, so common in such situations – attempting to project Al Faran as the creation of

Indian Intelligence. Both HUA and Al Faran in separate statements claimed Hamid Turki as their leader. The HUA was to pay rich tributes to Javed Ahmad Butt, its Chief Commander and leading negotiator, after his death in an explosion.

The Charar-e-Sharif Siege

Operating jointly, the terrorists belonging to the HUA, mostly foreign mercenaries and HUM (mostly Pakistani, led by Maj Mast Gul), succeeded in occupying Charar town and the Charar-e-Sharif shrine of Sheikh Nooruddin Noorani in early 1995.

They were subjected to a prolonged sieze by the SF. Finding no safe way out from their predicament, they resorted to a clever ploy to save themselves : These foreign, mercenary desparados set the shrine and major part of the town ablaze and escaped the cordon set up by the SF due to the ensuing mayhem and confusion. They had also committed several atrocities on the civilians, including the summary execution of two local Muslims.

Attacking Hindus and their Religion

HUA was always keen to foment communal strife in Kashmir, and never missed an occasion and a chance to spread the poison of Hindu – Muslim hatred. In 1994, they blatantly declared a ban on the Hindu pilgrimage to the sacred Amarnath temple, an annual feature in Kashmir. They made four demands : (1) Withdrawal of SF from the Hazratbal shrine; (2) opening of all mosques in the Jammu region; (3) rebuilding of all damaged mosques in India, and (4) withdrawal of security arrangements for Amarnath pilgrims.

The HUA threatened attack on the much-venerated ancient Vaishno Devi temple, near Katra, Udhampur district. It planned assassination of senior mainstream politicians like Ghulam Rasool Kar, PCC-I President and Mohd Syed Akhoon, NC MLA. The threat was brought home with two bomb blasts in Jammu on 20 and 26 July 1995, killing 19 Hindus and injuring another[82].

India : Dar-ul-Harb (Territory of War) and Must be Conquered

The terror leaders have not forgotten that not long ago the Muslims ruled over India and they will not let the terrorist mercenaries under them to forget the 'fact' either. The HUA leaders in Pakistan conceived the idea of a strong network to pave the way for restoring 'Muslim rule' over India. Delving deep into the Islamic history, they drew parallels with the battle of Uhud Prophet Mohammad waged against the Qureshis and the Múfti-e-Azam movement launched by Mehmood-ul-Hassan, Deobandi, against the British. Then they would cite the Reshmi Rumal Movement started by a disciple of Mehmood-ul-Hassan, named Mulana Obaidullah Sindhi who wanted to further promote the goal his mentor had perceived. After all, Sindhi had carried the decree of *jihad* in a silk hankerchief (= reshmi rumal) to the *Amir* of Afghanistan, declaring India as Dar-ul-Harb (= territory of war) – its implication being too obvious to need any amplification.

To go a little under the surface, Mehmood-ul-Hassan and Maulan Ahmad Hasan had formed an underground against the British. Both were imprisoned in Matta by the British, and later released. They joined the Indian National Congress on their return in 1919. Although the Jamaat-ul-ulemah-e-Hind cast its lot with India on the issue of partition, its counterpart in Pakistan (JUUI-Pakistan) still maintains that India is. Dar-ul-Harb[6] since it is ruled by non-Muslims, and not the Muslims. JUUI (Pakistan) has maintained links with Dar-ul-Ulom, Deoband, and Jamaat-ul-Ulemah-e-Hind.

If we are to go by the reports, Deoband and its edelogical proclivities have spawned anti-India holy warriors. Here is one instance of Faiz-ul-Wahid, *Amir* Jammu. Arrested on 23 August 1995 by J & K Police, he revealed that he was motivated to join the HKUM and to undergo arms training in Pakistan by a visiting Turkish national, Hassan Hussian Yalmaz in 1990 at Dar-ul-Uloom, Deoband. Faiz was a student at Deoband and Yalmaz an Afghan Mujahideen who had fought in Afghanistan. There were three other motivators, all fellow Bangladeshi students.

Completing arms training at Abu Badar camp in Afghanistan, Faiz returned to Deoband and claimed to have motivated 22 students from different Indian states for arms training in Pakistan/Afghanistan. Their break-down : West Bengal-4, UP-2 Rajasthan-2, Bihar-2, Tamil Nadu-2,Assam-1, J & K-1, Myanmar-2, Bangladesh-3, total 19.

Now, there is evidence of this unfortunate trend of teachings at two famed seminaries. In October 1994, Khurshid Ahmad, a resident scholar of Nadwat-ul-Ulemah, Lucknow, was killed in an encounter with police at Saharanpur (UP) while they were conducting an operation to rescue four foreign tourists kidnapped in New Delhi in September 1994. Yet again on 21 November 1994, Mohd Abu Bakar, a former student of the same Nadwat-ul-Ulemah, Lucknow, was also arrested in connection with this abduction case. The Tableegi Markaz in Nizamuddin, New Delhi, was used by the HUA for abduction of these foreigners.

Abductions : A Tool of Terror and Extortions

Abduction is oft-used tool to spread terror and extort huge sums of money under pain of death. This has happened all the world over, and within India, the secessionist and terrorist outfits in the North-East have perfected the art since 1947. The Muslim terrorists, too have used this tool to terrorise and extort.

Ahmad Omar Syed Sheikh, a British national of Pakistani origin, was arrested in Ghaziabad, UP on 31 October 1994. An Afghan trained HUA militant, Sheikh had masterminded the abduction of four foreign tourists in Delhi in September 1994. He also confirmed details disclosed by Faiz-ul-Wahid and added three states – Gujarat, Manipur and Delhi – to make up the deficiency of 3 in the total of 22 students motivated by Faiz at Dar-ul-Uloom, Deoband to join terror trail, as mentioned above.

After building the network, the HUA leadership had planned to conduct high-profile operations in New Delhi which, as some one put it, is crawling with the VIPs, both indigenous and foreign. These operations could involve abduction of VIPs and foreign nationals – British, American etc. The aim was to secure the release of HUA leaders detained in Indian jails. A group of HUA activists headed by Ilyas (Afghani) purchased two houses – one each in Ghaziabad and Saharanpur – and rented at least seven apartments in Delhi.

The arrest of some local criminals in July 1997 revealed that the HUA functioned under different names at different places. These included Alma-e-Tanzeem Movement and Lashkar-e-Babri in Ferozabad, Mathura, Muzaffarabad, Meerut and Agra.

Inter-outfit Nexus, Linkages, and Coordination

The HUA is a member of UJC and APHC. It has been insisting and demanding its inclusion in the Executive Committee of the APHC.

It is a founder member of the Shora-e-Jihad (SEJ), a body of five Pro-Pakistan outfits – HUA, HUM, Al Jihad Force (AJF), TUM, and AUM – formed in August 1996 to coordinate terrorist activities in J & K.

The HUA preferred to function in isolations, in general, from the local secessionist groups as also the political parties simply because of its basic mistrust of Kashmiri political leaders. (Or, does it find the latter too convinced of Kashmir's fortunes with India being beneficial to all concerned?). It has, therefore, avoided linkages at the political level confined its cooperation to the local units of the AJF, HUM, MM, ABQ, JKMLA and LET.

In April 1995, the HUA and HUM formed the 'Crush India Forum' at Anantnag to plan joint action against the Indian SF. The Forum faced some post-natal problems when HUM militants shot dead a prominent local leader, Mufti Jamaluddin, at Kupwara.

The ISI brokered a functional understanding between the LET, HUA, MM, and HUM in November 1995 and assigned different operational areas to these groups in the Poonch-Rajouri border belt. The aim obviously was to avoid inter-group clashes and consequent mutual recriminations. The HUA was to conduct operations in Poonch-Rajouri area and the JKMLA would provide logistic support to it.

The HUA and LET developed a working arrangement in the districts of Kupwara, Badgam, and Doda. In June-July 1995, the HUA had similar coordination with the Al Barq (Farooq Qureshi faction) in Badgam. But in early 1996, Qureshi joind the HUA with a sizeable section of the Al Barq cadre in POK due to differences with AG Lone. Then, Qureshi, alongwith HUA cadres, joined the Tehrik-e-Jihad (TEJ).

Even as the top leaders were quitting or being marginalised in quick succession, the outfit faced the problems over the inflow of funds. It had to borrow ammunition from the LET. This inevitably led to the down grading of its standing and status to that of a junior partner vis-a-vis HuM in the hierarchy of SEJ. The arrests and killings of important office bearers of the SEJ in 1997 possibly weakened the already tenuous coordination among its constituents. This perhaps persuaded the ISI to float the TEJ.

Taking over as Supreme Commander of the HUA in the late 1995, Sikander revived its old links with the IUM leader Hilal Haider to reduce or eliminate the domination of the HUM, inspite of the opposition from the ex-HUJI cadres in the fold of the HUA.

The attitude of various Mujahideen groups who had fought shoulder-to-shoulder with the HUA in Afghanistan had a significant impact in instigating insurgency in J & K.

Sending Arms into J and K

The HUA had inherited a huge cache of arms and ammunition from its precursor outfits – HKUM and HUJI. In specific terms, the heritage included the bounty of weapons captured from the Soviet Army staging a retreat in a hurry from the Khost area. Equally important was the output from a large number of local weapons factories, contributed by local tribal Chieftains in the Darah area of Pakistan.

Transporting/shipping the weapons to the launching camps near the LOC was achieved with consummate ease with the help of the ISI and Pak Army. Thence on, smuggling the weaponry into J & K across the LOC was an easy step, with the help of the guides and infiltrating militant cadres, and the fact is well established.

The Dissonance Within

Factional divisions between the HKUM and HUJI continued even after the two were merged to create HUA. Qazi Saifullah Akhtar, former Chief of HUJI was at logger heads with Fazal-ul-Rehman Khalili, the former HKUM Chief. They just could not reconcile themselves to the merger of their outfits.

To assuage Akhtar's feelings, he was appointed *Nazim* of the HUA in Tajikistan, and later, *Sarparast-e-Ala*. But without showing any interest, he continued distancing himself from the HUA. In fact, he started operating independently from Lahore.

Regionalism played a part in fomenting factionalism and consequent dissensions within the HUA. Akhtar, ex-*Amir*, HUJI, hailed from Pakistan Panjab while Farooq Kashmiri, over-all executive in-charge of HUA's operations in J & K, hailed from Poonch (POK). Even if the HUJI faction functioned under the banner of the HUA, its cadres resolutely kept consolidaling their independent identities by reopening their offices/training centres. This trend of defiance again is confirmed by the HUJI faction staging the kidnappings of the four foreign (western) tourists in Delhi in September 1994 and in Pahalgam in July 1995, and as if to make a point, subsequently, ignoring the directives of HUA leaders in Pakistan for early release of the hostages.

New Leadership, Combined Operations and Setback

On 17 February 1996, Javed Ahmad and three other HUA leaders – Ali Mohd Wani, Abu Hamid and Abu Hamza – were killed in an IED explosion at Nai Basti, Anantnag. Parvez Ahmad Baba then took over as Acting Chief Commander. Indicative of the intra-party differences, he was replaced by Nazir Ahmad Sodozey in a meeting of the Majlis-e-Amla held in Srinagar on 20 March 1996. In another quick change, the Majlis-e-Amba finally nominated Abdul Fazal as C-in-C.

In May-June 1996, HUA leaders forged a joint strategy with other outfits like HUM, JUM, TUM, and LET to sabotage the 1996 pool process in J & K for electing members to Lok Sabha. They intensified anti-Hindu violence in Doda district, aimed at fomenting and enhancing communal clashes in the Hindu-dominated areas.

'Liberated' Zones in Kashmir

The HUA and other constituents of SEJ had planned to establish three liberated zones in the Kashmir Valley wherein men and materials could be concentrated for launching attacks elsewhere. The zones : (1) Upper reaches of Daksum-Kapran (Anantnag); (2) Shaji Marg (Badgam); and Bandipore (Baramulla). The plans did not bear fruit, particularly because several of its prominent leaders, including three successive C-in-C fell in encounters with the SF (1997). The HUA, consequently, was on the backfoot.

The situation forced the HUA to divide itself in two units : foreign mercenaries under the banner of HKUM and local militants under local commanders of HUJI. On ground, HKUM alone was functionally capable. Obviously, the ISI had more faith in the 'foreign' freedom fighters than the local enthusiasts.

Differences Accentuated; and it all end in Ban

The hiatus between the foreign and local militants was increasing instead of getting blurred. Local cadres of HUA from Kupwara district, especially Gujjars located along the LOC, forced Farooq Qureshi to quit the HUA after some of its foreign militants killed a local militant of the HUA in Handwara in January 1997. The incident snowwalled into a major native-vs-foreigner issue within the outfit.

The final division came in April/May 1997 when over 200 Kashmiri youth joined Farooq Qureshi in POK. They later joined TEJ when it was formed by the ISI. TEJ primarily had cadres from the Muslim Mujahideen, Ansur-ul-Islam and the departing group from HUA.

Serious differences emerged between Haji Arif Hussain, ex-Chief Commander of Jammu Province HKUM (killed, 5 May 1997) and Aamir, ex-Chief Commander of HUJI (J & K) over Fazal's appointment as HUA Chief. To make the matters worse, Fazal also developed differences with Nazir Mahmood Sodozey, former Finance Chief, HUA (arrested 25 April 1996), over the local vs foreign mercenary issue.

It seems there was no signs of narrowing down of these differences, rather they were getting aggravated. This is what exactly happened when Fazal issued a statement on 29 July 1996 adversely commenting on the formation of the SEJ and HUA's participation in it. When Haji Arif Hussain took exception to this stance of Fazal, he was promptly expelled from the outfit, and subsequently replaced by Abu Ghazi, a Pak national.

Consequent to the American banning the HUA on 8 October 1997, its name was changed to Harkat-ul-Mujahideen (HKUM). The rechristening was first reported by a Pakistani Urdu daily, Lahore's *Qaid* on 12 December 1997.

2

Terrorist Outfits in Jammu and Kashmir

(HM, IUM, JEM, JKDEP, JKIF, JKJEI AND JKLF)

Hizbul Mujahideen (HM)

Formation	**April 1989**
Strength	1400, Pak-trained
Arms held	Around 200 weapons including 1,550 AK rifles, 55 LMG/UMG/SMG, 162 MG., 1000 small arms, 90 RL, 2000 hand grenades, 500 mines, assorted ammunition and explosive, sniper rifles and 5.45 Krin Krinvok SMGs.
Headquarters	Srinagar
Objectives	Secession of J and K through armed struggle and merger with Pakistan.
Sponsors	Pakistan, POK, ISI, JEI (J & K) JEI (POK).

Leadership

- Ghulam Nabi Nowsheri, Patron (Pak-based).
- Muhammed Yusuf Shah aka Syed Salahudden, Supreme Commander (Prom J & K, now based in Pakistan).
- Tanvir Aziz, Deputy Supreme Commander (POK-based).
- Abdul Majid Dar, C-in-C, J and K.
- Abdul Rashid Hajam, Deputy C-in-C and Divisional Commander (Baramulla and Kupwara)

Areas of Operations

- Kashmir Valley and Muslim-dominated pockets of Jammu, Bandipur, Sopore and Anantnag.
- Rest of India in the pattern of a Pan-Islamic organisation.

Foreign Links

Pakistan, POK, ISI, UJC, Pakistan (In fact, Salahuddin is presently Chairman of the UJC), Kashmir Jihad Committee, KJC (Pakistan).

Links with Political Parties/Groups

ABDR, AUI, AUC, TEJ, AJC, ATGR, KEJ, JEI (Pak), JKLF, AJF, MM, ABQ, JK JEI, BTFK (Sikh militant outfit), LET, HUA, TUM, SEJ.

Finances

ISI.

Other Equipment

Advanced communication systems/networks.

Publications It owns news agency, *Kashmir press International*, Rawalpindi.

Major Acts of Terrorism

- 23 Mar 90. NC-F leaders hanged to death—Anwar Khan, at Tangmarg', Baramulla and Mir Mustafa, former MLA.
- 11 May 90. Killed Sheikh Mansoor, MLA, Shopian.
- 21 May 90. Killed Maulvi Farooq, Chairman, AAC, Srinagar.
- 23 May 90. Abdul Sattar Ranjoor, CPI leader, killed by Mohammad Shafi Shabnam, Pulwama.
- 28 Aug 90. DN Chowdhary, Manager, Cement Factory, Rajpora, Pulwama, kidnapped and then killed.
- 10 Sep 90. Killed Abdul Rashid Dar, former MLA, Anantnag.
- 11 Jan 91. Shabnam Lone, daughter of AG Lone, abducted and later released, Srinagar.
- 16 Jan. 91. Blasted home of Inayatullah Kakroo, Pro NC-F businessman, Baramula.
- Feb. 91. (1) Killed Ghulam Mohiuddin Dar, Assistant Registrar, Cooperatives, Panchgama, Pulwama. (2) Killed Nazir Ahmed Wani, Former MLA of NC and Ghulam Qadri, District Secretary, Janata Dal.

- 27 Jul. 91. Abducted from home in Srinagar Mohammad Ashraf, DFO, Forest Department, released next day.
- 19 may 92. Abducted Master Ahsan Dar (Chief Commander, MEI and former Chief, HUM), released after 2 days.
- 13 Nov. 92. Three ABQ cadres, including its Deputy Chief killed by HUM at Surmarg Chak (Kupwara) in inter-group clash.
- 10 Apr. 93. Set fire to *Sanatan Dharamshala* and *Akhara* building in *Lal Chowk*, Srinagar, 200 shops, 50 houses, 10 hotels and a cinema hall destroyed; three dead.
- 17 June 93. Shamina Parveen, casual artiste of Doordarshan, Srinagar, abducted from Walalkadal, Srinagar; later killed.
- 23 July 93. Killed Dr. Ghulam Watri Ahangar in Srinagar (SGR).
- 25 Aug 93. Shot dead Harbans Singh Tulla, a prominent Sikh leader; Baramulla.
- 25 Nov. 93. Station Engineer, Doordarshan Kendra, Srinagar killed and his home damaged in a rocket attack; SGR.
- 26 Nov. 93. Six members of a Muslim family, including two women, killed at Huhama, Badgam.
- 26 Nov. 93. 6 members of a Muslim family, including an infant and two women, killed, Rangwar (Kupwara).
- 18 Mar 94. Wali Mohammad Ittoo, former speaker of J & K Assembly, killed in Jammu City.
- 27 Mar 94. Abducted and killed at Badgam, son-in-law of Abdul Ghani Veeri, former minister.
- 9 Apr 94. Killed at Murran , Pulwama, Ghulam Qadir Mir, Former MLA.
- 19 Jun 94. Abducted and killed Dr. Qazi Nissar; Dayalgam (Anantnag).
- 15 Jul 94. Killed Abdul Majid Banday (ex-MLA, Cong-I; Shopian).

- 17 Jul 94. Rocket attack on home of Haji Mohammad Abdullah, father-in-law of Ghulam Nabi Azad.
- 4-5 Aug 94. Attack on the house of Maulvi Attaullah Suhrawardi (ex-Minister, NC-F) in Doda town.
- 20 Sep 94. Attacked house of NC-F activist Mohammad Ibrahim Ghanai in Pulwama; his wife shot dead and grandson abducted.
- 22 Sep 94. Abducted/killed a prominent Janata Dal leader, Ghulam Rasool Reshi; Dangerpora, Pulwama.
- 4 Feb 95. 75-year old Munawar Wani shot dead, in Dodipora, Kupwara.
- 20 Feb 95. Abducted and gangraped Shakeela; later burnt alive.
- 25 Feb 95. 3 villagers shot dead when resisting abduction; Pattan, Baramulla.
- 16 Mar 95. Feroz Ahmad Darwas shot dead; Sumbal, Baramullah.
- 23 Apr 95. Manzoor Ahmad Dar abducted and killed; village Tohab, Pulwama.
- 26 Apr 95. Abducted and shot dead at Tarapora, Kupwara a prominent religious leader Mufti Jamaluddin.
- 26 May 95. (1) Killed at Batmaloo, SGR, NC-F activist Abdul Jabbar. (2) Shot dead NC-F Block President, Ghulam Ahmad Kaura; Rainawari; SGR.
- 1 Jun 95. Abducted Mrs. Tahira and her brother in Lal Bazar, SGR; released Tahira after rape and brother after torture.
- 5 Jul 95. Killed 3 Muslims; Rainawari, SGR.
- 7 Jan 96. 2 Muslims (businessmen) shot dead, their houses burnt; Frestabal, Pulwama.
- 17 Jan 96. Retired school teacher Ghulam Mohammad Dar shot dead at Massamapora (Badgam).
- 3 Mar 96. Abducted and killed Abdul Qayoom; Babhor, Doda.

- 3 May 96. Killed 3 Hindu members of Village Defence Committee; Sarar, Udhampur.
- 15 May 96. Prominent College teacher, Prof. B.A. Mattoo; Awanta bhavan, SGR.
- 4 Jul 96. Sarpanch of Kate village (Doda) Suresh Kumar abducted and killed.
- 17 Aug 96. Two Hindus shot dead; Chamsar, Udhampur.
- Oct 96. Killed Ghulam Rasool Lattoo, a Shia, NC-F polling agent, SGR.
- 20 Apr 97. Killed Abdul Samad, Janata Dal candidate in Banihal Assembly Constituency.
- 16 May 97. Shot dead two Hindu employees, Sheep Husbandry Department; Maharo, Udhampur.
- 15 Jun 97. Killed three Hindu teachers, including Principal, Government High School, Gharat, Udhampur.
- 8 Aug 97. Killed Mushtaq Ahmad, Surilgala, Udhampur.
- 12 Aug 97. Kidnapped and killed Ahad Naik; Hargam, Doda.
- 18 Aug 97. Ghulam Hassan killed by slitting his throat; Prahander Neel, Doda.
- 12 Oct 97. Killed three members of a Muslim family; Ramnagar, Udhampur.
- 28 Jan 98. Killed Dr. Syed Haider in Kinhama hospital.
- 12 Apr 98. Abducted, killed Riaz Ahmad; Gandoh, Doda; and Ghulam Nafi Hergo, Accountant, Block Development office.
- 18 Apr 98. 26 Hindus killed in Prankote, Dhakikote, and Ladla villages; some burnt alive; three houses and a shop set afire.
- 31 May 98. (1) Shot dead Ghulam Mohd. Wani (Block President, NC-F) and Mohammad Yusuf Ganai; Ganderbal, SGR (2) Abducted, killed Mohammad Afzal Dar, teacher and brother-in-law Mohammad Maqbool Dar, former Union MOS Home Affairs; SGR.
- 4-5 Jun 98. Killed Mohammad Abdullah Mir, NC activist; Ratnipora.

- 10-11 June 98. Killed four Muslims, including a woman, by throat slitting; Surankot, Poonch.
- 19 Jun 98. 25 members of a Hindu marriage party killed; Chapnari, Doda.
- 27 Jun 98. Shot dead Mohammad Ibrahim, Surankot, Poonch.
- 27-28 Jul 98. 17 Hindus, including two women, shot dead at village Harna.
- 20 Sep 98. Shot dead Abdul Ahad Wani; Banihal, Doda.

Origins

Having failed to win over the JKLF to its side, the ISI continued working through JEI (Pakistan) which subsequently succeeded in persuading Mohammad Ashraf Dar, Maqbool Allai. And Abdullah Bangroo (then with the JKLF) to float an outfit called the Al Badar (ABDR). In April 1989, JKJEI leaders renamed it Hizbul Mujahideen (HM). Master Ahsan Dar was nominated its Supreme Commander.

On the contrary, Imran Rahi, then Deputy Chief HM, claimed in an interview to the News, Pakistan (10 May 1991) that Ansar-ul-Islam (AUI), formed in 1986 was rechristened HM in 1988.

It has stayed steadfast in its goal of merger of J & K with Pakistan. Ali Mohd Dar, Deputy Supreme Commander of HUM (since killed in August 1998) in POK for long, was inducted into the valley in December 1997 to reorganise and mobilise HM cadres for terrorist actions.

Recruitment and Training

HM used the existing JKJEI network and infrastructure to drawn the valley youth into its fold. In December 1989, its leaders launched a massive recruitment drive, with Pakistan providing specialised arms training, arms supply, and financial help. With JEI (POK) assuring 50,000 trained Islami Jamaat-e-Tulba (IJET) cadres to operate under the HM banner, it emerged as a potent force in the valley.

In 1991, major outfits like the pro-JK PL Tehrik-e Jihad Islami (TEJI) led by Abdul Majid Dar, HAJC, and Alla Tigers (ATGR) merged with HM.

In late 1990s, the HM cadres accounted for 65 per cent of the violence in the Valley, primarily directed against 'pro-India' political parties/activists, 'informers', minorities and SF. It often resorted to brutal methods of torture and killings – gouging the eyes chopping off the limbs etc.

Salahuddin Takes Over HM

Heartened by the enhanced armed strength of HM and continuing support of Pakistan/Pan-Islamic fundamentalist organisations, JKJEI found it worthwhile to consolidate its control over the HM. Mohammad Yusuf Shah aka Syed Salahuddin (former Amir-e-Zila, Srinagar, JKEI), took over as Supreme Commander on 11 November 1991, replacing Master Ahsan Dar. As a result, there was some internal dissonance. While Dar was accused of misappropriating funds to the tune of Rs. 2 crores, his supporters were systematically disarmed. Dar himself was kidnapped (Kokarnag, May 1992). Finally, he raised a new terrorist outfit, Muslim Mujahideen (MM) and went over to POK to seek support for it.

The Salahuddin take over led to the increased activities of the JKJEI cadres as the overground arm of the HM. This civilian (overground) face of the (underground) HM was assigned the responsibility of motivating people, raising funds, collecting intelligence, and providing logistic and propaganda support for the HM.

Pak-based HM leaders, including Salahuddin, were actively collaborating with the ISI operations launched from Sialkot. To enable the ISI to mount major acts of sabotage in the Jammu region, the HM provided to it its cadres hailing from Rajouri and Poonch areas. ISI and HM jointly set up explosions in MAM Stadium on Republic Day 1995.

During the Charar-e-Sharif episode (Mar-May 1995), HM adopted a rigid stance. Its cadres, led by a Pakistani national, Mast Gul, refused India's offer of safe passage out of the shrine. The successful 'escape' of Gul through the SF cordon was flaunted as an example of HM's capacity to defeat India. The destruction of the shrine on 1 May 1995 and the township later did cause public anger against the HM.

Enthusiastic welcome to Mast Gul in POK and Pakistan reflected poorly on its image as a fighter against terrorism, among the comity of nations. ISI officials castigated Salahuddin in a UJC (= MJC) meeting and instructed him to refrain from any such moves that show Pakistan in a bad light. Was this admonition sincerely meant or a mere public posturing!

Linkages with Other Outfits

HM established links with Sikh extremist groups in Panjab through Manjit Singh Pyasa of Baramulla in 1990. Next year, Rajinder Singh Bittoo of BTFK met with HM leaders for securing help in executing trans-border operations through the Kashmir Valley. The Sikh extremists were also provided access to HM's radio station, Sada-e-Hurryat Kashmir in Pakistan.

In 1991-92 JKJEI made fervent efforts to involve JKJEI (Hind) and SIMI in providing logistic support to Sikh and Kashmiri Muslim terrorists (India be warned that Sikh secessionism is not dead).

HM has achieved and then maintained its predominant status in the J & K 'movement' through Shora-e-Jihad (SEJ), the umbrella militant *super tanzeem*, formed in July 1996. This new outfit, though Chaired by S. Hamid of JKPL-S, is effectively controlled by HM through Firdous Kirmani, HM Coordinator (killed 7-8 Mar 96). Simultaneously, Muttehida (= United) Jihad Council (MJC or UJC), representative body of all terrorist outfits in Pakistan, (Revived Dec 95) is also dominated by HM, as its Chairman, Salahuddin, has been made the Chairman of UJC too.

To avoid inter-group rivalries, HM tried to mend fences with the MM by making latter's Chief Commander, Bilal Siddiqui, as *Naib Amir* of UJC.

HM has working relations with LET, HUA, and TUM and other constituents of SEJ. In 1996, prior to the Indian General Elections, the ISI had allotted areas of operation for various terrorist outfits with one objective – disrupt the polls.

Ali Mohd Dar, Deputy Chief Commander of HM, participated in the 9th Annual Conference of Markaz Dawa-ul-Irshad/LET held at Muridke, 1-3 November 1996. So he did the 10th, an annual event (5-7 November 1997).

Inter-Group Clashes

Since the early 1990s, in order to have exclusive control over the terrorist movement in J & K, the HM adopted outmaneuvering tactics against its rivals, particularly the JKLF – the only outfit fighting for an 'independent' Kashmir, unlike the rest who all want merger with Pakistan. HM killed prominent JKLF leaders like Mohd Maqbool Malik, Dr. Abdul Ahad Guru, and Prof Abdul Ahad Wani. To besmirch its reputation and point it as a compromised outfit, it launched propaganda blitz that JKLF had reached an understanding with New Delhi. Two events further lent evidence to the accusation: release of Abdul Hamid Sheikh from detention and contacts between JKLF leadership and Rajesh Pilot, Union MOS for Internal Security. Any such rumour – accusation or assertion – can be a death of kiss for a terrorist outfit. But the JKLF survived, even prospered inspite of the canard. After a brief bull, clashes between the two outfits resumed. To wit, the JKLF resorted to armed moves to thwart attempts by HM to occupy/take over the Hazratbal Shrine, Srinagar.

Most prominent political leaders of all non-JKJEI persuation have been on the HM hit list. It made an abortive bid to kidnap Yasin Malik, JKLF leader on 2 June 1994. KJHC played the truce maker.

The killing of Dr. Qazi Nissar, a religious leader of Anantnag on 20 June 1994 brought inter group violence once again into sharp focus. Large processions were taken out by the locals where anti – JKJEI/HUM, anti Pakistani and pro – India slogans mere vociferously raised. The IUM openly charged HUM with the assassination, and released videos containing the disclosures of two eye-witnesses.

HM cadres killed many political workers during 1994-95. It constituted a separate wing, *Minority United Forum*, to target political leaders and activists. It had also issued death warrants against leaders like Chief Minister Farooq Abdullah and PCC-I President Ghulam Rasool Kar.

HM supported the ban imposed by HUA on the annual Amar Nath Yatra of Hindus, and took active part in enforcing it. It also demanded removal of the Hazratbal 'siege' by the security forces. When the SF dismantled their bunkers, HM tried to seize control of the shrine – propagating its pro-Pakistani ideology from the pulpit. Later JKLF leader Yasin Malik succeeded in displacing HM from the shrine.

There was certain demoralisation among its rank in late 1994 when the SF operations led to the arrest/killing of some important JKJEI/HM leaders. Salahuddin fled to POK to save his own life (November 1994), and proposed that all ranking leaders flock to POK for the same reason. Consequently, Ghulam Hassan (JKJEI) returned to the valley in June 1995 to lead the HM in the absence of Salahuddin and operated under the same name – Salahuddin.

There was cause for further demoralisation among the HM cadres: beside the SF operations, there was large public response to the appeals of Shabir Shah (then JKPL leader); then there was Pak Failure to mobilise sufficient international support on Kashmir at the UN General Assembly meeting in November 1994. But there was no let up in the pressure on HM. Its cadres became a target of attack from other groups. Then, the counter-insurgency groups like those of Kuka Parey (IUM) in Bandipur – Sonawari area, Shirir Khan (MM) in the Pattan area, and Nawaz Azad (MM) in Anantnag town challenged JK JEI/HM activists, and forced a retreat. Under the situation, it was no surprise when there was a heavy surrender of JKJEI/HM cadres to the SF in 1995.

Intra-outfit Dissonance

Mid – 1990s onwards, there were rumblings within the outfit – a very common feature in most of the terrorist and insurgent organisations: the leaders wallowing in 5-star luxury in safe havens, far removed from the scene of action – POK in this case. The lower rung cadres mere leading a life of privation, and always hunted by the SF. Some even thought of themselves as the cannon fodder! HUM was no different as far as this 'infection' was concerned.

The ongoing conflict between the hard-liners and the moderates in the JKJEI got aggravated with the moderate GM Bhat taking over as *Amir*. His policy of distancing the JKJEI from the 'culture of gun', and also in the process, disowning the HM, was endorsed by Salahuddin. But Abdul Majid Dar, a

Jamati and Deputy Supreme Commander, broke away with 4 – 500 supporters.

Situation End 1990s

The killing of Ali Mohd Dar in August 1998 was a big below to HM. It had earlier made a loud announcement about its arrival on the scene through Prankote massacre, April 1998 and Chapnari killings, June 1998 – felling 26 and 25 Hindus respectively – in collaboration with the LET.

Its strength plummeted to 1,400 in 1998 from 3,000 in 1996.

HM has started operating under different banners/names in different areas after 1998; *e.g.*, Far zandan-e-Millat, Mujahideen-e-Tulba, Pir Panjal Regiment.

As its finances were in precarious position, its leaders undertook a fund-raising 'pilgrimage' to ISI, Muzaffarabad. It also wanted a clarification on the emergence of TEJ as a rival which threatened its predominance in the field. There was surprise and shock for them from a different direction. The leaders felt let down when the ISI hinted a preference to Harkat-ul-Ansar (HUA) in matters financial and material.

Harkat ul-Mujahideen (HUM)

Like many other Islamist terror organisations, the Harkat ul-Mujadeen was a child of the US-funded jihad against the "Soviet aggression in Afghanistan." It was thus a Pakistan – based outfit which subsequently spread its wings into the "Jammu and Kashmir Jihad."

History of Harkat, Briefly

By 1991, the HUM had substantial presence in both Afghanistan and Jammu and Kashmir.

In Jun 1993, a Committee of clerics arranged for the Harkat to merge itself into a new organisation, the Harkat ul-Ansar (HUA). Maulana Azhar Masood Alvi, the terrorist who was to be released years later in return for the passengers/hostages on board Indian Airlines flight 814 in the infamous 1999 swap, was one of the key figures in this new group, HUA.

The Harkat ul-Ansar gained much international attention when it kidnapped European and US hostages in 1994 and 1995 in murderous efforts to secure the release of Azhar Masood.

Declared Terrorist Organisation by US : 1997

In 1997, the US declared HUA a terrorist organisation. To counter the US ban, the outfit fell back to its initial designation, and continued functioning as the HUM. A year later (in 1998), the US fired missiles at two of the HUM-run camps in Afghanistan.

Support to Taliban

Matters came to a head in 2001, when the Harkat extended support to the Taliban against the US. While Pakistan responded by proscribing the group, it continued to operate, adopting still another name that belonged to a new charitable organisation, the Al-Asar Trust. One faction, the Harkat ul-Majahideen Alami, carried out a series of strikes against French and US interests, as well as an attempt on the life of Gen Musharraf.

Active in India, Too

Besides Afghanistan and then Pakistan, Harkat operatives have also been increasingly active in India. In Mar 2007, police in Ahmedabad shot dead Pakistani nationals Imran Shahzad Bhatti and Mohd Iqbal, who are alleged to have been preparing to execute major strikes in western India. Days earlier, police in Lucknow killed Mohd Salim bin-Aziz, a Harkat terrorist who had served with the outfit in southern Kashmir.

Ikhwan-ul-Musalmeen (IUM)

Formation 1989

Strength 225 (including Pakistani elements)

Arms and Equipment Around 400 weapons including 250 AK rifles, 10 LMGs/UMGs, 150 small arms, 20 RL, 50 hand grenades, and quantities of assorted ammunition explosives; advanced communication systems.

Headquarters Srinagar

Objectives Liberation of Kashmir through armed struggle; self determination to decide Kashmir's future.

Sponsors Pakistan, POK, ISI.

Organisational Structure

- Apex : *Amir, Naib Amir*, Chief Commander, Deputy Chief Commander.
- Districts : District Commander, Deputy District Commander.
- Field formations include Sector Commands and Regiments.
- Seven Regiments : Khalid, Suleman, Umar, Mehrajuddin, Usman, Hyder, Bashir in Srinagar; Israel regiment exclusively entrusted with executing abductions.
- Women's Wing : Saidat-ul-Musalmeen

Leadership

- Bilal Ahmad Beg, Chief Commander.
- Niaz Ahmad Sofi, Deputy Chief Commander.
- Abdul Majid Lala, Representative in Pakistan.
- Kuka Parrey, leader.

Areas of Operation

J & K, POK, Delhi, Mumbai, Western UP.

Kathmandu, Kolkata, Bhagalpur.

Hyderabad (India).

Links with Political Parties/Groups

KLC, Saidat-ul-Musalmeen (its Women's Wing) and JKLF.

Foreign Links

- IUM (Egypt), Hashim Qureshi (JKLF leader operating from Netherlands); Haji Abdul Hamid (in the UK); Fundamentalist groups in Sudan.
- Has Units in POK, networks in Sri Lanka, Nepal, Bangladesh.

Finances

Pakistan, ISI, Local Collections.

Publications

Nida-e-Mashriq

Major Acts of Terrorism

- 11 Dec 89. One killed, seven injured in blast in Air Cargo Complex, Srinagar.
- 6 – 10 Apr 90. Kidnapped and killed Mushir-ul-Haq, Vice Chancellor, Kashmir University; HL Khera, General Manager, HMT factory; and Abdul Ghani, Personal Assistant to the VC; Srinagar.
- 3 Jun 90. Killed Dr. Gulshan Watali, brother of AM Watali, ex-DIG, J & K Police; Srinagar.
- 28 Jun 90. Killed two women; Darsu, Pulwama.
- 29 Jun 90. Killed Abdul Aziz, Additional DC, Srinagar.
- 6 – 8 Jul 90. Kidnapped Farooq Ahmad, son of the DC, Srinagar.
- 20 Oct 90. Blast in house of Mohd Yasin Shah, ex-MLA, NC (Farooq); Srinagar.
- 8 Dec 90. Looted Rs. 3.2 lakh from J & K Bank, Chini Chowk, Anantnag.
- 23 Feb 91. Six killed, 47 injured in blast in Jamia Mosque, Jammu.
- 27 Feb 91. Kidnapped Nahida Imtiaz, daughter, Saifuddin Soz, MP, NC (Farooq); released 8 Mar 91 in exchange for Mushtaq Ahmad Khan.
- 28 Jun 91. Kidnapped K. Doraiswamy, Executive Director, IOC; released 20 Aug 91, in exchange for nine militants.
- 13 Aug 91. Kidnapped Dr. S.L. Khosla, Manager, New India Assurance Company; released 15 Nov 91 in exchange for Nissar Ahmad Jogi.
- 6 Feb 92. Abducted Mohan Lal Peshin, Programme officer, Integrated Child Development Scheme.
- 16 Jun 92. Shot dead in house Nazir Ahmad Siddiqui, prominent businessman, and his wife; Qamar Wari, SGR.
- 2 Mar 93. Killed Habibullah Mircha, Naib Tehsildar, Handwara, Kupwara, and Ghulam Nabi Baba, retired Assistant Commissioner; both relatives of Ghulam Rasool Kar, President, J & K Congress-I; Sopore.

Origins

Bilal Ahmad Beg floated J & K Students Liberation Fund (JKSLF) in 1989 following differences with Yasin Malik, then C-in-C, JKLF. The JKSLF operated independently even as describing itself as a front of the JKLF (POK). It had shot into prominence through 'spectacular' acts like the kidnapping and killing Mushir-ul-Haq, VC, Kashmir University, and HL Khera, GM, HMT factory in April 1990.

To begin with, it had three main groups, each under Bilal Beg, Yasin Butt (later arrested), and Javed Ahmad Shala. Its influence was essentially confined to SGR city and Baramulla district.

Bilal Begwent to Pakistan in August 1990 via Nepal to seek enhanced financial help. He was persuaded to give up his pro-independence stance. At the same time differences between Beg and Amanullah Khan, Chairman, JKLF, widened, with each openly trading charges against other. This acrimony enabled JKSLF leaders, Beg and Butt, to convince the ISI to recognise their outfit's separate identity in J & K. The JKSLF was renamed Ikhwan-ul-Musalmeen (IUM) in April 1991.

The ISI started supporting the JKSLF to wean it away from the JKLF to weaken the latter's support base because it refused to give up its demand for independent Kashmir – an anathema to Pakistan. The aim behind their exertions was to deny publicity mileage to the JKLF which was trying to appropriate all the credit for the acts of the JKSLF.

Mid-1991, the ISI pressed Beg to become a member of the HUM-dominated TEHK but he withstood this all by threatening to expose ISI activities through the media, and to recall all IUM militants. Later, of course, Prof. GM Shah and Sheikh Rashid, Pak Industries Minister, prevailed upon the ISI to restore supplies to the IUM.

Kashmir Liberation Council (KLC) is Created

At a meeting in Muzaffarabad in January 1992, Bilal Beg. Dr. Ghulam Qadir Wani, patron, Islamic (or International?) Students League, ISL, and Mohd Yasin Butt, then Military Adviser, IUM decided to launch the Kashmir Liberation Council (KLC) as a conglomerate entity of like-minded organisations to fight for the 'rights' of the Kashmiris and to work for their future without involving India or Pakistan. The KLC was meant to be a 'secular' entity with the ISL as its students' wing. The real intention behind the formation of the KLC was to extend the influence of the IUM, through it (KLC) at the cost of JKLF which had been weakened following the arrest of its top leaders.

The KLC became operational on 20 May 1992 with Maulvi Abbas Ansari as its Chairman. To establish and flaunt its secular credentials, the IUM unconditionally released Mohan Lal Peshin, a Hindu State government official, from captivity. And for the very same reason, it also inducted Hriday Nath Wanchoo, a Hindu Human Rights activist and a noted trade union leader, as a member of its central committee. Wanchoo, however, was killed by the terrorists in December 1992.

Planning Big and Targeting VIPs

Planning was immediate and meticulous Bilal Beg and Yasin Butt despatched a tested IUM Cadre, Ishtiaque Hussain Mir, to Delhi to undertake the study and survey of the residence of ex-Governor J & K, Jagmohan, and examine its security arrangements. The *tanzeem* also secured photographs of Doordarshan Kendra (= National TV Centre) and a Power Plant as a part of target intelligence.

In compliance of the instructions from the ISI, the IUM created in April 1992 a cell in Delhi to target the VIPs and vital installations. The IUM also cultivated Muslims of Western up to foment communal strife.

To execute their planned violent acts, the IUM despatched a squad under Tanveer Ahmed Butt to Delhi on 13 April 1992. It was captured consequent to a raid on their hideout on 28 April 1992 and a large quantity of high explosives and detonators was recovered from it.

It was also discovered later that the IUM had also supplied requisite small arms, explosives, and funds to one Abdul Rauf of Meerut, a Pakistani-trained militant for violent operations in the neighbourhood–a highly, communally sensitive/valnerable area.

Mid – 1992, the IUM was again on the war path, issuing threats to eliminate the political leaders and their relatives, who were advocating the reinitiation of the political processes in the State. That they meant the threat seriously stood proved when they kidnapped and killed two close relatives of Ghulam Rasool Kar, the State Congress-I Chief as also shot a relative of Ghulam Nabi Azad, then a Union Minister, in March 1993.

On 1 May 1993, Mushtaq Ahmad, Intelligence Chief of IUM, planted a car bomb on the convoy route of the State Governor, Lt Gen (Retd) KV Krishna Rao. He was saved as the device exploded prematurely – killing Isreal Khan, instead.

Networking and Inter-Outfit Clashes

Under orders from the ISI, Bilal Beg travelled to Sri Lanka in early 1993, as also to Nepal and Bangladesh to establish a network linking it to various extremist groups in India, whose representatives were located in these countries, or operating from there. The functioning and networking of these organisations was proved by arrest of four militants with links to the IUM in Hyderabad and Kolkata in October 1993.

The three top IUM leaders – Bilal Beg, Sajjad Ahmad Kannu, and Rafiq Ahmad Wani – have used Islamabad as their Headquarters and Kathmandu as the operational base for India.

When Dr. Qazi Nisar was killed in Anantnag on 20 June 1994 by HUM terrorists, the IUM took the lead in exposing the JKJEI and HUM. It had videotaped the disclosures of two eye witnesses to the killing and released its clips to the media. The exposure aggavated the recrimination between the HUM and IUM militants. During a function at Jamia Mosque, Anantnag on 6 June 1995 to Commemorate the first death anniversary of Dr. Nissar, IUM activists openly criticised the APHC's failure to identify Nissar's assassin as promised. It also accused Hurriyat leaders of being scared of JKJEI/HUM cadres.

The success of the IUM cadres against the HUM resulted in the increased influence of Kuka Parrey in other areas, especially in the Anantnag district where he joined hands with the MM and inflicted heavy losses on the JKJEI/HUM. The conspicuous success and trend set by Kuka Parrey encouraged other militant groups, which had been subjected to harassment by the HUM, to undertake similarly aggressive action against the JKJEI/HUM.

Current Standing

Post – 1992, majority of top leaders of the IUM were arrested/killed, and consequently its activities were severely curtailed.

Despite the depleted and demoralised cadre, the IUM was able to take on the JKJEI/HUM in 1995 clashes in the Bandipore and Sonawari – Sumbal areas of Baramulla district. In the end, it succeed in forcing a majority of its opponents out of these areas.

Jaish-e-Mohammad (JEM)/Tehrik-al-Furqan (TAF)/Al Dawa

Formed	February 2000, Karachi
Strength	600-700
Arms held	LMGs, HMGs, Assault Rifles, Mortars, IEDs, Rocket Grenades
Headquarters	Islamabad; later moved to Bahawalpur
Objectives	Secession of J & K and merger with Pakistan
Sponsors	Pakistan, POK, ISI

Leadership

- Maulana Masood Azhar, Founder and *Amir*.
- Maulana Mohd Yousuf Ludhianvi, Co-Founder (Spiritual guide to two important Deobandi leaders : Maulana Fazl-ur-Rahman of the Jamaat-i-Ulema-i-Islam (JUI), and Maulana Azam Tariq of Sipah-e-Sahiba).
- Mufti Nizamuddin Shamzai, Co-Founder (Chairman, Majlis-i-Tawan Islami, Pakistan).
- Maulana Abdul Jabbar, *Nazim*, Military Affairs.
- Maulana Sajjad Usman, Finance Chief.
- Maulana Qari Mansoor Ahmad, Nazim, Propaganda.
- Hafiz Nisar Ahmad, Head, Publications.
- Omar Sheikh, Arms Instructor.
- Mushtaq Zargar, Head, Recruitments.
- Yousuf, Officer-in-Charge, Balakot Training Camp.

- Shamsuddin Haider, Spokesperson.
- Rana Farooq, Spokesperson, Muzaffarabad (POK).
- Maulana Mufti Mohd Asghar, Launching Commander.
- Mufti Mohd Uwais Kashmiri, Head, POK Affairs.
- Qari Zarar, Head, Punjab Affairs.
- Maulana Ghulam Murtaza, Officer-in-Charge, Punjab (Pakistan).
- Qari Mohd Sadiq, Head, Finance (Punjab).
- Maulana Abdullah Shah Mazhar, Chief Organiser, Karachi.
- Maulana Umar Hayat, Organiser, Rawalpindi.
- Sajjad Tehadi, Chief Commander, J & K.
- Abu Hijrat, Commander, J & K.
- Qari Azhar Mahmood, Launching Commander.
- Abdul Rehman Sindhi, Commander.
- Maulana Sanaullah Rind, Commander.
- Maulana Mazhar Shah, Leader.
- Dr. Abdul Razzaq, Leader.
- Mufti Jamil Khan, Leader.

Areas of Operations

J & K, Muzaffarabad, Balakot (POK), Pakistan (Punjab, Bahawalpur, Rawalpindi, Karachi, Islamabad.

Links with Political Parties/Groups

Pakistan, POK, ISI, JUI, HUJI, HUM, HUA, Sipah-e-Sahaba, Majlis-e-Tawan-Islami, Dar-ul-Ifta-e-wal-Irshad.

Sheikh-ul-Hadith, Dar-ul-Haqqania, Al Qaida, Taliban.

Foreign Links

Pakistan, ISI, POK, Al Qaida.

Finances

Pakistan, POK, ISI, Al Qaida.

Major Acts of Terrorium

- 19 Apr 2000 : First human bomb attack outside Indian Army's 15 Corps Headquarters, Srinagar.
- 1 Oct 2001. 39 killed when four terrorists attacked J & K Legislative Assembly Complex in Srinagar.
- 13 Dec 2001. Indian Parliament attacked by a group of five JEM terrorists. Eight Parliament staff members killed, New Delhi. All five terrorists also killed.
- 21 Dec 2001. Three women killed, one injured in Poshkreeri, Anantnag district.
- 12 Feb 2002. Omar Sheikh arrested in Lahore in connection with Daniel Pearle's abduction and murder; held guilty by Pak courts.

Origins

The Jash-e-Mohammad (= Army of the Prophet) (JEM) was formed by Maulana Masood Azhar on 4 February 2002 at a congregation in Binori Mosque, Karachi. He had been arrested on and been in the Indian jails since 10 February 1994. He was released on the last day of the 1999 in Kabul alongwith two other jailed terrorists in exchange of the hijacked passengers of the Indian Airlines Flight IC – 814. Three of these detained terrorists had the "honour" of being escorted to Kabul from Delhi airport by India's then External Affiars Minister Jaswant Singh in his plane. To repeat, the three were freed in Taliban's Afghanistan.

The goal of JEM was initially limited to "give an effective response" to the Indian SF in J and K. The JEM had the blassings of the chiefs of three major religious schools (= seminaries) in Pakistan :

- Mufti Nizamuddin Shamzai, Majlis-d-Tawan Islami.
- Maulana Mufti Rashid Ahmad, Dar-ul-Ifta-e-wal Irshad.
- Maulana Sher Ali, Sheikh-ul-Hadith Dar-ul-Haqqania.

Masood Azhar had his education in the Jamia Islamia attached to the Binori Mosque, Karachi, and came under the influence of HKUM leaders. The HKUM is one of the constituents of the Army of Islam and had fought alongwith

Osama bin Laden's Al Quaida against US troops in Somalia and Afghanistan.

After passing his *almia* (examination) in 1989 at the age of 21, he was assigned the task of bringing out a magazine, *Sada-i-Mujahid*, that covered the activities of the HKUM. When that outfit extended its activities to J & K, Azhar was entrusted the responsibility of mobilising Kashmiri youth to swell its ranks.

Azhar works for the HUJI, HKUM and HUA

On 29 January 1994, Azhar arrived Delhi via Dhaka on a Portuguese passport on his way to Srinagar. His passport identified him as Vali Adam Issa. His mission in Kashmir was to work for the merger of HUM and HKUM to create HUA.

By 1996, the HUA had emerged as a ruthless, dreaded terrorist outfit in J & K, next only to the LET. The HUA was responsible for murder of several UKUM leaders.

Splits Follow the Creation of JEM

Within a month of his release at Kabul, Azhar started appearing at the Binorimosque, Karachi, with Maulana Mohd.Yousuf Ludhianvi and Mufti Shamzia. On 4 February 2000, the three announced the formation of the JEM.

The cadres for the JEM had mainly been lured from the ranks of the HKUM, which caused bitterness between the two outfits, and worse for the HKUM, a split in it. Consequently, there were frequent violent clashes between the two over resource sharing. For a solution to the mutual recriminations, the two *tanzeems* submitted their respective cases to a *hakam* for arbitration. The 3-member arbitration panel of religious experts comprised :

- Mufti Rasheed Ahmad of the Zarb-e-Momin Jihadi Militia.
- Mufti Nizamuddin Shamzai of Binori.
- Dr. Sher Ali Shah.

The final decision was that the offices of HKUM in Punjab (Pakistan) captured by the JEM would be restored to the former, which in turn, would pay Rs. 40 lakh as its share of the division of assets. Despite the *hukam*, the two outfits have continued to clash.

Recruiting Drives; Introducing Suicide Bombers

JEM launched vigorous recruiting drives, organising a number of large rallies all over Pakistan in 2000. It received encouragement and liberal help from Lt Gen Mohd Aziz of the ISI. Consequently, it opened 30 offices in different villages of Punjab (Pakistan) and 90 units in Karachi itself.

JEM established a major training camp at Balakot in the NWFP, fit enough to train the cadres in batches of 800-1,000 at a time. Interestingly, overall command of this important camp was vested in Yousuf, a Christian convert from Sindh who was married to Azhar's sister. The talk about the zeal of a new convert!

JEM conducted its initial operations in J & K from its office in Islamabad. The HKUM weekly, Zarb-e-Momin, published a report saying that Masood Azhar has inaugurated another office at Vihari in Southern Punjab on 5 March 2000.

By July 2001, it had graduated to subject Chief Minister Farooq Abdulla to a vicious rocket attack. Luckily, he escaped uninjured. In December 2001, its terrorists launched two grenades attacks : at a bus stop at Kupwara, injuring 24 persons; and in a market place in Chadousa, injuring 16. More successful for them, in diabolical terms, was the operation in which they planted a bomb each in Qamarwari and Srinagar, which killed a total of 21 persons.

JEM is the first terrorist outfit that introduced *fidayeens* (= suicide bombers) in J & K as a part of its terror tool kit. On 1 October 2001, JEM terrorist terrorists attacked the J & K Legislative Assembly, killing 39 persons. Consequent to this act of terrorism, the US Administration initiated moves to ban the JEM and freeze its assets. But before the slow-moving wheels of the US democracy could get the ban approved from its legislature, JEM was able to mount most serious attack on Indian democracy's cradle – its Parliament – on 13 December 2001, which brought India and Pakistan to the brink, with their militaries glowering at each other in eye ball-to-eye ball confrontation across the common border, for months on end! The US ban materialised only after this sinister attack. Incidentally the JEM mounted this attack a mere 18 days short of the second anniversary of release of its founder by the Indian External Affairs Minister, Jaswant Singh.

Expecting a Ban and Inventing a New Name : JEM

The US had initiated a move to ban the JEM after it mounted an attack on the J & K Legislative Assembly on 1 October 2001. In an attempt to beat the actual ban, JEM renamed itself as Tehrik-al-Furqan (TAF) on 8 October 2001, in less than a week of US announcement about banning it. Some fast footwork, this! Incidentally, the rechristening came a day after Gen Mohd Aziz took over as Chairman, Joint Chiefs of Stall Committee on 7 October 2001. The TAF had Mufti Nizamuddin Shamzai as the Patron-in-Chief and Maulana Mazhar Shah as the Convender.

Mufti Shamzai is the cleric who had issued a *fatwa* of *jihad* against India on 1 July 1999 against the back-drop of the Kargil crisis in response to a request from the HKUM. The *fatwa* had directed all *Madrassas* in Pakistan to suspend teaching and despatch all students to participate in the *jihad*. He was also the one who had praised two former Chief of the ISI –Lt Gen Hamid Gul and Lt Gen Javed Nasir – as Allah's gift to the nation.

Nothing has changed for the JEM but for its name, despite the US ban on it. Its terrorist activities were hardly affected under the ban. Yes, may be to avoid causing any embarrassment to Pakistan President, its office was shifted to Bahawalpur from Islamabad.

Another source says its new name is Jamaat-ul-Furqan (JUF). The JEM has opened at least four major military training camps, located in Balakot, Muzzaffarabad, Hajeera and Manshera.[7]

J and K Democratic Freedom Party (JKDFP)

Formation	25 May 1998
Headquarters	Srinagar
Objectives	Solution of J & K Problem through peaceful means.

Leadership

- Shabir Ahmad Shah, President.
- Maulana Mohd Tariq, Working President.
- Mehmood Ahmad Sagar, Senior Vice President.
- Syed Salim Gillani, Vice President.
- Mohd Ibrahim Dar, Vice President.
- Hakim Abdul Rashid, Secretary (Political Affairs).
- Qazi Manzoor Ahmad, Secretary (Foreign Affairs).
- Rashid Mahmood, Secretary (Publicity).
- Sharif-ul-din Bani, Secretary (Human Rights)
- Manzoor Ahmad Ganai, Secretary.
- Yunus Tak, Secretary.

Areas of Operation : J & K

Links with Political Parties/Groups.

JKPL and APHC (Subsequently, it broke away from the conglomerate, which itself stands split into two parallel organisations, presently. Shabir Shah's PDF is working in lonely splendour in the Kashmir scenario of date. Only other organisation in the similar situation of functioning in lofty isolation is Yasin Malik's JKLF).

Origins

In 1995-96, J & K People's League (JKPL) saw a steady erosion of its support base, mainly because of internal squabbling. Expectedly, it split in February 1998 into two factions :

JKPL (Nayeem) and JKPL (Hamid)

About the same period, Shabir Shah had differences with the APHC leadership. To firm his hold on the JKPL, Shah established contacts with its old activists like Fazal-ul-Haq Qureshi who had left the Party either to set up their own outfits or had been rendered ineffective. He launched a vigorous membership drive to build his own loyal cadre.

In December 1996 Shah had proposed ammendments/ changes into the JKPL Constitution : (1) to enshrine the right to self determination and delete all references to 'establishment of Islamic rule' and 'accession to Pakistan'; (2) proposed a new name of the Party – All J & K People's League (AJKPL); (3) suggested a new flag with the contours of the undivided J & K State against a red, white, and green background to replace the Crescent and Star; (4) AJKPL to distance itself from Pakistan and militancy, and to have a secular outlook.

Given the Muslim majority he was addressing his secular vision to, it was a tall order. And expectedly, this did not fly. Three years later, in May 1998, Shabir Shah formed his own J & K Democratic Freedom Party (JKDFP), near identical twin to his AJKPL vision.

Shah created his Party despite tremendous pressure from Pakistan exerted through his POK-based lieutenant, Mahmood Sagar. Given all this, Sagar remained loyal to his beliefs as also to Shah who anointed him as Senior Vice President in the Party's hierarchy.

JKDFP's Goals

As its President, Shah declared the goals described below :

- The entire State of J & K, which includes all territories that constituted the State till 13 August 1947, is disputed and its political future is yet to be decided by its people.
- The disputed state is neither a border nor a territorial dispute between India and Pakistan, and no other country has the right to impose a solution on its people.
- For a permanent, peaceful and lasting solution of the J & K problem, it is essential that the people of the State be provided an atmosphere free from pressures, both external or internal. Both India and Pakistan are parties to the dispute.
- A meaningful dialogue can evolve a permanent, just and lasting resolution of the Kashmir problem in consonance with the aspirations of the people of J & K (pre-1947 configuration).

JKDFP's definition of 'J & K' with pre-1947 borders overlaps a similar objective in some other organisations like JEI and JKLF.

Shabir Shah opened offices throughout J & K to widen his party's support base.

Current Status

The JKDFP has not made any significant impact so far on the J & K politics – especially if its J & K means the pre-1947 Princely State. The road to this goal is long, unchartered and treacherous.

It had faced criticism because of its willingness to start a dialogue with India prior to considering any participation in the Assembly polls of September 2002. Pro-Pakistani elements and APHC leaders had promptly and expectedly painted Shabir and his Party as identifying themselves too closely with New Delhi line.

The JKDFP appeared, at one time, to have the potential of emerging as the rallying force for many in J & K who have suffered from continuous terrorism let loose by the Jihadi *jamaats* trained and instigated by Pakistan and its ISI, and have serious reservations over the APHC's hard liners, and worst of all, have developed certain cynicism about almost all actors relevant to the scene – terrorist outfits, agencies, and governments.

This may be a rather stark picture of the latter half of the 1990s. But certain new realities have entered the field viz Indo-Pak Peace Parleys commencing in January 2004, and Prime Minister Manmohan Singh's already having had two rounds of talks with most separatist elements. There is certain hope is the air but Pakistan's inability or unwillingness to keep its promise of not permitting any anti-India terrorist network on its soil seem to be coming in the way. In this situation, JKDFP is like any other player in the field densely populated by all kinds of separatist forces—hard liners, moderates, and opportunists—and Pro-India political parties continuously supported by Kashmiris in the polls against threats of bullets and violence from the Pro-Pakistan secessionist elements. Situation during the last decade, and particularly since the turn of the century will be discussed later in this work.

Jammu and Kashmir Islamic Front (JKIF)

Formation	October 1995
Strength	50
Headquarters	Srinagar
Objectives	Liberation of Kashmir through armed struggle; right of self-determination.
Sponsors	Pakistan, POK, ISI

Qrganisational Structure

- Apex : Chairman, Chief Commander, Deputy Chief Commander.
- District level : District Commander, Deputy District Commander, Area Commanders.

Leadership

- Bilal Ahmad Beg, Chairman (in POK since 1994).
- D Haider, Vice Chairman.
- Mehrajuddin Butt, Deputy Chief Commander.
- Javed, Member, Central Committee (in Pakistan).
- Shabir Jan Khan, Member, Central Committee (in Pakistan).
- Fayaz, Member, Central Committee (in Pakistan).
- Salim Butt, Former District Commander, IUM.

Operational Areas

J & K, Delhi, Gujarat and some other States in India; Kathmandu; Dhaka.

Foreign Links

Pakistan, POK, ISI.

Links with Political Parties/Groups

Member of Islamic Resistance Party; made inroads into Muslim pockets of Gujara, Rajasthan, and Maharashtra; developed links with Indian political parties/groups.

Finances

ISI

Major Acts of Terrorism

- 3 Jan 96. Seven killed, thirty injured in bomb blast at Sadar Bazaar, Delhi.
- 21 May 96. 13 killed, 40 injured in bomb blast at Lajpat Nagar Central Market, Delhi.
- 22 May 96. 15 killed, 30 injured in bomb blast in Dausa (Constituency of MOS for Internal Security, Rajesh Pilot), Rajasthan.

Origins

During 1994-95, Sajjad Ahmad Kannu, then Deputy Chief of the IUM, and Hilal Beg (also of the IUM) had differences with its leadership, especially with Niyaz Ikhwami and Mehrajuddin Butt. Niyaz removed Hilal Beg from the IUM in April 1995 alleging anti—movement activities in collusion with Iftikar Ansari, a local Congress leader.

Kennu was arrested, but he escaped. In June 1995, Kuka Parrey, then Deputy Chief of IUM, formed his own faction of the outfit by breaking away from it. The IUM was accused by the HUM of collaborating with the Indian SF. Kennu's escape too was seen the result of this instance by the HUM. Kenu himself was keen to stage some violent acts to establish his credentials with the IUM circles. He launched the J & K Islamic Front (JKLF) with himself as Chief Commander and Hilal Beg and Bilal Beg (in POK) as Deputy Chiefs. Later, Hilal Beg himself launched a parallel political entity and named it J & K Liberation Council (JKLC).

The JKLF ran indoctrination camp near Muzaffarabad for recruits from the Kashmir Valley and other parts of India.

Abdul Ghani aka Assadullah, on old activist of the AUM (later arrested in connection with the Lajpat Nagar bomb blast) was assigned the responsibility for publicity, press and Diaison work. In December 1995, Bilal Beg, Dr. Haider and Assadullah appealed for funds to strengthen JKIF to fight for the Kashmir cause. The outfit has an efficient communication network in the Valley to coordinate it activities and receive instructions from the leaders and pass them on to cadres in and outside Valley. The house and telephone of Farida Dar, on important woman activist of JKIF, were used frequently in this regard.

Two Pak nationals – Shamshad Haider and Javed Hussain– were motivated by the ISI and Bilal Beg to settle in Mumbai for carrying out violent acts of sabotage at its cinema hills, industrial locations and public places. The two were inserted in August/September 1997. Running out of luck, they were arrested in March-April 1998. During interrogation, they implicated Col Farooq of the ISI for detailed planning of this operation.

Bilal Beg Persuades Tiger Memon to Help

Bilal Beg roped in Abdul Hamid Hurrah, former Chief Commander of the IUM, Rafiq Ahmad Wani and Shabir Shah, in Pakistan since 1994, to strengthen his outfit. Bilal Beg tried but failed to get membership for the JKIF in MJC (Pakistan).

The chief accused of 1993 Bombay Blasts, Tiger Memon, living in Karachi and operating from their with the help of the ISI, played a crucial role in regrouping the JKIF with liberal financial help.

The Suspicions Persist

Mitha Sofi, Chairman IUM and Salahuddin, HM Supremo, were keen to ensure the closure of JKIF offices in Pakistan/POK as they suspected a deal between it and the Indian SF. On 28 January 1996, Sofi, then Chief Commander, IUM travelled to POK for talks with Bilal Beg, Chairman of JKIF to prevent clashes between their outfits. They failed to reach an understanding. Sofi and Salahuddin floated a new outfit, J & K Ikhwan-ul-Musalmeen to counter the JKIF, and occupied the Muzaffarabad office of the JKIF. That invited the attention of the Pak Police, resulting in the arrest of Sofi and his supporters. Their interrogation led to the raid on their offices and hideouts, which yielded a rich cache of arms. Utterly frustrated, Mitha Sofi joined the JKIF and returned to the Kashmir Valley in July 1996.

Acts of Sabotage in India

JKIF team sent to India under the leadership of Abdul Gani in 1996 was assigned to carry out blasts in and around Ahmedabad, Gujarat. The mission proved abortive as the intelligence reports led the police to their hideout, resulting in the arrest of the saboteur terrorists and recovery of high grade explosives.

JKIF was obviously determined to Wreak death and destruction on India beyond the confines of J & K. So they yet again planned a chain of explosions in New Delhi before and on the Republic Day (26 January) 1997. Fayaz Ahmad Shah was assigned the mission, and as is the ISI wont, he and his associates were to reach India via Nepal. As ill luck would have it (or may be, India's good luck), Indian intelligence was one up and they were arrested on 11 December 1996 in Kathmandu, along with 20 kg of deadly explosives. The Republic Day celebrations went off peacefully.

Earlier in 1996, JKIF was under pressure to perform or quit. It succeeded in exploding a bomb in Sadar Bazaar, Delhi on 3 January 1996, killing seven and injuring 30. Sajjad Kenu died in a similar explosion in Srinagar on 8 January 1996. These two successes restored the faith of the ISI and the JKIFI was given even more deadly missions in India, as detailed above even if both of these proved abortive – and embarrassing for ISI and Pakistan.

Nepal : A Helpless Country?

The ISI has found Nepal and its capital Kathmandu as helpful friends in carrying out its nefarious activities against India and to achieve its aim of grabbing J & K from her. It is not that Nepal is doing all this to harm India. It is just that security arrangements at Kathmandu leave much to desire, and this has often left India fuming.

So it should come as no surprise that the Pak ISI and so many terrorist outfits operating under its aegis have used Kathmandu as a transit point for their violent machinations in J and K, and other parts of India. The fact become self-obvious if one examines the sequence of events leading to terrorist operations in Delhi, Gujarat, and Rajasthan. Kathmandu-based Kashmiri businessman come handy and prove an asset in the hands of the ISI and other terrorist outfits. They are like 'safe houses' in a foreign land. One such businessman is Javed, a prominent JKIF leader who runs a carpet business in Kathmandu.

To wit, it is useful to remind us all that the Indian Airline flight had taken off from Kathmandu which was hijacked by the Islamic terrorist to Kabul, and consequently landed the NDA/BJP Government, and especially its External Affairs Minister Jaswant Singh into extreme embarrassment, some would say eternal shame, on the first day of the New Millennium.

J & K Jamaat-e-Islami (JKJEI)

Formation	1942
Strength	2,00,000 (including Pakistani elements).
Headquarters	Srinagar
Objectives	Establishment of an Islamic State (Nizam-e-Mustafa) and its merger with Pakistan.
Sponsours and Supporters today	Pakistan, POK, ISI

Organisational Structure

- Apex Body (Policy) : *Majlis-e-Shora* of 24 members.
- Majlis-e-Namaidgan : It is 90 – member body elected by 1300-odd *rukuns* or basic members. It is supervised by the Majlis-e-Shora.
- *Amir-e-Halqa*. He is also elected by the *rukuns*, and has authority over 5-6 villages.
- Rukun-e-Jamaat (= Parliament). Composed of all *tanzeem* levels, it is convened by the General Secretary.
- Chief Executive : *Amir-e-Jammaat*, assisted by General Secretary.
- Districts : *Amir-e-Zila / Nazim-e-Zila*.
- Tahsils : *Amir-e-Tehsil / Nazim-e-Tehsil*.

Leadership

- G..M. Bhatt, *Amir-e-Jamaat*; also *Nazim*, Falah-e-Aam Trust.
- SAS Gillani, *Amir-e-Jihad*.
- Mohd Ashraf Sahrai, *Qayum-e-Jamaat*.
- Tanveer Ahmad Tantry, *Amir-e-Suba*.

- Abdul Ahlad Thokar, *Nazim*, Public Relations.
- Nazir Ahmad Qureshi, Rabita Alam-e-Islami (representative ian Saudi Arabia).
- Dr. Mohd Ayud Thakur (representative in the UK and President, World Kashmir Freedom Movement).
- Ghulam Nabi Fai (representative in the US and Executive Director, Kashmir American Council).
- Dr. Mohd Yusuf Khan, President, Islamic Studies Circle.
- Syed Saiduddin, *Nazim*, Muslim Welfare Society.
- Sheikh Suleman, *Nazim*, Talim-e-Tarbiat.
- Abdul Hamid Fayaz, *Nazim*, Islami Tehrik-e-Tulba.
- Nazir Ahmad Kashani, Leader.
- Nazim-e-Auqaf, Leader.
- Fatima Shafi, Chief Banat-ul-Islam (Women's Wing)

Majlis-e-Shora

Major Leaders

- GM Bhatt
- Syedullah Tantrey.
- Mohd Ismael Bhatt.
- Ashiq Kashmiri.
- Hakim Ghulam
- Abdul Majid Fazli
- Ghulam Nabi Nausheri
- Mohd Ashraf Sahrai.
- Mohd Abdulla Sheikh.
- Sheikh Ghulam Hassan.
- Hakim Ghulam Nabi.

Areas of Operation

Kashmir Valley; Baramulla, Anantnag, Pulwama, Kupwara, Doda districts; POK; Pakistan.

Links with Political Parties/Groups

- Islamic Study Circle for religious teaching; Iqbal Memorial Trust recognised by Rabita-e-Alam-e-Islami which supervises schools in the Kashmir Valley (255; 33,000 students) with an Orthodox curriculum; Muslim Welfare Society and Falah-e-Alam Trust which manages the schools and the printing press.
- Youth Wing : Islamic Tehrik-e-Tulba.
- JKJEI circumvented Government ban in 1990 and opened new schools under the Falah-e-Alam Trust.

Foreign Link

Pakistan; ISI, JEI (Pakistan); Pan Islamic bodies like Rabita-e-Alam-e-Islami (Saudi Arabia); World Assembly of Muslim Youth (WAMY) Saudi Arabia; International Islamic Federation of Students Organisation (IIFSO), Kuwait; Ikhwan-ul-Musalmeen (IUM), Egypt; Muslim Students. Association of Uganda and America; International Muslim Association (IMA), New Zealand; JEI, Bangladesh.

Finances

Pakistan and ISI – Rs. 3 crore annually; covert funding by Pan-Islamic bodies; donations from West Asia; voluntary contributions in the form of *Ushar* and *Zakat*.

Publications

Urdu weekly *Azan* (banned in 1990); *Khudat;* Rah-e-Aman; *Shariat-ul-Nabi*, and *Hijrat*.

Beginnings, Role and Networking

A school teacher Pir Saiduddin established JKJEI in 1942. It was a unit of the JEI (Hind), Rampur, till 1947. During the 1947-52 period, the JKJEI was rather inactive. In 1953, it broke away from JEI (Hind) and JEI (Pakistan). Assuming an independent identity, it framed its own Constitution, and started concentrating its attention on the spread of *Wahabi Cult* of Islam. It rigorously built its cadre strength during the 1952-71 period, but opted to stay away from democratic poll processes.

The JKJEI supported militancy indirectly during 1988-89. Casting away any such pretence; it launched its own military wing, HUM in September 1989. This marked the formal start of this organisation's direct and active involvement in the J & K militant movement and the process of taking orders and instructions from the ISI. Within less than six months, it become the lead actor in the violent secessionist stakes in J & K, when it floated he Tehrik-e-Hurriyat Kashmir (TEHK) in February 1990 to unite all Islamic secessionist forces under one banner. On 16 April 1990, New Delhi banned the JKJEI for two years. Perhaps having second thoughts on the issue, the ban was not renewed when it expired on 12 December 1993.

The killing of Dr. Qazi Nissar, a religious leader of Anantnag, on 20 June 1993 did produce spontaneous mass resentment against the JKJEI/HUM duo and their violent activities. The two not only weathered the storm of criticism but also succeeded in sabotaging the investigation into Qazi's death through coercive tacties. More than this, the aggressive posturing by the JKEI/HUM after Qazi's death created a feeling of insecurity among the anti-JKEI secessionist leaders. Even the general public seemed to have been frightened, and many civilians in Anantnag district were made to pay fines and tender apology to the HUM for their 'anti-Movement' activities. The terrorists had for the first time succeeded in coercing into silence and abject submission not only the unarmed, innocent civilians but also sections of the armed secessionist outfits. The JKJEI/HUM gun had spoken violently and decisively. The years of propaganda, based on religious zealotry and ideological and fanatical extremism against the dar-ul-harb that was India had started showing the results for Pakistan, its operational arm, the ISI, and various secessionist outfits – all clamouring for merger of Kashmir into Pakistan. The 1989-90 was the defining years for the Indian polity, marking effective beginning of secessionist war unleashed by the Islami Jihad forces. In the years to come, the secessionist terrorism was to claim increasing toll in human, material, and cultural resources of India. A neighbour, an Islamic State had succeeded in not only fomanting terrorism within an Indian State but also exporting it across the border to that State and into wider areas of India beyond it.

To put it briefly if aptly, the JKJEI utilised the terror tactics of its armed wing, HUM, the financial resources of Falah-e-

Alam. Trust, the recruitment and subsequent indoctrination of the students of the Jamaat schools to foment and deepen anti-India sentiment of Muslims in the Kashmir Valley. It was meant to be a fell blow for the much-admired Indian secularism. At local level, it continued to support pro-Pakistan and pro-Wahabi tenets of Islam and simultaneously eroding the dominant centuries-old *Hanifia-Eitoadi* beliefs in the valley.

The international propaganda institutions that spread the anti-India agenda objectives of the JKJEI include activists like Dr. Ayub Thakur of the World Kashmir Freedom Movement (WKFM), UK, Ghulam Nabi Fai of Kashmir American Council (KAC), USA, and affiliated fronts which include the Council for Human Rights in Kashmir (CHRK) USA, and Kashmir Centre, USA.

Political Interlude and Invitation from Indian Prime Minister

Advised by the JEI (Pakistan), the JKJEI took part in the electoral politics in 1972 and secured five seats in the J & K Assembly. The Sheikh Abdullah government banned the organisation for the period 1975-77.

Persuaded by its secessionist orientation, it joined the Muslim United Front (MUF). As in 1972, it won some seats in the 1987 State Assembly elections as well.

The Islamic Study Circle, front organisation of the JKJEI, interacted with and influenced the government servants and the intellectuals. The Falah-e-Alam Trust, created in 1988 for supervising the chain of JKJEI schools claimed to be an independent body. But in reality, it was a front of the JKJEI and was guided and financed by it. GM Bhatt, an old time *rukum* of JKJEI, became its *Amir* in due course of time.

On 19 February 1991, the JKJEI responded favourably to an offer for talks by the Indian Prime Minister, Chandra Shekhar, to find an amicable settlement to the Kashmir issue. It set out pre-conditions bordering on to its secession from India. In May 1991, SAS Gillani, *Amir-e-Jihad* of JKJEI, wrote to Indian Prime Minister declaring that his organisation considered accession of J & K to India as 'temporary' and that a majority of people wanted a solution based on the UN resolutions. He advocated a tripartite conference attended by the representatives of India, Pakistan and Kashmir.

The letter and pre-conditions which they know were sure to be rejected out of hand was but one of the gambits the secessionists took resort to occassionally to fudge the issues or obfuscate the realities. In October 1993, Indian SF learnt that terrorists, including Afghan mercenaries led by Maj Mast Gull of Pakistan Army, were using the sacred shrine of Hazratbal as a sanctuary while indulging in violent acts of terrorism in Srinagar/Valley. The Army laid siege to the Shrine on 15 October, with the terrorists holed up within. To garner populist support on an emotive issue with the Muslim Community, Gillani a hard line secessionist, launched a compaign against the Army for laying siege to a holy shrine. He was of course arrested and siege was lifted after 32 days only after the besieged terrorists surrendered to the SF.

In another move to make political capital, the JKJEI declared a ban on the Amarnath Yatra (= pilgrimage) by Hindus in August 1994 and also demanded the removal of bunkers set up by the SF in the Hazrat Bal Shrine area. The intentions of the JKJEI became clear when it managed to instal a pro-JKJEI *imam* in the shrine after the bunkers were dismantled in the area. It was looking far beyond the immediate became clear again when it attempted to bring the Muslim Auqaf Trust into its fold that would enable it to exercise full control over its commercial properties and afford unquestioned access to large sums offered by devotees in Hazratbal and other important shrines in the valley. It also initiated populist schemes like hospitals in Srinagar for medical treatment at concessional rates. As is the fate of all such self-serving and opportunistic measures, none of the above-mentioned schemes/gambit bore fruit.

After his release on 30 September 1994, Gillani launched a compaign against the electoral process in J & K and exhorted people to continue with the jihad.

JKJEI at Loggerheads with Shabir Shah and APHC

Shabir Shah had been an inconvenience for the JKJEI as also for the APHC leadership. The large public response to Shabir's release on 14 October 1994 and his espousal of a peaceful solution of the Kashmir issue through negotiations caused certain discomfort – even consternation—among his JKJEI colleagues. When it tried to include Shabir in the APHC, it did not succeed as the 'inconvenient' man again set some preconditions not acceptable to others : the merger of all the constituents of the APHC into a single organisation; election of a single leader; and representation for Jammu and Ladakh regions in the APHC. The subsequent demand that he be provided a personal membership of the APHC and not as the leader of the JKPL, too was not acceptable to the JKJEI.

The JKJEI ranks were unhappy with the functioning of the APHC because of their perception of smaller parties getting more importance at the cost of the *Jamaatis*. There was heart-burning and resentment, too, over the nomination of Maulvi Umar Farooq and Maulvi Abbas Ansari as the APHC representatives/emissaries to promote the Kashmir cause as well as the APHC itself in Saudi Arabia, UK, and other countries. The two leaders took the overseas trip during the period 14 December 1994-13 February 1995. The JKJEI leaders were upset by the reports that Maulvi Ansari criticised their outfit during this trip, and stubbornly refused to meet the JKJEI supporters of the POK-origin in the UK.

Another issue of contention was the importance given by the APHC to the death of the non-JKJEI leaders like Qazi Nissar while hardly any sympathy was expressed at the killings of the JKJEI activists in inter-group clashes. The JKJEI leadership overruled the request of some of its own leaders to quit the APHC whose membership was seen as a tactical necessity.

Counter-Insurgency (CI) Groups vs JKJEI (Leadership)

The deployment of the CI groups in the latter half of 1994 and their targeted attacks on the JKJEI cadres led to their death in many cases. This, coupled with the failure of the ISI/Pakistan to intervene directly in Kashmir demoralised its cadres. Consequently, JKJEI leaders from Baramulla, Kupwara and Anantnag fled to the safety of Srinagar. To the dismay of its leadership, several paid advertisements appeared in the local press wherein some individuals expressed their dissociation with the JKJEI.

Hardliners vs Moderates in JKJEI

Now came the conflict between the hardliners and moderates which had its origin in the earlier history of the outfit. In 1991, JKJEI activists elected Hakim Ghulam Nabi, moderate, as its *Amir*. But the hardliners led by Ghulam Nabi Nowsheri, Deputy *Amir*, stationed in Pakistan, continued to control the affairs of the outfit – Hakim's election notwithstanding. The success of the CI groups aggraiated the hiatus between the hard liners and the moderates within the JKJEI. The moderates, including Saifuddin Qari and Nazir Ahmad Kashani proposed dissociation from the HUM. They reasoned that the militant activities had adversely affected their organisation and exposed its cadres to attack by the renegade CI outfits as well as the Indian SF. They were also concerned over the HUM conducting its operations 'without any knowledge' of the JKJEI. Early in 1995, the differences over the organisation's association with the HUM led to the resignation of Saidullah Tantrey from the post of *Amir-e-Suba*, Jammu.

The inability – it obviously could not be 'unwillingness' – of JKJEI to exercise control over HUM, its very own military wing and in a manner of speaking, its very own creation to serve its (JKJEI's) political objectives, led to a loss of face in public. It could not be a matter of pride for parents if their own child, howsoever unruly and obstreperous, does not even listen to them. This unhappy relationship had been seen by the public in the light of certain incidents/events in the past. During the Charar-e-Sharif crisis, for instance, JKJEI/senior leadership failed to persuade Mast Gul and his mercenaries to vacate the area even when there was full-throated public outcry again their presence and consequent violent actions. People in Kashmir Valley and the rest of the State noted this infirmity, the fault line, in the JKJEI-HUM equation. Expectedly, the hardliners led by Gillani criticised their moderate colleagues for not extending a helping hand to the Mujahideen who had made – and were still willing to make – ultimate sacrifices in the holy jihad. Gillani was showing his colours openly and defiantly. It was no surprise that after the turn of the century, he led his hardliners out of the APHC to constitute a parallel body under his won leadership – abandoning his life-long colleagues and loyal secessionist fraternity of Abdul Gani Bhatt, Maulvi Abbas Ansari and Maulvi Umar Farooq with the parent body.

ISI Gathers the Indian Secessionists at the Holy Mecca

The ISI convened a meeting in June 1995 of secessionist leaders from Pakistan and Kashmir to instruct and guide them on the secessionist path way. The JKJEI too sent its delegation to benefit from the 'received wisdom' of the secessionist anti-India forces after due deliberations. The Pak delegation was headed, and rightly so, by Nawabzada Nassarullah Khan, Chairman, Parliamentary Committee on Kashmir, and included top leaders of most *tanzeems* working for Pakistani objective of wresting Kashmir from India. Ghulam Nabi Fai, Executive Director, Kashmir American Council, was also in attendance.

The participants signed the Mecca Declaration reaffirming their resolve to continue the Kashmir struggle to find a solution in accordance with the UN resolutions and then, as a pro-forma practice, or habit, called upon the world body and international community to intervene in Kashmir.

The hardliners vs moderates issue dominated the Mecca meet also. Leaders like Ghulam Nabi Nowsheri and Nazir Ahmad Kashani believed that militancy by itself was inadequate to resolve the Kashmir issue and advocated some 'other' initiatives also. They complained about the lack of adequate support from Pakistan for their movement. But, the hardliners like Mohd Yusuf Shah and Gillani Won the day – securing the endorsement of continuing support to militancy. More importantly, hardline seemed to be the ruling ideology of the separatist leaders, for the simple reason that Gillani was nominated Amir-e-Jihad of the JKJEI at this meeting.

JEI (Pakistan) : Vaulting Ambitions for Muslim Homelands

JEI (Pakistan) had grandios objective of creating Muslim homelands in various parts of this country after dividing it into North and South India. A detailed presentation was made at Mecca. But JKJEI and JEI (POK) refused to buy such 'far fetched', if not 'hair – brained', plans – conceptually grand but low on practicability. After opposing it vigorously, the two asserted the struggles ought to be confined to J & K only.

JKJEI Regroups and APHC Disowns HUM

After the return of Abdul Majid Dar, former Military Adviser HUM, from Pakistan late 1995, the JKJEI/HUM started reorganising/regrouping of their activists/cadres in various parts of Kashmir. Early 1996, additional groups of foreign mercenaries were inducted into the field to augment the HUM strength to enable it to confront the CI groups more effectively.

In an attempt to emphasise its hold over the APHC, JKJEI virtually seized the Kashmir Awareness Bureau opened by the former in New Delhi for liaison with the diplomatic missions, by appointing Firdous Aseem (a JKJEI *rukun*) as its head. There were hardly any dissenting voices over this highhandedness. Desirous of widening its operational reach and political influence, the JKJEI sought interaction with national leaders like VP Singh, former Prime Minister, through JEI (Hind). It also announced its willingness to work towards a negotiated settlement of the Kashmir issue.

In 1996, the JKJEI vigorously agitated for and spearheaded the anti-election campaign initiated by the APHC. But once the elected NC government was installed in the State, the *Majlis-e-Shora* of the JKJEI decided on a two-prong strategy on 14-15 October 1996 meeting : (1) to avoid an unduly extreme posture against the Farooq Abdullah government; and (2) Simultaneously, to adopt a 'wait and watch' policy line on the issue. The thinking, possibly, behind this ambivalence was to see if the NC government could secure greater autonomy from New Delhi, as had been declared/promised by Abdullah in the NC election manifesto. The greater autonomy, in any case, was bound to advance even if indirectly, the cause of JKJEI itself, and subsequently pave the way for Kashmir's secession from India, and consequent merger with Pakistan.

When SAS Gillani replaced Umar Farooq as Chairman of the APHC, hardline domination of the amalgam was complete. The elevation of Gillani also suggested that the ISI no longer believed in Umar Farooq 'delivering' for Pakistan. The election of Gillani restored the hardline orientation to the Kashmir issue. Some of the other APHC leaders like AG Lone, Prof Bhatt, and Maulvi Abbas Ansari were also known to harbour similar views.

Sustained pressure from the SF persuaded the JKJEI to distance itself from militancy and to disown the HUM. It took this step essentially to protect its cadres and maintain its strength. Another significant move was the JKJEI allowing its cadres to quit the outfit if they so desired. This perhaps was meant to portray an image of a liberal outfit where its cadres enjoyed certain freedoms. It also pondered over the tactical gaims of initiating negotiations with New Delhi. Such a step was sure to present a 'constructive' 'prositive' image of itself, in contrast to the hardline one it carried.

In October 1997, the moderate GM Bhatt took over as *Amir* of the JKJEI. It was seen as a beginning of a moderate phase for it, even if briefly. After all, Bhatt had advocated a peaceful settlement of the Kashmir issue.

1998 Change in Stance : Was it Tactical?

Prior to the Foreign Secretary level talks between India and Pakistan in 1998, Pak authorities announced that they would also discuss Kashmir on behalf of the people of Kashmir. Struck by the implications of this announcement, Gillani issued an immediate rebuttal : The people of J and K had not authorised Pakistani authorities to negotiate on their behalf. This statement by Pakistan was a below to their self-esteem and pride. After all, APHC had been shouting from the house tops that it was the sole representative of the people of Kashmir. The motives behind this rebeuttal could be complex. It chose to downplay its enthusiasm for accession to Pakistan as a tactical move since it had alienated the pro-independence elements/lobby. It had, in fact, had engaged in a debate over the idea of an independent Kashmir vs a Palestine-like State. Or, was it a mere ploy to loudly declare its independ stance to counter the popular belief of the JKJEI being a pro-Pakistan outfit? Or still more simply, it was to tell Pakistan : "Please do not take us for granted."

A little later, the JKJEI used sympathisers within the ruling NC circles to exert pressure on Dr. Farooq Abdullah to pursue his greater antonomy plank a little more vigorously.

1998 : Pakistan Criticised for Offering Peace Talks with India

The ISI formed a committee, composed of Abdul Rashid Turabi, Ghulam Nabi Nowsheri and some others, to disrupt the 1998 Lok Sabha elections from the State. JEI (Pakistan) organised a 3-day, 23-25 October 1998 ijtemah (= gathering, congregation) in Islamabad, with an attendance of over 100,000, including 400 armed militants of the HUM. There, Turabi emphasised the importance of a unified jihad in concert with LET. Salahuddin harped on the need for merger of Kashmir with Pakistan, and asserted that struggle for Kashmir was also a war of survival for Pakistan. They also discussed in detail the alleged human rights violation by Indian SF. The HM set up stall with photographs and names of 'martyred' (slain) militants. Was it an obvious case of convincing the convinced?

The concluding day declaration reaffirmed their resolve to work for the liberation of Kashmir. Jihad fund collections at the congregations amounted to Rs. 50 crore, and 10 kg of gold.

Significantly, Qazi Hussain Ahmad chaired a special session of the *Majlis-e-Shora* at the venue which categorically criticised the Pakistan government for offering peace talks with India. They feared that would adversely affect the jihad in Kashmir.

Intra-outfit Differences : An Inevitable Bane

Despite the much flaunted unity at the surface, the JKJEI had usual inter-faction serious differences. Much before the onset of 1988 militancy, there were two distinct factions led respectively by Qari and Gillani. The had opposite views on the resolution of Kashmir issue. The tussle between the moderates and hardliners had continued even after the election of GM Bhatt to preside over the fortunes of the outfit. As *Amir-e-Jamaat*, GM Bhatt started consolidating his position by nominating like-minded moderates to office. In the 24-member *Majlis-e-Shora*, only six belonged to the Gillani group. Ghulam Mohd Mir, Baramulla was appointed *Nazim-e-Talimaat* (= Director, Education) of the Falah-e-Alam Trust, replacing Saifullah Sofi, Anantnag who was directly involved in active militancy.

GM Bhatt declared at a press conference in Srinagar on 14 November 1998 that JKJEI "is a politico-religious organisation with no linkages to militancy". This was vehemently opposed by hardliners like Hakim Ghulam Hassan Nabi and Ashraf Sehrai who asserted that any shift in the organisation's policy on militancy should get approval by the *Majlis-e-Shora*.

Bhatt's moderate stand also invited criticism from the APHC which summoned him on 18 November 1998 to explain his 'deviant' stance. Yasin Malik reportedly chided him for his pro-India stand. The APHC press release after the meeting, of course, talked of 'identity of views' between JKJEI and APHC – papering over the rough edges. The next day, 19 November, Gillani publicly castigated Bhatt for his policy of delinking militancy from the Kashmir struggle.

With Gillani's open criticism and angry outburst, the ideological differences spilled into public domain. A damage-control exercise had become an urgent necessity. An extraordinary meeting of the *Majlis-e-Shora* was convened for 5-6 December 1998. The press note issued at the end of the meeting suggested a victory for Bhatt : "The differences were discussed at length and the view emerged that the JKJEI had not deviated from its policy of acknowledging the Kashmir issue and seeking its resolution in a peaceful manner." As a sop to the hardliners, it also added, that the *Majlis-e-Shora* advised Bhatt and Gillani to work together.

J and K Liberation Front (JKLF)

Formation	1964 in Pakistan; 1988 in J & K.
Strength	150
Arms Held	Over 100 weapons including 75 AK rifles, 3 RLs and rockets, probably M-72 anti-armour weapons.
Headquarters	Muzaffarabad and Srinagar.
Objectives	Liberation through armed struggle of J & K, POK, Gilgit, Baltistan, Hunza, and Aksai-Chin and their subsequent reunification as an independent entity called Jammu and Kashmir
Sponsors	Pakistan, POK, ISI

Organisational Structure

- Apex : Supreme Revolutionary Command Council.

- Underground militant set up : C-in-C, Deputy C-in-C, Military Adviser at the Headquarters and Divisional/ District/Area Commanders.

Leadership

Amanullah Khan Group (POK-based).

- Amanullah Khan, Chairman.
- Dr. Farooq Haider, Vice Chairman.
- Raja Muzaffar, Vice Chairman and Chairman (Military Wing).
- Ghulam Mustafa Alvi, Finance Secretary.
- Afzal Jatalvi, Chairman (Diplomatic Wing).
- Master Afzal, Military Chief.
- Saifuddin, Officer-in-Charge, Transit Camps and Coordinating Chief (Muzaffarabad, POK).
- Ghulam Nabi War, coordinating Leader (Muzaffarabad, POK).
- Farooq Khan, Coordinating Leader (Kotli).
- Sardar Qadeem, Coordinating Leader (Rawalkot, POK).

Amanullah Khan Group (Kashmir Valley).

- Prof Maqbool-ur-Rehman, President.
- Riaz Ahmad Lone, Vice President.
- Abdul Qadir Rather Vice President
- Rashid-ul-Hassan, General Secretary.
- Farooq Ahmad Mr., Organiser.
- Dr. Zaffar Iqbal, Publicity Secretary.

Yasin Malik Group (POK-based)

- Aftaf Quadri, Chief of Political Wing.
- Daud Khan, Chief of Military Wing.
- Salim Haroon, Leader.
- Basharat Noorie, Leader.

Yasin Malik Group (Kashmir Valley).

- Yasin Malik, President.
- Mohd Rafiq Dar, Chief Commander.

Areas of Operations

- J and K PoK, Pakistan, UK

Political Parties/Groups

- Pakistan, ISI, Sikh terrorist organisations.

Foreign Links

Offices in UK, France, the Netherlands, Germany, USA, four Central Asian States, Pakistan.

Publications

Voice of Kashmir International (monthly), *Front Times*.

Major Acts of Terrorism

- 1 Aug 88. Blast in Telegraph Office and Amar Singh Club, SGR, by Bilal Siddiqui, Aijaz Dar and others.
- 17 Aug 89. Killed Mohd Yusuf Halwai, Block President, NC (Farooq), SGR.
- 14 Sep 89. Killed Tikka Lal Taploo, BJP State President, by Fiyaz Ahmad Dar, Ishfaq Majid Wani and Yasin Malik, SGR.
- 2 Oct 89 (Birthday Gandhiji). Killed a woman and infant, two injured in attack on family of Sub-Inspector Shabir Ahmad.
- 4 Oct 89. Killed NK Ganjoo, retired Session Judge, SGR; he had presided over the trial of Mohd Maqbool Butt, JKLF leader in 1967-68.
- 8 Dec. 89. Kidnapped Rubaiya Sayed, daughter of then Home Minister Mufti Mohd Sayed in Srinagar; released in exchange for five JKLF militants.
- 27 December 89. Killed Prem Nath Bhatt, a leading advocate in Anantnag by Manzoor Darzi, Aijaz Ahmad Mir and Mukhtiar Ahmad Khan.
- 9 Jan 90. Killed a Hindu, by Yasin Malik, Chanpora, Srinagar.
- 29 Jan 90. Killed two Hindus by Yasin Malik, Kralpora, Badgam.
- 13 Feb 90. Shot dead outside his house Lassa Kaul, Director, Srinagar TV Station, by Shaukat Bakshi, JKLF leader.

- 13 Feb 90. Killed Hanif Mohd, owner of Vikas Bakery by Farooq Ahmad Dar, Srinagar.
- 13 Mar 90. Shot dead Ali Mohd. Backoo of the NC, in Habbakadal, Srinagar.
- 19 Mar 90. Shot dead BK Ganjoo, Telephone Engineer, at his house in Kanikadal, Srinagar, by Mohd Salim Zargar.
- 20 Mar 90. Shot dead in his Srinagar office AK Raina, Deputy Director, Food & Civil Supplies.
- 14 Apr 90. Kidnapped and killed Sarla Bhatt, Hindu staff nurse at Sher-e-Kashmir Institute of Medical Sciences, Srinagar.
- 1 May 90. Killed Makhan Lal Táploo, prominent local BJP leader at Anantang by Aijaz.
- 20 Aug 90. Killed Parvez Qadiri, Conservator of Forests, by Javed Ali Mir and Manzoor Darzi, Anantnag.
- 6 Oct 90. Looted Rs. 1.18 crore from the J & K Bank, Anantnag.
- 27 Oct 90. Toreched 175 houses and 150 shops by terrorists in a bid to escape from SF, Chini Chowk, Anantnag.
- 23 Jun 91. Burnt alive three probationary officers of the LIC, in Nishat Bagh, Srinagar.
- 30 Nov 91. HUM attacked JKLF for killing of Ghulam Nabi Ghanai, prominent JEI leader in Sopore; inter-group clashes in the Soura and Ganderbal areas caused the death of ten JKLF and three HUM militants.
- 14 Mar 93. Abducted SAS Gillani, his son and son-in-law from Srinagar; released next day.
- 11 May 93. One killed, three injured in a rocket attack on the New Secretariat building in Srinagar.

Origins

Mohammad Maqbool Butt founded the JKLF in Peshawar in 1964, aimed at creation of an independent Kashmir, unifying under this entity the existing areas represented by Indian J & K, POK, Gilgit, Baltistan, Hunza, and Aksai Chain. Initially named J & K National Liberation Front (JKNLF), the outfit was rechristened J & K Liberation Front (JKLF) in 1971. Indicative of vast resources at its disposal, by 1983 it had opened offices in the UK, France, the Netherlands, Germany, the US (New York), and four Central Asian States, besides, of course, Pakistan.

The J & K unit of the JKLF was established in February 1988. Exactly 4 years before that, in February 1984, it had kidnapped and then murdered an Indian diplomat, RH Mhatre, in Birmingham (UK). On 5 September 1985, the British police arrested Amanullah Khan and seized some documents from him which revealed the JKLF plans to carry out blasts in a number of places in India and other countries. He was deported to Pakistan in the late 1986.

Pakistan-ISI : Early Plans for Subverting J and K

The arrival of Amanullah in Pakistan marked the resurgence of JKLF activities there, especially from January 1987 when Pakistan was occupied by the Siachen problem, consequent to India placing its troops there. Analysts agree that the launch of the 'proxy war' in Kashmir by Pakistan can be related to this period. Pakistan had been planning this 'war' ever since its independence and thus had the forty years of preparatory work behind this plan. It of course is obvious that Pakistan had made skillful use of religion to incite anti-India – in fact, anti—Hindu- sentiments in the Kashmir Valley.

So in 1987, the ISI wanted leaders of the JKJEI and JKLF to take up major offensive operations. The former had been weakened but JKLF agreed to take up the gauntlet. Pakistan initially made use of its (JKLF's) experience to motivate Kashmir Youth for arms training and subversive activities, to create and secure a toehold for itself in J & K. Subsequently, it would be expanded into a foothold to promote pro-Pakistan, and by implication, anti-India, militant outfits in J & K. That would be the time to show JKLF its place in the scheme of the tings as envisaged by Pakistan – and its operational hand, the ISI. The Pakistan Intelligence, spearheaded by the ISI, advised JKLF to soften its stance on independence and extend cooperation to the pro-Pakistan militant organisations. Carried away by its recent successes in acts of terrorism, JKLF had by then become a highly self-opinionated outfit. It obviously conveyed to Pakistan/ISI that it was not amenable to the pressures from them.

Seeing its stubborn refusal to show any spirit of accommodation towards its interests, Pakistan started indicating to JKLF as to who was the master of the show. The process of isolating it had earnestly begun. By 1990, JKLF had been painted in a corner, even if it was able to carry out individual acts of violence for another couple of years.

But Amanullah was not the person to give up easily. On 18 June 1990, he announced the formation of a "Provisional Independent Government of Jammu and Kashmir." It drew a sharp reaction not only from the ISI but also from pro-Pakistan non-Kashmiri elements in the valley like Dr. Farooq Haider.To chasten Amanullah, the ISI resorted to its ultimate stratagem: Splitting the defiant JKLF. It was a three-way split: JKLF (Amanuallah faction), JKLF (Dr. Farooq Haider faction), and J & K National liberation Army (JKNLA) under Hafiz Anwar Samavi. Thus JKLF (Pakistan) stood split into three entities, the so far bigger-than-life Amanullah heading only one of them. Two prominent leaders of JKLF made a patch-up bid soon after this split. They were Afzal Jatalvi, President, Foreign Zone of the JKLF in the UK, and Azmat Khan, Chief of the outfit in the USA. They arranged joint meetings among the rival leaders. These and some similar efforts made by others proved abortive. The man who practically lost it all was Amanullah Khan, the erstwhile undisputed supremo of the united JKLF – now defunct as an entity.

JKLF Spreads its Wings into J & K and Initiates Terrorist Activities

The J & K unit of the JKLF was raised in February 1988 by a group of four, popular known as HAJY (Hamid Sheikh, Ashfaq Wani, Javed Ahmad Mir, and Yasin Malik) Group. Its first group of recruits, expectedly and naturally, was sent to POK for arms training under an oath of allegience to the JKLF. Earlier, the Pakistan-based JKLF had inducted a number of activists into J & K, including Abdul Hamid (1984), Rauf Kashmiri (1988), and Ghulam Mohd Wani (1988) with the aim of motivating and recruiting young persons in the valley. It was not something happening in isolation. The chief puppeteer was active on both sides. Simultaneously, as the recruits were being despatched to POK, a group of secessionist Kashmiri youth, especially those belonging to the JKPL and the ISL who had supported the Muslim United Front in the 1987 Assembly elections, were recruited to take up arms against the Indian government. At a May 1987 meeting in Srinagar, some of them, including Bilal Ahmad Siddiqui, Humayun Azad, Abdullah Bangroo, agreed to initiate an underground movement with the blessing and active material support from Pakistan.

The JKLF is known to have resorted to violent terrorism from its very inception. In September 1966, a group of Pakistani militants under command of Maj Amanullah infiltrated into the Valley to incite and organise the local population to stage an uprising against the legitimate governments at Srinagar and by extension, at New Delhi and achieve independence for the Kashmiris. The outfit was also involved in several violent operations, including the killings of senior police officials (1966) and the hijacking of Indian Airline's passenger planes (1971 and 1976).

The violent blasts at the Central Telegraph Office, Srinagar, and Srinagar Club on 31 July and 1 August 1988, respectively were acclaimed by the JKLF as the beginning of the first phase of their struggle in J and K. It was obviously the lead actor till then. But the emergence of more pro-Pakistan groups like the HUM and with liberal financial and material help from the ISI beginning early 1990, led to the reduction in the JKLF terrorist activities and consequent dimunition in its standing and status. Besides this natural corollary to increased presence of other rival groups in the field, Pakistan-ISI had started well-planned moves to isolate and marginalise the JKLF in the late 1980s and had completed the process by early 1990, as discussed earlier here.

In the Valley, the JKLF was the one outfit that bore the brunt of anti-insurgency drive unleashed by the SF. Its leader Ashfaq Majid Wani was killed in 30 March 1990 encounter in Srinagar. Soon after this major blow came an equally severe next one : the arrest of its leading lights and determined fighters like Yasin Malik and Hamid Sheikh. In a short spell of unfortunate events, the JKLF was left bereft of its leaders, weapons, and ammunition.

The ISI was the only godfather they have to turn to in these hours of crisis. Javed Ahmad Mir, acting C-in-C of JKLF, visited Pakistan twice, November 1990 and March 1991, to seek urgent help necessary for survival of the outfit as a functional entity as also to restore it to its wonted status among the militant organisations. He met with ISI officials on his own, without involving JKLF (POK). Pakistan-ISI saw their chance, with the recalcitrant, once-defiant outfit on its knees-literally. Pakistan reiterated its insistence that it (JKLF-J & K) give up its pro-independence policy.

Internal Dissonance, Clashes with the HUM, and Attempts at Reconciliantions

Serious differences emerged between Amanullah and Javed Mir, as the former smelt that Javed and Aslam Qureshi were conspiring to remove him from the post of Chairman. The JKLF (POK) leadership despatched a 'high power' team of Parvez Ahmad Mirza and Rauf Kashmiri, both Senior Vice Chairmen and both belonging to the Farooq Haider faction, and Zahid Amin Qasif, Political Secretary, JKLF (Aminullah faction), to Kashmir to diffuse the crisis. But there seemed to have been no tangible results of these exertions.

In July 1993, a JKLF (J & K) delegation consisting of Javed Mir and Altaf Qadri, went to Pakistan on fake travel documents, via Kathmandu-Mumbai-Tehran route. Javed Mir urged the JKLF (POK) and ISI for substantial assistance as his outfit was under attack from the HUM. ISI reiterated its stand that JKLF give up its secular/pro-independence posture to receive any help from Islamabad. As a *quid pro quo*, the ISI was believed to have offered an immediate tranche of Rs. 2 crore and financial assistance of Rs. 50 lakh per month, apart from liberal quantities of military wherewithal.

At the August 1993 meeting of the JKLF Central Committee at Rawalpindi, Javed Mir moved to remove Amanullah, blaming him for his failure to maintain cordial relations with Pakistan-ISI and for misappropriation of funds. The charges were also supported by Pakistan-based JKLF leaders like Dr. Farooq

Haider, Mohd Maqbool Dar, Dr. Ghulam Nabi Bachha, Hafiz Anwar Somavi and Master Afzal. Javed proposed Yasin Malik as Chairman. The move failed to click because it required the concurrence of the National Zone Committee of the JKLF.

On his return in January 1994, Javed Mir attempted re-activation of the organisation and addressed a few public meetings also. Meanwhile, another dissident group led by Iqbal Qureshi broke away from the *tanzeem* to form the J & K Democratic Liberation Front (JKDLF) on the instigation of Hashim Qureshi.

In October 1993, JKLF militants occupied the Hazratbal Shrine and later the area was besieged by the SF. The militants surrendered on 16 November 1993. It was a serious loss of face for the JKLF which was gleefully exploited by its detractors, expecially the HUM.

Suddenly, there was a series of clashes between the JKLF and pro-Pakistan military outfits, especially the JKJEI/HUM combine, accompanied by a barrage of anti-JKLF propaganda, as if on a cue. Things became clear when the ISI encouraged the HUM to sustain the onslaught as the JKLF (J & K) had refused to budge from its policy of fighting for an independent Kashmir. It was paying a heavy price for it since Pakistan was hell-bent to force the change of its stance at any cost. Several top JKLF leaders like Maqbool Malik, Dr. Abdul Ahad Guru and Prof. AA Wani were kidnapped and then brutally killed by the HUM. It was a heavy price to be paid for a firmly believed principle.

Hashim Qureshi, a Netherlands-based JKLF leader, had convened a meeting in Nepal in August 1990 of representatives from various militant outfits. Adherents of 'accession to Pakistan' and 'independence for Kashmir' were both excluded to avoid inevitable clashes/conflicts during the meet. However, there was no indication that JKLF had abandoned its line at that point in time.

Amanullah once again tried reconciliation with JKJEI/HUM to end mutual attrition. A July 1992 joint statement issued in Muzaffarabad by HUM, JKLF and other outfits appealed to the warring *tanzeems* to stop fighting each other and engage SF instead. JKLF (J & K), on its part, had issued a statement denying all allegations of any secret parleys with Government of India or its representatives/agencies.

The JKLF and HUM leaders held six rounds of negotiations between May and November 1992 to forge an understanding, in part to comply with the July 1992 appeal, to prevent any further clashes between the two. In their last meeting on 2 November 1992 held at Badgam, the two warring side agreed to withhold their differing standpoints on Kashmir's future until India vacated J & K. The two sides also initiated confidence building measures like holding joint public meetings. But it was rather a tawdry, if make-believe patchwork, more suited and applicable to clever political elements, and it failed, as it was bound to. Consequently, the brutal clashes did not cease at the field level. The situation continued to be as it was before these 6-round parleys.

Failed Rejuvenation Attempts and Final (?) Split

The cornered and somewhat dejected JKLF leadership attempted constituting a new political platform, inviting intelligentsia and influential elements from the split community of its somewhat estranged loyalists. Early 1992, the Mahaz-e-Azadi (MEA) merged with the JKLF. As a conciliatory move – or, was it compensatory? – Bashir Ahmad Butt, acting President of the MEA, was appointed General Secretary of the JKLF.

Aimed at projecting its continued relevance and born-again 'activism', the JKLF launched a massive drive to mobilise masses to violate the LOC on 30 March 1992. It failed to mobilise any support which was anything but impressive. The JKLF issued a second clarion call to its cadres, supporters and sympathisers to assemble in thousands and cross the LOC into India on 24 October 1992. It was simultaneously a highly emotive but wrecklessly irresponsible call. In the unlikely exent of POK people reaching anywhere at the LOC after defying POK barricades, the Indian SF would have had no option but to fire at the people violating the LOC to cross into India. It could have been a ghastly bloodletting. But luckily, nothing of the sort happened in the event – indicative of the failure of the JKLF to prove its credentials as a mass movement, or even as a popular organisation. Firstly, it failed to draw any large number of people in response to its call – nowhere in thousands it had been repeatingly drumming about. A few hundreds who did assemble were not allowed to come anywhere near the LOC by the overzealous POK border militia—trembling at the scary thought of some of them getting killed at the hands of the Indian SF. So the second call, a belligerent if wreckless provocation for Indians, too was a flop, from all angles. Refusing to see realities of life, JKLF's Javed Ahmad Mir chose to castigate Sardar Abdul Qayoom Khan, then Prime Minister of POK, for his ambivalent stand on these two calls, and accused him of being insensitive to the sentiments of the Kashmiris. In fact, he was blaming Qayoom for the failure of his own outfit to achieve a massive mobilisation of the Kashmiris in response to both its calls issued in March and October of the year 1992. Some clever logic, this! It was an interesting way to shift attention away from meagre – very weak – response to JKLF's two fervent calls for masses to converge at various LOC locations to demonstrate its popularity and mass appeal among the people of POK, and in Pakistan, beyond its boundaries. It must have been rather frustrating for this *tanzeem* to get such a tepid response as opposed to an expected hurricane of humanity spilling across the LOC into J & K, sweeping all in its wake! Hence the dire need to find political scapegoats – Prime Minister Qayum in the instant case!

Now comes a landmark event – almost cataclysmic, if you will! Yasin Malik, released from jail on 17 May 1994, initiates moves to transform the JKLF into a political organ and delink it from terrorist pathways of wanton death and destruction. Yasin has not publicly spoken, explaining the metamorphosis. After all, he had several assassinations and inhuman murders to his name. Why this sudden change of mind? Had he seen the futility of it all? Was he convinced that any amount of violence will not yield results? Pakistan had initiated two – three, including the 1971 one – wars but failed to wrest Kashmir from India. A democratic India, resilient but firm in safeguarding its sovereignty and territorial integrity, will never bow down to forces of violence and unreason. Perhaps, but only perhaps, peaceful ways might have some chances of success – even if partial. But all said and done, it was a Mafioso turning Gandhian – and that should be welcome to us all – even to the blood-thirsty merchants of death that these mindless terrorists have reduced themselves into!

But this u-turn by Yasin, rather his transformation to a 'peaceful Jihadi' – an oxymoron, if the one ever existed – accentuated the differences between the JKLF and HUM. He publicly accused the HUM of being primarily responsible for inter group bloody clashes and consequent damage to the Kashmir cause. Expectedly, to ensure that the public spat does not assume ugly proportions, the APHC stepped in and attempted reconciliation between the two hostile outfits determined to pursue their respective objectives.

But that did not put an end to mutual rivalries and the two persisted in working against each other – most effectively illustrated by the happenings during the Hazratbal crisis. Needless to say, each was bent upon using the unfortunate crisis to advance its own political gains. On 6 August 1994, Malik took resort to hunger strike, demanding the dismantling of the SF bunkers in the Hazratbal shrine area. This gave birth to a disinformation campaign by the pro-Pak elements, alleging a tacit agreement between Yasin and New Delhi and that the hunger strike was a mere ploy to hoodink his opponents and befool the gullible public. The JKJEI/HUM combine, to sideline the peaceful protest of Yasin and to marginalise his JKLF, took active control of the Hazratbal issue which had till then been used by the JKLF as a rallying point to flaunt and promote its pro-independence policy – to the chagrin of its pro-Pakistan rivals. To strike him where it hurt the most, the KJHC declared the hunger-strike by Yasin, a true and good Muslim, as an un-Islamic act. Touched on the raw, Yasin started boycotting the APHC meetings. Not willing to let go of the opportunity, or may be he had been keenly awaiting such a one, Amanullah Khan nominated Javed Ahmad Mir, and subsequently Shabir Siddiqui, to represent the JKLF in the APHC. Concerned with his ultimate isolation, Yasin rejoined the Conglomerate on 11 August 1995. Even after this happened, mutual accommodation and inter-faction trust remained distant dreams.

The continued rivalry, resulting from the deep distrust, between Yasin Malik and Shabir Siddiqui, a confidante of Javed Mir, ultimately resulted in the formal split of the JKLF in J &

K on 19 September 1995. Three days later, Amanullah formalised it on 22 September by expelling Yasin from the JKLF and by appointing Shabir Siddqui and Basharat Raza as President and C-in-C, respectively, of the J & K unit of the JKLF.

The armed occupation of the Hazratbal shrine once again from 24 to 30 Mar 1996 by the Shabir Siddiqui faction of the JKLF presented another opportunity to the rivals to be one up on each other. The fiece firefighting between the ultras besieged within the shrine and the SF surrounding them resulted in the death of 33 terrorists, including that of leaders like Shabir Siddiqui himself and Basharat. It was not only a serious loss of face for the Amanulla faction but also led to the further marginalisation and credibility-deficiency of Amanullah Khan personally in the Kashmir Valley. Never the one to accept the blame personally, Amanullah blamed Yasin for the neutralisation – in fact, it was decimation—of his faction's leadership and appointed Ghani Naseem as its new Chairman. Yet again, rapprochment was attempted between the rivals by mutual friends but to no avail. In any case, by this time senior leaders like Bashir Ahmad Butt and GN Misgar had come to recent Yasin's proximity to Gillani of JKJEI and AG Lone of JKPC – leaders known for their staunch, Pro-Pakistan stance on the Kashmir's issue, and hence an anathema to Amanullah and his cahorts. Reciprocally, Yasin was even more suspicious of Javed Mir's closeness to Amanullah.

Fortunes of JKLF till the Late 1990s

Pressures from Pakistan-ISI combine and pro-Pak groups in J & K notwithstanding, the JKLF stubbornly stuck to its policy of an independent Kashmir as final solution of the problem. Its representatives created an uproar at the 15 October 1996 meeting of the Executive Council of the APHC in Srinagar over the Washington Declaration which laid down that the self-determination agreed upon in the UN resolution had only two options available to the state of Jammu and Kashmir : Its accession to either India or Pakistan. The Declaration had been jointly signed by the representatives of the APHC from J & K (Maulvi Umar Farooq) and POK and the absence of third option for an independent Kashmir was the cause of outrage expressed at the said 15 October 1996 meeting. Later, bowing to the pressures, the APHC issued a statement disowning the Washington Declaration.

Meanwhile, the JKLF (Yasin) attempted reestablishing contacts with the ISI through Altaf Qadri of POK, and even deliberated upon the resumption of militant activities. Rafiq Dar, Chief Commander, JKLF (Yasin) went over to Pakistan via Nepal early December 1996 to solicit help from the ISI. Dar also represented JKLF (Yasin) in the UJC in POK.

About 1997-98, there was certain decline in the fortunes of the JKLF (Yasin), and majority of its activities were carried out though the KJHC (more popularly, APHC).

3

Terrorist Outfits in Jammu and Kashmir

(JKPC, JKPL-R, JKPPE, JKUPL, JUM, JUMI, LET, MC, MEA, MJF, MM, PEI, SEJ, TEJ, TUM)

J and K People's Conference (JKPC)

Formed	1975
Strength	60,000 membership, including foreign elements
Headquarters	Srinagar
Objectives	Autonomy for J & K
Sponsors	Pakistan, POK, ISI

Organisational Structure

- Apex Body : Chairman, Vice Chairman, and a Central Working Committee.
- District Committees have Presidents.

Leadership

- Abdul Ghani Lone, Chairman (assassinated 21 May 2002).
- Sajjad Lone, Chairman.
- Ghulam Mohd Hubbi, Acting Chairman.
- Nizamuddin Butt, Vice Chairman.
- Pir Hafizullah Maqdoomi, General Secretary

Areas of Activity

POK; Kupwara, Baramulla, Badgam districts

Links with Political Parties/Groups

Constituent member, APHC; linked with JKJEI; HUM, TEJI, JKLF, Al Barq.

Foreign Links

Pakistan, POK, ISI, Kashmir American Council (KAC).

Finances

Pakistan, POK, ISI.

Publications

Chattan (Urdu weekly)

Origins and Networking

The JKPC was originally launched in 1975 by Abdul Ghani Lone to seek greater 'internal autonomy' for J & K as provided for in the Article 370 of the Indian Constitution. Later, it assumed an anti-New Delhi line by demanding restoration of the pre-1953 position, regarding the residuary powers enjoyed by the State. Later, Lone veered round to espousing a 'pro-independence' stance for Kashmir, which brought it closer to the JKLF. This similarity of the views on future of J & K was the cause enough for the JKPC to come on the streets and arrange demonstrations against the death sentence awarded to the JKLF leader Maqbool Butt in 1984.

A large number of young JKPC activists are believed to have received arms training under the banner of various militant outfits like TEJI, HUM, and Al Barq (ABQ).

The JKPC joined the Muslim United Front, an amalgam of religious/fundamentalist organisations in 1987. During the 1988-89 period, Lone was the leading figure to arrange financial assistance from Pakistan, essentially through *hawala* transactions. He was helped by some other members of his family also in securing these finances.

Lone patronised the ABQ as a tactical move and was in touch with the Pak agencies. Being a shrewd tactician, when the JKJEI/HUM posed a serious challenge to the other groups in J & K, Lone directed the JKPC cadres to entice the Shia and Hanifia militants from these outfits to neutralise/weaken their leadership, especially of the HUM. Since 1992, Lone had been in cahoots with the secessionist leaders like Maulvi Abbas Ansari, Gillani and Prof. Abdul Ghani who were persistently demanding the resolution of Kashmir issue in accordance with the UN resolutions.

The JKPC was one of the founder members of the APHC.

As indicated earlier, Lone had veered round to anti-India line on Kashmir and consequently, he refused to attend the conclave of former legislators of the state convened by the Government of India on 7 November 1992 at New Delhi to discuss the Kashmir issue. The IKPC had publicly refused to have any 'conditional talks' with India.

Forging International Contacts

Lone went to UK for medical treatment in February 1993 – ostensibly, that was the reason he offered on paper. The US was but a short hop from there. He joined Ghulam Nabi Fai, Executive Director of Kashmir American Council, to help the latter in his anti-India exertions. He pleaded with certain elements in US Congress and the Administration for Kashmir's secession from India. Returning home in 1993, he actively took part in the APHC activities and managed a reconciliation with the JKJEI/HUM.

When the Hazratbal shrine was occupied by the armed terrorists during October-November 1993, the JKPC used the incident to inflame local sentiment on religious extremism. He was arrested in October 1993 while leading a demonstration in Srinagar in support of the terrorists besieged by the SF within the shrine precincts. After his release, he joined forces with Gillani to disrupt electoral process in Jammu and Kashmir.

Lone visited New Delhi in November 1994 and met the envoys of the Islamic countries to project the APHC as the sole representative of the Kashmiri people. He also advocated plebiscite for determining the future of the J & K.

Going Down the Descent?

By the late 1990s, the JKPC was a diminished entity, its activists declining in numbers. Like some other outfits of its ilk, the JKPC too was becoming dependent upon the platform provided by the APHC for conducting activities, limited though they are in size and duration.

During the years when the APHC was hurtling down precariously towards a split between the hardliners (Gillani and his cohorts) and the moderates (Umar Farooq, AG Bhatt, Abbas Ansari, et al), Lone was swerving towards the latter – consequently, offering himself on the cross-hairs of the hardliners. It did not come as a surprise to the serious students of the changing inter-outfit equations in J & K when AG Lone was assassinated on 21 May 2002 while attending the function to commemorate the death anniversary of Maulana Mohammed Farooq, who was widely respected cleric of Kashmir. (Senior Farooq, father of Umar, who is current leader of the Awami Action Committee (AAC), was the founder of the AAC. Some analysts ascribe his elimination to the fact of Lone evolving a more accommodative stance towards the State Assembly elections that were due to be held in the late 2002.

Sajjad Lone, son of AG Lone, took over the leadership of the JKPC after the death of his father.

J & K People's League, Rehmani (JKPLR)

Formed	September 1974
Strength	850, including foreign members
Arms held	Over 50 AK rifles, some MGs
Headquarters	Srinagar
Objectives	Liberation of J & K through armed struggle and its accession to Pakistan
Sponsors	Pakistan, POK, ISI.

Organisational Structure

- Chairman, General Secretary, Chief Organiser, Secretary, Treasurer, and a 10-member Central Council.
- At the District and tehsil *levels*, Presidents and General Secretaries.

Leadership

- Mohd Farooq Shah, aka Rehmani, Chairman in POK
- GM Khan Sopori, Acting Chairman.
- Dr. Abrar Nasir, General Secretary.
- Hakim Abdul Rashid, ex-Chief Commander, Al Fateh Force, in POK.
- Irshad Sakal, Chief Organiser

Operational Areas

Baramulla and Chattar in J & K; Muzaffarabad, Sinkyari (Manshera) in POK.

Links with Political Parties/Groups

Pakistan, POK, ISI, JKJEI, KJF/TMEK, AJF, TEHK, AFF, HIZB, HMM, and IRF.

Foreign Links

Pakistan, POK, ISI

Finances

Pakistan, POK, ISI, local collections (extortion/protection money/donations).

Publications

Aflaq

Origins, Splits, ISI Links, and Failure to Unify

The JKPL split during 1988-89 period due to personality clashes between Mohd Farooq Shah Rehmani and Shabir Ahmad Shah. In February 1990, Rehmani alongwith Abdul Aziz Sheikh and Muzaffar Ahmad Shah, split the parent outfit to create a faction named after himself, JKPL (R) and a militant outfit he named as Tehrik-e-Jihad Islami (TJI). Sheikh was named the General Secretary of the JKPL-R. As differences cropped up with Muzaffar over the utilisation of funds, Rehmani again moved out to launche another outfit he named as Tehrik Muzahmat-e-Kashmir (TMEK) which was later rechristened as Kashmir Jihad Force (KJF).

On the other side, Shabir had also floated his own faction he named after himself, JKPL(S), with the Muslim Janbaz Force (MJF) as its armed wing.

Rehmani went over to Pakistan in September 1990 to reinforce his relationship with the ISI. Consequent to persuation and occasional armstwisting, the ISI orchestrated the merger of two factions of the JKPL – JKPL (R) and JKPL (S) – to form a united entity, literally called so : J & K United People's League (JKUPL). The two respective armed wings were also merged to create a single outfit, Al Jihad Force (AJF).

Like most forced marriages, this one too did not last long. Rehmani not reconciled to the merger and concerned over the ISI's projection of Shabir as the undisputed leader of the JKUPL, revived his JKPL-R in May 1992. An intense media war by the factions ensued.

There was friction in AJF too. The Rehmani loyalists, holding key positions in the joint military wing proved to be major irritants in its smooth functioning. In September 1993, a group of pro-Rehmani activists headed by Fazal-ul-Haq Qureshi floated the J & K People's Political Front (JKPPF). They also attempted revival of the TJI which had earlier merged with the HUM.

The appointment of Parvez Haider as Chief Commander of the AJF by the JKUPL leadership led to alienation of cadres who owed loyalty to Firdous Ahmad Baba, founder C-in-C of the MJF, and Aziz Sheikh in the AJF. The Rehmani faction, in turn, paying back the compliments, started trying to win over JKUPL cadres to its own fold. As if to complete the undoing of the ISI's exertions for unifying the factions, Babar Badar revived the MJF.

Early 1994, GM Khan Sopori, ex-JKPL Chief of Baramulla district, rebelling against the JKUPL/JKPL-S leadership, specifically againsts. Hamid, caused another split. In September 1994, GM Khan Sopori and Nasir Bakhtyar merged with the Rehmani faction.

The leaders of both factions of the JKPL had been accused of misuse and misappropriation of funds. The notable exception had been that of Shabir Shah. But unfortunately, a close confidante of this clean men, Nayeem Khan, was accused of siphoning of Rs 40 lakh for his personal ends. He later joined the MJF.

ISI Displeasure Helps Formation of the IRF

Rehmani, once a favourite of the ISI as Chairman of the TEHK, fell from grace when he was indiscreet enough to criticise Pakistani policies in J & K and consequent role of the ISI there. This led to the closure of the JKPL-R office in Rawalpindi and its subsequent shifting to Muzaffarabad. Financial support from the ISI ceased in 1994 since the JKPL-R was not afflilliated to any secessionist political party. But it had funds flowing in from local collections as also from the JEI (Pakistan) with which it had continued to have cordial relations.

In reaction/response to the ISI decision to discontinue funds/ arms support to them, the four affected outfits – Al Fateh Force (AFF), Jamaat-ul-Mujahideen (JUM), Hizbullah (Hizb), and Hizbul Momneen (HMM) – came together to create the Islamic Resistance Force (IRF) in June 1995. These outfits were not included in the Muttahida (= United) Jihad Council (MJC, also UJC), but were instructed by the ISI to maintain a separate identity.

The IRF and its constituents may not have been accommodated in the umbrella organisation due to certain specific policy parameters, but they were well looked after for they were still serving Pakistan's end game. So, the IRF was provided a joint office in Chattar, Muzaffarabad, and a common transit camp at Sinkyari, Manshera. The ISI had provided a monthly sum of Rs. 3 lakh to the IRF.

Revival Attempts Follow the Setbacks

The JKPL-R suffered a serious setback when top party leaders, including Javed Ahmed Shah and Mir Niazi withdrew from it in July 1995. Rehmani possibly suffered an erosion of his support base among the cadres due to his prolonged absence from the Valley, resulting in low level activities for the cause. It was yet to suffer another setback when one of its leaders, Mohd Yaqoob Sheikh, ex-Chief, Al Jihad, floated his own faction, named, as was the wont or fashion, after him, JKPL (Sheikh) in October 1997, with its office in Muzaffarabad.

Almost disappointed with the ISI, JKPL-R leaders pleaded with the APHC leaders like Gillani, Abbas Ansari, and Yasin Malik for help to revive their weakened outfit. They also were desirous of a berth in the prestigious APHC.

J & K People's Political Front (JKPPF)

Formed	August 1993
Headquarters	Srinagar
Objectives	Resolution of Kashmir issue through tripartite talks involving India, Pakistan and the people of J & K

Leadership

- Fazal-ul-Haq Qureshi, Founder Chairman.

- Ghulam Mohd Naikoo (former TEJI leader), General Secretary.
- Shakeel Bakshi (former JKLF Vice Chairman).

Areas of Operation

Kashmir Valley.

Links with Political Parties/Groups

JKPL(R), JKLF, TEJI, APHC.

Origins

Due to ego clashes with the leadership of the JKPL, Fazl-ul-Haq Qureshi, one of its founders, launched the JKPPF in August 1993. GM Naikoo of the TJI joined him, to become the General Secretary of the JKPPF.

The party spelt out a three-point programme for an amicable solution of the J & K issue :

- Seeking cooperation from the people and political parties in J and K.
- Mobilising public opinion in other parts of India.
- Launching international campaigns to pressurise both Islamabad and New Delhi.

Activities

Ever since its inception, the JKPPF has largely remained inactive, and issuing statements to the press has been its only activity. Naikoo welcomed the Indo-Pak talks held in January 2004. To make such talks meaningful, he suggested both countries recognise the Kashmiris as a party to parleys. Taking a moderate line, he appealed to the APHC leaders to reconsider their decision on *Kafan Bandho* (= Be ready to face death) and Operation Hurriyat Programme announced in the wake of the Hazratbal siege.

To begin with, the JKPPF leadership was vying with the APHC for providing an integrated 'peaceful solution' programme to resolve the J & K issue. They claimed the support of many militant organisations, including Mohd Altaf Khan Andrabi aka Azam Inquilabi's organisation. JKPL-R leaders lobbied with APHC leaders like Gillani, Abbas Ansari and Yasin Malik to garner their support.

The outfit staged a *dharna* before the Srinagar-based UN Military Observers Group on 24 October 1994 and presented a memorandum requesting the UN to intervene.

J & K United People's League (JKUPL)

Formed	September 1989
Strength	4000, including Pakistani elements
Headquarters	Srinagar
Objectives	Liberation of Kashmir through armed struggle
Sponsors	ISI

Organisational Structure

- Apex : Chairman, Vice Chairperson, General Secretary, and Central Committee
- Field : District/Tehsil Committees Presidents and General Secretaries.

Leadership

Has two factions

Shabir Shah Group

- Shabir Ahmad Shah, Patron.
- Mehmood Ahmad Sagar, President, Pakistan based.
- Mohd Shafi Zargar of Doda, Vice President.
- Advocate Abdul Salam Rather, Vice President.
- Haji Mohd Farooq Wani, General Secretary.
- Khalil Mohd Khalil Baga, Finance Secretary.
- Abdul Qayum Bedar, Publicity Chief.
- Mukhtiyar Ahmad Sofi, Public Relations Chief.
- Asgar Ali, Joint Secretary, Ladakh.
- Nayeem Ahamd Khan, Officer-in-Charge, Foreign Affairs.

Farooq Rehmani Group

- Farooq Rehmani, Founder, JKPL-R.

- Abdul Aziz Sheikh, Commander, Al Jihad Force (AJF).
- S Hamid, Commander, AJF.
- Bashir Ahmad Tota, General Secretary.
- Nissar Ahmad Sofi, Chief Commander, AJF.

Areas of Operations

Kashmir valley and Muslim-majority regions of Doda district in Jammu.

Links with Political Parties/Groups

JKPL-R/KJF and JKPL-S/MJF

Foreign Links

Pakistan, ISI.

Finances

ISI, POK, local collections.

Origins

The JKPL was launched in 1972-73 by Nazir Ahmad Wani, a prominent leader of Al Fateh, a pro-Pakistan Subversive outfit, defunct since 1970. The Pro-Pakistan Youth groups that merged to create the JKPL were : (1) Youngmen's League (student's wing of the Plebiscite Front); (2) Students and Youth League (Pro-Maulvi Farooq); and (3) Islamic Students Organisation (Pro-JKJEI).

Other prominent leaders of the JKPL were Nisar Khan, Ayoob Bhatt, Shoban Bhatt, Janhar Sheikh, Farooq Rehmani and Younus Tak. As most of these leaders were from Anantnag, the JKPL did have some influence in the district. The JKPL had close ties with the JEI in its formative years, but these weakened over the years.

Its leadership passed to younger people like Shabir Shah, Abdul Rehman, Mukhtiar Ahmad Waza and Imtiaz Ahmad during 1979-80. Subsequently, it extended its influence to Pulwama, Tral, Sopore, Doda, Bandipur, Srinagar and Badgam in the 1980s.

The JKPL has been opposed to any negotiations with India, and has been demanding the inclusion of Pakistan as a third party in resolving the issue. Keen for quick results, it formulated a 3-year plan in 1979 for liberation of Kashmir from India and constituted a cell at its headquarters to execute the Plan. The first year was earmarked for recruitment of the youth, the second for their arms training, and third for launching the guerrilla warfare in Kashmir to wrest it from New Delhi.

Mukhtiar Waza played the leading role in the recruitment drive and then organising the requisite training. In fact, himself was the Camp Commander, Muzaffarabad till 1989 to give practical shape to his ideas and create determined cadres to proceed with the planned liberation struggle. But before it could even achieve elementary success in its pet project, the JKPL got split in personality-based factions.

Splits, JK PUL, Fission, Fusion and Birth pangs.

Two factions of the JKPL were led by Farooq Rehmani (R) and Shabir Shah (S) and understandably named after them too : JKPL (R) and JKPL (S) respectively. Shabir group broke away from the JKPL essentially because of Rehmani's refusal to hold organisational elections and accommodate its leaders in the governing structure of the outfit. JKPL (S) was comparatively better organised compared to the JKPL (R), had determined and dedicated cadres with history of anti-India activities, and should come as no surprise if it has/had functioned as an effective and well knit operational group for over two decades since its inception.[9] Its military wing was named Muslim Janbaaz Force (MJF) and led by Parvez Haider, and later by Babar Badar.

Rehmani group, JKPL (R), had Abdul Aziz Sheikh as General Secretary. Its military wing was named Kashmir Jihad Force (KJF).

In December 1991, under pressure from the ISI, the factions merged to create the J & K United People's League (JKUPL). Their military wings, MJF and KJF, were also merged into new force called Al Jihad Force (AJF), and Abdul Aziz Sheikh was oppointed its Chief Commander.

When the JKUPL and AJF were formed as a result of merger of the factions, most of the more important appointments and position in the two were cornered by Rehmani and his faction leaders. That fact had caused considerable bitterness and consequent friction between the leaders of the JKPL-R/KJF and

JKPL-S/MJF. But despite the predominance of his group in the newly created, unified outfits, Rehmani had a cause to feel concerned, and deeply disturbed. He was feeling himself sidelined, even ignored by the Pakistani authorities, who were projecting Shabir Shah as the undisputed leader of the JKUPL—a position that he thought rightly belonged to him. In a manner of speaking, the reasons for friction and the consequent parting of ways between its two major constituent units were present from the early days of the creation of the JKUPL.

In March 1992, Rehmani asked Aziz Sheikh to force Shabir supporters to make 'voluntary' exit from the organisation. But at its Central Council meeting at Pulwama in April 1992, prominent leaders of the JKUPL and the erstwhile JKPL-R, including Aziz Sheikh himself, Abdul Rashid Hakim, Zahoor Ahmad Sheikh, and Manzoor Ahmad Malik opposed Rehmani's move. By implication, this was a precursor to the break-up of the JKUPL. In May 1992, in the wake of the Central Council meeting rejecting his motion, Rehmani and Javed Ahmad Shah reactivated the JKPL-R/KJF. With this decision, the JKUPL stood effectively divided.

In September 1993, another group of Pro-Rehmani workers led by Fazl-ul-Haq Qureshi, Ghulam Mohd Naikoo and Abdul Majid Pathan floated the J & K People's Political Front (JKPPF) and also made an abortive attempt to revive the militant outfit Tehrik-e-Jihad Islami (TEJI) which had earlier merged with the HUM. It was not the end of the splitting season.

Early 1994, another group of pro-Rehmani cadres led by Ghulam Mohd Khan split from the JKUPL and launched a parallel new outfit. Subsequently, the Khan group announced its merger with another splinter group, AJF (Bakhtiar) and KJF to form the Al Fateh Force (AFF) with Abdul Rashid Hakim as its Chief.

Shabir revives JKPL(S) and Falls Foul of APHC

Released from detention on 14 October 1994, Shabir Shah launched a drive to build an independent mass base for himself in all regions of the state and among all sections of its people. Early 1995, Shabir and Firdous Ahmad Baba, aka Babar Badar, revived the MJF. S Hamid, eager to marginalise Rehmani and his influential cohorts, was expecting a helping hand from Shabir to strengthen his hold on the JKUPL. His calculations went awry when APHC gave representation to the splinter factions of the JKUPL while he (S Hamid) wanted to be the sole representative of that organisation. In course of time, Hamid lost most of his cadres to Shabir, and subsequently, moved closer to the HUM and HUA, with the residue.

At a September 1995 meeting in Srinagar, Shabir revived the JKPL-S, his original faction, with a nod from the ISI. As an analyst put it, it was the formal divorce of an ISI – arranged, incompatible marriage which needed approval, in the South Asian tradition, from elders before, it could reluctantly be implemented in the 'larger' interests.

Shabir had an uneasy equation with APHC leaders, particularly Gillani (lately spelt as Geelani). AG Lone and Mohammad Yasin Malik were rather suspicious of his persistent moves to build on independent base for himself, ignoring the APHC. Shabir's insistence an merger of all constituents of the APHC, election of a single leader and offering representation to the Jammu and Ladakh regions in the APHC were the ideas totally alien to the Pro-Pakistan leadership of the APHC and hence totally unacceptable. Geelani was, of cause, the leading light of the rejectionist brigade.

APHC leaders were also peered at the singular importance granted to Shabir Shah by foreign dignitaries and envoys who often met him separately. Patience grew thin when he was received for one-on-one meeting by former Prime Minister VP Singh in May 1996 and US Ambassador to India, Frank Wisner, on 1 August 1996. Consequently, he was suspended from the primary membership of the APHC on 8 August 1996.

Shabir Parts Ways Finally and JKUPL Unified Again

In early 1998, history repeated itself and the JKUPL was again split into two factions, named yet again after their leading lights – Nayeem and S. Hamid. As a cynic chose to put it, giving the reasons for these unending splits : Ego clashes was the cause and multiplication was the name of game. While breaking away, the JKPL (Nayeem) accused Shabir Shah of misuse of funds. This was perhaps the very first time Shabir faced such an accusation, because he had maintained a reputation for honesty and personal integrity during his long stint in the field of militancy. Be that as it may, misuse/misappropriation of funds is a fairly routine accusation against Jihadi leaders engaged in the risky commerce of militancy "where retirement pensions are seldom claimed."

Following his differences with the APHC, Shabir Shah decided on a new political party due to erosion of his support base in the JKUPL/JKPL. He succeeded in getting the support of some of the prominent expatriate Kashmiri leaders in the US and the UK. To strengthen his hold and broaden his support base, he re-established contacts with old activists of the JKPL who had quit the party to set up their own outfits, like Fazl-ul-Haq Qureshi, or had become ineffective, like some older colleagues. Finally he launched a vigorous membership drive in all parts of the State for his yet to be named party. He had obviously planned all aspects of his new venture rather meticulously.

On 25 May 1998, the J & K Democratic Freedom Party (JKDFP) was launched with Shabir Shah as its President. Thus came the final parting of the ways with the APHC and all other secessionist organisations/groups in J and K. Another leader of his ilk is Yasin Malik, not a part of APHC, like Shabir Shah, but has ideological differences with him about the future of Kashmir.

Possibly realising the futility of splintered existence and convinced that there was "much weakness in disunity," the factions again merged to revive the good old 'mother' outfit, JKUPL, on 27-28 July 1998. Some of its leading positions decided upon are : (1) the detained JKPL leader Abdul Aziz Sheikh, Chairman; (2) Bashir Ahmad Tota, Vice Chairman; (3) Nayeem Ahmad Khan, General Secretary. The merger was hailed by POK-based JKPL leaders like Mohd Yaqoob Sheikh, younger brother of Abdu Aziz Sheikh, and Ghulam Rasool Sheikh.

The objective of the reunified party was to work for solution of Kashmir through the self-determination, the right granted to the people of J & K by the UNO, predicated on the peaceful means and based upon the principles of equality, brotherhood and humanity. Membership of the reunified party was open to all citizens of J & K, irrespective of religion and/or origin. Nayeem Khan announced to the press on 3 August 1998 that new leadership would sever its relations with the AJF, its one-time military wing, and more surprisingly, eschew militancy as a means to achieve its objectives.

Although the JKUPL was not a major player on the Kashmir landscape at that point in time, still it is worthwhile to record that it is third organisation, after the JKLF (led by Yasin Malik) and the JKDFP (led by Shabir Shah), to renounce the use of militancy and stress on the peaceful means to achieve its objectives – be they secessionist or independent Kashmir. We are living in interesting times.

APHC leaders, particularly SAS Geelani were known to be weary of – perhaps more 'accurately' hostile to – Shabir Shah's efforts to strengthen and broaden his support base independent of their conglomerate. But they were rather supportive of and even encouraged actively the reunification effort of various factions of the JKUPL; and understandably, were quick to admit it to the Executive Council of the APHC.

For all practical purposes, the latest *avatar* of the JKUPL remains a hypothetical entity. At the best, it is a remainder of the JKPL and its various incarnations – or is it 'editions'?

Jamaat-ul-Mujahidden (JUM)

Formed	December 1990/April 1991
Strength	30, including foreign elements
Arms	30 weapons mostly AK Rifles, a few LMGs, RLs and pistols.
Headquarters	Srinagar
Objectives	Merger of J & K with Pakistan
Sponsors	Pakistan, POK, ISI

Organisational Structure

- Majlis-e-Shora : Amir, Chief Commander, and Finance Chief
- Similar system down to the district level.

Leadership

- Ghulam Rasool Shah, *Amir*.
- Maulvi Abdul Haq, Former *Amir*.
- Ghulam Nabi Shah, General Secretary.
- Abdul Malik, C-in-C.
- Abdul Rashid Mir, Chief coordinator.
- Farid Beg, *Amir*, Public Relations.
- Ghulam Mohd Butt, Launching Chief.
- Nazir Ahmad Dar, Finance Chief.
- Manzoor Ahmad Shah (Representative in Pakistan).
- Abdul Wahid Mir, Chief Coordinator (in Pakistan).
- Nasrul Islam, Chief Coordinator (J & K).

Areas of Operations

Kashmir Valley, Kupwara, Srinagar, Pulwama.

Links with Political Parties/Groups

HUM, DEM, APHC, JKMC, TUM, HIZB, TKI, MJC, IRF.

Foreign Links

Jamaat-i-Ulema-i-Islam JUUI (Pakistan), ISI.

Finances

ISI, IRF, WKFM, local collections (extortion/protection money).

Publications

Mahaz-e-Kashmir.

Origins

The JUM is a breakaway group of the HUM. Due to his differences with Mohd Ahsan Dar, then C-in-C, HUM over the influence of JKJEI in the outfit, Hilal Ahmad Mir (Since Killed), formed Islam Ka Fauji Bazu in December 1990, renamed Jamaat-ul-Mujahideen (JUM) in April 1991. Earlier, Nasrul Islam and Ghulam Rasool had formed a parallel group called Shabab-ul-Islami. This was subsequently merged with the JUM.

JUM is opposed to the electoral process in the State of J & K.

Political Affiliation Must for Link with the ISI

After splitting with the HUM, Nasrul Islam of JUM sought military and financial assistance from the ISI for his outfit. Senior ISI officers in Muzaffarabad advised him to get JUM affiliated to a political organisation in the Valley before seeking financial/material support or undertaking terrorist actions.

To meet the ISI – demanded prerequisite, in February/ March 1992 Nasrul Islam managed to get the JUM affiliated to JKMC, a secessionist political organisation led by Prof. Abdul Ghani Bhatt, is its armed wing. But it proved a short-lived union because Bhatt, on his release from detention soon after this understanding rejected it since it was taken in his absence and without his approval. The JUM then negotiated with the TUM and Hizb for a merger, but all those exertions proved abortive.

Frustrated in its effort to find a political associate, the JUM launched its own political wing in March 1995, as a last resort to have its own political facade. It was christened Tehrik-e-Khilafat-e-Islam (TKI) with an 8-member Central Committee, and Mohd Yusuf Shah as its *Amir*.

Operations and Consequent Muzzling of Media

After it gained membership of the IRF in 1996, JUM activities picked up. On 23 October that year, it exploded a car bomb outside the MLA hostel in Srinagar, which killed two policeman. It again triggered an explosion on 3 January 1997 near a nursing home on Gupkar Road, Srinagar, which killed seven civilians and injured double that number. One of its women terrorists, Farhat of Rajbagh, and her maternal uncle exploded an IED in auto-rickshaw to target J & K Minister of State, Ali Mohd Sagar who was scheduled to travel on that route. But the Minister survived.

The JUM managed to penetrate certain sections of the State bureaucracy. Consequently, some of its leaders, arrested for terrorism, got released with the connivance of certain officials.

Besides its infamous, vociferous anti-India compaign, the JUM came to be known as the first terrorist outfit in the State to muzzle the print and electronic media, carrying an unrelenting campaign against the right to freely disseminate the news and reviews as they saw them. It opposed the telecaste in Feb-June 1993 of the well-liked Hindi serial *Bible Ki Kahaniyan*. It conducted a shrill, systematic campaign against the All India Radio/Doordarshan (AIR/DD), threatening to blow-up the station. It killed an AIR news reader, Mohd Shafi Butt in Srinagar on 2 October (Gandhiji's birthday) 1993 and abducted seven Air/DD employees, including an Assistant Director, although they were subsequently released.

The JUM also harassed the staff of the local dailies like *Srinagar Times* and *Al Safa*.

On 16 December 1996, it gave a *bandh* call to protest the 1971 dismemberment of Pakistan – independent Bangladesh was born that day – which was also supported by the IRF. Obviously, any stick is good enough to leat BEAT India with. (So they were blaming India for break-up of Pakistan, forgetting conveniently that it was the 'butchers' in the Pak Army uniform who repulsed the distraught Bengali majority out of the wedlock after 24-year old uneasy cohabitation).

On 5 January 1997, the IRF gave a *bandh* call to draw attention of the people to the 5 January 1949 UN Resolution granting the right of the Kashmiris to self-determination *after* laying down certain conditionalities to be met by the two sides before the start of the process (That Pakistan was and still is unwilling to meet these conditions is often forgotten not only by terror merchants like the IRF but also by well-informed if not well-meaning analysts and politicians).

The JUM considered the surrender of Hashim Qureshi, the hijacker of the 1971 Indian Airlines flight to Lahore, as an act of treason and had threatened action against him.

ISI Chaperoned JUM into Nepal

ISI led it into Nepal by hand. Intelligence has details of its operations on record. It was clear that the outfit operated in Nepal in cahoots with the ISI officials – 'operatives' would be a more accurate descriptions – posted in the Pak embassy in Kathmandu. It had opened a shop, appropriately called Satellite Communication Centre, in Thamel locality of Kathmandu, in early 1996, with STD, ISD, and fax facilities under the overall charge of Farooq Ahamd Ahangar. This shop, nay 'joint', provided all necessary infrastructural wherewithal for operations in the Kashmir Valley.

Ahangar left Kathmandu in August 1996 for the Valley, handing over the 'shop' to Riyaz Ahmad Shah. Subsequently, Ahangar closed shop, literally, and returned to POK.

JUM Quarrel with the APHC and Within Itself

Even while being its constituent, the JUM severely and publicly castigated the APHC when the OIC invited the latter to participate in the 7-9 September 1994 conference of its Foreign Ministers and it did. It passionately adumbrated that the APHC leaders had neither any moral right to represent the Mujahideen fighting bravely for the cause of Kashmir's freedom nor any justification for its claim of being the sole representative of Kashmir. The spat obviously left a trail of bitterness against the JUM among most of the terrorist outfits in the State. After all, no one needs to be reminded that almost all strident and determined groups, intent upon wresting Kashmir from India and its ultimate merger with Pakistan, are members of the APHC and have been functioning under this umbrella conglomerate for years. Even more, the APHC have represented anti-Indian terrorist organisations all over the world.

It needs to be emphasised that the JUM, among the smaller and less powerful terrorist, separatist outfits, was always tilting at windmills when ever it saw itself ignored, as if it were a major, if not the only one, secessionist formation fighting India. Its first instance was the public criticism of the APHC by the JUM because the former had agreed to attend the OIC Foreign Ministers conference in September 1994, just mentioned above. The same syndrome was visible – was it due to an innate sense of insecurity, or the inferiority complex of the weak? – whenever an individual terrorist leader or an organisation had its strength or influence on an ascending curve. Here follow two examples: The huge public response to and enthusistic public receptions for Shabir Shah after his release from detention seemed to have perturbed the JUM no end! So, the JUM took it upon itself to warn Shabir Shah on 5 November 1994 against building an independent political career for himself, and criticised him for behaving like Sheikh Abdullah – as if that in itself was a crime! The history repeated itself when Yasin Malik received a huge popular reaction from the people' and a loud acclaim from some academic circles on his release on 17 May 1995. So uneasy was the JUM leadership over this phenomenon that it accused the JKLF of some dark, shadowy underhand deal with New Delhi.

JUM was no stranger to intra-outfit recriminations – the usual bane of almost all terrorist outfits in J & K. It had faction fights over the leadership issue. Abdul Rashid Mir, alias Majrooh, brother of Nasrul Islam was opposed to the appointment of Muzaffar Mirza alias Asghar as the Acting Chief in the Valley, with the two factions trading allegations and counter allegations in a no-holds barred free-for-all. If the Majrooh faction accused Asghar of misappropriating JUM funds and associating with the HUM, the latter returned the compliments in equal vehemence – accusing Majrooh of having cornered huge funds for personal gratification and joining hands in unholy alliance with the JKPL-S and Dukhtran-e-Millat (DEM).

The mutual acrimony did not end with the inter-factional accusations flying thick and fast in the air. Majrooh even tried to enlist the support of the POK-based JUM leader, Manzoor Ahmad Shah to dethrone his rival, Asghar, to take control himself.

JUM : Not a lead Player

JUM leader from POK, Abu Rafia, participated in the 11th Ijtemah (= rally, gathering, congregation) of the LET at Muridke in November 1998 as a representative of the JUM (J & K).

To be truthful, the JUM has never managed to be counted among the front-ranking terrorist organisations like the JEM and LET.

Jumaat-ul-Mujahideen Almi (JUMI)

Formation	1990
Strength	130, including foreign elements
Headquarters	Islamabad/Muzaffarabad
Objectives	Establishment of Islamic supremacy in the world and liberation of Muslim minority areas through armed struggle.

Sponsors — Pakistan; POK; ISI; Pan-Islamic organisations; major industrialists of Pakistan; West Asia; JUUI/Tabligh-ul-Jamaat (Pakistan); HEI (Yunus Khalis Jamaluddin Haqqani, Afghanistan); Taliban.

Leadership

- Mufti Bashir Ahmad, *Amir-e-Ala*, Muzaffarabad.
- Abdul Sattar Salik, Nazim (Rawalpindi).
- Khalil-ul-Rehman, Dera Ismail Khan.
- Maulana Tayyab, *Imam,* Guru Mandir Mosque, Karachi.
- Quzi Hasibur Rehman, *Nazim*, Miran Shah.
- Qari Isaq, *Naib Nazim*, Miran Shah.
- Maulvi Mohd Iqbal, Nazim, Abbotabad.
- Javed Iqbal Afghani, Group Commander (Foreign Mujahideen in J & K).

Areas of Operations

J & K, Pakistan, Saudi Arabia, Afghanistan, West Asian Countries.

Links with Political Groups/Parties

Pakistan, ISI, POK, HKUM, HUJI, HUA, HEI.

Foreign Links

Mainly Pakistan and Afghanistan.

Origin

The Pan-Islamic JUMI was formed by Maulana Masood Kashmiri in 1990 after breaking away from HKUM, which itself was the result of a split in 1985 in the HUJI due to personality personality clash between the HUJI Chief Commander Maulana Fazal-ur-Rehman Khalil and its Amir Qari Saifullah Akhtar. At the time of formation of the HKUM, Maulana Kashmiri had sided with Maulana Khalil.

As the three outfits – HUJI, HKUM and JUMA – drew their cadres from among the youth of the Deobandi persuation, eminent Deobandis attempted re-unifying these three bickering outfits. The scholarly clerics succeeded in unifying two – HUJI and HKUM – of these three outfits into HUA, as the JUMA chose to retain its separate identity.

Fought in Afghanistan, and then in Kashmir

The JUMA fighters actively participated in the Afghan war against the Najibullah regime, when the HEI (Afghanistan) provided the logistic support to its cadres. The outfit had its own training camp in Pharsigund, near Yawar.

In the latter half of 1993, JUMA was to become one of the first outfits to induct foreign mercenaries, mostly from Pakistan and POK, into Kashmir.

The 1993-94 period proved hard time for the JUMA. Four of its cadres were arrested on 14 October 1993. Shahid Khan, an Afghan national and its Deputy Chief Commander in the Kashmir Valley, was killled in an encounter with the SF in 'Sopamarg'.[10] Its Chief Commander, Mohd Saghir, was killed in the Valley in an encounter during the second week of January 1994.

Lashkar-e-Tayyaba (LET)

Formed	1980
Strength	500 including the Pakistan and Afghanistan trained militants
Headquarters	Muridke, near Lahore (Pakistan)
Objectives	Establishment of Nizam-e-Mustafa in the world; merger of J & K with Pakistan; establish the rule of Allah the world over
Sponsors	Pakistan, POK, JAEH (Pakistan)—Hafiz Mohd Yahya Group.

Organisational Structure

* *Amir*
* Supreme Commander
* District Commanders

Leadership

* Hafiz Mohammed Syed (also spelt, Saeed), *Amir,* Finance Chief

* Zaki-ur-Rehman, Naib *Amir* and *Amir* in J & K
* Qari Abu Zar Atta-ur-Rehman, Chief Commander, Kashmir Valley
* Abdullah, Deputy Chief
* Amir Hamza, Publicity Chief
* Prof Mohd. Azam Cheema, Launching Chief and former *Amir* of MDM Training Centre.
* Hafiz Abdul Salam, former *Amir*
* Mian Nayeem, former *Amir*
* Prof. Zaffar Iqbal, Secretary, *Amir-e-Ala*
* Dr. Manzoor, former Chief of Military Wing
* Tameez-ud-din Lakhwi, *Amir* (POK)
* Haji Mohd. Azam (Poonch)
* Muzammil Butt (Doda)
* Mohd. Umair (Baramulla)
* Chaudhri Abdullah Khalid Chauhan (Bagh)
* Rafiq Akhtar (Muzaffarabd)
* Aftab Hussain (Kotli)
* Faisal Dar (Srinagar)
* Chaudhri Yusuf (Mirpur)
* Maulana Mohd. Sharif Balghari (Baltistan)
* Raja Mohd. Irshad
* Masood Lone

Areas of Operations

J & K, POK, Pakistan

Links with Political Parties/Groups

Pakistan, POK, ISI, ABQ, HUM, AFF, TUM, SEJ, ISYF (J & K), JKJEI (POK), HUA, HUM, MM

Foreign Links

Pakistan; ISI; militant outfits like IUM (Egypt); IRG (Algeria); Arab guerrilla groups operating in Pakistan; MJAH (UK, Pakistan); World Kashmir Freedom Movement (London).

Finances

Saudi Arabia, Kuwait, Pakistani industrialists of the Ahl-e-Hadis sect, ISI

Major Acts of Terrorism

* 5 Jan. 96	16 Hindus massacred in Barshalla, Doda
* 25-26 Jan. 97	17 Hindus massacred in Sumber, Doda
* 25-26 Jan. 97	25 Kashmiri Pandits massacred in Wandhama, Srinagar
* 24 June 97	Eight Hindus killed in Swari, Rajouri
* 18 April 98	7 Hindus massacred in Prankote, Doda
* 19 June, 98	25 Hindus massacred in Chapnari, Doda
* 8 Aug., 98	35 labourers massacred in Chamba district, Himachal Pradesh.
* 20 March, 2000	36 Sikhs massacred at Chhattisinghpora, Anantnag on the eve of President Bill Clinton's visit to India.
* 1-2 Aug. 2000	83 civilians killed in separate attacks in Kupwara, Doda, and Anantnag on the eve of talks held between the HUM and the Indian government
* 10 Aug. 2000	Three civilians killed, 42 injured in two bomb attacks in a gathering of SF in Srinagar.
* 22 Dec. 2000	Fidayeen squad attack army garrison in the Red Fort, Delhi, one killed, one captured.
* 16 Jan. 2001	A terrorist squad attack Srinagar airport; six of them killed.
* 22 Oct. 2001	Four fidayeen killed in an attack on Awantipora airbase.
* 15 Jan. 2002	Four terrorists arrested in New Delhi; 8 kg RDX recovered; had plans to disrupt Republic Day parade, 26 January.

* 20 Jan. 2002	Eight children, two men and one women killed in Behra, Poonch, terrorists were led by Mohd. Najeeb Salwa
* 22 Jan 2002	Mohd. Najeeb Salwa and his associates killed; Poonch
* 7 May 2002	Village Defence Committee members kill two cadres including a District Commander, Abu Abdul Qazi; village Dammi Lopara, Doda
* 2 Aug. 2002	15 civilians massacred in Shroti Dhar, Doda

Origins

The LET is the military wing of Markaz Dawa-ul-Irshad (MDI). The two are rather tightly knit and have an undistinguishable relationship in J & K militancy. That is the reason to discuss it together here.

The MDI was jointly founded by Zafar Iqbal and Prof Hafiz Mohd. Sayed (University of Engineering and Technology, Lahore) and Abdullah Azam of the International Islamic University in the 1980s. It is affiliated to the Jamat-Ahl-e-Hadis (Hadith) (JAEH), Pakistan and propagates the pan-Islamic Wahabi ideology.

The MDI has fought the Soviets in Afghanistan alongwith the Jamaat Al Dawa Ilal Quran va Sunna. The MDI believes the democracy is the tool of infidels. It has nearly 500 offices in Pakistan. After the Afghan War, it initiated the induction of its cadres into J & K.

LET cadres are drawn from this radical Sunni sect which believes in the sayings/rulings of the Prophet or the 'First Family' alone.

At a meeting held at Tehran in mid-1993, the LET forged an understanding with AG Lone, Chairman, JKPC and Tajmul Islam, *Amir*, Al Barq. This pact paved the way for the LET-JKPC-Al Barq cooperation and coordination in J & K operations. The MDI started the induction of its cadres under the banner of LET after the Tehran meeting.

The MDI/LET combine has emerged as a very well organised jihad group in J & K.

LET : Ways of its Training

The combine runs an arms training centre in Afghanistan's Kunnar province which can handle/train groups (of cadres) up to 600. The MDI has a training camp in Pakistan also, near village Nungal Sodham, removed 1 km from Muridke. In addition they have training camps in Kasur and Muzaffarabad as well.

It conducts two types of training for its trainees: (1) a 3-week basic course, called Daura Aam; and (2) a 3-month advanced course, called 'Daura Khas'.

LET has Worldwide Links

It is important for the Indian strategic community as also for Indians who have their heads deeply buried in the sand because of ideological compulsions or misplaced convictions flowing from so-called liberal mindset—some think it is a sickness that can truly be termed *liberalitis*—accepting in unthinking manner, a kind of mental bankrupty, the passionate outpourings from mushy peaceniks, particularly of Indian variety, to note carefully that the LET/MDI believe that "Kashmir is the gateway for the rescue of India's 125 million Muslims." Its objective is not the mere liberation of Kashmiri Muslims but also Indian Muslims from the Dar-ul-Harb, viz. 'Hindu' India, even if officially it is 'secular' nation.

To advance this cause, it has assiduously forged links with militant—more accurately, 'terrorist'—movements in Afghanistan, Bosnia, Palestine and Kashmir. Fundamentalists from Saudi Arabia, Kuwait, Cuba, the US, Nepal, Afghanistan, Kashmir, Nigeria, Myanmar and the Philippines have attended its hugely popular and massively attended annual conventions at Muridke, near Lahore.

Another faction of the Ahle Hadis (AEH) known as Markazi Jamaat Ahl-e-Hadith (MJAH), Lahore, patronises the TUM, a separatist outfit in the Valley. The Birmingham unit of the Jammat-e-Ahl-e-Hadith (JAEH) has been active in promoting the liberation of Kashmir.

Despite ideological differences over jihad, the MDI/LET has collaborative arrangements with the JKJEI (PoK), HUA, Al Barq and HUM. If it is a question of serving their visceral anti-

Indianism, these outfits can unite for the 'sacred' cause of wrenching Kashmir out of the Indian Union, keeing aside the ideological considerations.

Following the axiom that an enemy's enemy is a friend, the MDI/LET had/has established a nexus with the Pak-based Sikh terrorist leader Lakhbir Singh Rode and his organisation, the International Sikh Youth Federation (ISYF). Practising clever tactics, LET cadres in the guise of the Sikhs have been inducted into J & K via Nepal. The ISYF collaboration has been expanded and deepened to facilitate the expansion and wider spread of the LET-incitad terrorism network to other parts of India—to sabotage it from within, besides bleeding it through the well-nuanced policy of 'thousand cuts'.

Operational Highlights and Major Landmarks

The outfit heralded its presence in the J & K in February 1993 when it inducted its first group of 12 Pak/Afghan trained mercenaries into the State, in the Poonch sector. It held fire till the LET had inducted over 300 well-trained and equipped foreign (terrorist) mercenaries in Kupwara, Badgam, Doda, Rajouri and Poonch districts. Then it struck the first major blow. A gang of 50-60 ultras ambushed an army patrol on 29 October, 1994, killing/capturing five of them, including two officers.

Besides indulging in the mindless terrorism, the outfit does not forget its political agenda—disrupting the electoral, democratic process. The LET forged a Coordination Committee in early 1996 with three other like-minded *Tanzeems,* viz. the HUM, HUA and AFF, aimed at disrupting and stalling that year's Parliamentary (Lok Sabha) polls.

The TUM represents LET in the UJC. It is also a constituent of the Shora-e-Jihad (SEJ).

The MDI/LET pair clandestinely worked with the *madrassas* (= religious schools run by the Islamic clerics and charities, essentially, to teach Quran and *Shariat* to the young school children and boys) like the Al Mahadul Islamic, New Delhi and Tarim-ul-Islam *Madrassa,* Bareilly to plan and execute terrorist/ militant operations in J & K and rest of India. The diabolical plans hatched by the two included, at one time or other, the assassination of Indian Prime Ministers, Shiv Sena Chief Bal

Thackeray and surprise of surprises, even SAS Geelani, JKJEI and AG Lone, JKPC. For the puritans of the LET, even starkly anti-Indian fanatics like Geelani and Lone do not measure upto their parameters of visceral anti-Indianism.

The LET has planned and carried out some major attack in synch with the HUM. The atrocious massacre of 23 persons (all Kashmiri Pandits) in Wandhama, Srinagar on 23 January 1988 belongs to this category. To make a statement to the international community and convey a defiant message to Gen. Musharraf and his American overlords, the LET orchestrated a death dance of macabre proportions by staging the massacre of 36 Sikhs at Chhattisinghpora, Anantnag on 20 March, 2000 on the eve of President Bill Clinton's visit to India.

The LET flaunted its capabilities by staging several fidayeen attacks on the SF. The attack on 27 December, 1999 on the Headquarter of the Special Operations Group (SOG) was one example of such attacks, dubbed 'spectacular' by the press.

MUSLIM CONFERENCE (MC)

Formed	12 January, 1989
Strength	10,000
Headquarters	Sopore, Baramullah
Objectives	Independent J & K with Pre-1947 status
Sponsors	ISI, Sardar Abdul Qayoom Khan, former Prime Minister, now President, POK

Leadership

* Prof Abdul Ghani Bhatt, Patron
* Ghulam Nabi Sumji, President
* Iftiqar Hussain Jalili, Vice President
* Advocate Abdul Hamid, General Secretary

Areas of Operation

Kashmir Valley

Links with Political Parties/Groups

Pakistan, POK, ISI, Pasdaran-e-Islam (PEI) JUM, APHC, JKJEI/HUM

Foreign Links

Pakistan, POK, ISI

Origins

The Muslim Conference (MC) was launched on 12 January 1989 by Prof. Abdul Ghani Bhatt, a JKJEI activist, in protest against the 'weak kneed' policy of his outfit's leaders over the Kashmir issue and their failure to give a sustained boost to the Muslim United Front (MUF) in the valley. Interestingly, he was supported by a heavy weight politico from across the LOC, POK Prime Minister Sardar Abdul Qayoom Khan, who also assured the MC leadership of financial assistance.

Prof. Bhatt embarked upon the ambitious plan to unite all non-JKJEI, secessionist groups, including the JKPL, under the MC banner. He also contaited the leaders of various militant outfits (including Farooq Rehmani and Dr. Ghulam Qadir Wani), for the same over-arching aim. Simultaneously, he was also engaging Al Jihad, Al Barq, and Muslim Mujahideen to counter the onslaught from the powerful HUM.

The MC has received heavy funding from Pakistan, mainly through *hawala* transactions, since its very birth. But the vast resource base notwithstanding, the MC has failed to create a popular sentiment among the masses of common people, or even to build a strong and dedicated cadre.

But what was more damaging for the organisation was that top leadership, including Prof. Bhatt, Ghulam Sumji and Mushtaq Wani, was accused of misappropriation of funds by none others than their own middle level colleagues. Simply put, what it meant was that these three were no different than so many corrupt leaders heading other outfits, similarly mired knee deep in 'mud of corruption'.

Its Military Wing Proved a Disappointment

The MC launched the Pasdaran-e-Islam (PEI) in early 1990 as its armed wing. But unfortunately for it, the PEI remained largely inactive. As an alternative, the MC adopted JUM as its militant wing in September 1991, and about same time, Mushtaq Ahmad Wani was deputed as its representative in POK.

On his release in April 1992, Prof. Bhatt disowned the JUM, since it was appointed "without my approval", and in turn, adopted militant outfit MM as his armed wing. Mohd. Ahsan Dar, former chief of the HUM, was appointed to head the MM.

MC jains infighting within the APHC

After the APHC was constituted as an umbrella conglomerate, the MC activities came to be projected through the platform of the former, since it did not have an effective cadre of dedicated workers on the ground. Prof. Bhatt organised anti-India rallies and opposed the electoral process in J & K, something that was also an important plank in the agenda of the APHC.

He got marginalised in the APHC due to the domineering proaclivities of the JKJEI/HUM. As a result, he started boycotting the meetings of the APHC. He also developed significant differences with the JKJEI leaders in the APHC over the killing of his brother, Mohd. Sultan Bhatt, on 8 November, 1996. Sultan was allegedly killed by the HUM ultras.

With the inter-outfit equations frequently changing, dictated by the changing dynamics of the situation flowing from the strength and influence of different constituent at a given time, Prof. Bhatt had joined hands with the JKEI to marginalise Yasin Malik and his JKLF, in mid-1994 when he perceived Yasin as Creating an outonomous base for himself, independent of the APHC. The entire APHC leadership was against Yasin when he was engaged in a campaign, July-August, 1994, for removal of the Hazratbal siege (The issue has already been discussed in an earlier section).

Mahaz-e-Azadi (MEA)

Formed	May 1977
Strength	150
Headquarters	Srinagar
Objectives	Self-determination for Kashmiris; mobilise opinion against the Indian government; terrorise non-Muslims

Leadership

* Sofi Mohd. Akbar, Founder
* Mohd. Altaf Khan, Chairman
* Ghulam Mohiuddin Mandoo, General Secretary

Areas of Operations

Kashmir valley, especially Anantnag, Baramulla and Srinagar district.

Links with Political Parties/Groups

Pakistan, POK, ISI, JKLF, ISL, JKML, 'Operation Balakot', QMC

Foreign Links

Pakistan, POK, ISI, JKLF (UK)

Finances

Pakistan, ISI, POK

Origins : Courtesy Pakistan

Sofi Mohd Akbar, a prominent leader of the Plebiscite Front (PF), nearing obliteration, was opposed to the pact reached between Sheikh Abdullah and Prime Minister Indira Gandhi in 1975. During his April 1977 visit to Pakistan, Mohd. Yusuf Buch, Special Assistant to Premier Z.A. Bhutto, urged Akbar to float an organisation to rake up the J & K issue with a pro-Pakistan line. The very next month (on 15 May, 1977), Akbar just did that, and established Mahaz-e-Azadi with the help of some extremist elements of the nearly defunct PF. He called upon the Kashmiri Muslims to join him and continue the struggle for self-determination.

Understandably enough, the MEA has maintained a pro-Pakistan stance. In 1978, Akbar attempted establishing links with the UK-based JKLF leaders to work for the 'Common goal'.

Akbar vehemently opposed the death sentence awarded to the JKLF activist Mohd. Maqbool Butt in 1984. After his execution, the MEA staged protest demonstrations, burning the Indian flags and hosting the Pak flags.

Change of Leadership and its Objectives

Mohd. Altaf Khan took over as Chairman of the MEA after the death of Akbar in December 1987. Earlier, Aftab was the Chief Organiser of the ISL (now defunct) and had founded the J.K. Muslim League in 1982. He has undergone guerrilla warfare training in Pakistan.

In July, 1989, Azam Inquilabi, on his return to Kashmir Valley after an 11-moth stay in Pakistan, launched military wing of the MEA, and christened it as Operation Balakot (Op BKT).

It seemed, in the true traditions of such Islamic organisations, Inquilabi, the chief of the military wing of the MEA, had started calling the shots even in the parent organisation, MEA after creating Op BKT. He even changed the objective/goal of the MEA—from pro-Pak stance to pro-independence line. A document circulated in July, 1989 itself, possibly immediately after he had floated Op BKT, Inquilabi espoused the concept of an 'independent Kashmir', pushing away pro-Pakistan line followed earlier. Ironically, perhaps brazenly, he welcomed moral and material support from Pakistan—may be, in the same order. In the same statement, it was also adumberated that in case of a military threat from India, China or Russia, the independent Kashmir would enter into a confederation with Pakistan, Afghanistan, and Iran for self-defence. Some strategic thinking this, even when the very foundation of the conceptual framework is missing!

Declining Fortunes Lead to Change of Heart

Altaf Khan moved over to PoK in November 1990. Next year, Bashir Ahmad Butt, other MEA leader, joined the JKLF with his loyalists. Altaf returned to Kashmir in January 1995 and publicly espoused a peaceful solution to the Kashmir issue. This was obviously the result of his frustration in Pakistan whose leaders and agencies he accused of continuously neglecting the pro-independence leaders. He also accused the Pak government of being utterly insensitive towards the problems of Kashmiris.

Altaf's statement advocating peaceful solution to the Kashmir issue became a centre of controversy. The Al Jihad and Al Fateh Force severely criticised him for favouring a peaceful solution. But the JKLF welcomed his return to the Valley and expressed hope that the efforts of the 'genuine freedom fighters' would help in preventing the spilling of the Kashmiri blood.

Expectedly, pro-Paskistan leaders like Geelani and Dr. Mohd Sultan, both of the JKJEI and A G Bhatt were suspicious of Altaf's change of heart.

Later Altaf presented a "conservative peace plan" and floated Qaumi Mushwarati Council (QMC) in pursuit of a moderate approach. In October 2001, Altaf Khan joined hands with former J & K Chief Minister Ghulam Mohd. Shah for seeking a final solution to the Kashmiri issue.

MUSLIM JANBAAZ FORCE (MJF) ALSO JANBAAZ FORCE

Formed	December, 1989
Strength	100
Headquarters	Srinagar
Objectives	Secession of J & K through armed struggle
Sponsors	Pakistan, POK, ISI

Leadership

* Firdous Ahmad Baba (Babar Badar), Founder
* Mohd. Iqbal Kotwal, C-in-C (PoK-based)
* Tanvir Ahmad, Acting Chief
* Masrat Rafiqi, Deputy Chief
* Bashir Ahmad Shah, Finance Chief
* Yunus Tak, Military Adviser
* Adil Faridi, Representative of POK
* Abdul Hamid Wani, Commander

Areas of Operation

* Kashmir Valley and Muslim pockets in Jammu province, particularly Doda district
* Office in Muzaffarabad

Foreign Links

Pakistan, PoK, ISI, UJC (also, MJC)

Links with Political Parties/Groups

Coordinates with militant groups in J & K and the rest of India, especially Sikh extremist groups; constituent of the UJC

Finances

ISI, Kashmir Liberation Cell (KLC)

Publications

Sada-e-Janbaaz

Major Acts of Terrorism

* 18 June, 90	12 vehicles damaged in explosion in the State motor garages in Pratap Chowk, Srinagar
* 19 June, 90	Two jawans killed, eight others injured in rocket attack on the Duke Hotel, Srinagar
* 30 July, 90	Blast in J & K Bank, Civil Secretariat Branch, Srinagar
* 14 August, 90	Blast in temple on Lawrence Road, Delhi
* 14 Dec., 90	Attack on Indian Oil Depot, near Railway Station, Jammu
* 10 Jan., 91	Kidnapped Shabnam Lone, daughter of AG Lone, and her Sikh friend, Jasbir Kaur, alias Jassi; both released later.
* 22 March, 91	Six killed and 28 injured in blasts at Jamia Mosque, Jammu.
* 31 March, 91	Kidnapped two Swedish engineers working on the Uri Hydel Project; named John Ole Loman, Johan Janssen; both later released.
* 12 April, 91	Three killed, 11 injured in a blast at Railway station, Jammu.
* 23 Oct., 91	40 injured in a blast near Raghunath Temple, Jammu.
* 5 Dec., 91	Over 1.75 lakh wooden sleepers, worth Rs. 3 crore, destroyed in a fire at the State Forest Corporation Depot, Udyanpur village, Doda.

Origins

In December 1989, JKPL (S) floated its armed wing in J & K, and named it Farzandan-e-Millat (FEM). Babar Badar was despatched to POK for negotiations with the ISI to extend support to the FEM, which was re-named as Muslim Janbaaz Force (MJF). Later, another delegation, comprising Abdul Hamid Wani and Mohd. Akbar Lone, Lecturer, Regional Engineering College, Srinagar went to Pakistan to finalise the details of arms supply and financial help with the ISI. In return, the MJF leadership was directed to widen its network in J & K.

Large quantities of arms were inducted into the Kashmir Valley through the trainees, guidees, and couriers. Col Asad of the ISI arranged the requisite financial assistance through Hamid Wani. Arms and funds were supplied under an operation code-named 'Al Ghazi'. The training to the MJF cadres was imparted in the camps located in the area near the Afghan border.

MJF abducts Swedish Engineers

In 1991, the MJF joined some other outfits in earning earning notoriety when it kidnapped two Swedish engineers working at the Uri Hydel Project and kept them under prolonged captivity. The subsequent negotiations involving the Swedish emissaries, Pakistan-based MJF leaders and Pakistan officials resulted in the release of the hostages.

MJF : Enervation and Subsequent Revival

Hereafter followed the decline of the MJF caused by the arrests and killing of some of its top leaders. In December, 1991, under pressure from the ISI, and partly as a result of its misadventure related to the Swedish Engineers, MJF was merged with the KJF to create a united armed wing, named Al Jihad Force (AJF), to become the military arm of the JKUPL, the political conglomerated created by merging of various factions of the JKPL. So it was a twin unification in military as well political fields. But the unity was not to last long.

In 1993, at the instance of Shabir Shah, JKPL-S Chief, Babar Badar revived the MJF. In early 1994, Babar deputed Shabir Wani as representative to Pakistan, and resumed the recruitment of Kashmiri Youth, especially in the Doda district, for their arms training in Pakistan. Contacts were renewed with the ISI.

On release of Shabir Shah in May 1994, fresh exercise was set in motion to reunify the JKPL, AJF and MJF in order to optimise their operational effectiveness. But most of the AJF activists of Shabir Shah extended covert/overt support to the MJF.

Post-revival, the MJF remained active mainly in the Doda district. Indicative of an important departure from the erstwhile policy line, Babar Badar, along with Bilal Lodi of ABQ, Imran Rahi of HMM, and Ghulam Mohiuddin Lone of MM, launched the Forum for Permanent Resolution of Kashmir issue, which was prepared for an 'unconditional dialogue' with the Government of India.

Muslim Mujahideen (MM)

Formed	January 1993
Strength	250
Arms held	Around 70 weapons including 50 AK rifles, RLs, and seven sniper rifles
Headquarters	Baramulla
Objectives	Secession of J & K from India and its merger with Pakistan
Sponsors	Pakistan, POK, ISI, JKMC

Organisational Structure

- Appex: 10-member Supreme Command Council.
- Supreme Commander, two Deputy Chiefs, one Chief of operations.
- Districts: District Commanders.

Leadership

- Master Ahsan Dar, Supreme Commander.
- Shabir Ahmad Zargar, Deputy Supreme Commander (in POK).
- Javed Jehangir, Deputy Chief (in POK).
- Abdul Majid Dar, Chief of Operations and Arms Procurement.

- Madassar, aka Ubba Lohar, Farooq Launching Chief.
- Shabir Ahmad, aka Zargar, District Commander, Srinagar

Areas of Operation

Kandi belt of Baramulla and Badgam districts; Srinagar; Anantnag; Kupwara; Pulwama.

Links with Political Parties/Groups

Pakistan, POK, ISI, JKMC.

Finances

Pakistan, POK, ISI, local collections other Equipement.

Other Equipment Communication Sets

Origins

Master Mohd Ahsan Dar was removed from the post of Chief Commander of the HUM following his dogged opposition to the appointment and/or positioning of some untrained/inexperienced JK JEI activists/cadres in key posts of the outfit (that is, HUM). He had earned the wrath of the JKJEI over the execution of Muzaffar Mir (son of a JKJEI chieftain of Anantnag) and for killing a Muslim couple to settle personal scores. In addition to all these, the JKJEI also accused Ahsan Dar of misappropriation of party funds/weapons.

His position becoming untenable in the HUM, given these serious accusations, Ahsan Dar chose the well-trodden route of launching his own outfit in June 1992 with 250 of his trusted men, all experienced militents, who had quit the HUM with him. He named it Mujahideen-e-Islam (MEI). In July 1992, he met with Prof AG Bhat, President, MC, who agreed to own the MEI as a militant wing of his MC.

Ahsan Dar visited Pakistan in August 1992 and met Qayoom Khan, POK Prime Minister, to seek patronage for his outfit. Qayoom persuaded Dar to take over as *Amir* of the Al Mujahid Force (AMF), assuring him of all financial and material assistance. Ultimately and under advice of the ISI, the final arbiter in such situations, Ahsan Dar announced the establishment of the Muslim Mujahideen (MM) on 18 January 1993. It was an amalgamation of Mujahideen-e-Islam (MEI), Al Umar Commandos (AUC), Al must ot a Liberation Tigers

(AMLT) J & K Muslim Liberation Army (JKMLA), and Al Mujahideen Fil Islam (AMFI). He even tried, even if abortively, a merger of some other militant outfits like JUM, AJF, ABQ and Operation Balakot, as the ISI was rather concerned about debilitating inter-organisation clarhes.

Effort at settling the mess and POK connection

On the ground, MM cadres were positioned in Srinagar, Baramulla, Badgam, Anantnag, Kupwara and Pulwama. It coordinated its operations with outfits like the JKLF and AJF. But, on the other hand, it had frequent clashes with the HUM. Sardar Qayoom and Babar Badar, Chief of MJF, tried to knit the ABQ, MM, and MJF into a united whole as an effective alternative to the HUM.

Ahsan Dar again visited Pakistan in July 1993 to have his MM recognised by the UJC. He lodged a protest over continued support by Pakistani authorities to the AMF which was supposed to have merged with the MM, but that position stayed on paper and it in reality had not merged with the MM and continued to maintain its separate, independent identity.

Ahsan Dar was arrested in December 1996 on return from POK. Acceptedly, the arrest was a set back to the MM, but it still continues to have influence in the Kandi belt of Baramullah district.

Parban-e-Islam (PEI)/Hizbul Momineen (HMM)

Formed	1990 (PEI), HMM, 1992
Strength	50-100
Headquarters	Srinagar
Objectives	Liberation of Kashmir through armed struggle; merger with Pakistan
Sponsors	Anjuman-e-Ittehad-ul-Musalmeen

Leadership

PEI

- Sarwar Abbas Ansari, Patron (Pak-based).
- Aga Syed Hassan Al Mousavi, Patron.
- Syed Abbas Rizvi, C-in-C (Pak-based).
- Syed Shaukat Hussain Madani, Secretary.

HMM

- Ali Roza, Chief Patron.
- Maulana Abbas Ansari, Patron.
- Syed Sadiq Rizvi, Patron.
- Aga Syed Hassan Al Mousavi, Patron.
- Khwaja Qasim, Deputy Patron.
- Shuja Hussain, C-in-C (POK).
- Syed Aziz Hussain Rizvi, Chief Commander.
- Moh Yousuf Rather, Chief Commander.
- Basharat Abbas, Deputy Chief (Pak-based).
- Syed Maqsood Rizvi, Representative in Iran

Areas of Operation

Shia-dominated pockets in Srinagar, Badgam and Baramulla districts.

Links with Political Parties/Groups

- HUM, MJF, JKLF, TNFJ.
- Member, Ittehadi Forum; IRF.

Foreign Links

Pakistan, POK, ISI, Iranian fundamentalist organisations.

Finances

ISI, Iran.

Origins

Early 1990, the Shia minority in Kashmir found itself gripped by a feeling of insecurity due to targeted attacks on them by Sunni militants. The community formed a militant organisation for self-defence, known as Pasban-e-Islam (PEI), under the patronage of Anjuman-e-Ittehad-ul-Musalmeen (Pakistan).

The PEI leaders visited Muzaffarabad to explore the possibility of a 'protection' pact with MJF. It proved abortive since the Pak authorities wanted the PEI to join the HUM, something totally unacceptable to them. Consequently, the PEI leaders decided to join the JKLF.

The PEI also forged contacts with the Tehrik Nifaz Fiqa Jaffaria (TNFJ), a Shia *tanzeem* in POK. The latter organised arms training for PEI cadres in a camp near Pershawar. It also advised PEI leadership to set up a training camp of its own. The plan suffered a premature death since the ISI decided it could not afford or handle armed Shia-Sunni clashes in J & K.

The Inevitable Iran Connection

Aga Al Mousavi visited Iran in June 1991 to hold discussions with Iranian leaders. He is believed to have been advised by Alama Syed Ali Naqvi, a leader of the TNJF (Pakistan) to cooperate with the HUM. Consequently, Syed Maqsood Rizvi from Iran visited J & K, November 1991 to March 1992, to persuade Shia leader to adopt a pro-Pakistan line.

Since Anjuman-e-Ittehad-ul-Musalmeen claimed the PEI as its militant *tanzeem* in J & K, it was granted recognition by the UJC and ISI.

PEI Changes Name and Accepts HUM

In March 1992, the PEI rechristened itself as Hizbul Momineen (HMM) and accepted the Sunni-dominated HUM as a "brother *tanzeem*". Obviously, Mushtaq Rizvi's over 4-month stay in J & K was successful in wearing down the PEI's opposition and aversion to the HUM.

Several Shia leaders, including Maulvi Abbas Ansari, were uncomfortable because the JEI-HUM, the Sunni pair, were staunchly opposed to the Shiite beliefs. Subsequently, and understandably, the supporters/loyalists of Abbas Ansari revived the PEI.

Shora-e-Jihad (SEJ)

Formed	July 1996
Strength	5,000
Headquarters	Srinagar
Objectives	Liberation of Kashmir through armed struggle, and merger with Pakistan

Sponsors

- Pakistan, ISI

- Constituent Units: HUM, TUM, AJF, HUA, AUM. Each of them in turn has individual ISI and various other sponsorships.

Leadership

- S. Hamid (JKUPL), Chairman (earlier from AJF and JKPL).
- Pir Mohd Maqbool, Member.
- Abdul Rauf, *Amir-e-Ala* (from TUM).
- Firdous Kirmani, Coordinator (from JKJEI, HUM).
- Prof Abdul Hassan, Finance Chief (from HUA).
- Ghulam Hassan Khan, Member (from HUM).
- Mohd Zaman, Member (HUM Divisional Commander).
- Abdul Hamid Fayas, Member (from HUM).
- Abdul Hyder, Member (from HUM).
- Mohd Ashraf Laya, Member (from HUM).

Origin

In July, 1996 five militant outfits—HUM, AJF, TUM, HUA and AUM—created an umbrella organisation, Shora-e-Jihad (SEJ), to provide a 'single nodal point' to exercise command and control over the militant/terrorist operations in J & K, besides countering CI Groups in a coordinated manner. Having played a leading role in conceptualisation and creation of this conglomerate, S Hamid was logically elected its first Chairman.

The creation of SEJ was supported by another, similar conglomerate, the Islamic Resistance Force (IRF), and its constituents: AFF, JUM, HIZB and HMM.

SEJ: Its Major Political Exertious

The SEJ took off with opposing the 1996 Lok Sabha election process in J & K. In a well-planned and thoroughly-executed strategy, it identified and subsequently neuntralised (including physical elimination) 'anti-movement' activists and cadres who advocted secularism/mainstream politics. Interestingly, on 16 August 1996, the SEJ organised a function to pay tribute to Gen Zia-ul-Haq, the late military ruler of Pakistan on his first death anniversary. It was a statement made by the secessionists the Indian policy makers and saner elements in Kashmir must have made a note of. When they prepared and circulated a 'hit list' of political leaders and senior bureaucrats they made no efforts to conceal their intention or plans. This was brazenness unvarnished.

The SEJ imposed a ban on local newspapers like *Afaq* and *Nida-e-Mashriq* because it felt they did not give 'adequate' coverage to the militant activities. The media people held a voluntary strike in March 1997 to protest this ban.

It is no doubt that S Hamid was the founding Chairman of the SEJ, but it was actually controlled by the JKJEI/HUM. This was hardly surprising, not only because Firdous Kirmani of the HUM/JKJEI was its coordinator, but also because a huge majority of the top posts in the conglomerate were held by the TKJEI/HUM. After his death, five HUM leaders got appointed as SEJ office bearers, giving the pro-Pakistani hard-liners even a greater control over the conglomerate.

Dissentions Weaken the SEJ

In the course of time, the AJF, a founding member, was sidelined, with just two appointments in the SEJ pecking order. S Hamid, himself beset by difficulties even as its chairman, expressed his desire to relinguish the high office. He was persuaded to continue, in the larger interests of the movement, by the AJF and JKPL leadership, including Altaf Masoodi, Abdul Khaliq Sagar, Nayeem Khan and Ghulam Hassan Lone.

S Hamid was killed in April 1998. His demise marked the onset of the period of SEJ's dorment militancy. It was no longer the nodal point for insurgent anti-India activities.

Tehrik-e-Jihad (TEJ)

Formed	April 1997
Strength	550-600, mostly foreign mercenaries, Pak ex-servicemen.
Arms and	AK 47-130, LMGs-15, HMGs-10
Equipment	RLs-6, pistols-60, sophisticated rockets-8, including four of 107 mm dia.
	Advanced communication network
Headquarters	Muzaffarabad

Objectives — Liberation of Kashmir through armed struggle and its accession to Pakistan.

Sponsors

Pakistan, POK, ISI.

Organisational Structure

Two-tier

- Command Tier with Headquarters in Muzaffarabad (POK).
- Operational Tier (army pattern) in J & K

POK-based Command Tier

- *Amir-e-Ala, Syasi Amir, Amir-e-Maliat,* Publicity Chief, *Camp Amir, Naib Amir,* and *Launching Amir.*

Operational Tier

- Supreme Commander, Chief Commander, Military Adviser, and a Launching Chief.
- *Amir-e-Ala* supervises the TEJ; responsible for organising finances, arms, ammunition and logistics in coordination with the ISI.
- *Amir-e-Maliat* is responsible for financial management; assumed importance as JEJ has 'preferred' status.

Leadership

- Abdul Rashid Qureshi, *Amir-e-Ala* (based in POK).
- Mohd Altaf Wani, *Siyasi Amir* and Supreme Commander (presently in POK).
- Advocate Mushtaq Ahmad Wani, Publicity Chief (former member MM and MC).
- Qayoom, Supreme Commander (J & K).
- Sonaullah Khan, Chief Commander.
- Khalid, Military Adviser.
- Shah Nawaz, Launching Chief.
- Majid Dar, *Naib Amir*.
- Javed, Launching, Chief in the Valley.
- Jahangir Badar, Divisional Commander, Poonch and Rajouri.

Areas of Operation

Kupwara, Baramulla, Rajouri, Poonch, Tangdar (J & K); Muzaffarabad (POK).

Links with Political Parties/Groups

Pakistan, POK, ISI, MM, HUA, HUM, AMF, JKMLA, HIZB.

Foreign Links

Pakistan, POK, ISI.

Finances

"Most favoured" status accorded by ISI Origins

The 1996 ISI assessment disclosed that the internal disputes within the HUA were jeopardising operations in J & K. Sardar Qayoom, former Prime Minister of POK, and then its President was persuaded that his *tanzeems* like the AMF and AUI had ceased being effective. In January 1997, it was decided to merge the defunct outfitslike AUI, HIZB, JKMLA, and MM and provide a new thrust to the ISI-managed insurgency in J & K. Qayoom agreed to avoid public criticism of the ISI.

In April 1997, the ISI created the new *tanzeem*, Tehrik-e-Jihad (TEJ) by bringing in sizable section of HUA cadres, especially the Gujjars of Rajouri, Poonch, Kupwara and Baramulla districts as also of other areas along the LOC. The TEJ was led by Faroq Qureshi, a Gujjar and ISI favourite due to his reputation as a "launching expert."

Incidentally, the HUA was declared a Terrorist Organisation by the US on 8 October 1997.

Recruitment and Training

Mohd Hanif, TEJ District Commander, was advised to recruit committed Gujjar, Pahadi, and/or Bakarwal teenagers to serve as guides/porters. The ISI preferred guides from the border/LOC areas to those from the Valley who were deemed as unreliable. The guides were recruited under two categories: Full Guides and Half Guides. Full guides were entrusted with the responsibility of reaching men and materials to ultimate destinations such as the hide-outs in the Valley, target areas, or launch sites. They had to be totally reliable and trustworthy.

Half Guides were essentially meant for employment along the LOC, to facilitate the infiltration/exfiltration of the militants across it.

The ISI also inducted retired Pak Army personnel, mostly JCOs/NCOs, and foreign mercenaries into J & K. They often dominated the *tanzeem*.

The apprehended TEJ operatives in J & K disclosed that the operations in the Valley are some times planned, and always coordinated from Muzaffarabad by Maj Gen Nayeem Akhtar of the Pak Army. ISI's Sialkot office performs similar operational functions in the Jammu region.

In line with other outfits, and as planned and desired/directed by the ISI, the TEJ also has actively undertaken operations to disrupt/sabotage the 1998 Lok Sabha polls as well as national functions/celebrations to commemorate the Republic Day and Independence Day. In the same vein, they have often mounted attacks and exploded bombs at the people gathered to celebrate Hindu festivals.

The JEJ took over some of the training camps/launching bases located at Ashmuqam, Kel, Dudniyal and Lipa (POK) and Dardpora (Kupwara), which had been used earlier by Al Barq or HUA. The TEJ has successfully utilised the Gujjars and Pahadis for dumping arms and ammunition in large quantities at camps and bases mentioned above, as also some others located elsewhere.

Farooq Qureshi was an invitee at the 11th annual *ijtema* (= rally, gathering) of the LET/MDI held at Muridke on 4 November 1998.

Current Status: Comparatively Speaking

The TEJ does not seem to have lived upto the expectations of its masters—Pakistan and ISI. This was a cause of disappointment, particularly when it had operational understanding with the likes of the HUA and HUM.

At the best, it could be rated as moderately effective whereas more daring and sensational operations were executed by the outfits like Lashkar-e-Tayyaba and Jaish-e-Mohammed.

Tehrik-ul-Mujahideen (TUM)

Formation	June 1990
Strength	65, including 35 foreign militants
Arms	Over 45 weapons, including 25 AK rifles and 15 pistols
Headquarters	Badgam (Kashmir)
Objectives	Merger of Kashmir with Pakistan; promotion of Pan-Islamism
Sponsors	Pakistan; POK; ISI; Jamaat-e-Ahl-e-Hadis Ashvi (JAHA, POK).

Organisational Structure

- Apex: *Amir,* Chief Commander, *Naib Amir,* Operations Chief, Military Adviser, Intelligence Chief.
- Field Level: Divisional Commanders, District Commanders (one each for three districts of Valley), Regimental Commanders.

Leaderships

- Mohd Abdullah Tairi (President, Ahal-e-Hadis, J & K), Patron.
- Abdul Rashid, Chief Commander.
- Abdul Ghani Dar, *Amir-e-Ala* (in POK).
- Sheikh Jameel-ur-Rahman, Supreme Commander (in Bangladesh).
- Fida Hussain, Finance Chief and Deputy Chief.
- Aizaz Ahmad, Deputy Chief (in Bangladesh).
- Abdul Hafiz Chikkan, *Naib Amir*.
- Ghulam Hassan, Military Adviser.
- Shoukat Hussain Wani, Representative in SEJ.
- Shakur, Chief Coordinator (Finance, Logistics).
- Bashir Madani, Representative in Saudi Arabia.

Area of Operations

- Kashmir Valley, especially concentrated in Beeru belt of Badgam district, Ganderbal and downtown localities of Srinagar; Pulwama and Anantnag.

- Offices in Muzaffarabad and Jalalabad.

Foreign Links

Pakistan, POK, ISI, Saudi Arabia, Bangladesh, J & K Jamaat-e-Ahal-e-Hadis Ashvi (JAH, POK).

Links with Political Parties/Groups

Pakistan, POK, ISI, HUM, SEJ, LET, AEH, JKLF (Pakistan).

Finances

Pakistan, ISI, JHA (POK), local collections (extortions/protection money).

Origins

In June 1990, Yunus Khan, a confidante of Mohd Abdullah Tairi, President, J & K Jamaat-e-Ahal-e-Hadis (JAEH), formed the Tehrik-ul-Mujahideen (TUM).

Recruitment and Training

It drew cadres from youth belonging to the Ahal-e-Hadis (AEH) sect which believes in the teachings of the Prophet and the First Family.

From July 1990, the TUM started sending its cadres for arms training to Pakistan. It also opened its office in Muzaffarabad (POK) which was managed by Ghulam Mohd Ghani and Mohd Shah Wani.

Operations and Clashes with HUM

TUM's activities largely remained confined to Badgam and Anantnag districts. In 1993, the POK nationals also joined its operations. It created the new post of Operations Chief in April 1995 to increase its operational effectiveness in the Valley.

Its activists were directed to secure the support of the intelligentsia for the objectives of the TUM and its ongoing militant operations to achieve them.

Towards the late 1990, its relations with HUM started deteriorating. In April/May 1991, HUM ultras killed two activists of the TUM in Kupwara and Anantnag. The mutual hostilities led to the killing of the son of Abdul Qadir Wani, *Naib Amir-e-Ala* of TUM by HUM cadres. Even when subsequently the two became members of the umbrella organisation, SEJ, formed in

1996, the mutual blood-letting between them continued unabated.

Dissensions within

The TUM suffered initial setbacks due to personality clashes and ego hassles between Sajjad Mir and the POK-based Tamveer-ul-Islam. The things sank so low that in 1992, the latter discontinued providing help to the TUM unit in the Kashmir Valley.

In July 1993, Bashir Ahmad Sofi took over as the C-in-C, Kashmir Valley after the killing of Sajjad Mir. He visited Pakistan in October 1993 to investigate allegations of funds embezzlement against Islam, and to streamline the POK unit. Sofi then tried to mend the fences with Islam with the help of Tamizuddin (*Amir* of LET, POK) and some ISI officers. But all to no avail. Sofi then opened a separate office in Muzaffarabad by regrouping/redeploying loyal cadres.

Establishing a Nexus, and Reasons for it

The TUM was a founding member of the SEJ, and its objective in helping the creation of the conglomerate was to checkmate and subsequently marginalise the APHC, which was dominated by the JKJEI/HUM. After all, the founding Chairman of the SEJ, S. Hamid, was considered a close supporter of the TUM.

During his October 1993 visit to Pakistan, Bashir Sofi explored the chances of operational coordination with the LET and held discussions with Tamizuddin and Hafiz Mohd Saeed of the Markaz Dawa-ul-Irshad (MDI). Both *tanzeems* derived inspiration as well as support from the AEH. From 1995, the ISI started routing funds to the LET through the TUM/JAEH (J & K) channels. The TUM also commenced representing the LET's interests in the UJC.

Since its very birth, the TUM has maintained cordial relations with the JKLF (Amanullah) in POK.

Funding Goes International

The AEH emerged as the main channel for the supply of funds to various outfits (including TUM) in J & K from Pakistan and Saudi Arabia.

In July 1990, Sajjad Mir attempted revitalising the TUM and despatched its activist Bashir Sofi to Saudi Arabia for arranging additional funds. Bashir Madani of Pulwama has a carpet business in Riyadh. He was representative of the TUM in Saudi Arabia.

Then there were intelligence reports that Afzal Malik, a Pakistani in leather goods business, was the ISI conduit for the large scale hawala transactins. He used his extensive contacts in Saudi Arabia, Bangladesh, the UK, and the US to facilitate these transactions.

TUM's Tentacles in Bangladesh

During 1996, the TUM established linkages with the Bangladesh AEH Youth Association which helped it in its trans-border operations. It also managed to recruit a chain of sympathisers from among the ranks of the AEH Muslims in West Bengal, particularly in the border areas. They proved excellent guides and good porters for the trans-border movements.

Aijaz Ahmad Ahangar, former Chief Commander of the HUJI in the Valley, joined the TUM after his marriage to the daughter of Abdullah Ghazali, *Amir-e-Ala* of the TUM (in POK). Ahangar operates from the office of the AEH in Dhaka. When the CI operations by the SF became rather vigorous, and consequently risky for the terrorists/secessionists in the Kashmir Valley, the TUM leaders like Javed Ahmad, Operations Chief; Abu Moosa and Mohd Aslam, Divisional Commanders; and Zamilur Rehman, Chief Commander left the Valley for safer havens of Dhaka in October 1997.

When the SF completed their drive against the anti-national terrorists and the situation looked safer, the TUM despatched Mehrajuddin Hafiz to Dhaka in February 1998 as a special emissary of Supreme Commander Abdul Rashid to ask the Dhaka-based leaders to return to the Valley.

Nepal also Helps Indian Terrorists

Pakistani embassy in Kathmandu is known to help its anti-Indian activists/terrorists operating in Kashmir Valley with men, money, and materials. In subsequent phases, Pak diplomatic staff in Nepal extended their anti-Indian network of terrorism to Bangladesh territories as well.

The intelligence reports suggest that prominent TUM leaders, including Abdul Ghani Dar, frequently visited the Pak Embassy in Kathmandu. The Kathmandu network was extensively used to distribute funds received through *hawala* transactions for a number of terrorist/secessionist outfits. Thoughtfully enough, the Pak Embassy also set up some handicrafts emporia in Kathmandu to provide its staff and the transient terror operatives the functional cover so very essential in the given situation.

What was the modus operandi of executing the devious anti-India activities on the Nepalese soil? Most importantly, the TUM's Kathmandu base was used to ferry Pak explosives into Indian territory-generally through the services of the couriers crossing into Indian territory (UP and Bihar) over the open, mostly unmanned, Indo-Nepal border; and occasionally, if deemed fit/necessary/urgent, by air to distant destinations in India. Likewise, the base was also used for human traffic; the move of the TUM cadres/terrorists to and from Pakistan over the Indo-Nepal border for operations in India to foment secessionism and religious strife in India. Later, as mentioned above, the operational reach of its Nepalese Embassy was extended beyond India, into Bangladesh which Pakistan had coopted for its anti-India compaign. But let it be put on record that these under-cover operations suffered a temporary setback with the arrest of Mohd Shafi, First Secretary, along with the TUM activists. Besides, the international Community also came to know of the anti-India shenanigans of the Pak Embassy in Kathmandu. As for India, the arrests came as no news as it was aware of the activities of its intelligence sleuths posted by Pakistan in its Kathmandu Embassy for years on end.

Recent Setbacks and Current Status

In its early years, the TUM suffered a major setback when its founder, Yunus Khan and its then C-in-C, was killed in a 1991-encounter. He was succeeded by Mohd Salim Mir on his return from POK in July 1991.

The outfit suffered a string of major damages/losses in 1997 with the arrests/killings of its several senior leaders, starting with the arrest of its Finance Chief Ahmedullah Nahami in New Delhi in February on 23 March, Abdul Rehman, C-in-C and Bilal Ahmad, Operational Commander, were killed in Srinagar. The very next day, the TUM's senior-most functionary who represented it in the conglomerate SEJ, Shoukat Hussain Wani, was arrested in Srinagar. The misfortunes, heralded by the year 1997 did not end here. Three more senior leaders were in the bag before the year was out. Parvez Ahmad Bhatt and Maulvi Rauf were arrested in October. Then came the arrest of Nazir Ahmad, military Adviser, in the last month of the year 1997.

There was certain degree of demoralisation in the ranks of the cadres as also among its junior level leaders, mainly because of loss of so many senior leaders in 1997, and subsequent depletion in its strength. Low access to weaponry also was the contributory factor for the consequent low morale.

As for the current status, the TUM never occupied the top rungs among the insurgent formations in J & K. With its limited presence in the Valley, its activities have remained at a low ebb when compared to the three leading players in the secessionist/ terrorist field: HM, LET and JEM.

Intelligence reported that the outfit TUM shifted its leaders from Kashmir Valley to Bangladesh in the last quarter of 2006.

4

Pakistan's Machinations

For a perspective, it will be of help to have some idea about physical and some historical facts on Jammu and Kashmir.

Key Statisties

Date of formation

26 October, 1947.

Area	2, 22, 236 sq km, of which 78, 114 sq km is under Illegal occupation of Pakistan and is known as 'Pakistan Occupied Kashmir' (POK) in India and Azad Kashmir (Independent or Free Kashmir) in Pakistan. Of POK's 78,144 sq km, so-called Northern Areas sprawl over 72,495 sq km Islamabad directly rules the Northern Areas, having detached it from the POK, claiming that it was never part of Maharaja's Princely State of Jammu and Kashmir. It may not be out of place here to state that much tom-tommed Prime Minister and President of the POK exercise control over; mere 5,619 sq km of the area.
Capital	Srinagar (Summer) Jammu (Winter)
Population	10,143,700
Villages	6,652
Towns	75

LEGIS LATIVE BODIES

Legislative Assembly

It has 76 seats presently. Originally it had 100 seats, of

which 24 constituencies are in POK, under illegal occupation of Pakistan.

Legislature Council

It has 36 seats.

Chief languages	Urdu (official), Kashmiri, Dogri, Pahari, Balti, Ladakhi, Purig, Punjabi, Gujri and Dardi.
Major religions	
	Islam
	Hinduism
	Buddhism

Histroy of Pakistan's Perfidy

First a brief perspective on Kashmir's history. Legend has it that Kashyapa Rishi reclaimed the land that now comprises Kashmir from a vast lake. It came to be known as Kashyapamar, and later Kashmir. Emperor Ashoka introduced Buddhism to the Region in 3 BC. Subsequently the Valley became parts of empires of Kanishka and Mihiragula.

Around 7th century AD, a local dynasty, the Karkotas, believed to have been founded by Durlabhavardhana, ascended to power in the region. Kalhana, Kashmir's reputed historian, says this dynasty spread its wings in the reign of Lalitaditya – defeating Kanauj, the Tibetans and even the Turks in the Indus area. The dynasty came to an end in about 855. Then followed the Utpalas. The founder was Avantivarman. His son Sankaravarmana expanded the state's limits, annexing even a part of Punjab from the Gurjaras. At his death, Tantrins, a powerful military faction, emerged as virtual (military) dictators of the region. But ultimately, a group of Brahmanas elevated Yasaskara, a member of their order, to the throne of Kashmir. Yasaskara's line was succeeded by the dynasty founded by Parva Gupta.

The Hindu rule in Kashmir came to an end in the 14th century. Around 1339 or 1346, a Muslim adventurer named Shah Mirza seized power and assumed the title of Shams-ud-Din Shah. the Sultanate of Kashmir thus estalished ruled till about 1540 when a relative of Humayun, Mirza Haider, annexed Kashmir. He ruled Kashmir virtually as a sovereign, even if in theory he ruled on behalf of Humayun. In 1551, local nobles deposed Haider. Around 1555, the Chakks seized the throne. Kashmir ultimately became a part of the Mughal empire in Akbar's reign.

In 1819, Kashmir was annexed to the Sikh Kingdom of Punjab, and later on to the Dogra Kindgom of Jammu in 1846. That year, the treaties of Lahore and Amritsar that were signed at the conclusion of the first Anglo-Sikh war made Raja Gulab Singh, the Dogra ruler of Jammu, the ruler of an extensive Himalyan Kingdom. The State was under Dogra rule till 1947, when after a lot of hesitation as he was nurturing dreams of an independent state, he signed the instrument of accession with the Union of India after a short spell of high drama. The Rest as They Say is History

The above somewhat detailed account has been given in view of the latest claim made by Pakistan that Northern areas were not part of Jammu and Kashmir in 1947. For the present suffice it to say that the first 1947-48 Indo-Pak war on Kashmir ended with a cease-fire that become operative on the midnight of 1st January 1949, leaving 78,114 sq km of area of Jammu and Kashmir in illegal possession of Pakistan, and the illegal possession continues till date.

On 5 March, 1948, the Maharaja announced the formation of an interim popular government with Sheikh Mohd Abullah as Prime Minister. Since then, democracy has prospered in Jammu and Kashmir, bar the occasional hiccups. The last election in 2002 resulted in a Congress-PDP coalition ruling the State, with a rotating Chief Ministership. For the first three years, PDP's Mufti Saeed was the Chief Minister who yielded the Chair to Congress Party's GN Azad in November, 2005.

Pakistan's New Shenanigans (Claim) on Northern Areas

Pakistan's ambassador to Brussels has laid the foundation for diplomatic row by asserting new claims on the Northern Areas, a sprawling 72,459 – square kilometer tract of Jammu and Kashmir occupied in 1947. In a letter written to Baroness Emma Nicholson of Winter Winterbourne, the author of a recent European Pariliament report on Jammu and Kashmir,

Ambassador M. Saeed Khaled has claimed that the "whole of the Nothern Areas was not a part of Jammu and Kashmir state in 1947."

Equally surprisingly, Ambassador Khaled insists that the UN resolutions on the State "do not, in any manner, apply to any part of the Northern Areas." As such, he argues, "integration of the Northern Areas with Pakistan is also not prohibited an assertion sure to irk not only India but also many politicians in the sensitive forntier region.

It is some irony to see Pakistan making this claim, as the country's Supreme Court years before rebuffed this proposition made by Islamabad's civilian rulers (in 1994). More on it a little later.

Curiously, Pakistan's claim signifies a break with decades of established foreign policy position. Although it ceeded a small part of this region – 2,000 sq km to be exact – to China in 1963, "Pakistan has historically been ruluctant to formalise its de facto direct rule of the Northern Areas."[1]

Winterbourne, whose report is to be presented before the European Parliament plenary on 24 May 2007, has already sent a 7-page reply to Khalid, rejecting his claim. Says she : "I am unable to commend your Government's new position to the European Parliament." The Baroness, reply append's colonial era maps and treaty documents which make clear that Northern Areas were part of undivided Jammu and Kashmir."

Intriguingly, Pakistan's new claim flies in the face of that country's Supreme Court's verdict. In a September, 1994 judgement, the highest Court held that while the Northern Areas are "not part of Azad Kashmir as defined in the Azad Kashmir Interim Interim Constitution Act", the region was indeed "part of Jammu and Kashmir State" as it existed before 1947.

Why was Pakistan so far reluctant to formalise its de-facto direct rule of the Northern Areas? May be, Pakistani diplomats believed that India would use such on act to strengthen its case for institutionalising the status-quo in Jammu and Kashmir. If that be so, why this sudden change instance? Only Pakistan can explain, if at all!

An Obsession

Pakistan refuses to consolidate itself as a nation ever since its creation in 1947. Its obsession with Kashmir is pathological. Given the historical facts, it refuses to accept the facts of life and some somehow to grab Kashmir for itself. It has tried to keep the pot boiling through a variety of means. It keeps testing the waters to see if India's will to safeguard its territorial integraity and political will has flagged.

It has tried major aggressions and minor combat practices (like the 1947 tribal 'incursions' and 1965 Cutch/Kachh attacks). Having failed to reach its desideratum through arms route, under Musharraf it has launched 'peace offensive' through peace-process in 2004. This chapter briefly discusses Pakistan's strategy on forcing India at least out of the valley.

Jammu and Kashmir : Secessionist Terrorism

India as a nation has faced the spectre of terrorist violence from the very day of its independence. One can go even beyond that and say that India must be the only nation of its size and population that faced the threat of ethnic and religious violence even before it was bron! After all, it is a matter of history that certain princely States refused to join the still-to-be born India when London in its wisdom, or mischief, granted them the choice of joining India or Pakistan, or even to go for independence. The states that immediately grab your attention in this respect are Tripura, Junagarh, Hyderabad, a vast Hindu-majority state under a Muslim ruler, and Jammu and Kashmir, in contrast, a large Muslim-majority State under a Hindu ruler, to name at least four such States. A near civil war situation prevailed when the Nizam (= its ruler) of Hyderabad expressed himself publicly to join Pakistan. But for a quick, decisive masterly stroke, in the form of 'Police Action', by that Iron Man of India, Sardar Patel, the dangerous situation could have gone out of control, and consequently, India would have lost the strategically important state for ever.

In case of Jammu and Kashmir, its Maharaja continued dithering between joining India or proclaiming independence for his state till Pakistan marched in its Army under the guise of tribal raiders and forced his hands to sign the Instrument of

Accession with the Indian Union. By then the aggressors were already knocking at the doors of Srinagar airport. The Indian Army landing at the airport just at the proverbial eleventh hour saved the situation, and subsequently started rolling back the aggression. When the aggressors were still in control of the two-fifths of state's territory, the Indian Prime Minister Nehru in his political wisdom, some analysts assert under pressure from Sheikh Abdullah, ordered his military to cease fire. That territory till date not only remains under hostile occupation but has posed most serious threat to nation's integrity, flowing from Pakistan's vile machinations, and for the last two decades or so, through secessionist terrorism orchestrated and fuelled by Pakistan with some help from a number of fraternal nations.

India also suffered a threat from ethnic secessionism from certain tribes from its North-East region on the eve of its independence. The Nagas were the first to declare their independence a day before India's. Then followed Mizos, some Manipur and Tripura tribes. ULFA and Bodo rebellions were among the last to rock Assam. As of today, most of these are on the mend. The erstwhile rebel leaders are either ruling their states like the Mizos or Nagas, or are contemplating negotiations like the ULFA. Two groups of Naga leaders are still engaged in the final stages of negotiations with New Delhi. It can be said with a fair degree of certainty that no secession threat looms large in India's stratigically important North-East.

But a small minority of Muslim militant extremists, aided and abetted by Islamic terrorist groups the world over, are a source of anxiety to the Indian security planners. One need have no cause of concern on this score because the democratic India has shown great resilience in the past to face all such threats. It has the strength to overcome all such threats to its sovereignty and integrity in the long run. But what must be noted is that the nation has already paid a heavy price for the terrorist violence in the J & K for the last over 16 years. All the relevant statistics will be adduced later here to make the point. J & K is the only princely state of the Pre-1947 British India that is bleeding and suffering as a result of 'thousand cuts' policy practised by Pakistan against India in J & K. Therefore, it is necessary to have a brief look on its history and the route that terrorism has followed in that State. To understand the past is a pre-requisite to plan counter-terrorism and-insurgency measures to defeat the twin scourges.

Pakistan Exploits Religion to Reach 1989

It is clear to the students of history how eagerly – rathe obsessively – Pakistan wanted to take over Jammu and Kashmir by negotrations if possible, and by force if necessary. Its founder, MA Jinnah, tried all tricks in his armoury – negotiations with Maharaja Hari Singh, followed by thrreats of direct action. When persuation and coercion both failed, he tried to achieve his aim through his co-religionist Sheikh Abdullah, the uncrowned king of the Kashmiri people, who had waged the struggle for independence in Jammu and Kashmir as an inseparable part of the struggle of the Indian National Congress under the Mahatma to force Britain to quit India through peaceful means. When Jinnah failed to get his way even with Abdullah, Pakistan decided to wrest Kashmir from India through force of arms, starting with the so-called triblal raiders entering Kashmir in October 1947 to liberate their Muslim brethran for sake of *Umma*. It was a fiction Pakistan could not sustain for long. To cut it short, Pakistan made three (more accurately, two-and-a-half) wars to snatch Kashmir from India : 1947-49 and September 1965 were full-fledged aggressions, with a smaller one thrown in-between, viz April 1965 attempt to test the waters in Kutch.

Pakistan's Multi-faceted Policy to Grab Kashmir

Pakistan polity must be complimented for the single-minded perserveration it has exhibited ever since October 1947 to absorb/merge Kashmir in its territory after wresting it from India. A brief backgrounder is apt here for understanding the issues involved. But before that, a word on why it is "Kashmir issue", though officially, it is "Jammu and Kashmir issue".

Pakistanis simply imagined that being a Muslim-majority State, it was theirs by right. When Maharaja Hari Singh prevaricated, they were rather up set – almost flummoxed by his intransigenee. Of course, Pakistan forgot that for all the 567 Princely states, the rulers were to decide whether they would join India or Pakistan after the British quit. So when they could not work their magic on the Maharaja, or the Sheikh, they resorted to the use of force. The first Indo-Pak war ended with the issue being referred to the UN by Pt. Nehru. First, why it is Kashmir issue? There is no doubt that Pakistan is least interested in Hindu-majority areas of the composite State, namely, Jammu and Ladakh regions. But all its attention is on the Kashmir Valley, and in particualr, its crown jewel, Srinagar, whose only link with the outside world was the Srinagar-Rawalpindi Road. (Like wise, Jammu had no links with any part of post 1947 India. In pre-1947 India, its only link with the wider world was the Jammu-Sialkot Road. Besides the Muslim-majority factor, the other factor that favoured its merger with Pakistan was the fact of its physical links with its two major cities. Hence their deep anguish at the obstinate Maharaja's 'No' to Pakistan leaders.

Pakistan would have been quite happy if India had conceded the Valley to it. Yet again, it is a well-known fact, if not that well-publicised one, that it had agreed to the division of Valley between India and Pakistan, as a face-saving solution, after the prolonged Swaran Singh—Bhutto Parleys under the pressure of certain Western powers, subsequent to the 1965 War. The dividing line ran just south of Baramulla, this giving the town and area north to it right up to Uri border over to Pakistan. Some last minute hitch came in the way of the 'pact' being signed. All this naration is meant to stress the fact that Pakistan was at that time, and possibly even today, interested in the Kashmir Valley. So for it, it is essentially the Kashmir issue.

Now back to the Pakistan's multi-facted approach to achieve its goal of getting Kashmir for itself. While planning and waging these wars, Pakistan had been pursuing and conceptualising its stance on the other two prongs of its Kashmir prolicy : the strategy of negotiations and also playing up the religious vulnerability of the Kashmiri Muslims to Pakistan blandishment of ideological oneness between them and Pakistanis. The strategy was simple : what it could not achieve in the battlefield, it will get it on the negotiating table. Here Pakistani diplomacy must be offered kudos and bouqnets. It has persistently demanded that India must concede that Kashmir is a disputed territory. So India and Pakistan must hold discussions to resolve this dispute. So Pakistan won its case when Prime Minister Vajpayee and Musharraf agreed during their January 2004 Summit in Islamabad that the two nations would discuss all outstanding disputes between them, including Kashmir. Pakistan had scored a diplomatic victory over its bigger neighbour. So far (August 2006), the two countries have completed three rounds of talks, discussing six disputes, mutually agreed upon between them, and the fourth round has just started.

While fighting its wars with India, always started by it, and also simultaneously working on India to concede that Kashmir was a disputed territory between them, the Pakistan Government had not forgotten to make use of another potent weapon in its armoury : religious affinity between the Kashmiris and the Pakistanis.

From 1947 onwards, Pak propaganda has been bombarding the Kashmiris with the most potent refrain : Kashmiri Muslims are not and can never be safe in 'Hindu' India. To safeguard their religion, they must join Muslim Pakistan. Even reasonably educated Muslims are prone to be carried away by the pulpit. Pakistan persistently and single-mindedly continued inflaming the Kashmiri Muslim mind through a variety of means available to it : radio, TV, press, clerics and fundamentalist Muslim preachers sent in from across the borders and the coopted local elements among the intelligentsia, youth, and politicians like Prof. Abdul Ghani Bhatt and SAS Geelani. Besides this all, export of terrorism had been conceptualised at a very early stage. Sections of so-called "tribal invaders" werse settled within Kashmir during and after the 1947-49 misadventure and the process continues till date.

It was a well-planned infiltration to win the minds of the Kashmiris, and executed with elan, finesse, and single – focussed determination. To begin with it was an intermittent and sporadic stream of fanatics sent across the border – small and steady. But as it started yielding initial results, the tap was increasingly opened wider and wider. By 1989, sections of the Valley Muslims, including the youth, had been radicalised enough as to persuade Pakistan planners to bring every thing in the open. A study will prove that a good number of secessionist outfit, popularly called *tanzeems* in daily parlance, were created about this time.

There were certain attending circumstances in and around the region to help Pakistan to reap the windfall. The US and Pakistan weaponry had enabled the radical Islamists, Taliban, to take over a Country, Afghanistan, within a couple of years of pan-Islamic endeavour led by Pakistan. The Pak terrorist organisations had taken an important role in fighting and overthrowing the pro-Soviet current regime, enabling them to hone and perfect their terrorist methods and skills. Thereafter, it was a simple question of exporting that model of success just across the border to J & K. A large number of Muslims, hailing from majority of OIC nations, had been radicalised and prepared by the pulpit to join the jihad in Afghanistan. All of them were now ready to do the duty by their faith in Kashmir. At one time in mid-1990s, Muslims from 22 member-countries of the OIC were fighting in Kashmir under the ISI guidance and coordination. As if the fortune was similing on the Pakistan – ISI combine, after the Congress under Rajiv Gandhi lost the elections, the 1989 proved most unstable for the Indian polity.

A make-shift Prime Minister who ascendeded the 'throne' through a devious manipulation, leaving a bilious Chandrashekhar crying foul, proved unequal to the responsibility of defending India's interests, he was sworn to do. At the very first minor obstacle, only days after he took over, his Government stumbled. Some analyst believe, perhaps fairly, that India bowing to terrorist threats and releasing Rubaiya Saeed, daughter of the then Union Home Minister, was the original sin. India has not been able to look the terrorists in their face ever since that abject surrender. That single cardinal failure to act determinedly was a big boost for the terrorism in Kashmir, masquerading as a 'fight for justice'. All these factors to some extent, and in some way or other, gave heart to the merchants of death and destruction operating in Kashmir.

It is also worthwhile to record here the Pak stance on UN resolution of 5 January 1949, giving the right of self-determination to the people of Jammu and Kashmir. Pakistan had drummed it as a victory against India, heartened by a single postulation : when given an opportunity, Muslims will vote for merger with the Muslim Country, Pakistan. But some where along the way, the initial euphoria gave way to the sober ground realities. Jinnah had tried persuation with the Maharaja and the Sheikh, but failed. Then came the Pakistani aggressors, opressing, looting, beheading, and even raping the common citizenry that came their way in their 'victorious' march to Srinagar. This had fomented individual anger against the raiders and collective a version to Pakistan and its avaricious leadership. Popular leaders like the Sheikh fumed and thundered against the aggressors. In this scenario, Pakistan saw no chance for it to win the Kashmiris to its side in the UN-sanctioned plebiscite. So it made no move to create conditions that were pre-requisites for holding the plebiscite. The main one required Pakistan to vacate its troops from the areas of Jammu and Kashmir it had occupied forcefully as a result of an aggression. The plebiscite was then to be conducted under the Indian aegis. Though it kept shouting for the self-determination for the Kashmiris, it never took that one step that would enable India to hold the plebiscite. And Pakistan had its reasons to dilly-dally on that important issue.

People of J & K were solidly behind Shiekh Abdullah's National Conference. The Sheikh felt comfortable with India's secular polity, even if occasionally, he toyed with the idea of independence for his land. Even more importantly, rather omenously for Pakistan, a poll arranged by a US-based NGO in 1970s showed 63 per cent population of J & K voting their preference for India compared to 35 per cent for Pakistan. And this when Muslims are in majority in J & K. But Pakistan did draw some right lesson from this adverse popular vote. It redoubled its efforts at spreading its ideological agenda among the Kashmiri Muslims, and also increased the number of fundamental and militant elements it was sending across the border to foment religious conflict and political instability. The communal card came handy to it, and it was the ideal weapon in its hands to employ in a communally fragmented society like the one in J & K.

By the late 1980s, Pakistan authorities could discern the signs of visible success of its exertions to create anti-India sentiment among the sections of the valley population. It knew it was the right time to shout for steps to find solution for the 'Kashmir problem', and simultaneously up the ante by increasing militant violence to follow a two-track policy on Kashmir issue. By now it had seen the effectiveness of terrorist violence as a foreign polícty option, *a la* Afghanistan. If India does not respond 'suitably' to peace overtures, terrorism was always available as final weapon of resort.

This brief account of Kashmir situation from the 1947-49 aggression onward is necessary to understand why 1989 was a defining year for study of any aspect of J & K issue. But to study terrorism in Kashmir, this understanding is an absolute 'must'!

A Summing-up Before Detailed Study

Before taking up a detailed took at the two decades of terrorism in the valley—the 1980-89 decade, its initial phase, and the 1990-2000 decade, the virulent phase—and then the events after 'apocalyptic' Nine-Eleven, here are summed up the events in a capsule leading to these periods. First two self-serving peraptions. The incessan efforts to seize the State from India by means fair and foul and pattern of terrorist violence since 1989 – that defining year – are the results flowing from interplay of the twin self-generated perception.

- Being a Muslim – Majority State, Jammu and Kashmir naturally belongs to Pakistan. Its contiguity with the latter only reinforces the logic.
- The fact of its confidence and capability winning the day in Afghanistan against the Soviet Army and the Government backed by it, should be equally applicable in Kashmir. The success of *Jihad* in Afghanistan should be replicated with same felicity.

On India achieving independence, the Princely State of Kashmir acceded to India and Pakistan refused to accept the accession, arguing that the division of mother century was based on two-nation theory, and consequently, the State belongs to Pakistan. It was encouraged in its thinking on these lines by the action of the British officers in control of Northern Areas of the State like Gilgit and Hunza who unilaterally acceded to Pakistan without any authorisation from Maharaja Hari Singh, the ruler of the State. In fact, the Commander of State's Army, a Brigadier, sent by the Maharaja, was besieged by the troops under command of these British Officers, who subsequently made good his escape after months of struggle. The perfidy of these officers was in line with the more sinister perfidy perpetrated by the British Government and its Representative to UN at New York during the debate on the Kashmir issue brought before it by India. The recent study of primary documents by an Indian diplomat, C. Dasgupta throws more light on the early years of the Kashmir issue and related debate in the UN General Assembly, and more glaringly, on the perfidious role of the UK favouring Pakistan against India.[2] Dasgupta confirms emphatically what was already known in the knowledgeable circles that India's first Governor-General, Lord Mountbatten, "foiled his (Nehru's Indian) Government's instructions for preparing contingency plans for a counter-strike across the Pakistani border while prevailing upon Nehru to take the Kashmir issue to the UN." He points out that as Governor General, Mountbatten was not a figure as he was constitutionally expected to be, but exercised "very real executive power" as Chairman of the Cabinet's Defence Committee.

It is possible to have some sympathy with Pakistan's frustration over not getting either Hyderabad or Jammu and Kashmir for itself. It saw it in terms of India's high-handersness the fact of both states being absorbed into the Indian Union – one a Muslim-majority state under a Hindu ruler and the other a Hindu – majority one under a Muslim ruler. It was unable to see the ethics of the situation. But then ethics and morality do not have any place in the realm of Real politic! It is the objective situation and the national interests that count.

But seeing the happenings till date, it must be said to Pakistan's credit that it does not fail to take advantage of any opening, howsoever in small and insignificant, to turn the tide in its favour. Seeing an opportunity presented by India's somewhat diminished vigilance, its leadership did not think twice in forcibly occupying the barren heights of Kargil, with a more sinister design behind the adventure or misadventure, as it later turned out. With such a determined adversary, India cannot afford to lower its guards in any aspect of its security paradigm.

To resume the chronology of narration, the two wars of 1947-49 and 1965 failed to get J & K for Pakistan. Not only did the Kashmiris show any inclination to collaborate with the invaders, as Pak strategic planners had envisaged, they in fact developed on attitude of hostility towards them because of the atrocities unleashed by them on the local population. They in reality helped the Indian Military defeat the Pak 'hordes', often at the cost of their lives.[3] So, the participation of the local people was minimal. This fact was confirmed by Babar Badar, Chief of the Muslim Janbaaz force and captured by the Indian SF in 1996, when he disclosed what he was told by Maj. Assad of the ISI during his 1994 briefing : "In 1965, we should have taken Kashimiris into confidence. The infiltrators were actually outsiders and the masses had been taken by surprise."

The 1971 war handed down a resounding, nay a humiliating, defeat to the much-vaunted Pak Army. It also saw the birth of Bangladesh after more than two million East Pakistani Muslims were cruelly butchered by their own countrymen and co-religionists belonging to the Pakistan Army and other Central Government agencies.[4] What is more, in less than three decades, the two-nation theory, the raison de'etre behind carving of Pakistan out of India, was blown into smithereens by the cruel acts of commission and omission by the rulers of that very nation.

Having failed to wrest Kashmir forcibly through the instrumentality of wars, Pakistan, with its Army in a heightened sense of desparate and its political class in severe frustration, decided to take recourse to "unorthodox methods" in the 'war' for J & K. In defence parlance, it is known as 'low intensity conflict' (LIC), or, even low cost war. In an unvarnished truth, it is war by terrorist violence. It is low cost warfare for the perpetrator, but the one which bleeds the victim through thousand cuts. What is even more inhuman is the ghastly ways the terrorists, the frenzied, dehumanised, insensitive robot-like machines, kill the innocent people, including children and women.

Terrorist Activities : 1980-89

This decade marks the adoption of 'proxy war' or 'LIC' strategies by Pakistan, and increase in the terrorist/violent incidents. If earlier they were sporadic and irregular, now on, there was to be a spurt in frequency and magnitude of these incidents. As stated earlier, Pakistan concluded it had brought the situation in J & K, through its ceaseless exertions, to a point where sections of its population had become receptive to its ideological objectives. Another important development in this decade was formation of several militant/terrorist *tanzeems* to foment anti-India sentiment in J & K.

From mid – 1980s, Pakistan attempted cultivating Kashmiri leaders and coopt them for another round of invading/seizing J & K through internal disruption and sabotage – and a little shove from outside. Initially, Shabir Shah and his JKPL(S) were seen to have necessary base and potential for the job. But Pakistan leaders reportedly failed twice in calling him over to Pakistan.

As detailed earlier, the Pak leaders and Jihadi groups were confident, after seeing the back of Soviet forces in Afghanistan, to replicate the success in Kashmir against India. The fallacy lies in oversimplifying the existing situations in two different set of circumtances and ground realities. It errs in generalising and missing the difficulties in mapping one set of contemporary experiences to another dissimlar, indeed non-identical, set of conditions.

The deportation of Amanullah Khan from the UK to Pakistan in late 1987 led to the reorganisation of JKLF (Pakistan), as he was installed as its Chairman. In February 1988, Ishaq Majid Wani, Yasin Malik, Hamid Sheikh and Javed Mir set up JKLF (J & K), with its headquarters at Srinagar.

The 1987 J & K Assembly elections become a focus of major controversy. There were strong allegations of elections being rigged by the ruling NC party. Such controversies are not too infrequent in India's rumbustious democracy. But J & K being a sensitive state, unlike any other, the situation was exploited adroitty by political opponents of Chief Minister Farooq Abduall, especially the Islamic Students League (ISL). The Muslim United Front (MUF) had performed poorly, and the ISL attributed it to the electoral fraud and launched an agitation in the state. The State responed with arrest and imprisonment of several young activists. Pakistan sensed it as a good opening.

ISI operatives promised arms and training to these 'boys' to launch armed struggle against India. On release from custody, they were willing tools in the hands of the ISI. They went in droves across the LOC to the camps in POK, and received training in guerrilla warfare. The clerics in POK and the ISI puppetteers 'channelised the anger and frustrations of the youth into anti-India armed militancy as a religious duty. These youths on return were eager to form their own *tanzeems* – all indoctrinated and primed up for action. "When youth is available in such numbers, the person like Shabir Shah with his cautious attitude was hardly relevant to the situation."

Consequently, the first set of major terrorist acts took place in Srinagar soon thereafter. the Central Telegraph Office in Srinagar and the Srinagar Club were blasted on 31 July 1988.

During 1988-89, the JKLF (J & K) and the Muslim Janbaaz Force (MJF) became operational. The two were valley-based and ISI wanted a new *tanzeem* to operate in and from Jammu as and when necessary. ISI's Brig Farooq 'chose Babar Badar, MJF Chief, who hailed from Jammu and was in Pakistan for training' to raise the Jammu – based outfit. Initially Al Madad, it was later renamed Al Madad Algar Ali. It was tasked to disrupt the movement of the Indian Army units. It would delay the deployment of the Army in its operational role in J & K. That in turn would help Pakistan's war plans. Jammu is the main physical link between the Kashmir Valley and the rest of India.

The ISI strategy appears to be : *Have more tanzeems, not less, in J & K*. The possible reason could be the reduction of vulnerability since a smaller number of *tanzeems* could face high attrition, or be won over by India. Another reason could be the ability it affords the ISI to play one outfit against another, as and when necessary. It also enabled the ISI to practise the policy of wielding big stick against the recalcitrant tanzeems as and if required. It was good old policy of "Carrots for the loyalists and stick for the under-performing/non-performers." Yet again, a larger number of tanzeems could create confusion among the 'trackers' of intelligence agencies and the security forces. That should also explain the ISI resorting to frequent splitting/ splintering of the *tanzeems*. "One estimate places the number of terrorist outfits created by Pakistan-ISI, both of the permanent and transient variety, during the period 1980-99 at 150." The analysts confirm this pattern, of the "Terrorist Master" creating and dissolving cells/outfits at will, also practised in Lebanon, Palestine and the Philippines.

Knowing well that 'liberation' of Kashmir was not a viable goal in foreseeable future, ISI adopted the policy of causing Indian fatigue *a la* the soviets in Afghanistan. Consequently, the implication of this policy line was to let "India bleed by a thousand cuts", and it has been quite clear since 1989.

The JKLF (J & K) should have long realised that Pakistan would never accept its agenda of independence as a third option for solving Kashmir issue. When the ISI insisted that JKLF 'boys' take their orders from its officials, and not Amanullah, their Chairman, even staunch Pak supporters in the ranks of the JKLF, including its Srinagar Chief Ishaq Majid Wani, were deeply disappointed. The ISI intention was further made unambiguous when it insisted the outfit jettison its 'independence" agenda as the *quid pro quo* for continuation/ renewal of military and financial assistance to it. It indeed was naive of the JKLF to believe othewise.

The ISI employed all means at its disposal to split, weaken, or even choke the JKLF, if not physically eliminate it. The ISI marginalised several prominent JKLF leaders like Mohd Altaf Andrabi *alias* Azam Inquilabi and Maqbool Butt. Engineering splits was another weapon employed by the ISI. To wit, Mushtaq Ahmad Zargar, *alias* Latrum, a promising JKLF leader, deserted it and emerged as the leader of the AUM, a tanzeem believed to be aligned with Mirwaiz Mohd Farooq, the Chief priest of Kashmir.

A look at the history of the militant organisation will show fission was the order of the day, as if willed by a 'higher' power. Fusion always looked a distant dream. If ever fusion become a reality, it will sooner rather than later be revisited by fission which will be clear when one studies various tanzeem that follow. Some major splits in chronological order are mentioned below :

- HUM was carved out of the JKLF.
- Mujahideen-e-Islam out of HUM.

- MM out of AUM, which in turn was carved out of the JKLF.
- AUC out of the former Students Liberation Front of JKLF.

This was not all. Even the JKPL(S), Shabir Shah's faction of the JKPL, was not allowed to remain untouched. After all, he had once talked 'secularism' and peaceful solution to the Kashmir issue. So hardliners like Mushtaq-ul-Islam bade adieu to form the Pan-Islamic Hizbollah.

Inter-outfit rivalries and hostilities were rather sharpe in some cases. Ideological differences, and at times, even clashes, cost lives. Out of mounting pile of 'eliminations' and mutual attrition, the HUM emerged as a strong if ruthless *tanzeem*, practising 'strong arm' tactics – often walking over the dead bodies of its rivals. It literally rose through corpses of its 'enemies'. The victims included Shahid Bima, an MJF Area Commander in North Kashmir as well as JKLF ideologues like Mohd Maqbool Maulvi, Dr. Abdul Ahmad, and Prof. Ahmad Wani. It did not flinch even from besmirching the reputation and credibility of its ideological rivals. The HUM launched a strident campaign against the JKLF about it being against the libertion of Kashmir and that its leaders were in cahoots with New Delhi. So was targeted the MJF, in similar vien.

Now comes the Osama apparition looming large on the horizon. Al Qaida was created in 1988 by Osama bin Laden and Abdullah Azzam in Afghanistan. Both fought the Soviet Union, shoulder-to-shoulder with the CIA, ISI, and the Taliban – of course with the weapons supplied liberally by the US. After the withdrawal of the Soviets in 1989, Al Qaeda unleashed a vigorous campaign to take on the next set of "enemies of Islam." Its earlier ally and benefactor, America, was now on the enemy list, along with Israel, of course. The tools forged and the experience gained in fighting – and trouncing – the Soviet Union came in handy for the new battles.

Osama declared a *jihad* in Kashmir in 1989, simultaneously adding India as the third devil on the list of enemies of Islam! For anti – India *jihad* in Kashmir, Osama extended his support to the HKUM, HUJI, HUA, LET and JEM. This support is in line with his declared aim of estalbishment of Nizam-e-Mustafa in the *Ummah*, which incidentally includes India.

Thus ended the 1980-89 decade of *jihad* in India's Jammu and Kashmir, compelling India to expand its military presence to confront the menace. It suffered casualities larger in numbers than the preceding decade. The nation with the second largest Muslim population ended up on the 'enemies of Islam' list. As we shall see, the next decade is to see even more virulent form of the Islamic violence unleashed by the frenzied terrorists.

Shape of Terrorism : 1990-2000 Decade

The most important landmark or incident of the 1990-2000 decade was ascendance of the Jamaat-e-Islami (JEI), Pakistan in Jammu and Kashmir, with its virtual absorption of the Hizb-ul-Mujahidden (HUM) in its fold in the beginning of the decade to foster the mutual agenda of the spread of the Pan-Islamic fundamentalism in the state. It was indeed an excellent idea, perceived by the JEI (Pak) : the ideological content of the agenda at the intellectual plane was to be provided by the JEI while the coopted HUM would be the source of muscle power.

The very first step in this grand manoeuvre[(5)] conceptualised by the JEI (Pakistan) was to take over the HUM with the help from the ISI in 1990. The rest followed a explained above. The HUM, as a result, had the JEI apparatus and Muslim clergy network available to it to extend its appeal among the youth in the rural area of J & K. By 1993, the birth and subsequent efficient functioning of the JEI-HUM-ISI combine had made remarkable inroads into the Kashmir valley. The consequent spread of the Pan-Islamic fundamentalism forced the decline in the fortunes of the pro-independence and comparatively liberal formations in the ranks of anti-India separatist/secessionist forces. So the partial withdrawal of the enervated pro-independence and liberal elements from the landscape proved detrimental to the Kashmiri agenda which got sacificed at the altar of this more vigorously executed Pan-Islamic agenda at least partially. Analyst observed that even the Pakistan – patronised JKLF had serious problems in accepting the new platform – or the altered altar, so to say.

But unfortunately, the Hindutva fired Hindu Right played in the hands of such anti-India forces like this ISI-JEI-HUM combine with the demolition of the Babri Masjid on 6 December 1992. Consequently, the long-festering Ayodhya Temple-Mosque dispute grabbed the attention of the international community and media organisations the world over-remaining in the headlines for long time to follow. To avenge the demolition, the Islamic fundamentalist set off 'the Bombay blasts' of 12 March 1993 – or so some analysts felt. The blasts took heavy toll of human life, with 257 killed and 713 inured. Property worth 27 crore was destroyed.

The Indian investigation established collaboration between the Bombay underworld (popularly known as D Company, with 'D' universally understood to stand for 'Dawood Ibrahim') on the one hand and Pak agencies led and coordinated by the ISI, on the other. After due judicial processes, when India asked for the extradition of Dawood, Pakistan denied his presence there. This when Pak press has flashed his home address in Karachi as a major scoop. And expectedly, following in the foot steps of extremist Muslims in India and even some 'liberal intellectuals', Dawood's lawyers projected the blasts as a Muslim reaction to the demolition of the Babri in December 1992.

But the Bombay violence proved yet again the Pak propernsity to exploit any such tragic happening in India to its won advantage. It blamed India of turning its Muslim population into a convenient scape goat for all its failures on the communal front – its inability to forge harmonious relations between its two major communities. It also accused New Delhi of holding Pakistan responsible for all its domestic problems, as a reflex action. Holding ISI innocent of any involvement in India's internal affairs, it repeated the charges it had hurled at New Delhi when the Babri was demolished : India has failed to protect its Muslim minority and its sacred sites.

More significantly, the Bombay blasts convincingly laid bare the strong operational bonds between the criminal gangs like the D Company and the ISI. Ironically, these very things, and Pakistan's direct complicity in Bombay Blasts was disclosed by none other than Muneer Ahamd in his *Will Pakistan Break Down* (Lahore, 1997)? Muneer has the then President Ishaq Khan rebuking Prime Minister Nawaz Sharif over the ISI's involvement in the Bombay blasts; and for treating the Memon brothers of the D Company as State guests.

This was also about the same time, 1994, when Pakistan, Saudi Arabia, and the US were engaged in mid-wifery in the areas of Singesar, Maiwand district and Kandahar to help in the birth of the Taliban to fight the Soviets in Afghanistan. Or, may be they were godparenting the child. The Pakistani *madrasas* were the main breeding grounds for the new recruits, with a smathering – rather stiffening – from some Afghan guerrilla groups, e.g., HEI, joining in. The political support so vital for success of such endeavour, was provided by no less a person that Prime Minister Benazir Bhutto's Interior Minister, Maj Gen (Retd) Naseerullah Babar. He played a key role in the creation of the Taliban, with Mullah Omar as their publicity-shunning leader – later to be acclaimed as a recluse "who took direct orders from Allah."

In cahoots with the Taliban was the Al Qaeda –to prove even a bigger curse for the humanity for the years to follow. But in the early years of the anti – Soviet Jihad in Afghanistan when the Taliban took power there, the Al Qaeda and the Taliban enjoyed a symbiotic relationship. They jointly plied the drug trade as a major enterprise – exploiting its potential to the full for financial support for their terror network. The Taliban regime allowed Osama bin Laden to establish and operate his terrorist training camps on the Afghan soil, protected against any hostile attack, and guarded his drug stock piles. The Taliban leadership had established blood relationship with Osama.

To begin with, the ISI was the umblical cord between the Taliban and the Al Qaeda of Osama. Subsequently, the ISI helped Al Qaeda to test maters in the Kashmir insurgency consequently it became a link between the Taliban, Al Qaeda, and secessionist outfits in J & K; and continued playing that role in Afghanistan till the collapse of Taliban, and is still doing so in Kashmir. By now it is an established fact that the ISI orchestrates all anti – India subversive activists and terrorists within India and in its neighbourhood.

Now comes the major act of the international terrorism. Qaeda operative Ramzi Youssef of Pakistan bombed the World Trade Centre in New York on 26 February 1993. He was nabbed by the FBI in Karachi on 7 February 1995, the result of painstaking investigations and shadowing his movements for two years. It turned out that Egypt's Cleric Sheikh Omar Abdel Rahman was his spritiual mentor, who himself was arrested in New York, thereafter. As was to be seen in the years to come, this terrorist bombing was the harbinger of Qaeda's decision to target the US citizens and its assets, the world over : Dares Salam and Nairobi, 7 August 1998; New York and Washington DC, 11 September 2001 (the calacalysimic Nine-Eleven); and the collateral death of many non-US nationals. President Bush declared on Nine-Eleven : "America is under attack. ...We are at war." On the 5th anniversary of that attack, and after gearing up the nation to face the eveil with a variety of antiterror measures and raising several new establishments like the Department of Home Security, the President repeated : "We are still at war". The reputed journalists feel the US authorities are expecting a Nine-Eleven type threat in the near future. The only Super Power, after spending billions on the anti-terror front is yet not sure if it has plugged all the gaps in its security structure. Such is the all-pervading nature of the international terror, mainly perpetrated by the extremist elements in a single religion – a miniscule minority, undoubtedly, but enough to keep the entire world under seige, and on tenterhooks.

Osama issued one of his first declarations on 12 October 1998, putting the US and Israel on the "enemies of Islam" list, besides usual fulminations against Saudi rulers. It said :

> People of Islam
>
> It is the duty now of every tribe in the Arabian Peninsula to wage jihad and to cleanse the land from these Grusader occupiers. Their wealth is booty to those who kill them. My Muslim brothers, your brothers in Palestine and in the land of the two Holy places (= Saudi Arabia) are seeking your help and asking you to take part in the fight against the enemy – the Americans and the Israelis. They are asking you to do whatever you can to expel the enemies out of the Holy places of Islam.

Now comes the time when Osama cast his net wide. He had obviously plans to assume the leadership of the *Ummah* for waging jihad against its enemies the world over. With this aim in mid, he formed the World Islamic Front for Jihad against Jews and Crusaders (= Al Jabbah al Islamiya al Almiyah Li – Qital al – Yahud Wal-Salibiyyin), in February 1998. Having the Afghan jihad experience to back him – after all it had defeated the mighty Soviet Union – he now aimed high at the wide-spectrum targets which included:

- Liberation of the Middle-East from the 'clutches' of Israel.
- Ejecting the US from the Holy Land of Saudi Arabia.
- Over throw of the Saudi monarchy, and other corrupt governments.
- Uniting all Muslims under the umbrella of the *Ummah* to transcend national borders and establish a Caliphate-style government.

First to join as members of this 'Universal' organisation of Osama were the Al Jihad of Bangladesh and the Jamaat-ul-Ulemah of Pakistan. More than a dozen terrorist outfits in the Islamic world are known to have subscribed to Osama's 'cause' and had created a vareity of formal and informal linkages. Some of the members of this "rather strange and motley group of Islamic bed follows" are listed below :

- Egyption Islamic Group.
- Jihad Organisation in Yemen.
- Pakistani Al Hadith Group.
- Lebanese Partisans Group.
- Libyan Islamic Group.
- Bayt al Imam Group, Jordan.
- Islamic Salvation Group, Algeria.

While this decade withnessed the above-mentioned dramatic series of events in the Islamic world and beyond, the terrorist movement within Jammu and Kashmir too underwent a significant change in mid-1995. The Kashmiri Youth was rather reluctant to offer themselves for recruitment by the terror/ secessionist outfits. The internecine bloodletting among the hostile factions of a number of outfits had taken its toll of many a leader and enthusiastic young cadres. School dropouts and rowdy elements had begun to dominate some of the major outfits.

Rape had become rather common occurrence in the Valley while innocent civilians had fallen victims to suspicion and killed as 'informers'. These in discriminate acts of mindless, wanton viloence, and more so the violation of the young women caused wide-spread disillusionment and disappointment among the valley population. Even the sections, who were sympathetic towards these "freedom fighters", felt disgusted enough to condemn the senseless human misery wrought on the common man and the rape committed by them as all that damaged their 'cause' rather than advance it. Consequent to the reluctance of the Valley youth to offer themselves for recruitment, there was large scale induction of foreign, unemployed or unemployable "soldiers of fortunae" into the valley by the Pakistani mercenary outfits like the HUA. The overall management of this huge enterprise, of course, was in the hands of the ISI.

Meanwhile, there was change at the political helm in 1993-94. Benazir Bhutto replaces Nawaz Sharif as Prime Minister of Pakistan. It is for record that she was not particularly enthusiastic towards the JEI since it was an alliance partner in Sharif's Muslim League. But let there be no doubt that she too was as committed to its "casue" as her predecessor.

This was also the time that the famed Kashmiri Sufism, indigenous and tolerant , came under attack. The home-grown faith and teachings of the Sufi saints and *peers* were anathema to the terrorists, who under the guidance and tutelage of the JEI, were taught and prepared to spread the inter-communal hatred and consequent violence to achieve their goal of "freedom" which was impossiblle, may unthinkable, in the ambience of tolerance and harmony preached by the Sufism. Thus it was that saner voices of reason, tolerance, and harmony began to be muffled. In this atmosphere of intolerance, extremism and mindless violence, resulting from the Pak-exported and – inspired terrorism for the last half a decade, it should come as no surprise that the much-revered shrine of the venerated Sufi saint, Sheikh Nooruddin Wali, in Charar-e-Sharif was forcibly taken over by a group of militants of the Hizbullah outfooled by an Afghan/Pak militant, bearing the nick name of Mast Gul. Committing a blasphemous act, the terrorist burnt down the 300-years old *ziarat* (= sacred monument) in May 1995 during their stand-off with the SF, who had besieged them in the precincts of the Charar-e-Sharif. The incident is significant as it marks not only the onset of "spectacular acts" by foreign militants but also the use of foreign (Pakistani), non-State actors like the fundamentalist JEI.

Buoyed by a fresh influx of funds and arms from the ISI, JEI unleashed a flurry of vicious killings in J & K. Assuming a cover name, Al Faran, it staged a high-profile kidnapping in Pahalgam of six western tourists, hailing from Norway, UK and USA, during 4-9 July 1995. They beheaded the Norwegian but disclosed nothing about the fate of the others. Consequently, the US State Department declared it a terrorist organisation in October 1997. In Pakistan, the HUA resorted to a simple play of changing its name to circumvent the consequences of the US declaration. The HUA ceased to exist, as if by a slight of hand, assuming the name of Harkat-ul-Mujahideen (HKUM), its parent organisation, which incidentally had worked closely with the CIA in Afghanistan! A good case of wheels within wheels. Lo and behold, the be leopard simply changed its spots with the full knowledge of the government of the day in Islamabad.

The intelligence had confirmed the presence of Taliban terrorists in Kashmir. Later, credible information surfaced to indicate that Pakistan military units of Charat and Sahiwal divisions, deployed on the Pak-Afghan border, had supervised the Taliban's movement from Afghanistan to J & K. It is worth recording that Taliban were in power in Afghanistan. A Pakistani arrested by the Indian SF in February 2000, Javed Akhtar Abbasi, disclosed that he had gone to Kandahar in September 1997 as an emissary of Mast Gul to request for military hardware and other assistance from the Taliban Deputy Defence Minister, Maulana Naeem Akhoon. The Islamic outfits do not work within the borders of a single country, nor depend upon it totally for their operational wherewithals. Here is a Pakistani organisation operating in India, and seeking help from another Muslim Country, Afgthanistan. As is often claimed declared, a nation does not mean much to a Muslim, since *Ummah* is *the* nation – a world-wide entity for the international Muslim Community. Thus if the said emissary failed to receive the required help from Afghanistan, any of the remaining 44 nations of the 45-member OIC can be approached to meet this end. After all, did Pakistan not knock at the doors of the OIC against India on the Kashmir issue?

If the Taliban can fight in Kashmir, can the Qaeda be far behind? And it is Qaeda India has to beware of.

There were reports that possibly for operational reasons, Osama "preferred India as a transit point for the movement of activists of his Islamic Army from West Asia to Afghanistan."

To wit, a senior official's journey in April 1997 with his family to Kandahar from Yemen through Amirtsar (Punjab, India) was taken note of. What could be the reason behind this preference for Indian soil as transit point? Besides the operational factor mentioned above, he was also interested in testing the Indian waters for his plans for Kashmir, possibly in the near future. As if to prove the above postulation, Osama is believed to have paid a clandestine visit to the Valley in the first quarter of 1997 and held discussions with the senior leaders in Sopore and Shopian. Synchronising with Osama's visit, a Kashmiri doctor based in Saudi Arabia paid a 'financing' visit to the valley.

There are credible reports about Osama meeting with Kashmiri secessionist leaders in the Khost area around 12 June 1998 and, promising funds for the Kashmiri 'cause'. There were also connected reports to suggest that "a group of Kashmiri/Sikh terrorists is planning to enter India from Kandahar around 2 August 1998 to attack the US Embassy and its Consulates."

Now we return to the practice of the terrorists/secessionists staging something 'big' or 'spectacular' on the eve of India's Republic Day/Independence Day anniversaries to grab the headlines. To cite one instance, HUM cadres attacked four Hindu families in village Wandhama, near Ganderbal town on the night 25-26 January 1998. The carnage on the eve of the Republic Day left 23 dead – four children, nine women, and ten men. One Hindu boy, aged 14, was the only one to survive. Such barbarity displayed by the terrorists is rather impossible to ignore, forget or forgive. It is time some effective anti-terrorism policy is in place.

Mid – 1999 saw the Pakistani aggression in Kashmir's Kargil area. A detailed reconnaissance' comprehensive planning, and appropriate troop composition had been gone through before the Kargil war began in May 1999. Beginning with the so-called 'tribals' marching across the border in October 1947, Pakistan has never let go of an opportunity to stir the Kashmir cauldon for ulterior gains. They had stuck to this policy till the Kargil fiasco unmindful of the reality of India steadfastly safeguarding its territorial integrity, even after some initial set-back at times as the aggressors always have the initial advantage on the option of time and place for their evil designs. Having failed repeatedly to wrest Kashmir from India through the force of arms, Pakistan finally took resort to the negotiations table. The so-called peace process was launched through mutual consultations in January 2004. The third round of the Composite Dialogue stands interrupted because of the July 2006 carnage perpetrated by the terrorists on the Mumbai Suburban trains. This brief narration, prior to the Kargil war account, illustrates the Pak stance on Kashmir and India – aggessive, opportunistic, and grabbing. This is for a section of Indians – idealist, liberal, rationalist, head-in-the-sand and sleep-walkers – who are prone to and proud of equating India and Pakistan on the Kashmir issue.

Undoubteldy, Pakistan had a complex set of objectives – military and political – for the Kargil aggression, even if some scholars and analysts like to call it 'Kargil incursion'. If the aggressors had been allowed a permanent occupation of the Kargil heights, the entire Ladakh and troops in the area would have been cut off from the mainland, with dire consequences. Again on the military plane, further advance east by the occupation forces would have cut off the Siachen brigade. On the political plane, the terrorists would have had a field day, with the Indian SF stretched hopelessly between the Kashmir Valley and Ladakh. All this would have given Islamabad not only a major military victory but even a bigger political success against the arch enemy, India, something it has been thirsting/ lusting for ever since the loss of Bangladesh. It must be handed over to Pakistan : if it has failed to grab Kashmir from India through means fair or foul, it can't be blamed for not trying. Equally truly, it would be a mistake for Indians to forget that the man behind the Kargil aggression is today occupying Presidential Palace in Pakistan, and in military uniform.

As for the operations by India against the intruders, there certainly were initial difficulties. All aggressors have the initial advantage. In this case, they had the additional bonus because they were entrenched on the top of the hill features with sharp escarpment for the Indian troops to climb if the occupation force was to be evicted. So when the Indian troops mounted their operations to exict the intruders, they not only had to advance against the enemy perched on the top, but also engaged in hill climbing similtaneously – both under the hail of withering fire. It became even more of an up hill task literally for Indians as they did not have the air cover in the first few days of the war. But their doggedness, tenacity, and famed fighting skills saw the Indian military on the top, with the intruders pushed back into the POK territory they had come from in the first instance.

As for the Indian Air Force, its operational deployment got delayed due to certain decisions, or lack of them, at the top. But once they started operating, the airmen performed valiantly, facilitating the advance of the Infantry.

When less than 10 per cent of the Indian territory was still under the adverse occupation, Pakistan was provided a face saver by the US President. Prime Minister Nawaz Sharif had rushed to Washington to seek US intervention. President Clinton asked Prime Minister Vajpayee over to Washington, who befittingly refused to oblige. After a tense, terse 4 July 1999 meeting, Clinton told Nawaz to withdraw Pak troops from across the LOC. The diplomatese siad : On the advice of the US, Pakistan agreed to cease-fire and withdraw its troops. Pak military had suffered another serious setback. But as is its wont, Pakistan projected the defeat as partial vicotry because it "has succeeded in internationalising the Kashmir issue."

Two points need to be made about the Kargil 'war'. India made a political decision not to extend this war beyond eviction of the intruders. Indian troops and Air Force were under orders not to cross the LOC, much less the international borders – consequently, incurring/accepting much higher casualities. Due to reasons embedded in international diplomacy or domestic politics, India chose not to dub the Kargil conflict as a 'war'.

The Kargil war had an international dimension. It is believed that over 200 Taliban fighters of the elite 055 Brigade, while returning to Peshawar after the fall of Bamiyan, were diverted to Kashmir to take part in the Kargil conflict. Incidentally, the 055 Brigad had three broad geographical divisions :

- The Arabs from Egupt, Saudi Arabia, Yemen, Jordan, Algeria, Morocco, Sudan and Libya.
- The Central Asians from Tajikistan, Kazakhstan, Uzbekistan, Uighurs from China.
- The South/South-East Asians from Pakistan, Bangladesh, Indonesia, Malayasia and Philippines.

If the 1990-2000 decade saw the entry of the Pak JEI into Kashmir to give the separatist movement the Pan-Islamic orientation in its opening year, its last major incident, the hijacking of Indian Airlines Kathmandu-New Delhi Flight IC-814 with 154 passengers on board on 24 December 1999 by ISI-trained terrorists led by Ibrahim Azhar, also had Pak connection. Ibrahim's brother, Masood Azhar, who was one of three terrorists released from Indian jails in exchange of 154 passengers, founded the JEM at Karachi in February 2000. To impress the Indian authorities about their serious intent, the terrorists stabbed to death Rupin Katyal, one of the passengers, when the plane landed at Amritsar Later, his body was handed over in Dubai airport. Perhaps in a unique case, the three jailed terrorists to be released under a deal with the hijackers were escorted to the Kabul airfield by India's External Affairs Minister Jaswant singh in his own aircraft from New Delhi. His action was widely criticised. Jaswant has extensively covered the incident, explaining his side of the story, in a book released last month (July 2006). The other two of the three passengers, who were released in Kabul on the last day of the year 1999, were Omar Sheikh of the HKUM/HUA and Mushtaq Ahmad Zargar of AUM.

It is worth a note that the boarding passes of these terrorists (hijackers) were picked up by the American soldiers during the mopping up operations launched by them after the US intervention in/take over of Afghanistan, post-Nine-Eleven.

Two of the three terrorists realeased in the deal, viz Masood Azhar and Omar Sheikh, were in the headlines in January

2002, for the murder of Daniel Pearl, a *Wall Streat Journal* correspondent.

The ISI further extended its operational capability in J & K by creating some more *jihadi* outfits, including the LET, ABDR, and JEM. The foreign mercenaries formed the "strike" core of these outfits, to borrow a military term. These outfits drew youth into their fold offering competitive and attractive terms in the 'market place'. The practitioners of terror trade had adopted modern 'business management' model in recruiting and employing the young, ambitious activists. The ISI despatched the foreign mercenaries to J & K on two-year contracts with handsome salaries and attractive terminal benefits – in the manner of Soldirs of Fortune who specify their terms of engagement, usually going for the highest bidder.

The phenomenon had local application also. Secessionist ideology, in desparation to retain its relevance, was turning itself into a lucre of risky nature. This was 'commerical terrorism', if one may coin a term apt for the occassion and purpose, which benefited all the non-Indian players in the field. This mutually benefitting "terrorist commerce" is kept active and alive by Pakistani donors and Kashmiri recepients, if you will, especially in the areas of depressed employement opportunities and in the times when the tourism business has been badly hit by the terrorist business.

It must be emphasised that the ISI does not overlook any opportunity, possibility or section of the people to swell the ranks of the terrorist organisations. It did not forget to recruit Pakistan's own retired service men as also the criminals undergoing different kinds of sentences, and their subsequent induction into the Valley. Recruiting the latter category to do its bidding is generally termed the "Dirty Dozen" approach.

Kashmir under Greater Threat after Nine-Eleven

11 September 2001, popularly Nine-Eleven, was a cataclysmic event for the world – more accurately for the West, and especially for the US. But it also had its fallout for India's difficulties in Kashmir. Osama's was a larger than life presence over the international horizon—portentious and threatening, for one. An apparition foments greater phobia than the real thing.

Two, Osama's presence in Kashmir, directly or indirectly, was known to the intelligence agencies for quite sometime. Post-Nine-Eleven, he confirmed it personally. To put it more honestty, the world was a lot more unsafe in this (2001) decade.

Having kept the pot boiling during the 1990-2000 period, the terrorists got a shot in the arm as Osama's covert support to them in J & K became overt as he threatened the US with more deaths after Nine-Eleven if it continues its 'support' to India. This threat from Osama came on the air close on the heals of a similar threat from the JEM Chief Azhar.

Frist the Osama-speak. The videotaped statement, issued by Qaeda spkesman, Suleman Abu Ghaith, was aired in October 2001 by Qatar's Al Jazeera TV Channel. It was in this statement that Osama included India in the company of Russia, Serbia and Israel as "enemies of Islam." India had been put on notice. It now faced a bigger threat in Kashmir : ISI trained Pakistani terrorists had now been joined by the Islamic *jihadis* the world over led by Osama.

A little before this statement, JEM Chief Maulana Azhar, bristling at the freezing of his outfit's assets by the US on 11 October 2001, had fumed against India : "We warn them (Indians) to beware of *Mujahideen*. We will soon deal them a smashing blow to assert our authority. We will continue the struggle. We have not launched jihad at the dictates of anybody; and we will not stop jihad at any body's dictates too." The two sworn enemies of India – Osama and Azhar - could not have been more direct and explicit. India must take such threats seriously, if it has not already done so. It defies both belief and commonsense to learn that the JEM bank account in Pakistan had only Rs. 50,000! Obviously, it had enough notice to move the funds out of its bank account. But there is no prognostic cleverness involved here, nor any extra-ordinary intelligence snooping. The simple fact of the matter is that the US Administration had publicly declared its intention to ban the JEM months before the Congress could legislate the declaration into law.

Now follows the summary of the major terrorist incident in one year that followed the Nine-Eleven.

- 1 Oct. 2001, 38 killed in *fidayeen* (= suicide) attack on J & K State Assembly premises (JEM).
- 18 Oct. 01, Failed bid to assassinate two J and K ministers (HIZB).
- 22 Oct. 01, Failed attack on IAF base, Avantipur (LET).
- 30 Nov. 01, Killed 4 members of Village Defence Committee, Galyot, Udhampur district.
- 2 Dec. 01, Killed 7 civilians, Trinagal, Udhampur district.
- 13 Dec. 01, killed 9 civilian employees and guards as also all 5 terrorist attackers in Commando-style attack on Indian Parliament, New Delhi (JEM). It led the two nations to the brink twice in the coming one year.
- 20 Jan. 2002, 11 civilians killd in attack in Behra, Poonch district (LET).
- 22 Jan. 02, (outside J & K). Armed attack on the premises of the US Information Service (USIS) in Kolkata. Aftab Ansari, a representative of the HUJI, claims responsibility. He was later extradited to India.
- 4 March 02, abducted and killed 4 civilians, Morha Pathana, district Rajouri.
- 22 March 02, injured 35 in grenade attack, near Jamia Majid, Shopian town.
- 30 March 02, killed 7, injured 20 in *fidayeen* attack on Raghunath Temple, Jammu.
- 14 May 02, killed 18 Army family members and 10 civilians in *fidayeen* attack on family quarters of *jawans* in (Army) cantonment area, Kaluchak, Jammu district; 47 injured, 25 family member and 22 civilians. 3 attackers also killed, all Pakistani (LET).
- 19 May 02, injured 7 civilians in *fidayeen* attacks on two SF camps, Chasana, Udhampur district.
- 1 June 02, 18 injured including 17 civilians in grenade attack on a picket in Anantnag.
- 13 Julu 02, killed 27 Hindus in *fidayeen* attack in Kasimnagar, Jammu district (LET).

Army deployed along the LOC : January 2002

Army was moved to the LOC to stem the inflow of the militants/terrorists from across the border. That this unwanted and destructive infiltration did come down is shown by the two tables below.

Infiltration 5 months before January 2002 (August-December 2001)

Category	*Aug.*	*Sep.*	*Oct.*	*Nov.*	*Dec.*
Foreigners	218	151	158	101	1961
Locals	127	131	118	81	67
Total	345	282	276	182	228

Infiltration in 5 months after January 2002 (January-May 2002)

Category	*Jan.*	*Feb.*	*Mar.*	*Apr.*	*May*
Foreigners	21	39	111	143	122
Locals	12	21	33	66	43
Total	33	60	144	209	165

A scrutiny of these two tables shows that the number of infiltrations over the five-month period after the Army deployment compared to the 5-month period before it has dropped by about 45 per cent.

But it needs to be noted that the phenomenon of infiltration is weather-governed as well. This demands that the infiltration data for the period January-May 2002 be compared with the corresponding period of the year before. That will be a more genuine comparison for proper analytical study. The table below has the comparative figures for the two periods.

Infiltration Data for Jan-May Period of 2001 and 2002

Month	*Foreigners*		*Locals*		*Total*	
	2001	*2002*	*2001*	*2002*	*2001*	*2002*
Jan.	109	21	40	12	149	33
Feb.	78	39	26	21	104	60
Mar.	61	111	54	33	115	144
Apr.	93	143	56	66	149	209
May	125	122	54	43	179	165
Total	466	436	230	175	696	611

There does not seem to be any appreciable decrease in the inflitration numbers in 2002 compared to similar period during the year 2001. The following detailed observations should be a more accurate analysis as certain inferences can be drawn from the table above. The fact that both the Armies were deployed can be treated as a balancing out factor. Inferences follow :

- Over the comparable periods. January-may, the number of foreign infiltrators dropped only marginally, a mere 6.4 per cent – 436 against 466.
- In March and April 2002, there was a significant increase in foreigner unfiltration over the same months in 2001 – from 61 to 111 and 93 to 143 respectively for March and April of these two years. Both indicate an increase of 80 per cent.
- In January of these two years, the drop was significantly large, from 109 to 21, about 80 per cent. In February, the drop was 50 per cent.
- The levels of foreign infiltration was approximately same for the month of May of these two years.

Funding the Terror in J and K : Patterns and Major Sources

Most estimates place the ISI spending to foster and fuel the insurgent/terrorist violence in J & K at Rs. 200 crore per year. The amount goes to meet incentive payment, and expenditure on training, salaries, arms and ammunition, etc. There are other sources of funds also as shall be clear as we go along.

First the details on the ISI funds. It directly contributes nearly 25 per cent of the total of Rs. 200 crore. Another 40 per cent come from various Islamic groups world over. A mere 1 per cent of the amount comes from local collections – mainly through extortion, ransom payment, and other such blackmail tactics.

The despatch of money to the outfits active in India and its province of J & K in particular, is ramified in a tangled skein of networks. Documents seized from Al Jihad activists in India revealed that this outfit alone receives Rs. 1.5 crore every month from the ISI. It was sent through various religious trusts and welfare organisations. A variety of channels were used for the purpose : Courier services, centuries old *hawala* transactions –

secure, swift, and undocumented. Two prominent persons, Ghulam Nabi Fai (USA) and Dr. Ayub Thakur (UK), have been implicated in some of the *hawala* transactions/payments to some terrorists/outfits.

It is an open secret in Pakistan/POK that Prime Minister of POK runs Kashmir Liberation Cell, a front for the ISI to funnel funds to the terror merchants in J & K. Occasionally, Prime Ministers like Qayoom puts some money into this cell from the state's treasury. To wit, Qayoom's ADC, Col Farooq was caught once with his hands in the till – misappropriating the Kashmir "relief funds."

Once the earlier channels are found out to be what they actually are meant to be, the new one are put to use. Post-2000, the funds have been pumped into J & K mainly through certain front organisations of the well-established and widely-spread network of the JEI and the constituents of the United Jihad Council (UJC), popularly Kashmir. Jihad Council. Some of the front organisations of the JEI are : (1) Al Rashid Trust (2) Islamic Relief Trust (3) Public Relief Trust (4) Mehboob Alam Trust (4) Centre for Kashmir Studies (5) Iqbal Memorial Trust (6) Islamic Study Circle.

Then funds come as donations from various charities and Islamic organisations the world over, especially in the Persian Gulf area, the USA and the UK. Some of these are World Association of Muslim Youth, Rabita-e-Alam-e-Islami, World Kashmir Freedom Movement, Kashmir American Council (through GN Fai), Kashmir Study Group (through Farooq Katwaria, USA), and Friends of Kashmir, UK (through Dr. Usman). There are surely some others on the intelligence files but not yet in public domain.

The flow of funds to the terrorist outfits in J & K alone is placed between 5 and 10 crore monthly, or Rs. 60 to 120 crore annually. The main beneficiaries include the HUM, LET, JEM et al. During April 1999-March 2000 period, the HUM alone is believed to have received about Rs. 21 crore.

As is the case the world over, or nearer home, within the North-East, the multi-billion narco-trade also sustain terrororist-inflicited inhuman, violent excesses in J & K also. As is only to be expected, the ISI yet again is the conduit for such funds, as was disclosed by Shamshad Ahmad of Pakistan, who was arrested on 8 May 1998 in India. Further, the ISI leaves no avenues or opportunities unexplored/unexploited to destabilise India politically or economically. With eyes on disruption and sab of India's economy, the ISI occasionally keep pumping fake Indian currency (notes) through smugglers. On the tip off from the intelligence, the police and Army have been recovering huge amounts in fake currency in the areas contiguous to Indian shore-line, and sometimes in its interiors. The intelligence sleuths assert that against 10 such recoveries of contraband, 15 to 30 go unrecovered!

The 'open' nature of fund soliciting in Pakistan and POK by several terrorist organisation may come as a surprise to common run of Indians and also some mushy Indo-Pakistani Friendship Associations who want to keep their head firmly buried in the sands of delusion, but not to their newspaper-reading compatriots. The Indian press, particularly the English language, regularly carries stories from the Pak press about the advertisements issued by various *tanzeems* and organisations, with full addresses and bank account numbers, inviting and exhorting the public to liberally contribute to the Kashmir Jihad Fund.

But what should take the cake for sheer blatancy and chutzpa are public advertisements in the dailies and weeklies for the youth to come forward and join this or that *tanzeem*, with details of pay, perks, and sundry emoluments for the family in case of the brave son/father attaining martyrdom during his jihad for the Kashmir 'cause'. This was obviously in the knowledge of the Pakistan government, which in any case took the public stand that the fight in Kashmir was 'freedom struggle' and not terrorist activity, and Pakistan extended it full diplomatic, political, moral and economic support. Then there are dozens of NGOs and liberal bleeding hearts who are urging India to make peace with Pakistan as Musharraff is a reasonable man, has changed his stance on Kashmir, and more importantly, a common Pakistani, like his Indian counter part, sincerely desires peace. How one wishes these do-gooders knew better? How come any anti-India rabble rouser can have lakhs of

Pakistanis on the road, shouting and demanding 'death' for India. Then, at its annual convention at Muridke, the LET gets a million or so Pakistanis to hear and applause anti-India fulminations of its leaders, led by Saeed. The all spew brimstone and fire against India to the wild roar of cheering and applauding "India-loving" denizens of that "friendly" country, if we are to believe our ultra-liberal academics, journalists, and scholars. A very rough count should include Kuldip Nayar, Khushwant Singh, AG Noorani an Admiral, a national awardee but innocent old Lady and a daily newspaper each from Chennai and Kolkata for whom it is more important to 'understand' and project Pakistan's case on any important Indo-Pak issue to their Indian audience than overly worry about understanding and projecting Indian case. It is about time that these bleeding hearts understand that Pakistan's sole desire, fervently nurtured and frequently hoped for, is to see India dismembered (The point should rest here, as this is not the place or book for its further explication).

The last point in this part is about Pakistan willingly agreeing to the militant outfits like the LET handling and administering the relief and rehabilitation chores in the areas bordering the LOC, after the 2005 earthquake in POK. We will not go into the reasons for this lop-sided decision, but an honest understanding of its ramifications is called for, and its fall-out for Indo-Pak relations. One, this opportunity enabled the anti-Indian terrorist outfits to spread its tentacles wider and deeper among the devastated population. They not only garnered sympathy and support for their 'cause', besides of course their deep gratitude, but also tapped the out-of-work youth to swell their ranks. Two, and more importantly, the Pak government's easy option of letting the militant outfits handle the relief was a godsend for the latter to fill their coffers with 'easy' money through defalcation and misappropriation of vast quantity of funds meant for the relief of the devastated unfortunates.

Training of and Supplying Arms to the Terrorists

It was a given that Pakistan had elaborate arrangements for training and arming the militants for subsequent employment in J & K. In the late 1980s and early 1990s, elementary training was imparted under the aegis of the JKLF and it was 7-10 day capsule. A select lot from among these trainees were given additional-advanced-training lasting for a period of 4-6 weeks. By 2000, there were 200 training camps and an equal number of transit camps—meant for the temporary stay of the militants before their being pushed across the LOC into J & K—in POK, Pakistan and Afghanistan. It was obviously a vast network to cater for ever-increasing number of recruits/militants meant for the jihad in Kashmir.

Post-Nine-Eleven situation demanded of Pakistan to close these terror-training camps. India has been demanding their dismantling for years on end but without any visible success. Under the US pressure after Nine-Eleven and its intervention/attack on Afghanistan, Pakistan effected a U-turn in its Afghan policy—abandoning the Taliban, its very own creation. Otherwise, it would have been declared a "terrorist State" by Washington, the consequences of which it was not in a position to bear. As a result of the US pressure and mindful of the international situation resulting from the anti-West and anti-US aims of the terror war unleashed by Osama bin Laden on 11 September 2001, Pakistan President Musharraff publicly declared in January 2002 that "Pakistan will not allow any part of its territory to be used by the terrorists." The pledge was the demand of a difficult situation Pakistan was placed into, but how it was played out in the coming years is a story of duplicitous diplomacy and double standards in international affairs. For sometimes, it was a success story that went awry in the later year when the fires of terrorism threatened to engulf Pakistan itself. The details will be dealt with in a separate chapter. But for now, let it be recorded that Pakistan reportedly closed many of the terror training camps. Based on its earlier experience as opposed to the US expediency, India remained severely sceptical in this regard, knowing the ground reality rather well—and from close quarters. Some analysts criticised the Faustian deal struck by the USA with Pakistan following 11 September as hollow and contradictory, wishing good luck, of course, to the USA as it needed protection from its old allies and new-found friends in the global war aganist terrorism. Be that as it may, but the Indians should not make the mistake of forgetting Israel and its problems with the Palestinians!

The Pak Army got more directly involved in training the *mujahideen*, around 1994, planning more systematic and advanced training curricula for them. The literates were selected for courses lasting 3-6 months. Some brighter, tougher trainees were taken to the Pak Army Camps situated along the Indo-Pak border/LOC including Lipa and Atugam, for 6-9 months of higher training, ending with their participation in firing exercises. The recruits were also imparted good, strong religious indoctrination with generous doses/capsules of history of Islamic wars.

Mid-1990s, the JKLF had rented some rooms in Muzaffarabad, and called the complex as the Ayubi Training Camp. It was run by the JKLF Coordenator, Raja Muzaffar. It also served as a base to transfer recruits to different IST training camps in POK. The Ayubi was also used for launching trained militants into the valley. Similarly, the HUM had its offices in Muzaffarabad. All training camps/centres maintained forward camps near the LOC for the cross-border operations.

The Indian SF have seized, since the beginning of the organised militancy in 1989 till mid-2002, the following quantities of weapons :

- Over 21,000 AK series rifles.
- Over 2,000 machine guns.
- 8,456 pistols/revolvers
- 3,307 recokets
- 5,403 mines
- Over 3 million rounds of small arms ammunition.

This obviously is the tip of the iceberg.

The Cross-border Terrorism : Almost Continuous

When two democratic institutions of India came under terrorist attacks in 2001—the J & K Assembly on 1 October in Srinagar and Indian Parliament in New Delhi on 13 December—it was obvious that India's democracy was the target. The latter outrage was particularly taken seriously, compelling India ordering full mobilisation. Within two month, the Army was on its battle stations and other two services fully operationalised. The Vajpayee Government was twice on the cusp of ordering 'go' during 2002, according to a later report in the *India Today*. But in the event, this elaborate, costly exercise was reduced to being dubbed as "coercive diplomacy"—a permissible combat practice. In the process, the LOC came to be held by the military since January 2002, which has certainly paid dividends for the overall security scenario in the State.

The relations between Pakistan government and the terrorist/militant organisations mushrooming and freely operating in Pakistan has been a subject of some contention. Most analysts believe there are symbiotic relations between the two but Pakistan claims these outfits are autonomous. Indian agencies' interception of communications between them do not bear out the Pak assertion about autonomy. During the 26-27 July 2002 New Delhi visit by US Secretary of State Colin Powell, the Goverment released evidence to media from intercepted messages between 'central stations' in Pakistan and these terrorist outfits like Al Badar, JEM, LET, HUM and HKUM in the Kashmir Valley. The exchange was on regular basis. One intercept revealed plans about suicide bomber attack on India's Minister of State for External Affairs Omar Abdullah, during his visit to Mahore village, Udhampur district, in July 2002. Nothing of the sort came about. Some messages smelt of anti-Mushour of tenor. After all, post Nine-Eleven he had earned the wrath of so many terror-mongers.

It is significant that such messaging between these two entities have continued—their frequency fluctuating during different periods of time. The practice effectively falsifies the myth of autonomy enjoyed by these outfits as assiduously propagated by Islamabad, as also Pak claims of its inability to control these loose cannons on the militancy deck.

Now to the question of the continued cross-border terrorism from across the LOC as also the international border with Pakistan that renders India's fight against these terrorists less effective—if not totally ineffective. For this section, Pakistani inspired/supported terrorism in J & K is matter of immediate concern. A common man cannot understand—much less accept—India's inability to staunch the flow of these unwelcome, troublesome *jihadis* The popular refrain is : "Just seal the border. If Israel can do it, why not India?" Leaving aside the larger question and a certain flourish let us accept there are military and political reasons behind India's inability on this score. At the very outset, it needs to be emphasised that no nation, how soever powerful, can insulate itself within its border—be it the US against the Mexicans, Europe against the Africans and Asians, or India against the Pakistani and Bangladeshi citizens. A determined foreigner will enter a country, even risking his life if necessary.

Now we revert to cross-border traffic into J & K. From the tactical perspective, the effectiveness of the Indian Governemnt and its security apparatus in reducing/eliminating cross-border terrorism is circumscribed by certain factors. By its very nature, this circumscription can not be altogether done away with. By continuous endeavour, the flow can be controlled, and thus reduced. What are these factors? Adverse terrain, the absence/limited efficiency of sensor systems to detect infiltration, the sustained support of Pakistan, and presence of certain ideologically sympathetic elements within Valley are four of such factors. Even with the increased Army presence on the LOC, it controls it since January 2002), for "border management", a continuing residue of infiltration from across the LOC persists. Pakistan does not inject the militants into J & K over the LOC only. It has the option of flying them to India's neighbouring countries and then induct them into India either through its airports or over their borders with India into the states like UP, Bihar if they are coming from Nepal, or the states like West Bengal and Assam if they were flown into Bangladesh, in the first instance. Pakistan is also known to push the militants into India over the international borders into Rajasthan and Gujarat.

Due to a political decision, India does not allow its forces to adopt a policy of 'hot pursuit' while on the trail of the militants if they cross over into PoK/Pakistan. Israel is one country that practices the policy of "hot pursuit" effectively and vigorously.

It is only fair to assume that, from the "strategic" perspective, there are explicit political and military objectives behind the deployment of the Army on the borders. With this step, additional para-military forces are available for internal security duties within J & K. At the apex in the state is the Unified Command which has over-all charge of counter-terrorist and counter-infiltration operations, and it is headed by the state Chief Minister.

Pakistan has found export of terrorism as an important instrumentality of its foreign policy for dealing with India over Kashmir issue. It will not renounce the benefits of this success story in a hurry—its compulsions of joining the USA in war against the international terrorism notwithstanding. It is necessary, in this context, that Pakistan keeps improving the efficiency and effectiveness of its terror machine in India's J & K state, and as a part of its larger objective of dismemberment of India, into Indian territory beyond J & K. One imperative to ensure the strategic sustainability of its anti-India terrorist compaign in J & K is to periodically insert hardcore, foreign/non-indigenous mercenaries into it. There are reasons for this periodic 'booster dose', so to say. One, over a period of time, the native Kashmiri elements seem to be becoming non-cooperative, reluctant, inactive and at times, even hostile. Two, many of these mercenaries are on contract assignments and need periodic replacement/pullback. Three, the new products from the numerous training camps have to be inducted into J and K, along with some seniors, to offset losses and casualities. Pakistan is thus well-ahead and equipped with its plans of counteracting any expected attrition in the ranks of its "holy" warriors in J & K, and therefore India should be quite clear in its mind that Pakistan can sustain its terrorist campaign for indefinite future, as it has succeeded in doing ever since 1947 through a variety of clever if dubious means. Consequently, India should plan and be prepared to execute its couter-infiltration and counter-terrorism strategy for an indeterminate period.

Some experts on terrorism, including some military strategists, nurture the illusion of controlling if not altogether eliminating the Pak fomented pandemic from J & K in the medium-term future. The past experience does not support this prognosis/analysis. So it is time these well-intentioned but ill-informed Indians stop living in their delusionary world and come out with a more realistic and balanced measures to fight and defeat the jihadis including the fidayeen who have already hypothecated their mundane existence for a luxuriant life in *bahisht* (heaven), with due guidance and inspiration from a 'learned' cleric.

The contents of unclassified document, "Reforming the National Security System : Recommendations of the Group of Ministers (GOM)," released by the National Security Council Secretariat (NSCS) in Februay 2001, is in public domain for over 5 years by now. It had highlighted the need for refining the civil-military synergy and for effective implementation of the existing laws and power granted under them. In fact, the recommendations in paragraph 6.82 (*vii*) expects a composite group "to bring out a manual on civil-military interface incorporating practical measures for implementation" at both the formal and informal levels. One is not aware if it was as a result of recommendations made by this document, but eleven months after its release, the Army was deployed along the LOC, in January 2002. It is only reasonable to assume that the Army and civil administration in J & K have long been working, as advised and giuded by this 'manual'. If that is not the case, as some analysts assert, because of our lackadaisical attitude on matters of geo-strategic and security implications, it is not a day too early to produce this manual and act on it. One frequently hopes that all the other recommendations of the GOM, most being very practical, are being implemented with sincerity and persistence.

Some critics have castigated India for asking the US to advise/pressurise Pakistan to cut off all kinds of support to the terrorists, operating in J & K, including dismantling of their training camps and basis in POK/Pakistan. The reason is simple and straight forward : Why should India depend upon a third country to douse the flames of secessionist terrorism externally stoked by Pakistan? The supplicant status of a nation expected—and inspiring—to be a Super Power by 2030, is rather galling to the susceptibilities of Indian analysts and scholars. In the international communities, each nation must fend for itself in field of national security and counter-terrorism—all the talk of inter-dependence of nations in the globalised world notwithstanding. Why should any other nation singe its hands, taking India's chestnuts out of fire. Joining the global war against terrorism is important in the matters of exchanging relevant intelligence inputs, forging bilateral extradition treaties, use of Interpol where necessary, but to expect anything outside these parameters will really be unrealistic, or simplistic. To wit, let us take case of Indian expectations from world community, especially from the US. First, an issue of principles and ethics. As for the ethics, it is almost an unknown commodity in the sphere of international politics. As for the principles, it is fine to take about them in bilateral or multi-lateral treaties. They make for rhetorical flourish, or for the embellishment of the texts of such treaties. There is very little practical value of idealism in the world of real politik. All this is not indicative of cynicism, but reflective of ground realities. Again, in principle, all nations will condemn, and cast their vote against terrorism of all hues; and cross-border terrorism or export of terrorism will be particularly condemned even more harshly.

But there will be wide divergence of views while giving practical shape to these ideals/principles. Let us start at the beginning. The UN till date, after spending long hours of debating the subject through endless years and using reams and reams of paper recording the proceedings of these endless if acimonious debates, have failed to work out the definition of the term 'terrorism'/'terrorist', acceptable to all its members. Then comes the much-overused cliche of someone's terrrorist being another's freedom fighter. Now to the topic of Pakistan fighting a low intensity war with India through the use of the weapon of cross-border terrorism. This, of course, is an issue that seriously impinges on India's security paradigm. But it will be unrealistic of New Delhi to expect all the rest of them seeing it in the same light. Other countries are unlikely to have the commitment or intensity of purpose or suffering to feel sufficiently persuaded to effectively restrain Pakistan. Most nations will have their own policy compulsions or bilateral compromises to make. Forget about China, which is a close political ally of Pakistan, even the US today is a strategic ally of Islamabad, though the terminology employed officially is "non-NATO ally." Pakistan is a partner of USA in the latter's war against terrorism, especially Osama's Qaeda. Although it is acknowledged fairly widely, no nation because of compulsions of diplomacy or national interests talks about the double-game

Pakistan is playing on the question of sincere action against Osama and his Qaeda. It is well-known that the US President have privately told Gen. Musharrof that Pakistan is hoodwinking USA about its "sincere" efforts at tracking Osama and his senior activits of Qaeda, but in public it is sometimes, "Pakistan must do more against Al Qaeda in its NWFP" and more frequently the refrain is, "Pakistan is playing valuable role in anti-terrorist operations." On 10 September 2006, in a TV interview on the eve of the 5th anniversary of Nine-Eleven, US Vice President Dick Cheney profusely thanked Musharrof for his contributions in the field of countering international terrorism. A daily, dated 13 September 2006, confirming President Bush's intention of giving price concessions to Pakistan in the purchase of 38 × F-16s, ended up saying, "Bush talks often to Musharrof on phone."

It is worth an emphasis that each nation fights its own battles, despite the rhetoric otherwise!

The role of drug money to promote the terrorism by various organisations is widely known and exhaustively documented by the relevant UN agencies. There is empirical evidence to show that the infiltrating groups are composed of non-indigenous mercenaries, couriers and guides. The latter two categories are known to be actively engaged in drug smuggling into India for subsequent export to more lucrative destinations in various parts of the globe. These smuggling operations are in support of and for benefit to the ISI and drug syndicates. And it need not come as a surprise if the drug lords have the protection of not only of criminal elements of India but also of certain members of its political class. Thus the narcotic trade has security implications for India. Hence the need for concerned Indian authorities to redouble their country-wide efforts in the field of anti-drug campaign to weed out/reduce the damage/danger to the national security.

Armed Forces the world over in a democratic set-up have no power of arrest or detention over the civil population. But in an insurgency situation or to confront the terrorist violence, certain such powers have to be granted to the military to enable it to tackle the ultras effectively, without losing any time which will certainly be the case if it has to abide by the usual, time-consuming civil/criminal law procedures. Certain civil 'police' powers were given for the first time to the Armed Forces operating against the Naga insurgents in the mid 1950s. The North East example was replicated in some other regions of country also facing serious law and order/insurgency situation.

The Armed Forces (Jammu and Kashmir) Special Power Act, 1990 (No. 21 of 1990) was published in the *Gazette of India* on 10 September 1990, coming into force with retrospective effect from 5 July 1990. It vests the military with a spectrum of 'police' powers including those for search, seizure and arrest in the "disturbed" areas of J & K, so declared under this Act by the state government. Twelve districts have been declared "disturbed" : Jammu, Kathua, Udhampur, Poonch, Rajouri, Doda, Srinagar, Badgam, Anantnag, Pulwama, Baramulla and Kupwara. The Act requires the military to hand over the arrested persons and seized property to the nearest police station "without undue delay". The Act was passed for effective control of terrorist activities in J & K, especially because the state police had failed to act against the violent elements which is its primary responsibility. Some human rights groups have been voicing occasional criticism of the Army for violating basic rights of the people, especially those arrested by it for terrorist activities. Keeping in mind such criticism of Army, the infirmities and difficulties of police, and results achieved by the Army under this Act, or lack of these, it should be an constructive exercise to analyse the functioning of the Army personnel under this Act. In fact, such an analysis has already been carried out, but its details are not in public domain.

Intelligence inputs and their timely evaluation are useful tools in fight against terrorism. The need for better, actionable intelligence, securely disseminated in the shortest possible time, is even more important to reduce and eliminate infiltration by the SF in the terrian-challenged areas of J & K. Multiplicity of intelligence agencies is the bane most countries suffer from. To avoid wasteful duplication, and make effective and quick use of the intelligence gathered, better coordination both at operational and headquarters levels is the sine qua non. India cannot be unaware of the importance of the subject of intelligence. Chanakya dealt with it in his seminal book

Arthashastra. It is a fact well-known since his days that complete information will soldom be available. The governments will have to undertake decision-making under conditions of uncertainty because of lack of full information and consequently decisions will have to be based on available trends on the subject and national interest.

The use of air power has been a contentious issue in India post-1947 wars. The Indian Air Force was simply not used during the 1962 Chinese war due to a decision made at the very top. In Kargil war, the Air Force was not used in the initial stages—for whatever reasons. The air power can help and supplement the Army's effort to furter reduce the quantum of infiltration. If the Air Force is to be used effectively, efficient counter-measures against the threat of the Stinger missiles would be necessary. The fear of escalation, which was believed to be the reason behind India's reluctance to use the IAF in 1962, needs to be addressed in detail and won over. The escalation control must be handled in a planned manner. For targets in hilly areas and behind the cliffs, the cluster bombs have been found useful choice to dislodge and neutralise the holed up foreign infiltrators.

Some analysts suggest the mining of the infiltration routes to check the entry from across the border. This has its costs in terms of effect on the border 'commerce', 'family traffice', and human and animal casualities. The human rights groups will also raise hue and cry. But it must be weighed against the heavy loss of life and property caused by infiltrating terrorists, and also heavy deployment of troops to counter it.

From the statements by the senior civil and Army functionaries, the Army was initially employed in the 'offensive-Defensive' posture to handle potential conventional thrusts of the Pakistani Army. At a certain stage in 1990s. Army's Major objective became counter-insurgency/terrorism operations to reduce/eliminate infiltration across the LOC. The strategy and tactics for the two roles are distinctly different. It can be assumed the concerned Army authorities must have examined the turin-issues, based on the experience and ground realities. One possible result of the Army's analysis of the issues involved was raising of a new force, the Rashtriya Rifles, for exclusive deployment in J & K. Further refinement in the role and strategy of the Army in J & K was effected when it was deployed along the LOC in early 2002. As of today (August 2006), the SF seem to be happily placed for the role assigned to them.

The GOM Report cited earlier has a comprehensive section on "Border Area Development" and made wide ranging recommendations on meeting "the special needs of the border population" (Para 54.132 *et seq.*). The Report has also spelt out financial implications for its recommendations. New Delhi will have no problem on findings the needed resources. The counter-terrorism war also involves battle for winning the minds of the affected people. The implementation of the suggested measures would go a long way to enhance the security of the border population and secure their cooperation in achieving the objectives.

It is worth mentioning here that the Army is doing a great deal from its own resources to win this battle for head and heart. Under the well-conceived 'Operation Sadbahavana', it is providing educational and medical facilities to the local people. It provides financial help and employment opportunities to the victims of the terrorism. As a goodwill gesture it has adopted some orphaned children. Finally, through an annual 'Bharat Darshan' programmes, young boys and girls are provide an opportunity to inter act with Indians beyond the confines of J & K.

Even the extremists among the secessionists seem to be convinced that force of arms will not work against India. There were reports in August 2006 about differences between Syed Salahuddin, HuM Supremo, and his political mentor SAS Geelani, all because there were reports of the former expressing desire to take part in the Indo-Pak Peace Talks presently going on between the two countries at official and political levels. This was the role Geelani perceived as exclusively his which Salahuddin seemed to be usurping, howsoever, indirectly. Hence, the near-public spot. The other similar straw in the wind is Chief Minister GN Azad talking about ceasefire in the coming holy month of Ramzan, and inviting the separatists to reciprocate. Interestingly, the other two main political parties, PDP and NC, headed by Mufti Mohd. Saeed and Omar Abdullah, respectively, have supported Azad's move.

For record, third round of Indo-Pak Peace Talks is presently going on, temporarily suspended consequent to the July 2006 terrorist killings in Mumbai. Prime Minister Manmohan Singh, reaching Hawana this evening (14 September 2006) to attend the NAM conference, is scheduled to meet President Musharrof on its sidelines. This meeting might result in the resumption of the peace talks.

India is periodically criticised by strategic analysts and security experts for its inability to craft a coherent, firm anti-terrorism policy, even when it has been on the receiving end for long years. A number of reasons—political, religious, international ramfications—seem to be coming in the way. It is time, the experts assert, the political class gets its act together and forge a strategy with all possible consensus if possible, and alone if necessary, to staunch the bleeding the nation is watching helplessly. It is, indeed, urgently demanded by national security imperatives. It obviously has to be different from the episodic or reactive reponses seen over the last few decades. It assumes urgency, post-Nine-Eleven, because it makes India look like a nation not able to advance its democratic, secular, pluralistic interests while aspiring to be one of the six superpowers by 2030. Having said this all, it would be realistic—and closer to the unvarnished truth—to postulate that present UPA Government will not be able to deliver on the issue due to a variety of reasons, including the vote bank factor (The subject is discussed in detail elsewhere).

As a scholar puts it, India will continue to be a 'value threat' in our region, mainly because of it making a success with its democratic experiment. It is all the more a great achievement given its size, diversity in so many spheres of national life—linguistic, religious, social, ethnic and political—and large percentage under poverty line. Its democracy, noisy and rumbustious, is the envy of not only its regional neighbours but also of many Asian and African nations. Its 'value threat' for its regional neighbours lies in its fervent and deep adherence to some essential but difficult values in the contemporary times : secularism, pluralism, democracy and responsible/responsive civil governance. So in its lonely splendour, it stands out as a large island in an archipelago of 'counter value' regimes. India's cultural vivacity by itself is seen a threat in certain countries, especially its largest neighbour. A leading security analyst wrote some years back that a film like Pakeezah is perceived a bigger threat in Pakistan than the addition of couple of armoured divisions to the Indian Army's military muscle. The wide popularity enjoyed by a poster bearing superstar Amitabh Bachchan's photo in Pakistan compels Islamabad to ban its circulation (August 2006).

J and K Assembly Election : 2002

An Indian election is a noisy, colourful, boisterous, and at times even riotous affair. Certain amount of electoral violence occurs as India melds a variety of religions, cultures, languages, political parties, and aspirations in the long haul to make the demographic transition to a modern nation-state. If earned worldwide acclaim and accolades, the electorate in J & K deserves even bigger accolades for daring to go through the exercise in the face of terrorist threats of violent action against those who defy their call to boycott the voting. In the valley, people have voted at the pain of death, and at the very minimum, at the risk of losing their limbs. In the given circumstances, a little more violence in J & K with so many terrorist outfits violently targetting the candidates, voters, and electoral staff, and consequently the entire poll process, would have to be accepted/tolerated.

In this part, following three aspects of the 2002 polls are discussed :

- Terrorist violence during the Election Period.
- Election Commission's Statistics on voter turnout.
- 'Freeness' and 'fairness' of the polls.

Terrorist Violence in the Election Period

As is publickly known, most of the separatist groups in J & K have their affiliated military outfits, with a track record of terrorist violence. All of them are assiduously engaged in carrying out Pakistan's Kashmir agenda. All the outfits—secessionist and pro-independence—were violently opposed to the electrons 2002 and had loudly told the electors to stay within their houses. So it was natural that their violent opposition to these polls would be reflected in voter/candidates/polling staff intimidation through increase in the frequency and amplitude of terrorist episodoes.

The 2002 election was held in the limelight of international attention through the presence of a number of NGOs to see the fairness or otherwise of this poll process in J & K. In the months leading to the election, the NDA Government at the Centre had tom-tommed their resolve to ensure (the first?) free and fair polls in J & K. Polling was conducted in four staggered phases with the "best possible" security arrangements involving the BSF and para military/police organisations. The Army was kept a discreet distance away—just in case, as the last resort. Let it be on record that the election process as a whole was 'certified' as fairly free by most of the international observers. A detailed survey to judge its 'freeness' and 'fairness' was conducted by two Indian scholars. Its details will be discussed later.

The table below reflects the official figures on the fatal casualities in three categories—civilian, SF and terrorist—during the 6-week period before the date elections were announced by the Election Commission on 22 August 2002, and during the 6-week period over which the poll process was completed including the voting, on 8 October 2002.

Persons killed during the 6-week period each before and during the assembly polls 2002

Targets	*Killed in the Pre-Poll 6-weeks (7 July-22 August 2002)*	*Killed in the 6 weeks during the polls (23 August)-8 October 2002*	*Percentage increase during the poll period*
Civilian	137	179	30.6
SF	61	103	68.8
Terrorist	207	259	25.6
Total	405	541	33.6

As similar periods of 6 weeks before and during the polls have been chosen, the comparative figures during the two periods are relevent to understand the increase in killings by the terrorists during the latter period. Some relevant observations on the data in the table above follow :

- An increase of 34 per cent in the total killings during the poll period is significant in view of an enhanced security cover arranged jointly by the State and Central governments. It shows an efficient planning and coordination; strength of purpose and determination; and numbers deployed by the terrorist master-minds to achieve their objectives in any or all kinds of situation/s.
- The fact that the highest increase in the fatalities was in the SF ranks tells its own story. The human rights NGOs may take a note.
- The 30 per cent increase in the civilian fatalities is even more significant and important for the Indian democratic traditions. People outside J and K, and in particular, the arm-chair critics and ultra-liberal scholars, who usually find nothing right with their country or its democracy, must note that 44.08 per cent voters of J and K came out to exercise their franchise, braving the terrorists' bullets. These brave people—voters, candidates, party workers and polling booth staff—deserve a national salute. And to note, the voter turnout of 44.08 per cent is higher than the Indian average since the Independence which ranges between 36 and 39 per cent.
- It is worth a note that the smallest increase in the fatilities, 25.6 per cent, among the three categories is among the terrorist ranks.

Observers noted another feature of the terrorist violence during the 2002 polles : Ministers of the Farooq Abdullah Government and candidates/workers of the ruling National Conference were the prime targets of the terrorists/*tanzeems*. Mushtaq Lone, Law Minister of J & K, tops the list. He was killed when he was addressing an election rally on 11 September 2002 in Tikkipora, Lolab. He was killed by a burqa-clad male assassin who had positioned himself in the women's enclosure at the rally. An outfit, called Al Afreen, claimed the responsibility. It was later identified as a cover name of the LET. Next came a series of three abortive attacks on Ms Sakina Akhtar Ittoo, J &

K Minister of State for Tourism, in Anantnag district on 11, 15, and 21 September 2002, inviting a lot of publicity as well as adverse comments. Some dubbed these attacks as staged show, which seems to be too harsh on the lady. Several NC workers fell to the assassin's bullets.

Voter Turn Out : Election Commission's Statistics

The polling was held in four phases :

- Phase 1 — 16 September 2002
- Phase 2 — 24 September 2002
- Phase 3 — 1 October 2002
- Phase 4 — 8 October 2002

Despite the suffocating acrid clouds in the wake of terrorist's death-dealing violence, in the run-up to the polls, the people in the state turned out in amazingly high numbers, as detailed earlier here, and exercised their franchise—literally facing the bullets. Table below reflects districtwise statistics of voter turnout (VTO) for the years 2002 and 1996 polls as released by the Election Commission of India.

District-wise Voter Turnout (VTO) in Jammu and Kashmir Assembly Polls 2002

	1996			*2002*		
		VTO			*VTO*	
Districts	*Voters*	*Total*	*Percentage*	*Voters*	*Total*	*Percentage*
Kupwara	2,46,029	97,094	39.46	2,84,826	1,50,844	52.96
Baramulla	4,97,934	2,77,722	55,77	6,26,416	2,50,484	39.99
Srinagar	5,64,104	1,41,342	25.06	7,24,073	79,933	11.04
Badgam	2,68,504	1,77,763	66.20	3,15,414	1,45,031	45.98
Pulwama	2,38,872	1,25,888	52.70	2,76,489	72,411	26.19
Anantnag	5,13,586	2,44,452	47.60	5,86,741	1,44,339	24.60
Kargil	71,241	57,262	80.38	87,368	66,307	75.89
Doda	3,02,779	1,90,732	62.99	3,87,734	2,04,403	52.72
Udhampur	3,44,784	1,96,931	57.12	4,93,938	2,91,026	58.92
Kathua	2,86,197	1,80,386	63.03	3,61,680	2,42,916	67.16
Jammu	8,36,289	5,06,157	60.52	11,44,033	6,61,551	57.83
Rajouri	2,67,816	1,60,891	60.08	3,70,094	1,64,467	44.44
Poonch	2,02,904	1,41,654	69.81	2,56,909	1,34,043	52.18
Total	47,08,265	25,37,526	53.90	59,15,715	26,07,755	44.08

Some of the points of significance follow :

- For the whole state, the VTO is 44.08 per cent in 2002 against 53.90 in 1996.
- The highest 2002 VTO is in Kargil district at 75.89 per cent, and the lowest, expectedly, in Srinagar at 11.04 per cent.
- The 2002 elections have been seen by people of J & K, and the rest of the Indians as fairer and freer compared to that of 1996. For those who lay greater store by the word of foreigners, most of the NGOs and foreign correspondent turned out the same verdict.

Survey and Verdict by an Indian Duo

A survey to measure the 'freeness' and 'fairness' of the 2002 polls was conducted by two Indian scholars—Yogendra Yadav of the Centre for Study of Developing Societies, New Delhi and Rekha Chowdhury of the University of Jammu, Jammu. They had positioned local investigators in 77 of the 87 constituencies for three days, from day before to the day after the polling, to note irregularities, if any, and obtain the views of the voters.

They selected four major indicators to measure the degree of 'fairness' :

- Voter turnout, to see if the official figures are accurate/correct.
- Interest of 'average citizen'.
- Occurrence of common malpractices.
- Voter perception of 'fairness'.

The assess the 'free' aspect of the poll process, they selected the following indicators :

- Voter intimidation by SF and militants.
- Presence of militants at/near polling booths.
- Voter perception of fear and post-poll threats.

The survey's findings based on voter perception of 'fairness' and a comparison with earlier state elections are :

Perceptions of 'Fairness'

- 60 constituencies : 'Completely fair' to 'largely fair'—about 78 per cent.

- 11 constituencies : 'somewhat fair'—about 14.3 per cent.
- 5 constituencies : 'largely unfair'—about 6.5 per cent.
- 1 constituency : 'grossly unfair'—about 1.3 per cent.

Perceptions of Rigging

(a) Booth level

- 63 per cent : no rigging
- 10 per cent : 'massive rigging'—17 per cent in the Valley.

(b) Overall perception

- 90 per cent of the respondents felt that rigging was reduced; 65 per cent felt so in the Valley.

Citizen Participation

- Active interest : home visits by candidate's agents; attendance at election meetings; and active campaigning.
- Percentage response in Jammu region uniformly higher than in the Valley.
- Popular enthusiasm and citizen interest for J & K as a whole was equal to, and in some parameters, higher than for similar elections in the rest of India.

The survey concluded with finding that the 2002 Assembly polls were the "fairest of them all."

On the 'freeness' aspect of the polls, the survey's findings on 'voter intimidation' are :

Jammu and Ladakh

By Security Forces

- No coercion to vote in any of the 44 constituencies.
- Flag marches in 14 constituencies.

By Militants

- Visited 11 constituencies
- 'Advised' voters in two constituencies to refrain from voting.

Kashmir Valley

By Security Forces

- Forced voters to vote in 20 constituencies but did not favour a candidate or party.

- Staged marches in 37 of the 44 constituencies.

By Militants

- Visited 13 constituencies
- Advised voters in 10 constituencies to refrain from voting.

Analysts believe that fear of both the terrorists and the SF holds the key to 'freeness'. But the response of the respondents to fear from these two sources was markedly different. When asked about the threats from the terrorists, the reply was mostly silence, and at times, evasive. On the question about Army threat, the respondents were unduly vocal and loud. Both the responses are on expected lines, and understandable, reflective of the fact that people have no fears about openly criticising, even condemning, the soldiery. But it must not be forgotten that representative character of the survey is in doubt due to its skewed nature.

Regardless of its skewed nature, the survey has come to the tentative finding that, under the prevailing circumstances, there is a qualitative feeling—not a quantitative index—of a deficit in the 'freeness' factor.

Analysts must appreciate, as should the duo incharge of survey, that assessing the 'freeness' of holding elections under the threat of the gun is a mined territory—where even angels fear to trade, forget about the mere mortals. The findings of the survey are mentioned for their information value, however skewed these might be and for reasons understandable but beyond correction. And the scholars and researches like Chowdhury and Yadav must have freedom to do a job, even if the circumstances are far from ideal. Whether one agrees with their findings, and methodology employed to reach them, is not important.

The survey conducted by the two scholars also indicates that the EC's number on voter turn out are higher by 1.3 per cent than their assessment. As one is not privy to their methodology for the task in hand, nor its inherent margin of error, it is advisable not to comment on this "minor disagreement" over the number. But given the fact that EC is better equipped to determine the voter turn out, with its dedicated staff, its figures are likey to be closer to the facts. But in any case, the survey's numbers are in close agreement with the EC's.

One may cavil at its findings and methodology adopted by it, but it must be acknowledged that overall credibility of the J & K elections has been enhanced by this non-official, non-govermental survey. This is a significant gain because today there is a degree of scepticism and cynicism about whatever a government—any government—says or does.

It is an established fact that India's Election Commission has a world-wide reputation for independence and objectivity, and non-partisan approach to its task of conducting elections in the country ever since 1950. It is widely believed that the policy, practices, and procedures adopted, refined, and implemented by India's EC are right. So were they during 2002 poll in J & K. There was an all-round appreciation of the EC's work. Western countries, professing an adherence to 'democratic values' and 'civil society', were also seen to have been impressed.

The electronic voting machines (EVM) have been used earlier also in the Indian elections. But successful use of the EVM in the Urdu language was innovative, and a remarkable success story, especially in the interiors where the population was mostly illiterate. There is temptation to declare this 2002 achievement as a technological triumph when compared to the "utter uncertainty and comprehensive chaos" till the very last moments of the deadline for declaration of the result of the 2000 US Presidential election, when fortunately a State Governor and the US Supreme Court retrieved the situation for America. As a wag put it, the "result of the last Presidential election depended on a 'pregnant charade.'" There is perhaps some call for Indians to say, "three cheers for Indian democracy which succeeds even in the face of the gun-toting militants and their bullets."

The ruling NC failed to get a majority, though it emerged as the largest single party. The result led to the coalition era in

J & K, as is the vogue at New Delhi and in many States of the Union. The Congress and the People's Democratic Party of Mufti Saeed agreed on coalition arrangement, with each party candidate leading the government for 3 years each. The Mufti having completed his 3 years as Chief Minister, presently Congressman Ghulam Nabi Azad is occupying the chair. But it ought to be added that no Chief Minister, howsoever efficient, can provide good, responsive, development-enhancing governance to people of J and K till it is freed from the ravages of the terrorism. The Mufti did as good a job at the helm as was possible in the prevailing violent environment in the State. The same is true of Azad today (September 2006).

Pakistan's Desparation to Grab Kashmir : An Analysis

Pakistan never reconciled itself to the fact of Jammu and Kashmir's accession to India. At the time of the Partition, the ruler, Maharaja Hari Singh had offered to sign the standstill agreements with both the dominions. Indid refused but Pakistan signed one. In a hurry to clinch the issue of accession, Pakistan, even after signing the said agrrement, started employing strong-arm tactics against the state to force the Ruler's hand in its favour.

The state was connected to the erstwhile British India by road by the Rawalpindi-Srinagar and Sialkot-Jammu highways. Both the starting points were now in Pakistan. To take advantage of the states utter dependance on these two roads, Pakistan imposed a ban on despatch of essential commodites to the State. The blockade as expected, created a serious situation in the State as the rail and road communication, as mentioned above, ran through Pakistan in 1947 and Pathankot-Jammu-Srinagar route was no better than a Cart track.

Maj. Shah, Jinnah's Military Secretary made several trips to Srinagar to convince the Maharaja and the administration of the inevitability of the state's accession to Pakistan. Once he met Jammu and Kashmir's Prime Minister MC Mahajan with a sword in one hand and the Instrument of accession in the other. Mahajan stood his ground and the frustrated Shah returned emply handed. But they would not give up.

Then they tried a different approach. Maj. Shah met the Maharaja and conveyed Jinnah's personal assurances that his privileges, status and position would be protected and that he need not worry or bother about Sheikh Abdullah and his National Conference. When this politicking too did not work with the Maharaja, who perhaps was keen for an independent state, equidistant from India and Pakistan, Pakistan made preparations for fullscale invasion. Pakistan had its reasons, or so they thought.

Pakistan sought accession not only for religious grounds, but also for political and strategic reasons. Jinnah wanted more territory for his Pakistan for he was not happy with what he had been awarded finally. He had publicly spoken of getting a 'moth-eaten' Pakistan. It was believed Lord Moutbatten too was keen that the Maharajah should join Pakistan. This was to ensure the long term strategic interests of the West, which would have preferred a Kashmir under the Pakistani control and for understandable reasons.

Blockade had already created a difficult situation for the state when the information on border raids reached Srinagar. The Maharaja made fervent appeals to the British Prime Minister to intervene and save his state from certain disaster. But there was no response. Finally, he made appeals to Pakistan, which fell on deaf ears. Then he sent a personal telegrame to Jinnah, asking him to stop raids, or, "I would seek friendly assistance to safeguard his state's integrity and honour of his people." It all fell on deaf ears once again. Meanwhile, the tribals from the NWFP, as Pakistan described the invaders, were marching well within the state's boundary.

"Operation Gulmarg"

Main column of raiders crossed over into Jammu and Kashmir from Garhi Habibullah, a small border town, and captured Muzaffarabad, a district town on 22 Oct. 1947. Advancing to Uri was easy as it had no forces. Then they reached Baramulla 26/27 October, despite some resistance from the state forces. They sacked Baramulla, wasted much precious time in loot, rape and murder of the local residents. It in fact proved their undoing, as the same day, the 27th, the first few units of the Indian Army, airlifted from Delhi, had landed at the Srinagar airport.[8]

Indian Army units intercepted the raiders just on the outskirts of Srinagar, advanced to Barmulla and recaptured it for India. This was initial phase of Operation Gulmarg, an ill-conceived Pakistani venture in more ways than one. It ensured that the Maharaja signed the Instrument of Accession with India. Left to himself, he might have waited much longer to choose between India and Pakistan. Now he had no choice. India had refused to intervene till he signed the legal agreement. But for that document and in its absence, India will technically be committing on aggression.

The next phase of the Op Gulmarg saw Indian and Pakistani armies locked in a longdrawn mid-intensity war. It was during this phase that Nehru was accused of not permitting the Indian Army to go beyond a certain line in Jammu and Kashmir. The Brigade Commander, in command of troops, was to write later (in a book he authored) that his troops were sitting at Uri for months and there were no order to resume the advance. As the subject is not germane to this book, it should rest here itself.

Finally the war ended with the UN-supervised ceasefire on 1 January 1949. This left two armies facing each across the arbitrarily drawn Ceasefire Line (CFL), causing unnatural division of Jammu and Kashmir as it followed no geographical or administrative boundaries. It needs to be recorded that the CFL was drawn on actual ground positions held by the armies. The CFL was converted into Line of Actual Control (LOC) at the post-Bangladesh-War Shimla Agreement.

Even if Op Gulmarg failed to achieve its main aim, still it resulted in some major strategic gains for Pakistan. By annexing vest areas in northern and Western Jammu and Kashmir, Pakistan not only succeeded in gaining a permanent foothold in the State but also creating defensible topographical boundaries which provided depth to some vital areas inside Pakistan.For record, area under illegal occupation of Pakistan (POK) is 78,500 sq. km. out of total area of Jammu and Kashmir of 2,22,200 sq. km. Northern Areas alone account for 74,500 sq. m. of the total area of POK. Pakistan has floated a new fanciful theory about the Northern Areas just the other day—24 May, 2007. Details a little later.

A serious look at the map of Pakistan and contiguous areas of the POK leaves no doubt in a discerning mind the strategic and operational significance of the latter for Pakistan. By capturing this area (of POK) and holding on to it since 1947-48, Pakistan obtained the following advantages for itself:

* Areas from Hajipir bulge to Kotli and Mirpur provide (strategic) depth to Rawalpindi-Islamabad-Gujarat-Jhelum-Mangla Dam belt. In addition, these areas have literally opened a window of opportujnity for further intrusions into Uri, Gulmarg, Poonch, Rajouri, Nowshepra and Chhamb sectors.
* Occupation of Muzaffarabad-Bugina-Neelam Valley areas provides depth to Abbotabad-Attock-Peshawar belt.
* Occupation of Gilgit-Skardu-Burzil and Kamri passes created depth for the strategic passes on the Karakoram range, provided link with Chinese Xinjiang and made the construction of the strategic Karakoram highway viable and safe. The areas of Burzil-Kamri passes provide ready-made bases for infiltration into Gurais-Talal Valley. Skardu and adjacent areas provide routes of ingress into Ladakh through Skardu-Bagicha and Khapalu-Siari-Turtuk routes. The latter incidentally is the only worthwhile route of ingress to Siachin from POK.
* By occupying Northern Kashmir, an overland route to Afghanistan was denied to India.

It is not certain if Pakistan military leadership of that time foresaw these advantages, or it was incidental gain due to a premature 'ceasefire'. What is more likely perhaps is that the British generals then in command of Pakistani Army pointed out strategic and tactical advantages of holding on to these occupied areas at all costs.

An analyst, perhaps in generous frame of mind or, may be, a born pro-Pakistani, suggests that "it is however evident that Pakistan's quest for Jammu and Kashmir is not purely 'emotional'." With the passage of time, frustration because of repeated failures to grab Jammu and Kashmir and need for public support, gave the Kashmir issue an emotional-political colour, which over a period of time became an abiding obsession. Consequently, since the 1950s Pakistan's foreign policy has largely been dictated by the Kashmir factor. Massive economic and military support from the US between 1950-62 was sought mainly to redress the adverse military balance vis-a-vis India, with on eye on Jammu and Kashmir. This policy has continued till date. Obsession of parity with India, a country five times larger and the fifth largest economy in the world, in all fields, especially in military hardware, might have ruined in Pakistan—losing its eastern half to Bangladesh—and may destroy it in future too—uprisings in the NWFP and Baluchistan—has been its abiding article of faith. The latest confirmation of the same has come from a US study, published in May 2007. Most of the aid Pakistan received from the US as its 'frontline partner' in its "war on terrorism"—over $ 5 billion from 2002 to 2006—has gone into purchase of arms meant to be used against India, just in case, and not arms and technologies that could be useful to employ in its counter-terrorism battle.

A world on the change in Pakistan's stance on the Northern areas. The EU report on Jammu and Kashmir, prepared by Baroness Winter bourne and published in draft form in 2006, was presented to the European Parliament plenary on 24 May 2007. It was approved by a vast majority. Pakistan had officially raised many objections on the report's contents which it thought were anti-Pakistan in their import, which its author had rejected with due deliberatio. This does not concern us here. Shortly before the Report was due to be submitted to the European Parliament, Pakistan officially wrote to the Baroness that the Northern Areas were not part of the state of Jammu and Kashmir before 1947. The Baroness rejected this claim with the British India period maps and various treaty documents.

What has intrigued the analysts and scholars is Pakistan's decision to formalise this defacto arrangement. What could be its reasons for this decision to get the issue included in the Report. After all, for decades the Northern Areas have been ruled directly by Islamabad, having been separated from the

POK through a government notification. Why this tearing hurry for formalistaion of a de-facto arrangement. The analysts were at their wits' ends to ascribe any worthwhile reasons for this decision till the full text of its official communication to the Baroness was made public. With it, its motives were crystal clear—and perhaps to clever to be missed.

In the official communication, Pakistan claimed that the Siachin glacier, presently under active discussion with India, was part of the Northern Areas. Its aim was to present India with a *fait accompli*, one the EU had accepted its proposition. But not only did the EU part Pakistan's proposition of the Northern Areas not being part of the State of Jammu and Kashmir, it also ruled against the Siachin being part of the Northern Areas. But it must be given to Pakistan : It can never be faulted for not trying!

Pakistan Attempts again in 1965

India's 1962 debacle rekindled Pak hopes of settling Kashmir through the force of arms. Having been demoralised by the humiliating defeat, Indian military had been rendered unfit to defend Kashmir, or so Pakistani security establishment thought.

An ingenuous plan, Op Gibraltar, was rustled up: Armed infiltration to create on upsurge in Jammu and Kashmir, which will tie down Indian Army reserves in the state; and then comes the coupe de grace in the shape of an all-out offensive. In this destabilised state, reaching Srinagar would not be a problem—at least, not two difficult.

So the armed infiltrators were unleashed in August, 1965. Op Gibraltar floundered at the very first stage because of lack of support of the Kommon Kashmiri. There was no upsurge in the horizons. But there was some recompense in the south. A major offensive, Op Grand Slam, in the Jammu region did achieve limited success but failed in its aim of cutting off vital logistics jugular to Poonch and Rajouri sectors. War ended in a costly stalemate for Pakistan, after India opened a new front in Punjab. By the time ceasefire became effective on 23 September 1965, Pakistan's moral and political stability stood shaken. Eventually, both Bhutto and Field Marshal Ayub

Khan had to quit, Gen Yahya Khan declared himself Pakistan President in 1969.

Tashkent Agreement that brought about the ceasefire restored the status quo ante on the pre-war positions even in Jammu and Kashmir. This neutralised some of the major tactical advantages Indian Army had secured in various sectors. Withdrawal from the Hajipir bulge, in particular, was a major tactical setback.

The 1971 War : A Balance Sheet

The major theatre of war was in the east. As a matter of a clearcut political decision, India decided on restraint in the West, may be, not to ruffle the international opinion.

For obvious reasons, Pakistan in 1971 was on the defensive in Jammu and Kashmir. Some analysts expressed surprise that India took no advantage of the favourable situation to, at least, capture areas/positions returned to Pakistan in 1965—bar in the Kargil sector. In fact, very little of consequence happened in Jammu and Kashmir in 1971 except a limited Pak offensive to secure a foothold in Chhamb sector that fizzled out. Indian commanders, it seems, were sitting idle in the State even when Pakistan faced a major military defeat in the East.

Humiliating military rout in 1971 operations and consequent emergence of Bangladesh as an independent nation was indeed a major setback for Pakistan. Bhutto had few bargaining chips when he came to face Indira Gandhi at the 1972 Shimla Conference. Under the circumstances, he had to make a radical departure from his country's past positions. "This (Shimla) Agreement changed the basic stance on Jammu and Kashmir so far held by Pakistan". The Agreement, besides other matters, stipulated :

* Differences to be resolved "by peaceful means through bilateral negotiations."
* The existing ceasefire line (CFL) to be redefined as determined by field commanders of two armies and would be called LOC, Line of Actual Control. Both sides pledged to respect "The LOC without prejudice to the recognised position of the other."

* UNIMOG was not to be involved in disputes or violations of the LOC, as these matters were to be settled by bilateral negotiations at the appropriate levels.

The UNCIP resolutions of 1948 and 1949 had already been abandoned by both sides in 1965, and in 1972 there was no mention of self-determination. It was however agreed that representatives would meet to discuss ways and means to establish durable peace including "a final settlement of Jammu and Kashmir."

It needs to be said however that with 1971 debacle, Pakistan was however down but not out. It licked its economic and military wounds for a while and did succeed in making a rapid recovery from these traumatic experiences. By the 1980s, Pakistan's armed forces were, once again, well-equipped and trained. So on to the 1980s.

The 1980s : Pakistan is back at its Old Game

By 1980s, having equipped its armed forces to be a match for India, Pakistani rulers were planning, after investing a lot of thought, new instruments to poke and provoke India to determine its limit of tolerance and patience. Gen Zia created a new all-service intelligence organisation, which came to be so well-known by its acronyms ISI (Inter Service Intelligence), with expertise and professional training to launch covert operations. Suffice it to say, soon it gained a reputation to train, equip, and launch terrorist outfits across the LOC, and in due course of time, the Pakistani rulers, military as also civilian, used it to topple inconvenient governments and to top it all, even to manipulate election results in their favour.

The Soviet intervention in Afghanistan came to Pakistan's help, creating an opportunity for the country and its military to feather their nests. Liberal military and economic aid gave Pakistan a semblance of political stability and its military a rank opportunity of rekindling its dreams of another go at 'Kashmir'. By then, the nation and its military had an additional reason to seek/risk a war with its eastern neighbour : avenging the 1971 humiliation and loss of its eastern wing! By 1986, Pakistan had gained a very valualble, experience of training and launching vast 'army' of Islamist fighters/Mujahideen against the Soviet troops operating in Afghanistan. On the material side, the Pakistani Army had stashed away a huge quality of arms and ammunition, suitable for subversion and terrorist operations, from the liberal US supplies meant for use against the Soviets in Afghanistan. With these two assets under its belt—the experience of training and launching terrorists/militants and abundant physical assets for their use—Pakistan was yet again ready to embark on a new venture in Jammu and Kashmir.

It needs to be noted that this time, Pakistan had adopted an innovative option of low intensity conflict—known to the military mind by its acronym : LIC. Having failed to achieve its objective through costly classical warfare, it goes to Pakistan's credit that it changed tack and adopted LIC. Obviously, it had not changed or abandoned its aim of 40 long years, but refused to repeat its past blunders. How did it go about the job ? In the 1980s, particularly in its latter half, Pakistan sponsored and promoted separatism and terrorism in India's province of Jammu and Kashmir as delineated here :

* Close coordination was established between JKLF and Punjab extremists in the UK and Pakistan.
* Religious fundamentalism was propagated in small but lethal dozes to promote separatism and communal ideology.
* Training and indoctrination of select leaders from the Kashmir Valley was arranged to create dedicated militant cadres subsequently.
* Political unrest was fomented and loyalties of local police and government servants were methodically subverted.
* Large number of youth exKashmir Valley and Poonch sector were given extensive training in the use of automatic weapons, sabotage, and attacks on security forces. They had started issuing automatic weapons and explosives to these 'trained' recruits, rather Islamist fighters.
* Special teams were trained to organise agitations and hartals, and to engineer incidents to damage the secular and democratic image of India.

As mentioned above, a humilitated and truncated Pakistan has nurtured an ambition to teach India a lesson—by avenging the 1971. It had to match India by paying it back in the same coin. It saw its opportunity in 1985-86 and started preparations for its plans to destabilise India with spreading disaffection and subversion in Jammu and Kashmir to begin with. One analyst says the first phase of the LIC was launched in 1987 and was perhaps completed in 1989. "The first phase political objectives of throwing out the Farooq Abdullah Government by plunging the State into political and economic chaos was accomplished through agitations against the Indian Republic and employing tactics of fomenting subversion and selective acts of terrorism. Governor Jagmohan's Government too was got rid of by similar but more intensified terrorist violence. Inaction of the Abdullah government earlier and ill-conceived whiplash reaction of Jagmohan later, gave an added momentum to the Pak ambitions."[9]

This analysis, if not motivated, at least lacks balance and objectivity. The government is blameworthy either way : If it shows restraint, it is guilty of 'inaction'. If it acts effectively, the charge of 'whiplash reaction' is laid on its door. There was nothing like a phase-wise launching of Pakistan's plans to destabilise India, starting with Kashmir. The main factor behind Pakistan's success in initiating Islamist terrorism in Kashmir was changing tack after the 1971 humilation, realising that wars could not bend India. It was two decades of propagating religious extremism and spewing of anti-India and Hindu venom that some Kashmiris in the valley were ready for terrorist violence. It is as simple as that.

Notwithinstanding the above, it is still interesting to read the outputs of theorising scholars and analysts. The one qoted above says the first phase ended in 1989. "This confrontation however failed to graduate to insurgency, even though it was successfully transformed from mere terrorism to a violent struggle between the 'people' and the state."

It is obviously misreading the situation and misinterpreting the term 'people'. It is a small band of Kashmiri, Muslims confined to the valley around Srinagar, who are carrying out terrorist activities on the bidding of their masters in Islamabad, and particularly the ISI. The 'people' are represented by those Kashmiris who cast their votes in the democratic elections at the pain of death. It was heartening to see more people voting in the 2002 Assembly polls, in terms of percentages than in so many other states of India.

The fact of the matter is that Pakistan sponsored insurgent/terrorist violence started in 1989 and has taken a heavy toll in human lives. Islamist succeeded in getting militants from 22 Islamic countries. But for the last four to five years, security forces are having upper hand over the terrorist. With Pakistan itself realising the futility of terrorist violence, it has joined India to launch a peace process, even if the extreme rightists like Geelani are spitting venom even on Musharraf.

It may be hazardous to offer any dateline on this issue being solved, but what can be safely said is that the worst is over. Of course, the unthinkable can always happen.

Notes

1. Praveen Swami, *Hindu*, 24 May, 2007.
2. Dasgupta, C. (2002).
3. Maqbool Sherwani was killed, nailed to the stake, by the Pakistani hordes for misleading them to gain time for the advancing Indian troops to reach Baramulla, thus saving the town for India. This Author had the honour of meeting the martyr's father at his house in Baramulla and bowed his head at the grave of Maqbool in salute to his sacred memory in 1962. May Allah bless the good and great Maqbool and his family.
4. It took over three decades for Pakistan to express regrets—not apology, it be noted—to the people of Bangladesh, over that 1971 horrendous genocide, during the July, 2002 visit to Dhaka by Gen. Musharrof.
5. The Americans want us to spell it as 'maneuver'.
6. Surely, the BJP—led NDA, first time in power at the Centre, did not mean to convey that all the polls held earlier in Jammu and Kashmir were not free and fair.
7. Courtesy Santhanam *et. al.* 2003, p. 43.
8. Here the author can just not resist the temptation of mentioning the fact that is a matter of pride for him, and his Sikh Regiment. 1 Sikh (First Battalion, the Sikh Regiment, to mention its proper designation) from his Regiment was the first unit of the Indian Army to land at Srinagar.
9. Karim, Afsar, 1991.

5

Present Situation in Jammu and Kashmir (Currents and Cross-Currents)

This chapter deals with various aspects of the present situation in Jammu and Kashmir, with currents and under-currents impacting against each other. First come some select terrorist outfits active in the State.

Some Active Terrorist Outfits

1. Hizb-ul-Mujahideen(HM)
2. Jaish-e-Mohammad(JEM)
3. Lashkar-e-Tayyaba(LET)
4. Students Islamic (SIMI)
   Movement of India

"Hizb not Linked to Al Qaeda", Says Salahuddin : 4 Jan 2007

Syed Salahuddin, Supreme Commander of Hizb-ul-Mujahideen (HM) and Chairman of the United Jihadi Council (UJC), an umbrella organisation of 19 militant groups operating in Kashmir, has denied any link between the Al Qaeda and his outfit. He made the following points :

- "It is not in our interest to side with Al Qaeda because we are not fighting only for Muslim Kashmiris but for all Kashmiris, including non-Muslim.
- "The US introduced the name of Al Qaeda after 9/11. It was not popular among the Muslims till then. I never heard of the Al Qaeda during Afghan jihad.
- "India has always tried to establish links between the HM and the Al Qaeda and Taliban but both groups emerged only in 1990s.

- "We started our struggle more than a century ago and the Al Qaeda and HM came into existence only in the '90s."

Asked if the people involved in the 7/7 London bombing, had any links with the HM, the Muzaffarabad based terror Chief said his outfit was operating in Kashmir only.

It is obvious that he is denying the links fearing adverse repercussions of an open, unambiguous admission.

Jaish Regrouping : *Daily Times* (Pakistan) : 22 Apr 2007

Jaish-e-Mohammad (JEM) – the jihadi outfit responsible for the hijacking of IC-814 in 1999 to Kandahar, the 13 Dec 2001 attack on Indian Parliament and two attempts at Gen Musharraf's life – is reorganising itself under its new commander Mufti Abdul Rauf, younger brother of Maulana Masood Azhar.

The JEM has been banned by Pakistan besides being categorised as an unlawful terrorist group by India and the US.

Pakistani paper, *Daily Times* of 22 Apr 2007, says : "Jaish has established a transit camp in Islamabad for its activists coming from southern Punjab and travelling to Kohat where another camp has been set up."

The Islamabad camp will serve as a base for JEM's propaganda campaign and distribution of pamphlets in tribal areas.

Sources told the Daily that Rauf is spearheading the reorganisation of the JEM. He had appeared on the scene after Azhar went underground following the two suicide attacks on President Musharraf.

Pakistan had banned Jaish in Jan 2002 soon after the Parliament attack had led to a massive troop mobilisation on the either side of the Indo-Pak border.

Although JEM's activities have declined in Kashmir after its commanders were killed in a series of police actions in south Kashmir's Shopian area, its reorganisation inside Pakistan will have serious fall-out in the Valley. "In fact, the outfits effort to revive its network in the valley hit a hurdle last week when Sopore police arrested three of its commanders who had silently been reorganising the group in north Kashmir since they returned after graduating from a Surat Madrassa in 2004.

Jaish appeared over the militancy map of Kashmir soon after a group of Pakistani militants hijacked an Indian Airlines (IC-814) plane on its way to New Delhi from Kathmandu and diverted it to Kandahar in Dec 1999 where the then Taliban government supported the act. After the India-Afghan (Taliban) – hijackers talks, Azhar, alongwith the British Sheikh Umar Sayeed and a Kashmiri militant leader and Al-Umar Chief Mushtaq Zargar were flown to Kandahar by the then Indian External Affair Minister Jaswant Singh and later released in exchange of passengers and crew of Indian Airliner. And soon after his release, Azhar split his group from the HUM, setting up JEM and vowing to intensify attacks in Kashmir.

"JEM Investing in Legal Business" : US Report : May 2007

As the US State Department-released "Country Reports on Terrorism" yield detailed information on various aspects of world wide terrorism, there is deeper cause for concern for countries like India. The JEM is found to be investing in legal businesses to fund its terrorist operations. The revelation shows it following in the foot-steps of outfits like Al Qaeda and LET. First a word on the latter.

Typically painstaking and given the through-going ways in executing tasks entrusted to it, the American investigative agencies, in the days following 9-11, set out to look into possible suspicious investments in the stocks of airlines and the insurance companies. Evidence suggested that entities with prior knowledge had gambled on these stocks crashing in the aftermath of the attacks on the World Trade Centre. Stock markets in the US and Germany, in particular, were under scrutiny. It was suggested that Al Qaeda and its front agencies were making "legitimate" money through such channels to fund future terrorist action. Even if the case could not be conclusively proved but, still, it did reveal the sophisticated nature of modern terrorist syndicates.[1] For all their medievalism, jihadi groups such as Al Qaeda and LET are deft practitioners of globalisation, employing modern communications technology and international funds flow to their advantage. In light of this information, even if not unprecedented, the findings in the US 2007 Report – that JEM is investing in commodity and real estate markets so as to "mains tream" its assets, prevent government seizures, and multiply returns – are positively alarming.

Being South Asia's largest economy with one of the world's best performing stock markets and a real estate sector that has grown exponentially in the last three years, India, understandably, is on the radar of the JEM's portfolio managers. This is an entirely new threat from terrorism, which is not physical and cannot easily be detected by human searches and armed action. Investments in financial markets enable the terrorist outfits to convert loose, illegal cash into legally earned and verifiable wealth. Then the insiduous flow of this (sanitised) blood money corrodes country's economy, surely if slowly, which is not even easily noticed. This is even more sinister and detrimental then flooding the country with huge amounts of fake currency.

The worry does not end here, with the ill-gotten money converted into legitimate, but it is the starting point. It must be understood and known how this black-turned-white money is put to use by the merchants of death. It is easy to see that not every terrorist-promoted business entity can be detected and effaced. In the US and Europe, Al Qaeda and its cohorts over the years have installed numerous sleeper cells. These agents are well-ensconced as small businessmen, dealers for big producers, local retailers, and so on. In India, too, numerous instances have surfaced of Pakistani terrorists entering this country and, while waiting for the command to execute the assigned (destructive) strike, setting up small shops and workshops. While cumulative effect of all these may well be substantial, but it still comes nowhere near what large-scale investments in the financial markets can achieve. The latter, for example, can destabilise the indices with one blockbuster move, in a bloodless act of economic terrorism. They can buy influence in a company or a sector by making targeted investments, and creating space for blackmail. Even worse than that, they offer scope for windfall earnings for terrorist outfits and agencies.

How does India counter/defeat this looming threat to its economy, and security. Initiatives like 'Know Your Customer', under which the banks, mutual funds and investment houses are asked to ensure water tight verification of their clients, are a beginning. Another can be moving to a business and financial system that makes cash transactions less and less viable. Property market is an apt example. In acity like Delhi, 40 to 80 per cent of the value of plot of land or an apartment is paid in cash. This is an avenue any criminal, not just a terrorist, would only be too happy to exploit.

An analyst feels this 2007 Report should also caution the UPA Government on another score – its naive if ill-conceived plans to experiment with the "Islamic banking" demanded by certain sections of the Indian Muslims. It must be put to sleep, he suggests.

Besides this 'financial' jugglery by the JEM, the 2007 Report also have some other findings that need attention. It trashes Musharraf regimes' claim to have destroyed terrorist camps operating from its territory. "In anticipation of asset seizures by Pakistani Government, JEM withdrew funds from bank accounts and invested in legal businesses such as commodity trading, real estate and production of consumer goods."

Incidentally, in Feb 2007, National Security Advisor MK Narayanan stunned stock markets and politicians alike in India by claiming in Munich that "incidents of terrorist outfits manipulating the stock markets to raise funds for their operations have been reported. Stock exchanges in Mumbai and Chennai have reported that fictitious or notional companies are engaging in stock market operations. Some of these companies were later traced to terrorist outfits.

Narayanan had said that the legitimate businesses that terrorist groups were engaged in included restaurants and shipping. The US Report, which suspects that Qaeda could be funding Jaish, has also termed five other India-based groups, named below, as "groups of concern" :

- Communist Party of India (Maoists).
- ULFA
- Harkat-ul-Jihad-i-Islami (HUJI)

- Hizbul Mujahideen.
- Jamaat-ul-Mujahideen.

More significantly, the Report also calls the bluff of Fazl-ul-Rahman, the radical Deobandi cleric who has been working hard on an image make over : Passing off as a peacemonger. The Report says that one of the anti-India terror groups, Harkat-ul-Mujahidden, is aligned with Rahman's faction of Jamaat-ul-Ulema-i-Islam.

On Musharraf regime's claim of crackdown on terror groups, the Report is categoric that outfits like Jaish continue to operate "openly" in parts of Pakistan despite the government's "ban". It goes on to state that "most of JEM's cadre and material resources have been drawn from Pakistani militant groups HUJI and HUM. JEM collects funds through donation requests in magazines and pamphalets, and Al Qaeda is suspected of providing funding."

The US statement is significant, because it means that groups like JEM and LET, despite being regressive and having a primitive mindset, are quite adept at harnessing not just modern technology but also modern market instruments to execute their agenda. Gone are the days when LET merely put up donation boxes in Pakistani towns and cities. In fact, if the ultimate goal of terrorist groups is to have a world that is fit only for the 12th century, terrorists are making very profitable use of the instruments of the 21st century.

Their terror savvy now matches their financial savvy. After 9-11, countries had instituted a crackdown on Hawala transactions. The terrorists got wise and entered the legitimate business world. Real and fake ATM cards are now in circulation as are indications that terrorists groups are (now) using legitimate banking channels to fund terror operations.

The favourite "safe locations" for terror funds are in Dubai and the UAE. These funds are moved in almost unrecognisable, and unexceptionable amounts through banking channels to areas and operatives where the next terrorist attack is to happen. Keeping track of this or even intercepting these "hot" funds is the cutting edge of the counter-terror operations all over the world.[2]

The Report designated three Pakistan-based terrorist groups – HUM, JEM and LET – as "foreign terrorist organisations", prohibiting US residents from extending material support to them.

The Report released on 30 April 2007 made some other points of significance :

- Pakistan FATA have become safe haven for Al Qaeda terrorist and other extremist insurgents since the fall of the Taliban in Dec 2001. Despite Pakistan's efforts to establish governance there, the tribal areas contrinues to be safe havens for terrorists and source of instability for Pakistan and its neighbours.
- Three Pakistan-based terror outfits—JEM, LET and LEJ (Lashkar-e-Jhangvi—have been retained in the State Department's List of Terrorist Organisation.
- The failure of the tribal leaders in FATA to fulfil their promises to the government under the terms of the North Wazristan agreements of Sep 2006 led to insurgent infiltration into Afghanistan.
- Pakistan remains a major source of Islamic extremism and a safe haven for some top terrorist leaders. Credible reports estimated that as many as 900 Pakistanis lost their lives in more than 650 terror attacks in 2006, with another 1,500 people seriously injured. Pakistan has experienced attacks from international terror networks such as Al Qaeda and its supporters. Attacks occurred with greatest frequency in the regions bordering Afghanistan : Baluchistan, the NWFP, and the adjacent FATA.
- Despite having some 80,000 troops in FATA, including Army and Frontier Corps (FC) units, the government of Pakistan have been unable to exert control over the area.
- In South Asia, Afghan attacks were up by 60 per cent. Pakistan and India both had few ever attacks.
- JEM continues to operate openly in parts of Pakistan despite President Musharraf's 2002 ban on its activities. The group is well funded, and is said to have tens of thousands of followers who support attacks against

Indian targets, the Pakistani government and sectarian minorities.[3]

LET Terrorists Mutilate Villagers : Jun 2006

This outfit excels in spreading terror and its brand is no longer limited to suicide attacks. LET is now mutilating and killing people and burning property of those it suspects of having helped security forces capture its cadre.

In a gory act of revenge, and to ensure its demonstrative effect, LET terrorists slaughtered a 65-year-old man and chopped off the tongues, noses and ears of two others. The ultras also left 11 others brutally injured in Nehoch-Dunga village of Gulabgarh area of Mahore tehsil of Udhampur district on the night 15/16 Jun 2006.

All this display of inhuman brutality because the LET believed the villagers had helped security peronnel eliminate three Lashkar terrorists on 23 April and had to be taught a lesson. This, of course, is second such incident in Udhampur district after the LET terrorists massacred 13 Hindu villagers on 30 April, 2006.

Hameed, one of the injured admitted in Government Medical College in Jammu, said seven militants descended into the village and barged into the house of Abdul Ahad. He continued: "They dragged him out, gathered other villagers at gunpoint at one place and started beating them ruthlessly with canes, boots, and rifle butts. Terrorists slit Ahad's throat in front of the villagers because they suspected he had informed the forces about the hideout of Lashkar terrorists killed in April."

The horror and trauma of the helpless villagers did not end here. "Then, they brutally chopped off Roshan Din and Ghulam Rasool's noses, ears, and tongues with sharp weapons." Subsequently, they nearly beat Hameed, Fatima Bi (wife of Abdul Ahad), Mohd Shafi, Mohd Yusuf and Ahmad Din to death – all the while turning a deaf ear to the hapless villagers' plea for mercy and compassion.

The terrorists set ablaze over a dozen cattle sheds and hutments before disappearing into the shadows.

Reasi SSP JL Sharma told the press the next day (16 June) that a special company of police and troops of 59 RRBn were rushed to the spot on 16 June and all the 11 injured were shifted to Mahore hospital initially. Later, seven seriously injured among them were airlifted to Government Medical College.

LET Terrorist Escapes from Jail : 14 Dec 2006

A Lashkar-e-Toiba militant—Rafiq Ahmad Sheikh alias Mudasir Gujri—involved in several dreaded attacks, including one on a Congress rally in May 2006 and carrying a reward of Rs. 5 lakh on his head, has escaped from the Kot Bhalwal Jail, Jammu and Kashmir High Court was informed by the police. The court had asked the State Police earlier this week to submit case diaries etc. regarding Sheikh after his mother filed a petition seeking court's intervention into disappearance of her son from the jail.

HM Asks Kashmiri Youth not to Join Forces : 14 Dec 2006

The frontline militant outfit, Hizbul Mujahideen (HM) asked Kashmiri youth to stay away from seeking employment in armed forces or face dire consequences. Its spokesman Junaid-ul-Islam told Kashmir News Service that recruiting Kashmiri youth in Army is a conspiracy hatched by India and his outfit "can go to any extent to scuttle it."

LET Terror Shadow on SAARC Meet : 31 Mar 2007

A few days before the SAARC sunmit is to begin in New Delhi (3-4 Apr 2007), an intelligence intercept has set alarm bells ringing for the security agencies. The message discussing a possible attack in the city targeting the sunmit is seen as a serious threat. Eight heads of state/government are due to attend the summit.

A senior source said : "The intercept discusses possible infiltration of the terrorists into the country via the sea route. It is being seen as a serious threat in the wake of recent seizure (Feb 2007) of arms and explosives by the Indian Coast Guard near the southern coast in which five persons were arrested."

The intercept is especially worrying for the security establishment as it bespeaks of Islamic and Sikh terrorists collaborating in executing the attack. It refers to a meeting held at the residence of Resham Singh Babbar, a prominent leader of Babbar Khalsa International (BKI), the outfit responsible for twin blasts in Cinema Halls in the capital in 2005. The meeting, held in the first week of March, was attended by the members of BKI, Muslim Sikh Council (UK), LET and JKLF.[4]

The detailed information garnered by the intelligence apparatus is rather amazing in expanse and depth. And it is obvious that only a small, not-so-sensitive detail has been passed on to the media. According to the intelligence, at the meeting, Tagi Ali, a frontman for the Lash operations in India, sought assistance from Resham Singh of BKI in escorting Sayyed Hassan Jawed from Karachi, Mohd Azhar from Lahore, and Sahibzada Ahmed Khan from Pakistan, alongwith two others, to reach the port of Mumbai on 1 April.

According to the plan, a part of the group has been directed to go to New Delhi and target the Summit. Two men will stay back in Mumbai and plan an attack on oil and gas installations there at the same time.

Intelligence agencies reports indicate that these terrorists have been especially trained to be human (suicide) bombs when need be. They have been directed to leave for Kashmir after carrying out the attacks.

"Over a month after the Samjhauta train blasts, this is another attempt by the terrorists to derail the peace process," a police officer said.

LET Ideologue Supports Geelani : Apr 2007 (Fulminations of a Frustrated Terrorist)

LET ideologue Hafiz Mohd Sayeed, who is also the chief of Jamat-ul-Dawa (JUD), has said that "the entire Pakistani nation" is with Syed Ali Shah Geelani, a Hurriyat hardliner whose 22 Apr 2007 rally in Srinagar was largely attended and led to the arrest of four of his party leaders.

Sayeed, was quoted on the JUD site as having told a Friday (27 Apr 2007) congregation in Liaquat Bagh, Rawalpindi, that the Indian government had registered cases against Geelani and his associates for 'unfurling Pakistani flag' at his rally, so the people of Pakistan must send a message to Geelani that the entire Pakistani nation was with him and "would sacrifice everything for the freedom of Kashmir."

Some of the significant utterances are summed up here :

- Sayeed criticised the Pakistan government, saying it was damaging freedom struggle in Kashmir.
- "The government talks of building a dam, but where would the water come from? First of all, you here to liberate Kashmir for that."
- Pakistani's founder Mohd Ali Jinnah had described Kashmir as Pakistan's jugular, but the present rulers were undoing the freedom movement there."
- Citing Rahul Gandhi's recent remarks that his family divided Pakistan and created Bangladesh, Sayeed said : "With the facts that are coming to the fore, there remains no reason to establish friendly relations with India."
- "There were external and internal conspiracies against Pakistan, so the nation should dissolve differences between the Sindhis, Balochs, and Pathans to unite under jihad."
- "The US is threatening Iran but the real danger is to Pakistan and other Islamic nations."

LET Terror Module Busted : J & K Police Claim : May 2007

Kashmir police on 1 May claimed it had smashed a LET module which was involved in a series of violent acts, including the bombings carried out at the residence of the moderate, separatist leader Mirwaz Farooq and headquarters of his faction of APHC in Jan 2007.

IGP, SM Sahai (Kashmir Range), addressing a press conference at Srinagar on 1 May said : "13 persons, including a woman, involved in the terror network, have been arrested, so far. In this process, this module got paid not only by the LET, but by the HM terror outfit as well for executing their nefarious directions purely for pecuniary benefits. This showed the extent to which the terrorism here has been criminalised.

Some important points from the statement he was reading from :

- "An alarming example of criminalisation of terrorism was revealed during this investigation when it was found that a woman, Rafiqa had conspired with members of this terrorist group to have her second husband Manzoor Ahmad Ganai eliminated. There is a srong suspicion this woman had got her first husband eliminated in the same manner.

- "However, their ring leader Abu Tahir, who is a Pakistani militant in charge of Lashkar operations in Baramulla district, is still at large. He is known to be hiding somewhere in Baramulla district and a manhunt for him is underway.
- "The module operating under the name 'Sidiqi Group' had been assigned to target Hurriyat Conference (Mirwaiz) leaders and activists, police officials and those helping the security forces in their anti-militancy operations besides carrying out grenade explosions at public places and crowded areas, including on the eve of reopening of the Durbar, the biannual office move here (Srinagar) next week.
- "Module must identify places for possible fidayeen (suicide) attacks by Lashkar commanders.
- "The group was also involved in criminal acts and the lone arrested woman, Rafiqa Akhtar, who is from Pattan area of Baramulla, had planned to physically eliminate her second husband, Manzoor Ahmed Ganai, and had sought the Group's help to execute it. The police is investigating the possible involvement of the group in the murder of her first husband sometime ago.
- "3 × AK rifles, 12 magazines, 100 AK rounds, two pistols, two hand grenades and four pouches were seized from the group.

LET Threat to "1857 Celebrations" in Delhi? May 2007

Delhi police intensified its vigil early May 2007, fearing that certain LET terrorists could be in Delhi to carry out a terror strike at the 150th anniversary of the India's First War of Independence in 1857, which culminates on 11 May, when the 'Jang-e-Azadi' march that set off from Meerut arrives at the Red Fort, Delhi. This function will be attended by the President, Vice-President, Prime Minister and other dignitaries.

The apprehensions are compounded by the fact that the Delhi Police has been unable to track down an accomplice of three LET terrorists arrested eleven days back at the popular shopping arcade, Dilli Haat, in south Delhi, sources said on 9 May 2007. The accomplice, identified as Raj, who gave the slip to the police at the Haat, is said to be the contact person for the LET in Delhi and had brought to Haat one of the three arrested persons, a Pakistani national identified as Abu Qasim.

The police suspect Raj could be hosting more terrorists who may be awaiting an apportunity to strike, especially the 150th anniversary of the 1857, celebrations.

Finding Raj is important because he was tasked with hiding Qasim in Delhi after receiving the explosives from the two Kashmiri Lashkar operatives : Shafaqat Iqbal Mir and Shabbir Ahmed.

Significantly, all of them were working on the orders of Abu-al-Kaama, the mastermind behind the 2005 Pre-Diwali blasts in Delhi.

Senior police officers had not ruled out the possibility of a terror plot to target the Red Fort at the time of arrest of these three ultras at the Haat. Special Cell sleuths had seized 2 kg of RDX, three electronic detonators, an electric timer and two hand grenades from the three during their arrest at the Haat.

Another worrying factor was the information received by the police that Raj know well the topography of Delhi and could have been assiqned a terror mission.

Incidentally, a sketch of Raj, based on information given by the three LET ultras, was prepared and released by the police on 30 April. Half a dozen police teams have conducted raids at various possible hide-outs of Raj in the neighbouring Gurgaon, Faridabad, Noida and Ghaziabad in the NCR area.

Another report said that Raj had also been assigned to activate over 20 LET sleeping agents and carriers lodged in different parts of the country for suicide attacks.

What is Hyper-active LET's Agenda in India? Early 2007

LET is an enigma for India, if one goes by the certificate of 'good conduct' issued to it recently by none less than *Mujahid-*

e-Awwal (for jihad in Kashmir) of Pakistan, Sardar Mohd Qayyum Khan during end-Apr 2007 visit to New Delhi! He says "it was never a terrorist outfit, and it has ceased its activity (whatever it be?)." The question is : What is the value of a 'good conduct' certificate issued to a sibling', even by a Qayyum?

But examining its activities over the last few years, it is easy to see that it has emerged the serious most threat to India's security as far as the terrorist outfits go.

A look back in history is always good. In this particular instance, it should be instructive to re-read what the head of LET's military operations, Zaki-ur-Rahman Lakhvi, told *The Nation* on 9 April, 1999, four weeks before the first shot was fired by the Pakistani Army in the Kargil war : Proclaiming that another war was already imminent, he said: "we have extended our network in India and carried out attacks on Indian installations successfully in Himachal Pradesh last year. To set up a Mujahideen network across India is our one target. We are preparing the Muslims in India and when they are ready, it will be the start of the disintegration of India."

Grim words these, and reflective of equally grim determination to destroy India through Islamic Jihad! One can be reasonably certain that Indian intelligence must have made a note of this stark threat in its computers/records, but how seriously it was taken one has no means to know or comment. After all, intelligence agencies and their functioning are beyond the ken of ordinary mortals. But even if its ramifications were studied by Indian intelligence, it apparently failed to prevent the havoc let loose by the LET and its operatives/modules in India during the last couple of the years, and in particular in 2006. Alternatively, in spite of its best counter-terrorism effort, it failed to prevent the LET-incited violence.

At least one journalist[5] had taken a serious note of Lakhvi's words and found Indian authorities too waking up to the significance and seriousness of these words in the midst of an intense Islamist terror campaign directed at its major cities in 2006 and onwards.

Mumbai police have asserted that Lakhvi's subordinates planned the 11 July 2006 serial bombings in the city, financed their architects, and trained the perpetrators.

But key questions remained unanswered. What is the Lashkar's agenda in India? Who are its leaders and what is their relationship with the Directorate of ISI? Most important of them all, is the military regime of Gen Musharraf an enemy of Lashkar's jehad, or, in fact, its author? There are no firm answers to most of these questions. Both the marienettes who physically enact the Lashkar's jehad in India and the masters who hold the strings are out of sight. "Like the audience of Indonesian Wayang Kubit thaeatre? We may follow the story only through the shadows the puppets cost."

But fortunately, Mumbai police's investigations into the 11 July blasts have enabled us to go beyond the art of watching the shadows. They have not only revealed the substantial facts but have also given the chance to the serious observers to know something about the lineage of the LET – in the distant past.

Mumbai police found out that the 11 July serial bombers trained at a five-room building on the Multan Road in Bahawalpur. Building is a "fortress", as Police Commissioner A.N. Roy says. Two Bahawalpur residents, contacted by the highly-respected Indian fortnightly Frontline from Chennai, did give a fair descriptive details about this Lashkar facility, leaving no doubt that the well-guarded building did exist. This, in a manner of speaking, is the starting end of the 11 July blasts.

Ensconced in this building is a man, known to his students as 'Baba' (= endearing and respectful epithet for a grandfather). 'Baba' is the man, says the Mumbai police, a Lashkar operative, who taught the men who executed the serial bombings their tradecraft.

'Baba', whose real name is Mohd Azam Cheema' was born into a lower-middle-class family in 1953. He went on to teach Islamic religious studies at the Government Municipal Degree College in Faislabad (earlier Lyallpur). During his tenure there Cheema came into contact with a circle of far-Right Professors at the Department of Islamiat (Islamic culture and religion) in Lahore Engineering University. It is important to prominently record the names of these Ultra-Rightists :

- Hafiz Mohd Saeed
- Zafar Iqbal

- Hafiz Abdul Rehman Makki
- and some others.

(The students of the present Islamic extremism and terrorism will immediately recognise at least two of these names! More on it later, in this narrative).

These scholars linked to the ultra-conservative Jamaat Ahl-e-Hadis sect were engaged in setting up what was then called the Markaz Dawa wal Irshad. Spread on a 160-acre campus near Lahore donated by former Pakistan President Gen Mohd Zia-ul-Haq, the Markaz in essence was a platform to draw recruits for the anti-Communist jehad in Afghanistan.

By 1986, aided by generous contributions from the ISI, the CIA, and Osama bin Laden's close aide, Abdullah Azam, the Markaz had set up the foundations of its new armed wing : Lashkar-e-Taiba (also Toiba, and more correctly and accurately. Tayyaba), 'Let or LET' being more popular acronym. The LET cadres were trained at camps in the Afghan provinces of Kunnar and Paktia. By 1989, though, factional feuds among Islamist groups in Afghanistan led the Lashkar to shut down its facilities there. Now a more ominous turn of events as far as India is concerned.

Having bailt up an army of Islamist fighters, imbued with extremist ideology of jehad, the LET turned its energies—expectedly—eastward. From its very outset, the Lashkar was clear about its objectives. Nothing will lay them out more unambiguously than these ringing words of Saeed, written as far back as 1999 : "The jehad is not about Kashmir only. It encompasses all of India." An eminent scholar Yoginder Sikand expands the theme more clearly, if ominously, for India : "The Lashkar strategic goal is to extend Muslim control over what is seen as having once been Muslim land, and, hence, to be brought back under Muslim domination, creating "the Greater Pakistan by dint of jehad."

After leaving Afghanistan in 1989, Lashkar set out seriously on preparations to realise its wider, and more ambitious project of 'subjugating' India. By 1993, necessary infrastructure was in place to realise the dream of Islamisation of 'Hindu' India – its latest ideological mission.

Even as the LET carried out its first major military operations in Jammu and Kashmir, the terrorist group demonstrated its desire to act on a larger stage. On the first anniversary of demolition of the Babri Masjid, Lashkar operatives Jalees Ansari, Azam Ghauri and Abdul Karim "Tunda" carried out a series of bombings across North and West India. While Ansari was soon arrested, Ghauri and Karim went on to set up elaborate Lashkar network in alliance with the now-proscribed SIMI.

Working under the overall command of Lakhvi, Cheema is believed to have been assigned the task of enhancing the capabilities of these networks. His exertions, however, seems to have achieved litte. In July 1998, the Delhi police arrested Abdul Sattar, a resident of Pakistan's Faisalabad district who had set up a covert terror cell in the town of Khurja. A year later, the Jammu and Kashmir police broke up a cell run by another Pakistani, Amir Khan, with operatives in Maharashtra, UP, Haryana and Delhi. Mohd Ishtiaq, son of a shopkeeper from Kala Gujran in Pakistan's Jhelum district who had risen to become one of the Lashkar's top field operative, was also arrested.

Curiously, despite its grand polemic and bellicose posturing, then, the Lashkar had little to show for its efforts beyond Jammu and Kashmir. After 1999, the pressure on the outfit become intense. The newly-formed JEM, with which the Lashkar competed for both cadre and resources won accolades among the Islamists with a series of increasingly spectacular strikes, culminating in the Dec 2001 attack on the Parliament House. It is obvious that cheema had expended the enormous assets at the Lashkar's command, with little to show for it.

It is obvious that it needs to revive its fortunes and regain its position among the top terror mongers of the subcontinent. Interrogation records of Abdullah Mujahid, a terrorist arrested from Afghanistan in Jul 2003 and now held in GITMO bay reveals that LET reached out to its old friend's in Al Qaeda for help. At a Feb 2003 meeting at LET's Murid ke headquarters, Mujahid was appointed chief of operations against India. A veteran of jehad in Afghanistan, Mujahid had been put in charge of security for the city of Gardez after the fall of Taliban regime. However, he was removed from office on the suspicion of colluding with the Taliban and al-Qaeda; and could, as far as is known, never take up his new assignment with the Lashkar. The Lashkar had to look elsewhere for renewal.

On Way to Regain Old Reputation?

In mid—Sep 2006, two LET ultras and the soldiers exchanged fire across the main market street in the small north Kashmir village of Sumlar. Houses and shops were destroyed in the firefight. The sprawling Bandipora forests, home to the largest concentration of the LET cadre in Jammu and Kashmir, lie about a 100 metres beyond the ruins. It was to this area that terror group's command now turned to – commanders who, whlive Cheena, had seen real fighting.

Mohd Muzammil, if that be his real name, and Abu Alqama, still known only by his chosen *nom de guerre*, were to present themselves as the leaders of the next phase of the Lashkar's jehad.

Ever since it began its operation in Jammu and Kashmir, the Lashkar's c mmanders had to contend with some serious odds. One major diffiently was the absence of a well-established over-ground network, of the Kind the Jamaat-e-Islami had provided to the Hizb-ul-Mujahideen (HM). In Pakistan, the Lashkar was able to draw on the resources of the Jamaat Ahl-e-Hadis. But while the group's presence in Jammu and Kashmir dated back to at least 1923, the ultra-conservative organisation had won relatively few followers.

In fact, its assault on the traditional religious values/practices provoked a hostile backlash from mainstream clerics. "Several Ahl-e-Hadis activists were physically attacked." Sikand has recorded, "a social boycott was instituted against them; they were turned out of their localities; and, being branded as apostates, they were refused entry into the mosques." The Ahl-e-Hadis remained "a largely elitist phenomenon, with its core support base among a limited section of the urban lower middle and middle class."

Lashkar leaders in the Bandipora area, as in other parts of the state, used fear to over come their lack of legitinacy. Opponents of the jehad were merilessly silenced. In 2002, soon after he was elected Sarpanch of Sonarwani village in defiance of Lashkar fiat, Ghulam Hassan Khan received a bullet through the arm. He, of course, was among the lucky ones. Ghulam Ahmad Wani, local accountant who refused to conduct the marriage riots for a terrorist, was tortured to death in the forests. Ghulam 'Lola' wani, a small-time politician, was beheaded in the middle of the village. "We could all hear him screaming", recalls Khan, "no one wanted to be next."

At once, the Lakshar's field commanders made adroit use of patronage to draw new recruits. Some were won with cash and others with mafia-like favours. Mohd Isaaq, one of the Lashkar's top ethnic-Kashmri operatives, joined the outfit soon after his wife eloped with Sher Khan, a member of a powerful pro-India militia, "Isaak wanted to be paid compensation of Rs. 20,000", recalls Arigam villager Noor Alam Mir, "but Sher Khan would not pay. He had a gun, so Isaak got one of his own from the Lashkar." Sher Khan was shot dead by the Lashkar in 2003, while he was playing cricket with the children in the village field.

Muzammil soon demonstrated that the assets Lashkar had built up in Jammu and Kashmir could be used to hit targets across India. In Sep 2002, he supervised the storming of Akshardham Temple in Gandhinagar. Manzoor Zahid Chowdhury, a Jammu and Kashmir-based Lashkar operational commander was ordered to despatch two Pakistani nationals to carry out the attack. Lashkar cadre in Ahmedabad, working under Muzammuil's overall command, facilitated the final strike.

Among Muzammil's best-known operations was a Jun 2004 plot to assassinate former Union Home Minister LK Advani. A Pune resident, Javed Sheikh and his Mumbai-based girl friend Ishrat Jehan Raza, were tasked with conducting two Pakistani nationals to Ahmedabad for the strike. Sheikh was also involved in a separate Lashkar plan to bomb the Bombay Stock Exchange. An ethnic Kashmiri medical student in Pune, Manzoor Ahmad Chilloo, was tasked by his Lashkar controllers in Srinagar with liaising between Sheikh and the operatives who would have carried out the Mumbai attacks eventually.

Investigations into 2005 serial bombings in New Delhi demonstrated similar networks at work. Abu Alqama, who had charge of the Lashkar's operation in Jammu and Kashmir, tasked a Bandipora-based commander code-named Abu Huzaifa and his immediate subordinate Abdul Rehmani 'Mota' to execute the strike. Tariq Ahmad Dar, a Srinagar-based pharmaceuticals salesman was then charged with its physical execution. Abu Alqama is also believed to have had charge of an abortive bombing operation in Mumbai in Jan 2006. Khurshid Ahmad Lala, Arshad Badru and Mohd Ramzan Qazi were arrested from a safe-house in the city, where they had stored detonators brought in from Jammu and Kashmir.

Some Questions on 11 July Blasts Remain Unanswered

Were the Mumbai serial blasts Cheema's effort to restore his 'honour' and his place in Lashkar hierarchy? Or, was he just a minor part of the conspiracy, responsible only for training the actual perpetrators? We do not know, and that is not the only question that remains unanswered, says an analyst.

Just why did Lashkar committed so many Pakistani nationals to the operation when it had operatives within India to carry out the strike; why men were trained in Pakistan for a month when their role was to place bombs in trains; why the perpetrators chose to stay on in India when they could have crossed the border into Nepal and Bangladesh. All these are questions to which the investigators seen to have no answers. Key members of the Lashkars western India operations who might have insights to offer, such as Rahil Ahmad Sheikh, Fayyaz Ahmad Kagdi and Zabiuddin Ansari, are believed to have long escaped to hideouts in Bangladesh and Pakistan.

Unless the still-nascent Indo-Pakistan joint counter-terrorism mechanism throws up new evidence, credible answers may never emerge. It is unlikely that the Pakistani Lashkar operatives involved in the serial bombings were known to their Indian counter-parts by anything other than their Arabic 'Kunyats' – *nom de guerre* drawn from the names of the companious of Prophet Mohammad.

Such little information is of little more value than none at all. For instance, Mumbai police officers claim a dead body discovered from one bomb site is that of a Lahore-based Lashkar operative named Salim – "an assertion so vague as to be useless." On the other hand, it also must be accepted by the journalists and analysts who sit and pass judgemental verdicts on the police investigations and consequent patch-work of the 'facts' put together painstakingly by them that it is always easy to pick holes on these 'facts' and findings on one ground or the other. May be a certain balance and circumspection is necessary when sitting in judgement.

As far the blanks and shortcomings in the investigative field, one thing is rather clear : Pakistan's covert services could fill in the blanks if they ever chose to do so. But going by the track record so far, and the empirical evidence available, it is most unlikely to happen – ever! Leaving aside the mass of scholarly work on the issue, independent eye-witness accounts demonstrate the Lashker's close links with the ISI.

Journalist Ghulam Hasnain, writing in *Time* magazine's 5 Feb 200 issue, described how he watched Lashkar operatives monitoring wireless transmissions from their field units on a Fidayeen suicide-squad attack on Srinagar airport. During the attack, he wrote, a colonel-rank ISI officer called to ask for details of the operation. Hasnain noted that other "militant groups in Pakistan can listen in to the same frequency. So can the Pakistan's military." So, of course, can the communications-intelligence experts in India's covert services—one reason why Pakistan's claim that Lashkar operates outside its control receives so sceptical a hearing in New Delhi.

It is not only India that dismisses as untrue Pakistan's routinely and repeatedly offered claims of LET's training infrastructure, including camps, having been closed/dismantled. Much of the world does the same. Official reports released by the US Department of State, notably, have been dismissive of similar claims by Islamabad. In mid-2006, the BBC's News night programme released the contents of a confidential research paper prepared by the military-funded Defence Academy. "Indirectly", the paper asserted, "Pakistan (through the ISI) has been supporting terrorism and extremism, whether in London on 7/7 or in Afghanistan or Iraq."[6] Western states, it asserted, had chosen to turn "a blind eye" towards the problem, and its solution : Requiring "Pakistan to move away from Army rule and for the ISI to be dismantled."

Prime Minister Manmohan Singh said recently, as he and his predecessors had done earlier, "Pakistan will have to walk the talk." For him, as for Prime Ministers before him, the real question is how India can best push Islamabad do deliver on its promises.

The difficulty in achieving this desideratum should not be under estimated. Even the US, with billions of dollors shoving into its kitty, could not push Pakistan beyond a certain point. Even after Pakistan publicly whittlingly down its counter-terrorism drive, White House continues its monthly doles to it. Of course, Bush must have his reasons for this munificence. There is an unfortunate angle for India to this American munificence. A US research has disclosed (May 2007) that a major share of aid, in cash or kind, given by Washington to Islamabad for counter-terrorism purposes, has been used by the latter in fighting India.

In contrast to Pakistan's interest in fighting terrorism in Iraq and Afghanistan, especially the latter, where it took a U-turn in its foreign policy under threat of being "bombed back into the stone age", Pakistan has certain foreign policy objectives and ideological/emotional sentiments at play in Jammu and Kashmir. It has, for long decades used terrorism in the state from across the border as a policy instrument. It has not only sponsored the terrorism here but refused to do anything that could lessen pressure on New Delhi on this account. Having failed to bend India to do its will through its repeated aggressions, Pakistan chose to shift to 'peace process.' All the while, it has not allowed its main/ultimate weapon (of extremism/terrorism) to get rusty. It has kept it in shape ...just in case! Majority of Indians, including and especially, its Leftists, Liberals, eliter, and some political parties who practice vote bank politics, choose to ignore this 'fatal' reality, winking at the harsh realities of life!

India must never forget the threat posed to its very existence by the terrorism sponsored and supported from across the border, and especially by the hardliners like the Geelanis and the Saeed-led LET, even in the face of the charm offensive mounted by Musharraf through his favourites – minions, to some – like former President and PM of the POK Sardar

Qayyum (during end Apr 2007 visit to New Delhi) and present PM of POK Attique Ahmad Khan (in his intervew to *Asian Age*, dated 22 May 2007).

SIMI Leaders Choose the Date for Surrender : Jun 2006

Here is a factual narration of surrender by the President, SIMI's UP unit Mohd Aamir, in a daily[7] dated 3 Jan 2006 :

- "With charges as serious as treason, masterminding the 16 Mar 2006 riots in Kanpur, UP State SIMI President Mohd Aamir would always have been a dream catch.
- "And so it was that after being on the run for five years, the top militant surfaced in a luxury car on 24 Apr 2006 outside the Becongunj police station. With a celebrated politician in tow, the most-wanted man sat with the senior police officers to plan his surrender.
- "Hours later, every one concluded that a surrender at the police station was damaging for the police's image. So Aamir spent the night enjoying police hospitality and surrendered before a metropolitan magistrate (VI) the next day."

The above reads like a surrealist event in a mystery novel. The fact that all this is a real life story makes it serious, as it reflects poorly on India's lackadaisical approach to tackling and confronting head on the serious issue of long standing terrorism this country has been subjected to and it has paid heavy price for this non-serious attitude towards the menance.

At the end of this drama, rather farce, of surrender, the man who spent the last year (2005) in a terror sanctuary in Bangladesh slipped unnoticed into Barrack six of Kanpur Jail.

Almost similar is the manner of surrender of District SIMI President Salman Ahmad and Hizb-ul-Mujahideen militant, Mohd Zubair. They secured bails and disappeared without trace. They were named for instigating the 16 March riots and executing serial blasts. The conducive climate for these two surrenders was provided by the UP State government in Mar 2006 when it refused to extend the ban on SIMI that the Centre had proposed considering the evidence placed before it by the intelligence agencies. It needs recording that Chief Minister Mulayam Singh Yadav personally gave a clean chit to SIMI, declaring that in his State it was not a terrorist organisation. This, when the Union Home Minister Patil had publicly declared SIMI to be a terrorist outfit and asked UP to extend ban on it! Or, was it also for public consumption?

So, Aamir's surrender was planned in Delhi in Mar 2006 when the government showed signs of going soft on SIMI—may be for political reasons, or as some one would put it less delicately, for vote-bank considerations. After all, a shrewd politician and a wrestler to boot knew in Mar 2006 that he would be facing the toughest wrestling bout in his State's political arena in a years time!

Sources say Aamir was asked to get in touch with a political leader, and the latter in turn left it to the police to finalise the surrender modalities. At the advice of police, Hamir surrendered in a Kanpur riot case (No. 20/01), in which he is the prime accused among 37. A non-bailable warrant was issued to help him escape the spotlight.

The case against Aamir is based on the confessions of Hizb militants Mumtaz Ahmad, Wasif Syed and Ghulam Gilani, the three who had set off the blasts.

They testified that Aamir had sent them for training across the border, and on their return, he gave them the explosives and equipment to execute the blasts. The police then fiercely guarded Aamir's surrender – never putting it on record. They did not even try to seek his remand in Mar 2007, or thereafter, "which had shocked the intelligence agencies.

In a interview to a daily on 2 June 2006 in the Court campus, Kanpur,[8] he made the following points :

1. After getting bail in most cases, only the treason case slapped by Bajaria police is left. "By Allah's grace I shall sail through it."
2. When asked about his 'famous surrender' and reasons behind it, Aamir was more than a bit surprised about the news being leaked out.
3. But he was frank enough to name another accused in the 16 March riots case, Dr Abrar Ahmad, as the man who arranged his surrender. Dr. Abrar, however, denied it.

4. What does he expect from the State Government? His answer : "It should withdraw the treason case. LK Adwani and Rajnath Singh are responsible for our ordeal. We were all falsely implicated. One day, Allah will answer all our prayers against these oppressors."
5. Does he still idolize Osama bin Laden the same way that SIMI cadres used to before the ban? Aamir promptly counters : "Laden is not a terrorist. He is just an enemy of the United States, not India. He is doing great service to humanity by taking America head on. America should realise that it is the number one killer of humanity. This is my view and it does not matter to me how my opinon is taken."
6. He denies that "SIMI has helped." But he reiterates his loyalty to the outfit. "My association with SIMI changed my life. I understood my religion well. SIMI made me a good community man."

Now follows in brief the profile of this outlaw – Mohd Aamir :

- He is President of SIMI's UP unit.
- He shot into lime light in 1999 after organising the Ikhwan Conference.
- This conference proved to be the launch pad for many militants.
- Years later when the State was rocked by blasts in Kanpur, Lucknow, Faizabad and Agra, Aamir figured high on the wanted list.
- He is reported to have sheltered many top Hizb cadres. One among them was Kala Kashmiri, who was subsequently shot down in Punch Sector, Jammu and Kashmir.

This account of Aamir, and also of SIMI in UP, is reflective of another unfortuante face of the Indian polity : the games politicos and political parties play with the serious subjects like terrorism and insurgency. At times, personal and party interests take precedence over national ones. All parties must join their heads to work out on effective counter-terrorism policy.

Fighting Terrorism and Insurgent Violence

This part deals with the problems faced by the counter-terrorism forces, price paid during the conflict and the allied issues. The most bizarre entry in this should be the item where in the BJP announces cash reward for civilians who kill terrorists. This part leads with that item

Most important entry belongs to the analysis of the counter-insurgency situation during the year 2006.

BJP Offers Cash for Kills : An Irresponsible Act, June 2006

> "Kill a terrorist and take home Rs. 1 lakh. And if you die fighting the terrorists, your family gets Rs. 2 lakh."

This is the gist of announcement made by the opposition BJP at Jammu on 8 June, 2006. It launched a Satyagraha on the 7th to protest increasing terrorist-related incidents and selective killing of Hindus in the State.

BJP National General Secretary Vinay Katiyar made the above statement at Jammu on the second, day of the Satyagraha in the presence of senior party leader Sahib Singh Verma. He made it clear that soldiers do not qualify for the prize money. He added: "The government pays cash relief when nationalists fall prey to terrorism But the BJP will ensure an award to those who eliminate terrorists to restore, peace and harmony... The Satyagraha will not stop till the government concedes to our demand for more sophisticated weapons to the Village Defence Committees (VDCs) and more Army presence in militancy-hit areas in the State".

Later in the day (8 June), the party workers, headed by Verma, took out a protest rally demanding that Doda, "recently in the news for the massacre of more than 30 Hindus", be handed over to the Army. They courted arrest outside the Civil Secretariat.

It is not easy to be judgemental on such issues. But one does find that this offer by the BJP is an attempt at playing politics with as serious an issue as insurgency. The other two demands (additional troop deployment and handing over Doda to Army) are normal, usual stuff of democratic process and electoral politics.

Who Suffer More? Hindus or Muslim? Avoidable Question

The BJP asserted early June 2006 that more Hindus than Muslims have fallen to terrorist bullets. But the State Government said the facts speaks otherwise.

The records show that 40,493 people, including terrorists, security forces and civilians, have been killed between 1 January 1990 and 30 April 2006. Of these, civilians number 16,010, of whom again 14,237 or 88.9 per cent are Muslims. Kashmiri separatists or even leaders say the number of deaths is higher, more than 100,000.

Reportedly, the first victim of militancy in the Valley was a Muslim, Mohd. Yusuf Halwai of Khankah Mohalla in Srhygar. He was shot dead on 20 August 1989 for putting on the lights on Independence Day, defying the JKLF's call for "black day".

There are several reasons why more JVJuslims have been killed by terrorists in the Valley. To start with, terrorists first targeted the Kashmiri Pandits—beginning with Ne£l Kanth Ganjoo, the judge yho ordered the execution of JKLF founder Mohd. Maqbopl Butt—not only for being associated with India but also for being a non-Muslim The increase in the violence led to more and more Pandits leaving the Valley, unable to live in the atmosphere of fear. With the number of Hindus dwindling, the Muslims became the clear majority in the Valley.

But when it came to furthering their cause, the militants were just ruthless with the Muslims, who they found to be informers.

Security forces too have had their share of blame, in the killings. Often, they were known to react in panic when faced with massive pro-Azadi processions and fire indiscriminately at crowds shouting anti slogans, in the fear that the demonstrations were providing cover to armed militants. Scarity personnel have also been known to react in anger and seek revenge on losing their comrades to militants.

Yes, militants did use crowds as coyer to throw grenades or fire at security pickets, patrols and vehicles. The resulting cross-ljire left thousands of civilians dead, most of them Muslims. Terrorists have also & killed co-religionists for being informers. Many of these informers later became counter-insurgents who targeted militants as well as their families. There have also been instances when militants, in retaliation, wiped out the families of counter-insurgents.

Besides these, there are instances of incidents, when militants have missed their intended targets. And in the process they killed more civilians than security forces, their primary targets.

Summary of Killings : Data about J & K

Killed between 1 January 1990 and 30 April 2006

A.	Total	40,493
B.	Civilians	16,010
C.	Muslims (88.9 per cent of B)	14,237
D.	Hindus (11.1 per cent of B)	1,773

Annus Horribilus : 1996

- The year witnessed 1,424 militancy—related deaths, the most in any year since 1990.
- 1305 Muslims were killed, the most in any year.
- 119 Hindus were killed, which is less than the 2000 figure of 199 Hindu fatalities.

Massacre

The term 'massacre' started being used from 1993 to describe minority killings. In comparison to Muslim deaths, Hindu deaths always grabbed more attention. Some of the more prominent massacres are listed here.

• May 2002	37 soldiers and their families killed in Kaluchak
• August 2002	96 people, including 35 Amarnath pilgrims, killed in six massacres across South Kashmir and Doda.
• July 2002	29 Hindus killed in Jammu
• March 2003	24 Kashmiri Pandits killed in Nadimarg

- May 2006 — 22 Hindus killed in Doda
- Prominent individuals — Murders of DD Director Lass a Kaul and Deputy Director (Info.) P.N. Handoo, and Judge (retired) Neel Kanth Qanjoo—who had ordered execution of JKLF founder Mohd. Maqbool Butt.

It was obviously an irresponsible assertion by the BJP to claim that more Hindus have died in Kashmir than Muslims. It was strange, implied the BJP, considering Hindus are the minority in the State. But the official death census, even thougji reportedly not yery reliable, shows otherwise—the BJF assertion is far from the facts. Even then, one difference needs to be noted : Hindus are killed for -being Hindus and Muslims are sometimes killed for being informers and mostly accidentally in the crossfire.

More Efficient Crowd Control

The BSF announced (15 October 2006) "it has now developed an improved version of teargas shells, 10 times more potent than the ones in use presently. The new shells, developed by it at the BSF's Tear Gas Unit (TGU) at Tekanpur, near Gwalior, fylP, uses a new chemical, stronger and more irritating but less toxic than the older ones. It will be much less liable to be defused by using a wet cloth.

The TGU has also developed plastic tear gas shells which will disintegrate as they hit the ground, thus making it impossible for prptestors to lob them back at the police or security forces.

"There is a huge demand for these teargas shells from police forces, as they have emerged as a favourite crowd control weapon. Teargas minimises fatalities as there is more emphasis on human rights nowadays", said BSF Director General A.K. Mitra. The new shells will not cause any permanent damage, but a great deal of temporary discomfort to those who face' them.

These shells are part of the paramilitary force's modernisation drive. Other crowd control devices developed by the TGU include dye-markers, which will emit coloured fumes, that will stain the clothes of the protestors, and small plastic shells for use against women agitators.

Analysts feel the new teargas shells may prove useful — and more effective—in dispersing the violent crowds which frequently stage demonstrations' on the Srinagar roads. They may not deter the terrorists, but will definitely deter their supporters.

Army's Kill Ratio up : 22 October, 2006

In J & K, the Army has achieved an attrition ratio of 8 to 1—the force kills eight terrorists before a soldier lays down his life. In the past six years, the ratio varied between 5.4 to 6.75 to one. Army Chief J.J. Singh says, "we are losing less lives." He adds the Army is not engaging terrorists in head-on combat but surgical strike, launching operations with least collateral damage.[10]

Army Jawan Kills his Commander

A soldier SC Bahra on 31 October, 2006 fired several shots at his Commanding Officer Lt. Col. Saket Saxena of 28 Rashtriya Rifles "at Dara near Srinagar's Harvan after the latter refused to grant him leave". The Colonel succumbed to injuries in the hospital. After faring at the officer, Bahra fried to kill himself but was overpowered by his colleagues. He has been taken into custody.

This is the fifth such incident in Jammu and Kashmir during the last ten days. It has the top brass extremely worried over growing stress levels in the military ranks which have been resulting in suicides and fragging— killing of fellow soldiers.

A senior retired officer analyses the tragedy. There has been manifold increase in commitments of the Army due to its prolonged deplayment on Internal Security (read, anti-terrorism) duties..... The living conditions of the Army in the field are rather primitive—living in cramped bunkers without any facilities under constant fears of terrorist strikes.... Command failures could be another reason..."[11]

This tragic incident is included here to indicate the variety of ways a nation 'undersiege' pays for terrorist demons.

Counter-Insurgency Operations in J & K : An Analysis : January, 2007

India's security forces have been engaged in anti-insurgency operations from the days of country's Partition, starting with the late October 1947 Pak. invasion of the valley. But in more specific Jerms, Pakistan sponsored and instigated insurgency took off in its more sinister form in late 1980s. Before a detailed look on the relevant issues in the year 2006. a brief analysis of the situation in general terms.

Maintaining an Indian Army tradition : Officers leading from front

It is a glorious tradition of the Indian Army officers are tajight to lead from the front. They continue doing so, even if paying a heavy price! 23 December 2006 encounter between the militants hiding in Behrampur village. near Patan in Baramulla district, 27 km. from Srinagar and 29 RR troops led by their CO Col. G.S. Sarna occupied the headlines in the dailies. In the fierce battle Col. Sarna was killed[12] while three of his soldiers Were wounded. A top commander of LET too lay dead.

Most such counter-insurgency operations are on intelligence tip off—intelligence-driven so to say. Just two weeks earlier, on 15 December 2006 Maj Manish Pitambre had led a similar intelligence-driven operation in Bijbehera in South Kashmir. He killed Hizbul's most wanted Sohail Fazal but laid down his own life too in the battle.

Is the Army paying heavily for its restraint ?

Soon after these operations was to come the Army Day (15 January) 2007. A senior Army analys[13] indulges in loud thinking : "why should Col." Sarna and Maj Pitambre have been killed at all in cqunter-insurigent operations in December 2006? Both led bold and daring raids to take out top terrorist commanders. No doubt they will get suitable gallantry awards. In the past too, several officers have surrounded villages and flushed out militants holed inside a hut or a home. In some cases, battle raged for 48 or 72 hours, two to four militants engaging scores of security forces. So long was the wait in some cases that militants managed to escape."

It is, of course, well known that most of these operations are intelligence driven and pfficer-led—invariably at the level of Commanding Officers and/or Company Commanders. Heroism in battle and leading from the front are laudable values and tacties, surely it is time Indian Army learns to conduct these operations 'surgically with minimum loss, of human life. It is indeed the time to dispel the notion, as nurtured in some western academic and analytical circles, that "life in India comes cheap". It is not that the Indian Army is unaware of the need to conduct such operations with minimum loss of lives, or unwilling to change its operational doctrines and tactical practices to adopt the concept of surgically taking out the insurgents/terrorists ensconced in a village or a house—a normal practice with the Israeli, US or EU countries' armies.

What is not well known is that the Indian Army—any by extension, other branches of security forces—is working under severe constraints imposed by concern for civilian life and damage to destruction of property? Human rights activists and other relevant NGOs may be hyperactive of late, but the Indian Army has been sensitive toward the need for avoiding collateral damage since the days it launched action against the Phizo-lod Nagas in early 1950s—its first counter-insurgency operations. But in all its operations against the insurgents/terrorists in Naga Hills, Mizo Hills, Jammu and Kashmir and Punjab, Indian Army has seldom employed punishing airstrikes or even gun ships to destroy the known hostile hide - outs or militant concentrations. But it is time to change track and plan the employment of precision munitions to take out the terrorists. Surgical strikes are in vogue today the world over and Indian Army's diffidence to use them or Ministry's reluctance to allow the Army to resort to them are totally in-comprehensible.

In a democracy, the civil supremacy is an acknowledged reality of life, and that is as it should be. But to the utter consternation of military High Command, even the military operations became justifiable in 1993 in Jammu and Kashmir. Interference in counter-terrorism operations was taken to the bizarre extreme during, the 1993 Hazratsiege when the Srinagar High Court ordered that the besieged terrorist be fed *biryani* and *korma*. Such decisions, analysts wrote, lionised the terrorists. The longer the siege or operations consequent to such court orders, and/or for any other reasons, the greater the gain and glory for the terrorists who are under the media spot-light. Such publicity is indeed the thing the terrorists hanker after and as a former British Prime Minister Margaret Thatcher put it, it is the oxygen that sustains them.

Price India Pays for Jammu and Kashmir Insurgency

Since 1990, Indian Army has suffered 117 officer fatalities and 282 non-fatalities in similar counter-insurgency operations in J and K. These figures, obviously, do not include Jawans and JCOs on the Kargil martyrs' list. It must be recorded that one Kargil is being fought every 16 months. What is more worrisome, even horrendous, is the fact that the Indian Army has lost more lives in Jammu and Kashmir than all the wars and counter-insurgency operations elsewhere in the country since 1947. The question needs to be reasked : Does India care for the lives of its nationals—its martyrs, its heroes of war?

Is India insensitive to avoidable loss of life in Combat

Some analysts put this question in bolder relief. The rhetoric not withstanding, it seems' only, too true that saving soldiers' lives when they are fighting for the nation and face fatal daggers during the combat is not (our) country's priority! "Till not so long ago, soldiers did not have bullet-proof jackets. Even today they are available to 70 per cent of troops engaged in counter-terrorism operations". Is only ttye MOD responsible for this lapse? What about the military top brass?

The soldier (popularly known as 'Jawan' today, even if earlier, he was matter-of-factly a '*sipahi*') is so row a priority commodity that it was only two months ago that some tentative thoughts on modernising the Infantry—man—the chief battle winner still in the continent even if thq Air Force or the Artillery are busy claiming the honour—were given "while (literally) zillions are being spent on new machines".

Army gained excellent successes in 2006

Notwithstanding the said handicaps the soldiers operate under in the Valley, "the situation there was never better than in 2006".[14]

Army uses an expressive phrase to describe its counter-terrorism strategy : An iron fest in a velvet glpve! The transformation is easy to discern. Srinagar was once under Army control for counter-terrorism operations. It was transferred to the BSF some years ago, and in 2006 CRPF took over the responsibility. Here are some figures indicative of the change—for the better in 2006.

- Till 25 December 2006, 123 terrorists had been killed in 42 attempts at infiltration during the year (2006).
- The level of violpnce in 2006 was lowest in four years.
- In all, 560 terrorists were killed, 408 apprehended and 195 had surrendered.
- Impressive recoveries were made by the Army.

  -798 rifles, 335 pistols and 138 other weapons.

  -7,254 grenades.

  -3,131 kg of explosives, sufficient to make 350 mamoth lEDs. "^^ **Common Kashmiris are disillusioned with terrorists**

Even in 1947, the Kashmiri had seen the true face of Pakistan and its armymen who had committed aggression on the valley in the guise of the frontier tribesmen : they committed rape and rapine in the valley, worst sufferers being the Kashmiris of Baramulla and its surrounding villages. In the succeeding two to three decades, some mshmiris were turned into hard-line anti-Indians under persistently vicious extremist propaganda barrage unless had by Pakistan, its agencies including the ISI and infiltrators sent from agross the LOC. In the recent years, even those hard l lines have started turning away from the falsehoods spread by the Pakistanis, their acolytes and the Pak-sponsored terrorist outfits.

While hardcore anti-Indian elements led by the likes the AliJShah Geelani are undoubtedly there, but their ranks are dwindling. Their strengths may be pegged at a few thousand : those, who gathered to accord a 'warm' welcome to Geelani at Srinagar on 22 April 2007 on his return to the Valley after his kidney operation at Mumbai, could be a reasonable representation of his hard-lines anti-India dichards in the

Valley. To sum up the situation as of today (April 2007) : while some hardcore elements of Geelani's UK are there who are inveterate anti-Indians, the realists recognise the change 'in 'ground reality. The things are likely to get better, not worse. There are certain indicators available that presage the change : the Gujjar women taking up guns to depend themselves in Hill kaka areas than to meet all .their whims and fancies in meek surrender; people coming forward in some places to inform the Army posts abput the presence of the ultras in their neighbourhood; and 5000 Kashmiri youths quencing for 100 vacancies is spmething unprecedented in the valley's Vecent history.

Attrition ratio improving even in the absence of counter-terror policy

Attrition ratio is an important factor in any counter-terrorism operations; the formula is simple : Higher the better. The Army lost 76 soldiers in 2006, achieving an attrition ratio of 1:7.2, a near all-time high. In sharp contrast is Pakistani Army's Waziristan record of 1:1.43.

Achieving an attrition ratio of 1:7.2 should be no cause of complacency for Indian Army. Losing 76 soldier is a high cost. It is time to think afresh—'out of box' ideas, to use a currently favourite cliche—on the ways to reduce casualties in Jammu and Kashmir. The Army and IAF top brass must put their heads together to disillusion the terror leadership about its claims of "low-cost high- gains operations" in the Valley. They of course can't be faulted for such assertions, as guerrilla warfare or hit-and-run tactics employed by the terrorists are universally dubbed as Low Intensity (Conflict LIC), as it admittedly extracts a high cost from a conventional army engaged in counter-terrorism operations. The military must think through some innovative ideas on the issues.

One that immediately comes to mind is surgical air strikes, routinely employed by the countries faced with insurgency or militancy situations. US , UK/EU countries have been criticised essentially because of avoidably high collateral damage caused as a result of such surgical strikes. Perhaps, for this very reason, there is strong public opinion, even aversion, against any use of this method against the terrorists—be it in J & K or in the

North-East But advances made by relevant technologies and availability of precision, almost pin-point, weapons should persuade Indian authorities, both civilian and military, to take recourse to air- strikes in the counter- insurgency battles. But analysts and critics see little chance of such an "innovation"—it indeed will be one for our country—being tried as India does not have, as they claim, a coherent well-thought-through counter-terrorism policy in place.

Even if the Executive approves of such a policy, one can be sure there will be issues of coordination between the Army and the IAF. Some feel the latter may not easily come round to the use of its air craft such secondary roles for the Army-led operations. At the end of it all, there is always a fervent hope that the two services can craft a joint strategy on the subject in the national interest! It is the time that the Indian counter-terrorism strategy envisions the pro-active use of not only helicopter guns hip but also fighter aircraft, against the insurgents in Jammu and Kashmir, and also in the North-East if necessary at a future time.

Here is a brief summary of record of employment of the IAF. Since the Independence, it has been employed in offensive role twice in the North-East in 1955, in Arunachal Pradesh in 1956, and Mizoram in 1966. Helicopter gunships, but never fighters, were used all of five times in J & K. But in Srilanka, these were used freely.

Israeli experience deserves a look

Israel is known to use its Air force effectively in precision attacks. The Israeli Defence Forces (IDF) earned a well-deserved reputation for its Entebbe action—a text book operation, if there was ever one.

The Israeli counter-terrorism doctrine has identified three operational parameters: Intelligence, planning and precision for pin-point fighting. Contrary to popular perception, the IDF is quite sensitive to unintended non-combatant casualties, legitimacy, appropriate and proportionate use of force and international opinion. Previously the Israeli Air Force (IsAF) accounted for 35 per cent of kills in counter-terrorism operations. The 2005 figure was 70 per cent, rendering ground forces less relevant!

Because of precision-guided missiles/munitions the ratio of terrorist to civilian killed has increased from 1:1 to 12:1. But the key to targeting is intelligence. The IsAF, which has taken the initiative away from Special Force's, is now involved in 80 per cent of operations. With real time intelligence and surgical use of Hellfire missiles from Apache helicopters, IsAF accounted for 100 terrorists and 12 civilians killed. Not a single soldier was lost.

The operative part of Israeli experience is: "Not a single soldier was killed." Given their respective situations, histories, and geo-strategic imperatives, India cannot follow Israel and copy its methods. But India can certainly frame and execute a more purposeful, resolute and no nonsense counter-terrorism policy. It should, at lost 100,000 Indian in the J & K, North-East and Punjkab theaters and rest of the country, display a resolve and shed an image of namby-pamby, soft State. Its tolerance threshold for taking casualties is unacceptably high. When India is spiring to be a super power, a member of the UN Security Council, ana even the international community accepts that its economy will be third largest in the world by 2035 AD, next only to the US and Chinese, it is time it behaves like a confident nation. India should stop being supine and think of adding some supine to its counter-terrorism posture.

As a first step, it should declare publicly that India intends to pursue the policy of 'hot pursuite' against terrorist fleeing the Indian soil into any direction. It is time the country does something to wash off the smear and taint that got attached to its image after the policy of surrender during the Kandahar hostage crisis. If that was BJP-led NDA, the present dispensation, the Congress-led UPA is a shade worse. It removed the NDA-enacted anti-terrorism laws from the statue book. It cannot brace itself to act tough against the Bangladeshi infiltrators who are posing a serious threat to country's sovereignty and integrity in over 20 border districts of Assam and West Bengal, and also seem to be incapable of adopting any effective anti-terrorism policy because of its minotiry-appeasement proctivities, driven by vote-bank considerations. India cannot expect to have an effective policy against the terrorism till the Indian Polity coalesce into competitive formations led by the Congress and the BJP and the rest reduced to insignificance. A tall order, indeed, but there is no other way to save the country.

Some alternative strategies are needed to be considered immediately. As a first step, the cost-effectiveness of standoff aerial capabilty on selected targets in special case, substituting assault by ground troops by using precision weapons must be tested in Jammu and Kashmir, in May 2002, during operation Prakram, AF employed surgical strikes to eliminate Pakistani Army incursions in Machchal sector at Lunda Post Point 3260.

In short, a pro-active policy

In the past, the top brass in the IAF and the Army said the Government would not allow the offensive deployment of the helicopters as it was concerned that could up the ante. On the other hand, there were reports about the inter-services differences coming in the way of optimum gains from deployment of the war machines, including helicopters. Why, even in the Kargil war, IAF is believed to have taken, six days to fly into help the Army's battles after the Government cleared its operational deployment. In fact, the political and military establishments must explain as to why casualty reduction strategies were not thought through earlier and introduced by way of innovative measures.

The military must make a care for a new effective, surgical strategy that would act as a deterrent for terrorists holding villages and institutions to ransom. The political Executive must clear this proactive policy late services carry it out in practice. Given history of Pakistan's over Kashmir, it is not a day too early to adopt a deterrent policy in dealjng with the terrorism sponsored from across the border. Does it need to be stated in so many words that being offensive and pro-active in matters of natibnal security is no offence.

Kashmir Terrorism: Price Paid (March 2007 : Government Figures

A government report released on 26 March 2007 put the total fatalities in J & K between January, 1990 and mid-February, 2007 at 42,147. This is in sharp contrast to a figure of more than 80,000 worked out by the Human Rights and Civil Society organisations. Be that as it may, here is break-down of the Government figure.

1. Total deaths caused by Islamist terrorist in J & K	42,147
• Militants	20,647
• Security Personnel	5,024
2. Civilians killed	
• By militants	11,221
• In explosions caused by grenades and IED planted by Ultras	1,678
• In cross firing incidents between security forces and terrorists	3,404
• In the clashes between the terrorist outfits	173
• Number of members of the Village Defence Committee's who were killed fighting the terrorists	127
3. Highest number of security personnel killed in a year (2001)	613
• It dropped to 182 in 2006	
4. Incidents of violence	
• Such incidents had gpne down considerably over the years particularly after a thaw in relations between New Delhi and Islamabad in the wake of the composite dialogue process initiated by the two countries.	
• Highest number of civilians killed in a single year, 1996, the year elections were held in the State after a gap of 7 years	1,438
• Highest number of Army and para-military personnel killed in the period January 1990-mid-March 2007	3602
• J & K Police personnel killed since January 199 till mid-March 2007	537
• No. of Special Police Officers killed in the said period	438

5. Number of militants surrendered 5,024
   - Between January 1990 till mid March 2007 3,877
   - Highest number for a year (1996) 655
6. No. of militants arrested
   - Since January 1990 (till mid-March 2007) in the counter-insurgency operations 18,600
   - Most of them were released on court orders, recommendations of screening committees or Human Rights Cells.
   - Number still held under judicial custody 365
   - Still detained under Public Safety Act 497
   - Lodged in State jails 413
   - In jails outside the state 84
7. Number injured during the entire period
   - Total 33,885
   - Civilians 21,659
   - Security Personnel 12,124
   - Militants 102

Expectedly, and not surprisingly at all, figures estimated by the others (non-Government entities are much higher than the 42,147 given out in the fact sheet released by the State Police. According to the J & K Coalition of Civil Society (JKCCS), more than 80,000 people have rost their lives in the violence. While the Mirwaiz Umar Farooq—led moderate Huravat says the number of detenues in jails runs into thousands, the hardline Hurriyat led by Geelani asserts that the number of dead is more than 100,000.

"Luck runs out for Doda Terrorists" : April 2007

This is the headline of a story, datelined 17 April 2007. It says : "No guns, no bullets, not even the obsolete 303 rifles. People living in far-hung areas of Doda, District Jammu (and contiguous to Chamba district of Himachal Pradesh) have abandqned these weapons of self-defence against terrorists and taken recourse to (Gandhian) non-violent, gastronomical means to tackle, heavily-armed ultras who often barge into their houses, seeking food and shelter.[15]

Villagers, who have endured terror for the past 15 years, started using dehydration tablets supplied to them by the police to mix with the food and drink when the terrorist came calling!

This new strategy to deal with the ultras repently led to the killing of two top LET men (a foreign mercenary and a district commader). SSP Manohar Singh told the daily that these tablets given to the villagers were used successfully.

"Is police brutality blocking surrenders"? April 2007

It is indeed a sad question but it seems to have a kernel to truth in it? This story from a daily[16] makes this unpleasant and unfortunate truth a plausibility.

Abu Bhai (name changed, the reporter tells his readers), a LET terrorist, has many close shaves with death in the past decade. But the realisation that it was no *jihad* but just a money and power game and awareness of Pakistan's designs of a Kashmir and Kashmiris, soon downed upon him .

For some time now, Abu Bhai—a terror in the dense jungles of Kishtwar and Anantnag who had picked up the gun over ten years ago—have been deliberating over his surrender. His girl friend was instrumental in his change of heart, even if he once again wanted to lead a normal life. At the last moment, Abu again changed his mind. Now he does not want to give up arms courtesy Doda police. This is disclosed in a story datelined Kishtwar (Doda), 29 April, 2007.

The latest change of heart is also attributed to his girl friend, who vehemently told Abu : "Do not surrender to Irfan. If you have to surrender, do so before the Army, not before the police."

Irfan, interestingly, is a policeman in the area who was suspended a couple of days ago for an alleged custodial death in his police post and also for allegedly raping the sister of the victim" The region has already witnessed violent protests, with the villagers blocking Thatri-Kishtwar National Highway (NH) 1B.

Not only Abu, but scores like him, fed up with the gun, were keen to surrender. But not any more. Now they dread to do so in these areas "which Jammu and Kashmir Chief Minister GM Azad's home town."And if some of them do surrender, police beats up, their relatives mercilessly for their surrender before Arm authorities and not before them, the villagers of Kither, Jangalwar, Thatrhi, Palmar and Keshwan have alleged.

Behind this brutal conduct of the Doda police towards the relatives of the surrendered militants in the Kishtwar region is a very interesting incident/episode.

On the right bank of the Chenab as one travels to Kishtwar, an unmetalled road—one shies away calling it a dirt track for obvious reasons—meanders upto the Chief Minister's home in Soti village, some 30 km from the NH 1B. Though heavily infested with militancy, the Chief Minister's brothers, sisters and causins live at Soti.

Having taken over 18 months ago, Chief Minister Azad order massive development works in his home district, including the 30 km long Thathri—Soti road. And the contract for building this road went to his younger brother Ghulam Mustafa Bhat Azad. As is the practice in these areas where the ultras rule me roost, a dreaded terrorist Ashiq Hussam alias Khubeb, *Tehsil* Commander UM, demanded his commission. After some resistance, he had to pay at the pain of death. Coining to know the fact of this payment, the Chief Minister went berserk and ordered the Doda police to go after Ashiq Hussain and produce him dead or alive.

Knowing that the police was in hot pursuit, Ashiq Hussain surrendered before the Army which, the villagers testify, has good reputation in the area. Now it was the turn of the District SP go berserk, as the militant had chosen to surrender before the Army, and not his police. The surrenderee's brothers, cousins, father and all other relatives were mercilessly thrashed for the mortal sin committed by the former.

It was bound to have its adverse fall out Bilal Bhat, a resident of village Gundoh, says : "There are other youths of the area involved in militancy who were keen to surrender after Ashiq. But seeing the fate of his family, they have changed their mind." In more specific terms, the villagers say there were "eight boys who had followed Ashiq into militancy and looked upon

Ashiq as their mentor. They were keen to surrender after Ashiq did so. Seeing the police attitude, they too changed their minds."

Resentment is believed to be brewing up against the police high-handedness in not only Gundoh but other neighbouring villages also. The relatives of some active militants are ruefully saying : "perhaps, now we will persuade our boys to surrender not in Doda district but in some other region where they will not face any similar threat from the vindictive police."

J and K Government Issues 'Most wanted' Terrorist List : April 2007

The Jammu and Kashmir Government "has recently submitted to the Centre a list of 120 'most wanted' militants sheltering in the POK, and Pakistan after engineering acts of terror in the state, and requested it to take up this issue with Islamabad", a senior state intelligence source told the media on 24 April, 2007. The latest revised list was handed over to the MHA during a review meeting at New Delhi.

The fact that the militants are taking shelter in POK and operating from there is proof enough that Pakistan actively aiding and obetting terrorism in Jammu and Kashmir.

Of the 120 militants, 39 are Pakistani nations, while the rest, 81 are Kashmiri. The district distribution of the 81 are :

Poonch – 60

Baramulla – 1

Srinagar and Rajouri – 4 each

Anantnag – 5

Pulwama – 3

Udhampur – 2

Badgam and Doda – 1 each.

Some important happenings and incidents: May 2006 to May 2007

Here follow some select events and incidents in the insurgency/terrorism-affected Jammu and Kashmir during the period May 2006–May 2007.

Pathribal 'encounter'? An unfortunate case : May 2006

The CBI filed a charge-sheet against five Army men—four officers (including Brig Ajay Saxena, the senior most officer named as an accused by the CBI, who was then colonel) and a JCO—on 14 May 2006 in the fake Pathribal encounter and the case was listed for hearing on 24 May.

The CBI has alleged that the five accused killed five innocent civilians at Pathribal village in Anantnag district on 25 March 2000, on the pretext that they were the "terrorists" responsible for the grisly massacre of 36 Sikhs in Chittisinghpora in South Kashmir.

The accused, in turn, contend they are being singled out and victimised for an operation conducted jointly by the Army and the J & K Police. But the CBI, however, has given a clean chit to the then Anantnag SSP, Farooq Khan, who has now been reinstated and posted as SSP Rajouri after remaining suspended for three long years.[17]

The five accused, named by the CBI are listed below :

- Brig (then Colonel) Ajay Saxena.
- Lt Col Brajendra Pratap Singh.
- Maj Saurabh Sharma.
- Maj Amit Saxena.
- Subedar Idris Khan.

A daily[18] learns Brig Saxena has written a letter to the Director General Military Operations (DGMO), Lt. Gen Madan Gopal, pointing out :

- Armymen have been singled out for "harassment ignoming, humiliation, agony and financial strain" over an operation conducted jointly by the Army and J & K Police.
- The operation was ordered by a senior Army officer (a Brigadier, Commander of a Rashtriya Rifles Sector) on the basis of information provided by SSP Anantnag Farooq Khan.
- Outlining the circumstances of Pathribal encounter, the letter said it took place in an area notified as a Disturbed

Area under the Armed Forces Special Powers Act (AFSPA), 1990. The accused are entitled to protection under this Act.

- The two of the five persons killed in the (encounter) operations were on the list of active overground workers maintained by the Rashtriya Rifles (RR) and the CBI probe revealed that a third among the dead also had terrorist links.
- During the relevant period—when Col (now Brigadier) Saxena Commanded 7 RR Battalion (Bn)—the unit received over 50 awards, including a dozen Seva Medals. In two years, 7RR Bn eliminated 78 militants.
- The CBI charge sheet has serious operational ramifications for the future of counter-insurgency operations since it would create distrust in the rank and file about verbal orders and posed a threat to the lone Kashmiri accused whose intelligence inputs had led to the elimination of 40 terrorists.

Sushma Saxena, Brig Saxena's wife, has also written to the Army Chief's wife, Anupama Singh, who is President of the Army Wives' Welfare Association (AWWA). Saying she was expressing the views of all five officers who stand indicted by the CBI, Sushma Saxena wrote : "If our husbands are prosecuted in this case, then every husband who is fighting in the valley in the future is also liable to face such action. All our husbands have done is obey orders and carry out operations based on information provided by a Senior Commander and the J and K Police.

Defence Minister Pranab Mukherjee on 15 May (2006) said his Ministry was studying the CBI chargesheet and seen the appeals made by the wives of the five accused.

Even if the legal panel of CBI has ruled that the Agency does not require sanction for prosecuting Army officers because killing of innocent persons in a fake encounter cannot be taken as discharge of "official duty", the Army is preparing to challenge that view in the Srinagar Court.

The Army's counter is that the Pathribal encounter was a joint Police-Army operation, carried out on intelligence provided by the J and K police and that the trial would jeopardise further joint counter-insurgency operations.

Another interesting fact has come to light about Farooq Khan, now reinstated (May 2006) after remaining suspended for three years. Khan, an IPS officer of the 1994 batch, was given a clean chit by the CBI in 2005, the Mufti Sayeed Government refused to reinstate him. The Azad-Government reversed that decision of its predecessor (the Sayeed Ministry) and reinstated Farooq as SSP Rajouri.

Pathribal 'Fake' encounter : Why police exonerated?

While the CBI has chargesheeted only Armymen (four officers and one JCO) for Pathribal fake encounter of 2000, a daily[19] finds that in fact the J and K police too played a major role in it.

- The FIR filed by the 7RR Bn described the fake encounter as a "joint operation" with J and K police.
- Daily diary reports of Sherbagh police post clearly indicates that on the orders of the then Anantnag SSP Farooq Khan, a SOG (Special Operations Group) party was sent for a "secret operation". In fact, ASI Bashir Ahmed wrote about the "secret mission" in his departure report.
- Tajinder Singh, then Dy SP (SOG), Anantnag, and Col Ajay Saxena explained the "joint RR-police operation" with the help of an extensive site map to the then Union Home Minister LK Advani, giving graphic details about the killing of five Pak-based Lashkar terrorists who were behind the massacre of Sikhs in Chittisinghpora.
- Advani congratulated the police and Army for the operation and even had a group picture taken with the police and Army officers. Cash awards were also announced for the officers.
- Kashmir Zonal police Headquarters issued a press statement, claiming that five Lashkar terrorists responsible for the Chittisingpora massacre had been eliminated in a joint RR-police operation. The then Union Home Secretary Kamal Pandey gave a similar statement at a press conference in New Delhi.

- Mohd. Yaqoob Wagay alias Chatti Guru, a local milkman, was picked up a few days after the 20 March 2000 Chittisinghpora massacre by the police for allegedly "guiding" the killers to the village. Union Home Secretary Kamal Pandey announced his arrest in New Delhi and the police and RR claimed that based on Wagay's "leads", they had killed five Lashkar terrorists.
- Nine months later, Anantnag police admitted that the police had no corroborative evidence to chargesheet Wagay and that they have reduced the charge from the multiple murder to "trying to breach peace (Cr PC 107/ 151)".
- Once the CBI established that the five killed in the joint police-RR operation were actually civilians, the question is : who picked up these civilians? The J and K police itself established that a Maruti Van was used to ferry one of the victims, Zahoor Ahmad Dal, from Anantnag. This was a seized vehicle, in the custody of the police!

It should indeed be of interest to hear CBI for its reasons to let the state police off the hook, if it was a'fake' encounter, in fact, at Pathribal.

Attacks on Tourists in J and K in 2006

Tourism had picked up during 2005 and was on the upswing by mid-2006 to the total delight of the Kashmiris plying this trade. It was the precise time the terrists chose to blow the whistle. The attacks on the tourists are listed below :

- 25 May. 5 Gujarati tourists killed, 6 injured in grenade blast at Batpora, Zokoora.
- 31 May. Tourist bus attacked; 21 injured.
- 12 June. Blast at main bus stand in Jammu; 1 killed.
- 12 June. 9 Nepali labourers attacked in Badro-Yaripora village in South Kashmir.
- 21 June. Bus with Amarnath pilgrims near Bihama-Ganderbal attacked.
- 24 June. Grenade lobbed at Dashnami Akhara building at Budshah Chowk; one civilian killed, ten injured.

- 11 July Grenade attacks at five places in Srinagar killed 8, including 6 tourists and injured 35.

Militant's SIM Card registered in the name of a Jawan

Police intelligence disclosed at Jammu on 25 October 2006 that a SIM card, seized from Hizb-ul-Mujahideen (HM) militant Altaf Chowdhary on the 23rd "is registered in the name of Naresh Kumar, a jawan of Rashtriya Rifles (RR) from Samba area and presently posted in Sopore belt of Baramulla district.

"It was possible that forged documents were used to get the SIM card but we want to investigate the entire racket," the police said. This revelation has added a new dimension to the nexus between criminals and militants lodged in Kot Balawal jail.

On the 19th, a mobile phone belonging to Harkat-ul-Ansar militant Ruhail Hashmi was seized. The service provider was asked to hand over all the documents related to the two SIM cards that were being misused by the ultras from inside the jail.

Kashmir Sex Scandal

Early in 2006, Srinagar was agogwith a high-profile sex scandal involving politicians, bureaucrats, police officers and businessmen. The rumours were flying thick and fast and every day, whispers were adding new names to the already long list.

Such scandals certainly are not the monopoly of the Kashmiris, or even of Srinagar as the capital of the State. These are the regular, if occasional, staple of the media, print and visual. Even a routine happening of this kind can be magnified into an attention-grabbing affair for weeks, nay months, on end in Jammu and Kashmir due to politics of rivals for milking it for narrow political gains and because of the eagerness of certain Islamist outfits to refurbish their puritanie image and extremist ideology.

Taking advantage of the situation, the Dukhtran-e-Millat (DEM) activists took out protest marches against the scandal and demanded the arrest of the 'culprits'.

Taking the law into their hand, the DEM activists raided some houses which they dubbed as brothels, run by their owners with the complicity of the police officials for favour in cash or kind. Some suspected "prostitutes and call girls" were dragged in public and beaten up.

Some accused were arrested by the police to be tried in the local courts. Fearing that they may not get fair trial in the charged atmosphere of the state, as also danger to their life and limb, they requested the court to shift the case outside the state. The trial was shifted to Chandigarh.

9 Oct. 2006 Accused denied bail

A court in Chandigarh denied bail to 13 accused in the Kashmir sex scandal. District and Session Judge BS Mehndiratta concurred with the prosecution's argument that many of the suspects were influential persons and could try and delay the trial proceedings if released.

13 of the 14 accused in the case are presently lodged in Chandigarh's high-security Burail Jail, where they were moved from Srinagar following a direction by the Supreme Court.

Mobile Phones in Jail

Jammu and Kashmir government on 29 October 2006 asked for the attachment of the SP of the Kot Bhalwal jail on the outskirts of Jammu to the prison department headquarters in connection with the smuggling into jail of mobile phones.

All six accused in 2002 Jammu Temple attack acquitted

The Principal Sessions Judge, Jammu on 30 October 2006 acquitted the six men accused of the 2002 fidayeen attack on the Raghunath Temple in which 11 people were killed.

On 30 March 2002, two armed militants had forced their way into the Temple after hurling granades in Raghunath Bazar damaging shops and vehicles They fired indiscriminately, killing many devotees on the spot. The security forces eliminated the ultras in a counter-attack.

The Judge observed that there was sufficient material in the file and the case diary dated 14 April 2002 against Virender Sharma, from whom a huge quantity of arms and ammunition was recovered but "it is astonishing to find that he had not at all been arrayed as accused in the present case." He ordered that a notice be issued to the investigating officer to explain why Sharma was not made one of the accused.

No case against Abdullah, says AG

On 30 Oct 2006, Attorney General Milon K Banerji refused to give his consent for initiating criminal contempt proceeding against former Jammu and Kashmir Chief Minister Farooq Abdullah for his remarks "that if Parliament terrorist attack convict Mohd Afzal Guru is hanged, the judges who convicted him can be murdered."

The AG said Abdullah's remarks did not scandalise the judiciary in general or the Supreme Court in particular and it was nothing but his personal view.

A Delhi-based advocate, Rajesh K Gogna, had sought his consent, as required under the statutory provisions to initiate criminal contempt proceedings for Abdullah's comments on a TV Channel recently. Gogna said he would challenge the AG's decision before the Supreme Court.

Twin Blasts Rock Valley : 14 November 2006

Two deafening blasts in Srinagar and Baramulla on the 14th sent grim reminders of terrorism to Foreign Secretaries of India and Pakistan who began a two-day talks in New Delhi the same day to find ways of establishing peace and eradication of terrorism in the region.

At least 19 civilians and 13 security personnel including an Army Major—Amit Arvedi—were injured in the blasts. Hizb-ul-Mujahideen, the indigenous militant outfit that is fighting the security forces for the past 17 years, claimed responsibility for the attacks.

The deadlier blast took place in Srinagar's bustling Karan Nagar locality around 4 PM. Militants had parked an explosive-laden car outside a well-guarded CRPF formation (target of the attack) and triggered the IED fitted inside it. They first lobbed a grenade and then triggered the IED a few seconds later. 22 peopel including four CRPF and five local police personnel were injured in the blast, whose sound could be heard in a 5-km periphery.

Earlier in the day, at 1-45 PM, the terrorists targeted a military convoy in another blast at Khanpora locality of Baramulla district, when it was on its way to uri from Baramulla. They triggered the IED that injured six civilians and four soldiers including a Major.

Kashmir has moved away from inclusive, tolerant Islam

In Nov. 2006 an unidentified gunman hurled a grenade at a procession of worshippers in south Kashmir led by Abdur Rashid Dawoodi, a prominent cleric of the Barelvi sect, killing five people—four of them children—and injuring over 30.

The incident brought into the open the simmering sectarian schism, which over the past two decades has become the undertone to the valley's Sufi Islamic homogeneity. The period of turmoil was critical. For not only did Kashmir slide headlong into unremitting chaos but its social landscape also witnessed a sweeping crisscrossing of different political ideologies and drift towards a new Islamic orthodoxy.

It was the 1990s that witnessed most of the cataclysmic changes, wought in by the rise in virulent violence perpetrated by the terrorists—majority of them from across the border. In these years, seminaries and madrassas, influenced and inspired by the Deobandi thought/ideology, sprang up all over the Valley. "A rough estimate puts their number about 450-500."[20]

The *Madrassas* in the valley may have steered clear of militant struggle and its ideology—even if some analyst dispute this proposition and averment—their effect on Valley's traditional religious orientation has been far reaching. To put it in another way, the Valley has lost its syncretic beliefs and traditions, obviously at gun point. Consequently, "thousands of students graduating from these institutions have started preaching the "pure intrinsic Islam" in line with the interpretation of Hazrat Abu Haneefa, originator of Islam's Hanfia school of thought followed by the Deobandis. They look down upon the inherent Sufi leanings of the people who visit shrines and seek blessings of the saints which they deem as generally antithetical to the spirit of monotheistic Islam, which does not tolerate a worshipful attitude towards even the prophet, leave alone saints.

The message of the hard-line Islam is not lost on the people, which in fact has resonated in the ears of the Kashmir's new generation bred under the shadow of a rough Kalashnikov culture. It is an accepted fact that "a decade and a half on, Deobandi Islam has come to dominate the religioscape of the valley. Mufti Abdur Raheem, the grand Mufti of North Kashmir, proudly admits so : "Most Muslims in Kashmir belong to the Deobandi thought."

But this resurgence in religious orthodoxy has been in conflict with the traditional Kashmiri Islam, influenced by the Sufism. In fact, the Kashmiri Islam is called "Rishut"—named after the indigenous saints of Kashmir who are called *rishis* (It needs to be recorded that the venerable ancient Hindu saints and sages were generically known as *rishis*. The leading *rishis* of valley are Sheikhul Alam Sheikh Nooruddin Wali, Sheikh Hamza Makhdoomi, Hazarat Bulbul Sahib, and Hazarat Naqshbandi Sahib. The Rishis preached devotion to God and the Prophet and insisted the values of tolerance and harmony. So, the Kashmiris, particularly women, frequently visit the shrines where they seek the saints blessings and their intercession in the fulfillment.

But Deobandi Islam, as already mentioned, generally discourages this (obeisance to the Rishis) as being violative to the basic tenets of their religion. And they are not alone in doing so. Over the past two decades the Valley has also witnessed the imperceptible rise of the Jamiat Ahle Hadith, an apolitical religious group, which believes in the supremacy of the Quran and Sunnah, unmediated by any religious scholar. Jamiat, according to its Chairman Moulana Showkat, now owns about 600 mosques and five major Darul ulooms. One of them located at Batamalu in Srinagar is affiliated to Madina University in Saudi Arabia. "We have a membership of one million Muslims in the State, most of whom are well-read", says Moulana, who was shot at by an unidentified gunman recently.

If some analysts assert that the spread of Ahle Hadith is the result of "the circumstances of the past two decades", the Maulana disagrees. He attributes this spread to the spread of education in the Valley.

But the sweep of Deobandi Islam is rather extensive. It envelopes the Valley's dominant religious and political movements, from the Tabligul Islam to the Jamaat-i-Islami. In fact, the Jamaat, Jammu and Kashmir's leading religious, political as well as secessionist organisation, has been the Chief propagator of the Deobandi thought in Kashmir. The Jamaat has been active in Kashmir since the late 1940s, but its influence did not seep down to the grassroots until the 1980s, the valley's last peaceful decade before the onset of the armed separatist struggle in 1989.

Jamaat influence also started from its schools, which by 1980 had proliferated all over the valley. That is, despite being denied state patronage by National Conference leader Sheikh Abdullah, who had even unsuccessfully moved to close them down. But the Jamaat must get the credit for the fact that its schools set up under its party organ Falah-i-Aam Trust don't teach religion only. They were and still are in step with modern education.

But on the other hand, *madrassas* in Kashmir are only a recent phenomenon. They set up base only in the 1990s when Kashmir was in the firm grip of the separatist militancy. So their coming can be connected with the separatist militancy. At a more broader level, these *madrassas* can be seen as part of the geo-political situation in the sub-continent, particularly its Afghanistan components. Some analysts link the spread of these madrassas and connected separatism with the successful completion of anti-Soviet jihad in Afghanistan when the Islamist fighters were diverted to the PoK and Kashmir areas.

But in the past few years, the valley has experienced a renewed groundswell for its sufi roots. Interestingly, large sections of the population, particularly in South Kashmir, once the stronghold of the Jamaat-i-Islami, have returned to the influence of Barelvi thought propagated by Abdur Rashid Dawoodi.

Like Sufism, Barelvi Islam does not forbid its adherents from seeking the blessings of saints which has traditionally been the way of life for most Kashmiris. This is also seen as the reason for its fast spread. Thus the attack on the procession of worshippers—which the separatist outfits claim was the handiwork of the Indian agencies—is seen as a reaction against the resurgence of Sufism. This clash of canons has serious implications for the valley's prevailing political and religious alignments.

This nascent resurgence of Sufism notwithstanding, the situation in J and K is rather unhappy and will remain so till

Pakistan continues supporting secessionist fundamentalism against India.

Jamaat-i-Islami, Kashmir (School of Islamic thought)

Founded in the late 1940s, it started chiefly as a religion propagation party, which rose to become an influential political cadre-based party of the State, with steadfast separatist ideology. It drew its strength from its schools set up in every nook and corner of the State.

It participated in the State's electoral process but it hardly managed to get more than a few of its candidates elected to the Legislative Assembly. But in 1990, Jamaat members led by Syed Ali Shah Geelani resigned from the Assembly and joined the outright separatist struggle that broketout in the late 1989.

Jamiat Ahle Hadith (School of Islamic thought)

The apolitical religious group has been active in the Valley since the second quarter of the 20th century. Founded by noted Islamic scholar Moulana Anwar Shah, the group was formally registered in 1958 under the J and K Society Act. Presently, it owns 600 mosques and five major Darul Ulooms in the Valley, one of which, Alquliat-u-Salafia, located at Batamaloo in Srinagar is affiliated with the Madina University.

It is the only religious group which also has a Darul Uloom in Turtuk situated along the LoC in the Ladakh region of J and K. Its present Chairman, Moulana Showkat, claims his Jamiat has a membership of one million Muslims across the state.

The Deobandi School

This is the predominant school of the valley, which follows Imam Abu Haneefa's interpretation of the Quran and the Sunnah. The Deobandis own approximately 150 Darul Ulooms across valley and 400 *madrassas*. "Most Muslims in Kashmir belong to the Deobandi thought," claims the Grand Mufti of North Kashmir Mufti Abdur Raheem.

Over the years, the Deobandis have come to wield a significant influence on the Valley's religious and political life. Its main offshoots in Kashmir are Jamaat-i-Islami and Tablighi Jamaat.

It is worth mentioning that it were the Deobandi *madrassas* that produced the Taliban—the most fanatical of Islam. They earned infamy in Afghanistan, as its rulers, by not only denying education to women and imprisoning them within the four walls of their houses but also by blasting the statue of the Buddha to smithreens—an act of vandalism unknown to the civilized world.

Incidentally, the Bandipora mosque is the largest Deobandi institution in Kashmir.

Tablighi Jamaat

An offshoot of the Deobandi school, it has been active in Kashmir for the past several decades. Its adherents are essentially concerned with the propagation of Islam among Muslims. Unlike Jamaat-i-Islami, it has no political agenda and does not believe in a cadre-based structure.

It held its largest congregation in Kashmir at Srinagar's Eidgah in 1988 which was presided over by Inamul Hassan, the then national head of the Tablighi Jamaat. Though no accurate estimates exist, Tabligh is one of the fastest growing organisations in Kashmir.

A jawan and a militant killed : 9 Dec. 2006

Rashtriya Rifles troops, on a tip-off that militants were holed up in a house at Banola village of border district of Poonch in J and K, encircled the house. In the ensuing firefight, Sep Virender Kumar and a militant were killed, while another jawan was injured. A civilian, Mohammad Sharief, who had accompanied the troops, was also killed in the encounter.

'Kill troops and get cash reward' : HM : 9 December 2006

After the recent threat by Kashmir's self-styled terror group G-4 to the youth against joining Army, the Hizbul Mujahideen (HM) has announced cash reward of Rs. 1 lakh for killing an armyman or an agent of the special operations group of police. In a letter written from the PoK, HM "Supreme Commander" Syed Salahuddin has promised Rs. 2 lakh to a militant "who kills armymen deployed at a post." The informers will be rewarded with Rs. 10,000 if they give information on security forces.

Analysts see this announcement on rewards for killing Armymen as a counter to the State's policy of giving cash rewards to the militants who surrender before the security force and join the national mainstream. The policy has already seen to be paying dividends as over 110 militants have surrendered this year (till 5 Dec. 2006) in Uri in Baramulla sub-sector. This obviously has the terror leadership worried. Hence the counter-measure.

Four people including two militants killed : 11 Dec. 2006

Four people, including two militants—Mohd. Shafi, an HM commander and an "A" category militant and "B" category Ghulam Hassan Sheikh alias Nadeem, alias Zafar—of HM were killed during a joint operation by the troops of Rashtriya Rifles (RR) and Special Operations Group (SOG) at Sofigund Tral Village of Pulwama district.

Militant held with explosives : Jan. 2007

A suspected LET militant, Iftikhar, was arrested with 2.5 kg of RDX by the Delhi police near the Seelampur Metro Station on 25 January 2007. He came to Delhi by the Sampoorna Kranti Express from Patna where he had been handed over the explosives by a LET conduit who had brought it from Nepal. He was ordered to hand over the consignment to another LET conduit in Delhi. When he was waiting for the latter, he was nabbed by the police.

He reportedly revealed that he did two training stints in terrorist camps in PoK. He remained in touch with his handlers and received instructions from them through the Internet. He has also visited Dhaka/Bangladesh. The police fanned out in the city "to trace the other members of the module that had been sent to create disturbances during the Republic Day (26 January) celebrations."

The police disclosed that its Special Cell had in March 2005 smashed a LET module by killing three terrorists in an encounter and arrested six others. During their interrogation, the latter disclosed the name of one of their men, Iftikhar Alam, a resident of Gaya in Bihar. They made repeated attempts to trace and arrest Iftikhar but had failed. But on the 25th, their luck turned, as these explosives were meant to be used on 26 January.

Besides the RDX, the police also recovered two detonators and a timer.

We won't give up Kashmir : A Page from History : 25 March 1957 (50 years ago)

Pakistan President Gen Iskander Mirza warned at Karachi, in his nationwide broadcast on Pakistan's first republic day anniversary : "Indo-Pak relations would be further embittered if India continues to be unreasonable on Kashmir. Our most vital problem continues to be that of Kashmir. Pakistan's relations with India depend solely on the issue of Kashmir."

Terrorists stealing Armymen's identity Cards : April, 2007

It was May 2006 that ultras dressed as policemen had breached security and opened fire on a Youth Congress function in Srinagar, convened to celebrate Rajiv Gandhi's birth anniversary and killed/injured 7/21 people. The intelligence is now concerned that the militants using the stolen identity cards of Armymen could wreak similar havoc.

The concern is natural given the fact that as many as 67 mobile SIM cards recovered over the last three months from captured militants in Jammu and Kashmir by the State police were procured by the former by using the fake identity cards of Army personnel. That is not all. In a bizarre incident, with serious implications for national security, an entire batch of 87 identity cards belonging to armymen below the rank of officers has mysteriously. It was disclosed by sources close to the MoD in March 2007.

To start with, two such SIM cards were recovered from inmates in Kot Balawal prison, Jammu, in Dec. 2006.

Congress leader shot dead : April 2007

After a bull of over two months in Kashmir Valley, another political leader (senior Congressman and a businessman) Jan Mohd. Kakroo was shot dead and his security guard injured on 1 April 2007 when they came out of a shrine at Khawaja Bagh in Baramulla district of north Kashmir.

The terrorist outrage is obviously a setback for loud and persistent demand for troop withdrawal/reduction in the Valley by the PDP father-daughter duo. Just two days back (on 29 March), the centre had agreed to set up three panels to look into the PDP's demands, including the repeal of the Armed Forces Special Powers Act. State Congress Vice President Abdul

Gnai Vakil, describing Kakroo's killing as reply to those who are trying "to create an impression that all is well here", said : "The incident proved that PDP was not right in demanding troop reduction." Sayeed mouthed the usual platitude : "The killing shows the frustration of the terrorists, and it was perpetrated on a day when the messenger of peace Prophet Mohammad was born."

Indian jehadis get bounty to marry PoK girls : April 2007

Marrying into families based in PoK brings in big moolah for mercenaries who hail from J and K and are being trained in PoK camps for jehad against India.

- Rs 30,000 (Pak currency) for marrying a local girl.
- A handsome monthly allowance of Rs. 4,500.
- These two rewards are in addition to the pocket expenses and other remunerations militants of Indian Kashmiri origins receives while they are in PoK.
- Most of the Kashmiri youths in HM and LET have married in PoK with their Pakistani mentors arranging a "free of cost marriage" in Muzzaffarabad.

These are the facts culled from an intelligence report (made public on 4 April 2007) based on the questioning/debriefing of LET militant Hussain Shah "who surrendered in Doda in February 2007."

The report says the bounty offered to Kashmiri youth to marry a local girl is intended to break the ranks of HM which is a predominantly Kashmiri outfit with most of its cadres drawn from the Valley. In contrast, the LET is dominated by the Pakistanis with almost 90 per cent of its militants being Pakistani nationals.

Shah, a resident of Chareel tehsil in Doda district, had crossed over to PoK in May 2004 and had been trained in several LET camps and also treated in a hospital controlled by the LET when he had developed a knee injury while undergoing this training in PoK.

Pakistan ISI still plays an active role as its officials organise a 2-week special map-reading training programme at a camp located at Kotli, in Deena forests on the banks of the Jhelum near Mirpur.[21]

The report also speaks about the militant camps having been pushed into the more interior areas to avoid detection by an overwhelming presence of foreign forces on Pakistani soil.

It also confirms what is already a common knowledge : LET has become self-sufficient in generating funds for its operations. Most of its funds come from the Arab countries.

Shah's inputs speak volumes about the marginalisation of the HM in the Pak-controlled jihad in Kashmir. This may further add to the frustrations of the Kashmiri youth who now feel they have little role in Kashmir.

24 Militants surrender in Jammu and Kashmir : 20 April 2007 [Returnees from PoK]

24 militants surrendered before the GoC, 19 Inf. Div., Maj. Gen. Ramesh Halgali in Baramulla on 20 April 2007.

They (surrenderees) owed allegiance to the Hizb-ul-Mujahideen (HM), the Tehrik-e-Jahad (TEJ), the Hizbe-e-Islami (HEI), and the Kashmir Revolutionary Force (KRF).

Defence spokesman Col. A.K. Mathur said emotional scenes were witnessed as the militants met their family members. Many of them had crossed over to the other side of the LoC at an early age. Some important points from Col Mathur's statement released on the occasion are summed up here :

- "All of them were forced to crosss over to PoK six to eight years ago. They joined jehad by compulsion due to circumstances and not by choice. But they have realised the futility of jehad. Hundreds of lives have been ruined, families shattered and only darkness engulfs the horizon of PoK (felt the militants).
- "The surrenderees unequivocally spoke of growing disillusionment amongst the Kashmiri militants.
- "There is widening rift between the local and foreign militants. They were forthright in admitting that they feel safe and free in India and want to expose Pakistan's false rhetoric in support of Kashmiris.

- "They have also confirmed that terrorist infrastructure in PoK is intact and flourishing. Pakistan's involvement in abetting militancy in Jammu and Kashmir in terms of moral, financial and material support from across the LoC remains undiminished."

Surrender of 24 militants : Army is getting results : 19 April 2007

A day before the surrender on 20 April 2007, a daily, known for its prowess in investigative journalism, came out with some interesting and relevant facts about the event. Some perceptive and informative details are excerpted here from its story datelined Srinagar, 19 April 2007.

- "The violent game of hide and seek between infiltrating militants and the Army on the LoC has been replaced with a peaceful cross-over by groups of Kashmiri militants returning home. And the Army is going to host a mega surrender ceremony and a "reunion with the families" at its Rampur brigade in Baramulla (district). Tomorrow 24 Kashmiri militants will officially lay down arms.
- "This farewell-to-arms story has an interesting twist. Sources reveal that the Army has established well-knit contacts across the LoC to help the "disenchanted" and "home sick" among the thousand young Kashmiri men, who had trekked across for arms training in the early 1990s, return. In fact eight militants had surrendered in a similar manner in March 2007 in Uri.
- Col Mathur told the daily : "They (militants) have been crossing in small groups for the last few days. We had prior information that these militants wanted to surrender and we let them in. They sent us a message that they wanted to surrender to avoid a situation where troops would mistake them for infiltrators."
- "Although Col Mathur said these militants had run away from their camps, sources reveal that the Army has developed a network of its own men in PoK who are constantly helping in these surrenders. A source privy to this operation told the daily : 'The first contacts across

were established during the earthquake (in 2005) when the LoC was virtually unmanned for several days. The men who are working for the Army, in fact, become guides for these militants, ensuring them of a peaceful reunion with their families here. And it seems to be working.'

- "The Army has organised a surrender ceremony at its Rampur Brigade where these 24 militants would lay down arms before Maj Gen. Ramesh Halgaly. GoC, 19 Divison. The Army has also invited parents of these militants and a reunion function would follow the surrender.
- "The Jammu and Kashmir Police have a list of around 1,000 Kashmiri men who had crossed over for arms training in 1990s. A number of them has married and settled down there now. Majority of them do not want to join militancy (said a senior police officer). This has been a huge problem for us because their parents want travel documents to go and meet them. Once these men start returning after their surrender to the army at the LOC, it will help to resolve the long-standing problem."

"Pak Army stopping surrender of militants" : 29 April 2007

The Pak Army is keeping a close watch on militants in 52 training camps across the LoC to ensure that they do not surrender to Indian authorities, senior Army officers said 29 April 2007. "Despite the ongoing peace process, the training camps across the border are still operational and hundreds of trained militants are ready to find their way into the Kashmir Valley."

Over 700 Kashmiri youths who have been trained in training camps in PoK are ready to infiltrate into the Indian side, the source disclose. Intelligence agencies say that out of 52 training camps in Pakistan and PoK, five of them are in Muzaffarabad alone.

Brig Narinder Pal Singh Hira, Commander 12 Inf Bde, says : "The Indian Army has a list of Kashmiri boys who crossed the LoC and are in constant louch with their parents to motivate their wards to surrender. The Pak Army is keeping a close eye on the militants to thwart their efforts."

"Kashmir Jihad will continue" : Hafiz Saeed : 6 May 2007

Jamat-ud-Dawa Chief Hafiz Saeed on 6 May 2007 said that Jihad (= holy war) in Indian Kashmir continue without a break. Addressing a news conference at Islamabad, Saeed said : "Our mujahedeen (= holy warriors) have not halted operations in Kashmir. Jihad will continue. The main aim of the Jihad is to get rid of the Indian rule. Until we achieve this goal, there is no reason to stop Jihad. The other option is that India should itself withdraw." Some Brazenners, this!

He rejected the US report that Pakistan was a safe haven for banned LET and other Jihadi organisations. "Pakistan Government is now with the US rulers. They are killing or arresting Mujahideen but providing no shelter to them.

He declared the recently enforced Women Protection Act (WPA) against the Islamic norms, Quran and Sunnah (= teachings of the Prophet Mohammed) and against the constitution of the country. He urged the government to abolish the law (WPA) immediately. He claimed they held 11,512,703 people's signatures during his party's signatory campaign against the WPA.

During the campaign, more than 30,000 women across the country out of total signatories voted against the WPA. He asked Chaudhry Shujaat Hussain, head of the ruling Pakistan Muslim League (Qaed); PMO-Q, and Wasi Zafar, Minister for Law, Justice and Human Rights to fulfil their promise of having the WPA revamped.

In the next phase of signatory campaign, he said, the JUD would get signatures of more people in order to give strength to his anti-WPA drive.

"If the government will not take out WPA, then the JUD will take its signatory campaign inside the Parliament in order to develop understanding of parliamentarians against the bill, Saeed warned.

Decline in influx of terrorists Pakistan : Report : 10 May 2007 (Costs of terrorism)

With the onset of summer and the melting of the snow on

the mountain passes, though there should be an increase in infiltration from across the border, mercifully there has been a decline in the infiltration from across the border in Jammu and Kashmir this year (2007) as compared to last year (2006).

"The infiltration for the period Jan-March 2007 was 39 as compared to 59 during the corresponding period last year," said an official release dated 10 May 2007. Some other comparative figures from the official report are summarised below :

- No. of infiltrations in J and K

  Oct 2006-Mar 2007 148

  Apr 2006-Sep 2006 405

- No. of security forces killed

  2006 151

  2005 189

  2004 281

- No. of terrorists killed

  2006 593

  2005 917

- No. of terrorism-related incidents

  During 2006, number was lower by 16 per cent compared to 2005

- No. of civilians killed

  Number lower by 30 per cent in 2006 as compared to 2005

  389 in 2006 and 557 in 2005

- No. of security personnel killed

  Number lower by 20 per cent compared to 2005.

- No. of grenade attacks

  2006 226

  2005 152

  49 per cent increase in 2006 over 2005.

Now a word on financial implications of the insurgency in Jammu and Kashmir. Since the onset of militancy in the State in 1989, the Central Government has reimbursed a whopping Rs. 3,591.64 crore to the State Government from 1989-90 to 2005-06 for security related expenditure (SRE). Which is the total amount of money incurred by the state in its fight against terrorism during these 16 years.

The money is used for various purposes including hidden costs for surrenders, money for sources etc. For the financial year 2006-07, the revised budgetary allocation under the SRE head was Rs. 165.10 crore while Rs. 120 crore was earmarked for Relief and Rehabilitation.

Moreover a sum of Rs. 18.64 crore had also been disbursed to the government of Himachal Pradesh during the period 1999-2000 to 2005-06 for meeting the SRE in its bid to contain spill-over terrorism from J and K to Himachal Pradesh.

PEACE PROCESS : A STATUS REPORT

Whether as a result of pressure from the international community, especially the West led by the US and UK, or because of their own faith in bilateral solutions to their problems, India and Pakistan seem to be seriously engaged in the "peace process" to untangle so many issues/disputes bedevelling their relationship.

Besides the official channels, which are presently going through the fourth round of the "Composite Dialogue", starting May 2007, more than one back channel and a plethora of NGOs too are claiming to be calming the ruffled feathers.

It is not that there are no rough patches on the way—Geelani's extremism for one. Then PDP keeps upping the ante by demanding demilitarisation first, followed by disbandment of the village defence councils.

Jammu and Kashmir : Politics of Troop Deployment : March 2007

It is widely believed the world over that the politicians could do anything for strengthening their vote-bank. But it will be unfair on Indian political class to credit them with more banality and mendacity than their counterparts in the rest of the world. It is reasonably fair to aver that the former would not play politics with national interests to garner some additional votes under any situation. But a section of opinion holds sincerely 'that is exactly what the Father-Daughter Duo of the PDP have been doing over the last few weeks (Feb-March 2007) by demanding the troop-pull out from some of the Jammu and Kashmir areas". This section felt that even if the crisis created by the threat-laced demand for lower security profile were defused without any major concessions, what had been enacted over a couple of weeks in Mar 2007 "was a political drama at its shameful worst".

It was suggested that rather than rejecting it outrightly—as Chief Minister Azad had, indeed, courageously done—the Centre and the Congress-led UPA coalition accorded legitimacy to the debate by inviting and entertaining Mufti, trying to both pacify him and provide a face-saver. It matters little that if no troop pull out (or thin out) or re- deployment followed, he ought to have been told that the threat veiled or brazen to withdraw from the State's Coalition Government scared no body and he and his party were at liberty to quit. It, of course, is clearly understood that the PDP is seeking to fill the political space vacated by the insurgents whose strategy and machinations have been thwarted by the very security forces whose withdrawal it was now passionately demanding. It may be a clever political stance, but it certainly is not in national interest.

So the message that should have gone out from New Delhi was that the loss of a state government was of little consequence when compared with the national risk involved in any politically-driven security compromise.[22]

An opportunity has obviously been lost to make it unambiguous to the insurgents, and their sponsors and supporters across the LOC, that India stood firmly behind its security forces, doing a very difficult job efficiently and effectively for the people of the country and that, New Delhi would do nothing that saps the morale of soldiers and their officers performing a national duty.

Instead, the Government decision provided an opportunity to put force levels and deployment strategy on the political agenda. If the Congress hawked it as a political victory by not conceding the demand for troop thin out, the BJP went on the other extreme in its less-than-responsible attempt to make its own assessment and level charges of "surrender".

Some analysts perched on the other side of the fence assert politics is not the game of black and white. There are a lot of gray shades in-between. Then there is that averment by the Mandal Messiah VP Singh : Politics is the art of reconciling the opposites. If a little concession, not of substantial nature, can save the Coalition, it is worth it. They like to call it 'pragmatism'.

A blunt refusal even to discuss the Mufti demand would have forced PDS out of the Government and collapse of the Azad Ministry would have been inevitable. Whatever its other consequences, seen and unseen, the PDP would have added to its popularity, claiming to be the "voice of Kashmiris". Yet again, certain responsible entities in the West, including the EU and US Government, Human Rights and some other NGOs, have repeatedly blamed the Indian security forces of human rights violation. Seen in this light, there does seem to be some merit in offering some sops to the PDP. In hind sight, it may be seen as a clever move by Prime Minister and Congress President to thwart the PDP in its drive to become a threat in electoral politics. It is no great secret that anti-New Delhi stance always benefits political parties in the Valley. PDP success itself in the 2003 Assembly poll proves the point. The perceived pro-New Delhi stance can result in a party's undoing. Farooq Abdullah's loss in 2003 is the other side of the PDP's performance.

At the end of seeing both sides of the issue, it is important to make a self-obvious point. The unprincipled tactics and demands by the politicians or their parties is bound to impact the soldier fighting the mindless perpetrators of violence on the innocent, helpless civilians. The men conducting counter-insurgency operations are fully conscious that they are walking on a tight rope which remains taut only so long as the nation appreciates their problems and fully backs them. They and their leaders are sensitive to the shifts in the winds, and are not totally unaware of the political realities, as their forebears might have been in the years after the 1947. "They would have taken in stride, as they have done since that year, much of what the local politicians have recently hurled at them, but it assumes a different dimension when their traducers are given "sympathetic" treatment in New Delhi. The discussions with the Mufti over the last few days (between 18 and 23 March 2007) must erode the troops morale and simultaneously boost that of the militants."[23]

Terror data go against troop cut: 1 May 2007

The ground realities in Jammu and Kashmir are against any possibility of troop cut as actively demanded by the PDP. Troop reduction is unlikely to materialise even after a month of Prime Minister Manmohan Singh brokering a fragile political truce between the two main ruling coalition partners—the PDP and the Congress.

As many as 111 terrorist-related incidents were reported in a month (April 2007) since the Prime Minister set up three high powered committees to address the PDP's demands for troop pull out, vacation of civilian properties occupied by security forces and repeal of the AFSPA.

Having consistently linked troop withdrawal to the level of militancy at any given time, the Centre cannot ignore the latest data, argue senior military officers.[24]

Defence Minister AK Antony has clearly ruled out any troop reduction in the given situation. The Prime Minister Manmohan Singh himself sent a message home at the 24 April Round Table Conference and his talks with PDPs Mufti Sayeed at the end of March 2007 : "Deployment of security forces will be in direct relation to the extent of militancy".

Data collected by security agency reveals that terrorism-related violence has hit 16 of the 22 Jammu & Kashmir districts, with varying gravity, leaving 41 terrorists, 21 civilians, and 7 security persons dead in April. Relative peace in the remaining six districts, including two in Ladakh, is attributed to their demographic composition that does not suit the militancy.

The sensitivity of the troop withdrawal issue that strained the PDP-Congress ties prevented the security officials from speaking on record, says a reporter. Those who spoke on condition of anonymity said the "police has effective intelligence but not manpower and ability to strike in the interiors." As a result, without the Army, the 60,000-strong Jammu and Kashmir police, together with its 24,000 SPOs (Special Police Officers), would be lost in the State's hostile terrain made up of thick forests, plains and hills with near-negligible road links.

"In some areas, it takes 3 to 5 days to reach a tehsil headquarters from a district headquarters".

It is clear from this one factor that fighting insurgency is not an easy proposition in the state, particularly in the distant, inaccessible interiors. But it was essentially because of close coordination and cooperation between the state police and central paramilitary and military forces that the "security forces in the recent years have had the upper hand in the fight against terrorism, with two to five militants killed or apprehended each day." Stressing the obvious, a senior analyst asserted: "We will lose the advantage if the troops are pulled out."

However, the vacation of civilian properties—hotels, schools, public parks and dak bungalows—by the security forces is proceeding apace in a planned way. In Srinagar alone, they have cleared out from 24 hotels.

"Disband the VDC" : PDP : 22 April 2007

Hardly a couple of weeks after the demilitarisation controversy in the State raked by the People's Democratic Party, a major coalition partner in the Congress-led state Government, was put to rest by Prime Minister Manmohan Singh, who constituted three committees to examine the demand, the two coalition partners are again on a collision course.

Two days ahead of the 24 November 2006 third round table conference, on Kashmir, the PDP President, Mehbooba Mufti, has now raised a fresh crisis by demanding the dishandment of the Village Defence Committees (VDCs) in the State.

There are presently over 3,700 VDC, in the whole of Jammu and Kashmir, of which 1,500 are in the Doda district alone and their number—and popularity—seem to be growing. And Mehbooba had demanded their disbandment while addressing a public meeting in the Doda district, at Kishtwar, a few days ago.

Chief Minister Azad categorically rejected the demand, declaring instead the VDCs would be further strengthened, and where ever necessary. "Will be assisted by Special Police Officers (SPOs)".

Incidentally, each VDC consists of eight members who are given a weapon each by the State. Azad said the VDCs "have done a good job in tackling militancy".

Geelani spits his usual fire : 22 April 2007

Soon after returning to Kashmir after revoking from his renal surgery from Mumbai where he had gone for treatment some three months back, the hard line separatist leader, chief of his faction of APHC, Syed Ali Shah Geelani on 2 April 2007 addressed "a mammoth gathering of 40,000 people at the martyrs' graveyard in Edgah, down town Srinagar". His speech comprised his usual rankings, repeating his well-known hard line utterings :

- Amid the pro-Pakistan and pro-freedom slogans, Geelani ruled out all the temporary solution and said the right to self-determination was the "only solution" to the Kashmir issue.
- With the jam-packed ground, 77 year old Geelani asked the people to repeat with, "no status quo, no autonomy, no self-governance, no softening of borders, only right to self-determination".
- Kashmir would never witness peace, unless each and every soldier returned to barracks.
- He thought the Third Round table conference, scheduled for 24 April 2007, was a wastage of time.

"The main attraction of the really was flags of the LET and HM outfits which were seen flying from different directions".

An FIR was filed at Safakadal police station against Geelani by the police for holding a meeting without prior permission and raising of anti-national slogans at the venue.

Things are moving : Some interesting Kashmiri visitors and their significant statements: end April-May 2007.

Sardar Mohd. Abdul Qayum Khan

The man who initiated the India-Pakistan War 1947 comes to New Delhi bearing a message of peace. "Mujahid-e-Awwal (= First Revolutionary) as Sardar Abdul Qayum Khan's followers call him, is the first holy warrior. In 1947, Qayum, then an officer in the British Indian Army, initiated a military thrust into

Poonch that sparked off the first India-Pakistan (1947-49) war. His forces, made up of tribal irregulars and military personnel, were among the most successful of the columns that almost succeeded in seizing Jammu and Kashmir for Pakistan.[25]

In the subsequent years, Qayum went on to become POK's Prime Minister and President. He still remains among the most influential voices in its politics, six decades on. Qayum was in New Delhi for an intra-Kashmir Conference attended by politicians from either side of the LOC. They had gathered in an effort to undo the history Qayam helped make.

During his stay at New Delhi (27 April-3 May 2007), Qayum met the following Indian leaders :

- Prime Minister Manmohan Singh.
- Leader of Opposition L.K. Advani.
- J & K Chief Minister Ghulam Nabi Azad.
- Saifuddin Soz : Union Minister of Water Resources.
- He was accompanied by J&K Panthers Party Chief Prof. Bhim Singh.

Mohd. Qayum at the ORF seminar/discussion : 28 April 2007

Mohd. Qayum said on 28 April 2007 that the Hurriyat should not boycott talks with New Delhi if the Kashmir problem has to be solved. "Unless they sit and discuss things, problems cannot be solved". He was replying to questions at the Observer Research Foundation (at New Delhi) on the boycott of the third round table conference on Kashmir by the Hurriyat.

Qayum also made a passionate appeal to the Indian Government to offer safe passage to Pakistani terrorists in the valley to return home. But he was silent on similar demands for safe passage and amnesty by India to the Kashmiri youth who crossed over to POK but were now disillusioned.

Giving a clean chit to Gen. Musharraf, he said there were no training camps in POK.

Revealing a soft corner for Lashkar-e-Tayyaba, he said its operatives were "misunderstood". "They are motivated by religion and have no political motives. Their camps have been dismantled". This, when the Indian MOD report, released in March 2007, says infiltration has to stop and Pakistan should take decisive action to destroy terrorist infrastructure including camps, launch pads and communication network of terrorist groups.

Qayum, who fancies himself as Mujahid-e-Awwal (= Fighter No. 1) for the Kashmiri cause, said the blame game must end if the peace process has to make any headway. He called for dialogue between Kashmiri leaders on both sides of the LOC. Criticising the earlier attitude of both India and Pakistan of viewing such meetings with suspicion, he said, "Heavens won't fall if Kashmiri leaders of both sides meet."[26]

For another daily[27], Qayum seeking "safe passage" for militants in Jammu and Kashmir to return home, was adding a new dimension to the issue of militancy in the state. "Militant Camps in Pakistan have been dismantled. But may be some belonging to the LET school of thought are still (there) on that side (Jammu and Kashmir), waiting for a safe passage home (POK)", he said.

Matter was already under discussion with the Indian Government "at various levels", he said. "We are ready to accept them. Instead of keeping the irritant there, it is better they are moved home across the LOC."

Here are some more points he made:

- Asked about the criticism that "India has not responded adequately to Gen. Musharraf's proposals on Kashmir, he said, "I think India has responded quite adequately given the difficulties they have to face, they have sufficiently responded."
- If the CBMs were followed with trust, "we can travel the distance earlier than we thought of."
- On solution to Kashmir issue, he said, "anything that saves Kashmir and the Kashmiris should be acceptable". But he stressed on the people to people contact, saying this did not have to wait for "the solution", which has not yet been found in 60 years. "People can bring political and moral pressure on politicians."

- He praised Musharraf for stopping activities in militant camps in Pakistan. "Musharraf should get credit, only he could do it. There were no camps in POK, he said. As for the camps on Indian side, he felt "most would still be there."
- He defended LET, which India holds responsible for major acts of terrorism in the recent past, and said: "LET has no political motives, only religious ones. It has ceased its activities."
- Speaking like a good Pakistani for once, according to this author, he said: "In any case, he did not agree with the term 'terrorism' to describe movement like the one in Kashmir". "This was coined after 9/11," he argued, saying he had been part of it himself at one point of time. He did, however, agree that there were "some acts of terrorism."
- Asked about the Talibanisation of Waziristan, Qayum conceded that this affected the peace of the country, "but this has no direct bearing on Kashmir."
- He was critical of the Emma Nicholson report, saying this was based on pre-conceived notions.

Panthers Party leader Prof Bhim Singh, who had organised the group's visit to India for Intra-Kashmir Conference, said "borders can become irrelevant only if the people on both sides are made relevant."

Those who attended the discussion included the Centre's interlocuter on Kashmir NN Vohra and former J and K Governor GC Saxena.

Interview to Praveen Swami, The Hindu : 30 April 2007

Q. You have repeatedly suggested during this visit that the borders in J&K be made irrelevant. Is not it necessary to first have an agreed border before it can become irrelevant?

Ans. Let us put it this way : the idea of irrelevance is meant to free up the movement of the people and trade across both sides of Kashmir. Without doubt, we will have to agree on a border. However, we can begin dismantling restrictions prior to that decision.

Q. Irrelevance as a concept, concerns some policy makers in India, who say without an agreement on the border, it will allow Pakistan to press its claims at a later stage—to use the free movement of people', as it were, to strengthen its political hand. What would be your response to this line of argument?

Ans. I agree that it is a matter of great concern that the status of a territory that existed prior to the independence of India and Pakistan continues to hang in limbo six decades later. This situation cannot be allowed to persist. The problems, though, is that me have been discussing the final status of Kashmir for all these decades. Nothing has been achieved. So, let us forget about finality. Let us deal with the problems as it exists. One problems is jihadi activity. Another problem are the hardships faced by people in their day-to-do lives. Let us try to deal with these problems one-by-one. Even this is difficult enough because, unfortunately, the antagonism that caused the problem is still in place. Both in India and Pakistan, the legacy of Partition persists.

Q. So, in your view, is the problem in Kashmir tied up with the larger problem of communalism in South Asia? It is interesting to hear you say this, because Sheikh Mohd. Abdullah once said that Kashmir's Muslims would meet the same fate as Muslims in some other parts of India had done during partition.

Ans. Yes, the situation in Kashmir is the outcome of far larger history. Ultimately, the fate of the people of Kashmir is enmeshed with that of the region. But it is important to note that we cannot be made hostages of this larger conflict. During a recent meeting with President Musharraf, I said that any solution that would save the lives of Kashmiris would be acceptable'. Any solution.

Q. Some hardline leaders would oppose it. Both the HM Chief Yusuf Shah and Islamist leader Syed Geelani, have rejected the kinds of compromise you are advocating.

Ans. Every one—India, Pakistan, the various Kashmiri leaders—have their public postures and commitments.

Ultimately, the bottom line is that we have to accept realities. We cannot, for one, have independence. There were good reasons why the UN resolutions on Kashmir excluded this possibility, it remains impracticable today. Second, India will not, under any circumstances, accept one more partition. Third, in the present world situation, the major powers will not accept the emergence of a new Muslim majority state. I may or may not like these three realities, but I have to work within this framework. So I ask those who reject dialogue and compromise—What is your alternative?

Q. Presumably, continuing to fight! This is what some jihadi leaders, and Geelani, say.

Ans. Jihad for what purpose? To what end? As you know, I talked of Jihad in 1947. I not only talked about it, but also put my life on the line, fighting for what I believed in—unlike some of those calling for it today. We secured some of our objectives. Others we did not. We stopped when limits of what could be achieved had been reached. We did not engage in mindless violence.

Q. Your characterisation of violence seems a little at odds with what you said at a recent seminar at New Delhi—that the LET is a religious group, not a terrorist organisation, that it had fought the British during the freedom struggle.

Ans. Let me clarify what I said, because I see it has been misunderstood by many in India. I have often held discussions on the LET with many of those worried about the organisation—the Europeans, the British. My purpose is to reach out to the group, and persuade it to come on board the peace process. Nothing is achieved by putting some one in a corner. There are many sane, reasonable people in the Lashkar, with whom there have been some fruitful conversations. Let us leave it at that now.

Q. Could you tell us a little bit about your own alternative? What is your vision of the future?

Ans. Well, my solutions is this: let there be peace, freedom of movement, and trade.

Then, let us see what is possible. I do not want to get involved in a public discussion of the specifics of a solution. There is a lot of dialogue going on now behind close doors, and I think it is best that these discussions stay secret. You are probably too young to remember this, but even Sheikh Abdullah had proposed a kind of condominium proposal, involving India, Pakistan and Kashmir. Some people seem to be talking about the same sorts of things today.

Q. Sheikh Abdullah had, among various other proposals, advocated a confederation of India, Pakistan and Kashmir during his May 1964 visit to Pakistan. Gen. Ayub Khan, Pak military ruler, rejected it. He thought the proposal would "undo the Partition and place the Hindu majority in a dominant and decisive position."

Ans. Politics in our part of the world is based on suspicion and mistrust. People are always ready to believe the worst : it is our fitrat (= basic character/trait). If anyone tries to do anything good, there are a dozen people' poised to heap abuse on him. Prime Minister Manmohan Singh is in this position. President Musharraf is in the same position. In Pakistan, there are people shouting, "do not trust India? Fine, trust no one. But accept that you must move forward. We are neighbours. We cannot shift to some other neighbourhood. We can be good neighbours, or squabble endlessly. What future do we wants? In India and Pakistan, we are very good at talking endlessly about the past, while outsiders go about making our future. Is that really what we want?[28]

Intra-Kashmir Conference: 30 April 2007 : New Delhi

Calling for "general amnesty" to all those in jails, participants of the "India-JK heart-to-heart talks" appealed to the parliamentarians and civil society of India and Pakistan to take the peace process to its "logical end."

This was the second round of such talks and a joint statement was issued at the end of it, which was read out by former POK Prime Minister and President Mohd. Abdul Qayum Khan. Some salient points from the statement are summed up here:

- It recommended that old historical links between the two sides of Kashmir, including "pony, road and rail routes" which existed before 1947, should be reopened.

- To further facilitate the movement across the LOC, it recommended that the arrangements for travel, which existed before 1956, should be restored. Qayyum said that earlier Deputy Commissioners on the two sides had the authority to issue travel documents.
- The POK leader, without using the terms like "militants" or "safe passage", said that "those suffering in jails or still present in J and K may be given an opportunity to return home". Asked pointedly if he meant militants, Qayum said it also included political detainees.
- "General amnesty to those still in jails will provide them a chance to start a new life. It will promote the peace process."
- "Coordination committees of legislators, women, youth and students shall be constituted shortly to strengthen the dialogue among the people on either side of the LOC". Asked if leaders of the APHC will be involved, his reply: "There could be meetings of prominent personalities on the two sides."
- Answering queries, Qayum, who was accompanied by J&K Panthers Party Chief Bhim Singh, said the situation "will see a significant change if there was no obstruction to the movement of people and trade flourished between the two parts of the State."
- Responding to the query about the reported reaction of the UJC, he claimed there was no contradictions in his statements which may have been mis-reported or misunderstood.
- He suggested that those wielding guns should also be involved in the dialogue process.
- Rejecting the possibility of independence of Kashmir, he said it was nearly impossible to conceive a new independent Muslim majority state in the present geo-politics and it would require opening agreements concerning the Partition.

Qayum at Press Conference : SAFMA : 30 April 2007

At a Press Conference organised by South Asia Free Media Association (SAFMA), Qayum criticised the APHC for boycotting the recent (24 April 2007) Round Table Conference (RTC) saying they were wrong to do so. Many proposals discussed at the RTC would be beneficial to the people of the state, he said.

Some other views/points from this Press Conference:

- He claimed independence for Kashmir was not practical. "Option of independence was not available to the people of Kashmir nor was it possible to have one more partition.
- Fully backing the ongoing dialogue between India and Pakistan, he indicated that he favoured the Sheikh Abdullah proposal of confederation between India, Pakistan and Kashmir.
- He emphasised that the (dialogue) process was more important than the solution.
- Asked about the existence of a terror infrastructure in POK, he said militant camps existed in Pakistan and POK before 11 September 2001 but there was no trace of these now as far as he knew.
- He favoured "safe passage" for the militants from across the LOC, who want to return home.
- He hit out at the Jihadi elements, saying that their activities were communal in nature and only concerned with money. Such forces also have links with official agencies.
- Asked if Gen. Musharraf was losing his hold on power, he replied in the affirmative and made an interesting point: "It was because people want a change in regime every five years, like in India."[29]

One more interview of Qayum : 6 May 2007

Two interviews have already been covered in detail. This is the last one in a daily of 6 May 2007.[30] It will be covered very briefly, for the points not discussed earlier, or to lay emphasis on points already covered in the earlier two interviews.

Sardar Qayum is the supremo of the ruling Muslim Conference in POK. Involved in the tribal incursions in Kashmir in 1947, Qayum has reoriented his policies according to the times.

Q. How do you see the Indo-Pak peace process?

Ans. The peace process is moving in the right direction, able it slowly. They al be it drawn the outlines but the pace is slow. Lest it becomes redundant and people lose interest in it, the process needs to be stepped up. I have been insisting on concentrating on the process and making it successful. That will automatically lead to a decision.

Q. Why are there hurdles when leaders talk about easing travel curbs across the LOC?

Ans. There are governments within governments. Nobody really knows how many agencies are at work. That is why things take so much time. Something which can be done in 10 minutes takes a year. For instance, there are so many restrictions for people wanting to travel by the bus between Srinagar and Muzaffarabad that it is easier to get passport than meet those requirements.

Q. India has ruled out redrawing of boundaries.

Ans. We have not discussed boundaries at all. Kashmir has no boundaries but control line that is taken as boundary.

Q. India is concerned about cross-border terrorism.

Ans. There is no such thing as terrorists. These people were considered to be freedom fighters before 9/11, but that day changed the complexion entirely throughout the world for any movement, individual or collective. This went to the benefit of Indian authorities and politicians. Camps in Pakistan were closed before 9-11. Similarly, other training camps comprising Kashmiris were also curtailed because the movement had achieved the purpose of highlighting the Kashmir issue. The presence (of militants) is now limited to volunteers who were already inside Kashmir on the Indian side and did not return.

Q. How do you look at suggestions for converting the entire Jammu and Kashmir into a free trade zone?

Ans. This ought to have been done long ago. I had offered to the then Chief Minister of Jammu and Kashmir in 1971 for visits on both sides and opening trade routes.

Q. What is the best way to end violence in the state?

Ans. Let the people believe that meaningful peace process is afoot. Ninety nine percent people carrying weapons will automatically drop them if there is no problem. You need to give a substitute. The simple thing is that the peace process should be stepped up and once trade and exchange of people takes place openly, I think there will be no cause for any militant activity.

Q. Is it time for cease-fire in the state?

Ans. Yes, there should be a ceasefire.

Qayyum's remarks irk UJC : 29 April 2007

The UJC, an amalgam of several militant outfits on 29 April criticised former POK Prime Minister Sardar Qayyum's remarks on Kashmir issue as "Condemnable utterances". Qayyum had on the 28th disfavored independence as a solution to the Kashmir problem and asserted that the Hurriyat was not the "true representative" of the people of the state.

Reacting to Qayyum's seeking "safe passages" for militants form Jammu and Kashmir to POK, UJC spokesman Syed Sadaqat Hussain said that: "It seems, he (Qayum) apprehends that freedom of Kashmiris will bring an end to his family rule". Hussain added further:

- "Though Mr. Qayyum is terming armed resistance as an impediment in the so-called peace process, we need to remind him that he has the distinction of being the first mujahid and firing the first bullet, which enabled him to enjoy power for the past 59 years.
- "In the beginning, Mr. Qayyum had formed an outfit Al-Jihad force and had accumulated huge amounts in the name of the outfit from Europe and Islamic countries."

Hussain did not stop here. He went further, equating Qayyum with the late Sheikh Abdullah: "He gives one statement in POK and other in New Delhi and Europe for pleasing his bosses there. He is adopting the same policy that Sheikh Abdullah had."

Indian separatists upset over Qayyum's utterances: 5-6 May 2007

Sardar Qayyum's observations during his 28 April-3 May 2007 India visit that independence for Kashmir was no option available—thus out of question—and that UN resolutions on Kashmir had become obsolete, has been seen as a snub to the Srinagar-based hardliners among the separatists who steadfastly refuse to relent on the issue.[31] Qayyum had even made it clear that he did not relish the separatists, including the leaders of both the factions of the APHC, of JKLF's Yaseen Malik and JKDFP's Shabhir Shah, boycoting the Round Table Conference (RTC) convened by the Prime Minister on 24 April 2007.

Qayyum's plain speaking must have been particularly repulsive to the separatists and terrorist outfits who have been feeling let down by their erstwhile patron and supporter—Musharraf's Pakistan. On second thoughts and essentially as a face-saver, APHC's Chief Umar Farooq now wants the Prime Minister to convene a separate RTC for the recessionist and separatist leaders. As is known, Geelani will not even attend such a conference—supposing the Prime Minister calls one, of which there is little hope.

Stand alone Geelani gave the call for a J&K bandh on 5 May. But the call evoked little response in Jammu Division. Acting tough, the State Government on the same day (5 May) stopped the Safar-e-Azadi (=journey for independence or freedom) of JKLF leader Yaseen Malik, who had planned a tour of the State, especially its Muslim-dominated areas to seek independence for Kashmir.

Chairman of Pakistan-based UJC Syed Salahuddin has declared that the terrorist outfits will continue their fight.

The separatist outfits have come under attack from the mainstream parties also, as their violence also adversely affect the tourist trade, the mainstay of common Kashmiris.

The Opposition BJP warned the Congress-led UPA government not to fall in Musharraf's trap and act tough with the separatists and militants.

State Congress Chief Peerazada Syeed accused the separatists of double standards: Why are they shy of attending Prime Minister's RTC when they had held a series of meeting with President Musharraf in Pakistan and with every visiting Pak leader and officials at Pak Embassy at New Delhi? Their obvious aim is to keep the Kashmir pot boiling through such tactics.

The violent actions by the separatists scare away tourists from the valley. Hotelines and tourist trade businessmen have been complaining that cancellations of bookings have started pouring in. They are not the only ones to suffer as a result. The common Kashmiri is the worst sufferer, as it affects his livelihood. Unmindful of his sufferings, terrorists regularly step up violence during tourist season every year, and often specifically target the tourists. It is an irony that notwithstanding all this, they claim to be fighting for him.

Back in Pakistan : Qayyum sticks to his guns : 4-5 May 2007

Faced with a volley of questions by an accusing Pakistani media over his statements during his 28 April-3 May 2007 visit to India, Sardar Qayyum stuck to his guns, saying the truth about cross-border militant training camps could not be hidden, nor could anyone find fault with his desire for peace in Kashmir, and his view that the UN resolutions were obsolete.

Returning from New Delhi on 3 May, the former Prime Minister of POK drove straight to meet the media in Islamabad, presumably to clear the air over his statements in India that have been slammed by Kashmiri Opposition parties in Pakistan. Some important excerts follow:

- "It is a fact that there were training camps [for militants] in Pakistan and in Azad Kashmir. It was in the open. We cannot keep something like this under wraps. The Americans can give you all the details about these camps. These things cannot be kept hidden in this day and age. We should speak the truth, or we will be exposed as liars.
- "But I was misreported as having said these were terrorist training camps, while I had stressed the camps were for freedom fighters. I had also pointed out that President Musharraf had closed down the training camps and that there was no more infiltration into India.
- "My purpose in India was to attend an intra-Kashmir 'heart-to-heart' dialogue, where I asked for free movement of Kashmiris, intra-Kashmir trade and peace.

- "We have wasted 50 years in discussing a final solution, and got nothing in return but bloodshed and suffering for Kashmiris. There should be no more discussion on this. Rather, we should focus on tackling the situation on the ground in Kashmir, where people are dying. If we focus on the process, improve the atmosphere, it will lead to the solution by itself. No one can disagree with my point-by-point demands for free movement, trade and peace.
- Asked about Indian "inflexibility" on General Musharraf's famous four point proposals, Qayyum shot back: "They gave me a visa even though they considered me as Enemy No. 1. Is this not flexibility?"
- Qayyum praised Prime Minister Manmohan Singh. "He is on the right track towards finding a solution to the Kashmir issue. My impression is that a good environment is being created for a solution to Kashmir (problem) and to take the peace process forward, and the Indian Prime Minister is making all efforts. The Round Table Conference (RTC) discussed all the issues and I think they are serious. They are working on demilitarisation, on opening of routes, so these are within the parameters suggested by President Musharraf."
- "The APHC should have attended the New Delhi RTC, because no Kashmiri should refuse an opportunity to present his point of view."
- The UN resolutions on Kashmir are obsolete. They were only recommendations. Do you want to keep harping on them until last Kashmiri is killed." This was his counter-question to a reporter who questioned him on the subject.
- As the reporters pressed him about India's 'unyielding' stand, he urged Pakistanis to stop thinking of India "as a municipal committee" which had "not done this or that". Describing India as "10 times a bigger county", he said it would have to keep its "own commitments" in mind before taking any step and could not be pushed around.

- "There is no question of India trapping Pakistan in a peace process. We fail ourselves on many occasions, and blame India for nothing."

Sardar Qayyum's India visit: A Critique

The visit of Sardar Mohd. Abdul Qayyum Khan, Mujahid-e-Awwal, should be seen as some kind of landmark in the long contentions history of Kashmir dispute between India and Pakistan, which dates back to almost-the partition. It was the first time that an ageing[32] Pakistani leader of his vintage and eminence visited India and made some observations on "the" issue of Kashmir which were severely criticised by Kashmiri Opposition parties in Islamabad and the terrorist outfits of Pakistan and POK—besides the separatist leaders of Jammu and Kashmir.

Some of these statements and assertions were essentially against the grain of Pakistan's stance on Kashmir:

- Independence is not the option available as solution to the Kashmir issue.
- UN resolution on Kashmir were obsolete.
- Terrorist training camps did exist in Pakistan/POK, though he replaced the term "terrorists" with "freedom fighters".
- He pleaded for free movement of people across the LOC, intra-Kashmir trade and peace, and "the rest will follow", he said.
- He castigated APHC for boycotting the 24 April Round Table at New Delhi.
- He praised Prime Minister Manmohan Singh's efforts to find a solution of Kashmir issue, and said "he is on the right track".

All this while, he talked and sounded like a genial, wise Kashmiri who has seen it all, more so the futility of pursuing a path of violent confrontation till someone asked him about terrorism. "This was where he stumbled, and revealed his true colours and in doing so, exposed President Musharraf's thinking on Jammu and Kashmir", wrote an analyst[33] about the visit of Qayyum.

Before proceeding to put the Qayyum visit under the scanner, a word on his past life and political achievements. He took part in Pakistan's so-called tribal invasion of Kashmir in 1947, and subsequently rose to become POK's Prime Minister and President. As a spokesman of UJC, angry with his statements in India, put it: "He and his family have been ruling POK as a family business." But for some strange reason when he decided to pursue on independent line of thinking on Jammu and Kashmir in 2001, Gen. Musharraf ensured that the Sardar, despite his electoral victory, did not become the Prime Minister. Musharraf was so miffed at his remarks against his rule that he did not allow even the Sardar's son, Mohd. Atique Khan, to become the Prime Minister. The things are obviously different now or else the Sardar and his delegation would not have stepped out of Muzaffarabad.

The fact that the General has mended fences with the Sardar was obvious from the latter's effusive praise of the President in public. Even more interesting was the way he chose to explain people's disillusionment with Gen. Musharraf. "Yes, they want a change every five years as in India".

More important, and beyond personal equations, is the fact that the Qayyum of 2007 was articulate, self-assured and spoke authoritatively about the changed stance of Islamabad on certain aspects of Indo-Pak relations such as obsoleteness of UN resolutions, initiating of measures like free movement, trade and peace, and his optimism about peace process. He may not have out-Kasuri-ed Kasuri—"You will hear positive news within a week"—in this respect, but he spread hope among his audience. There were pronouncements on Pakistan's changed stance on several aspects of Kashmir issue by Pak leaders Musharraf downwards, but it was the first time that these were pronounced on the Indian soil with such articulation. It may not be off the mark if some analysts aver that Qayyum had not only been briefed thoroughly by the Foreign Office of his country, but he had personal blessings of Musharraf himself. If the General had castigated Gilani for his extremist views, Qayyum castigated APHC for boycotting the RTC. Even more surprising was his comment on the mindless violence. His piece be resistance came when a reporter insisted on the need for jihad. "Will you continue until the last Kashmiri is killed."

Certain criticism of his utterances can only be expected. After all, he did not come here to give 100 per cent solace to Indians. Hence the specific comments of an Indian analyst:[34]

"More intriguing was Sardar's stand on Jihadis. He argued that there was need to review the terminologies used in identifying those who are fighting for their rights. He said they were not terrorists or jihadis. To his credit, he chose not to call them 'freedom fighters'. He denied the existence of terrorist camps in POK. What he chose not to elaborate was that most of the terrorist camps were either shut down by the Musharraf Government under American pressure or were damaged in the Oct. 2005 earthquake. He, of course, was completely oblivious of the presence of Jamaat-ud-Dawa (JUD) camps in the region. JUD is the parent body of the LET."

One thing that was self obvious from his interviews and statement was the fact of LET being close to his heart. It was with certain affection that he usually spoke of it:

"It had fought the British.... It has ceased its activities." So a word on the realities of LET should be in order—to draw a true and authentic picture.

The LET, in fact, had swung into action immediately after the earthquake, setting up a chain of mobile dispensaries, hospitals, and rehabilitation centres across the region at a time when Pakistan Army was more seriously engaged in plugging the breached defences and possible damage to the Kahuta nuclear complex. The LET remained active in the area for several months carrying out extensive rescue and relief operations, winning accolades from Gen. Musharraf as well as the people it helped to stand on their feet. The LET utilised the opportunity to network with Kashmiri militant group leaders like Syed Salahuddin and Yaseen Malik, who was accorded a public reception in Muzaffarabad. LET also raised substantial contributions from different parts of the world. To cite one example of its fund-raising capacity, within days of the earthquake, the outfit bought a mobile operation theatre worth Rs. 5 crore.

About the LET, Qayyum said it was an organisation which was most misunderstood. To him, it was not a terrorist organisation, but a religious body with specific objectives. He refused to say/accept that "the LET's sole objective is to target India". For him, it is an old organisation, in existence even before the Afghan jihad. To Indians, nothing could be, more removed from the truth. To state the fact, the LET was set up in 1986-87, at the fag end of the Afghan Jihad, by Osama bin Laden's ideologue, Abu Azzam, and two religious scholars from Pakistan, Hafiz Sayeed and Zafar Iqbal.

The Qayyum-LET link, undoubtedly goes back to the outfit's terrorist campaign in Jammu and Kashmir. The LET had set up several launching pads in the POK for terrorist operations in India. In 1999, the LET used these launching pads and many other camps and routes to lead the infiltration into India's Leh-Kargil sector—a vanguard (or part) of Pakistan's larger attack to occupy India's strategically important Kargil heights to cut off supply and maintenance routes of Indian forces deployed in vast region of Ladakh to protect the Indo-China and Indo-Pakistan borders. A year after this aggression was repulsed, LET Chief Hafiz Saeed and Qayyum shared a platform at a conference in Muzaffarabad where Sayeed said it was "the duty of the armed forces of Pakistan to cross the bloody (boundary?) line for the liberation of their Kashmiri brethren". Sayeed further declared that peace talks should only begin after the Indian troops were ousted from Kashmir, and that all Mujahideen groups, including the Hizbul Mujahideen (HM), would strengthen mutual coordination and cooperation to continue jihad till the liberation of Jammu and Kashmir.

Qayyum said in his speech: "Jihadis should get together and not fight separately. The LET should join hands with the HM."

The Conference ended with a recruitment drive for Jihad in Jammu and Kashmir. This is the reason for Qayyum's ambivalence about defining a 'terrorist'. Obviously, he prefers the term 'jihadi'. Likewise, during one of his interactions with the press during New Delhi visit, he was boath to call them 'terrorists', even if he abstained from anointing them as 'freedom fighters'.

But he must be given due credit for his articulation of Pakistan's new approach to find a solution to the vexed Kashmir issue—renouncing violence, even if it be in theory or as a ploy to entice gullible Indians in miasma of 'pious intention' of that country's never say die military leadership led by the ISI: "It is time to give up violence because we (have) achieved whatever we could by the gun." He was in the forefront of using gun to persuade India to the negotiating table on Jammu and Kashmir. "Having achieved our objective, we should give up the past and strive for peace." It needs to be emphasised that this is uncannily similar to what Gen. Musharraf, the architect of the Kargil aggression, has been saying for the past two years (2005-07) even as he refused to shut down terrorist groups like the LET.

For this very reason, some Indian analysts have chosen to dub Qayyum as 'His Masters voice', echoing what the Pak military establishment wants to convey to the opinion-makers in New Delhi. It is obvious thus that Musharraf's scheme is to create a smoke screen of peace and reproachment with India while keeping the option of jihad alive in Jammu and Kashmir. Sardar Qayyum, Mujahid-e-Awwal, is one of the pawns in the new game on Jammu and Kashmir being set up by the Pakistan Army.

Whether Qayyum is a pawn or an articulate actor for his country is not an important issue. But the fact remains that all Pakistani leaders, led by Musharraf and including his over-optimistic Foreign Minister Kasuri are speaking this language of peace ad nauseam. May be, having failed to 'wrench/snatch' any further territory of the State from India through repeated wars and then continuing acts of terrorism, they have come to repose some faith in the "peace process" and are just trying to extract some 'face-saving' gains from their 'goodman' Prime Minister Manmohan Singh who has repeatedly ruled out any territorial concession to Islamabad. Let us rest our discussions on the visit of the ageing Mujahid-e-Awwal at this point.

Undoubtedly, Qayyum's was an important visit to New Delhi concerning the issue of Jammu and Kashmir, which is still experiencing considerable terrorist violence. It was natural to devote fair amount of space to discuss various ramifications of this visit, his statements and interviews during his stay, reaction of Indian and Pakistani media and terrorist outfits on either side of the LOC. An interesting feature of his utterances in New Delhi is that he was criticised in both India and Pakistan—even though for different reasons.

A heartening change: Women pick up guns to defend themselves against the Islamist militants

In a heartening development, people have picked up guns themselves to defend themselves against the depredations of the ultras. More importantly, it were the Gujjar women who led the way in this courageous fight against the once-dreaded terrorists.

Subsequently, in some places men too followed their lead.

Gujjar women pick up guns against terrorists: March 2007

A reporter of a daily[35], writing from the twin villages of Marah-Kulali in Hill Kaka ranges in Surankote Tehsil, located near the LOC in the border district of Poonch in Jammu Division of J&K State, pens this evocative, if challenging, introduction to a heartening story of 'Gujjar woman courage' in a lonely, distant and 'forlorn' place:

- "As dark approaches, Munira Begum, a young tribal Muslim Gujjar woman, shuts the door of her small house and prepares to cook the evening meal. As she starts to light the fire, there is a violent knock on the door. Instantly, Munira picks up a gun kept near the chulha (=hearth). Despite a pounding heart, she remembers to cock the rifle and readies her finger on the trigger. In these hills swarming with terrorists (mostly foreign), a knock at any door after dark, brings terror and fear in the lives of the villagers. For this is the time, when terrorists operating in these areas come looking for food, shalter and other worldly comforts.
- "As the knock grows louder, with baited breath and heightened tension and her hand still firmly on the trigger of the rifle, Munira readies herself to take on the unwelcome visitors. In earlier days she would have had no choice but to fulfill the demands for food and other needs of the guntoting militants. Not any more. As she gets closer to the door, she asks sternly, 'who is it?'

  "Me open the door".

Having recognised the voice, she opened the door with a sigh of relief. Reshma Bi has come for some urgent work. Interestingly, Reshma too has a rifle slung across her shoulders as she treads the half-kilometer from her house to Munira's.

For too long now, Munira and other women of this village had faced the brunt of terrorism and remained its worst victims. The yearning for peace and the desire to lead tranquil lives without terrorist violence has moved these Gujjar women to pick up courage—and the gun—against the abominable beasts called terrorists. It is heartening to learn that these brave women have formed an all-women brigade : the first Women Village Defence Committee in the state of Jammu and Kashmir.

As one approaches her village by a serpentine access road, the tall and slender Gujjar women can be seen standing on their roof tops sporting rifle on their shoulders. It indeed must be a pleasant surprise—and an exhilirating experience for a town-bred generation—to come face to face with these simple but courageous women sporting a rifle on one shoulder and a boby on the other, busy carrying out the household chores.

Munira's anguish poured out for the ears of a daily's reporter in her (local) Gojri dialect which is worth recording: "Aawane sann te mengne sann roti, gusal vste paani, pepsi. Asan bada mushqil waqt dekhya (The terrorists, entering our house, demanded food, shelter, hot water for bathing, pepsi etc. In all these years, we witnessed turbulent times and suffered a lot).

The excesses of foreign terrorists on civilians and sexual assaults on local women became increasingly intolerable. Munira's mother-in-law Saden Bi, takes over to fill in details: "When militants descended on our homes, they would ask the menfolk to step out of the houses. If our main resisted, they were beaten up. There was an enormous amount of uncertainty in our lives."

This was not the end of the trauma for these helpless women. These visits framed the vulnerability of these women. Saden Bi recalls. "The dignity and honour of our daughters was at stake. In some households the menfolk work in Saudi Arabia, or in towns of Surankote and Poonch, leading behind the women who live alone. Three years ago, terrorists killed a local priest when he resisted his wife's rape. Around the same time, an old man in the area was killed when he resisted the militants who attempted to snatch a grazing lamb from his herd."

Such stories can be multiplied, if more victims—both men and women—of terrorists' excesses (in the fields of sexual molestation, blood thirst, greed and monetary banalty, and love for rapine) are given a chance to speak out. To wit, an elderly woman who cooked for the terrorists was killed when she asked this gun-toting group to keep their guns away after they had forced themselves inside her house.

Here is Poonch SSP Shiv Darshan Singh Jamwal, exalted over the related developments: "That was a turning point as many men from these villages who were in Saudi Arabia, including the slain priests brother, went to the holy shrine of Mecca and vowed to avenge these killings. They returned and helped the security forces constitute the first ever Women Village Defence Committee in Poonch."

Incidentally, this was also the time when Army had launched Operation Sarpvinash in Hill Kaka area to flush out the militants who had ensconced themselves well in the biggest militant hideouts ever discovered in the 17 year long insurgency in Jammu and Kashmir. The gravity of the situation—and horrendous dimensions of threat posed to India's national security by the fortress like hideouts built by the insurgents in this not-so-remote area—could well be imagined from the fact that the Army units had to use artillery fire in this operation, during which at least 150 foreign militants were killed.

The auother cannot resist the temptation to add these footnotes to this exhilirating development in the Hill Kaka area of Jammu and Kashmir State:

- A complimentary copy of this news story should be sent to Arundhati Roy who is carrying out a vicious campaign against 'Salwan Judam'—an anti-insurgency campaign launched by the State Government of Jharkhand, under which the relatives of the tribals who are killed and raped by the Naxals are given arms to defend themselves. Roy might be a great author, but she is innocent of nation's security concerns. In any case, this one-book wonder is reducing herself to a writer of tracts.

- Second complimentary copy should go to the father-daughter due of the PDP who should learn what a great job women Village Defence Committee (Women VDC) is doing in Hill Kaka. They will stop clamouring for disbandment of all the VDCs in the state.
- Third complimentary copy should go to the Chief of Dukhtran-e-Millat who are presently engaged in a passionate campaign against some brothels—real or imaginary in Srinagar. That outfit should shift focus to the sexual escapades of the terrorists in Jammu and Kashmir, who are playing with the honour and dignity of the entire Kashmiri womanhood.

A heartening change : locals subdue ultras : April 2007

An erstwhile bastion of militants, the Prankote belt of Reasi district of Jammu and Kashmir, is now practically a free zone, reports a daily dated 29 April 2007.[36]

The credit for this heartening change must go to the valour of the locals, mostly Gujjars, who have picked up weapons to prevent the entry of the militants in the belt.

The belt, a cluster of several villages, is one of the most inaccessible parts of the state. Reaching the Prankote area involves more than 8 hours of tough walk from a point on the nearest Reasi-Arnas motorable road.

Prankote grabbed the national media headlines under horrendous circumstances. 28 civilians were brutally murdered on the 17/18 April 1998 night. The news of the gruesome slaughter reached the authorities 10 hours later. And it took more than 24 hours for the security personnel to reach the site of the ghastly massacre, which provoked mass migration of civilians. Over 3,000 people from various villages migrated from the remote hills to the low lying areas of Reasi district.

But the majority of the local communities decided to stay on and fight the mindless militants. "After a long drawn-process, the local population has finally succeeded in driving out militants."

Interestingly, the first challenge against the militants by the local citizens was offered through the locally-made 12 bore guns—popularly known as "country-made" weapons.

Abdul Rashid, who heads a group of local men fighting the militants, says matter-of-factly that sometime back there was little opposition to the militants as they forcibly entered the homes and stayed on for days. After years, the residents of the eleven villages in the belt are experiencing freedom but the threat to their lives still remains. The villagers, who have become a headache for the militants, are on their hit list.

In the surrounding belt, Jehangir, area commander of the HM, has been the longest surviving militant. His 22-strong cadre have frequently threatened the local population. In Dec. 2006 there was an attack by the militants in the belt which injured a civilian, but it was finally repulsed. In Feb. 2007, the militants again made an attempt to cause casualties, but were frustrated yet again.

Atique Mohd., a 24-year-old youth who had confronted the militants in February, puts it honestly : "By the severity of attack, we can well gauge the determination of the militants to eliminate us but we are also motivated and there is no room for being complacent. For us the battle against militancy is far from over and therefore any negligence would mean certain death. Most of the attacks occur at night and therefore one among us always remains awake in respective areas."

Fortunately, the commendable resistance put up by the civilians in Prankote area has not become the object of criticism by 'limosine liberal' and Leftist intellectuals as the 'Salva Judum' has in the distant Chhattisgarh.

Another heartening instance : Women lead resistance in a hotbed of militancy : Mahore : May 2007

A daily[37] of 20 May 2007 carry a story of women leading resistance in a hot bed of militancy in Jammu and Kashmir. The Mahore women told the journalist : "Social diktats forced us to take to arms."

A remote and inaccessible area, Mahore in Reasi district had remained a hotbed of militancy for the last one decade. It was an important high way route for militants to reach other parts of the State. But now the women in this hilly, militancy-infested belt of the State are in the vanguard of resistance against militants.

But much has changed here after the women took to the arms.

20-year-old Praveen Akhtar puts it straight from her heart :

"We picked up weapons after militants tried to impose social dictate on us, and tried to curtail our freedom. There were two options : our succumbing to diktats and changing our life styles. Or, the difficult one of rebelling against them. We opted for the latter. We have snatched our freedom."

As these women learnt the use of rifles, mostly army-discard 303 rifles, they gained confidence, and opposed the militants veil campaign.

Praveen Akhtar's statement and resolve reflected therein are confirmed and supported by Neelu Devi : "We have always been equal partners with men and therefore we are keen on preserving our much-cherished freedom."

Now comes even more heartening revelation consequent to their brave action of deifying the 'dreaded'—a term often thrown in casually but unfailingly by the press while describing all and sundry terrorists/ultras anywhere.

Apart from resisting social diktats, women have given a jolt to militancy in these areas. It seems unbelievable, but it reads and sounds true : "A writ of fear runs among the militant ranks, and no one dared to attack the villages here or even pass through this belt in the last few months. As the ranks women fighting the militants swelled, they, along with the men, outnumbered the militants active in the belt—22. There are 300 locals in the villages of Mahore."

Ghulam Nabi of Tuli brings out another interesting facet of this brave story : Women the worst victims took up the cudgels to begin with. He says : "Many men picked up weapons, encouraged by the fact that women successfully rebelled against the militants. The anger against militants was more among women, who were the worst victims of their diktats."

There is a similar story related earlier of Gujjar women going about their daily chores with rifles slung across their slender but strong shoulders. Now this equally heartening story. Will the trend catch on?

TERRORISTS ALSO KEEP CHANGING AND THINKING AFRESH

It seems terrorist outfits also keep thinking afresh and changing their tactics and strategies as demanded by the circumstances.

Islamic Terrosists Pushing Islam Towards Intolerance

Islam has produced *sufis* and saints like Chishti of Ajmer, Nizamuddin of Delhi, and Baba Farid of Punjab (just to name three only) who have preached interfaith harmony and mutual respect among various religions. Such traditions in Islam draw their followers and adherents from other religions also, especially the Hindus, alongwith the common Muslims, of course.

The Islamist terrorists have never had any use for such liberal strains and tolerant traditions of Islam. They proved this in a telling manner on 10 Nov., 2006 by targeting a religious congregation led by Maulana Abdul Rashid Dawoodi, in Palwama district. That much-vaunted Kashmiriyat too came under attack by this wanton act is of minor import. Many analysts, in any case, did not lay much store by this amorphous, unduly publicised and highly adumbrated concept by its votaries, in the manner of its twin,Punjabiyat. In any case, it was buried fathoms-deep when the terrorists forced lakhs of Kashmiri Pandits out of their homes in the valley—turning them refugees in their own country.

But the larger issue here is the intolerance displayed and spread by the terrorists in the valley (and elsewhere). The provocation for targeting his congregation was the growing popularity of Maulana Dawoodi, who reportedly belongs to the Barelvi School of (Islamic) theology. The preacher draws sustenance from the Sufi tradition of Islam, which has its deep roots in the Valley (as in some other parts of India).

Unlike the Maulana, the terrorists take inspiration from a militant form of Islam which the Saudis have been overtly and covertly encouraging. Known as the Wahabi School of Islam, it seeks to dissociate the religion from the little Islamic traditions that have flourished in Kashmir since time immemorial.[38]

The Wahabis are more doctrinaire as they claim to be solely guided by the Holy Book and other scriptures. Not many people seem to know or realise that in Kashmir, Islam gained its strength through the patrons of *sufism* and other mystic forms of religion.

The terrorists have never displayed any appreciation/ sympathy to the *sufi* traditions of the *State*, because they desire Islam to be a monolithic religion that does not countenance saints and *gurus*. But this is not the first time that the terrorists have attacked a sufi congregation or a shrine. Over a decade ago, in mid-1990s, they showed their utter contempt for such traditions when they forcibly occupied and subsequently burnt down the 14th century shrine dedicated to the patron saint of Kashmir Noor-ul-Din Wali, at Charar-e-Sharief.

Maulana Dawoodi became on anathema to the terrorists since he preached a more tolerant form of Islam, which can coexist with other religions in a multicultural society like Jammu and Kashmir's. And for good measure, his school of Islam also encouraged shrine worship all of which is anathema to the terrorists—avowed practitioners of puritanic/hard line Islam, popularly known as Wahabite or Wahabist Islam which was founded by Abdul-Wahhab (1703?-92?) and flourishes in Saudi Arabia. Expectedly, his teachings was bound to Maulana Dawoodi on the hate-list of the terror-merchant. Consequently, he was in their firing line on 10 Nov. 2006. It does not matter to them that while targeting the preacher, they killed four innocent children and injured over 35 equally-innocent people, who had flocked to the local masjid (= mosque) to hear a religious discourse—incidentally delivered by the Maulana that day. Nothing could be more condemnable then this wanton act of cruelty against a 'soft targst'.

Analysts read meanings into the timing of the attack, coming as it did a week before the foreign secretary-level talks were due to start between India and Pakistan in New Delhi. It can be seen as a warning—and a violent one at that—that the two countries cannot ignore the wishes of the militants/terrorists in any deal or understanding they might arrive at! But it should be equally clear, aver the analysts, that terrorists' machinations cannot be allowed a free run—as seems to be the case so far! The Government must henceforth adopt a more pro-active approach to deal with the terrorist violence and mayhem than it has been able to do so far.

It is widely acknowledge that India, a country that has suffered the ravages and destruction (human and otherwise) wrought in by terrorist, particularly of Islamist variety over the last three decades, beginning 1989, has failed to conceptualise and execute on effective counter terrorism policy. Whatever be the reasons—political mendacity and banalty, vote-bank politics or chicanery practised by individual leaders—is not relevent. It is already late in the day, and India must act fast and furious.

"Enter, Kashmir's New Fidayeens" : Jan 2007

A reporter from Srinagar writes on 3 Jan 2007: "Security forces operating in strife-torn Jammu and Kashmir can take it easy even though there has been an increase in 'fidayeen attacks' in Srinagar—because they are now taking place in the virtual world."[39]

But these, indeed, are trying times for Kashmir! Because, in the entertainment-starved valley, youngsters with a "passion to carry out suicide attacks" are finding an outlet in video/games.

Games such as Delta Force, War of Freedom, Guns Versus Bombs, Midtown Madness, and Commandos' War Game are increasingly popular among youngsters in the age group of 12 to 20. The names of the games, as it were, are common to the terminology in use among the militant groups and separatists. To wit, the game Delta Force owes at least some of its popularity to the fact that it is also the moniker of the elite counter-insurgency Delta Force that operate in Doda. Likewise, "War of Freedom" is an expression often used by separatist Kashmiris to define their struggle.

A Kashmiri youth Gowhar Nazir, 18, of Srinagar's Habba Kadal locality, once a hot bed of separatist insurgency explains: "The modified versions of games such as Delta Force Part II show how to carry out suicide attacks."

Mudasir Zerger is rather direct and says matter-of-factly, "These are games in which we can wage virtual war against the Indian occupation of Kashmir. You carry suicide attacks without getting injured. The excitement is worth the cost of the game." Zerger, of Bohri Kadal, was confiding his thoughts to the daily's reporter.

Delta Force, the game, for example, invites the players to kill 11 commandos. "The commandos, in this game, can use machine guns, tanks, grenades and rockets, and yet the player has to get them all", says an excited Nazir, who finds the game thrilling. "The last commado left standing becomes invisible energy 40 seconds to make it more difficult for the player but I have won at least 50 times", concludes Nazir. He bought the game for Rs. 500.

But many are worried, as students are not attending classes in schools and colleges because they go gaming instead. Zahid Bazaz, (7), who plays Commandos War Game regularly, visits the Blue Sky Game club in Srinagar every other day. He spent even his tuition fee (Rs. 300) to purchase his favourite game.

A well-known psychiatrist of Srinagar Dr. Akash Yousuf offers his take on this destructive passion for this terrorism-encouraging video games: "Their passion for these games stems from the reality they have been exposed to...They have only seen crackdowns, curfews, killings ...hence the love for such games ...most children in Kashmir are already suffering from Post Traumatic Stress Disoroder (PTSD) and these games will affect their mental health adversely" The Doctor concludes, almost justifying this death-wish inclination: "The youngsters are attracted to this 'virtual blood bath' because they do not have access to other forms of entertainment."

This daily's above story is rather sad for more than one reason! Not only is Dr. Yousuf not exceedingly honest in his diagnosis of this fatal attraction among the Muslim Youth of the valley, even the reporter rests content asking no awkward or inconvenient questions of Zerger, Nazir or even Dr. Yousuf, and ends up with a popular cliche: "Cry, beloved Valley, yet again. ...

Some simple questions for Dr. Yourself: "The Valley youngsters only witness Army crackdowns, never bodies of innocent men, women and children brutally tortured and decapitated? They never saw the terrorists occupying a mosque, a holy shrine of a Sufi Saint, or killing a Muslim just emerging from a mosque after offering prayers? They are unaware of the reasons for Army's counter-terrorism operations! Why can't these youngsters visit scenic spots in and outside Srinagar, or go trekking in the forests or on the mountain tops? Are they unaware of cinema houses in the valley, or 24-hour TV Channels"?

May be, the Doctor or the Reporter have their self-imposed restraints! Possibly, and at least subconsciously, the both are aware of potential threat of a fatwa from an obscure *maulvi* or a *mulla*! And worse still, they can never ignore a shower of bullets from some enraged militant! To be charitable, may be, the daily in question has certain guidelines for its reporters to be on the side of discretion.

To sum it up, all human beings operate within certain paradigms imposed externally or internalised.

Nepali Maoist Held in J & K: A First: Feb 2007

Defence PRO Lt Col AK Mathur told the press on 13 Feb 2007 that a Nepali Maoist, Pasang Lama, a resident of Humla district near Kathmandu, was arrested by the Army in Baramulla. This was the first time that a Nepali Maoist had been arrested in Kashmir for having links with the terrorists there. Mathur gave the following information about Pasang:

- He was acting as a conduit between the Pak ISI, Nepali Maoists and insurgents of North-East. He used to purchase arms from Kashmiri ultras and sell them to Nepali Maoists at a profit.
- He was active over the past five years and was constantly in contact with the LET terrorists. They were planning to induct Nepali Maoists into the Valley to learn the making and planting of IEDs.
- In Delhi, Pasang stayed in G Block, Laxmi Nagar (East Delhi) on the Vikas Marg. He was a frequent visitor to Kashmir and had recently stayed in Srinagar for three months. He used to visit far-flung villages to make deals. He was acting in the guise of a shawl dealer."

His interrogation revealed that in Mar 2007 he made a huge purchase of arms (AK-47 assault rifle's, hand granades and some rocket launchers) from the Kashmiri ultras for Rs. 4,77,000. The consignment was delivered to him in New Delhi in a fruit truck, and his friend Kunjup Tsering took it to Nepal. After this success, he returned to the valley to strike another deal. He had been helped by one Younis Ahmad of Srinagar.

He was trapped when Ahmad and Pasang were lured to Baramulla for a fake arms deal, which was finalised for one AK-47 (Rs. 60,000), four hand grenades (Rs. 200 each) and one pistol (Rs. 30,000). This time, Pasang was to see the weapons in Baramulla, pay half the amount in advance and the rest when he gets the consignment in Delhi.

Pasang came to see the weapons with a bearer cheque of Rs. 20,000 Lal Chowk Branch of Vijaya Bank, with cheque No. 879867 dated 30.12.2006 drawn in favour of Ramesh. The entire transaction was recorded on video camera and Pasang was arrested by the Army. His aide Ahmad, who was called to another place was also arrested with an amount of Rs. 50,000.[40]

Pasang's links with an advocate of Jammu and Kashmir High Court are also under scanner. The call details from Pasang's Delhi mobile could also help nab other culprits.

MHA 2006 Report Sees Shift in Terrorist Strategy: Apr 2007

The MHA Report 2006 sees a shift in the militants' strategy: using Overground workers to target tourists and pilgrims. While there were fewer fidayeen and car bomb attacks in 2006, more grenades were thrown through the outsourcing as explained above.

The MHA assessment said the Pak-based and ISI-sponsored LET, ABDR and HM continued to attack *soft targets*.

But *infiltration declined morginally* because of heightened surveillance and more focussed counter-operations on the LOC. As many as 593 terrorists, including over 50 senior commanders, were neutralised during 2006, the document said.[41]

Militants' New Strategy: Outsourcing Terrorism: Apr 2007

The militant's think-tanks and planners seem to be wellprepared to face and overcome the difficulties that may come in the way of their plans, policies and operations to reach and realise their objectives. Its latest example was disclosed by the J and K police on 10 Apr 2007: Outsourcing of terrorism.

Infiltration from across the border has dwindled (if not dried up) and the militant numbers show a steep dip across the Kashmir valley, but security agencies are faced with this new challenge of outsourcing of violence by the terrorists.[42]

The *modus operandi* is simple: "militants are frequently recruiting 'youngmen with a clean slate' to hurl grenades, plant IEDs, commit target killings and then get back to their routine lives." Since many of them have no record, hence are not on the security radar. All this renders their detection that much difficult.

DGP, J & K Police Gopal Sharma talked to a daily about the problems created by this new challenge and some related issues: "Outsourcing of grenade and IED attacks has changed the complexion of militancy substantially. It is now a very local affair, and is amenable to a localised response. Militants choose the outsourcing as these new 'actors' are insiders, neither going across the border for arms training nor going underground to commit the violent acts. Their motivation is the macho image associated with violence, or pure indoctrination. Money, of course, is also a major attraction given that majority of them are from poor, divided families."

He further added, "There are instances where we are supporting the families of these youngmen after they were arrested only because we don't want militants to come, support them and create' new networks."

There were reports of 39 boys having been recruited in Sopore. The police did not arrest them and after necessary identification called in their parents "so that they can get to their children before the militants could."

In fact, this shift in militants' tacties is visible on the ground as well. Most of the intelligence agencies' estimates place the number of active militants in the State between 1000 and 1200. In the Valley, most of them are concentrated in hubs like the Bandipore forest in north Kashmir; the upper reaches of Tral and Shopian; Panzgam-Wachi-Nain Batapore in Pulwama in South Kashmir; or the mountains of Lolab Valley near the LOC. Only a few are found operating in towns and Srinagar city. The DGP gave examples of some recent arrests that prove the trend.

Azad Ahmad Wani, 18, of Gojwara in Srinagar who had worked as a salesman, was arrested with a pistol after investigations revealed that he had allegedly killed seven policemen across Srinagar during 2006. In all these cases, Wani had driven across Srinagar city centre on a bicycle and returned home after shooting the policemen. Police allege Wani ferried money, weapons and even militants from Bandipore and Tral to Srinagar.

Wani had dropped out of school in class IX because of poverty. His parents divorced, leaving his mother and sisters to fend for themselves. His mother Hamida Bano, a cancer patient, rented a room in her house in down town Gojwara to a man who claimed to be a fruit merchant. This tenant, in fact, was a Pakistani militant, Ansar. He got Wani, then 14, in touch with JEM militants without disclosing their identity.

Soon, Ansar was arrested by the police which raided Wani's house and recovered arms from the room. His ailing mother was booked because she was the only adult in the family. Wani was hired by the JEM after they visited him several times at a shop he worked at. Angry over police action against his mother, Wani agreed to carry out the strikes on behalf of Jaish. After his arrest, the family lost the only source of their income. Although Wani was sent to jail, the police support the family so that "militants do not come and exploit their situation".

Mohd Afzal Rather, 20, was arrested while trying to hurl a grenade at a vehicle near Srinagar's Tourist Reception Centre. A Class XII student, Rather got acquainted with a Pak-trained militant who used to frequent his neighbourhood. Police says he was soon given arms training and assigned to hurl grenades in Srinagar. He was also allegedly involved in a target killing in Sopore. His father, Nazir Ahmad Rather, police says, suffers from brain cancer, and the family crisis meant nobody kept a vigil on his activities.

Similar is the story of Sameer Haqani, 18, from Sheikhpora in Badgam. Arrested with a grenade in Nawgam, Haqani is serving time in a Jammu prison. Police say his family is poor, divided by a dispute between his parents. After Haqani's arrest, police cracked a bigger militant network and recovered EIDs rigged to mobile phones. Police said the militant strategy was to "outsource" planting of these bombs, too.

Tariq Ahmad Baba, 22, a resident of Pattan, was arrested after militants sent him to Srinagar to throw grenades at selected targets. Baba had no previous record of any involvement in militancy. Police say he was not even their radar because of his "absolutely good behaviour" in his village. Now he is in custody at Karan Nagar police station.

The abve account not only discloses how militants exploit the poverty and adverse circumstances of a family to snatch away their son from its folds to use him for their sinister motives, but also the fact of police acting as good samaritan even if the aim is to ensure that the family in question does not slip into the clutches of the terrorist outfits.

The security forces must also work out new ways to counter the outsourcing practices embraced by the Islamic outlaws.

J & K Ultras Seek Maoists Help: Apr 2007

Kashmiri Islamic terrorists are quick to explore new avenues if they seem to be heading for a dead end to reach their desideratum. With the Pakistani support for right to self-determination of Kashmiri people fading away, they promptly sought the Indian Maoist's cooperation to achieve their political goal.

A series of meeting took place between the leaders of LET and JEM and the CPI (Maoists) for complementing the movement of Kashmiri right to plabiscite as envisaged in the UN resolution. The former asked the Maoists to open their "shops" in the Valley to actively back this demand.[43]

As if the cooperation is already in operation a recent raid on some hideouts of the ultras yielded some Maoist literature on the issue of 'nationality', wherein the Maoists declare their favourite theme: Right of self-determination for all "oppressed nationalities".

Analysts are skeptical about the success of Maoists in the valley, where the 'class struggle' is hardly relevent as in some other part of the country, but they can exploit the situation to politically weaken India in the State.

MHA officials are concerned that the Maoists could impart vital training to the Kashmiri militants in mine blast techniques that they themselves learnt from the LTTE.

Though the presence of Communists in the Valley is ageold, but after the advent of separatist movement, there were few takers for the ideology of class struggle among the Muslim society of the valley.

Aware of this not-so-happy a history in the Valley, the Maoists have started seeing dreams of fresh hope: With the dwindling support of Pakistan to the Kashmiri insurgents, a scope for a fresh movement may emerge and they can exploit both the econmic divide and the popular slogan like 'right to self-determination' for creating their own support base.

Luckless Pandits : Refugees in their own Country

One cannot easily imagine the plight of the people who have been rendered homeless refugees within their own country.

Kashmiri Pandits: Living through their Memories: May 2007

Kashmiri Pandits experienced the 'Partition' twice. During both these cataclysmic events, the first a reality and the second one a virtual reality, Kashmiri Pandits came to Delhi. The first wave in 1947 was part of a larger influx from areas that were awarded to Pakistan. In 1990, more than 100,000 Pandits left the valley, running for their lives. This was in consequence to the Islamic terrorists targeting the Valley Pandits and killing them mercilessly. Seeing no saviour around, most of them flocked to Delhi.

For the older generation, which had to abandon their lives' work, the transition has been devastating. They were depressed for years. One of that generation says: "More or less, we have reconciled to the fact that there is no going back. The place may be beautiful, the water may be sweet, the weather may be 22, but you cannot live there" Memories are all they have!

A member of the younger generation, in his 30s, is matter-of-factly on the issue. "I am glad they left Kashmir when they did because life had become unbearable in the Valley. May be, it is pessimistic of me, very fatalistic of me, but I have no inclination to go back" He talks bitterly of militancy that caused thousands of Kashmiris to flee their homeland. "For my generation, move to Delhi was expected ...we had to go for work. But we did not expect to be shut out completely, in this manner."

To make up for the loss of their homeland, the community has set down strong roots. They have built temples like the Hari Parbat Temple in Faridabad, mirroring the one left in Kashmir, and a popular magazine, *Kashmir Samachar* keeps the community connected.

But while the memory lives through the grand parents and parents, the newest generation, born or raised in Delhi, know their part only through stories.

Some Painful Facts

- Kashmiri Pandits' estimated strength living in Delhi 500,000.
- No. of years since the terrorists forced them out of the Valley:17

Luckless Pandits Continue Leaving Kashmir: May 2007

"While there are talks at political and social forums about the return of the Pandits, the ground reality is that only 7,000 of them are now left in the Valley", said the President of Hindu Welfare Society (HWS), ML Bhatt on 16 May 2007. This Srinagar-based Society was formed in 1994 for the cause of those who preferred to stay back.

So the silent migration is still on, which has left only 7,000 Pandits in the Valley as of Mar 2007 against 13,000 in 2002. These 7,000 are residing in 270 pockets of villages and towns, including 63 families in Srinagar, 23 in Badgam and 18 in Matan.

According to the Census conducted by the HWS, following the mass exodus of the Pandits from 1989 to 1990 during

Governor Jagmohan's rule, 25,000 Pandits were left in 1991 as they had decided against migration. These 25,000 of 1991 figure have now been reduced to a mere 7,000, most of them poor and uneducated lot from the rural and backward areas. These hapless 7,000 stayed back risking their limbs and lives simply because, they had no means to leave.

Close on the heels of the recent visit of 25-old Kashmiri Pandits to the valley, who are presently residing at Mishriwala and other refugee camps, Bhatt said the MLA of the Bomai constituency tried to encash the situation by honouring them at a public function and announcing that these men would soon be bringing back their families to the Valley.

Bhatt also pointed out that members of his Society had also met with Congress President and UPA Chairman Sonia Gandhi in October 2006, requesting her for compensation to a ten poor families residing in the refugee camps in Srinagar and Matan. She had then instructed her party's state affairs' incharge Ambika Soni to do the needful, but nothing has happened till now, during the last seven months.

Are things Looking up in Jammu and Kashmir

Some analysts feel optimism in the air. Do the following developments justify the hope?

Autonomy or Self-Rule: Jammu and Kashmir Debate 2006

This is an old debate in the State, going back to pre-1947 period when Sheikh Abdullah-led movement was agitating for genuine power for people from the Ruler, Maharaja Hari Singh. Poste-1947, leaving aside Sheikh's arrest and reinstatement, the real thing started when Farooq Abdullah had a unanimous resolution passed by the State Assembly during the NDA Rule (1998-2004) at New Delhi and the Vajpayee Ministry rejected it without ceremony. This debate got a fresh lease of life when Indo-Pak peace talks started in 2004 and Gen Musharraf started talking about self-rule for Jammu and Kashmir.

Here we discuss the mid - 2006 edition of the debate between the National Conference (NC) and People's Democratic Party (PDP). The PDP's idea of self-rule "is altogether different from the concept of greater autonomy of the NCP", said Mr. GH Mir, former minister and a member of the committee consituted by the PDP for drafting the document on self-rule.

He explained (Jammu. 8.10.06) self-rule idea did not seek the abolition of the jurisdiction of the Election Commission, the Supreme Court and the Comptroller and Auditor General of India in Jammu and Kashmir. Neither did they favour the change of nomenclature of the Chief Minis to the Prime Minister and the Governor to the Sadr-i-Riyasat. But they supported an elected Governor though the electoral college for electing the constitutional head of the State was yet to be discussed and determined. If that was done, the people from all the three regions of the State would have the satisfaction of having a man from their own State as the Governor.

On the economic front, the PDP wanted to ensure the economic sustainability for the people of the State which could be achieved if Jammu and Kashmir was constituted into a trade-free zone, with powers to enter into trade agreement with any country.

The self-rule document of the PDP, presently under finalisation, favoured an elaborate discussion on the Indus Water Treaty of 1960 in the light of its adverse impact on the State's economy and its people. Since the Treaty could not be scrapped, the annual loss suffered by the State because of it needed to be assessed and the State accordingly by New Delhi. Once the compensatory amount started coming into the state's coffers, it will start marching partly in the direction J of economic resurgence and self-reliance.

Mir said, 'Apne Log, Apne Raj' concept could meaningfully satisfy the aspirations of the people.

Asked by the pressmen if PDF Patron Mufti Mohd Sayeed,

scheduled to visit New York from 29 October 2006 as member of the Indian O n cro delegation to the UN General Assembly, would circulate the document on self-rule among the deplomats and others on the sidelines of the General Assembly session, Mir said : "Why should he carry copies of the documents? Once it was ready, it had to be discussed with the government." Was there need to discuss it with Islamabad? "It was for the government to do that," was the reply.

A brief discussion of all such issues is deemed necessary since they often lead to a contentious atmosphere in the state which can then be twisted and exploited by the vested interests to vitiate its calm and peace. And that is something the anti-Indian elements and terrorists look for and a wait eagerly to foment more violence in the troubled State.

NC Pulls Out of Working Groups and RTCs

The National Conference (NC) announced 24 October 2006 that, henceforth, it would not take part in the meetings of the Working Groups (WGs) and Round Table Conferences (RTCs). The decision was taken by the NC, said its Chief Omar Abdullah, in view of the "failure of the Centre in ensuring zero tolerance to human rights abuses in the state."

The decision of the NC, the single largest party in the Assembly even though it is in the opposition, should be seen as a serious setback to the Centre's efforts to resolve the Kashmir issue. When asked if the NC would reconsider its decision if some assurance was given by the Centre, Abdullah said. "We are not saying we want the meetings to be boycotted, but we have suspended our participation .... The NC wants actual changes on the ground, which are not visible at the moment."[44]

Working Groups announced by the Prime Minister during his last visit to the State have as yet not been constituted, and two rounds of the RTC have already been held

Musharraf's 4-point Formula to Resolve Kashmir Issue : Dec 2006

The General in a TV interview said "his country is ready to withdraw its claim on Kashmir provided his 4-point formula was accepted for the resolution of Kashmir issue.

- Softening of borders between two parts of Kashmir.
- Demilitarisation of the whole Kashmir region.
- Free movement of the people. *I*
- Joint surveillance of the region by India, Pakistan and representatives of Kashmir.

The Musharraf formula continues to draw flak from hardline separatist circles in Kashmir. Chairman of a faction of APHC Syed Ali Geelani is the latest to criticise General. He said on 7

Dec : "The formula exhibits General's lack of confidence in his own people. This is clearly an Indian agenda and boils down to status quo in the disputed region. It was turn on Pakistan's 60-year stand on Kashmir. ... Post-9/11, Gen Musharraf has developed a timidity syndrome... He is afraid of the US and fearful of growing economy and military might of India."

But Geelani's rivals in the separatist camp have taken an entirely different stance on General's formula. "It is a good beginning, and would pave the way for the peaceful resolution of Kashmir issue", said the former APHC chairman and senior leader of Mirwaiz—led faction, Prof. Abdul Ghani.

Mirwaiz Visits North Ireland: Dec 2006

Mirwaiz Umar Farooq, 32, Kashmir's Chief Muslim cleric and Chairman of his faction of APHC, left for Belfast on 10 Dec 2006 to study the Good Friday Peace Agreement. The week-long trip has been sponsored by the British Commonwealth and Foreign Office.

During his stay in Belfast, he would meet the leaders nf.various political parties including Sinn Fein's Gerry Adams as also leaders of the Democratic Unionist Party, the only big political party of Ireland which had opposed the Agreement.

He said he was keen to find a negotiated settlement of Kashmir issue. It was precisely with this objective in mind that his APHC faction was in the process of studying the recent peace agreements arrived directly or through international mediations on other vexed issues across the world, such as the Dayton Peace Accord on Bosnia and Herzegovina.

Jammu and Kashmir : Is Reconciliation Round the Corner : Apr-May 2007

This seems to be the season for political soothsayers on the prospects of India and Pakistan reaching an agreement on the solution of the Kashmir issue. If we are to go by Pak Foreign Minister Kasuri's excessive optimism, solution is a matter of weeks, if not days, he said in Mar 2007. For demands of realism on such politically sensitive issues, Indian Prime Minister had to officially say that there is no such solution on the table and we do not see the things in the way as some people across the border see them.

Despite this note of caution from the Prime Minister and a kind of disclaimer issued by him, the BJP still decided on a warning to him against any secret understanding with Gen Musharraf to come to a hasty, patch work agreement against India's declared policy.

Again, it is a known fact that a plethora of NGOs and individual do-gooders are active in the peace-making field besides more than one officially-sanctioned back channels. In this crowded field, it is no surprise that the print media too have decided to join the fun and prognosticate a "reconciliation rush."[45]

The analyst says "with India and/Pakistan fast on a reconciliation path, mostly through back channel diplomacy on the Kashmir dispute, a new response is emerging from both separatist and mainstream political groups in Jammu and Kashmir."

If political groups are organising public meetings/rallies, mainly to remain "relevant" to the new emerging realities, the separatist outfits are miffed with the State Government for either disallowing or disrupting their public gatherings.

Statistically speaking, in Apr 2007 alone, nearly five dozen meetings were organised by the political groups and the parties - mostly pro-India - led by the mainstreamers like the NC, Congress and POP. On the other hand, we see JKLF Chief Yasin Malik bitterly telling reporters in Srinagar on 7 May : "Police did not allow us to conduct our mass contact programme - Safar-e-Azadi (= Journey of Freedom) - last weekned. The Government not only allows but also facilitates rallies (of mainstream politicians) in Kashmir. But our gatherings are being targeted."

The new waive of public meetings by parties like NCP, Congress, PDP etc seems to be election—oriented as well, as the Assembly polls are due in 2008. These meetings, analysts believe, simultaneously create more and more space for political manoeuvring at a time when there is a strong feeling in the establishment that this is the ripe time for consolidating the gains in the security situation during the last few years in the form of demilitarisation - at least progressively.

With increasing public interaction, the state parties should find it easier to reconcile with the ongoing peace process.

Political Analysis : Is Jigsaw Puzzle Falling in Place? Early 2007 (Crystalgazing on Kashmir's Future)

If military analysts were looking closely at the J & K situation through the framework, of the counter-insurgency operation during the year 2006, their civilian counterparts were looking at the Kashmir polity through a political prism. In Dec 2006, one of them puts it colourfully and imaginatively, if not with great clarity and precision:[46]

> "Behind the veils of secrecy, the shapes and colours of Jammu and Kashmir's future are starting to reveal themselves. Two governments, their covert services, terrorists, politicians and a small circles of mediators seem to have succeeded in gathering together pieces of Jammu and Kashmir peace puzzle from the far corners to which they were flung by the violent jehad that began in 1990. No one outside this magic circle of peace makers - and perhaps not even they - seems to have much idea of just how the final picture will appear. Yet it is impossible not to discern that history is, in fact, being made."

It may not be out of place here to mention the fact that too many people are engaging themselves in mediatory efforts to help India and Pakistan to find a solution to the vexed Kashmir issue - or is it "dispute"? Yet again, while Pakistan keep talking of the need to involve a third party in the dispute, India is equally emphatic in rejecting any third party .n role in the issue. Even then, despite India's emphatic rejection, too many foreign - based think - tanks and influential individuals keep insisting on offering their services for mediatory roles, and even working out one solution after another to resolve the dispute. Then there are seminars galore, here, there and everywhere, to discuss and offer solutions on the issue to New Delhi and Islamabad. Not to speak of the foreign individual and institutional dogooders, even certain governments particularly the US, UK and the EU, continue offering their services, of of course in the name of 'facilitatory role', being aware of the Indian sensitivity on the question.

Like the foreign field, the domestic one too is replete with the do-gooders offering their services to find solution to the Kashmir issue. Only a few are mentioned here. One is led by a former Naval Chief, now a peacenik, who mostly seem to be supporting Pakistan on the Kashmir issue and a 'Gandhian' Lady who usually accompanies the Indian and foreign dignitaries visiting the Mahatma's mausoleum. One remembers, yet again, Lt General who, speaking at a seminar in Delhi in Aug 2004 that "you should be hearing about final solution of Kashmir, on which I have been working on for years, within months if not weeks!" We are still waiting. These two should be good enough illustrations of the NGOs and individuals bending their energies on solving the Kashmir issue. Then there are Track Two diplomacy active in the field.

This somewhat longish but no less relevant aside can't be allowed to rest without mentioning the "exertions" of Pak Foreign Minister Kasuri who, besides mouthing inanities—made popular by his loss Gen Musharraf—like "the two countries must show statesmanship", "both countries must show flexibility," etc., occasionally indulges in very suggestive and alluring kite flying through statements which are rather graphic, almost titillating. Two should suffice for this account. In Feb 2007, he said "we are discussing a proposal with India on Kashmir, whose details are known to only four people in Pakistan." The newspapers were busy for the next week identifying these "four" Pakistanis. In mid-Apr 2007, he came out with such a stunning statement, "Mutually agreed solution will be publicly announced within days", that Indian Prime Minister had to issue a contradiction of sorts, "Certain statements made across the border are not within our knowledge."

Picking up the narration and returning to the political crystal gazing, an important development was that the long-stalled working group on Centre-State relations set up by the Prime Minister Manmohan Singh began its work in New Delhi on 13 Dec 2006. In coming months, the Working Group, chaired by Justice Saghir Ahmad, will hear submissions from parties such as the Congress, the POP, the CPI (M) on their vision for the future. Even though the NC has chosen to boycott the proceedings, citing concerns about continued human rights violations in the State, the Party's past proposals on the autonomy for the State will certainly inform the discussions.

President Musharraf, in turn, has expressed his willingness to drop all Pakistani claims to Jammu and Kashmir if four conditions are met:

- Autonomy or self-rule, presumably on both sides of the LOC.
- Free movements across the LOC.
- Joint supervision, a still undefined idea that presumably will expand existing mechanism for border management, water regulation and trade to other areas of interest.
- Phased demilitarisation, linked to a de-escalation of violence.

Pakistan's military ruler seems to be preparing his people for a settlement wip short of that country's stated demands. Foreign Office spokesperson Tasnim Aslam had recpatly surprised the audience at her press conference by declaring *suo motto* that Pakistan had never laid formal claim to Jammu and Kashmir, an assertion mat is factually accurate but "is also certain to generate a furore in Pakistan." Some reports suggested Gen Musharraf's ideas are not different, in their broad-strokes emphasis, to the content of a secret paper handed over to Islamabad by Manmohan Singh's government for exploratory discussions on how far India could go.

On its part, APHC (Umar Farooq or Moderate) has been driving increasingly closer to ideas such as self-governance, a formation fairly similar to NC's demand for autonomy or PDP's call for self-rule. At a press conference in early Dec 2006 in Srinagar, APHC leader Abdul Gani Butt sought "a debate over self-governance at the people's level to develop a broader consensus in this part of Kashmir and that (Pakistan-occupied) part of Kashmir." Intriguingly, he argued that rejecting the self-governance idea would end up marginalising secessionist voices. "We must collectively show India and Pakistan that the peace path passes through Kashmir", he asserted, "or else we may be swept aside."

The year 2006 saw the lowest level of violence since the 1989. A little less 1000 people died in the fighting in the state, putting the conflict below the threshold of common sholarly definition of what constitutes a war. Even then it will be too early and too optimistic for any analyst to say that India has seen the end of the tunnel. Formidable challenge of ending terrorist violence remains, "and a failure could only too easily undo all that has been achieved so far."

The perils of effusive optimism can be seen by citing just one instance. In Oct 2006, Mohd Ashraf Shah, a top Hizb-ul-Mujahideen (HM) commander, a Divisional Commander, told a confidant a few days before Eid, "Next week, this war will end" Less than two months later, Shah's bullet-ridden body lay inside a safe house (28 November, in Srinagar) he had been using since August for a series of meetings with polticians linked to the ruling PDP to work out a peace deal with the HM. His sincere exertions had ended in bling alley. His gory end reflected the inability of Shah and his ilk to compel terrorist groups to join the peace process, forsaking arms they are so used to wielding for years and years.

In the summer of 1991, soon after he had completed his final-year school education, Shah abandoned his home in the South Kashmir village of Jablipora (also, Zabalpora), and his aspirations of becoming a doctor, to train at a HM terror camp near Muzaffarabad in PoK. By 2001, he was leading the HM's terror operations in Rajouri and Poonch, operating under the code name 'Sohail Faisal'. He took charge of the strategically vital South Kashmir division - the HM's strongest and most affluent command - after his predecessor Shabbir Bhaduri, was killed in a Feb 2005 encounter.

Shah soon displayed his exceptional covert warfare skills, forging an alliance with the LET that facilitated a series of successful car-bomb attacks across southern and central Kashmir. His cadre demonstrated extreme brutality that was increasingly needed to put down growing public anger against terrorism, beheading suspected informers, shooting dissenters, and even bombing "anti-Islamist Sufi clerics."

But privately, Shah had been sending grim messages to his boss, HM Amir-i-Jihad Mohd Yusuf Shah, who operates using the vain glorious *nom de guerre* Syed Salahuddin, after the 12th century warrior who liberated Jerusalem from the crusaders.

He told the latter : "HM cadres were demoralised and desperate; we must listen to our friends in the POP, put a ceasefire in place, and come to the negotiation table."

It was obvious that Shah's masters were listening to what their field commanders had to say. It is clear from the points made by Salahuddin in an interview to the Srinagar-based Current News Service on 27 Aug 2006:

- HM is ready to announce a truce even today, but for that India will have to accept our three conditions.
  1. Prisoners should be released unconditionally.
  2. Strength of the troops should be cut down to the pre-1989 level.
  3. Human rights violations should be stopped.
- "I took up the gun as a last resort. I would be happiest person if guns on both the sides stop roaring."
- He seemed willing to drop his demand, conveyed through intermediaries to the RAW (India's external covert service) for talks in a West Asian country, saying "what is important is not the venue but the) agenda of the talks."

In the interview, he dropped several long-standing pre-conditions for a ceasefire : India respect the right of self determination of Kashmiris; affirm thafno solution is possible within the constitution; withdraw all forces; and join a 3-way dialogue with Pakistan and jehadis.

The language of the 27 August interview seemed to offer a breakthrough. Even as mainstream politicians urged New Delhi to meet the HM half-way, Salahuddin backtracked. Three days after the interview was given, United Jihad Council (UJC) spokesperson Syed Sadaqat Husain told the Srinagar-based Kashmir News Service that the HM Chief "had not offered a cease fire." Husain claimed that Salahuddin, "while responding to a question said that the UJC does not believe in [initiating [a] ceasefire for the sake of [a] ceasefire." All the old preconditions remained in place, he asserted.

Interestingly, Salahuddin remained silent, evidently shouted down by Islamist hardliners. More importantly, hours before

Husain's comments, the chief secessionist leader of them all, Syed Ali Shah Geelani political patron of the HM, had dismissed the ceasefire proposal with contempt. At a rally, he hailed the sacrifice of "martyrs to a just and sacred cause." Geelani also rejected the HM's cell for two APHC factions to join hands, "unity can only be forged with thóse ppople who support our demand for the right to self-determination."

It bears emphasis that while Divisional Commander Shah was pushing for an Bid cease fire, his Amir-i-Jehad had adopted comparatively softer line on so many aspects of the issue in his August interview :

- For the first time, he said the HM was ready to discuss with New Delhi a solution other than the UN-mandated plebiscite.
- He even suggested the HM would be willing to contest an internationally supervised election.

It needs to be understood that this softening of the HM's stance on the Kashmir issue had its reason, nay compulsions : changed circumstances in Pakistan. Friction between the UJC and its patrons in the ISI Directorate become public in Mar 2006, when 18 top jehad commanders staged an unprecedented public protest in Muzaffarabad, which followed an ISI decision to terminate monthly subsidies, ranging from Rs. 400,000 to Rs. 3000,000 to Islamist terror groups operating against India.

Mohd Ashraf Shad (of the HM) led the protests, sharing the platform with the following leaders of some other outfits.

• Mohd Zaki-ur-Rahman	LET
• Abdul Rahman	JEM
• Maulana Farooq Kashmiri	HUM
• Mushtaq Ahmad Zargar	al-Umar(AUM)
• Bilal Ahmad Beig	J and K Islamic Front
• Bakht Zamin Khan	ABDR

During these protests, UJC spokesperson Mohd Kalimullah told an Indian fortnightly[47] : "Protestors want Musharraf to reverse policies that dishonoured a war in which 100,000 Kashmiris have sacrificed their lives. Unless he announces that

Pakistan's political and moral support for the *Mujahideen* in Kashmir will continue, our leaders will remain on hunger strike. We will not back down."

But warnings from the ISI led the protesters to call off the protests. Even though terrorist groups continued to mount large-scale offensive operations against India, they failed to secure any additional funds and weapons.

An investigation by Pakistan's *Herald* magazine, the details of which ^ ^ were published in Aug 2006, said there was a mood of lethargy and disorientation" at jehadi training camps.

By May 2006, the UJC was apoplectic about Pakistan government's "weak and apologetic" policies on Jammu and Kashmir, as well as the "pointless moderation" of secessionist politicons. The UJC was obviously frustrated, when it said : "Some so-called moderates are playing political showmen and keep knocking at New Delhi's door. They are part of Indian cunnmgness." Clearly, the terrorist coalition was in trouble.

Salahuddin was aware of what was going on. Under intense pressure from the US to dismantle the infrastructure of Islamist terrorist groups in Pakistan, Musharraf simply could not afford to continue to subsidise the jehad in Jammu and Kashmir. He had his compulsions, and accordingly had formulated certain strategies : to use peace settlement with India, bearing the imprimature of the APHC (Umar Farooq's, obviously), against outfits such as the HM. The peace deal will allow Musharraf to crack the whip against terrorists without raising a serious battle within Pakistan. To the individuals like the Chief of HM, the next step was self obvious : Unless the HM leadership cut its own deal, and soon, it would be left out in the cold.

It was with such cold calculations that Mohd Yusuf Shah had offered a ceasefire in his August interview, which he subsequently - as detailed above - could not deliver. For one, HM's allies in the UJC had no political stakes in Jammu and Kashmir, and therefore little to gain from joining the peace process. A joint statement issued by the front organisation of the LETfAUM and the Jammu and Kashmir Islamic Front attacked the HM for making "pointless calls for ceasefire." Without the support of these groups, a ceasefire was pointless. The Lashkar, after all, had demonstrated its military capability to undermine any movement towards peace during the Ramzan ceasefire of 2000, when violence against civilians rose to record levels. The ISI, then as now, refused to rein in the Lashkar under its well-argued policy : dismantling the jehad would relieve all pressure on India to make concessions on the Kashmir issue.

By October, Yusuf Shah was forced to revert to his earlier positions, and he did so with a vengeance. He not only rejected "any thing under the Indian constitution," but also described plans for self-rule - a formulation that had secured the support of Musharraf - as a "document of slavery."

While this rejectionist posture was driven in part by the HM's need not to alienate its allies in Pakistan, it was also due to serious internal problems. For a ceasefire to work, its central leadership "have to be able to compel its field cadre to locate to predetermined positions and then to punish ceasefire violators. However, its highly criminalised field units were making cash hand-over from extortion and organised crime - and the cash-strapped central leadership could not complain. In turn, field units themselves were deeply divided, often due to ego hassles. Its southern division commander bitterly resented the fact that his subordinate in Poonch, Mohd Yunus, was made the overall commander for Jammu and Kashmir.

There were reasons for this out-of-tum promotion for Yunus. He had served as the Amir-i-Jihad's chauffeur in Pakistan and came from a family with a long history of service to the Islamist Jamaat-e-Islami, and these links counted more than pure combat experience.

In the wake of southern division commander's death, the political divisions in the HM command on dialogue had mainfested themselves down the terror group's command structure. There was a stalemate on the question of selecting Ashraf Shah's successor. HM leaders were unable to take a decision in Nov 2006 on the competing claims of hawks and doves to succeed the killed terrorist - Divisional Commander Shah. It was no surprise that Javed 'Seepan' Sheikh, an Anantnag-based policeman-turned-terrorist "who strongly favours dialogue, and Pulwama District Commander Parvez Dar, a hard liner who favours escalating, violence, have put in claims to lead the HM's largest unit". A second meeting to decide on the succession issue had to be called in December, and meanwhile Tral-based District Commander Hanif Khan was appointed acting divisional commander.

What is the situation on the peace process front? It may not be trotting, but it is certainly moving forward - even if by inches. Third round-table conference was held on 24 Apr 2007. Expectedly, even the Umar Farooq - faction of the APHC chose to stay away. Its main agenda was to examine the recommendations made by the working groups.

It is interesting to study the stance of three main political actors -NC, Congress and PDP - on the peace process..Each of these perfectly understands that it holds out enormous dividends - but also great risks. How?

- Should the NC be able to advertise a final settlement as indication of its autonomy plank, the Party would region its status as the natural party of government in Jammu and Kashmir. One needs to remember that as the ruling party, it had the State Assembly pass a very comprehensive resolution on autonomy - even though parts of it were totally unacceptable to then ruling coalition of the NDA.
- PDP is well aware that conjuring up a successful peace deal offers it the hope of reaching out of its South Kashmir strong held and challenging the NC state-wide. At the same time, it does not want it to happen when the Congress, its coalition partner, is in the saddle. It is too big a prize to leave it to others. That, perhaps, is the reason that it is complicating the issues one after the other : First the damand for the troop pull out and then disbandment of Village Defence Committees (VDC's).
- Undoubtedly, the Congress, in both Srinagar and New Delhi, is equally aware of the sheer size of the peace prize. Yet none can risk seeing its adversaries walk away with the reward.

For the secessionist outfits, the stakes are even higher. A senior secessionist" leader explained his quandry to a fortnight : "Pakistan's decision to endorse slogans such as self-governance and autonomy leaves us with no space at all. We have been left with no room for manoeuvre, for the mainstream parties have already taken up the slogans that we would have adopted as compromise." As a result, there is intense positional struggle within the secessionist ranks for what space remains. JKLF leader Yasin Malik's decision to set up an office in down town Srinagar was seen as a direct attack on Mirwaiz Farooq's constituency and provoked a violent backlash.

Mirwaiz Farooq has his own constraints to open a full-scale dialogue with New Delhi. Too fearful of his personal safety, he will venture into this dialogue only if the HM is on board. Recently, "he cancelled a scheduled meeting with New Delhi's official interlocutor, NN Vohra, after news leaked to the media, and then petulantly insisted that any further talks will take place 'only with the Prime Minister." He is well aware that he must move forward or face irrelevance.

Interestingly, PDP President and MP from Anantnag Mehbooba Mufti "used a recent conference in Cairo to brief the APHC Chairman on her Party's self-rule proposals. This meeting, analysts suggest, holds out the prospect of future alliances cutting across secessionist-mainstream lines.

There seem to exist so many potentially hopeful signs or possible ways out but still it is doubtful if any of these mainstream players and others have the tools needed to deal with the problems confronting peace-making : the criminalisation of the HM and the ISI's unwillingness to shut down the Islamist armies (and the terrorist training infrastructure) it gave birth to. Then, what is the way out? RAW is known to have maintained discreet channels of communications with the HM leadership in Pakistan and a Government of India envoy is believed to have held at least one round of discussions in New York with a prominent Islamist leader. But it is more than clear that the key to peace lies with Islamist, not New Delhi.

Pakistan, for the present, seems willing to nudge the HM towards the dialogue table. Judging by the increasingly acid polemic directed by both the HM and the LET at Musharraf, "it seems probable that they understand the peace process as a means of delivering euthanasia." Yet, Musharraf has proved unable or unwilling to act against their physical infrastructure and leadership hierarchy, which is a cause of serious concern not only for the moderate civil society within Pakistan but also, even more of a serious concern for India across its borders and the US and the EU in the distant lands.

This is the ramification of unchecked terrorism in Pakistan. And when it is sponsored and nurtured by the ISI, its meanings become even more sinister. It is not coincidental that India keeps telling the world that Pakistan is not doing enough to crush and eliminate the evil within its borders and the US and the EU intelligence agencies and think tanks periodically confirm the Indian averment. To avoid pushing Musharraf too hard and in the inttesTbf appropriate public diplomacy the White House, the State Department and the Pentagon desist making public assertions on this issue but he gets rap on his knuckles in personal/private meetings and discussions with the US President, Defence Secretary and Secretary of State.

Whatever the public postures, it is indeed the fact of life that we are at a crucial cusp of terrorism reality—the world is certainly not out of woods. Many amongst the ranks of Islamist terror groups, and their friends and sympathisers in the Pakistan's military, are looking forward' to a time when the US loses interest in Afghanistan; when pressures on Islamabad eases; when the jehad may flower again. It needs to be said that these are not the dying - wishes of the Islamists and the ISI top

brass, even the reputed think-tanks, scholars, journalists and strategic observers see the oncoming situation in a similar vein. Even more importantly, the ground realities not only in Afghanistan but also in Iraq point to a 'disaster' as for as the 'War on terrorism' is concerned.

Taking Afghanistan first, nothing is happening there that should cheer the US, NATO or Afghan military leaders. Southern and eastern Afghanistan is almost with the Taliban and the Al Qaeda fighters—the 'holy' warriors. Today (mid May 2007), two months after the NATO and Afghan troops launched their much-tom-tommed offensive, there are not very many worthwhile anti-Taliban achievements in their kitty. In fact, with certain trapidatious, they are all waiting for the Taliban spring-

2007 offensive. What is worse, inspite of repeated demands for additional troops by the NATO command in Afghanistan, the European nations led by France have been steadfast in their refusal to oblige. Taliban also know that foreign troops cannot operate in Afghanistan beyond a certain point in time. After that, they see the 'deluge'. "Afghanistan, then, will fall into the Taliban hands like the proverbial nine pins", assert some analysts. It is not without any reason that Pakistan has not gone beyond a point in its anti-terrorism drive against the— Taliban and even Al Qaeda, especially in the areas neighbouring the Afghan borders. In any case, for the very reason, Pakistan has never given up terrorism as an instrument of foreign policy against India and Afghanistan.

Now to Iraq, where the US is even in worse situation. Augmentation of its forces there, by 40,000 troops, has failed to bring any cheer to President Bush and his senior advisers. Bush has plummitted to his lowest ever popularity rating, 28 per cent, in May 2007. The Democrats, egged on by some anti-Bush Republicans, are hell-bent in laying down 2008 as troop pull out limit for US troops. How long will or can Bush keep vetoing such Congress-opproved resoutions? Not only is Iraq already deep in 'civil war' situation, the US forces have failed to check and rein-in the Sunni Islamic terrorists, who are in a minority, wreaking havoc on the majority Shia areas through physical, car-bomb and/or I— suicide bomb attacks. Bush's position seems to be becoming unviable by the day - if not by the hour.

It is not that the US and the NATO forces have not achieved any success in their anti-terrorism operations in Afghanistan and Iraq. They certainly have. But these are more of headlines-grabbing nature than of any deeper significance. Two instances of such success, that immediately come to mind, are the elimiantion (and killings) of Abu Ayyub al-Masri, Al Qaeda head in Iraq, on 1 May 2007 and of Dadullah, the chief beheader of Taliban and a terrorist close to Mullah Umar, the Taliban Chief in Afghanistan, on 12 May 2007.

It must be realised that producing successors to the al-Masris and the Dadullahs is not a problem for their respective outfits. What should be more worrisome to the world at large is that producing Islamist fighters, the 'Holy' worriors, including the suicide bombeers, is not an unsurmountable problems for the mullahs and their extremist mentors. In fact, they have perfected this art of mass-production of such 'Holy'. warriors, citing some Quranic injunctions which other Islamic scholars assert are the misinterpretations of their actual meanings.

Thus, some analysts feel, the Islam, a great religion of peace and harmony, and its Holy Book, the Quran, have been hijacked by the extremists in its fold for their own motives. It is these extremist Islamists the world should be wary about. Even of greater consequence is the impact of the sinister ideology of this miniscule minority of Islamist extremists on the huge moderate majority of their co-religionists. At a certain stage of their destructive journey the former is going to target the huge majority of Muslims within their country, and subsequently across its borders. Some empirical instances should be instructive here and of interest to layman. When after years of struggle, the Fatah was certainly if slowly moving towards an understanding, precedent to a final agreement, with Israel, the extremist Hamas comes into power and instantly upsets the peace apple cart. Yet again, when coalition-ruled Lebanon was dreaming of stability and prosperity, especially after the Syrian forces had ended their decades of occupation of Lebanon, the Hezbollah invites a counter-attack by Israel after a foolish act of aggression by its fighters. After the costly war, the terrorist Hezbollah launched an all-consuming agitation against the Lebanese Government.

The two examples of the Islamist extremist fringe plunging the moderate Muslim millions into death and destruction, should suffice here. In a wider context, Islamist fighters are engaged in terrorist warfare in 72 countries of the world. The international Islamic community must ponder over this unfortunate phenomenon and find a way to retrieve this extremist fringe for saner options. The Prophet has said killing one innocent man is to kill the entire humanity. With such lofty and humane tenets of religious philosophy, how does one explain, much less justify, the mass murder and merciless, brutal beheadings of innocent the world over by the extremist fringe of Islamists?

This somewhat extended discussion on the larger issue of Islamist extremism and terrorism the world over is considered apt and called for in the limited and narrow canvas of terrorism in Jammu and Kashmir. The reason? In the final analysis, Islamist terrorism will subsequently have bloodied and violent impact on the situation in Jammu and Kashmir. In fact, the two cannot be separated, or isolated, in different geographical entities. As of today, according to one estimate, Islamist fighters from 22 countries are helping the secessionists/terrorists in Jammu and Kashmir. Situation in Pakistan is no different if one goes by repeated warnings and calls by president Musharraf to the "foreign terrorists" to leave the country. An apt example of Islamist double-speak come from Mogadishu, Somalia. The chief of the Somali Islamic Courts Council (SICC), while condemning the US for interference in the internal affairs of Somalia and demanding withdrawal of its support, military and material, to Ethiopian troops fighting the insurrectionists and Islamist terrorists in Mogadishu/ Somalia invites the Holy warriors from all Muslim nations to join the anti-US jehad in Somalia!

Now we return to the peace process in Jammu and Kashmir, the main issue under discussion here. The fourth round of composite talks, an Q important and major constituent of the Peace Process, is due in May \ 2007. Even though no substantive progress have been made during the previous three rounds on important issues like Sir Creek, Siachen, and even the Kashmir issue, still some important CBMs on travel across the LOG and contacts between people from Jammu and Kashmir and the POK have been initiated.

Let the last word on the subject of peace process rest with the analyst quoted above : "Prime Minister Manmohan Singh and President Musharraf said in Apr 2005 the peace process between India and Pakistan is 'now irreversible'. In fact, experience has shown that it is incredibly fragile. Now is the time for Pakistan to move forward and for India to push as hard as it can - or risk seing history brutally reversed.

Jammu and Kashmir : Intra-Party Churning and Inter-party Realignments : Mid 2007

Even if some analysts doubted any usefulness of the peace-process, initiated by two neighbours, and others (especially like the BJP and its acolytes were suspicious of the very intentions of the UFA Government, things seem to be moving in Jammu and Kashmir, even if their direction is not yet clear. When the fourth round of the composite dialogue has just get under way in (early) 2007, certain amount of churning is descernible with the political parties. Even more importantly, there seems to be some inter-party re-alignment. Simply put, parties are trying to occupy some space created by the peace process. Therefore, if some parties are trying to move centre stage, like the POP, others are concerned with their being rendered irrelevant, like the Mirwaiz faction of the APHC.

Before examining the boil within the mainstream parties like NC. Congress and PDP, it is interesting to start with a look at the Geelani led APHC, which held a much-talked about rally at Srinagar on 22 April, 2007, just two days before Prime Minister's Round Table Conference on Jammu and Kashmir.

The rally was held at the Bihisht-e-Shohida-e-Kashmir, the Srinagar graveyard where many of those militants/secessionists who died fighting the state these two decades are buried. The Lashkar banners were conspicuously displayed/held high by its supporters. There were abundance of sloganeering for Azadi (= freedom, independence). An analysts who was present there, wrote : Banners emblazoned with the, Lashkar-e-Taiba's crossed scimitars-and-Quran logo fluttered outside the Srinagar graveyard (the venue of the rally). "Lashkar ayi, Lashkar ayi (the Lashkar are coming)", shouted the crowd that had massed there for Islamist patriarch Syed Ali Shah Geelani's 22 April Rally."[48]

The crowd was raising abusive slogans against Prime Minister Manmohan Singh and Chief Minister Ghulam Nabi Azad. "Policemen stood by and watched" The rally, billed as the largest Islamist (separatist) gathering in the recent years, served to demonstrate the growing aggression of the far right in Jammu and Kashmir. If it was meant to show the strength of the hard-line faction of the Geelani-led APHC, the observers felt, it was a message directed not as much at New Delhi as at the Geelani competitors and rivals vying for separatist space!

An analyst put it more colourfully, if ominously, "the rally has underlined that APHC Chairman Mirwaiz has a hammer hovering over his head, and the time to jump off the anvil is running out."

APHC (Mirwaiz) seems to be under siege from more than one adversaries. As the rally shows, Mirwaiz, despite his exalted position in state's religious hierarchy, is losing out to Geelani.' Some feel that aided by the failure of secular politicians to oppose religious reaction, neo-conservative Islamists have been increasingly successful in shaping the form and content of political mobilisation in the state.

One should join issue with this particular line of thought. Such analysts are unable or unwilling to know better. The fact remains that the extremist fringe of Islamic ideology has always had upper hand in the Islamic world. And it is particularly so today. Not to discuss the issue at too great a length, let us cite only a few instances where the hardline fringe is in ascendance over its moderate majority : Indonesia, Bangladesh, Pakistan, Iran, Palestine, and most ironic of it all, Ataturks's Turkey. To blame the secular politicians for this ascendance of the fundamentalism in Islam is being ignorant, or less than honest, or at the best, self-serving. Let us end this with a warning : It is the huge moderate majority of the Muslim world that will ultimately be facing threat from its extremist fringe. What would be worse is that the Islam, a great religion of peace, will itself be a sufferer from its own miniscule minotiry advocating Shariat rule interpreted in most illiberal terms.

Returning to the main narrative, it is also noteworthy that even the unionist (pro-India) politicians are also demonstrating their growing reach and influence. To cite an apt example, Chief Minister Azad, not known to have only any popular mass base in this—his own-state—drew crowds in excess of 15,000 at recent rallies in Kulgam and Bandipora.

But the entity in the throes of a crisis is undoubtedly APHC. It not only faces external danger from its split-away faction led by Geelani, it also seems to be suffering from internal crisis—dissent and differnces among its leading lights on the policy matters. In inner party meetings, APHC leader Abdul Gani Butt is believed to have strongly argued for the outfit to join Prime Minister's RTC discussions. That is the only way it can retain its relevance in the affairs of the state—and country. But fervently argued that multilateral engagementoffers the best means of marginalising the hardline Islamists—common enemy of both the APHC and Unionist formations.

As far back as 1998, Butt had argued the case for a multilateral dialogue involving both secessionist and mainstream parties—a concept not dissimilar to the process now being pushed forward by the Prime Minister.

But certain degree of mistrust among the major constituents of the APHC has impeded forward movement. Butt's close links with state's, businessman Mohd. Iqbal Bukhari, have, in particular, raised suspicious among others in the APHC. The Bukhari family, whose interests include a dominant share of the State's pesticide business, threw its weight behind the PDP last year. After PDP President Mehbooba Mufti renounced official protection as part of party's efforts to push its case on demilitarisation, the conveniently turned to Bukhari's son, Altaf Bukhari, for the use of his police security detail and jeep in its stead.

Leaders like the Mirwaiz believe, rightly or otherwise, that Butt is pushing the case for joining a multilateral dialogue, with New Delhi on behalf of the PDP. Butt's critcs argue if the APHC joins the RTC process, it will lose its status as sole spokesperson of the secessionist constituency in the State. In that case many of its members could defect to the ranks of the PDP, which has already made a significant inroads amongst supporters of Jamaat-e-Islami and Hizbul-Mujahideen.

Besides, there is some change in stances on certain issues in various political parties. APHC is uncertain about the dividends its participation in elections might yield. Like some other pro-dialogue secessionists, notably Mohd. Yasin Malik, the APHC has seen its key slogans stolen by mainstream parties. While PDP has appropriated issues like demilitarisation and self-rule, the Congress and NC have been increasingly vocal on issues of human rights and cross-LOC links. Yet again, the autonomy resolution passed by the State Assembly on behalf of the then ruling party, NC, is still on its agenda. Bar leaders like Bilal Gani Lone, who has an independent popular base in Kupwara, or the Mirwaiz himself, there are few in the APHC who could win an election on their own strength—a bitter truth the coalition finds it difficult to tackle with or admit publicly.

There is another outfit facing similar problem of irrelevance looming large over its identity, in the manner of the APHC. It is the Hizb-ul-Muhahedden (HM). The two could be unexpected allies. Once Jammu and Kashmir's most feared terror group, the HM, like the APHC, is facing an existential problem. Both are fearing irrelevance in the coming years. Even though the HM has long opposed Mirwaiz Farooq—elements from the outfit were responsible for the assassination of the cleric's father, Mohd Farooq—it now has good reasons to make its peace.

HM's situation is rather sad as of date. In Jan 2007, HM chief Yusuf Shah received a grim briefing on the state of play in his outfit. Only 621 cadre, he was told, were now available at the HM's three major traning camps in the PoK: the Qayoomabad and Shaheed Burhan-ud-Din facilities in Manshera and Shaheed Salim in Batrasi. Only 20 new recruits had arrived at the camps from Jammu and Kashmir in all of 2006, a small fraction of outfit's combat losses.

Records of the briefing, obtained exclusive by a daily,[49] show how sharp the erosion of the outfit's military capabilities has been. Just one consignment of eight Klashnikov assault rifles could be despatched across the LOC in 2006, down from 28 in 2005. While 40 kg of military grade explosives were sent to the HM combatants in 2005, not a single consignment could be shipped in 2006. Yet again, whereas 165 hand grenades were shipped across the LOC in 2005, just 50 could be delivered in 2006.

As if this was not bad enough, the outfit's financial infrasturcture is in ruins. From the 2005-06 winter, Pakistan's ISI had slashed the HM's monthly grant of Rs 3 million. After 18 prominent jihad commanders staged a public hunger strike in Muzaffarabad in Mar 2007, a maintenance flow was authorised. However, the flow was inadequate even to meet the HM's annual commitments to the families of the cadre killed in combat: estimated at Indian Rs. 27 million, according to the documents obtained by the mentioned above.

Shah was told during the briefing that morale among the cadres had deteriorated sharply. There had been several violent clashes between cadres in the three Camps. On one occasion, cash was looted from the main office in the Burhan-ud-Din camp. Some effort had been made to address morale by intensifying religious education: about hundred cadre had been sent to Jamaat-e-Islami-run institutions in Lahore and elsewhere. But this, the HM briefing notes record, had done little to stem the rot. Dozens of HM cadre had married local women and set up home in Muzaffarabad; others had negotiated private deals with Indian military intelligence and surrendered.

All of this, interlocuters engaged in secret dialogue with senior HM commanders say, has convinced the terror outfit that it must come to the negotiations table—or be extinguished. As a result, fissures between the HM and other terrorist outfits have been increasing.

While the HM counts Geelani as its mentor and political spokesperson, it did pass notice that there were hardly any slogans in its support at the 22 April rally. It may not be reflective of a rupture, but it certainly suggested cooling off between the chief secessionist and his one-time acolytes.

Given its unhappy situation, the HM is still not ready to give up arms—something New Delhi has made a precondition for talks. HM leaders' fears are well-placed: without their combat quotient, they will have no chance to compete with long-established and well entrenched mainstream politcal players who have either ruled or are ruling the State. The HM obviously have distaste of being 'also-rans'. But with every passing day, it is also becoming clear that equivocation is an unsustainable option. It must choose—and fast.

Emerging situation and Hard options

What lies ahead? Where do we go from here? In a dynamic situation, inactivity and indecision are luxuries that could prove too costly for the state and the country at large. Challenges, internal and external, must be faced squarely. The time for pussy-footing is over. India, and by extension Jammu and Kashmir, has come to be known as 'soft state' while dealing with terrorism. India is accused, perhaps rightly, of not crafting a coherent, counter-terrorism policy for reasons of vote-bank politics and excessive sensitivity towards Muslim sentiment within the country. All that fellows one ghastly act of terrorism after another are meaningless and mushy statements but no meaningful, resolute action. The same inanity is repeated every time, when recredescence of terrorist violence. Look at the way the US acted after one act of terrorism on 9 Sep. 2001 and what all new counter-terrorism measures were instituted, including setting up a new department of Homeland Security. Some of the measure may be deemed as harsh by some human rights activists and a variety of professional whiners, the glaring fact is that there has been no repeat of 9/11, not even a minor act of terrorism. But the US has not lowered its vigil. They keep arresting some suspects periodically.

Now coming to the State Government, Srinagar does not seem to be any better than New Delhi when it is question of taking firm measures against merchants of terrorism.Though the Army, aided by the State police and central para military forces, have gained an upper hand against the Islamist terrorists the battle is far from over. As far as the State Government is concerned, it must ensure that the law is enforced. There was a lot left to desire in handling the 22 April rally and its aftermath. If the state Government has often thwarted the rallies of some secessionist leaders, why was Geelani's allowwed? It was ridiculous to hear the state policy saying they had no information about the rally, and worse, "no permission of the state Government was taken to hold it." What were state's convert agencies doing?

Worse was yet too come. Despite the anti-national and inflammatory slogans at the rally, wide display of the banned LET banners, and open display of weapons, only four associates of Geelani were arrested. The chief secessionist was arrested by police only ofter the furore in the Parliament. Why cannot the Islamist separatist like him be put in jail—and thus out of public circulation?

Yet again, fails to understand why the Government has failed to proceed against the extremist figures like Asiya Andrabi, chief of the Dukhtran-e-Millat, who have repeatedly used violence to enforce their extremist view of Islam. Indulgence shown to people like Geelani and Asiya is a sad commentary on the state's will to maintain law and order and encourages more acts of violence.

As for external challence, it comes from Pakistan where Islamist forces sympathetic to Geelani have been gathering strength.

While the outfits like the HM suffered from the shrinking of direct ISI funding for jihad in Jammu and Kashmir, groups like the LET are prospering, having survived the challenge. With its sprawling West Asian and European financial networks, the LET has now emerged as the principal voice of the jehad. Intervitaly, this muscle has strengthened separatists like Geelani. As such, India needs to push Pakistan for more vigorous action against the LET.As has been metioned elsewhere, India has failed to parsuade or force Pakistan to proceed against the anti-Indian terrorist outfits beyond a point. For all intents and purpoes, all training infrastructure of these outfits is existing and can be used as and when needed to be.

Finally, and more importantly, certain inter-action among the mainstream parties and secessionist, is called for. To wit, an analyst feels politicians like Azad must help the APHC and HM understand that a multilateral dialogue is in their own interest. "Pushed by a complex set of social and political forces, any of the young people who a decade ago might have been drawn to the APHC or the HM are today turning to the Lashkar – something that ought to worry not just the Indian State and its supporters, but ethnic Kashmiri secesionists as weel.

So, how does one see political landscape in short and medium-term perspective? It is likely that mainstream parties, because of "their strong roots among broad-based mass constituencies opposed to Islamists (purveying extremism and intolerance) as well as the support of the state apparatus, will survive the new challenge." But the same cannot be prognosticated for the APhC and HM, who seem to be losing out to the APHC (Geelani) and the Muridke – base Pakistani terrorist outfit LET. Unless the two make immediate course correction, they "risk being blown away by the brewing storm."

As this peice practically opened with the Geelani rally on 22 Apr 2007, it should end with the 21 May rally of the APHC (Mirwaiz).

Asking New Delhi to build a consensus for resolving the Kashmir issue on the basis of Pakistani President Musharraf's four-point formula, moderate Hurriyat Chairman, on expected lines, made proforma criticism of India : India lacked political will to resolve Kashmir issue.

He also appealed to the militants to support the peace process, and ruled out participation in elections, saying they were no solution to problem; history was witness to it.

He was sepaking at a rally organised on the death anniversary of his father, Moulvi Mohd Farroq, and Abdul Gani Lone, who were gunned by militants on 21 May 1990 and 21 May 2002, respectively. APHC organises a rally every year on their death anniversary.

The rally was held a month after Geelani's and at the same spot. So comarisons were invevitable : one observer noted the Mirwaiz rally was just like any recently organised by the mainstream parties. It was agreed it paled in comparison to the much larger and more boisterous 22 April rally.

Even then, he said only his Hurriyat represented the aspirations of the people, and not mainstream parties such as the NC, PDP and Congress, Referring indirectly to Geelani, he said, "by adding more and more graveyard, you cannot achieve the goal. you need to have a vision. India's case is weak, and ours is strong. It is our responsibility to talk."

The Mirwaiz said he was ready for election if it were held across the LOC in "Azad Kashmir, Gilgit, Baltistan, and this part of Kashmir", and not the ones held here for power sharing.

Senior leaders Moulvi Abbas Ansari, Abdul Gani Butt, Agha Hassan, and Bilal Lone also addressed the gathering.

DATELINE : SELECT EVENTS AND ACTS OF TERRORISM

This part has two datelines

- Dateline : Events and Incidents
- Dateline : Acts of Terrorism.

Both lists are illustrative, not exhaustive. Only some select events and acts of terrorism have been included for general information of the readers.

Following these two time lines are five latest developments in Jammu and Kashmir covered appropriately under "Stop Press".

Dateline : Events and incidents

Date	Event/Incident
Mar 2006	Militants chop off two Teenagers' Fingers Mashak and Mubarak, the two school going teenagers, incurred the wrath of militants because they did not respond to their demand for new recruits for the terrorist outfits, and had their fingers cut off as punishment. Militants dragged out Mashak, 16, from his village Tajipura in Kulgam district on 6 March and chopped off two fingers from his right hand. In a similar incident, on 7 March a group of 6-to-8 militants pulled out Mubarak, 19, from his home in Katrash village in Kulgam District and cut off his two fingers. Sources said the chopping off was done in front of the villagers for demonstrative effect, as also with the intention of teaching them a lesson. It was a deliberate ploy to convey a message to the villagers that they better obey their dictates, or else face the consequences. Two years ago in a similar incident, ultras had chopped off the nose and ears of a woman, suspecting his brother to be an Army informer. Are such atrocious actions by the miltants indicative of their frustration, and desparation? Kashmiris too have become disillusioned with the militants and their

Date	Event/Incident
	wanton infliction of pain on the common man. An Army officer said : "In fact, the number of militants surrendering is also steadily mounting because of their falling morale." Here are some figures that do not need any explanation. • Number of militants who surrendered in J and K in 2005 — 81 • Number of militants who surrendered in 2006 (till March) — 45 • Militants who laid down arms till Mar 2006. — 15
Jun 2006	**Terrorists Resort to Narco-terrorism** Taking a leaf out of fellow jehadis in Afghanistan, terror outfits in J & K too have diversified into narcotic trade to fund their campaign of death and destruction. Thousands of hectares of the Kashmir Valley have been brought under illicit opium cultivation under the patronage of terror groups, who are faced with fund crunch of sorts since the international scrutiny forced their patrons in Pakistan to cut down on lavish funding. On 1 Jun 2006, when a Narcotics Control Bureau (NCB) team with some help from the State police was engaged in an operation to destroy a part of this crop in five villages of Sopian in Pulwama district of South Kashmir, they came under fire from a band of suspected jehadis. It was only with the additional protection provided by Army soldiers that the NCB squad could carry out its assigned task.

Date	Event/Incident
	The squad destroyed illicit poppy over an area of 1,750 *bighas*, estimated to be about 2,600 kg – worth at least Rs. 6 crore.
	It was not the first time that the NCB destroyed illicit crop in J and K. In mid-2004, the agency destroyed poppy crop spread over 167 hectares in Anantnage and Pulwama districts.
	Pakistan, under US pressure, has frozen the bank accounts of outfits already banned by the US and UN and those featuring on their list of "terrorist organisations." Pakistan was also forced to impose restrictions on fund collection by these outfits.
10 Jun 2006	One person was killed and six injured when the Army opened fire on thousands of demonstrations in Kupwara who were protesting against the alleged desecration of the Quran and a mosque at Zirhama village on 9 June. Soldiers of the 17 Dogra "had reportedly entered the mosque with their shoes on, broke almirahs and threw out copies of Quran.
Night 15/16 Jun 2006	**LET Terrorists Mutilate their Victims**
	In a gory act of revenge, LET terrorists slaughtered a 65-year-old man and chopped off the tongues, noses and ears of two others. They also left 11 others brutally injured in Nehoch-Dunga village of Gulabgarh area of Mahore tehsil in Udhampur district on the night 15/16 Jun 2006.
	All this brutality, because the LET ultras believe the villagers have helped security personnel nab three of their ranks on 23 April.

Date	Event/Incident
17 Jun 2006	The state police claimed to have achieved a major breakthrough by busting a Hizb module, with the arrest of five terrorists : three by Budgam police and two by Srinagar police. This helped the police in cracking some recent (past six weeks) cases, which are mentioned here. • Five grenade explosions since Jan 2006. These were the Zakoora bus explosion and the other four at Kothi Bagh, Maisuma, Badyari Chowk and Qamarwari in Srinagar • Car-blasts case that took place at four spots in Srinagar, and mastermind (Mohd Amin from Mochua village) in this case had been arrested. A mechanic by profession, he used to prepare cars for the militants to carry out such blasts. His method : by converting fuel tanks and filling them with explosives. Cars prepared by Amin were blasted at the TRC crossing, Bemina bypass, Rawalpora and airport road on different occasions.
18 Jun 2006	A senior militant, LET "Commander" Mushtaq Ahmad, alias Abu Saif, surrendered with his arms and equipment (one AK rifle', two magazines, 37 rounds, two grenades and some other belongings which he had brought with him from across the LOC) before DIG Rajouri-Poonch Range MA Anjum; Maj Gen GM Nair, GOC Dah Division; and SSP Rajouri Farooq Khan. He had recently crossed over to this side of LOC after spending six years in POK terrorist camps

Date	Event/Incident
	Meanwhile, security forces recovered 1.5 kg explosives.
21 Jun 2006	On a tip off, the Rashtriya Rifles troops launched a massive combing operation in the forests near Kalaroos and Karnah in the border district of Kupwara. They finally busted a 6 ft × 4 ft underground hideout built close to a nulla bed. The search yielded a large cache of arms and ammunition which included one Sniper rifle, three AK-47 rifles, two AK-56 rifles, one 9 mm pistol, two single barrel rifles. Other ammunition and explosives seized included the following. 1. A 107 mm shell. 2. Three 60 mm mortar bombs. 3. Two Under Barrel Grenade Launchers (UBGL). 4. Five rocket propelled grenade rounds. 5. Five rocket propelled grenade boosters. 6. 12 hand grenades. 7. 12 kg IED. 8. Two RCDS. 9. Six pencil IEDs. 10. 20 electric detonators (No. 33). 11. 35 electric detonators (No. 27). 12. One radio set ICOM. 13. 800 AK-47 rounds. 14. 20 Sniper rounds. 15. Five rounds of 9 mm ball pistol. 16. 15 rounds of 40 mm mortar. 17. Two binoculars

Date	Event/Incident
	18. One 82 mm mortar sight.
	19. One sniper sight.
	20. Five magazines for Sniper rifles.
	21. One magazine of 9 mm pistol.
	22. Ten magazines of AK rifles.
30 Aug 2006	The J & K police claimed to have unearthed an Al-Badr module responsible for killing security and police personnel (CRPF-2, BSF-2, and three police men) by arresting three militants of the outfit. State DGP Gopal Sharma told the press that the personnel of the CRPF, BSF and State police were targeted by these militants in a coordinated manner in recent months.
17 Dec 2006	**Pak Militants Lead Jammu Jail Siege** Violent clashes, led by Pak militants and other foreign mercenaries in captivity, erupted inside the high-security Kot Bhalwal Central Jail near Jammu early on the 17th Uneasy calm was restored in the jail premises only after hours of pitched battles the hardcore terrorists fought with the law enforcers. The situation inside the jail was on the boil for the last couple of days following strict enforcement of the jail manual by the authorities. For sometime now, there has been a CID inquiry on at this jail over the reports that hardcore militants "are 'armed' with SIM cards and cellphones." The clashes were triggered by the jail staff's attempt to carry out a thorough search inside the jail barracks to recover the illegal materials from the convicts lodged in the jail. 21 detainees, including top militants belonging to the HM and JEM outfits, and

Date	Event/Incident
	15 police personnel were injured during the day-long pitched battle the inmates fought with the securitymen.
	The police and the CPFP men had to resort to a baton charge and tear gas shelling to get the situation under control. No firing was ordered by the police.
	JAIL TARGETED : SOME PAST INCIDENTS
Oct 2006	
	Former Jail Superintendent Sheikh Mohd Rashid seizes mobile handsets and SIM cards from the jail inmates.
Dec 1999	
	JEM Maulana Masood Azhar was freed to secure release of hijacked passengers aboard IC-814 flight.
Jun 1999	
	Pak militants attempted a jail break by digging a 180-feet long tunnel.
	Time-to-Time Clashes
	Such clashes between local and foreign militants are fairly common.
Night	Four JEM Terrorists (Bashir Ahmad Ponnu, Fayaz
4/5 Feb 2007	Ahmad Lone, Abdul Majid Baba and Shahid Gafoor) were arrested near Ranjit Singh flyover, near the Connaught Place, in Delhi, after a 25-minute encounter. The police fired 20 rounds in retaliation to 12 rounds fired by one of the militants, the only one of the quartet with a weapon.
	They were planning a repeat of the serial blasts that rocked Delhi on 29 Oct. 2005 on the eve of the Deewali that year.

Date	Event/Incident
7 Mar 2007	In a joint operation by troops and police, two militants were killed in the Kangurnar and Sogam areas of Kupwara district in North Kashmir. From the identity cards recovered from their bodies, they were identified as Abu Shaheen, alias Shaheen Afghani, chief of the HUM, and Tahir Saqib. Two AK rifles, six magazines, ammunition and a radio set were recovered from the site.
	In another joint operation, one ultra of the HM, Shabir Ahmad Khanday, was arrested from the Awantipora area of Pulwama district in the South Kashmir.
	During search operations, the security forces seized one pistol, one magazine, a wireless set, three hand grenades, one AK 47 magazine and 61 rounds from the forest area of Khadi, Sogam in Kupwara district.
	On 6 March, three AK magazines, six RPGs, eight UBGL rounds, one hand grenade and 15 AK rounds were recovered at Langiote near the LOC in Poonch district.
	The security forces during a search at Khanetar in Poonch district recovered a Pika gun, and also busted a hideout. Some edibles were also recovered.
	A CRPF jawan died under suspicious circumstances at its camp near Shiraz cinema, Khanyar. He was identified as Showkeen Singh of 96 Bn, CRPF. The police is investigating to ascertain the cause of death.
1 Apr 2007	**Time Not Right For Troop Pull-out : Chief Minister**
	A day after Chief Minister GM Azad made clear that firm steps would be taken to deal

Date	Event/Incident
	with militancy, senior Congress leader Jan Mohd Kakroo was gunned down as he stepped out of a shrine after prayers at 7.30 AM. The shrine is located in Khwaja Sahib Mohalla, Baramulla. Azad rushed to the town after learning of the killing. He told the press : "For a long time, we have been telling our coalition partner PDP that this is not the time for troop reduction. In the last three days militants have shown what they want. First they killed five labourers in Rajouri, next day set off a bomb which left 13 injured in Kishtwar, and now this killing (on 1 April)." A militant outfit, Shuhda Brigade (= Martyrs Brigade) claimed responsibility through its spokesman. Abu Katba who said, "Kakroo was killed for being a Congress functionary. The PDP, passionately demanding troop pullout, also condemned the killing, with its Patron Mufti Mohd Sayeed saying : "Kakroo's murder is an inhuman act."
4 Apr 2007	**Hizb Issues Fresh J & K Threat : 4 Apr 2007** The HM, Jammu and Kashmir's frontline indigenous militant outfit threatened to target "700,000 Indian citizens in Jammu and Kashmir" unless harassment of Kashmiris and discriminatory treatment meted out to Kashmiris in various parts of the country stopped. In a statement to the local news agency CNS, the Hizb spokesman Junaid al-Islam regretted that the Kashmiri Muslim students, traders and travellers continue to be beleaguered by the police and "communal and rogue" elements across India.

Date	Event/Incident

The statement comes in the wake of reports that 28 Kashmiri students were detained by the Karnataka police "following a clash between two groups of students at Gausia Engineering College at Ramnagram near Bangalore earlier this week."

Chief Minister GM Azad had written to various chief ministers in India, requesting them to ensure that the Kashmiris are not harassed for such minor incidents.

"The detainees have since reportedly been sent into police remand by a local court."

The parents of the detainees held protest demonstrations along the streets of Srinagar on 4 April, demanding that their "innocent" wards be freed immediately.

According to police and local newspapers (of Srinagar), a Kashmiri and a Bihari student clashed over some issue within the college campus some days ago.

22 Apr 2007 **Geelani Returns and Holds a Public Rally**

Bursts of separatist sentiments are often timed with peace overtures by New Delhi, as Syed Ali Shah Geelani, the longtime hardliner secessionist, underscored on 22 April – just two days ahead of the Prime Minister's Round Table Conference (RTC) on the 24th – at a largely attended (huge?) public rally at Srinagar's Eidgah dotted with the graves of Kashmiri militants.

Coming on the eve of the RTC, an analyst felt, Geelani's show of strength, marked by pro-Pakistan sloganeering and lusty flaunting of the HM and LET banners was his way of asserting the clout these

Date	Event/Incident
	secessionist outfits and his own faction of the APHC wield in the separatist spectrum vis-a-vis the Mirwaiz-led (moderate?) faction of the APHC. The ailing Geelani, who had just returned to Kashmir after a two-month medical treatment in Mumbai, not only turned down Prime Minister's invitation for the 24 April RTC but handed down acerbic criticism to Pak military leadership for discussing the Kashmir solution short of the Un-mandated plebiscite. Significantly, Geelani's muscle-flexing, coincides with the growing demand and clamour led by the PDP and supported by the NC and CPI(M) for troop reduction and for the separatists and militant outfits being invited to join in the Indo-Pak Kashmir parleys. Even more, the NC and PDP want Pakistan-based HM Chief Yusuf Shah's involvement in the dialogue. New Delhi is cautious lest such a gesture at a time when the military has an upper hand in the counter—insurgency drive in the State is construed as a sign of weakness. What some observers assert is that New Delhi's evolving peace initiative on Kashmir is yet to infuse confidence in even moderate separatists to stick their neck out for a walk the talk with the Centre. Afraid of the gun at their temple, the Mirwaiz APHC is only waiting for the HM to move to the negotiating table. Undoubtedly, they will be there with them. (Ramesh Vinayak, *India Today*, 7 May 2007).
29 Apr 2007	Ex-militants using muscle and influence to help their 'vested interests.'

Date	Event/Incident
	A former militant and counter-insurgent and now a councillor, was arrested on 29 Apr 2007 after his guards opened fire on villagers protesting against his getting a road laid along a certain route. Police said, "Papa Kishtwari, an *Ikhwan* commander before he became a councillor after winning election, has been using his influence to have a road laid under a 'small-roads project' to pass along a hillock in Pampore on which stood some hutments and a shrine."
	Sardar Khan, SSP, Awantipore said, "The villagers had come out to protest this, and when they saw Papa Kishtwari approach, they tried to attack his vehicle. His guards opened fire, injuring some villagers. We rushed to the spot and arrested him."
	Mehraj-ul-din Kakro Deputy Commissioner, Pulwama, gave more details : "In the morning, a bulldozer had arrived, and that was resented by the local people, resulting in the incident. Having vested interests in the project, he pushed it through on the pretext of helping the local people. Kishtwari had built some shops after encroaching upon the road, which were demolished by the authorities. Presently, encroachments by Saif Neelam, proprietor of a major Kashmiri business house, were under demolition."
	Of late, there is interesting development witnessed in the Valley – a paradigm shift in the militancy. "Some militants and former militants are offering their muscle and influence", say several police officers.
	Kishtwari, whose real name is Ghulam Rasool Shah and used to operate in South Kashmir as an important deputy of the

Date	Event/Incident
	better known counter-insurgent commander and founder of the *Ikhwan* (counter-insurgency outfit supported by the State Government) Kuka Parrey. Villagers accuse Kishtwari of extra-judicial killings during his days as the Ikhwan commander. By way of a backgrounder, Kishtwari had been a junior officer in the CRPF before he deserted it to join the militant outfit Al Jihad after the outset of militancy in the late 1989. Police records disclose he was arrested in 1993, and released after 21 mouths in jail to join the counter-insurgent *Ikhwan*. It is but common knowledge among the local Kashmiris and several police officers would testify the fact that many members of this government-supported counter-insurgency outfit (*Ikhwan*) have joined politics or become toughs – and musclemen – for the political parties, of course, at a price. Shades of the Pappu Yadavs and the Raja Bhayyas of Bihar and UP, here in Kashmir! (*Source :* Muzamil Jaleel, *Indian Express,* 30 Apr 2007)
Apr-May 2007	'Bakerwals' revive a tradition : Head for summer destinations. A welcome change is being witnessed in the far-flung areas of Jammu and Kashmir as the 'Bakerwal' tribes revive their tradition of moving to the upper reaches of mountains during summer. This was not possible during the past six years due to militancy. After all these years, there is an activity in the remote meadows of Chassana situated

Date	Event/Incident
	on the edge of the Pir Panjal in Reasi district, as the Bakerwal clans are heading for their summer destinations. The movement of bakerwals on this route had died down over the years as the heights of Kosernag on the Pir Panjal had become the favourite haunt of the gun-toting ultras, who aften targeted the Bakerwals.
	Atta-ullha Khan tells a journalist : "It is after six years that my clan has resumed the tradition of moving to the heights. Many of us had chosen to dispense with the tradition as we became soft targets of militants who would enter our *dhoks* (summer huts) and rob us of our sheep and goats. They also forced us to become informers."
	The disruption in their routine has indeed ruined some of them. Testifies 45-year-old Mohd Ramzan : "We were [forced to be] on the streets and have become beggars. The presence of militants reportedly declined, we heard. So we decided to take the route again. Five years ago, I had a flock of 1,000 sheep but now I am left with 70. However, the risk to our lives exists as three local militants of the HM are still active in the belt. Vallage Protection Committees in the area have proved a big deterrent for them. Our tribe takes this route to move to the higher reaches in the summer and we retrace our steps when snow caps these heights in winter."
	The farthest these tribes go during summer is Drass area of the Ladakh region – the second coldest inhabited place on earth after Siberia.

Date	Event/Incident
	Drass incidentally, is the first stop as one crosses the Zogila (la = pass) heights from Kashmir valley.
	Bakerwals ply animal husbandry for sustaining themselves. Goat and sheep meat is their staple food. The animals are used for commercial purposes also.
	They complain that authorities have not done enough to improve their socio-economic conditions.
	The concept of mobile schools, where the teachers would travel with their charges and the scheme is supposed to have been officially sanctioned, is still non-existent for many tribes who have not even heard of it.
20 Apr	
10 May 2007	**They Keep Crossing LOC at Any Opportunity : Apr-May 2007**
	The Army apprehended two Pakistani militants of LET outfit in North Kashmir : Mohd Yasin, 18 from Lahore and Mohd Akhtar-ul-Islam, 21, from Sialkot.
	They were part of a 7-member group of Pakistani youth who got one to three months army training at Aksa near Muzaffarabad in the POK. The seven had crossed over to this side of the LOC between 20 and 21 Apr 2007.
	The two told the media at the Kilo Force head quarters of GOC Maj Gen Rajinder Singh that they had been forced to undergo arms training at Aksa. Yasin said he was forcibly kept and trained for a month in a camp in Jammu and Kashmir before going across. Akhtar admitted he was paid Rs.

Date	Event/Incident
	10,000 before crossing the LOC and was also assured of more money for his relatives once he joins the ranks across the border.
	The GOC said the group was launched on 16 April, and with the help of a guide they crossed the LOC during 20-21 April. One was killed in one encounter and others managed to escape. Two of the latter died when they slipped into a *nullah*. Their bodies were recovered between 23 April and 4 May. One of the escapees was killed in another encounter. "The last two, talking to the press, will be handed over to the police", he said.
7 May 2007	Warrant against LET militant (Red Fort shoot-out case)
	A Delhi court issued production warrant against Ashruddin, a LET terrorist involved in the Red Fort shoot-out who had been earlier declared a proclaimed affender. He was caught later in Lucknow and is now facing trial under the POTA.
	Chief Metropolitan Magistrate (CMM) of Tis Hazari court has issued a warrant to bring the ultra from Lucknow to Delhi to face the trial in the Red Fort shoot-out case. Delhi Police, with this warrant, will bring the accused to Delhi.
	The POTA case is in its final stages and a decision is expected within a month. There are 22 accused in the Red Fort shoot-out case.
	The LET militants snaked into the Red Fort on 22 Dec 2000 and fired indiscriminately on the guards of 7 Raj Rif stationed there, killing two jawans (Abadullah Thakur and

Date	Event/Incident
	Uma Shankar) and a civilian (Ashok Kumar).
8 May 2007	**Border Residents Want Ceasefire to be Permanent** Almost four years after guns fell silent along the LOC due to ceasefire between India and Pakistan, people in the border township of Mendhar, who suffered most due to hostility between the two countries, are heaving a sigh of relief (Shariq Majeed, *The Tribune*, 9 May 2007). Before (November) 2003, residents of Mandhar (just a few kilometers from Kotli district of POK) lived in a constant fear of getting killed due to heavy firing from across the border. Many villagers lost their lives in shelling before the ceasefire, and there was huge loss of property as well. Hundreds of animals were also killed in the shelling in Mendhar and its adjoining areas, including Balakote, Mankote Sagra and Gaulad. With guns having fallen silent along the LOC, people's fear has lessened if not vanished, which will happen only if there is permanent peace between two countries. Truce, by its very nature, cannot be permanent. Before the truce, people would rush home after 5 PM, fearing the worst in case they got caught in the shelling, but the markets now remain crowded till late in the evenings. Mohd Sajid of Gaulad voices the sentiments of all people living in the border belt : "Four years ago, our minds were constantly in the grip of fear. But now we are living in

Date	Event/Incident
	peace – those fears being distant if bad memories. But only friendship between the two countries will bring permanent peace to us. And we keep praying for that friendship."
	Months before the truce was agreed upon, Rifiq Khan, a *numberdar* of adjoining village of Balakote, died when a shell hit him. Even if the villagers of Balakote still recollect that shocking incident, they pray against the repetition of such incidents – wistfully wishing for a permanent cease fire.
10 May 2007	**UN Offices Closed in Tehsil Bagh, POK**
	Mounting violence and increasing attacks against humanitarian workers have forced the UN to close its offices in Pakistan's Tehsil Bagh (POK) region for two weeks.
	An UN statement said the decision had been taken "in view of the current security situation and the prevailing tensions."

DETELINE : ACTS OF TERRORISM

Date	Killed/injured	Details
21 May 2006	$\frac{6}{22}$	Four days ahead of the Prime Minister's second round table conference on Kashmir, terrorists struck in Srinagar, killing six including two policemen and injuring 22 others including the State DGP in an attack on a Youth Congress Rally at Sher-e-Kashmir Park.
12 Jun 2006	$\frac{9}{9}$	Casting a cloud of fear over the annual Amar Nath Yatra that began

Date	Killed / injured	Details
		just two days ago, the terrorists killed eight labourers of a brick kiln at *Darpath* Badro after segregating them. Five among the dead were Nepalis and three Biharis. They had been abducted only in the morning.
12 Jun 2006	1/29	The above outrage came hours after unidentified assailants tossed three hand grenades in quick succession in Jammu's general bus terminus, killing a bus conductor and injuring 29 persons, including a woman and girl.
15 Jun 2006	7/6	Seven persons, including two militants were killed, while six others were injured in several incidents of violence at different places in the State, namely – (1) terrorists detonated a powerful IED planted in a scooter on the Srinagar-Uri highway at Baramulla, injuring three. (2) Gunmen shot dead manager of a petrol pump (Pervez Ahmad Butt) at Laroo, Anantnag and a former militant (Azad Ahmad Dar) at Mirpora (3) one former militant each came under attack at Safa Kadal, Srinagar (Bilal Ahmad) and at Sopore, Baramulla district (Abdul Rashid Khan). (4) Security forces gunned down two militants of the Pak-based LET in two different

Date	Killed / injured	Details
		encounters at Ghatak Nallah and Malai Top Surrando in Doda district.
22 Jun 2006	2 / 15	Terrorists tossed a grenade at the house of a holy man, *darvaish* Abdul Ahad, alias Ahad Baba, in Sopore, North Kashmir, killing 2 of his devotees and injuring 15, even as the saint himself escaped unhurt. This was the second attack on the *Darvaish* since the time militancy took root in the state. The ascetic lives a simple life and sits in on iron cage clad in rags, while his devotees, belonging to different faiths, sit around him. Former Cabinet Minister and the Tangmarg MLA Ghulam Hassan Mir condemned the attack : "Ahad Baba is a revered saint not only in Sopore but in the entire State and to attack such a personality is an assault on humanity." It is indeed gratifying that a MLA finds courage to condemn the terrorists' wanton acts of violence even when this has implications for his personal safety in an atmosphere of intolerance and narrowmindedness created in the state by these very inhuman killers of common men.

7.10.06

A young officer, Lt N Parthiban, son of a retired Army officer, Maj V Natarajan of the Signals, was killed in an encounter with the militants on the LOC. Belonging to 5 JAK LI, he had phoned his parents only on the 6th, stating that his team had killed some militants and he himself shot dead three of them. Maj Natarajan had served in Kargil during the war and retired last year.

Coming from Pammal near Tambram, he passed out of the Officer Training Academy, Tambram (Chennai) in March 2006. Several College mates of the martyred officer thronged his house as his body was flown in on the 8th.

8.10.06

A group of militants sneaked into India from across the LOC. Picked up on the surveillance equipment and asked to surrender, the intruders refused. In the ensuing gun-battle in the area of Doba Nallah (near Choprian Ban, Saujian Sector) in Poonch district, three Pak infiltrators of JEM were killed. The troops arrested six overground workers of the ultras. In the clash, Soldier Rahul Kumar of 4 Bihar was also killed.

A huge cache of arms and ammunition, including 3 × AK rifles, 10 × AK magazines, 9 Chinese grenades, 5 UBGL grenades, one UBGL launcher, 2 wireless sets, one mobile phones, one GPF and 268 AK rounds, besides one blanket, three pouches, two bags and one binocular were recovered from the encounter site.

8 Oct 06

On the 7th, gunmen killed a dental surgeon, Dr. Mushtaq Ahmad Shah, after abducting him while on way to his home at Zachaldara in the Handwara area of Kupwara district. The bullet-ridden body of Dr. Shah, who works at Longate, was recovered by police from Nowpura in the Sopore area of Baramulla district in North Kashmir.

8 Oct 06

Three boys – Ajaz Ahmad Mir (11), Altaf Ahmad Mir (15) and Ishfaq Ahmad Mir (16) – were wounded when an explosive device went off near their house at Chattinbandi village in the Bandipora area of Baramulla district.

10 Oct 06

A Rashtriya Rifles battalion provided/fitted artificial limb to the victims of terrorist attacks, at a camp organised at Bandipora, Kupwara district.

10 Oct 06

After lasing nine infiltrators in two major foiled infiltration bids across the LOC in Gurez and Poonch sector during last two days, LET militants killed four army men including a JCO near Surankot in Poonch district, when they were conducting search operations to trace out a militant hide out in remote Chamraid Andarwali *dhoke* in Surankot in the wee hours. One LET ultra, believed to be a Pakistani national was also killed.

Date	Killed / injured	Details
4 Jun 2007	6 / –	Six militants, including four Pak ultras; at remote Gool area (Udhampur) and Banihal area. 58 Rashtriya Rifles and J & K police.
20 Mar 2007	6 / –	Four LET terrorists and two army men (Capt Hudson and L/NK Bawan Singh) were killed in a gun battle at Diver Inderbagh village in Lulabh pocket of frontier district of Kupwara. The troops belonging to 2 Para, 18 RR and State police had surrounded a militant hide-out on a tip off.
30 Mar 2007	5 / 4	**5 Hindu labourers killed by terrorists** Gun men in Army uniforms and some wearing *bandanas* as well shot dead five Hindu labourers and wounded four others at Panglar village, *Kala* Kote area of remote region of Jammu and Kashmir's frontier district of Rajouri. Panglar is some 50 km from district headquarters.

Date	Killed / injured	Details
		In a pre-dawn attack, gun men barged into the house of a Muslim resident at Panglar and after regregating his Hindu tenants, shot them dead at point blank range.
8 May 2007	10 / 7	Seven militants, two security forces and one civilian killed and seven injured in encounters at : • Lone Harray, Kralpora, Kupwara district in North Kashmir. • Chogal, Handwara in Kupwara district. • Lashidat, Kamkadi, near the LOC in Kupwara district. • Sangran, Kralpora in Kupwara district. Five suspected militants were apprehended and quantities of arms and ammunition seized during search operations by the security forces.
		'Stop Press'

Now follow five latest and significant developments in the State.

Ten HUM Militants Surrender : 5 Jun 2007

Ten militants of the *Harkat-ul-Mujahideen* outfit, including a self-styled Divisional Commander Barkat Ali – hailing from Bharti village of Bhallesa – laid down their arms on the morning of 5 Jun 2007 before Chief Minister GN Azad at Doda. State's DGP Gopal Sharma and the Chief Secretary too were present on the occasion.

With this surrender, the HUM outfit has been wiped out from Doda district, claims SSP Doda Manohar Singh. He told a daily : "All surrendered militants were locals, fed up with bloodshed and destruction. Some of them were active since long. This surrender is a big blow to the HUM. For past some months, the police has been interacting with the relatives of the active militants, who in turn motivated their children to lay down their arms and surrender."

Sources disclosed all the ten militants had surrendered before the security forces the previous evening at Bhallesa in the Bhaderwah area of Doda. They were taken to Doda on the 5th morning for laying down arms before the Chief Minister. Incidentally, Bhallesa is the native place of Azad and most of the surrenderees belong to that belt.

Those who surrendered include the following :

1. Barkat Ali, Divisional Commander, active since 1993.
2. Abdul Gani, alias Hamid, District Commander.
3. Fighters : Javed Iqbal, Alam Hussain, Manzur Ahmad, Akhtar Hussain, Ghulam Hussain, Inayatullah Khan, Talib Hussain, and Jan Mohd.

The weapons and equipment handed over by them are listed here :

1. AK 47, self-loading .303 and NSAS rifle.
2. One pistol.
3. A satellite phone and nine radio sets.
4. Huge quantity of ammunition.

Qaeda CD : J and K Jihad is doorway to India : Early Jun 2007

Al Qaeda has pledged to wage jihad on India through Jammu and Kashmir, considering in the "doorway" for the crusade planned against "infidels, apostates and hypocrites", besides "enemies in the guise of friends" and those "who misguide and dampen the spirits of the Muslim nation whatever their name and creed might be."

This has been quoted, by a daily[50], from a written statement delivered to a Srinagar based news agency, Current News

Service (CNS), by an unidentified courier on 8 Jun 2007. The statement in Urdu came with a CD of more than 15 minutes' duration, showing a masked gunman named Abu Ibrahim al-Asim reading out the same statement before a camera. The statement, as per his claim, was from the *amir* (chief) of Al Qaeda fil Hind (= Al Qaeda in India), Abu Abd al-Rehman al-Ansari, pledging that jihad to be fought in India would be based on *"Khalis tawheed"* (= pure Unitarianism).

The statement about the launch of the Al Qaeda in India comes after 11 months of a similar statement announcing the setting up of Al Qaeda in the State. The launch was publicised by making a telephone cell to the CNS on 13 Jul 2006. The caller had identified himself as being the spokesperson of the new outfit, Abu al-Hadeed. "It had engrossed the officials of various intelligence agencies and other law-enforcement authorities here (in Jammu and Kashmir) as well as the media within and outside the country." But soon the authorities came out with a definite "no" to the presence of Al Qaeda in Kashmir, even though the statement did not say if the new group has any relationship with the Osama bin Laden-led al-Qaeda or not.

That statement had said that the Al Qaeda Jammu and Kashmir's objectives and philosophy would be spelt out shortly and had asked Indian Muslims to take up jihad as a means for seeking salvation and for the sake of Islam. It too had mentioned the name of Abu Abd al-Rehman al-Ansari as being the *amir* of the outfit. Spokesman Abu al-Hadeed had quoted him as saying : "We will come to you again soon with the objectives and philosophy of the Al Qaeda Jammu and Kashmir.

But the promised 'objectives and philosophy' were never made public and that remained the first and last statement from the outfit. Pro-Independence JKLF leader Mohd Yasin Malik had publicly vowed to fight the "incursion", believing it would be harmful to the interests of the people of the state. The other separatist groups and leaders maintained silence on the issue.

The latest proclamation charges that "pre-meditated conspiracy" hatched at the international level has turned the ongoing "jihad" in Jammu and Kashmir into a dispute over a piece of land between India and Pakistan and a clash of interests of various nations. "Apart from the global infidelity and its adherents, some enemies in the guise of friends are involved in this monstrous game plan", the statement quotes Al Ansari as saying.

It identifies both factions of the separatist Hurriyat Conference alliance as being the culprits and, surprisingly, even does not spare the United Jihad Council (UJC) the Muzaffarabad-based alliance of Kashmiri Islamic outfits headed by HM "Supreme Commander" Syed Salahuddin.

"The role being played by the UJC is worse than that of Hurriyat Conference factions as it not only indirectly endorses its plans and policies but also obeys every diktat issued by secret agencies even if that goes against the principles of Islam and those strictly followed by our ancestors and the virtuous". This is frome the statement.

Without naming Pakistan, the statement accuses it of being party to the erection of a 12-feet-high barbed fence along the de facto border dividing Jammu and Kashmir and as part of mutual understanding with India, persuading the youth to accept monthly stipends and other benefits to "keep them away from jihad".

This report on Al Qaeda CD should end on a word of caution for the nation's security managers and intelligence agencies : They should not be in a hurry to dub such CDs as unauthentic. After all mere absence of evidence about Al Qaeda's presence or some active incidents of terrorism by its operatives cannot be taken as definitive conclusion that it has no presence here. They should patiently be waiting for months, if not years, before awarding any such certificate publicly. It is better to be certain than be surprised in such high-stakes situations.

Kashmiris 'Celebrate' a Terrorist's Killing : Jun 2007

"In the past when a terrorist was killed in Jammu and Kashmir, people would take to the streets to protest against the security forces. These days it seems you are as likely to find residents handing out sweets in celebrations and women spitting on the body instead."[51]

These observations are by a visiting reporter about the change in attitude of the locals on the killing of terrorists in the state. It appeared in a daily of 8 Jun 2007. How the people's mindsets are changing on the issue was illustrated by what happened after Atta Mohd, a tehsil commander of the HUK "was killed recently by the security forces" in Doda : villagers in Gandoh in Thathri district distributed sweets.

23-year-old from Bonjowa in Doda had been active in Guganda, Suranga, Kunthal and other areas of Gundoh tehsil, having joined HUM as a teenager in 2000. He attended a terrorist training camp in Muzaffarabad in POK and was known as an IED expert who had been involved in a number of terrorist incidents including the murder of Special Police Officers (SPOs).

Atta Mohd had become a hated figure in the village where, they say, he harassed, molested and raped local women and tried to extort money from the villagers.

Safdar Hussain, a militant from Gugada, Kara, tehsil Thathri, who surrendered to the Army, said, "He was involved in three or four murders of the villagers."

A First in Afghanistan : A Kashmiri Dies Fighting with Taliban Against US Forces

A Teenagar, Aijaz Ahmad Malla, who vanished from his house in Patushahi village of Bandipora area in North Kashmir six years ago has been reported killed in a fire fight with the US troops in Afghanistan.

He is the first Indian known to have participate in the Taliban-led jihad in Afghanistan.

Malla was reported missing on 12 Jul 2001, had joined the HUM and died in a skirmish in southern Afghanistan on 29 May 2007.

On 12 Jul 2001, his parents told the local police that their son had been kidnapped by "unindentified gunmen." Malla was just 11 years at the time.

Thus ended this 17-year-old jihadi's six-year-long journey with the HUM in the bad lands of Afghanistan – entering the history books as the first Indian (Kashmiri) to do so.

Seven months after he disappeared from Patushahi, Malla called home to say that he was at a Harkat training camp near Mansehra in Pakistan's NWFP. In subsequent years, he called home every few months to reassure his family that he was safe.

Last Phone Call

In the last two years, Malla called thrice to report that he was participating in forays across the Pak-Afghan border. Last of these calls came two months ago, says one of his brothers Asiq Ahmad. "I am again going to fight the infidels in Afghanistan and do not know if I will come back alive. Pray for me", Malla told his ageing father Ghulam Mohd Malla.

It is unclear just what motivated Malla, who apprenticed as a carpet-weaver under his father, to join the Harkat. None of his seven siblings, interestingly, appears to have been drawn to Islamist causes. Asiq serves in the 11 Secrurity Battalion of the Jammu and Kashmir Police while Pervez Ahmad is a constable in the CRPF. Arshid Ahmad runs a pharmacy, Manzoor Ahmad just completed his under graduate studies, and the two youngest children – Khalid Ahmad and Irshada Bano, are still in school.

It should not be on uphill task for any one to understand what motivated Malla to join the jihad. It is forced kidnapping from his home to begin with. Under pain of threat to his own person and other members of his family, Malla, like countless others, is compelled to stay in the Harkat camp initially. Then a Mullah/Maulvi is let loose on him with sermons about his duty as ordained by Allah to fight the infidels of the world led by the Chief Satan America. Finally he is painted the picture of luxurious life that is awaiting him in the *bahisht* (= heavens) even if he gets killed in jihad. With passions of religious ideology fully inflammed, the subject is no more a thinking, normal human being. He is a hate-filled destructive robot, all set to blow himself up for the cause of Islam as interpreted for him and dinned into his ears by the bigoted maulvis/mullahs. His death is not the end of story for his mentors—the mis- interpreters of a great religion of peace like Islam. When a Malla is killed, which he is bound to be because of the path of violence forced on him, the personal tragedy is further exploited to spread the venon against the infidels in a well-practised rhetoric and standerdised oration well-patented by now – to extract the last ounce of propaganda by the extremist Islamists who have determined to wipe out all infidels the world over to establish the rule of Shariah unchallenged and uninterrupted anywhere.

To return to the specifics, this is how the Islamists in Jammu and Kashmir moved to capitalise on Malla's death, advertising it as a sacrifice for their global campaign. Soon after the Urdu-language *Kashmir Uzma* and Islamists carried obituary notices on Tuesday, 5 June, hardline Islamist Syed Ali Shah Geelani held a *"gaibana janaaza"* – ritual last rites for those presumed dead. At the "gailbana janaaza", Geelani accused Gen Musharraf of being "an agent of George Bush."

Harkat's History

Like so many other Islamist terror organisations, the HUM was a child of the US-funded jihad against the Soviet Union. By 1991, it had a substantial presence in both Afghanistan and Jammu and Kashmir.

In Jun 1993, a committee of clerics arranged for the HUM to merge itself into a new outfit Harkat-ul-Ansar (HUA). Maulana Azhar Masood Alvi, the terrorist released from jail in return for the safety of the hostages on board Indian Airlines flight 814 in 1999, was one of the key figures in this new group.

The HUA gained international attention when it kidnapped European and US hostages in 1994 and 1995 in murderous efforts to secure Azhar Masood's release. In 1997, US declared it a terrorist organisation, which led the group to resume calling itself the HUM. A year later, the US fired missiles at two Harkat-run camps in Afghanistan.

Support to Taliban

Matters came to a head in 2001, when the HUM provided support to the Taliban against the US. While Pakistan responded by proscribing the group, it continued to operate using the cover of a new Charitable organisation, the al-Asar Trust. One faction, the Harkat-ul-Mujahideen Alami, carried out a series of attacks against French and US interests, as well as an attempt on the life of Gen Musharraf.[52]

Harkat operatives have also been increasingly active in India. In Mar 2007, police in Ahmedabad shot dead Pakistani nationals Imran Shehzad Bhatii and Mohd Iqbal, who are alleged to have been preparing to execute major strikes in western India. Days earlier, police in Lucknow killed Mohd Salim bin-Aziz, a Harkat terrorist who had served with the outfit in southern Kashmir.

One can only hope that security managers in India keep their Pakistani counterparts informed about such cases where Indian nationals have been trained in Pakistani/POK territory for jihad in Aghanistan or Jammu and Kashmir.

Rise in Surrender by Militants

The trend of increasing surrender by terrorists, witnessed in Jammu and Kashmir in 2006, is catching up this year (2007) too, with 50 surrenders till Apr 2007, according to Central intelligence figures. Para

As many as 30 terrorists surrendered before the security forces in Apr 2007, including mass surrender by 24 ultras at Baramulla.[53] The figure for the correspondent month (April) in 2006 was 25 and in 2005 was seven, according to central intelligence agencies. The State Police figures for Apr 2007 in also 30.

Senior security officials say the recent trend of surrenders suggests that most of the terrorists laying down arms come from Hizb-ul-Mujahidden.

The reasons for the increasing trend of surrendering by terrorists include disillusionment with the Pakistani propaganda, and humiliation at the hands of terrorists from across the border.

Year Wise Surrender Figure

Agency	*2006*	*2005*	*2004*	*2003*
Central Intelligence Agencies	202	83	137	111
Jammu and Kashmir Police	190	64	137	119

NOTES

1. Editorial, *Pioneer*, 3 May 2007.
2. *Times* of *India*, 2 May 2007.
3. US 2007 Country Terror Reports, excerpted by Rajeev Sharma *Tribune*, 2 May 2007.
4. Rahul Tripathi, *Times of India*, 31 Mar 2007.
5. Praveen Swami, *Frontline*, 20 Oct 2006.

6. It is for note that the paper has ignored India even though it is the worst sufferer of the Pakistan-sponsored terrorism. May be, it is because of the simple fact that in India neither western civil population nor troops are at the receiving end! It seems Indians, of course, do not matter, at least not to the researchers concerned.
7. Haidar Naqvi, "In UP, terror has government patron", *Hindustan Times*, 3 Jun 2006.
8. *Ibid.*
9. Arun Joshi (with inputs from Rashid Ahmad, Zorawar Singh Jamwal and Tejinder Singh Sodhi), "They are wrong, more Muslims killed in J and K", *Hindustan Times*, 9 Jun 2006.
10. *Hindustan Times*, 23 Oct 206.
11. Brig Harwant Singh, *Hindustan Times*, 1 Nov. 2006.
12. The next day's newspapers carried the story of Col Sorna's death on 23 Dec 2006 with a note of personal poignancy. He had talked to his wife on phone on the 22nd and she was to join him on the 24th with their two children! This is the life with all its uncertainties for on Army man – and his family.
13. Maj Gen (Retd) Ashok Mehta, "Soldiers' lives are precious", *Pioneer*, 10 Jan 2007.
14. *Ibid.*
15. Kavita Suri, *Statesman*, 18 Apr 2007.
16. Kavita Suri, *Statesman*, 30 Apr 2007.
17. *Times of India*, 16 May 2006.
18. Ritu Sarin, "Blame J & K cops, not just us for Pathribal : Brigadier tells DGMO", *Indian Express*, 15 May 2006.
19. *Indian Express*, 15 May 2006.
20. Riyaz Wani, "Clash of Canons", *Indian Express*, 10 Dec 2006.
21. Pradeep Thakur, *Times of India*, 5 Apr 2007.
22. Editorial, "Deployment politics" : Militant's morale booster", *Statesmen*, 28 Mar 2007.
23. *Ibid.*
24. Vinod Sharma, *Hindustan Times*, 2 May 2007.
25. This highly exaggerated, and somewhat self-serving claim, understandably appears in the 1 May 2007 edition of the *Hindu*, the daily which is normally sympathetic to Pakistani stance on the Indo-Pakistan issues.
26. Rahul Singh, *Hindustan Times*, 29 Apr 2007.

27. *Indian Express*, 29 Apr 2007.
28. Praveen Swami, *Hindu*, 1 May 2007.
29. PTI, *Hindustan Times*, 2 May 2007.
30. Prashant Sood, Tribune, 6 May 2007.
31. SP Sharma, *Tribune*, 6 May 2007.
32. It does not speak well of the Indian press and its correspondents/journalists that the age of this 'ageing' leader remained unmentioned, and thus unknown to their readers. No one seems to have had time ar inclination to find out this simple factual information from the distinguished visitor, or his staff.
33. Wilson John, "A Pawn Comes calling", *Pioneer*, 2 May 2007.
34. *Ibid.*
35. Kavita Suri, *Statesman*, 29 Mar 2007.
36. Luv Puri, *Hindu*, 29 Apr 2007.
37. Luv Puri, *Hindu*, 20 May 2007.
38. Editorial, "Sufis and Saints : Not so new targets of terrorism", *Tribune*, 13 Nov 2006.
39. Kavita Suri, *Statesman*, 4 Jan 2007.
40. Tejinder Singh Sodhi, *Hindustan Times*, 14 Feb 2007.
41. PTI, *Indian Express*, 1 May 2007.
42. Muzamil Jaleel, *Indian Express*, 11 Apr 2007.
43. Akhilesh Suman, *Pioneer*, 11 Apr 2007.
44. Cited, Rakesh Rocky, *Indian Express*, 25 Oct 2006.
45. Aziz Hussain, *India Today*, 21 May 2007.
46. Praveen Swami, "Treading through a minefield", *Frontline*, 29 Dec 2006.
47. *Frontline*, Chennai, 29 Dec 2006.
48. Praveen Swami, "Between the hammer and the anvil", *Hindu*, 3 May 2007.
49. *Ibid.*
50. Yusuf Jameel, "Qaeda : J and K doorway for jihad on India", *Asian Age*, 9 Jun 2007.
51. Kavita Suri, "Kashmir terrorist deaths come as a relief now", *Statesman*, 8 Jun 2007.
52. Praveen Swami, "(First Indian) Kashmiri killed in Afghanistan" *Hindu*, 8 Jun 2007.
53. Rakesh K Singh, *Asian Age*, 12 Jun 2007.

TERRORISM IN NORTHERN INDIA

TERRORISM IN NORTHERN INDIA

JAMMU AND KASHMIR AND THE PUNJAB

(In Two Volumes)

(Volume 2)

COL. VED PRAKASH

KALPAZ PUBLICATIONS

DELHI-110052

Terrorism in Northern India

Rs. 1800 (Set)

© Col. Ved Prakash

ISBN: 978-81-7835-703-4 (Set)
ISBN: 978-81-7835-735-5 (Vol. 2)

All rights reserved. No Part of this book may be reproduced in any manner without written permission.

Published in 2008 in India by
Kalpaz Publications
C-30, Satyawati Nagar,
Delhi-110052
E-mail: kalpaz@hotmail.com
Phone : 9212729499

Laser Type Setting by: Quick Media, Delhi
Printed at : G. Print Process,Delhi

Contents

Contents

6

Some Important Documents

The Jammu and Kashmir problem dates back to the 1947 Partition of India. This chapter adduces some appendices which provide some relevant information on this problem. It also has some documents concerning the India-Pakistan problem on the State.

Appendices	Subject
A	Known Training camps for Kashmiri Militants in PoK
B	List of New Training camps and Forward Staging Posts in Pakistan and PoK.
C	Analysis of Militancy Based on Population Pattern and Affiliation of the Population.
D	Instrument of Accession: Article 370 and Commitment for Plebiscite.
E	The Resolution of the UN Security Council of August 13, 1948.
F	Agreement between Military Representations of India and Pakistan Regarding the Establishment of a Cease Fire Line in the State of Jammu and Kashmir.
G	Various UN Resolutions on J and K : 1948-1971.
H	Proclamation of War of Liberation : OP GIBRALTAR 1965.
I	Tashkent Declaration 10 January 1966.
J	Shimla Agreement, 3 July, 1972.
K	Text of Kashmir Accord (February 1975).
L	Select Bibliography.
M	Political Views of Pakistan/PoK on Islamabad's Direct Rule over the Northern Areas.

Appendix 'A'

KNOWN TRAINING CAMPS FOR KASHMIRI MILITANTS IN POK

Pok

- Aliabad
- Arza
- Athmugam
- Bagh
- Betal Pul
- Bhatapora
- Bhimber
- Chhattar
- Chinari
- Dhani
- Domel
- Garhi
- Gilgit
- Gojra Fort
- Haji Pir
- Hajira
- Hallan Shumali
- Hollapd Jungle
- Jabri
- Jari Khas
- Kamri
- Kel
- Kotli
- Lahabad Pur
- Leswa
- Lipa
- Makri
- Mang Bajri

- Mangla
- Mirpur
- Muzzaffarabad (Match Factory) and Sharkot Lines
- Nausheri
- Palandri
- Rawalkot
- Saphota
- Shahkot
- Shardi

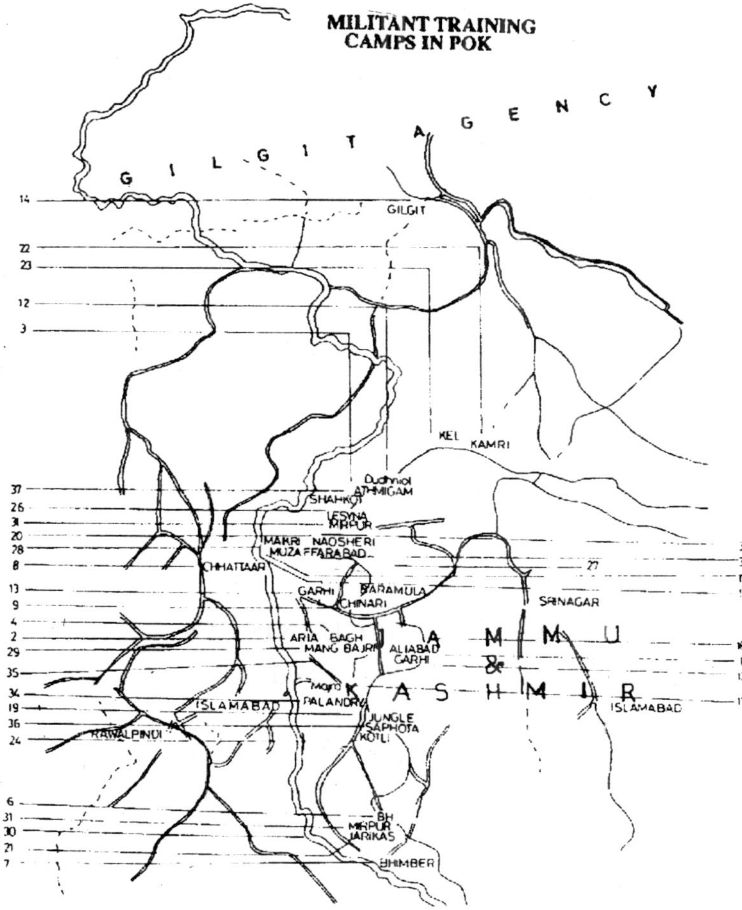

MILITANT TRAINING CAMPS IN POK

Appendix 'B'

LIST OF NEW TRAINING CAMPS AND FORWARD STAGING CAMPS IN PAKISTAN AND POK

Training Camps

- Muzzaffarabad (10 Camps)
- Garhi Dupatta
- Peshawar
- Ilaqa Gair (on Pakistan Afghanistan border)
- Gund Khost
- Kotli
- Attock
- Garhi Habibullah
- Mirpur
- Abbotabad
- Bagh
- Rawalakot

Staging Posts

- Khojabandi
- Lipa valley
- Dudhnial
- Kel
- Tejian
- Nekrun

CAMPS IN AFGHANISTAN

• Al Badar	Training in handling small arms for 45 days.
• Al Badar II	Training in automatic weapons, mortars ambushes, raids and explosive devices for 30 days.
• Al Badar III	Commando and specialised training for 60 days.
• 8 other camps	Location not know.

Appendix 'C'

ANALYSIS OF MILITANCY BASED ON POPULATION PATTERN AND AFFILIATION OF THE POPULATION

Demographic Pattern

The total Muslim population of Kashmir valley is above 30 lakhs. The breakdown being approximately:

(*a*) Shias — below 1,00000

(*b*) Sunnis — 29,00000.

There are six districts in the Kashmir valley, their demographic pattern is shown below:

Dist	*Muslims Shias / Sunnis*		*Hindus (before Migration)*	*Sikhs*	*Others*
Kupwara	NK	97.5%	2%	0.4%	0.1%
Baramulla	11%	87%	1.5%	0.3%	0.2%
Srinagar	26%	64.5%	8%	1.4%	0.1%
Budgam	32%	54.5%	2.8%	0.6%	0.1%
Pulwama	NK	95%	2.5%	1.6%	0.9%
Anantnag	NK	95.6%	3.8%	0.5%	0.1%

Age Structure

	ANE Below 20 Yrs.*	*Between 21 to 25 Yrs.*	*Between 26 to 35 Yers.*	*Above 35 years*
Fully Trained	40%	47%	12%	1%
Partly Trained	28%	31%	27%	14%

Economic Background

	Rs. 500 to Rs. 1000	*Rs. 1000 to Rs. 2000*	*Rs. 2000 & Above*	*Dependent*
Trained	68%	11%	2%	19%
Partly Trained	52%	21%	11%	16%

Education Factor

	Illiterates	*Under Matric*	*Under Graduate*	*Graduate and above*
Trained	21%	44%	29%	6%
Untrained	22%	40%	25%	13%

*ANE—Anti National Element

Professions

	Labourers	*Petty Traders*	*Students*	*Agriculturists*	*Govt. Servants*
Trained	42%	14%	19%	22%	3%
Partly Untrained	25%	18%	17%	21%	19%

Motivational Factors

Under Duress	—	35%
Persuasion	—	28%
Allurement	—	22%
Ideology	—	16%
Other reasons	—	9%

Conclusions

- Statistics indicate that fundamentalism is the main motivating factor for militancy.
- Due to overwhelming Muslim majority in all areas, there can be no resistance move from the minority communities.
- 87% of the trained militants are below the age group of 25 years.
- Both the trained and partly trained militants are either illiterate or under matric.
- Most of the trained and partly trained militants belong to the weaker sections of society.
- Only about 16% of the total population is supporting militancy on ideological grounds. 1/3rd of the militants are being coerced to join the ranks of militancy.

Major Militants Organisations and their Areas of Influence

Kupwara Dist	—	JKHM, Al-Barq and JKLF
Baramulla Dist	—	Al Jehad, IUM, JKLF and JKHM
Srinagar Dist	—	Al Umar, JKLF, JKHM, Al Jehad and IUM
Budgam Dist	—	JKHM, JKLF and IUM
Pulwama Dist	—	IUM, JKHM and JKLF
Anantnag Dist	—	JKLF, Al Jehad, JKHM

Other Militant Outfits Active in J&K

People's League

Hizbullah, Hizb-Islam, Hizb-ul-Jehad

Harkat-i-Mujahidin

Zia Missionary Force, Tehrik-a-Islami

Al Karbala, Al Khomeni

Operation Bala Kote, Mehaz-e-Azadi

Dukhtran-e-Millat (Women's Organisation)

Muslim Gurrilla Tigers

Zarb-i-Kaleem

Islamic Students League

General Pattern of Militant Activities

Initially the activities of militants centred around urban areas. Subsequently due to greater deployment and superiority of Security Forces, the anti-national elements were forced to move to rural areas. With the Security Forces enlarging their area of operations to rural areas, the militant activity has shifted back to urban areas.

At no one point of time, the anti-national element activities have been carried out throughout the valley. These have been confined to penny pockets. This has been done with an aim to divert the attention of Security Forces and to release pressure on the anti-national elements operating in particular areas.

Present Situation

- Due to the above reasons, militants have not been able to keep their arms caches at chosen places as they are on the run.
- The core leaders of militant outfits have been unable to provide effective leadership or evade the army dragnet easily.
- This has resulted in anti-national elements putting up disjointed operations against the Security Forces.
- The ground realities indicate that the rural population is pro-independence, whereas, the urbanities favour accession to Pakistan.

- Locals of Gurez and Tangdhar valleys have remained neutral.
- Areas of Sopore, Kupwara, Baramulla have served as staging centres for infiltration exfiltration and coordinating hub centres.
- The nerve centre of militancy has always been Srinagar as the majority of the militant leaders are based here.
- Significant percentage of the people in Anantnag and Badgam support militancy actively.
- Isolate militancy and choke it in urban areas.

Appendix 'D'

INSTRUMENT OF ACCESSION: ARTICLE 370 AND COMMITMENT FOR PLEBISCITE

In 1947, the J & K state was one of 562 (or so) princely states and these were divided in three categories. There were 140 major states out of which Jammu and Kashmir was one. The rulers of the Indian states were part of the British Indian Empire which consisted of eleven provinces and the Indian princely states.

The mechanism for joining the new dominions was adopted from Government of India Act of 1935 which provided for joining India or Pakistan through an Instrument of Accession. It was not specified that the Rulers would have to take the wishes of their subjects into account before joining either of the dominions. It was under these provisions the Maharaja of Jammu and Kashmir opted for India.

The text of the Instrument of Accession executed by Maharaja Hari Singh is appended. (Appendix 'D'). The main point which should be noted however is: Through this instrument of accession, the state handed over only three major powers to the Union of India *viz.*, Defence, External Affairs and Communication.

This format of accession was applicable to all major states and was not peculiar to J & K. The following Articles in the Instrument of Accession executed by Maharaja Hari Singh should be noted because they were special.

PARA 7: Nothing in this instrument shall be deemed to commit me in any way to acceptance of any future constitution of India or to fetter my discretion to enter into arrangements with the Government of India under any such future constitution.

PARA 8: Nothing in this instrument affects the continuance of my sovereignty in and over the state, or, save as provided by or under this instrument, the exercise of powers, authority and rights now enjoyed by me as Ruler of this state or the validity of any law at present in force in the state.

(Kashmir at this stage was governed by Jammu and Kashmir Constitution Act of 1939 and the instrument of accession was not without certain conditions which safeguarded the Maharaja's position. However, the Instrument of Accession was unconditional. Therefore it was in no way legally provisional or subject to the wishes of the people or heirs of the J & K state. There should be no question of negotiating on the validity of accession of the State to India.)

Article 370

In June 1949 J & K State like any other erstwhile princely state sent four representatives to the Constituent Assembly. However, Sheikh Abdullah made it clear that their association with India would be based on *Article* 7 of the Instrument of Accession. This was accepted and thereby a special status was conceded. Article 306A was thus adopted in the draft constitution of India which became Article 370 in the final constitution.

Article 370 in its application granted only limited powers to the Centre in that laws could be made only in respect of Foreign Affairs, Communication and Defence. The Article also provides for protection of State subjects. In legal terms the following excerpts from Article 370 are noteworthy.

1. The power of Parliament to make ..... Laws shall be limited to:

(*i*) those matters ... which in consultation with the government of the State are declared by the President to correspond to matters specified in the Instrument of Accession.

(*ii*) such other matters... as with the concurrence of the government of the State, the President may by order specify.

Provide further that no order which relates to matters other than those referred to in the last preceding proviso shall be issued except with the concurrence of the government.

Article 370 has generated major controversies since its very inception. In the present circumstances whether Article 370 is retained or scrapped is of little relevance. It is obvious, however, that the whole relationship between Centre and the States requires revision. In these circumstances Article 370 or other similar provisions like 371 and the sixth schedule of our constitution may be automatically revised.

The following points should be noted in regard to the Instrument of Accession:

- The plebiscite question and Article 370 of our constitution has no connection with the validity of Accession.
- Accession was final but not without conditions laid down by the Maharaja in Articles 7 and 8 of the Instrument of Accession.
- From December 1964 onwards a series of constitutional amendments were effected which eroded Article 370 greatly. Articles 356 and 357 of the Constitution were made applicable to J&K now. These amendments enabled the Centre to assume the government of the state and exercise legislative powers; these articles thus enabled the Centre to institute President's Rule in the state. The nomenclatures of 'Sadr-e-Riyasat' was changed to Governor and was now to be nominated by the centre.

The prime minister of J & K was now to be named 'Chief Minister' like in any other state of the Union. Moreover, now four Kashmiri representatives in the Lok Sabha (Lower House of the Indian Parliament), who had been hitherto nominated by the State Legislative Assembly, were to be elected directly by the people of the State. Thus Article 370 was gradually eroded over a period of time and the hue and cry against Article 370 has little relevance today.

Plebiscite

Question of plebiscite arose from the commitment Lord Mountbatten made on behalf of the Government of India on 27 October 1947 in reply to Maharaja Hari Singh's letter sent with the proposals of the Instrument of Accession. Relevant points of Mountbatten's reply are reproduced below :

> "In special circumstances mentioned by your Highness my Government has decided to accept the accession of Kashmir state to the Dominion of India. Consistently with their policy that, in case of any state where the issue of accession should be decided in accordance with the wishes of the people of

> the State, it is my government's wish that, as soon as law and order have been restored in Kashmir and her soil cleared of the invader, the question of the state's accession should be settled by a reference to the people."

It should be noted, that the word plebiscite or self-determination was not used in this communication. Nehru however made many statements in this regard (quoted earlier). He talked of a UN supervised plebiscite on the floor of the Parliament also.

> "In order to establish our 'bonafides' we have suggested that when the people are given the chance to decide their future, this should be done under the supervision of an impartial tribunal such as the United Nations Organisation. The issue in Kashmir is whether violence and naked force should decide the future or the will of the people."*

India did commit itself to holding a UN supervised plebiscite as per UN Security Council resolutions (13 August 1948 - Part III) and UNCIP Resolution 5 January 1949, Para 1, 2 and 3 subject to conditions laid down in Part II Truce Agreement A of the UN resolution of 13 August 1948. The main conditions on which India accepted the UNCIP resolution in 1948 should however also be noted :

- Assurance by UNCIP that Pakistan would be excluded from all affairs of Jammu and Kashmir.
- Azad J & K would not be recognised.
- Sovereignty of J & K government over the entire territory shall not be brought into question.
- Pakistani troops would be withdrawn from all parts of J & K.

The main conditions of UNCIP resolution for plebiscite were never fulfilled by Pakistan; in fact they fought shy of 'plebiscite' because they feared it would carry the whole of J & K to India. Later India allowed the matters to drift and finally discarded the idea of the plebiscite as the following statements made by Mr. Krishna Menon and Mr. M.C. Chagla in the Security Council, at different times, clearly indicate.

In January 1957 Mr. Krishna Menon stated the following in the Security Council (763th meeting) regarding the plebiscite:

> "If an offer is made and it is not accepted at the time it is made, it cannot be held for generations over the heads of those who made it."

In 1964 Mr. M.C. Chagla stated in the Security Council (1088th meeting 5 February 1964) "I wish to make it clear on behalf of my government that under no circumstances can we agree to the holding of a plebiscite in Kashmir."

Pakistan's insistence on self-determination as the basic condition of Indo-Pak talks on J & K issues are really not relevant after several decades and two wars over J & K. Pakistan of course never recognised J & K's accession to India. In Mr. Liaqat Ali's words it was a fraud. He said :

> "We do not recognise this accession. The accession of Kashmir to India is a fraud, perpetrated on the people of Kashmir by its cowardly ruler with the aggressive help of the Indian government."

LETTER OF 26 OCTOBER 1947, FROM MAHARAJA SIR HARI SINGH TO LORD MOUNTBATTEN, REQUESTING THE ACCESSION OF THE STATE TO INDIA

My dear Lord Mountbatten,

I have to inform Your Excellency that a grave emergency has arisen in my State and request the immediate assistance of your Government. As Your Excellency is aware, the State of Jammu and Kashmir has not acceded to either the Dominion of India or Pakistan. Geographically my State is contiguous with both of them. Besides, my State has a common boundary with the Union of Soviet Socialist Republics and with China. In their external relations the Dominions of India and Pakistan cannot ignore this fact. I wanted to take time to decide to which Dominion I should accede or whether it is not in the best interests of both the Dominions and of my State to stand independent, of course with friendly and cordial relations with both. I accordingly approached the Dominions of India and Pakistan to enter in to a standstill agreement with my State. The Pakistan Government accepted this arrangement. The Dominion of India desired further discussion with representatives of my Government. I could not arrange this in view of the developments indicated below. In fact the Pakistan Government under the standstill agreement is operating the post and telegraph system inside the State. Though we have got a standstill agreement with the Pakistan Government, that Government permitted a steady and increasing strangulation of supplies like food, salt and petrol to my State.

Afridis, soldiers in plain clothes, and desperadoes with modern weapons have been allowed to infiltrate into the State, at first in the Poonch area, then from Sialkot and finally in a mass in the area adjoining Hazara district on the Ramkote side. The result has been that the limited number of troops at the disposal of the State had to be dispersed and thus had to face the enemy at several points simultaneously, so that it has become difficult to stop the wanton destruction of life and property and the looting of the Mahura power house, which supplies electric current to the whole of Srinagar and which has been burnt. The number of women who have been kidnapped and raped makes my heart bleed. The wild forces thus let loose on the State are marching on with the aim of capturing Srinagar, the summer capital of my Government, as a first step to overrunning the whole State. The mass infiltration of tribesmen drawn from distant areas of the North-West Frontier Province, coming regularly in motor trucks, using the Mansehra-Mazaffarabad road and fully armed with up-to-date weapons, cannot possibly be done without the knowledge of the Provincial Government of the North-West Frontier Province and the Government of Pakistan. Inspite of repeated appeals made by my Government no attempt has been made to check these raiders or to stop them from coming into my State. In fact, both the radio and the Press of Pakistan have reported these occurrences. The Pakistan radio even put out the story that a provisional government has been set up in Kashmir. The people of my State, both Muslims and non-Muslims, generally have taken no part at all.

With the conditions obtaining at present in my State and the great emergency of the situation as it exists, I have no option but to ask for help from the Indian Dominion. Naturally they cannot send the help asked for by me without my State acceding to the Dominion of India. I have accordingly decided to do so, and I attach the instrument of accession for acceptance by your Government. The other alternative is to leave my State and the people to free-booters. On this basis no civilised Government can exist or be maintained. This alternative I will never allow to happen so long as I am the ruler of the State and I have life to defend my country. I may also inform Your Excellency's Government that it is my intention at once to set up an interim government and to ask Sheikh Abdullah to carry the responsibilities in this emergency with my Prime Minister.

If my State is to be saved, immediate assistance must be available at Srinagar. Mr VP Menon is fully aware of the gravity of the situation and will explain it to you, if further explanation is needed.

In haste and with kindest regards,

Yours sincerely,

Hari Singh.

INSTRUMENT OF ACCESSION OF JAMMU AND KASHMIR STATE

The following is the text of the Instrument of Accession executed by the Ruler of Jammu and Kashmir State on 26 October 1947.

Whereas the Indian Independence Act, 1947 provides that as from the fifteenth day of August 1947, there shall be set up an independent Dominion known as India, and that the Government of India Act, 1935, shall, with such omissions, additions, adaptations and modifications as the Governor-General may be by order specify be applicable to the Dominion of India; and whereas the Government India Act, 1935, as so adapted by the Governor-General provides that an Indian State may accede to the Dominion of India by an Instrument of Accession executed by the Ruler thereof :

Now, therefore,

I, Shriman Indar Mahandar Rajrajeshwar Maharajadhiraj Shri Hari Singhji, Jammu Kashmir Naresh Tatha Tibbet adi Deshadhipathi, Ruler of Jammu and Kashmir State, in the exercise of my sovereignty in and over my said State Do hereby execute this my Instrument of Accession and

1. I hereby declare that I accede to the Dominion of India with the intent that the Governor-General of India, the Dominion Legislature, the Federal Court and any other Dominion authority established for the purposes of the Dominion shall, by virtue of this my Instrument of Accession, but subject always to the terms thereof, and for the purpose only of the Dominion, exercise in relation to the State of Jammu and Kashmir (hereinafter referred to as "this State") such functions as may be vested in them by or Under the Government of India Act, 1935, as in force in the Dominion of India on the 15th day of August 1947 (which Act as so in force is hereafter referred to as "the Act").

2. I hereby assume the obligation of ensuring that due effect is given to the provisions of the Act within this State so far as they are applicable therein by virtue of this my Instrument of Accession.

3. I accept the matters specified in the Schedule hereto as the matters with respect to which the Dominion Legislature may make laws for this State.

4. I hereby declare that I accede to the Dominion of India on the assurance that if an agreement is made between the Governor-General and the Ruler of this state whereby any function in relation to the administration in this State of any law of the Dominion Legislature shall be exercised by the Ruler of this State, then any such agreement shall be deemed to form part of this Instrument and shall be construed and have effect accordingly.

5. The terms of this my Instrument of Accession shall not be varied by any amendment of the Act or of the Indian Independence Act, 1947, unless such amendment is accepted by me by an Instrument supplementary to this Instrument.

6. Nothing in this Instrument shall empower the Dominion Legislature to make any law for this State authorising the compulsory acquisition of land for any purpose, but I hereby undertake that should the Dominion for the purposes of a Dominion law which applies in this State deem it necessary to acquire any land, I will at their request acquire the land at their expense or if the land belongs to me transfer it to them on such terms as may be agreed, or in default of agreement, determined by an arbitrator to be appointed by the Chief Justice of India.

7. Nothing in this Instrument shall be deemed to commit me in any way to acceptance of any future constitution of India or to fetter my discretion to enter into arrangements with the Government of India under any such future constitution.

8. Nothing in this Instrument affects the continuance of my sovereignty in and over this State, or, save as provided by or under this Instrument, the exercise of any powers, authority and rights now enjoyed by me as Ruler of this State or the validity of any law at present in force in this State.

9. I hereby declare that I execute this Instrument on behalf of this State and that any reference in this Instrument to me or to the Ruler of the State is to be construed as including a reference to my heirs and successors.

Given under my hand this twenty-sixth day of October, nineteen hundred and forty-seven.

Hari Singh Maharajadhiraj of Jammu and Kashmir State

ACCEPTANCE OF INSTRUMENT OF ACCESSION OF JAMMU & KASHMIR STATE BY THE GOVERNOR-GENERAL OF INDIA

I do hereby accept this Instrument of Accession. Dated this twenty-seventh day of October, nineteen hundred and forty-seven.

Mountbatten of Burma Governor-General of India.

Appendix 'E'

THE RESOLUTION OF THE UNITED NATIONS SECURITY COUNCIL OF AUGUST 13, 1948

The United Nations Commission for India and Pakistan, having given careful consideration to the points of view expressed by the representatives of India and Pakistan regarding the situation in the state of Jammu and Kashmir; and—

Being of the opinion that the prompt cessation of hostilities and the correction of conditions of the continuance of which is likely to endanger international peace and security are essential to implementation of its endeavors to assist the Government of India and Pakistan in affecting a final settlement of the situation;

Resolves to submit simultaneously to the Governments of India and Pakistan the following proposals :

Part I: Cease-fire order

(*a*) The Government of India and Pakistan agree that their respective High Commands will issue separately and simultaneously a cease-fire order to apply to all forces under their control in the state of Jammu and Kashmir as of the earliest practicable date or dates to be mutually agreed upon within four days after these proposals have been accepted by both Governments.

(*b*) The High Commands of the Indian and Pakistani forces agree to refrain from taking any measures that might augment the military potential of the forces under their control in the State of Jammu and Kashmir. (For the purpose of these proposals forces under their control shall be considered to include all forces organised and unorganised, fighting or participating in hostilities on their respective sides).

(*c*) The Commanders-in-Chief of the forces of India and Pakistan shall promptly confer regarding any necessary local changes in present dispositions which may facilitate the cease-fire.

(*d*) In its discretion and as the Commission may find practicable, the Commission will appoint military observers who, under the authority of the Commission and with the co-operation of both Commands, will supervise the observance of the cease-fire.

(*e*) The Government of India and the Government of Pakistan agree to appeal to their respective peoples to assist in creating and maintaining an atmosphere favourable to the promotion of further negotiation.

Part II : Truce Agreement

Simultaneously with the acceptance of the proposal for the immediate cessation of hostilities as outlined in Part I, both Governments accept the following principles as a basis for the formulation of a truce agreement, the details of which shall be worked out in discussion between their representatives and the Commission.

A

1. As the presence of troops of Pakistan in the territory of the State of Jammu and Kashmir constitues a material change in the situation since it was represented by the Government of Pakistan before the Security Council, the Government of Pakistan agrees to withdraw its troops from the state.
2. The Government of Pakistan will use its best endeavor to secure the withdrawal from the state of Jammu and Kashmir of tribesmen and Pakistani nationals not normally resident therein who have entered the State for the purpose of fighting.
3. Pending a final solution, the territory evacuated by the Pakistani troops will be administered by the local authorities under the surveillance of the Commission.

B

1. When the Commission shall have notified the Governments of India and Pakistan that the tribesmen and Pakistani National referred to in Part II, A, 2 hereof have withdrawn, thereby terminating the situation which was represented by the Government of India to the Security Council as having occasioned the presence of Indian forces in the state of Jammu and Kashmir, and

further that the Pakistani forces are being withdrawn from the state of Jammu and Kashmir, the Government of India agrees to begin to withdraw the bulk of its forces from that state in stages to be agreed upon with the Commission.

2. Pending the acceptance of the conditions for a final settlement of the situation in the State of Jammu and Kashmir, the Indian Government will maintain the lines existing the moment of the cease-fire the minimum strength of its forces which in agreement with the Commission are considered necesary to assist local authorities in the observance of law and order. The Commission will have observers stationed where it deems necessary.

The Government of India will undertake to ensure that the Government of the State of Jammu and Kashmir will take all measures within its power to make it publicly known that peace, law and order will be safeguarded and that all human and political rights will be guaranteed.

C

Upon signature, the full text of the truce agreement a communique containing the principles thereof as agreed upon between the two Governments and the Commission, will be made public.

Part III

The Government of India and the Government of Pakistan re-affirm their wish that the future status of the State of Jammu and Kashmir shall be determined in accordance with the will of the people and to that end, upon acceptance of the truce agreement, both Government agree to enter into consultations with the Commission to determine fair and equitable conditions whereby such free expression will be assured.

U.N.C.I.P. RESOLUTION OF JANUARY 5, 1949

The United Nations Commission for India and Pakistan, having received from the Governments of India and Pakistan, in communications dated December 23 and December 25, 1948, respectively, their acceptance of the following principles which are supplementary to the Commission's resolution of August 13, 1948 :

1. The question of the accession of the State of Jammu and Kashmir to India or Pakistan will be decided through the democratic method of a free and impartial plebiscite.
2. A plebiscite will be held when it shall be found by the Commission that the cease-fire and truce arrangements set forth in Parts I and II of the Commission's resolution of August 13, 1948, have been carried out and arrangements for the plebiscite have been completed.
3. (a) The Secretary-General of the United Nations will, in agreement with the Commission, nominate a Plebiscite Administrator who shall be a personality of high international standing and commanding general confidence. He will be formally appointed to office by the Government of Jammu and Kashmir.

   (*b*) The Plebiscite Administrator shall derive from the State of Jammu and Kashmir the powers he considers necessary for organizing and conducting the plebiscite and for ensuring the freedom and impartiality of the plebiscite.

   (*c*) The Plebiscite Administrator shall have authority to appoint such staff of assistants and observers as he may require.
4. (*a*) After implementation of Parts I and II of the Commission's resolution of August 13, 1948, and when the Commission is satisfied that peaceful conditions have been restored in the State, the Commission and the Plebiscite Administrator will determine, in consultation with the Government of India, the final disposal of Indian and State armed forces, such disposal to be with due regard to the security of the State and the freedom of the plebiscite.

   (*b*) As regards the territory referred to in A-2 of Part II of the resolution of August 13, final disposal of the armed forces in that territory will be determined by the Commission and the Plebiscite Administrator in consultation with the local authorities.

5. All civil and military authorities within the State and the principal political elements of the State will be required to co-operate with the Plebiscite Administrator in the preparation for the holding of the plebiscite.

6. (*a*) All citizens of the State who have left it on account of the disturbances will be invited and be free to return and to exercise all their rights as such citizens. For the purpose of facilitating repatriation there shall be appointed two Commissions, one composed of nominees of India and the other of nominees of Pakistan. The Commissions shall operate under the direction of the Plebiscite Administrator. The Governments of India and Pakistan and all authorities within the State of Jammu and Kashmir will collaborate with the Plebiscite Administrator in putting this provision into effect.

   (*b*) All persons (other than citizens of the State) who on or since August 15, 1947, have entered it for other than lawful purpose, shall be required to leave the State.

7. All authorities within the State of Jammu and Kashmir will undertake to ensure, in collaboration with the Plebiscite Administrator, that :

   (*a*) There is no threat, coercion or intimidation, bribery or other undue influence on the voters in the plebiscite;

   (*b*) No restrictions are placed on legitimate political activity throughout the State. All subjects of the State, regardless of creed, caste, or party, shall be safe and free in expressing their views and in voting on the question of the accession of the State to India or Pakistan. There shall be freedom of the press, speech and assembly and freedom of travel in the State, including freedom of lawful entry and exit;

   (*c*) All political prisoners are released;

(*d*) Minorities in all parts of the State are accorded adequate protection; and

(*e*) There is no victimization.

8. The Plebiscite Administrator may refer to the United Nations Commission for India and Pakistan problems on which he may require assistance, and the Commission may in its discretion call upon the Plebiscite Administrator to carry out on its behalf any of the responsibilities with which it has been entrusted.

9. At the conclusion of the plebiscite, the Plebiscite Administrator shall report the result thereof to the Commission and to the Government of Jammu and Kashmir. The Commission shall then certify to the Security Council whether the plebiscite has or has not been free and impartial.

10. Upon the signature of the truce agreement the details of the foregoing proposals will be elaborated in the consultations envisaged in part III of the Commission's resolution of August 13, 1948. The Plebiscite Administrator will be fully associated in these consultations.

Commends the Governments of India and Pakistan for their prompt action in ordering a cease-fire to take effect from one minute before midnight of January 1, 1949, pursuant to the agreement arrived at as provided for by the Commission's resolution of August 13, 1948, and by the foregoing principles.

Appendix 'F'

AGREEMENT BETWEEN MILITARY REPRESENTATIVES OF INDIA AND PAKISTAN REGARDING THE ESTABLISHMENT OF A CEASEFIRE LINE IN THE STATE OF JAMMU AND KASHMIR

1. Introduction

A. The military representatives of India and Pakistan met together in Karachi from 18 July to 27 July 1949, under the auspices of the Truce Sub-Committee of the United Nations Commission for India and Pakistan.

B. The members of the Indian delegation were : Lieutenant General S.M. Shrinagesh, Major General K.S. Thimayya, Brigadier S.H.F.J. Manekshaw. As observers: Mr. H.M. Patel, Mr. V. Sahay.

C. The members of the Pakistan delegation were : Major General W.J. Cawthorn, Major General Nazir Ahmad, Brigadier M. Sher Khan. As observers : Mr. M. Ayub, Mr. A.A. Khan.

D. The members of the Truce Sub-Committee of the United Nations Commission for India and Pakistan were: Mr. Hemando Samper (Colombia), Chairman; Mr. William L.S. Williams (United States); Lieutenant General Maurice Delvoie, Military Advisor; Mr. Miguel A. Marin, Legal Advisor.

II. Agreement

A. Considering :

1. That the United Nations Commission for India and Pakistan, in its letter dated 2 July, 1949 (Annex 25). invited the Government of India and Pakistan to send fully authorized military representatives to meet jointly in Karachi under the auspices of the Commission's Truce Sub-committee to establish a ceasefire line in the State of Jammu and Kashmir, mutually agreed upon by the Governments of India and Pakistan.

2. That the United Nations Commission for India and Pakistan in its letter stated that 'The meetings will be for military purposes; political issues will not be

considered," and that 'They will be conducted without prejudice to negotiations concerning the truce agreement";

3. That in the same letter the United Nations Commission for India and Pakistan further stated that: "The ceasefire line is a complement of the suspension of hostilities, which falls within the provisions of Part I of the resolution of 13 August 1948, and can be considered separately from the questions relating to part II of the same resolution."

4. That the Governments of India and Pakistan, in their letters dated 7 July 1949, to the Chairman of the Commission, accepted the Commission's invitation to the military conference in Karachi.

B. The delegations of India and Pakistan, duly authorized, have reached the following agreement:

1. Under the provisions of Part I of the resolution of 13 August 1948, and as a complement of the suspension of hostilities in the State of Jammu and Kashmir on 1 January 1949, a ceasefire line is established.

2. The ceasefire line runs from Manawar in the south, north to Keran and from Karan east to the glacier area, as follows:

   (*a*) The line from Manawar to the south bank of the Jhelum River at Urusa (inclusive to India) is the line now defined by the factual positions about which there is agreement between both parties. Where there has hitherto not been agreement, the line shall be as follows:

      (*i*) In Patrana area; Kohel (inclusive to Pakistan) north along the Khuwala Kas Nullah up to Point 2276 (inclusive to India), thence to Kimi (inclusive to India).

      (*ii*) Khambha, Pir Satwan, Point 3150 and Point 3606 are inclusive to India, thence the line runs to the factual position at Bagla Gala, thence to the factual position at Point 3300.

(*iii*) In the south of Uri the positions of Pir Kanthi and Ledi Gali are inclusive to Pakistan.

(*b*) From the north bank of the Jhelum River the line runs from a point opposite the village of Urusa (NL 972109), thence north following the Ballaseth Da Nar Nullah (inclusive to Pakistan), up to NL 973140, thence northeast to Choota Qazinag (Point 10657, inclusive to India), thence to NM 010180, thence to NM 037210, thence to Point 11825 (NM 025354, inclusive to Pakistan), thence to Tutmari Gali (to be shared by both sides, posts to be established 500 yards, on either side of the Gali), thence to the northwest through the first "R" of Burji Nar to north of Gadori, thence straight west to just north of Point 9870, thence along the black line north of Bijidhar to north of Batarasi, thence to just south of Sudpura, thence due north to the Kathaqazinag Nullah, thence along the Nullah to its junction with the Grangnar Nullah, thence along the latter Nullah to Kajnwala Pathra (inclusive to India), thence acrose the Danna ridge (following the factual positions) to Richmar Gali (inclusive to India), thence north to Thanda Katha Nullah, thence north to the Kishanganga River. The line then follows the Kishanganga River up to a point situated between Jargi and Tarban, thence (all inclusive to Pakistan) to Bankoran, thence northeast to Khori, thence to the hill feature 8930 (in Square 9053), thence straight north to Point 10164 (in Square 9057), thence to point 10323 (in Square 9161), thence northeast straight to Guthur, thence to Bhulpathra, thence to NL 980707, thence following the Bugina Nullah to the junction with the Kishanganga River at Point 4739. Thereafter the line follows the Kishanganga River to Keran and onwards to Point 4996 (NL 975818).

(*c*) From Point 4996 the line follows (all inclusive to Pakistan) the Jamgar Nullah eastward to Point 12124, to Katware, to Point 6678, then to the northeast to Sarian (Point 11279), to Point 11837, to Point 13090, to Point 12641, thence east again to Point 11142, thence to Dhakki, thence to Point 11415, thence to Point 10301, thence to Point 7507, thence to Point 10685, thence to Point 8388, thence southeast to Point 11812. Thence the line runs (all inclusive to India) to Point 13220, thence across the River to the east to Point 13449 (Durmat), thence to Point 14586 (Anzbari), thence to Point 13554, thence to Milestone 45 on the Burzil Nullah, thence to the east to Ziankal (Point 12909), thence to the southeast to Point 11114, thence to Point 12216, thence to Point 12867, thence to the east to Point 11264, thence to Karo (Point 14985), thence to Point 14014, thence to Point 12089, thence following the track to Point 12879. From there the line runs to Point 13647 (Karobal Gali, to be shared by both sides). The ceasefire line runs thence through Retagah Chhish (Point 15316), thence through Point 15889, thence through Point 17392, thence through Point 16458, thence to Marpo La (to be shared by both sides), thence though Point 17561, thence through Point 17352, thence through Point 18400, thence through Point 16760, thence to (inclusive to India), Dalunang.

(*d*) From Dalunang eastwards the ceasefire line will follow the general line Point 15495, Ishmam, Manus, Gangam Gunderman, Point 13620, Junkar (Point 17628), Marmak, Natsara, Shangruti (Point 17531). Chorbat La (Point 16700). Chalunka (on the Shyok River), Khor, thence north to the glaciers. This portion of the ceasefire line shall be demarcated in detail on the basis of the factual position as of 27 July 1949 by the local commanders, assisted by United Nations Military Observers.

C. The ceasefire line described above shall be drawn on a one-inch map (where available) and than be verified mutually on the ground by local commanders on each side with the assistance of the United Nations Military

Observers, so as to eliminate any no-man's land. In the event that the local commanders are unable to reach agreement, the matter shall be referred to the Commission's Military Advisor, whose decision shall be final. After this verification, the Military Advisor will issue to each High Command a map on which will be marked the definitive ceasefire line.

D. No troops shall be stationed or operate in the area of the Burzil Nullah from south of Minimarg to the ceasefire line. This area is bounded on the west by the ridge leading northeast from Dudgaikal to Point 13071, to Point 9497, to Point 13466, to Point 13463, and on the east by the ridge running from Point 12470, to Point 11608, to Point 13004, to Point 13976, to Point 13450. Pakistan may, however, post troops on the western of the above ridges to cover the approaches to Kamri Bal Pass.

E. In any dispositions that may be adopted in consequence to the present agreement troops will remain at least 500 yards from the ceasefire line except where the Kishanganaga River constitutes the line. Points which have been shown as inclusive to one party may be occupied by that party, but the troops of the other party shall remain at a distance of 500 yards.

F. Both sides shall be free to adjust their defensive positions behind the ceasefire line as determined in paragraphs A through E, inclusive, subject to no wire or mines being used when new bunkers and defences are constructed. There shall be no increase of forces or strengthening of defences in areas where no major adjustments are involved by the determination of the ceasefire line.

G. The action permitted by paragraph F above shall not be accompanied or accomplished by the introduction of additional military potential by either side into the State of Jammu and Kashmir.

H. Except as modified by paragraphs A to G, inclusive, above, the military agreements between the two High Commands relating to the ceasefire of 1 January, 1949 shall continue to remain operative.

I. The United Nations Commission for India and Pakistan will station Observers where it deems necessary.

J. The delegations shall refer this agreement to their respective Governments for ratification. The documents of ratification shall be deposited with the United Nations Commission for India and Pakistan not later than 31 July, 1949.

K. A period of thirty days from the date of ratification shall be allowed to each side to vacate the areas at present occupied by them beyond the ceasefire line as now determined. Before the expiration of this thirty-day period there shall be no forward movement into areas to be taken over by either side pursuant to this agreement, except by mutual agreement between local commanders.

In faith whereof the undersigned sign this document in three original copies.

Done in Karachi on 27 July, 1949.

For the Government of India:

(Signed) S.M. SHRINAGESH

For the Government of Pakistan:

(Signed) J. CAWTHORN

Major General

For the United Nations Commission for India and Pakistan:

(Signed) Hemando SAMPER

M. DELVOIE

Apppendix 'G'

VARIOUS UN RESOLUTIONS ON J & K : 1948-1971

Resolutions of the Security Council on the India-Pakistan Question, 17 January, 1948 to 2nd December 1957

1. 38(1948). Resolution of 17 January, 1948 (S/651)

The Security Council.

Having heard statements on the situation in Kashmir from representatives of the Governments of India and Pakistan.

Recognising the urgency of the situation.

Taking note of the telegram addressed on 6 January, 1948 by its President to each of the parties[1] and of their replies thereto[2], in which they affirmed their intention to conform to the Charter of the United Nations.

1. Calls upon both the Government of India and the Government of Pakistan to take immediately all measures within their power (including public appeals to their people) calculated to improve the situation, and to refrain from making any statements and from doing or causing to be done or permitting any acts which might aggravate the situation;
2. Further requests each of those Governments to inform the Council immediatley of any material change in the situation which occurs or appears to either of them to be about to occur while the matter is under consideration by the Council, and consult with the Council thereon.

Adopted at the 229th meeting by 9 votes
to none, with 2 abstentions
(Ukrainian Soviet Socialist Republic,
Union of Soviet Socialist Republic).

17 January, 1948

2. Resolution 39 Adopted by the Security Council at its 230th Meeting, 20 January, 1948 (S/654)

(Original text: English)

The Security Council

Considering that it may investigate any dispute or any situation which might by its continuance, endanger the maintenance of international peace and security; that, in the existing state of affairs between India and Pakistan, such an investigation is a matter of urgency.

Adopts the following resolution :

A. A Commission of the Security Council is hereby established, composed of representatives of three members of the United Nations, one to be selected by India, one to be selected by Pakistan, and the third to be designated by the two so selected.

Each representative on the Commission shall be entitled to select his alternates and assistants.

B. The Commission shall proceed to the spot as quickly as possible. It shall act under the authority of the Security Council and in accordance with the direction it may receive from it. It shall keep the Security Council currently informed of its activities and of the development of the situation, it shall report to the Security Council regularly, submitting its conclusions and proposals.

C. The Commission is invested with a dual function :

(1) To investigate the facts pursuant to Article 34 of the Charter;

(2) To exercise, without interrupting the work of the Security Council, any mediatory influence likely to smooth away difficulties; to carry out the directions given to it by the Security Council; and to report how far the advice and directions, if any, of the Security Council, have been carried out.

D. The Commission shall perform the functions described in Clause C :

(1) In regard to the situation in the Jammu and Kashmir State set out in the letter of the representative of India addressed to the President of the Security Council, dated 1 January, 1948, and in the letter from the Minister of Foreign Affairs of Pakistan addressed to the Secretary General, dated 15 January, 1948; and

(2) In regard to other situations set out in the letter from the Minister of Foreign Affairs of Pakistan addressed to the Secretary-General, dated 15 January 1948, when the Security Council so directs.

E. The Commission shall take its decision by majority vote. It may allocate among its members, alternate members, their assistants, and its personnel such duties as may have to be fulfilled for the realisation of its mission and the reaching of its conclusions.

F. The Commission, its members, alternate members, their assistants and its personnel shall be entitled to journey, separately or together, wherever the necessities of their tasks may require, and, in particular, within those territories which are the theatre of the events of which the Security Council is seized.

G. The Secretary-General of the United Nations shall furnish the Commission with such personnel and assistance as it may consider necessary.

20 January, 1948

3. 47(1948). Resolution of 21 April, 1948 (S/726)

The Security Council,

Having considered the complaint of the Government of India concerning the dispute over the State of Jammu and Kashmir.

Having heard the representative of India in support of that complaint and the reply and counter-complaints of the representative of Pakistan.

Being strongly of the opinion that the early restoration of peace and order in Jammu and Kashmir is essential and that India and Pakistan should do their utmost to bring about a cessation of all fighting.

Noting with satisfaction that both India and Pakistan desire that the question of the accession of Jammu and Kashmir to India or Pakistan should be decided through the democratic method of a free and impartial plebiscite.

Considering that the continuation of the dispute is likely to endanger international peace and security.

Reaffirms its resolution 38 (1948) of 17 January, 1948;

Resolves that the membership of the Commission established by its resolution 39 (1948) of 20 January, 1948 shall be increased to five and shall include, in addition to the membership mentioned in that resolution, representatives of .... and ..... and that if the membership of the Commission has not been completed within ten days from the date of the adoption of this resolution the President of the Council may designate such other Member or Members of the United Nations as are required to complete the membership of five.

Instructs the Commission to proceed at once to the Indian subcontinent and there place its good offices and mediation at the disposal of the Governments of India and Pakistan with a view to facilitating the taking of the necessary measures, both with respect to the restoration of peace and order and to the holding of plebiscite, by the two Governments, acting in cooperation with one another and with the Commission, and further instructs the Commission to keep the Council informed of the action taken under the resolution; and, to this end.

Recommends to the Governments of India and Pakistan the following measures as those which in the opinion of the Council are appropriate to bring about a cessation of the fighting and to create proper conditions for a free and impartial plebiscite to decide whether the State of Jammu and Kashmir is to accede to India or Pakistan :

A. Restoration of peace and order

1. The Government of Pakistan should undertake to use its best endeavours :

(*a*) To secure the withdrawal from the State of Jammu and Kashmir of tribesmen and Pakistani nationals not normally resident therein who have entered the State for the purpose of fighting, and to prevent any intrusion into the State of such elements and any furnishing of material aid to those fighting in the State;

(*b*) To make known to all concerned that the measures indicated in this and the following paragraphs provide full freedom to all subjects of the State, regardless of creed, caste, or party, to express their views and to vote on the question of the accession of the State, and that therefore they should co-operate in the maintenance of peace and order.

2. The Government of India should:

(*a*) When it is established to the satisfaction of the Commission set up in accordance with the Council's resolution 39 (1948) that the tribesmen are withdrawing and that arrangements for the cessation of the fighting have become effective, put into operation in consultation with the Commission a plan for withdrawing their own forces from Jammu and Kashmir and reducing them progressively to the minimum strength required for the support of the civil power in the maintenance of law and order;

(*b*) Make known that the withdrawal is taking place in stages and announce the completion of each stage;

(*c*) When the Indian forces have been reduced to the minimum strength mentioned in (a) above, arrange in consultation with the Commission for the stationing of the remaining forces to be carried out in accordance with the following principles :

(*i*) That the presence of troops should not afford any intimidation or appearance of intimidation to the inhabitants of the State;

(*ii*) That as small a number as possible should be retained in forward areas;

(*iii*) That any reserve of troops which may be included in the total strength should be located within their present base area.

3. The Government of India should agree that until such time as the Plebiscite Administration referred to below finds it necessary to exercise the powers of direction and supervision over the State forces and police provided for in paragraph 8, they will be held in areas to be agreed upon with the Plebiscite Administrator.

4. After the plan referred to in paragraph 2(a) above has been put into operation, personnel recruited locally in each district should so far as possible be utilised for the re-establishment and maintenance of law and order with due

regard to protection of minorities, subject such additional requirements as may be specified by the Plebiscite Administration to in paragraph 7.

5. If these local forces should be found to be inadequate, the Commission, subject to the agreement of both the Government of India and the Government of Pakistan, should arrange for the use of such forces of either Dominion as it deems effective for the purpose of pacification.

B. Plebiscite

6. The Government of India should undertake to ensure that the Government of the State invite the major political groups to designate responsible representatives to share equitably and fully in the conduct of the administration at the ministerial level while the plebiscite is being prepared and carried out.

7. The Government of India should undertake that there will be established in Jammu and Kashmir a Plebiscite Administration to hold a plebiscite as soon as possible on the question of the accession of the State to India or Pakistan.

8. The Government of India should undertake that there will be delegated by the State to the Plebiscite Administration such powers as the latter considers necessary for holding a fair and impartial plebiscite including, for that purpose only, the direction and supervision of the State forces and police.

9. The Government of India should, at the request of the Plebiscite Administration, make available from the Indian forces such assistance as the Plebiscite Administration may require for the performance of its functions.

10. (*a*) The Government of India should agree that a nominee of the Secretary-General of the United Nations will be appointed to be the Plebiscite Administrator.

(*b*) The Plebiscite Administrator, acting as an officer of the State of Jammu and Kashmir, should have authority to nominate his assistants and other subordinates and to draft regulations governing the plebiscite. Such nominees should be formally appointed and such draft regulations should be formally promulgated by the State of Jammu and Kashmir.

(*c*) The Government of India should undertake that the Government of Jammu and Kashmir will appoint fully qualified persons nominated by the Plebiscite Administrator to act as special magistrates within the State judicial system to hear cases which in the opinion of the Plebiscite Administrator have a serious bearing on the preparation for the conduct of a free and impartial plebiscite.

(*d*) The terms of service of the Administrator should form the subject of a separate negotiation between the Secretary-General of the United Nations and the Government of India. The Administrator should fix the terms of service for his assistants and subordinates.

(*e*) The Administrator should have the right to communicate directly with the Government of the State and with the Commission of the Security Council and, through the Commission, with the Security Council, with the Governments of India and Pakistan and with their representative with the Commission. It would be his duty to bring to the notice of any or all the foregoing (as he in his discretion may decide) any circumstances arising which may tend, in his opinion, to interfere with the freedom of the plebiscite.

11. The Government of India should undertake to prevent, and to give full support to the Administrator and his staff in preventing, any threat, coercion or intimidation, bribery or other undue influence on the voters in the plebicite, and the Government of India should publicly announce and should cause the Government of the State to announce this undertaking as an international obligation binding on all public authorities and officials in Jammu and Kashmir.

12. The Government of India should themselves and through the Government of the State declare and make known that all subjects of the State of Jammu and Kashmir, regardless of creed, caste or party, will be safe and free in expressing their views, and in voting on the question of the accession of the State and that there will be freedom of the press, speech and assembly and freedom of travel in the State, including freedom of lawful entry and exit.

13. The Government of India should use and should ensure that the Government of the State also use their best endeavours

to effect the withdrawal from the State of all Indian nationals other than those who are normally resident therein or who on or since 15 August 1947, have entered it for a lawful purpose.

14. The Government of India should ensure that the Government of the State release all political prisoners and take all possible steps so that :

(*a*) All citizens of the State who have left it on account of disturbances are invited, and are free, to return to their homes and to exercise their rights as such citizens;

(*b*) There is no victimisation;

(*c*) Minorities in all parts of the State are accorded adequate protection.

15. The Commission of the Security Council should at the end of the plebiscite certify to the Council whether the plebiscite has or has not been really free and impartial.

C. General provisions

16. The Governments of India and Pakistan should each be invited to nominate a representative to be attached to the Commission for such assistance as it may require in the performance of its task.

17. The Commission should establish in Jammu and Kashmir such observers as it may require in the performance of its task.

18. The Commission should establish in Jammu and Kashmir such observers as it may require of any of the proceedings in pursuance of the measures indicated in the foregoing paragraphs.

19. The Security Council Commission should carry out the task assigned to it herein.

Adopted at the 286th meeting.[1]

The five members of the United Nations Commission for India and Pakistan were : Czechoslovakia (nominated by India on 10 February 1948); Belgium and Colombia (appointed by the Council on 23 April 1948); Argentina (nominated by Pakistan on 30 April 1948); United States of America (designated by the President of the Council on 7 May 1948, in the absence of agreement between Argentina and Czechoslovakia on the member to be designated by them)

21 April, 1948

4. 51 (1948), Resolution of 3 June 1948 (S/819)

The Security Council,

1. Reaffirms its resolutions 38 (1948) of 17 January, 39 (1948) of 20 January and 47 (1948) of 21 April 1948;
2. Directs the United Nations Commission for India and Pakistan to proceed without delay to the areas of dispute with a view to accomplishing in priority the duties assigned to it by resolution 47 (1948) :
3. Directs the Commission further to study and report to the Security Council when it considers it appropriate on the matters raised in the letter of the Foreign Minister of Pakistan, dated 15 January 1948,[1] in the order outlined in paragraph D of Council resolution 39 (1948).

Adopted at the 312th meeting by 8 votes to none, with 3 abstentions (China, Ukranian Soviet Socialist Republic, Union of Soviet Socialist Republics).

3 June, 1948

5. 80 (195). Resolution of 14 March 1950 (S/1469)

The Security Council,

Having received and noted the reports[2] of the United Nations Commissions for India and Pakistan established by its resolutions 39 (1948) of 20 January, and 47 (1948) of 21 April 1948.

Having also received and noted the report of General A.G.L. McNaughton[3] on the outcome of his discussions with the representatives of India and Pakistan which were initiated in pursuance of the decision taken by the Security Council on 17 December, 1949.[4]

Commending the Governments of India and Pakistan for their statesman like action in reaching the agreements embodied in the United Nations Commission's resolution of 13 August,

1948[1] and 5 January, 1949[2] for a cease-fire, for the demilitarisation of the State of Jammu and Kashmir and for the determination of its final disposition in accordance with the will of the people through the democratic method of a free and impartial plebiscite, and commending the parties in particular for their action in partially implementing these resolutions by (1) the cessation of hostilities effected 1 January, 1949, (2) the establishment of a cease-fire line on 27 July, 1949, and (3) the agreement that Fleet Admiral Chester W. Nimitz shall be Plebiscite Administrator.

Considering that the resolution of the outstanding difficulties should be based upon the substantial measure of agreement on fundamental principles already reached, and that steps should be taken forthwith for the demilitarisation of the State and for the expeditious determination of its future in accordance with the freely expressed will of the inhabitants.

1. Calls upon the Governments of India and Pakistan to make immediate arrangements, without prejudice to their rights or claims and with due regard to the requirements of law and order, to prepare and execute within a period of five months from the date of this resolution a programme of demilitarisation on the basis of the principles of paragraph 2 of General McNaughton's proposal[3] or of such modifications of those principles as may be mutually agreed;

2. Decides to appoint a United Nations Representative for the following purposes who shall have authority to perform his functions in such place or places as he may deem appropriate:

(*a*) To assist in the preparation and to supervise the implementation of the programme of demilitarisation referred to above and to interpret the agreements reached by the parties for demilitarisation;

(*b*) To place himself at the disposal of the Governments of India and Pakistan and to place before those Governments or the Security Council any suggestions which, in his opinion, are likely to contribute to the expeditious and enduring solution of the dispute which has arisen between two Governments in regard to the State of Jammu and Kashmir;

(*c*) To exercise all of the powers and responsibilities devolving upon the United Nations Commission for India and Pakistan by reason of existing resolutions of the Security Council and by reason of the agreement of the parties embodied in the resolutions of the United Nations Commission of 13 August, 1948[1] and 5 January 1949[2];

(*d*) To arrange at the appropriate stage of demilitarisation for the assumption by the Plebiscite Administrator of the functions assigned to the latter under agreements made between the parties;

(*e*) To report to the Security Council as he may consider necessary, submitting his conclusions and any recommendations which he may desire to make.

3. Request the two Governments to take all necessary precautions to ensure that their agreements regarding the cease-fire shall continue to be faithfully observed, and calls upon them to take all possible measures to ensure the creation and maintenance of an atmosphere favourable to the promotion of further negotiations.

4. Extends its best thanks to the members of the United Nations Commission for India and Pakistan and to General A.G.L. McNaughton for their arduous and fruitful labours.

5. Agrees that the United Nations Commission for India and Pakistan shall be terminated, and decides that this shall take place one month after both parties have informed the United Nations Representative of their acceptance of the transfer to him of the powers and responsibilities of the United Nations Commission referred to in paragraph 2 (c) above.

Adopted at the 470th meeting by 8 votes to none, with 2 abstentions (India, Yugoslavia).[1]

14 March, 1950

6. 91 (1951). Resolution of 30 March 1951 (S/2017/REV. 1)

The Security Council,

Having received and noted the report of Sir Owen Dixon, the United Nations Representative for India and Pakistan[2], on his mission initiated by Security Council resolution 80 (1950) of 14 March 1950.

Observing that the Government of India and Pakistan have accepted the provisions of the United Nations Commission for India and Pakistan resolutions of 13 August 1948[3] and 5 January 1949[4] and have reaffirmed their desire that the future of the State of Kashmir shall be decided through the democratic method of a free and impartial plebiscite conducted under the auspices of the United Nations.

Observing that on 27 October, 1950 the General Council of the 'All Jammu and Kashmir National Conference' adopted a resolution recommending the convening of a constituent assembly for the purpose of determining the 'future shape and affiliations of the State of Jammu and Kashmir'; observing further from statements of responsible authorities that action is proposed to convene such a constituent assembly and that the area from which such a constituent assembly would be elected is only a part of the whole territory of Jammu and Kashmir.

Reminding the Governments and authorities concerned of the principle embodied in its resolutions 47 (1948) of 21 April 1948, 51 (1948) of 3 June, 1948 and 80 (1950) of 14 March, 1950 and the United Nations Commission for India and Pakistan resolutions of 13 August, 1948 and 5 January, 1949, that the final disposition of the State of Jammu and Kashmir will be made in accordance with the will of the people expressed through the democratic method of a free and impartial plebiscite conducted under the auspices of the United Nations.

Affirming that the convening of a constituent assembly as recommended by the General Council of the All Jammu and Kashmir National Conference' and any action that assembly might attempt to take to determine the future shape and affiliation of the entire State or any part thereof would not constitute a disposition of the State in accordance with the above principle.

Declaring its belief that it is the duty of the Security Council in carrying out its primary responsibility for the maintenance of international peace and security to aid the parties to reach an amicable solution of the Kashmir dispute and that a prompt settlement of this dispute is of vital importance to the maintenance of international peace and security.

Observing from Sir Owen Dixon's report that the main points of difference preventing agreement between the parties were:

(*a*) The procedure for and the extent of demilitarisation of the State preparatory to the holding of a plebiscite, and

(*b*) The degree of control over the exercise of the functions of government in the State necessary to ensure a free and fair plebiscite.

1. Accepts, in compliance with his request Sir Owen Dixon's resignation and expresses its gratitude to Sir Owen for the great ability and devotion with which he carried out his mission;

2. Decides to appoint a United Nations Representative for India and Pakistan in succession to Sir Owen Dixon;

3. Instructs the United Nations Representative to proceed to the subcontinent and, after consultation with the Governments of India and Pakistan, to effect the demilitarisation of the State of Jammu and Kashmir on the basis of the United Nations Commission for India and Pakistan resolutions of 13 August, 1948 and 5 January, 1949;

4. Calls upon the parties to co-operate with the United Nations Representative to the fullest degree in effecting the demilitarisation of the State of Jammu and Kashmir;

5. Instructs the United Nations Representative to report to the Security Council within three months from the date of his arrival on the subcontinent; if, at the time of this report, he has not effected demilitarisation in accordance with paragraph 3 above, or obtained the agreement of the parties to a plan for effecting such demilitarisation, the United Nations Representative shall report to the Security Council those points of difference between the parties in regard to the interpretation and execution of the agreed resolutions of 13 August, 1948 and 5 January, 1949 which he considers must be resolved to enable such demilitarisation to be carried out;

6. Calls upon the parties, in the event of their discussions with the United Nations Representative failing in his opinion to result in full agreement, to accept arbitration upon all outstanding points of difference reported by the United Nations Representative in accordance with paragraph 5 above, such arbitration to be carried out by an arbitrator, or a panel of

arbitrators, to be appointed by the President of the International Court of Justice after consultation with the parties;

7. Decides that the military observer group shall continue to supervise the cease-fire in the State;

8. Requests the Governments of India and Pakistan to ensure that their agreement regarding the cease-fire shall continue to be faithfully observed and calls upon them to take all possible measures to ensure the creation and maintenance of an atmosphere favourable to the promotion of further negotiations and to refrain from any action likely to prejudice a just and peaceful settlement;

9. Requests the Secretary-General to provide the United Nations Representative for India and Pakistan with such services and facilities as may be necessary in carrying out the terms of this resolution.

Adopted at the 539th meeting by 8 votes to none, with 3 abstentions (India, Union of Soviet Socialist Republics, Yugoslavia).

30 March, 1951

7. 96 (1951). Resolution of 10 November, 1951 (S/2392)

The Security Council,

Having received and noted the report of Mr. Frank Graham, the United Nations Representative for India and Pakistan[1] on his mission initiated by Security Council resolution 91 (1951) of 30 March, 1951, and having heard Mr. Graham's address to the Council on 18 October 1951.[2]

Noting with approval the basis for a programme of demilitarisation which could be carried out in conformity with the previous undertakings of the parties, put forward by the United Nations Representative in his communication of 7 September, 1951 to the Prime Ministers of India and Pakistan.[3]

1. Notes with gratification the declared agreement of the two parties to those parts of Mr. Graham's proposals which reaffirm determination to work for a peaceful settlement, their will to observe the cease-fire agreement and their acceptance of the principle that the accession of the State of Jammu and Kashmir

should be determined by a free and impartial plebiscite under the auspices of the United Nations.

2. Instructs the United Nations Representative to continue his efforts to obtain agreement of the parties on a plan for effecting the demilitarisation of the State of Jammu and Kashmir;

3. Calls upon the parties to co-operate with the United Nations Representative to the fullest degree in his efforts to resolve the outstanding points of difference between them;

4. Instructs the United Nations Representative to report to the Security Council on his efforts, together with his views concerning the problems confided to him, not later than six weeks after this resolution comes into effect.

Adopted at the 566th meeting by 9 votes to none, with 2 abstentions (India, Union of Soviet Socialist Republics).

10 November 1951

8. 98 (1952). Resolution of 23 December, 1952 (S/2883)

The Security Council,

Recalling its resolution 91 (1951) of 30 March, 1951, its decision of 30 April, 1951, and its resolution 96 (1951) of 10 November, 1951.

Further recalling the provisions of the United Nations Commission for India and Pakistan resolutions of 13 August, 1948[1] and 5 January, 1949[2] which were accepted by the Governments of India and Pakistan and which provided that the question of the accession of the State of Jammu and Kashmir to India or Pakistan would be decided through the democratic method of a free and impartial plebiscite conducted under the auspices and the United Nations.

Having received the third report, dated 22 April 1952[3]. and the fourth report, dated 16 September 1952[4], of the United Nations Representative for India and Pakistan.

1. Endorses the general principles on which the United Nations Representative has sought to bring about agreement between the Governments of India and Pakistan;

2. Notes with gratification that the United Nations Representative has reported that the Governments of India and Pakistan have accepted all but two of the paragraphs of his twelve-point proposals;[5]

3. Notes that agreement on a plan of demilitarisation of the State of Jammu and Kashmir has not been reached because the Governments of India and Pakistan have not agreed on the whole of paragraph 7 of the twelve-point proposals;

4. Urges the Governments of India and Pakistan to enter into immediate negotiations under the auspices of the United Nations Representative for India and Pakistan in order to reach agreement on the specific number of forces to remain on each side of the cease-fire line at the end of the period of demilitarisation, this number to be between 3,000 and 6,000 armed forces remaining on the Pakistan side of the cease-fire line and between 12,000 and 18,000 armed forces remaining on the India side of the cease-fire line, as suggested by the United Nations Representative in his proposals of 16 July, 1952[1], such specific numbers to be arrived at bearing in mind the principles or criteria contained in paragraph 7 of the United Nations Representative's proposal of 4 September, 1952.[2]

5. Records its gratitude to the United Nations Representative for India and Pakistan for the great efforts which he has made to achieve a settlement and requests him to continue to make his services available to the Governments of India and Pakistan to this end;

6. Requests the Governments of India and Pakistan to report to the Security Council not later than thirty days from the date of the adoption of this resolution;

7. Requests the United Nations Representative for India and Pakistan to keep the Security Council informed of any progress.

Adopted at the 611th meeting by 9 votes to none, with 1 abstention (Union of Soviet Socialist Republics).[1]

23 December 1952

9. Resolution Adopted by the Security Council at its 765th Meeting, on 24 January 1957, concerning the India-Pakistan Question

The Security Council,

Having heard statements from representatives of the Governments of India and Pakistan concerning the dispute over the State of Jammu and Kashmir.

Reminding the Governments and authorities concerned of the principle embodied in its resolutions of 21 April, 1948 (S/726), 3 June, 1948,[4] 14 March, 1950 (S/1469) and 30 March, 1951 (S/2017/Rev. 1), and the United Nations Commission for India and Pakistan resolutions of 13 August, 1948 (S/1100, para 75) and 5 January, 1949 (S/1196, para 15), that the final disposition of the State of Jammu and Kashmir will be made in accordance with the will of the people expressed through the democratic method of a free and impartial plebiscite conducted under the auspices of the United Nations.

1. *Reaffirms* the affirmation in its resolution of 30 March, 1951 and declares that the convening of a Constituent Assembly as recommended by the General Council of the 'All Jammu and Kashmir National Conference' and any action that Assembly may have taken or might attempt to take to determine the future shape and affiliation of the entire State or any part thereof, or action by the parties concerned in support of any such action by the Assembly, would not constitute a disposition of the State in accordance with the above principles;

5. Decides to continue its consideration of the dispute.

24 January, 1957

10. Resolution adopted by the Security Council at its 774th Meeting on 21 February, 1957 concerning the India-Pakistan Question

The Security Council,

Recalling its resolution of 24 January 1957 (S/3779), its previous resolutions and the resolutions of the United Nations Commission for India and Pakistan on the India-Pakistan question.

1. *Requests* the President of the Security Council, the representative of Sweden, to examine with the Governments of India and Pakistan any proposals which, in his opinion, are likely to contribute towards the settlement of the dispute, having regard to the previous resolutions of the Security Council and of the United Nations Commission for India and Pakistan; to visit the subcontinent for this purpose; and to report to the Security Council not later than 15 April, 1957;

2. *Invites* the Government of India and Pakistan to co-operate with him in the performance of these functions;

3. *Requests* the Secretary-General and the United Nations Representative for India and Pakistan to render such assistance as he may request.

21 February, 1957

11. Resolution Adopted by the Security Council at its 808th Meeting, on 2 December, 1957, concerning the India-Pakistan Question

The Security Council,

Having received and noted with appreciation the report (S/3821) of Mr. Gunnar V. Jarring, the representative of Sweden, on the mission undertaken by him pursuant to the Security Council resolution of 21 January, 1957 (S/3793).

Expressing its *thanks* to Mr. Jarring for the care and ability with which he has carried out his mission.

Observing with appreciation the expressions made by both parties of sincere willingness to co-operate with the United Nations in finding a peaceful solution.

Observing further that the Governments of India and Pakistan recognise and accept the provisions of its resolution dated 17 January 1948[1] and of the resolutions of the United Nations Commission for India and Pakistan dated 13, August 1948 (S/1100, para. 75) and 5 January, 1949 (S/1196, para. 15), which envisage in accordance with their terms the determination of the future status of the State of Jammu and Kashmir in accordance with the will of the people through the democratic method of a free and impartial plebiscite, and that Mr. Jarring felt it appropriate to explore what was impeding their full implementation.

Concerned over the lack of progress towards a settlement of the dispute which his report manifests.

Considering the importance which it has attached to the demilitarisation of the State of Jammu and Kashmir as one of the steps toward a settlement.

Recalling its previous resolutions and the resolutions of the United Nations Commission for India and Pakistan on the India-Pakistan question.

1. *Requests* the Government of India and the Government of Pakistan to refrain from making any statement and from doing or causing to be done or permitting any acts which might aggravate the situation and to appeal to their respective people to assist in creating and maintaining an atmosphere favourable to the promotion of further negotiations;

2. *Requests* the United Nations representative for India and Pakistan to make any recommendations to the parties for further appropriate action with a view to making progress toward the implementation of the resolution of the United Nations Commission for India and Pakistan of 13 August, 1948 and 5 January, 1949 and toward a peaceful settlement;

3. Authorizes the United Nations representative to visit the subcontinent for these purposes;

4. Instructs the United Nations representative to report to the Security Council on his efforts as soon as possible.

2 December, 1957

1. Resolution 210 (965) of 6 September, 1965

The Security Council,

Noting the report of the Secretary-General, on developments in the situation in Kashmir since the adoption of Security Council Resolution 209 (1965) on 4 September, 1965 calling for a ceasefire.

Noting with deep concern the extention of the fighting which adds immeasurably to the seriousness of the situation.

1. *Calls upon* the parties to cease hostilities in the entire area of conflict immediately, and promptly withdraw all armed personnel to the positions held by them before 5 August, 1965;

2. *Requests* the Secretary-General to exert every possible effort to give effect to the present resolution and to resolution 209 (1965), to take all measures possible to strengthen the United Nations Military Observer Group in India and Pakistan, and to keep the Council promptly and currently informed on the implementation of the resolutions and on the situation in the area;

3. *Decides* to keep this issue under urgent and continuous review so that the council may determine what further steps may be necessary to secure peace and security in the area.

Adopted unanimously at the

1238th meeting.

2. Resolution 211 (1965) of 20 September 1965

The Security Council,

Having considered the reports of the Secretary-General on his consultations with the Governments of India and Pakistan.

Commending the Secretary-General for his unrelenting efforts in furtherance of the objectives of Security Council resolutions 209 (1965) and 210 (1965) of 4 and 6 September, 1965.

Having heard the statements of the representatives of India and Pakistan.

Noting the differing replies by the parties to an appeal for a ceasefire as set out in the report of the Secretary-General, but noting further with concern that no cease-fire has yet come into being.

Convinced that an early cessation of hostilities is essential as a first step towards a peaceful settlement of the outstanding differences between the two countries on Kashmir and other related matters.

1. *Demands* that a cease-fire should take effect on Wednesday, 22 September 1965, at 0700 hours GMT, and calls upon both Governments to issue orders for a cease-fire at that

moment and a subsequent withdrawal of all armed personnel to the positions held by them before 5 August, 1965;

2. *Requests* the Secretary-General to provide the necessary assistance to ensure supervision of the cease-fire and the withdrawal of all armed personnel;

3. *Calls on all* States to refrain from any action which might aggravate the situation in the area;

Decides to consider, as soon as paragraph 1 of Council resolution 210 (1965) has been implemented, what steps could be taken to assist towards a settlement of the political problem underlying the present conflict, and in the meantime calls on the two Governments to utilize all peaceful means, including those listed in Article 33 of the Charter of the United Nations, to this end;

5. *Requests* the Secretary-General to exert every possible effort to give effect to the present resolution, to seek a peaceful solution, and to report to the Security Council there on.

Adopted at the 1242nd meeting by 10 votes to none, with I abstention (Jordan).

Decision

At the 1244th meeting, on 22 September, 1965, the President made the following statement on behalf of the Council:

We note, of course, the report of the Secretary-General. We have heard the statements of the Minister for Foreign Affairs of Pakistan and the representative of India. The Council expresses its satisfaction that the cease-fire demanded in its resolution 211 (91965) of 20 September 1965 has been accepted by the two parties and calls upon the Governments concerned to implement their adherence to the cease-fire call as rapidly as possible and in any case not later than 2200 hours GMT on 22 September, 1965.

3. Resolution 214 (1965) of 27 September, 1965

The Security Council,

Noting the reports of the Secretary-General.

Reaffirming its resolutions 209 (1965) of 4 September, 210 (1965) of 6 September, and 211 (1965) of 20 September, 1965.

Expressing its grave concern that the cease-fire agreed to unconditionally by the Governments of India and Pakistan is not holding.

Recalling that the cease-fire demand in the Council's resolutions was unanimously endorsed by the Council and agreed to by the Governments of both India and Pakistan.

Demands that the parties urgently honour their commitments to the Council to observe the cease-fire, and further calls upon the parties promptly to withdraw all armed personnel as necessary steps in the full implementation of resolution 211 (1965).

Adopted at the 1245th meeting.

Decision

At its 1248th meeting, on 27th October, 1965, the Council, pursuant to its invitation to the representatives of India and Pakistan to participate, without vote, in the discussion of the question, decided, in the absence of the representative of India, to invite the representative of Pakistan to take a seat at the Council table, it being understood that the representatives of India was invited to take a seat at the Council table at any time if he so wished.

4. Resolution 215 (1965) of 5 November, 1965

The Security Council,

Regretting the delay in the full achievement of a complete and effective cease-fire and a prompt withdrawal of armed personnel to the positions held by them before 5 August, 1965, as called for in its resolutions 209 (1965) of 4 September, 210 (1965) of 6 September, 211 (1965) of 20 September, and 214 (1965) of 27 September, 1965.

1. *Reaffirms* its resolution 211 (1965) in all its parts;

2. *Requests* the Governments of India and Pakistan to cooperate towards a full implementation of paragraph 1 of resolution 211 (1965); calls upon them to instruct their armed personnel to co-operate with the United Nations and cease all military activity; and insists that there be an end to violations of the cease-fire;

3. *Demands* the prompt and unconditional execution of the proposal already agreed to in principle by the Government of India and Pakistan that their representatives meet with a suitable representative of the Secretary-General, to be appointed without delay after consultation with both parties, for the purpose of formulating an agreed plan and schedule for the withdrawals by both parties; urges that such a meeting take place as soon as possible and that such a plan contain a time-limit on its implementation; and requests the Secretary-General to report on the progress achieved in this respect within three weeks of the adoption of the present resolution;

4. *Requests* the Secretary-General to submit for its consideration as soon as possible a report on compliance with the present resolution.

Adopted at the 1251st meetings by 9 votes to none, with 2 abstentions (Jordan, Union of Soviet Socialist Republics)

4 September, 1965 to 5 November, 1965

5. The Security Council Resolution on Cease-fire, 22 December, 1971

The Security Council,

Having discussed the grave situation in the subcontinent which remains a threat to international peace and security.

Noting the General Assembly resolution 2793 (XXVI) of 7 December, 1971.

Noting the reply of the Government of Pakistan on 9 December, 1971.

Noting the reply of the Government of India on 12 December, 1971.

Having heard statements of the Deputy Prime Minister of Pakistan and the Foreign Minister of India.

Noting further the statement made at the 1617th meeting of the Security Council by the Foreign Minister of India containing a unilateral declaration of a cease-fire in the western theatre.

Noting Pakistan's agreements to ceasefire in the western theatre with effect from 17 December, 1971.

Noting that consequently a cease-fire and a cessation of hostilities prevail.

1. *Demands* that a durable cease-fire and cessation of all hostilities in all areas of conflict be strictly observed and remain in effect until withdrawals take place, as soon as practicable, of all armed forces to their respective territories and to positions which fully respect the cease-fire line in Jammu and Kashmir supervised by the United Nations Military Observation Group for India and Pakistan;

2. *Calls upon* all Member States to refrain from any action which aggravate the situation in the subcontinent or endanger international peace;

3. *Calls upon* all those concerned to take all measures necessary to preserve human life and for the observance of the Geneva Conventions of 1949 and to apply in full their provisions as regards the protection of the wounded and the sick, the prisoners of war and civilian population;

4. *Calls for* international assistance in the relief of suffering and the rehabilitation of the refugees and their return in safety and dignity to their homes and for the full co- operation with the Secretary-General to that effect;

5. *Authorizes* the Secretary-General to appoint if necessary a Special Representative to lend his good offices for the solution of humanitarian problems;

6. *Requests* the Secretary-General to keep the Council Informed without delay on the developments relating to the implementation of this resolution;

7. *Decides* to remain seized of the matter and to keep it under active consideration.

22 December, 1971

Appendix 'H'

PROCLAMATION OF WAR OF LIBERATION OP GIBRALTAR 1965

The Revolutionary Council of Kashmir proclaims :

Brave Kashmiris,

ARISE for now is the time.

We have suffered long enough under the oppressive and treacherous rule of impostors and enemy agents.

Long enough have we allowed the traitors, to further the enemy designs.

Remember that a Hindu despot who ruled over us, in utter disregard of the wishes of the people, sold us to India in 1947. This was the second sale of our land through a fraudulent and ignoble deed which brought the might of the cursed Indian Army into our beautiful and peaceful land.

Betrayed though we were, we fought the enemy on every inch of our sacred soil. And we should have won but for the intervention of the United Nations who obtained an undertaking from India that we will exercise our inalienable right of self determination under a free and fair plebiscite.

The United Nations was duped and so was the whole world. India dishonoured her international pledge shamelessly and with utter contempt for world opinion.

She played for time to occupy our land. Since then every day that has passed has been a day of misery and every night a night of crime. You know what acts of cruelty, sacrilege and barbarity the enemy has been perpetrating under the shadow of guns and bayonets.

For years our great leaders SHEIK MOHAMMAD ABDULLAH and MIRZA AFZAL BEG have been languishing in Indian prisons but their determination to throw off the yoke of Indian Imperialism remains unflagging.

We have seen our children butchered but every drop of their blood has illumined the path of our struggle.

Our women were dishonoured but in their agony they sanctified the course of our freedom.

Our brave fighters lost their lives but their dying calls stirred the hearts of their compatriots.

The will of our people remains unbroken; their united might unshaken.

The enemy is on the run. We will not rest content till we have chased him out of our land.

The time has come for us to deliver the final blow and hereby we take a solemn pledge to take up arms once again and continue the fight till:

(*a*) The usurpers are expelled out of our land;

(*b*) Our leaders now in jail are freed; and

(*c*) The will of the people is allowed to determine the future of our land.

The Revolutionary Council which consists of patriots of unimpeachable integrity and men of unswerving faith, has set up today the National Government of the People of JAMMU and KASHMIR which decries as here under:

From TODAY :

(*a*) All alleged treaties and agreements between the imperialist Government of India and Kashmir stand annulled and are no longer binding on us;

(*b*) The National Government of JAMMU and KASHMIR formed by the Revolutionary Council of KASHMIR is the sole lawful authority in our land;

(*c*) Only the National Government will be legally competent to receive taxes and public dues from the people of the state;

(*d*) Any KASHMIRI national who wilfully cooperates with the Indian Government or their puppet administration in occupied KASHMIR will be treated as traitor and dealt with as such;

(*e*) Every national of the state of JAMMU and KASHMIR who may be employed either by the imperialist Indian Government or its puppet administration, in civil or military capacity, shall support the freedom movement of the Revolutionary Council in every possible way;

(*f*) The National Government will issue orders and decrees on the KASHMIR National Radio representing the 'Voice of KASHMIR';

(*g*) Any national of KASHMIR who impedes the freedom movement or disobeys any order or decree of the National Government will be dealt with as a traitor.

The Revolutionary Council appeals to the world to support this freedom movement.

Now is the time for countries who have pledged themselves to help all freedom movements against imperialism to come to our assistance.

We have nothing against the people of India but their Governments have established a record of treachery and dishonesty in the world. We expect all sane and freedom-loving elements in India and particularly the brave Sikhs, the South Indians and the Rajputs who have always given us moral support to lend us active assistance.

The people of Pakistan have stood by us in our fight. To our regret they have not done as much as we expected of them. Now is the time for them too to join us in our struggle for life and liberty.

Let the nations of the world remember that if we go down the light of freedom will be extinguished for ever.

And above all, you the people of Kashmir, you are the ones who are on trial. You are the ones who must win this war for the sake of coming generations, for the sake of freedom and for the sake of the glory of your motherland.

Arise : now or there will be no tomorrow:

Important Ingredients of OP Gibraltar 1965

The important ingredients of *Op Gibraltar* in 1965 which are given below would make it obvious that these tactics are still being followed by the insurgents in 1993-94, their source being the same.

- Destruction of bridges and disruption of lines of communications;

- Raids on ammunition and supply dumps;
- Attacks on formation and unit Headquarters;
- Ambushing of convoys and patrols;
- Distribution of arms and ammunition to local civilians across the Cease Fire Line and enrolling them as Razakars;
- Creation of situations which would paralyse the J & K administration and encourage an open rebellion in the state.

Appendix 'I'

TASHKENT DECLARATION, 10 JANUARY 1966

The Prime Minister of India and the President of Pakistan having met at Tashkent and having discussed the existing relations between India and Pakistan, hereby declare their firm resolve to restore normal and peaceful relations between their countries and to promote understanding and friendly relations between their peoples. They consider the attainment of these objectives of vital importance for the welfare of the 600 million people of India and Pakistan.

I

The Prime Minister of India and the President of Pakistan agree that both sides will exert all efforts to create good neighbourly relations between India and Pakistan in accordance with the United Nations Charter. They reaffirm their obligation under the Charter not to have recourse to force and to settle their disputes through peaceful means. They considered that the interests of peace in their region and particularly in the Indo-Pakistan sub-continent and, indeed, the interests of the peoples of India and Pakistan were not served by the continuance of tension between the two countries. It was against this background that Jammu and Kashmir was discussed, and each of the sides set forth its respective position.

II

The Prime Minister of India and the President of Pakistan have agreed that all armed personnel of the two countries shall be withdrawn not later than 25 February 1966 to the positions they held prior to 5 August, 1965, and both sides shall observe the cease-fire terms on the cease-fire line.

III

The Prime Minister of India and the President of Pakistan have agreed that relations between India and Pakistan shall be based on the principle of non-interference in the internal affairs of each other.

IV

The Prime Minister of India and the President of Pakistan have agreed that both sides will discourage any propaganda directed against the other country, and will encourage propaganda which promotes the development of friendly relations between the two countries.

V

The Prime Minister of India and the President of Pakistan have agreed that the High Commissioner of India to Pakistan and the High Commissioner of Pakistan to India will return to their posts and that the normal functioning of diplomatic missions of both countries will be restored. Both Governments shall observe the Vienna Convention of 1961 on Diplomatic Intercourse.

VI

The Prime Minister of India and the President of Pakistan have agreed to consider measures towards the restoration of economic and trade relations, communications, as well as cultural exchanges between India and Pakistan, and to take measures to implement the existing agreements between India and Pakistan.

VII

The Prime Minister of India and the President of Pakistan have agreed that they give instructions to their respective authorities to carry out the repatriation of the prisoners of war.

VIII

The Prime Minister of India and the President of Pakistan have agreed that both the sides will continue the discus sion of questions relating to the problems of refugees and evictions/ illegal immigrations. They also agreed that both sides will create conditions which will prevent the exodus of people. They further agreed to discuss the return of-the property and assets taken over by either side in connection with the conflict.

IX

The Prime Minister of India and the President of Pakistan have agreed that the sides will continue meetings both at the highest and at other levels on matters of direct concern to both countries. Both sides have recognized the need to set up joint Indian-Pakistani bodies which will report to their Governments in order to decide what further steps should be taken.

The Prime Minister of India and the President of Pakistan record their feelings of deep appreciation and gratitude to the leaders of the Soviet Union, the Soviet Government and personally to the Chairman of the Council of Ministers of the U.S.S.R. for their constructive, friendly and noble part in bringing about the present meeting which has resulted in mutually satisfactory results. They also express to the Government and friendly people of Uzbekistan their sincere thankfulness for their overwhelming reception and generous hospitality.

They invite the Chairman of the Council of Ministers of the U.S.S.R. to witness this Declaration.

10 January, 1966

Appendix 'J'

SHIMLA AGREEMENT 3 July, 1972

Agreement of Bilateral relations between the Government of India and the Government of Pakistan

1. The Government of India and the Government of Pakistan are resolved that the two countries put an end to the conflict and confrontation that have hitherto marred their relations, and work for the promotion of a friendly and harmonious relationship and the establishment of durable peace in the sub-continent, so that both countries may henceforth devote their resources and energies to the pressing task of advancing the welfare of their peoples.

In order to achieve this objective, the Government of India and the Government of Pakistan agreed as follows :

1. That the principles and purposes of the charter of the United Nations shall govern and relations between the two countries.
2. That the two countries are resolved to settle their differences by peaceful means through bilateral negotiations or by any other peaceful means mutually agreed upon between them. Pending the final settlement of any of the problems between the two countries neither side shall unilaterally alter the situation and both shall prevent the organisation, assistance or encouragement of any acts detrimental to the maintenance of peaceful and harmonious relations.
3. That the prerequisite for reconciliation, good neighbourliness and durable peace between them is commitment by both the countries to peaceful co-existence, respect for each other's territorial integrity and sovereignty and non-interference in each other's internal affairs, on the basis of equality and mutual benefits.
4. That the basic issues and causes of conflicts which have bedevilled the relations between the two countries for the last twenty-five years shall be resolved by peaceful means.

5. That they shall always respect each other's national unity, territorial integrity, political independence and sovereign equality.
6. That in accordance with the charter of the United Nations they will refrain from threat or use of force against the territorial integrity, political independence of each other.

(II) Both Governments will take all steps within their power to prevent hostile propaganda directed against each other. Both countries will encourage the dissemination of such information as would promote the development of friendly solution between them.

(III) In order progessively to restore and normalise relations between the two countries step by step it was agreed :

(*a*) Steps shall be taken to resume communications, postal telegraphic, sea, land including border posts and air links including over-flights.

(*b*) Appropriate steps shall be taken to promote travel facilities, for the nationals of other country.

(*c*) Trade and co-operation in economic and other agreed fields will be resumed as far as possible.

(*d*) Exchange in the fields of science and culture will be promoted.

(IV) In order to initiate the process of the establishment of durable peace, both the Governments agreed that :

(*i*) Indian and Pakistani forces shall be withdrawn to their side of the international border.

(*ii*) In Jammu and Kashmir, the line of control resulting from the ceasefire of December 17,1971 shall be respected by either side. Neither side shall seek to alter it immediately, irrespective of mutual differences and legal interpretations. Both sides further undertake to refrain from the threat or the use of force in violation of this line.

(*iii*) The withdrawals shall commence upon entry into force of this agreement and shall be completed within a period of thirty days.

5. This agreement shall subject to satisfaction by both countries in accordance with their respective constitutional procedures, and will come into force with effect from the date which the instruments of ratification are exchanged.

6. Both Governments agree that their respective heads will meet again at a mutually convenient time in the future and that, in the meanwhile, the representatives of the two sides will meet to discuss further the modalities and arrangements for the establishment of durable peace and normalisation of relations, including the questions of repatriation of prisoners of war and civilian internees, a final settlement of Jammu and Kashmir and the resumption of diplomatic relations.

Indira Gandhi — Zulfikar Ali Bhutto

Prime Minister Republic of India — President Pakistan

3 July, 1972

Appendix 'K'

TEXT OF KASHMIR ACCORD (FEBRUARY 1975)

Agreed conclusions which led to Sheikh Mohammad Abdullah's accord with Mrs. Indira Gandhi, Prime Minister, and his subsequent assumption of offices as Chief Minister in February, 1975.

1. The state of Jammu and Kashmir which is a constituent unit of the Union of India, shall, in its relation with the Union, continue to be governed by Article 370 of the Constitution of India.

2. The residuary powers of legislation shall remain with the State; however, Parliament will continue to have power to make laws relating to the prevention of activities directed towards disclaiming, questioning or disrupting the sovereignty and territorial integrity of India or bringing about cession of a part of the territory of India or secession of a part of the territory of India from the Union or causing insult of the Indian National Flag, the Indian National Anthem and the Constitution.

3. Where any provision of the Constitution of India had been applied to the State of Jammu and Kashmir with adaptations and modifications, such adaptations and modifications can be altered or repealed by an order of the President under Article 370, each individual proposal in this behalf being considered on its merits; but provisions of the Constitution of India already applied to the State of Jammu and Kashmir without adaptation or modification are unalterable.

4. With a view to assuring freedom to the State of Jammu and Kashmir to have its own legislation on matters like welfare measures, cultural matters, social security, personal law and procedural laws, in a manner suited to the special conditions in the State, it is agreed that the State Government can review the laws made by Parliament or extended to the State after 1953 on any matter relatable to the Concurrent List and may decide which of them, in its opinion, needs amendment or repeal. Thereafter, appropriate steps may be taken under Article 254 of the Constitution of India. The grant of President's assent to such legislation would be sympathetically considered. The same approach would be adopted in regard to laws to be made by

Parliament in future under the Proviso to Clause 2 of the Article. The State Government shall be consulted regarding the application of any such law to the State and the views of the State Government shall receive the fullest consideration.

5. As an arrangement reciprocal to what has been provided under Article 368, a suitable modification of that Article as applied to the State should be made by Presidential order to the effect that no law made by the Legislature of the State of Jammu and Kashmir, seeking to make any change in or in the effect of any provision of Constitution of the State of Jammu and Kashmir relating to any of the undermentioned matters, shall take effect unless the Bill, having been reserved for the consideration of the President, receives his assent; the matters are :

(*a*) The appointment, powers, functions, duties, privileges and immunities of the Governor, and

(*b*) The following matters relating to Elections namely, the superintendence, direction and control of Elections by the Election Commission of India, eligibility for inclusion in the electoral rolls without discrimination, adult suffrage and composition of the Legislative Council, being matters specified in sections 138, 139, 140 and 50 of the Constitution of the State of Jammu and Kashmir.

6. No agreement was possible on the question of nomenclature of the Governor and the Chief Minister and the matter is therefore remitted to the Principals.

Mirza Mohammad Afzal Beg G. Parthasarathi

New Delhi

November 13, 1974*

Appendix 'L'

SELECT BIBLIOGRAPHY

Abdullah, Sheikh M., "Kashmir, India and Pakistan", *Foreign Affairs*, April 1965.

Akbar, M.J., *Kashmir Behind the Vale*, Viking, 1991.

Bamzi, P.N.K., *Kashmir and Power Politics: from Lake Success to Tashkent*, Delhi, 1966.

Bamzi, Prithvi Nath Kaul, *History of Kashmir*, Delhi Metropolitan Book Company, 1962.

Fazl, Abul, *Ain-i-Akbari* Delhi: (reprinted) Oriental Books reprint Corporation, 1977.

Hodson, H.V., *The Great Divide: Britain, India, Pakistan,* Hutchinson, London 1969.

India, Government of, notes, Memoranda and letters exchanged between the Governments of India and China. September-November 1959 and Note on the Historical Background of the Himalayan Frontier of India. White paper II, New Delhi 1959. (Excerpts Examined)

Indian Defence Review, New Delhi: July 89 and subsequent issue.

Jagmohan, *My Frozen Turbulence*. Allied Publishers, New Delhi, 1991.

Karim, A., *Counter Terrorism: The Pakistan Factor*, Lancer Paper 2, 1991

Korbel, J., *Danger in Kashmir*, Princeton, 1954.

Krishna Rao, K.V., *Prepare or Perish*, A Study of National Security, Lancer, New Delhi, 1991.

Appendix 'M'

POLITICAL VIEWS OF PAKISTAN/POK

(Excerpted from Azad Kashmir Writ Petition against Pakistan on the Jurisdiction of Northern Areas)

22. On announcement of independence of the subcontinent on June 3, 1947, the Muslims of the State demonstrated their voice in favour of accession of the State to Pakistan. *On July 19, 1947,* the Muslim Conference, in its meeting held in *Srinagar,* declared its desire to accede to Pakistan. The decision of the Muslim Conference, in the shape of its resolution, is reproduced :

(1) This meeting of All Jammu and Kashmir Muslim Conference Convention expresses its satisfaction and congratulates the *Qualde-Azam* for his achievement.

(2) The people of the Indian States expected that they would walk shoulder to shoulder with the people of British India in the attainment of freedom. On the partition of India the people of British India have obtained independence but the announcement of June 3, 1947 has strengthened the hands of the Indian Princes and unless the Princes respond to the call of the times, the future of the people of the Indian States is very dark. There are only three ways open to people of Jammu and Kashmir State:—

1. To accede to India, or
2. To accede to Pakistan, or
3. To remain Independent.

The Convention of the Muslim Conference has arrived at the conclusion that keeping in view the geographical conditions, 80 per cent Muslim majority out of total population, the passage of important rivers of the Punjab through the State, the language, cultural racial and, economic connection of the people and proximity of the borders of the State with Pakistan, are all facts which make it necessary that the Jammu and Kashmir State should accede to Pakistan.

23. It is relevant to recapitulate the scheme of independence of the subcontinent to enable to appreciate the conflict of Kashmir, relevant to the proposition under consideration. The

political forces in the subcontinent were divided into All India Congress (hereinafter referred to as Congress) and All India Muslim League (hereinafter referred to as the League). The leadership of Congress pursued independence of the subcontinent as one unit. Conversely, the League demanded creation of Pakistan by partition of India. Efforts were made at diplomatic and political levels to attain conciliation between the rival leadership of the subcontinent, but without success. Thus, in the light of demand of the rival parties, the scheme of independence of the subcontinent was pronounced by the British Government through the Viceroy of India, on June 3, 1947. The scheme was given a statutory form in the name of the Independence Act, 1947. The Act was promulgated by the British Parliament for setting up two Independent dominions, viz.,

1. Indian Union and
2. Pakistan.

Thus, both the dominions were to emerge on August 15, 1947 as successor to the Government of British India. The partition of the subcontinent was to take place on the basis of two-Nation theory, meaning thereby that the Muslim majority areas were to form part of Pakistan and the rest that of the Indian Union.

24. Prior to the Independence Act, the Government of India Act, 1935 envisaged a scheme of accession of Princely States to the British India. On the same pattern and style, advice was tendered by the Viceroy of India to the Princes. He addressed the Chamber of Princes in Delhi on July 25, 1947. The Princes were advised to accede to either of the dominions of their choice. Nevertheless, it was advised that while deciding the question of accession, the rulers should keep in view :

(*i*) the geographical proximity;

(*ii*) the welfare of the State; and

(*iii*) the views of majority of the people of the State.

25. The rulers of the States of the subcontinent somehow decided the accession of their States to either of the dominions, except the Nizam of Hyderabad and the Maharaja of Kashmir State.

26. The proposition under consideration is an off-shoot of the Kashmir dispute, as the ruler of the State failed to take timely decision by acceding to either of the dominions before August 15, 1947. The decision was delayed deliberately to reduce the majority of the Muslim population by resort to large scale genocide on the pattern of States of Kapurthalla, Faridkote, Patiala, Bharatpur, Alwar and Gwalior. In all these States, a preplanned extensive campaign of genocide was directed against the Muslim population. An identical drama was to be staged in southeastern part of Jammu, Kathua and Akhnoor; action of genocide was initiated by the State forces, assisted by bands of Sikhs and Hindus. A wave of terror thus ran throughout the State. In such a situation, the Muslims of the State, particularly the ex-soldiers who had served in the second world war, organised themselves into small units and decided to make a final bid for liberty. Thus, several thousands of Muslims of the State, particularly in the areas of Poonch and Mirpur, decided to struggle against the brute forces of the State. In lieu of their sacrifices, areas of district Mirpur, Kotli, Rawalakot, Bagh, Poonch, Gilgit, Baltistan and Frontier areas were liberated. The Muslim forces set up an Azad Government on October 24,1947, which took over the administrative control of these areas, in addition to freedom movement. The administrative control of Gilgit, Baltistan and Frontier areas was taken over by the Pakistan Government. This action was subsequently ratified by an agreement executed between the Government of Pakistan and the Azad Government of the State of Jammu and Kashmir, endorsed by the President of All Jammu and Kashmir Muslim Conference, in April, 1949. Since then, the administrative control of the areas has been continuously with the Government of Pakistan. As the people of these areas were not associated with the administration nor they were given due representation in the Assemblies, it was realised, with the passage of time, that these people were deprived of their basic human rights, including the right of representation and administration. Thus, an effort was made to seek redress of their grievances at other hand, as a deception, on August 12, a Standstill Agreement was proposed both to India and Pakistan. Pakistan accepted the proposal whereas India avoided it, on the pretext of direct negotiations at the ministerial level.

33. As the Pakistan Goverment and leadership was deeply occupied in the establishment of administration of the new dominion, settlement of refugees and other national issues, an organised genocide of the Muslims of the State was planned by fanatic Hindu and Sikh forces. Trained Hindu and Sikh gangsters were brought in the State. They were distributed arms. Muslims were disarmed. Additional military cantonments and posts were established in Jammu, Kathua, Samba, Mirpur and Poonch, and entire frontier common with Pakistan territory was sealed. In the first week of September, large scale genocide operations were started. The Muslims in Samba, Kathua, Udhampur and Jammu were subjected to sudden attacks. Over a quarter of a million were killed and more than a quarter million were forced to migrate to Pakistan. Times *of London,* in its publication of October 10, 1948, reported :

> "Over a quarter million Muslims were massacred in Jammu Province alone. The orgies of bloodshed were initiated by the hired gangsters imported by the State administration, with State troops looking on as unconcerned spectators, at times and on occasions by the troops themselves with the Maharaja heading them at quite a few places".

34. On apprehending the nefarious designs of the Maharaja and the State authorities, the Muslims of the State were alarmed. In a state of terror, they organised themselves. The lot who had served in the second world war, raised regiments and undertook an armed struggle against the forces of Maharaja. They were reinforced by the neighbouring Muslims from the Punjab, North-West Frontier Province and tribesmen. Mirpur, Bhimber, Kotli, Bagh, Rawalkot, Pallandari and Muzaffarabad were liberated. Rajouri and Mehndar, except Poonch city and areas surrounding Naushehra, were also occupied by the freedom-fighters. Gilgit, Baltistan and Ladakh were also eventually liberated by the local people of the areas, assisted by Gilgit Scouts and the Muslim soldiers of the State army. On October 24, 1947, a revolutionary Government was formed. The revolutionary Government assumed the charge of armed struggle and also undertook the establishment of administration to restore law and order in the liberated territory.

35. Maharaja Hari Singh, who deserted Srinagar, took refuge in Jammu. On giving a final touch to the conspiracy already undertaken, *the accession of the State* was announced with India. The Governor-General of India acknowledged the accession provisionally, with the condition that on restoration of law and order, the question of future of Jammu and Kashmir shall be determined by its people in exercise of their free will *through a plebiscite* under the auspices of the United Nations. The Government of Pakistan lodged a strong protest against the fraudulent accession of the State with India. The Indian Prime Minister, through telegraphic messages addressed to the Prime Minister of Pakistan, assured the settlement of future of the State by a reference to its people. The Indian Prime Minister invariably endeavored to convince Pakistan that the ultimate future of the State shall be settled by the people of the State. As the dispute could not be settled bilaterally, it was taken to the Security Council, by India. In the Security Council, India reiterated its claim to the accession, but at the same time, committed that the people of the State were the sole arbiter of their fate and future and they alone shall be able to decide their destiny. The Security Council, vide its resolutions, guaranteed that the Kashmir problem shall be settled by a plebiscite under the United Nations' auspices. The United Nations Commission for India and Pakistan reiterated the unanimously accepted resolutions of the Security Council in their own detailed resolutions unanimously passed on August 13, 1948 and January 5, 1949. These resolutions were also endorsed by both India and Pakistan.

72. On second thought, India manoeuvre to frustrate the resolutions of the Security Council and the United Nations Commission for India and Pakistan by holding elections to the Constituent Assembly of the Indian-occupied part of the State, and manipulated its endorsement of the alleged accession made by the last ruler of the State. Pakistan promptly invited attention of the Security Council to the conspiracy of India in collaboration with the leaders of the Indian held part of the State, and exposed the scheme of India to integrate the State with the Indian Union, to frustrate the resolutions of the United

Nations. The Security Council summoned its meeting and examined the complaint of Pakistan. It unanimously resolved on March 30, 1951:

"Having received and noted the report of Sir Owen Dixon, the United Nations Representative for India and Pakistan, on his mission initiated by the Security Council resolution of March 14, 1950.

Observing that the Governments of India and Pakistan have accepted the provisions of the United Nations Commission for India and Pakistan resolutions of August 13, 1948, and January 5, 1949, and have reaffirmed their desire that the future of the State of Jammu and Kashmir shall be decided through the democratic method of a free and impartial plebiscite conducted under the auspices of the United Nations.

Observing that on October 27, 1950, Council of "All Jammu and Kashmir National Conference" adopted a resolution recommending the convening of a Constituent Assembly for the purpose of determining the future shape and affiliations of the State of Jammu and Kashmir.

Observing further from statements of responsible authorities that action is proposed to convene such a Constituent Assembly and that the area from which such a Constituent Assembly will be elected is only a part of the whole territory of Jammu and Kashmir.

Reminding the Governments and authorities concerned of the principle embodied in the Security Council resolutions of April 21, 1948, June 3, 1948 and March 14, 1950, and the United Nations Commission for India and Pakistan resolutions of August 13, 1948, and January 5, 1949, that the final disposition of the State of Jammu and Kashmir will be made in accordance with the will of the people expressed in the democratic method of a free and impartial plebiscite conducted under the auspices of the United Nations.

Affirming that the convening of a Constituent Assembly recommended by the General Council of the "All Jammu and Kashmir National Conference" and any action that assembly might attempt to take to determine the future shape and affiliation of the entire State or any part thereof would not constitute a disposition of the State in accordance with the above principle.

73. Second attempt was made by India on identical lines in 1956. It once again manoeuvred to get the purported accession by the ruler, stamped the Assembly of the State, to perpetuate aggression and usurpation of the State. Pakistan, again, invited attention of the Security Council the conspiracy and emphasised that India may stopped from perpetuating its hold on the State defeating the United Nations' resolutions. The Security Council once again rose to the occasion reiterated its earlier stand, in the shape of its resolution passed on January 24, 1957. The resolution was passed in the following terms:

The Security Council

Having Heard statements from representatives of the Governments of India and Pakistan concerning the dispute over the State of Jammu and Kashmir;

Reminding the Governments and Authorities concerned of the principle embodied in its resolutions of 21 April 1948, 3 June 1948, 14 March 1950, and 30 March 1951, and the United Nations Commission for India and Pakistan resolutions of 13 August 1948 and 5 January 1949, that the final disposition of the State of Jammu and Kashmir will be made in accordance with the will of the people expressed through the democratic method of a free and impartial plebiscite conducted under the auspices of the United Nations:

Reaffirms the affirmation in its resolution of 30 March 1951 and declares that the convening of a Constituent Assembly as recommended by the General Council of the "All Jammu and Kashmir National Conference" and any action that Assembly may have taken or might attempt to take to determine the future shape and affiliation of the entire State or any part thereof, or action by the parties concerned in support of any such action by the Assembly, would not constitute a disposition of the State in accordance with the above principle:

Decides to continue its consideration of the dispute."

74. It is evident from the language of both the resolutions that The Security Council steadfastly adhered to its resolutions passed on April 21, 1948, June 3, 1948, March 14, 1950 and

March 30, 1950 and to the United Nations Commission for India and Pakistan's resolutions of August 13, 1948 and January 5, 1949. It affirmed that the final disposition of the State of Jammu and Kashmir will be made in accordance with the will of the people, expressed in the democratic method by free and impartial plebiscite conducted under the auspices of the United Nations. As a caution, it denounced the proposed attempt of the Assembly and National Conference of taking any step to determine the future shape and affiliation of the entire State or any part thereof in derogation to its resolutions. It warned that any attempt to determine the future shape or affiliation of the entire State or any part thereof would not be accepted and it would not constitute a disposition of the State in accordance with the principle enunciated in the resolutions.

75. Pakistan, at all levels, adhered to the aforesaid pronouncements of the Security Council. Therefore, no idea or scheme which is derogatory to the well considered and consistent policy of Pakistan may be entertained at any stage. By allowing integration of Northern areas to any Province of Pakistan would tantamount to negation of the Pakistan's stance at home and in the Security Council. At first, such a derogatory step may appear beneficial to some minds, but in the larger interests of Pakistan and particularly the future of Jammu and Kashmir State, no sane person would allow disintegration of the State in any manner. This is so, as indirectly it fell in line with the Indian policy to deny the right of self-determination to the people of Jammu and Kashmir by integrating the territory under its control with the Indian Union, by striking finally the hammer of servitude and subjugation on the people of the State.

76. It will not be useless at this juncture to lift the curtain from the Indian conspiracies to mislead the world opinion, to retain its hold on the State, right from the time the formula of partition of the subcontinent was announced. It may not be forgotten that the Indian leaders, despite making their individual and collective commitments, at all levels, to hold plebiscite in the State, concocted and fabricated grounds to delay the proposed plebiscite to keep the State in their fold. We propose to expose these conspiracies by reference to an independent source. Professor Alastair Lamb, in his celebrated treatises

"KASHMIR A DISPUTED LEGACY", edition 1991, recorded full account of political developments in the State. By dint of his deep study and research in various archives, including India, exposed the political developments which took place in late 1946 and 1947. He invited attention of the scholars interested in the Kashmir problem, to see how the Prime Ministers were changed, one after another, within a short span of time and Justice Mehr Chand Mahajan (he was member of the Boundary Commission, nominated by India) was installed as Prime Minister of Kashmir on September, 18, 1948. This was a crucial time in the subcontinent and particularly in the State, as the liberation forces within the State had already swung into action. At the relevant time, he was a sitting Judge of East Punjab High Court. He obtained leave to assume the assignment on persuasion of Patel and sanction of Jawahar Lal Nehru. Alastair Lamb described all the relevant events in chronological order, as they enveloped the political scenario at the time. He highlighted the hypocracy of Indian leadership, in his own words, and we extensively quote the relevant excerpts:

> Immediately after the departure from the State of Jammu and Kashmir of Major-General Scott on 22 September (and now safer from British observation) some active steps taken to strengthen links with by providing Srinagar airfield were India with wireless equipment to make it more suitable for bad weather operation. Arrangements were made for the supply of extra arms and ammunition to the Jammu and Kashmir State Armed Forces through an Indian Military adviser. Lt. Col. Kashmir Singh Katoch (a regular officer in the Indian Army, who was a scn of Janak Singh, then Prime Minister of Jammu and Kashmir, and related to Maharaja Hari Singh) who was established in Srinagar beginning of October (and who remained there throughout the accession crisis); and by the middle of the month, war material was being flown in to the State in significant quantities. Staff preparations were made for Indian troop concentrations at Madhopur in the Pathankot Tehsil near the Jammu border as potential reinforcements for the State Army. The improvement of the road from Jammu to Indian frontier in

the direction of Pathankot, begun around the time of the transfer of power, was accelerated and telegraphic lines of communication were expanded. Batra, the Deputy Prime Minister of the State, was now in regular contact not only with Sardar Vallabhbhai Patel but also with Baldev Singh, the Defence Minister in the Government of India. No doubt there were other links between Srinagar and New Delhi: for example : D.P. Dhar, a young Kashmiri Brahmin (Pandit) who was beginning his political career, certainly possessed close contacts at the higher level of Indian political life.

All this activity, recorded in considerable detail in the first volume of Sardar Vallabhbhai Patel's correspondence which was published in 1971, makes it clear that both Sardar Vallabhbhai Patel and Baldev Singh were heavily engaged in the planning of some kind of Indian military intervention in the State of Jammu and Kashmir, if only on a contingency basis, by at least 13 September 1947; and that by the third week of October a substantial foundation for such an operation had been laid ..." (Page 130)

'The Sikh Maharaja of Patiala, for example, in the first two weeks of October 1947 provided his colleague in the State of Jammu and Kashmir with a battalion of infantry and a battery of mountain artillery from his own State Armed Forces; perhaps this had been discussed when the Maharaja of Patiala visited Srinagar in July, 1947. When Indian troops finally intervened in Jammu and Kashmir on 27 October, 1947 they found, apparently to their surprise, Patiala gunners already guarding the vital Srinagar airfield, where they had been encamped since at least 17 October. The Patiala infantry were stationed in Jammu as reinforcements for the garrison of the Maharaja's winter capital. How these troops were transported is not known : it is possible that they were moved as part of the supply convoys despatched to Jammu and Srinagar by the Government of India in reply to the alleged Pakistani "blockade". Shortly after the formal intervention of the Indian Army the Maharaja of Patiala, Yadavindra Singh, came to Jammu to command his contingent in person.

In that by October, 1947 the Patiala State forces had by the terms of the State's accession to India (as part of the Patiala and East Punjab States Union) on 5 May, 1947 come under the control of the Government of Indian Union at the moment of the Transfer of Power, this deployment of Patiala State troops raises a number of questions which have yet to be answered, not least how they actually managed to reach the State of Jammu and Kashmir without the fact being reported to the senior British commanders still in the service of the Indian Army (who would surely have informed Mountbatten had they known). The arrival of such exotic forces could hardly have escaped the notice of the Indian Army observer in the State. Lt. Colonel Kashmir Singh Katoch)..." (Page 131)

"If Mahajan's account of his travels is true, and he was quite emphatic that he refused to return to the State until Srinagar airfield was firmly in Indian hands (reflecting both the Maharaja's determination that Indian assistance should physically arrive before he finally committed himself to handing power to Sheikh Abdullah and, one must presume, Mahajan's personal reluctance to run the slightest risk of falling into the hands of Pathans), then it would appear that the Indian intervention actually took place before the formalities of Accession had been completed..." (Page 136)

If we accept the chronology indicated by Mahajan rather than V.P. Menon, then it rather looks as if the Maharaja's original formal (as opposed to the various covert arrangements) request for Indian military aid, advanced on his behalf by Batra on 24 October but not accepted by the Indian side, made no reference to Sheikh Abdullah being given office, an idea which the Maharaja found extremely distasteful; and it is probable, moreover, that accession was not offered at this stage. The Sheikh Abdullah feature, discussed by Nehru with Sheikh Abdullah himself on 25 October, was surely finalised at the meeting at Nehru's house on the 26 October already described. A draft letter would have then prepared for the Maharaja's signature, that letter published as having originated from him on 26 October though, in fact, it was only brought to him in Jammu on the following day along with Mountbatten's acceptance of its terms. This charade, of course, of which Mountbatten must have been aware (unless he had been shown a fraudulently signed letter from the Maharaja, and perhaps, Menon had lied to him about a journey to Kashmir with Mahajan on 26 October), would have required a measure of falsification of the record both as to chronology and as to origination of the proposals. As we have seen in Chapter 4, such manipulations of documentation were not unknown in the British Government of India's conduct of political matters. The actual Instrument of Accession (which made no mention of the crucial Sheikh Abdullah element and was, therefore, in the context of the moment just a formality) was, in fact, no more than a printed form, not unlike an application for a driving licence, with blank spaces left for the name of the State, the signature of the Maharaja and the date: and it also captioned a printed form of acceptance which required dating and signature by Mountbatten as Governor General. It would have presented no great difficulties to arrange for Mahajan to carry back to Jammu with him on 27 October such a form, to be predated 26 October, with the Governor-General's acceptance already signed and dated 27 October, for the Maharaja to sign at a moment convenient to him"... (pages 136 and 137).

In his recent interview with Amera Saeed, appeared in esteemed English Daily *(MUSLIM)* of Islamabad, on Friday, November 27, 1992, he further highlighted the truth of bogus and fraudulent Instrument of Accession. Relevant portion is :

"The problem we have got now is that somebody is lying through his teeth, because here we have a whole set of documents which are dated the 26th (of October 1947) and accepted by Mountbatten on the 27th, and which can't possibly have been signed on the 27th. And then when we look at the documents and we wonder that they are, anyway. Because, what was produced was a printed document relating to accession during the British period. It can't possibly be the document that Mountbatten's people are talking about, because Mountbatten, in the discussions, of which we have several records of the accounts on the 26th, when he says we must have this accession, says 'Let an instrument of accession be drafted'.

"Now this is standard form, printed for August, with August crossed out, and October put in, which can't possibly be what they are talking about. So I think and this is the most important discovery I have made that there was no document at all. I was in the India Office Library a month ago, and I met a Professor Husnain, who has been an archivist of the Jammu and Kashmir State, and he says that they have been looking for the past forty-three years to find the original Instrument of Accession and never found it! There isn't one! When you come to think of it, having got the Indian troops in, why sign?"

77. We may also add the list of events leading to fraudulent accession manoeuvred by India, by reference to utterance from the horses mouth. Mohan Krishen Teng, a Hindu author, in his book *"KASHMIR ARTICLE* 370", recasted the political events, points of difference between the Kashmir leadership and Indian rulers, the pressure on Kashmir leadership and its ultimate succumbing to pressures. This evidence corroborates the analysis to Professor Alastair Lamb. We may liberally quote the relevant excerpts as :

> "Hari Singh did not commit himself to accept any future Constitution of India. However, he reserved the right to enter into agreements with the Government of India under any future constitution of India. The instrument of accession did not effect the continuance of the sovereignty of the Ruler in and over the State or the validity of any law in force in the State, save as provided by or under the Instrument of Accession." (Page 45)

> "The Conference leaders insisted that the obligations undertaken by the Maharaja, by virtue of the Instrument of Accession were subject to their approval. Therefore, they did not accept the accession of the State, as it was envisaged by the State Department or the Maharaja. In fact, they visualised the accession of the State as an administrative arrangement which was arrived at between them and the Government of India, not between the Maharaja and the Government of India.

> The Conference leaders, had before the partition of India, committed themselves to united India, which they had presumed would be based upon reorganisation of the British India and the Indian States into autonomous political identities, mainly based upon the reconciliation of communal balances. The partition had, however, destroyed the basis of Indian unity the Conference leaders had visualised and liberated the two Dominions from the constraints any

communal balances imposed upon them. The Constituent Assembly of India had opted for a Union of India based on the secular integration of the people of India rather than the recognition of communal balances and federal autonomy. In broad terms the conference leaders took the position which underlined :

(*i*) the Jammu and Kashmir State was a Muslim majority State and in order to protect Muslim identity, it could not be brought within the political organisation of India, which is dominantly Hindu;

(*ii*) the existing arrangements between the Maharaja and the Government of India could not form the basis of the constitutional organisation of the State or determine the future of the State's constitutional relations with the Dominion of India;

(*iii*) the future Constitution of the State and the constitutional relations between the State and the future federal organisation of India would be determined by fresh agreements between the Interim Government and the Government of India;

(*iv*) the stipulation of the Instrument of Accession would be treated as redundant to the extent such stipulations brought the State within the jurisdiction of the Dominion of India.

The National Conference leaders pledged their support to the accession of the State, but they refused to accept the secular integration of the State in the federal organisation of India. That claimed that the Jammu and Kashmir State was a Muslim majority State and as such it could be placed in the Indian political organisation only on the basis of communal balances, as a separate and autonomous political entity, which did not form a part of the constitutional organisation of India." (Pages 47 and 48)

"While the Indian leaders were trying frantically to find a solution of the problems in the State, and remove the Maharaja, Sheikh Muhammad Abdullah threw a bombshell in their midst. In a press statement, he gave to an influential English newspaper "Scotsman" he pleaded for the independence of the State. "Accession on either side cannot bring peace", Abdullah stated. "We want to live in friendship with both Dominions. Perhaps a middle path between them, with economic cooperation with each, will be only way of doing it. But an independent Kashmir must be guaranteed not only by India and Pakistan, but also by Britain, the United States and other members of the United Nations". Sheikh Muhammad Abdullah added further, "During the communal riots in the Punjab after partition, we tried in our humble way to stem the wave of fanaticism. That is why I urged we should wait before deciding our affiliation. I pleaded with both Dominions to help us first to win internal emancipation before asking us to choose! India replied by refusing to make a standstill agreement with the Maharaja; Pakistan did not do so. When during the crisis India accepted the Maharaja's accession. Pandit Nehru insisted that it was only provisional and that people must decide later". (Pages 51 and 52).

78. The aforesaid events fully coincide, without reservations, that any attempt at regional integration of any part of the State would not only negate the principle of right of self-determination promised to the people of Kashmir at the forum of the United Nations, rather it shall be suicidal to the Cause as a whole. The tremendous sacrifices of Cashmeres may go waste. A sane approach to the proposition, therefore, would be to desist from integrating the Northern areas to any Province of Pakistan, unless the future of the State, as a whole, is settled in exercise of right of self-determination as promised.

We may add another reason in support of our contention by reference to the provisions of Pakistan Constitution. In consistent with the policy, the framers of the Constitutions of the Islamic Republic of Pakistan in 1956, 1962 and 1973, made an express provision in the Constitutions in respect of the State of Jammu and Kashmir. Article 257 of the present Constitution of Pakistan postulated :

> "When the people of the State of Jammu and Kashmir decide to accede to Pakistan, the relationship between Pakistan and that State shall be determined in accordance with the wishes of the people of that State."

These provisions are consistent with the policy of Pakistan in relation to the Kashmir State. It is clearly postulated that the State of Jammu and Kashmir, as such, is a single entity.

Its future is yet to be determined in the light of the terms and of the act of accession. An open scope of terms and conditions of accession have been deliberately preserved by the framers of the Constitution. Therefore,

(*v*) When more than one meaning may be construable, such significance may be given to the provisions which are most close to the scheme and structure of the Constitution;

(*vi*) Constitution or statutes may be construed to maintain its harmony; and

(*vii*) Preamble of the Constitution may be helpful to construe the scope of objectives and intent of its framers.

92. In the light of the grund norms applicable to interpretation and construction of Constitution, as listed above, next, we advert to the scheme, objectives and character of the Azad Jammu and Kashmir Interim Constitution Act, 1974. It is undenied that the structure, position and status of Azad Jammu and Kashmir is unique among the comity of Governments and States in the world. Likewise, the scheme, structure and position of its Constitution is equally unique. This is so as the political status, as it emerged on constitution of the modern state in 1846; its status at the time of independence in 1947; the emergence of dispute pertaining to its accession; the dispute over its future status being still on the agenda of the Security Council; passing of various resolutions by the Security Council and the United Nations Commission for India and Pakistan, divided defence control on one part of it under India and the other part under Pakistan, presence of two Governments, one in the Indian controlled area and the other in the liberated area, are unparallel to any other State in the world in 20th century.

93. Another noticeable characteristic feature of the Constitution Act pertains to the style and character of the Government. Under Section 2, the term "Government" has been defined as 'the Azad Government of the State of Jammu and Kashmir'. In order to give true meaning to its definition, the scheme of Constitution envisaged various institutions, including:

(*i*) the President;

(*ii*) the Prime Minister (with Council of Ministers);

(*iii*) the Legislature;

(*iv*) the Council;

(*v*) the Supreme Court and the High Court;

(*vi*) the Chief Election Commissioner;

(*vii*) the Auditor General; and

(*viii*) the Council of Islamic Ideology.

It has its own national flag and national anthem. The Azad Government has a dual character as its fabric is blended with federal and unitary form of Government.

94. In consequence of the upsurge of the masses against the oppressor ruler and liberation of large areas, it was resolved to form a provisional government, with the claim of Government of whole of the State. The provisional Government was announced on October 24, 1947, with its capital seat at Pallandari in Poonch. The declaration issued by the provisional Government on this emergence contained the background of the liberation movement, liberation of part of the State and the objectives in view, for formation of the provisional government. The declaration being of vital importance, is reproduced:

> "The Provisional Azad Government, which the people of Jammu and Kashmir have set up a few weeks ago with the object of ending intolerable Dogra tyrannies and securing to the people of the State, including Muslims, Hindus and Sikhs, the right of free self-Government has now established its rule over a major portion of the State territory and hopes to liberate the remaining pockets of Dogra rule very soon. In view of these circumstances it has been reconstituted with Mr. Ibrahim, Bar-at-Law of Poonch as its provisional head, and its headquarters have been moved to Plandari in Poonch.
>
> The new Government represents the united will of the Jammu and Kashmir State to be free from the rule of the Dogra dynasty which has long suppressed and oppressed the people.
>
> The movement of liberty which has culminated in the formation of the present provisional Government has a long history dating from 1929.Thousands of Jammu and Kashmir people, including members of all communities, have suffered death and imprisonment in the cause of this

movement. One of its forms was the Quit *Kashmir Movement* launched in the Kashmir valley last year.

It will be recalled that Pandit Jawaharlal Nehru as a friend of the suffering people of Indian States went to help this movement at the time but was not allowed to enter the State territory under the orders of the ex-Ruler Hari Singh. The tyrannies perpetrated by the Raja and his officials and his troops on the people increased with the increase in the, desire of the people for freedom and self-Government.

Recently a prominent Hindu patriot, who wanted to proceed to Karachi and New Delhi to represent the intolerable conditions in the State to our neighbouring Dominions of Pakistan and India was arrested by the ex-Ruler's officials.

The united will of the people has, however, overcome the organised violence of the Ruler's armies. He and his so called Prime Minister have fled from Kashmir and will perhaps soon flee from Jammu as well.

The Provisional Government, which is assuming the administration of the State is most emphatically not a communal Government. It will include Muslims as well as non-Muslim in the provisional Cabinet which will serve the people, the temporary purpose of restoring law and order in the State and enable the people to elect by their free vote a popular legislature and a popular Government.

The Provisional Government entertain sentiments of the utmost friendliness and goodwill towards the neighbouring Dominions of India and Pakistan and hopes that both the Dominions will sympathise with the people of Jammu and Kashmir in their efforts to exercise their birthright of political freedom. The Provisional Government is further anxious to safeguard the identity of Jammu and Kashmir as political entity. The question of accession of Jammu and Kashmir to either Dominion can only be decided by the free vote of the people in the form of a referendum. The Provisional Government will make prompt arrangements for this and hopes to invite independent observers to see that the question is decided by the free will of the people."

It is evident from the Declaration recapitulated above that the character of the Azad Government was provisional till the liberation of whole of the State. It is represented by the united will of the people of Jammu and Kashmir to attain freedom from the Dogra dynasty. The united will represented all communities residing in the State. An undertaking was also given that the Provisional Government shall safeguard the identity of Jammu and Kashmir as political entity and that the question of accession of the State to either Dominion was to be decided by the free vote of the people in the form of free plebiscite.

95. As the war of liberation was in progress, no Constitution was framed immediately after the formation of the Provisional Government and the administration was run with the help of Rules of Business. The first Rules of Business were framed in 1948. These were supplemented in 1950. With the understanding that the future of the State was to be determined in a free plebiscite as guaranteed by the resolutions of the Security Council and the United Nations Commission for India and Pakistan; no need was felt to give democratic shape to the government and its institutions. As time passed on, it was realised that the Government will be given a democratic character. Thus, in 1960, limited franchise was introduced in the shape of Azad Jammu and Kashmir Basic Democracies Act, 1960. The President was elected by the electoral college comprising the Basic Democrats directly elected in Azad Kashmir and from refugees of the State settled in Pakistan. A Council representing the natives of Azad Kashmir and refugees settled in Pakistan was also constituted of elected representatives. As the desired purpose was not served, it was demanded that the national institutions may be given a true representative cover by introduction of the system of adult sufferage. The demand was accepted. The Azad Jammu and Kashmir Government Act, 1970 was promulgated. By virtue of the provisions of the Act, the President of Azad Jammu and Kashmir was elected by the electorates directly. A Legislative Assembly was also formed by its directed elected members.

In 1974, it was deemed expedient to introduce parliamentary form of Government, to harmonise it with the system prevailing in Pakistan. The Act of 1970 was modified and reenacted in the shape of the Azad Jammu and Kashmir Interim Constitution Act, 1974.

Haider, Subedar-Major Babar Khan and Wazir Walayet Ali formed a provisional Government, headed by Subedar Raees Khan. On November 3, 1947, flag hoisting ceremony took place at Gilgit in Scouts Lines where all civil officers of the State (Jammu and Kashmir) saluted the Pakistan flag. *On November 3, the charge of Gilgit was handed over to the provisional Government.* Brigadier Ghansara Singh was removed from Gilgit to Pakistan and was released on January 15, 1949 at Suchetgarh. In para 117 of his memoirs, he listed the main causes of fall of Gilgit agency. As one of the causes, he described that Mirs of Hunza and Nagar, who were State guests in Srinagar before return to Gilgit, had openly told the Chief Minister that they will establish Pakistan in Gilgit if the State opted for India and that Muslim officers of the State, posted in Gilgit, were very keen to establish Pakistan. They joined hands with the British officers for the purpose."

106. The other relevant authority on the point is Colonel (Rtd) Mirza Hassan Khan, who recorded his own memoirs in the name of "Story of Freedom Movement". In his memoirs, Colonel Mirza Hassan Khan disclosed the details of the revolution in Gilgit and Northern areas. He recapitulated the manner of revolution, its impact and achievements, including the tactics of overpowering and capturing Ghansara Singh, the Governor of Gilgit, to establish a revolutionary Government.

107. We may also quote some relevant excerpts from the speeches made by Sir Muhammad Zafarullah Khan, Foreign Minister of Pakistan, in the Security Council on January 16, 1948, in its 228th meeting, as listed in the "Documents on Kashmir Problem" by M.S. Deora and R. Grover, volume 1, published in 1991, at pages 177, 208 and 217 :

> "We now turn to the State of Kashmir itself. This State was purchased by the great-grandfather of the present Ruler of Kashmir from the British East India Company in 1846 for 7,500,000 rupees. Roughly, this is less than $2,500,000.
>
> The population of Kashmir is distributed communally as follows : In Kashmir proper, apart from Jammu, 93.5 per cent are Muslims, 62 per cent of the population of Jammu are Muslims. In the combined Jammu and Kashmir State,

78 per cent are Muslims. The total population is approximately 4,000,000.

Gilgit, which is the high mountain region in the Northwest, a part of which borders on the USSR, is entirely Muslim. The total area of the State, which is largely composed of high mountains and barren hills, is 82,000 square miles. The region is famous for its beauty. The people of this State are similarly famous. Their high artistic talents are well known. What is not fully known is the depths of misery to which they have been reduced by a century of unmitigated tyranny and oppression under Dogra rule until it is difficult to say which is the greater tragedy to a Kashmiri: his life or his death. Death often provides release from the unbroken chain of suffering, misery and privation which begins in the cradle and ends only in the grave." (Page 177)

"The two Governors-General met at Lahore and had a long discussion on 1 November. The upshot of the discussion was that the Governor General of Pakistan made the following proposals to the Governor-General of India for the acceptance of the Indian Dominion:

1. To put an immediate stop to fighting, the two Governors-General should be authorised and vested with full powers by both Dominion Governments to issue a proclamation forthwith, giving forty-eight hours' notice to the two opposing forces to cease fire. The *Governor General of Pakistan has no control over the forces of the provisional Government of Kashmir* or the tribesmen engaged in the fighting, but he will warn them in the clearest terms that if they do not obey the order to cease fire immediately, the forces on both Dominions will make war on them." (Page 208)

"It is not the so called raiders, but the people of Kashmir, who are fighting against heavy odds to end Dogra tyranny and to prevent Kashmir from falling into the hands of the Indian Dominion.

The Azad Kashmir forces are almost wholly composed of the sons of the soil, and even foreign observers have testified that, wherever they have gone, they have been welcomed as forces of liberation."

We are avoiding, for the purpose of brevity, to quote other sources as, in our estimation, the aforesaid leading authorities provide ample proof in their analysis, to hold that the Northern Areas were liberated by the people of the State.

108. The other condition pertains to the administration of the Government. Reference to the word "Government" in the definition, obviously pertains to the Azad Government. The Azad Government has been defined, as noticed elsewhere, as the Government of the State of Jammu and Kashmir. Therefore, the area of jurisdiction of the Government spreads throughout the State. Such a definition has been rightly assigned keeping in view the objectives of the Liberation Movement and its ultimate end, as noticed in the first declaration made by it.

109. The word "administration" is quite relevant in this context. Its meaning and scope are, therefore, to be construed in its dictionary meaning. In Black's Law Dictionary, the word "administration" has been defined as :

> "Management or conduct of office or employment; the performance of the executive duties of an institution, business or the like. In public law, the administration of government means the practical management and direction of the executive department, or of the public machinery or functions, or of the operations of the various organs or agencies."

The spirit of meaning of the word "administration" extends to performance of executive duties of the Government. The executive functions of the Government are, next, to be examined from the provisions of the Constitution itself. Section 19 of the Act envisages the extent of executive authority of the Government. It is reproduced:

19. Extent of executive authority of Government.

(1) Subject to this Act, the executive authority of the Government shall extend to the matters with respect to which the Assembly has power to make laws.

(2) The executive authority of the Government shall be so exercised as :

(*a*) not to impede or prejudice the responsibilities of the government of Pakistan in relation to the matters specified in sub-section (3) of section 31; and (*b*) to secure compliance with the laws made by the Council.

(3) Notwithstanding anything contained in this Act, the Government may, with the consent of the Council, entrust, either conditionally or unconditionally, to the Council, or to its officers functions in relation to any matter to which the executive authority of the Government extends."

It is evident that the executive authority of the Government envelops all matters with respect to which the Assembly has power to make laws. It is also assigned the responsibility to ensure compliance with the laws made by the Council. In other words, the executive authority of the Government extends to all subjects in respect of which the Assembly has power to make laws and the Council also makes laws in exercise of its jurisdiction. This takes us further to the legislative authority of the Assembly.

110. Section 31 of the Act deals with legislative powers of the Assembly and the Council. It provides that both the Council and the Assembly shall have power to make laws :

(*a*) *for the territories of Azad Jammu and Kashmir* ;

(*b*) *for all State Subjects* wherever they may be; and

(*c*) for all officers of the Council or, as the case may be, the government wherever they may be.

Under sub-section (2), clause (*b*), the Assembly has the power to make laws with respect to any matter not enumerated in the Council's Legislative List. Under the provisions of subsection (1)(*b*) and subsection (2)(*b*), the powers of the Assembly to make laws travel beyond the horizons of Azad Jammu and Kashmir. As a matter of fact, the Assembly has been empowered to make laws for all State Subjects, irrespective of their place of destination, and all residuary matters which have not been included in the Legislative List of the Council. In other words, the executive authority of the Government extends not only within the limits of Azad Jammu and Kashmir but to all such places and areas where the State Subjects reside, work for their earnings or carry their profession and business.

111. The term "State Subject" has been defined under Section 2. It means :

"A person for the time being residing in Azad Jammu and Kashmir or Pakistan who is a 'State Subject as defined in the late Government of the State of Jammu and Kashmir Notification No. IL/84, dated the 20th April, 1927, as amended from time to time."

In the Notification, the term "State Subject" has been defined as :

"THE STATE SUBJECT DEFINITION NOTIFICATION, DATED, THE 20TH APRIL, 1927. No. I-L/84. The following definition of the term "State Subject" has been sanctioned by His Highness the Maharaja Bahadur (vide Private Secretary's letter No. 2354, dated, the 31st January, 1927, to the Revenue Member of Council) and is hereby promulgated for general information :

The term "State Subject" means and includes:

CLASS I. All persons born and residing within the State before the commencement of the reign of His Highness the late Maharaja Gulab Singh Sahib Bahadur, and also persons who settled therein before the commencement of Samvat year 1942, and have since permanently residing therein.

CLASS II. All persons other than those belonging to Class I who settled within the State before the close of Samvat year 1968, and have since permanently resided and acquired immovable property therein.

CLASS III. All persons, other than those belonging to Classes I and II permanently residing within the State, who have acquired under a rayatnama any immovable property therein or who may hereafter acquire such property under an ijazatnama and may execute a rayatnama after ten years' continuous residence therein.

CLASS IV. Companies which have been registered as such within the State and which, being companies in which the Government are financially interested or as to the economic benefit to the State or to the financial stability of which the Government are satisfied, have by a special order of His Highness been declared to be State Subjects.

NOTE I. In matter of grants of State Scholarships, State lands for agricultural and house building purposes and recruitment to State Service, State Subjects of Class I should receive preference over other classes and those of Class II over Class III, subject, however, to the order dated 31st January 1927, of His Highness the Maharaja Bahadur regarding employment of hereditary State Subjects in Government service.

NOTE II. The descendants of the persons who have secured the status of any Class of the State Subjects will be entitled to become the State Subjects of the same class. For example if A is declared a State Subject of Class II his sons and grandsons will ipso facto acquire the status of the same Class (II) and not of Class I.

NOTE III. The wife or a widow of a State Subject of any Class shall acquire the status of her husband as State Subject of the same Class as her husband, so long as she resides in the State and does not leave the State for permanent residence outside the State.

NOTE IV. For the purpose of the interpretation of the term 'State Subject' either with reference to any law for the time being in force or otherwise, the definition given in this Notification as amended up to date shall be read as if such amended definition existed in this Notification as originally issued."

It is evident from the aforesaid definition of the term "State Subject" that all persons who were born within the State before the reign of Maharaja Gulab Singh and those who settled therein before 1942 and resided permanently, were State Subjects of Class I. Those who settled in the State before the close of 1968 Bikrami and resided permanently, on acquisition of immovable property, enjoyed the status of State Subjects of Class II. All those who acquired immovable property under a rayatnama or ijazatnama and resided in the State continuously, were placed in Class III as State Subjects. Class IV pertains to registered companies in the State.

112. It is undenied that at present or at the time of promulgation of the Interim Constitution Act, 1974, the Azad Government was not exercising administrative control over the Northern Areas, but the fact remains that the Northern Areas, immediately after liberation, were linked with the rest of the

liberated territories. In view of communication difficulties and limited sources, the administrative control was delivered to the Pakistan Government. The Pakistan Government having no legitimate sanction to hold the administration, felt advised to secure such sanction from the legitimate authorities in Azad Kashmir. It appears that, in such situation, it was deemed expedient to execute an agreement between both the Governments to legitimatize the administrative control. Thus, the impugned agreement of April 28, 1949 was secured to rectify the doubtful legitimacy of administrative control. Be that as it may, the fact remains that the natives of the Northern Areas being State Subjects, both the Assembly and the Council were eligible to make laws in respect of them in exercise of their powers under Section 31(1)(b) and the executive authority of the Government, as noticed under the provisions of Section 19, equally extended to those areas. Thus, the scheme of law introduced under the Interim Constitution Act covered the administrative jurisdiction of the Government in respect of the Northern Areas. In this view of the matter, the jurisdiction of this Court, as noticed in Section 44 (2) (a) (i), (b) (ii) and (c), squarely extended to the Northern Areas.

It is evident from the aforesaid provisions that the Legislative Assembly has been defined as the Legislature of Azad Jammu and Kashmir. In its literal sense, by accepting the contention of the learned Deputy Attorney General, representing the Government of Pakistan, the representation in the Assembly has to confine to the liberated territories under the effective administrative control of the Government. In other words, lite rally, the extent of territories under the effective control of the Government may be the five districts (Muzaffarabad, Bagh, Poonch, Kotli and Mirpur). It is undenied that the Assembly represents whole of the State, including liberated territories (excluding Northern Areas). Representation to the Indian occupied part of the State has been provided through the refugees from the Provinces of Kashmir, Jammu and other areas, settled in Pakistan. Six members are elected from amongst the refugees from Kashmir Province and six from Jammu and other areas from amongst the refugees, settled in Pakistan. The constitution of the Assembly, prima facie, corresponds to the jurisdiction of this Court, as enunciated elsewhere.

121. It is noticeable that one of the members of the Assembly represents the State Subjects residing abroad, (outside Pakistan) throughout the world. It is undenied that such a member has been elected twice from the State Subjects residing in the United Kingdom. The present Assembly is also represented by a member who resides and carries on business in the United Kingdom.

122. By accepting a narrow and rigid meaning of the term "Azad Jammu and Kashmir", the structure of the Assembly raised at the time of enforcement of the surveillance of the Commission, over the territory evacuated by the Pakistani troops, pending a final solution of the Kashmir problem. Three things emerge from the language used by the Commission, as it refers to:

(*i*) The territory evacuated by the Pakistani troops;

(*ii*) its administration by the local authorities; and

(*iii*) under the surveillance of the Commission.

Referrence to "evacuated territory" obviously means the territories of the liberated parts of the State of Jammu and Kashmir. This is supported by reference to evacuation by the Pakistani troops. Therefore, no doubt can be entertained with respect to identification of the evacuated territory.

Clause (3) of Part II, 'A', refers to "local authorities". This reference is obviously to the Azad Government and its administrative structure. The status of Azad Government has remained under controversy for the last 43 years, at different levels. One view is that the term "local authorities" refers to the provisional Government of the State of Jammu and Kashmir, in the light of its declaration made on its reconstitution on October 24, 1947. The counter view is that the use of the term "local authorities" has reduced the status of the Azad Government to that of a Municipal Committee. Both the views, prima facie, find support from the structure and status of the Government with reference to exercise of its executive authority and in the light of the ordinary meaning of the term "local authorities". It may not be out of place to refer here that the nomenclature and infrastructure of the Azad Government was made and raised during the life time of the founder of Pakistan,

Quaid-e-Azam Muhammad Ali Jinnah and under the supervision of the Prime Minister, (late) Liaquat Ali Khan. The Government was headed by the President with a Council of Ministers, including the Defence Minister. In addition to its executive duty, it controlled and supervised the Azad Kashmir Regular Forces comprising 35 regiments or more. It was In this view of the matter that Governor General of Pakistan (Quaid-e-Azam), in his first conference with the Governor General of India, on November 1, 1947 at Lahore, clearly accepted that he had "no control over the forces of the provisional Government of Kashmir". The Foreign Minister of Pakistan, while addressing the Security Council, on January 17, 1948, by reference to the fighting forces against the Indian and Dogra army in the State, highlighted that:

> 'The people of Kashmir were fighting against heavy odds to end Dogra tyranny and to prevent Kashmir from falling into the hands of the Indian Dominion.
>
> The Azad Kashmir Forces were almost wholly composed of the sons of the soil and even foreign observers testified that wherever they went, they had been welcomed as forces of liberation."

The aforesaid position raised the status of the Government as a de facto Government for the whole of State and not an ordinary local authority of the status of Municipal Committee, as presented by the counter view. It appears that the Government of Pakistan was equally anxious over the use of the words "administration by local authorities" in the liberated territory. It felt constrained to refer the matter to the members of the Commission for clarification. Thus, reference was made to the United Nations Commission for India and Pakistan. It was answered in positive manner, in a meeting held on September 2, 1948. Mr. Josef Korbel, a senior member of the Commission, who spoke for other members, elaborated the meaning of the term "local authorities" as:

(*i*) "By local authorities" we mean the Azad Kashmir people, though we cannot grant recognition to the Azad Kashmir Government."

(*ii*) "We have gone so far as we could to meet the point of view of the Azad Kashmir people. We have tried to deal with the de facto situation. But we cannot lose sight of the fact that the *State ofJammu and Kashmir still exists as a legal entity. We have to respect its sovereignty."*

It was further added :

"We agree that there will be no change in the existing administration of Gilgit."

129. The Government of Pakistan issued a press communique on January 16, 1949 in respect of the clarification sought from the Commission relating to various phraseologies used in the resolution of August 13, 1948. It is reproduced:

(*ii*) The Commission further explained in its letter of 19th September, 1948, that *the area in the occupation of forces under the overall control of the Pakistan High Command would remain in the occupation of the Azad Kashmir Forces.* The Commission stated categorically that its Resolution of 13th August "does not contemplate the disarmament or disbanding of the Azad Kashmir Forces."

(*iv*) Pending a final solution, the *territory evacuated by the Pakistan troops would be administered by the "local authorities" under the surveillance of the Commission.* It was explained by the Commission that the term, *"local authorities" meant the "Azad Kashmir Government"* although the Commission could not and did not accord recognition to that Government. It was further explained that "surveillance" did not mean actual control or supervision, and that the Commission's sole aim would be to ensure that the "local authorities" did not violate the ceasefire and truce agreements. The Commission also explained that it did not contemplate surveillance of the *Gilgit* Administration which was temporarily in charge of a *Political Agent of the Pakistan Government.* The Commission also made it clear that the Maharaja's Government would not, under any circumstances, be permitted to interfere with or to send any military or civil officials to *the territory under the control of the "local authorities".*

(*v*) The Government of India undertook to ensure that the Government of State of Jammu and Kashmir would make known that peace, law and order would be safeguarded, and that all *human and political rights*

> *would be guaranteed.* The Commission expected *that similar action would be taken by the "local authorities" in the area evacuated by Pakistan troops".*

It is manifest from the explanations advanced by the members of the United Nations Commission for India and Pakistan, that the term "local authorities" was used deliberately to acknowledge de facto status of provisional Government of the State of Jammu and Kashmir. The Azad Government, according to the resolution, was accepted as the lawful authority to administer the liberated territories. Thus, the authority and right to hold the administrative control of the liberated territories on this side of the ceasefire line fully vested in the Azad Government and none else. The resolution was accepted both by India and Pakistan in addition to other members of the Security Council. Therefore, it is an internationally acknowledged position that the liberated territories have to be governed by the Azad Government till the final solution of Kashmir issue.

130. The term "evacuated territory" was also construed by the Commission in its explanation sought by the Government of Pakistan, on September 2, 1948. The clarification was given as:

> 'The term "evacuated territory" means the area which is under the control of Pakistan High Command, including for this purpose the Pakistan Army, the Azad Kashmir Forces and tribesmen."

131. It is of interest to note that on the situation emerging on the evacuation of Pakistan troops from the liberated territories a very material question arose In respect of maintenance of law and order. Such question attained importance as in the other part of the resolution, pertaining to withdrawal of Indian army. It was postulated that the Indian Government agreed to withdraw the bulk of its forces from the State. By reference to "withdrawal of bulk" of forces, it was explained that a minimum strength of Indian forces would be retained in the State to look after law and order. As a counter measure, on this side of the ceasefire line, Azad Forces were to stay intact to assist in maintenance of law and order by the Azad Government. An explanation was sought from the Commission

with respect to the maintenance of Azad Kashmir Forces. In meeting held on August 31, 1948, Mr. Josef Korbel explained:

> "The Commission has made no demand either for the disarming or the withdrawal of the Azad Forces."

This position was reiterated in paragraph 2(C) of the letter of the Commission addressed on September 19, 1948. It was explained:

> "The resolution does not contemplate the disarmament or disbanding of the Azad Kashmir Forces."

132. The clear legal position which emerge from the aforesaid exposition is:

(*i*) Azad Kashmir Government enjoys a de facto status in the United Nations;

(*ii*) Authority of the Government to administer the liberated territories has been acknowledged; and

(*iii*) Azad Kashmir Forces were to stay.

133. The interpretation of the term "Azad Jammu and Kashmir", when examined in the light of the scheme of the Interim Constitution Act, keeping in view the historical background of liberation movement, the Kashmir dispute on the floor of the United Nations and settlement of the dispute through a free and impartial plebiscite under the United Nations' auspices, as agreed in the United Nations resolutions, it has to be accepted that the extent of administrative control of the Government spreaded over all the liberated territories. Inclusive of the Northern Areas of the State. Likewise the jurisdiction of this Court extend to all the liberated territories which formed part of the State of Jammu and Kashmir, all State Subjects wherever they may be, and all persons performing functions in connection with the affairs of the State (inclusive of Azad Jammu and Kashmir).

134. It is a celebrated rule of interpretation of Constitution or a statute that when the meanings of a word or term are not clear enough and are not found in consonance with the scheme of the Constitution or the statute, or are otherwise found in conflict when used in the same meaning and context in other parts of the statute, in such situation, the word "and" used in a

particular context was likely to be substituted and read as "or" and vice versa. This was deemed essential for harmonious meaning of the term or phrase, as the case may be and in order to save rather than to destroy the provisions of the statute. Both the words "and" and "or" are used interchangeable, so as to advance the purpose and objective of the provisions of the statute. This view finds ample support from Crawford's Interpretation of Statutes. At pages 3223 it is postulated as:

> "In ordinary use the word "or" is a disjunctive that marks an alternative which generally corresponds to the word "either". In face of this meaning however the word 'or' and the word "and" are often used interchangeable. As a result of this common and careless use of the two words in legislation, there are occasions when the court, through construction, may change one to the other. This cannot be done if the statute's meaning is clear or if the alteration operates to change the meaning of the law. It is proper only in order to more accurately express, or to carry out the obvious intent of the legislature, when the statute itself furnishes cogent proof of the error of the legislature, and especially where it will avoid absurd or impossible consequences, or operate to harmonise the statute and give effect to all of its provisions ....

Following the aforesaid rule of interpretation in order to attain objective significance of the word "and" used in the definition of the term "Azad Jammu and Kashmir", it is permissible to construe the word "and" as "or". Such an approach is compatible with both, (i) the literal and (*ii*) the liberal approach of interpretation of Constitution, as it is not a static but organic in nature. This leads to the effect that it is permissible to read the word "and" as "or". The definition of the term "Azad Jammu and Kashmir" has to be read as *"the territories which have been liberated by the people of that State or are for the time being under the administration of government."* Such an interpretation obviously suits to the scheme of the Constitution. The phraseology "are for the time being under the administration of Government" is to be construed disjunctively and not conjunctively.

135. The aforesaid analysis of the proposition relating to territorial jurisdiction of this Court, as conceived within the framework of the Interim Constitution Act, coupled with the acknowledged de facto status of Azad Government in the Act and international forum, leads to the conclusions :

(*i*) that this Court has been conferred jurisdiction by the Act for Azad Jammu and Kashmir and beyond, to the extent and in connection with the affairs of the State (Jammu and Kashmir);

(*ii*) in relation to all State Subjects, wherever they may be; and

(*iii*) to enforce Fundamental Rights conferred by the Act.

136. The proposition relating to administrative control of the Azad Government received attention of this Court in Brigadier (Rtd.) Muhammad Aslam Khan's case, decided by Mr. Justice Sardar Muhammad Sharif Khan, in Civil Arbitration No. 1, 2, 3, 4A of 1967, on March 20, 1976. The leading facts of that case were that Brigadier (Rtd.) Muhammad Aslam Khan secured lease of forest compartments falling on the Indian side of the Ceasefire Line. In view of the locality of the leased area, the matter was referred to the Government of Pakistan for its approval. It was examined by the Law Department of Pakistan and Ministry for Kashmir Affairs. On their approval, lease was granted vide agreement executed on November 13, 1963. There was a conflict on account of extraction of timber as on account of firing by the Indian army in the leased area, some workers were killed. In such situation, the Azad Government (lessor) terminated the lease unilaterally. The matter was referred to the arbitrator as agreed upon in the lease agreement.

Among others, the Government raised the objection that since the lease area was lying on the other side of the Ceasefire Line and the Government had no authority over that area, the forest standing thereon was beyond its effective control, as such the agreement was against public policy and void ab initio. The objection was repelled in the following manner :

> 'This is an admitted fact and there can be no denial to it by the Government that the Government has a de facto possession of the area under lease over which a portion of

the timber leased is still lying and it has been fully established by production of evidence along with the production of record that the area in dispute though on the other side of the Ceasefire Line, is in effective possession of the Azad Government of the State of Jammu and Kashmir. The administration of this Government is found exercising its full authority over the people of that area who are even subject to payment of land revenue to the administration of the Azad Government. *This Government is for the whole of the State though for the time being it is illegally deprived of a large part of the State by force, yet any area over which it can extend its control, it will be deemed that that area lies within the administrative control of the defendant-Government and as such leasing out the forest from that area under the effective control of the administration of this side, cannot be termed as an illegal act of the Government opposed to public policy. It is on record that the Forest Department as well as the Revenue Department have dealings all over the area in question across the Cease-fire Line.*

"Any part of the State which comes under the administration of this Government in any way, it will be deemed that a legal right has vested in this Government to deal with that part of the State in conduct of its business. This has been the stand of the Government itself while dealing with the Brigadier in execution of the agreement and for this point of view, even the opinion of the Law Department of the Government of Pakistan was also favourable obtained by the Government."

The Government feeling dissatisfied with the above finding of the learned Judge, preferred an Inter-Court appeal before a Division Bench of this Court. The Division Bench comprised of Mr. Justice Sardar Said Muhammad Khan J (presently Chief Justice of Azad Jammu and Kashmir) and Mr. Justice Sardar Muhammad Asharf Khan, Additional J (presently Judge of the Supreme Court). The point relating to effective control of the Government over the leased area was seriously canvassed on behalf of the Government. Mr. Justice Sardar Said Muhammad Khan, who delivered the verdict of the Court, on March 19, 1981 (in Civil Appeal No. 26/76, titled "Azad Government Vs. Brigadier Muhammad Aslam Khan", observed:

Another point urged by the learned Counsel for the appellant was that both the agreements were against public policy and as such, the agreements as well as the award were illegal. He has propounded the theory of 'Public Policy' on the ground that the area which was leased out in the instant case, was situated on the other side of the ceasefire line and there was not only an uncertainty with regard to the execution of the lease agreement but there was danger that relations between the two States would be jeopardized and even the lives of citizens of the State were at stake because the Indian forces might have launched an attack at any time, when the work of extraction of timber was carried on by the labourers in the lease area. The learned Counsel has argued that the agreement was ab initio void because the Government, the lessor, had no legal authority to control the area which was *on the other side of the Cease-fire Line. We are of the view that the Indian occupation of part ofJammu and Kashmir State against the popular will of the people of the State does not make Cease-fire Line or so-called Control Line a barrier to Azad Jammu and Kashmir Government to take any benefit from the territory.*

144. Paragraph 4 of the preamble of the Interim Constitution Act, 1974, reads:

AND WHEREAS, in the discharge of its responsibilities under the UNCIP Resolutions, the Government of Pakistan has approved of proposed repeal and reenactment of the said Azad Jammu and Kashmir Government Act, 1970, and authorised the President of Azad Jammu and Kashmir to introduce the present Bill in the Legislative Assembly of Azad Jammu and Kashmir for consideration and passage;"

It is manifest from the aforesaid provisions of the preamble that the Act was enforced in Azad Jammu and Kashmir by its Assembly with the approval of the Government of Pakistan. Approval of the Government of Pakistan was deemed necessary in view of its involvement in the affairs of Azad Jammu and Kashmir in the light of its responsibilities under the UNCIP Resolutions.

145. Section 31 of the Act relates to the legislative powers of the Council and the Assembly. Subsection (3) envisages that neither the Council nor the Assembly shall have the power to

make any laws concerning the respective subjects described there. In it is reproduced:

"(3) Neither the Council nor the Assembly shall have the power to make any law concerning.

(*a*) the responsibilities of the Government of Pakistan under the UNCIP Resolutions;

(*b*) the defence and security of Azad Jammu and Kashmir;

(*c*) the current coin or the issue of any bills, notes or other currency; or

(*d*) the external affairs of Azad Jammu and Kashmir including foreign trade and foreign aid."

Other relevant provisions are laid down in Section 56 of the Act. These are reproduced :

"56. Act not to derogate from responsibilites of Pakistan. Nothing in this Act shall derogate from the responsibilities of the Government of Pakistan in relation to the matters specified in subsection (3) of Section 31 or prevent the Government of Pakistan from taking such action as it may consider necessary or expedient for the effective discharge of those responsibilities."

III. *Division of functions between the Government of Pakistan, the Azad Kashmir Government and the Muslim Conference.*

A. Matters within the Purview of Pakistan Government.

(*i*) Defence. (Complete control over A.K. Forces).

(*ii*) Negotiations with U.N.C.I.P.

(*iii*) Foreign Policy of A.K. Government.

(*iv*) Publicity in Pakistan and foreign countries.

(*v*) Coordination of arrangements for relief and rehabilitation of refugees.

(*vi*) Coordination of publicity and all arrangements in connection with the plebiscite.

(*vii*) All activities within Pakistan itself with regard to Kashmir such as procurement of food and civil supplies, transport, running of refugee camps, medical arrangements etc.

(*viii*) All affairs of the Gilgit and Ladakh areas under the control of Political Agent at Gilgit.

B. Matters within the Purview of A.K. Government.

Policy with regard to administration in Azad Kashmir.

General supervision of administration in Azad Kashmir.

Publicity with regard to activities of the A.K. Government and its administration.

Advise to H.M. without Portfolio with regard to negotiations with U.N.C.I.P.

Development of economic resources of A.K. area.

C. Matters within the Purview of Muslim Conference.

Publicity with regard to plebiscite in A.K. area.

(*i*) Field work and publicity in the Indian occupied area of the State.

(*ii*) Organisation of political activities in the A.K. and the Indian occupied areas of the State.

(*iii*) Preliminary arrangements in connection with plebiscite.

(*iv*) Organisation for contesting the plebiscite.

(*v*) Political work and publicity among Kashmir refugees in Pakistan.

(*vi*) General guidance of the A.K. Government.

(*vii*) Advice to H.M. without portfolio with regard to negotiations with U.N.C.I.P.

Sd/	I agree to this in so	Sd/
(MOhammad Ibrahim) President, Azad Kashmir Govt. concerns	far as this the sphere of activities of the M.C. Sd/ (Ghulam Abbas) President All Jammu and Kashmir Muslim Conference.	(M.A. Gurmani) Minister without Portfolio, Govt. of Pakistan.

It is evident from the provisions of the agreement that various administrative and political functions concerning the liberated territories of the State, the liberation movement and Kashmir dispute in the United Nations, were bifurcated and assigned to different authorities, privy to the arrangements settled in the agreement. The Azad Kashmir Government was assigned primarily the responsibility and functions of supervising the administration in Azad Kashmir area. The first part contained various subjects, described therein, which were entrusted to Azad Kashmir Government.

The second part, postulated in Part III, was relevant as by virtue of that part of the agreement, the sphere of administrative jurisdiction was divided among the component parties to the agreement. The matters assigned to the Government of Pakistan were listed under caption 'A'. These subjects were eight in number. It contained the responsibilities of the Government of Pakistan in respect of all affairs of Gilgit and Ladakh, the area, at the relevant time, under the control of Political Agent at Gilgit.

152. The aforesaid arrangement was accepted as a matter of policy, by the parties, in view of the situation of Kashmir dispute, the tempo of liberation movement and the importance of administration in the liberated territories. This policy continued till 1970, when an Act of the Government was enforced on September 5, 1970. Prior to the aforesaid Act, the administrative business of Azad Kashmir was carried through the Rules of Business enforced from time to time. The first Rules of Business, available on record, were enforced on December 28, 1950.

153. By virtue of these rules, the administration of Azad Government was regulated, classified and distributed among various heads of Departments of the Government, including the appointment of President, Ministers, Civil Servants etc. The head of the Government was the Supreme Head who was empowered to nominate the President and the Council of Ministers. The President and Council of Ministers were collectively responsible to the Supreme Head. The legislative authority vested in the Council but no law was framed and enforced unless it received the assent of the Supreme Head. The

legislation emanated either from a Minister, Chief Administrative Adviser or heads of Departments. It was examined by the Secretary General and Legislative Department and was sent, for its approval to the Supreme Head.

Petitioners have challenged the propriety of the authority administering the Northern Areas, in addition to their complaint of depriving them of fundamental rights, representation in the Government and other national institutions for the last 45 years, the proposition raised in the petition squarely bring the case of the petitioners within the scope of the provisions of Section 44.

189. Respondent No. 1, in its written statement, has failed to explain as to why the residents of the Northern Areas were not integrated with Pakistan or with rest of the liberated territories of Azad Jammu and Kashmir. No reason has been given for failure to provide Fundamental Rights and representation to these people for the last 45 years. In absence of any positive explanation, it is permissible to assume that in view of the proximity of international boundaries of former Soviet Socialist Republic, Afghanistan and China, these areas were considered sensitive from the defence point of view. In view of its exceptional geographical location and proximity of the countries of immense supremacy, it was deemed in the national interest to avoid disturbance of status quo. Otherwise, we are not in possession of any reasonable and just cause for denying the basic rights, including the right of representation, to these people. The international scenario has been changed in the last couple of years. The Russian aggression in Afghanistan has been repulsed and Afghanistan is blessed with its independent sovereign status. The former Soviet Socialist Republic has been split and disintegrated into various States. The neighbouring States of Central Asia have assumed their independence. Their status as such, has been acknowledged internationally, as they have become members of the United Nations. Likewise, signing of Sino-Pak Border Treaty between China and Pakistan has also dispersed the apprehension of political intervention in the Northern Areas. Therefore, *under the present conditions, it is no* more *a sensitive region from the defence point of view. Its position is identical to the rest of Azad Jammu and Kashmir.* At this stage, if there is any apprehension of threat of

aggression, it is only from across the Cease-fire Line and that is common and identical to all the liberated territories. The responsibility of defence and security of Azad Jammu and Kashmir and Northern Areas equally rest on the shoulders of Pakistan Defence Forces. Therefore, in absence of any marginal sensitive position of either of the area from the defence point of view, there is least justification to keep the people of Northern Areas deprived of their basic rights and detached from the main-stream.

Next, we pass on to the provisions of Section 4 of the Interim Constitution Act.

190. Section 4 relate to Fundamental Rights, Subsection (1) postulates that any law or any custom and usage having the force of law, in so far as it is inconsistent with the rights conferred by this Section, shall, to the extent of such inconsistency, be void. Subsection (2) further provide that no law shall be made which takes away or abridges the rights so conferred and any law made in contravention of this subsection shall, to the extent of such contravention, be void. That brings to the conclusion that :

(*i*) the existing laws or custom or usage having the force of law, in so far as they were inconsistent with the rights conferred under Section 4(4), to that extent, were void; and

(*vii*) that detachment of Northern Areas from the rest of Azad Jammu and Kashmir tantamount to violation of the Resolutions of the Security Council of March 30, 1951 and January 24, 1957;

(*viii*) that the Azad Government represented the whole of the State of Jammu and Kashmir. Its such status (de facto) has been acknowledged by the United Nations;

(*ix*) that the jurisdiction of High Court extends to all matters relevant to the affairs of Azad Jammu and Kashmir, and the State as a whole in respect of all State Subjects, wherever they may be;

(*x*) that in view of the scheme of the Interim Constitution Act, the resolutions of the Security Council and the United Nations Commission for India and Pakistan, and the responsibilities assigned to and accepted by the Government of Pakistan, in connection with the defence and security of Azad Jammu and Kashmir (including Northern Areas), reflect that the Government of Pakistan is amenable to the jurisdiction of this Court; and

(*xi*) that the State Subjects residing in the Northern Areas have been deprived of the benefits of fundamental rights, enshrined in the Interim Constitution Act, during past, without lawful authority. These rights are admissible and exercisable by them in the manner and style as they are being enjoyed by their compatriots in Azad Kashmir.

194. The conclusions listed in (i), (ii), (iii), (iv) and (v) of the preceding paragraph, find no answer in the written statement of respondent No. 1. In paragraph 9 of written statement, it is admitted as true that the Northern Areas do not form part of the territories of Pakistan as defined in the Constitution of 1973. However, it is explained on account of that omission, it may not be concluded that the said areas are part of the territories of Azad Jammu and Kashmir. The explanation is self-contradictory when it is accepted that these areas are not part of Pakistan, then it does not lie in the mouth of the respondent to deny the geographical status of the areas for their being part of the liberated areas of the State. Be that as it may, the fact remains that these areas are admittedly not part of Pakistan. Likewise, the respondent has failed to explain as to why the residents of these areas may be kept deprived of the benefits of fundamental rights, civil liberties and right of their representation in the Government and other national institutions. In absence of an express answer to the averment it has to be believed that the respondent has impliedly admitted the claim of the petitioners in that respect.

202. It is, therefore, not right to suggest that no declaration and direction in the shape of quo warranto may be made against the Government of Pakistan. All that is required is the satisfaction of legitimate authority to do an act, in accordance with law.

203. The State of Jammu and Kashmir is presently divided by the Ceasefire Line. It is well acknowledged that the

sovereignty of the State vest in the State Subjects, who unequivocally uphold and respect the entity of the State. They are engaged in earnest pursuit of freedom from the obdurate, aggressive Indian Union. The cherished goal of their liberty is, prima facie, to be attained through the acknowledged democratic method of fair and free plebiscite, under the auspices of the United Nations. Until the status of the State is determined, in order to run the administration of liberated territories. Interim Constitution Act, 1974, with approval, has been enforced. All the authorities entrusted with different assignments and functions are enjoined to act in compliance with the provisions of the Act. We have recapitulated the detailed history of the Northern Areas, their legal status and the circumstances surrounding the present position. *We therefore, hold that no legitimate cause has been shown by the respondents No. 1 and 2 to keep the Northern Areas and their residents (State Subjects) detached from Azad Jammu and Kashmir, under separate and arbitrary administrative system and deprive them of fundamental rights.*

204. We accordingly accept the petition and direct :

(*i*) (*a*) the Azad Government to immediately assume the administrative control of the Northern Areas and to annex it with the administration of Azad Jammu and Kashmir;

(*b*) the Government of Pakistan to provide an adequate assistance and facility to the Azad Government in attainment of the said objective.

(*ii*) the residents (State Subjects) of the Northern Areas shall enjoy the benefit of the fundamental rights conferred by the Act. 1974. They shall be provided representation in :

(*i*) the Governmentl

(*ii*) the Assemblyl

(*iii*) the Councill

(*iv*) the Civil Services; and

(*v*) other national institutions, in due course of law.

(*iii*) Azad Government shall take steps to establish administrative and judicial set up in the Northern Areas within the framework of the Interim Constitution Act.

References

(NOTE : quantification of various outfits is difficult to assess).

*1. JKHM—Jammu and Kashmir Hizbul Mujahidin.
2. JKLH—Jammu and Kashmir Liberation Front.
3. IUM—Ikhan-ul-Muslimeen.
4. *M.J. Abbas in Kashmir *Behind the Vale,* p. 124.
5. RDSC, 1948, p. 1.
6. SCORS, 1948. Supplement for November 1948, pp. 64-5. 39 Draft resolution submitted by the representative of Belgium.
7. 3. RDSC 1948, pp. 2-3.
8. The drafty resolution was voted on paragraph by paragraph. No vote was taken on the text as a whole.
9. RDSC, 1948, pp. 8-9.
10. See Official Records of the Security Council, Third Year, Supplement for November 1948, Document S/11000, annéx 6.
11. RDSC, 1950, pp. 1-3.
12. Official Records of the Security Council, Third Year, Suplement for November 1948, Document S/1100: *ibid.*, Fourth Year, Supplement for January 1949, Document S/1196; and *ibid.*, Fourth Year, Special Supplement No. 7.
13. *Ibid.*, Fifth Year, Supplement for 1 January through 31 May, 1950, Document S/1453.
14. *Ibid.*, Fourth Year, Resolutions and Decisions of the Security Council, 1949, p. 7.
15. *Ibid.*, Third Year, Supplement for November 1948, Document S/1100, para 75.
16. *Ibid.*, Fourth Year, Supplement for January 1949, Document S/1196, para 15.
17. *Ibid.*, Fifth Years, Supplement for 1 January through 31 May, 1950. Document S/1453, p. 14.
18. *Ibid.*, Third Year, Supplement for November 1948, Document S/110).. para. 75.
19. *Ibid.*, Fourth Year, Supplement for January 1949, Document S/1196. para 15.
20. One member (Union of Soviet Socialist Republics) was absent.
21. RDSC, 1951, pp. 1-4.
22. See Official Record of the Security Council, Fifth Year, Supplement for September through December 1950, Document S/1791 and Add.1.

23. *Ibid.*, Third Year, Supplement for November 1948, Document S/1100, para, 75.
24. *Ibid.*, Fourth Year, Supplement for January 1949, Document S/1196, para 15.
25. RDSC, 1951, pp. 5-6.
26. Official Records of the Security Council, Sixth Year, Special Supplement No. 2. Document S/2375.
27. *Ibid.*, Sixth Year, 564th meeting.
28. *Ibid*, Sixth Year, Special Supplement No. 2, Document S/2375, annex 1.
29. RDSC, 1952, pp. 1-2.
30. *Ibid*, Seventh Year, Special Supplement No. 2. Document S/2611 and corr. 1.
31. *Ibid.*, Document S/2783 and Corr. 1.
32. *Ibid.*, annex 1.
33. RDSC, 1952, pp. 1-2.
34. See Official Records of the Security Council, Third Year, Supplement for November, 1948, Document S/1110, para 75.
35. *Ibid.*, Fourth Year, Supplement for January 1949, Document S/1196, para 15.
36. *Ibid*, annex 3.
37. SCORS, January, February and March 1957, p. 4.
38. *Ibid.*, annex 8.
39. One member (Pakistan) did not participate in the voting.
40. Official Records of the General Assembly, Third Session, Supplement No. 2. chap. 5.
41. SCORS, January, February and March 1957, p. 9.
42. SCORS, October, November, December 1957, pp. 21-2.
43. *Official Records of the General Assembly, Third Session, Suppement* No. 2, chap. 5, sect. C.
44. *The Hindu*, 23 December 1971; *U.N. Weekly Newsletter*, 31 December 1971, pp. 1. and 3.
45. This accord though signed in November 1974, is refered as the 1975 Accord.
46. Subheading added for easy understanding.
47. Pat of Socio-Political Study: Pakistan and POK.

PUNJAB

7

Terrorism in Punjab : 1978-93
The Traumatic Years

India arguably has the dubious distinction of a nation suffering longest under terrorist attacks. Terrorism/insurgency in the North-East and Jammu and Kashmir has earlier been discussed in this book. The terrorism experienced in Punjab in the past and potential worrisom situation presently are discussed in the following three (4 to 6) chapters.

1. Terrorism in Punjab.
2. Terrorism in India: Beyond North-East, Jammu and Kashmir and Punjab.
3. Naxal/Maoist insurgency in India.

Punjab: The Traumatic years 1978-93

After India's North-East and Jammu and Kashmir, Punjab was the third state/region to suffer the trauma and tribulations of an active and intense terrorist campaign launched by the extremist elements among the Community and actively supported by Pakistan.

Before discussing the genesis and causes of this 15-year long traumatic period in its recent history, here follow some important information on key statistics and historical perspective on the "Land of Five Rivers" (that is Punjab).

Key Statistics

Capital	Chandigarh
Area	50,362 sq. km.
Population	24,358,999
Principal Languages	Punjabi
	Hindi
	Urdu

Religious Denominations

Sikhs	54.40 per cent
Hindus	44.10 per cent
Christians	1.50 per cent

History of the Punjab

Punjab was the site of the Indus valley civilisation. Archaeological excavations all over the state have revealed evidences of the cities belonging to that civilisation that also included Harappa and Mohanjodaro, which are now in Pakistan. The Mahabharata contains rich descriptions of Punjab. It is also believed that parts of the Ramayana were written around the Shri Ram Tirath Ashram near Amritsar and that it was in the forests of what is today Punjab that Luv and Kush, the sons of Rama grew up.

The Rig Veda was composed here. Numerous cultural and educational centres were established in the region during the vedic and later epic periods.

A few years before the birth of Buddha (556 BC), the armies of Darius I, King of Persia, had arrived in Punjab and made the area a protectorate of the Persian Empire. In 327 BC, Alexander invaded Punjab, defeating Raja Paurava. In subsequent centuries, there were more invasions from the north. This happened during the rules of the Mauryas, the Sungas, the Guptas and the Pushpabhuti.

Cutting to more recent times, the Sikhs established their dominance in the region by 1764-65. Ranjit Singh led Punjab into a powerful kingdom and also added the provinces of Multan, Kashmir and Peshawar. After Ranjit Singh's death, Punjab passed into the hands of the British East India Company in 1849. It later became a province of the British India—more appropriately, British Indian Empire. Thus it was nearly a hundred years that it remained as such.

The 1947 Partition saw Punjab divided into two—the smaller Eastern part allotted to India. On 15 July 1948, eight princely states of East Punjab—Faridkot, Jind, Kalsia, Kapurthala, Malerkotla, Nabha, Nalagarh and Patiala—were grouped into a single political entity designated PEPSU (Patiala and East

Punjab States Union). On 1 Nov. 1956, as a result of recommendations of the States Reorganisation Commission (SRC), PEPSU was merged into Punjab.

The Sikhs were unhappy because their demand for a Punjabi Suba (=Punjabi-speaking state) had not been conceded. They mounted an agitation in 1960s. Consequently, the Punjab created on 1 Nov. 1956 was divided on linguistic basis. On 1 Nov. 1966, its Hindi-speaking parts were demerged from it and formed into a new state, Haryana. Simultaneously, Punjab's northernmost districts/parts were transferred to Himachal Pradesh.

In fact, "Punjabi-speaking state" has a past, which deserves a brief discussion. At the time of India's Independence some Sikh leaders had demanded 'Khalistan'. The logic was simple: The Hindus got Hindustan (India, or Bharat), Muslims got Pakistan, what did Sikhs get?

Post-Partition, the Sikhs were concentrated in India in East Punjab. Sikh leaders demanded a Punjabi language majority state, which would have accommodated most Sikhs. Fearing that a Punjabi-majority state might lead to a separatist Sikh movement, the Government opposed the demand. Even when the SRC did not concede the demand, there was strong resentment against the 'injustice'. After all, even during the British rule, the Congress had been demanding the linguistic division of the country. Why did even the SRC make an exception in the case of the Punjabi language? As stated above, finally the demand was conceded on 1 Nov. 1966.

A little over a decade after the birth of a Punjabi-speaking state, there was a separatist movement for Khalistan. Thousands of Punjabis mere killed during the 15 years (1978-93) of blood letting. The violence also claimed the life of a serving Indian Prime Minister, followed by the reprisal killing of some 3,000 Sikhs in Delhi and other areas in the country. It is not easy to determine if this happened by certain design or was it the result of combination of circumstances.

This chapter is laid out in four parts :

1. Backgrounder-Punjab.
2. Terrorist groups in Punjab.

3. Pakistan factor in Punjab and Jammu and Kashmir : Discussed together as they are interlinked because Pakistan is common player between the two.
4. Course of Khalistan Movement : A critique.

BACKGROUNDER-PUNJAB

The genesis of the terrorist movement in Punjab was rooted in a long and continuous process of decline in which intricate and often unscrupulous political manoeuvres systematically undermined democratic processes in the State. After Independence and the tragedy of Partition, political parties in Punjab continued to pursue a divisive politics that laid inordinate emphasis on the separation of communal identities, and that resulted in the 'reorganisation' of the Punjab State on 'linguistic' lines. This meant its trifurcation in 1966 into a Sikh majority Punjab and Hindu majority Harayana and Himachal Pradesh. The 'reorganisation', however, failed to create the necessary basis for a communal vote, and the share of the 'Sikh parties', specifically the Akali Dal, remained well below 30 per cent through the late Sixties and the Seventies, with more than half the Sikh population unequivocally rejecting their ideology and methods of communal mobilisation. The Akalis were, consequently, never able to do better than to cobble together unstable coalitions in Punjab. At the same time, the 'secular' formations, including prominently, the Congress (I), also adopted the politics of alternating communal incitement and appeasement, as they made a bid not only for the popular vote, but equally for the control of the religious affairs of the Sikhs through the Shiromani Gurudwara Prabandhak Committee (SGPC), the body that administered Sikh religious affairs and places of worship. This incendiary mix of unprincipled politics and the manipulation of religious identities and institutions gradually brought the lunatic fringe of the Sikh far right to the centre stage of the State's politics, pushing it into the spiral of violence that was to consume 21,469 lives in a little over a decade of strife, before the movement for 'Khalistan' was comprehensively defeated in 1993.

The incident to which the genesis of the terrorist movement in Punjab is traced, occurred in April 1978. The 13th of April marks the birth of the Sikh Khalsa, and had been chosen in that year by the Nirankari sect to hold its annual convention at Amritsar. The Nirankaris are accused of apostasy by the Akalis and by other fundamentalist Sikh groupings. A gang of a few hundred members of the Akhand Kirtani Jatha led by Jarnail Singh Bhindranwale and Fauja Singh attacked the Nirankari convention. There was a long history of such clashes, but on this occasion, 13 Sikhs were killed, including Fauja Singh, along with three Nirankaris. Over the next six years, until his death in June 1984, Bhindranwale was to propagate a creed of unadulterated hate, mobilising the political frustrations of the Sikhs from a fundamentalist religious platform. Despite his virulence, he was propped up by the 'secular' Congress (I) in the SGPC elections of 1979, though only 4 of his 40 candidates won. He also canvassed for Congress (I) candidates in the General Elections of 1980.

In the meanwhile, the 62 Nirankaris, including the head of the sect, Baba Gurbachan Singh, charged in connection with the killing of 13 Sikhs in the 1978 clash had faced trial and were acquitted on the grounds that they had acted in self defence. This was evidently an unsatisfactory resolution of the issue, and in April 1980, Baba Gurbachan Singh was shot dead in Delhi. The first information report (FIR) named twenty persons for the murder, including several known associates of Bhindranwale. With the government failing to act against Bhindranwale, his killer squads struck again, this time claiming the life of another proclaimed 'enemy of the Sikh *Panth*', Lala Jagat Narain, the proprietor of the Hind Samachar Group, publishers of the popular daily, *Punjab Kesri,* and a bitter critic of Bhindranwale. This resulted in a flurry of deceptive moves, apparently to arrest Bhindranwale, countered by a succession of manoeuvres to help him escape the consequences of his actions. Eventually, however, he barricaded himself inside the heavily fortified Gurudwara Gurdarshan Parkash at Chowk Mehta. What followed was a farce that made the a laughing stock of the Punjab Police and transformed Bhindranwale into a veritable icon among the Sikhs. The Gurudwara was surrounded by the police, but no attempt was made to arrest Bhindranwale. Instead, senior officials went in to 'negotiate a surrender', and Bhindranwale declared that he would 'offer himself for arrest at 1:00 pm on September 20, 1981, after addressing a 'religious congregation'.

His terms were meekly accepted. At the appointed hour, he emerged to harangue a large crowd of his followers armed with spears, swords and a number of firearms. Among those present were a prominent Akali leaders. Having aroused the rabble to a pitch, Bhindranwale 'surrendered' to the police. Even as he was taken away, the mob opened fire on the police, a pitched battle ensued, and 11 persons were killed.

The very same day, three motorcycle-borne 'storm troopers' opened fire in a market in Jalandhar, killing four Hindus and injuring twelve. The next day, one Hindu was killed and thirteen people injured in Tarn Taran. For 25 days, violence exploded all over Punjab, while Bhindranwale was held in custody, not in jail, but in the ample comfort of a government circuit house. These incidents included the hijacking of an Indian Airlines plane to Lahore. On October 15, Bhindranwale was a free man again, after the then Home Minister, without the benefit of any inquiry or judicial process, announced to Parliament that Bhindranwale was not involved in the murder of Lala Jagat Narain.

Bhindranwale now appeared invincible. With truckloads of men armed with sophisticated automatic weapons, he stormed across the Punjab, and even through the nation's capital, with impunity. When the government hesitantly arrested one of his close associates, Amrik Singh, the President of the All India Sikh Students Federation (AISSF), on July 19, 1982, Bhindranwale decided to move into sanctuary of the Golden Temple complex. What followed was a continuous sequence of sacrilege and desecration, as the holiest shrine of the Sikhs became the centre of terror in Punjab.

It was not Bhindranwale alone who operated out of the Golden Temple. Bibi Amarjit Kaur, the widow of Fauja Singh who had died in the 1978 clash with the Nirankaris, had at that time itself entered the Temple with another member of the Akhand Kirtani Jatha, and had created a terrorist group, the Babbar Khalsa, who were responsible for a multitude of heinous crimes over the next decade and a half. These crimes included, according to the boast of the Babbar Khalsa's chief assassin, the murder of 35 Nirankaris. A troubled entente existed between the Babbars and Bhindranwale's forces. A third armed group had come into existence in the Golden Temple complex around the faction–ridden offices of the SGPC in Guru Nanak Niwas.

Between 1981 and 1983, the terrorists had killed 101 civilians, with 75 of these killed in 1983 itself. They included A.S. Atwal, a Deputy Inspector General of Police, who was killed in broad daylight at the main gate of the Golden Temple complex in April 1983. His bodyguards simply fled in the face of the attack, and a police post nearby was abandoned. The killers danced a celebratory *bhangra* over the dead body, and then sauntered back into the Temple. A steady stream of tortured and mutilated bodies began to appear in the gutters behind the *Guru Nanak Niwas* –Bhindranwale's 'temporary residence'. Fearing an attempt by the government to arrest him, Bhindranwale then moved into the Akal Takht, and began fortifications. Between January 1, 1984, and June 3, 1984, the terrorists killed 298 persons on commands that emanated from the headquarters that had been established in the Golden Temple. On June 3, 1984, Prime Minister Indira Gandhi ordered the Army to clear the Temple, and the hastily executed Operation Bluestar virtually destroyed the Akal Takht and damaged many other revered buildings within the complex. More than a hundred Army officers and men died in the Operation, and over 550 innocent civilians were killed in the cross fire. The damage Bluestar did was incalculable, and it was compounded by Operation Woodrose, the Army's 'mopping up' exercise all over Punjab, intended to clear extremist elements from all Gurudwaras in the State. Mistrustful of the State Police, and lacking credible intelligence sources, the indiscriminate sweep of Woodrose pushed many young men across the border into the arms of welcoming Pakistani handlers. And then, even as Woodrose drew to an end, the evil was incalculably compounded by the pitiless massacre of Sikhs in what were perceived to be Congress–I government–sponsored riots of November 1984 in the wake of Prime Minister Indira Gandhi's assassination by two of her own Sikh security guards.

Operation Bluestar and the November 1984 massacres have been described by K.P.S. Gill as "the two most significant victories for the cause of 'Khalistan'... not won by the militants, but inflicted.... upon the nation by its own Government... These two events, in combination, gave a new lease of life to a movement which could easily have been contained in 1984 itself."

After the army, it was the turn of the 'political solution'. The Rajiv Gandhi government, having, in its first days, remained a mute spectator to the anti-Sikh riots, decided to force the ravaged State through a hasty and ill-timed election. Negotiations were initiated by the central government in mid–1985. The Akalis, led by Harchand Singh Longowal, assisted by S. S. Barnala and Balwant Singh (of whom Longowal and Balwant Singh later fell to assasins), showed great eagerness to reclaim their hold on events in the State. But the Centre's 'strategy' went well beyond the 'moderates' in the Akali Dal, and the government also initiated a dialogue with representatives of the All India Sikh Students Federation (AISSF), at that time a frontline terrorist grouping. The talks with the AISSF, however, broke down on trivial differences, mainly because of the Centre inclination in favour of the Akalis. However, the elections eventually took place – but only after Longowal's assassination on August 20, *1985*. Sympathy and the lack of any serious opposition in the September elections brought the Akali's to power now led by Barnala, with a sweeping *majority* (73 out of 117 seats).

One of the first acts of the Barnala government was the appointment of the Bains Committee, which released, *en masse*, over 2000 extremists at that time under detention. The impact on terrorist violence was palpable – not only because those who were released simply resumed their activities, but also because others saw in this act a restoration of the immunity they had enjoyed in the pre–Bluestar phase. 1985 had seen a total of 63 civilians and eight policemen killed by militants. As the Bains committee began its work, in just the first three months of 1986, 102 civilians and 10 security men fell to the terror.

Barnala also surrendered the Golden Temple to the terrorists once again. The shrine was restored to the Akali controlled Shiromani Gurudwara Prabandhak Committee (SGPC) on January 22, 1986. In less than a month, the terrorists, led by the Damdami Taksal, were in complete control. By the end of April, a '*Panthic* Committee' had been constituted to coordinate all terrorist activities, and a 'Declaration of Khalistan' was issued by the Committee from the Golden Temple (April 29, 1986). A day later, the Barnala government ordered a mock search in the Temple with ample advance notice. Not unexpectedly, "no one of note was caught", but the incident was sufficient to provoke a split in the Akali Dal, and, from that point onwards, Barnala's existence was entirely dependant on the Congress–I's support. During Barnala's tenure of a little over 19 months, the lives of 783 civilians and 71 security men were lost to terrorist violence.

The violence escalated continuously as both the political and the police leadership failed consistently to define an unambiguous response to terrorism. The sophisticated Kalashnikov assault rifle [the AK–47], supplied by Pakistan's covert agencies, was introduced into the terrorist armory in May 1987, and terrorism entered a completely new and deadlier phase. The impact was immediate and dramatic. The scale of killing was directly connected with the gun-power available to the terrorists – and did not recede to the pre-1987 level until the terrorists were finally crushed towards the end of 1992. By comparison, the Police were poorly equipped with World War II vintage .303 rifles, or the equally obsolete bolt-action 7.62s. The Central Reserve Police Force (CRPF) was marginally better off, with 175 Self Loading Rifles [SLRs] per battalion. But even the SLR was no match for the sheer lethality of the Kalashnikov.

Nevertheless, the police had begun to commit itself for the first time in this long-drawn war. Between May 1987 and April 1988 terrorists killed 1533 people in Punjab (a monthly average of over 127), including 109 policemen. In turn, 364 terrorists were also killed. But the vacillating and directionless policies of the government, and the complete inability, indeed visible reluctance, of the State to impose the rule of law – even in cases of the worst acts of terrorism and where the perpetrators were apprehended by the police – swelled the ranks of terrorist forces. Terrorism, which had, in the past, largely been restricted to the districts of Amritsar and Gurdaspur, now had another four districts – Hoshiarpur, Jalandhar, Ludhiana and Faridkot – firmly in its clutches.

The government, however, persisted in its opportunistic quest for just any kind of deal with the terrorists to the very end. On March 4, 1988, 40 high profile prisoners – the Jodhpur Detenues, including Jasbir Singh Rode – were released in a 'goodwill gesture' as part of a compromise with terrorists. They simply walked into the Golden Temple, where Rode was installed as the *Jathedar* (head priest) of the Akal Takht and the terrorists began to build up internal defences within the Temple around the *parikarma*. The terrorist response to the Government's 'goodwill gesture' was unequivocal. An unprecedented 288 people – including 25 policemen – were killed in March and another 259 [including 25 policemen] in April.

With nothing left to trade, and 2866 lives [2207 civilians, 177 policemen, 482 terrorists] lost to between October 1985 and April 1988, the Centre decided that it was finally time to enforce the laws of the land. This time, however, it was not the army that was called in. Operation Black Thunder was executed squarely under the charge of the Punjab Police – backed up by the elite anti–terrorist force, the National Security Guard [NSG] and para–military forces. Its objective was identical to that of Operation Bluestar – to clear the Golden Temple of the entrenched terrorist forces. Unlike Bluestar, however, this was achieved in a clean, economical and near-bloodless action, executed under the fullest glare of the media – both national and international – within a week between May 11 and May 18, 1988.

Though only a fraction of the terrorists operating in the State were apprehended during Black Thunder, the Operation generated crucial structural transformations in the terrorist movement. After the macabre exposures relating to the activities of the extremists in the Temple, the movement for Khalistan could never recover the facade of religiousity that had attended it in its early years, and became increasingly and manifestly criminalised. Moreover, the *Gurudwara* as sanctuary and safe–house for terrorists and their leaders ceased to exist. Divested of the sanctuary of the Golden Temple and the Gurudwaras, the leadership was forced to live life as fugitives in the Punjab countryside; on the one hand, their own deeds exposed them, and on the other, the deeds of their followers compromised them even further, since they were now believed to be condoned, even encouraged, by these leaders.

Immediately after Black Thunder, an enormous exercise to reorganise the Punjab Police was carried out, transforming a force that was widely perceived as demoralised, cowardly and incompetent, into the spearhead of the successful counterterrorism campaign that was to follow.

In the days following Black Thunder, however, the terrorists ravaged Punjab. 343 civilians were slaughtered in May alone. They included 30 migrant labourers working on the Sutlej–Yamuna canal in Ropar district; another 45 migrant workers gunned down in Punjab and Himachal Pradesh; and 20 killed in a bomb blast outside a temple in Amritsar. These reprisal killings were a demonstration that Black Thunder had not decimated their numbers in significant measure, nor undermined their capacity to strike at will.

But the police made demonstrations of its own. The swift redeployment and reorientation of forces bore immediate results, and the civilian casualty rate fell rapidly. The first six months of 1988 had seen 1266 civilians killed – an average of 211 casualties a month, in the second half of 1988, 688 civilians were killed – a high figure, but nevertheless a radical improvement –with the monthly average down to 114. The terrorists, moreover, began paying a heavy price. On July 12, 'General' Labh Singh, the head of the Khalistan Commando Force (KCF), at that time one of the most active terrorist gangs, died in an exchange of fire with the police. Avtar Singh Brahma, another dreaded terrorist, was among the 68 terrorists killed that month.

By January 1989, the terrorists had been pushed into a thin strip along the border, with over 70 per cent of their strikes restricted to just three of the twelve districts in Punjab – Gurdaspur, Amritsar and Ferozepur. This proportion was to remain a constant throughout 1989 and well into 1990.

It was only natural to focus attention on this area. In March 1989 a massive composite Special Operation – bringing together the forces of the Punjab Police, the CRPF and the Border Security Force (BSF) – was launched in the entire Mand area (a patch of marshland primarily lying in the Amritsar and

Ferozepur districts, but flowing over into Kapurthala and Jalandhar as well), Ajnala, Jandiala, Tarn Taran and Batala (along the river Beas). Cordon-and-search combing operations became a regular feature in this terrorist heartland, yielding a steady stream of arrests and seizures of arms, ammunition and explosives, and mounting pressures on the extremists that they found it progressively harder to bear. The impact was compounded by highly focused intelligence-based operations, as well as by the effective use of 'spotters' – captured terrorists who helped identify former associates. By May 1989, the anti-terrorist drive had completely blunted the capabilities of leading terrorist groups to strike at soft targets. The organisations that that had been reduced to a negligible presence included the Khalistan Liberation Organisation (KLO), the Bhindranwale Tiger Force of Khalistan (BTFK) and the Babbar Khalsa, the last of which had perhaps the most dedicated and resourceful, and the most dreaded, cadres.

The top terrorist leadership – the two 'Panthic Committees', one that was eventually headed by Dr. Sohan Singh [Panthic Committee (SS)], and the other dominated by Gurbachan Singh Manochahal and Wassan Singh Zaffarwal [Panthic Committee (M)] – was by now based entirely in Pakistan, and exercised only loose control over their increasingly criminalised 'followers'. Beyond making various 'statements' to cadres in India and issuing exaggerated threats of reprisal against those who were 'defaming' the movement through acts of extortion, rape and the murder of innocents, this leadership in exile did nothing about the wave of extortion and crime that was unleashed against the civilian population in the State by the proliferating gangs claiming allegiance to them. Violent turf wars broke also out between various gangs. There was already a deep and basic difference at the highest level of leadership, divided as it was between two irreconcilable 'Panthic Committees' (a third 'Panthic Committee', propped up by the Damdami Taksal, was also to emerge later, in September 1989). Pakistani handlers had made repeated attempts to mediate in order to bring about some sort of rapprochement between these groupings, but were entirely unsuccessful. The basic conflict, however, centered around control over the narcotics trade and gun-running.

The terror in the State had, till this point, been absolute. Public cooperation with the police was meagre, and even in the case of orchestrated public executions by small terrorist gangs, there was virtually no protest or resistance from the people at large. But all this began to change towards the middle of 1989. Since at least some of the police weaponry had been upgraded after Black Thunder, there were a substantial number of discarded .303 rifles available in police armouries. A Village Defence Scheme (VDS), and a system of appointing Special Police Officers (SPOs) was devised to arm and train volunteers in vulnerable villages to resist terrorist action at the local level. By April 1989, 2350 weapons had been distributed in 451 villages, and the VDS was to play a significant role to the very end of the war against terrorism.

There were other signs, small but nonetheless significant, of the turning tide. On June 6, a bus was hijacked by terrorists near village Talwandi Ghowan, PS Kathunangal, in the Majitha Police District, Amritsar. The Hindu passengers were forced off the bus and were about to be executed, when two Sikhs, Avtar Singh and Rajwant Singh, intervened to save their lives. They were shot dead, and two other passengers were seriously injured. The incident generated a great deal of revulsion against the terrorists among Sikhs in Punjab. Then again, just a month later (July 7), when a terrorist opened indiscriminate fire in the Tarn Taran bazaar, he was over-powered and beaten to death by the shopkeepers – an event virtually unimaginable even a few months earlier in this heartland of the terrorist movement.

By July, moreover, a number of hard-core and listed terrorists had moved out of the Punjab and set up operations in the Terai region of Uttar Pradesh, not as a measure to expand their areas of operation, but to escape the increasing pressures in Punjab.

The pressure also forced a change in tactics and weaponry. Militants in Punjab were advised to increasingly resort to the more surreptitious device of the timed or remote controlled plastic explosive device rather than the AK-47, which required them to be present at the moment of execution. Explosive handling became an integral part of training in the camps across the border after April, and some of the first significant seizures of plastic explosives and sophisticated timing devices were made in May 1989.

The flood of weapons in the State also assumed new and disturbing proportions. Till this point, weapons acquisition had to be financed by the terrorists themselves through extortion and narcotics smuggling. Suddenly, in July, messages were sent out that weapons "which had accumulated in Pakistan for which no payment is to be made" could be acquired by the simple expedient of sending "large numbers" of terrorists across the border.

The augmentation of the terrorist arsenal led to a substantial escalation of terrorist activities. But civilian casualties were held down throughout 1989, even as the losses inflicted on the terrorists, and by them on the police, mounted. Pakistan was strenuously and openly directing the terrorist campaign at this stage, to the extent that terrorist training camps were being organised eifen within 75 metres of the international border (in the Ferozepur sector). Border crossings remained a continuous and daily occurrence along the 533 kilometre long international border Punjab shared with Pakistan, and could never really be effectively checked, despite 122 kilometres of fencing that had been erected by August 1989.

By the end of the third quarter of 1989, a fairly high rate of civilian, terrorist and police casualties notwithstanding, the militants had been pushed inexorably into a corner. Almost 76 per cent of all terrorist incidents in 1989 were contained within four police districts along the border (out of a total of 15 police districts at that time): Majitha, Tarn Taran, Batala and Ferozepur. More significantly, of the fifteen police districts in the State, 10 were only marginally affected by terrorist activities, with several months in the year passing without a single killing there. At the end of the year, four of these districts had an average civilian casualty rate of *less than* two a month; in another six districts, casualties ranged between 2-5 a month. It was only in the four 'core districts' that the average rate ran into the double digits.

Even within these districts, the terrorists' sway was not absolute. By the 4th quarter of 1989, just 13 police stations accounted for nearly 65 per cent of all terrorist crime [and 64 per cent of civilian casualties] in these critical districts. And out of the 217 police stations in the entire State, nearly half the killings had taken place within the jurisdiction of just these 13 police stations.

Politics, however, intervened once again. A general election was now imminent, and a deeply discredited regime at Delhi, swamped under charges of corruption and nepotism, and lacking entirely lacking in a clear perspective on Punjab, decided to press ahead for elections in the parliamentary constituencies in this State as well.

The All India Sikh Students Federation had, by now, decided to complement its underground activities with an over-ground role. It combined with Simranjit Singh Mann's pro-militant United Akali Dal [UAD], and the extremist front organisations swept the poll, with 10 of the 13 seats going to candidates backed by the alliance. Before demitting office, Rajiv Gandhi ordered the release of Simranjit Singh Mann, and of Harminder Singh Sandhu and Atindar Pal Singh of the AISSF. All cases against them were arbitrarily dropped to give expression to what was then, perhaps, a proposition unique to Indian justice administration, that a man elected to Parliament may not be tried for any crime that he may have committed.

The V. P. Singh government that took oath of office on December 6, 1989, brought with it preconceptions, attitudes and a pervasive confusion that surrendered the initiative to the terrorists even before they engaged. The defining incident with regard to this Government's policy on terrorism occurred within the first week of its installation. The daughter of the newly appointed Home Minister was kidnapped in Kashmir (on December 11, 1989) by what was then an incipient terrorist movement in that State. The government's response was absolute capitulation – and, within days, Kashmir simply exploded into a full-blown insurgency that is yet to be brought under control. The message to extremists all over the country was abundantly clear: this government had neither the will nor the understanding to define and implement a cogent and resolute policy against terrorist violence.

While the government dithered, terrorist–affiliated overground organisations initiated an unprecedented secessionist campaign that was to reverse all the gains of the preceding years. For over five years (since Bhindranwale's death) the movement had been divested of a public voice, speaking only the language of the bullet and the bomb. But now elected Members of Parliament spoke openly of 'Khalistan'. A closely coordinated and aggressive programme of agitations and demonstrations, with a high level of coercive mobilisation, was simultaneously launched in collaboration with escalating terrorist activities.

This incendiary mix of politics, religion and intimidation culminated in a campaign of disruption that pinned down ever-increasing numbers of security personnel, progressively reducing the force available for operational duties. This strategy of quasi-political mobilisation was backed up by a massive and well-coordinated campaign by another group of terrorist front-organisations masquerading as human rights activists. 'Fact finding committees' comprising sympathisers or pro-militant politicians were set up after each police operation. At a time when an average of over 200 people were being killed in a month by the terrorists, these 'human rights' activists insisted that every action by the security forces was an unjustified 'excess' or an 'atrocity'. It was an extraordinary and highly successful campaign.

Worse still, the terrorists now directed a virulent and intensifying campaign of intimidation and murder against the security forces, especially in the lower ranks. The year 1990 alone saw 506 policemen killed – a majority of them while they were at home on leave. 19 members of their families were also killed by the terrorists – a number that was to rise sharply to 134 in 1991, as the terrorists made the families of policemen their favoured soft target in a concerted bid to demoralise the force.

The mounting tide of violence and open political subversion was compounded by irrational and arbitrary force withdrawals by the V.P. Singh government. The bogey of Assembly Elections in the State was, moreover, kept constantly alive throughout this phase, perpetuating an element of political uncertainty and constant political jockeying between both the over-ground and underground militant groupings. It was only in September, with the extension of President's Rule, that the question was briefly settled, only to be reopened shortly thereafter by the Chandrashekhar government that replaced V.P. Singh.

Meanwhile, the scope of political activity among parties and organisations of (relatively) moderate propensities had been completely eliminated. On May 14, the terrorists made an attempt to kill Gurcharan Singh Tohra, the SGPC President – and a 'moderate' Akali only if the definition was stretched to its very limits – on the Ludhiana-Patiala highway near village Pahwa. Tohra, an ex-MLA, H. S. Rajia and a gunman were injured, while the driver of the vehicle died on the spot. Rajia succumbed to his injuries in hospital. Less than a month later, Balwant Singh, an ex-Finance Minister of the State, was gunned down in Chandigarh. The traditional Akali parties simply went into hibernation, and no other national or regional party had, at this juncture, a functional State wing in Punjab.

After eleven months, the V. P. Singh government collapsed under the weight of its own internal contradictions, and the new Prime Minister, *Chandrashekhar,* heading a minority government with outside support from Rajiv Gandhi's Congress-I, was to preside over another vacillating regime for a further *seven months.*

The Army was inducted into the State in November in what was called Operation Rakshak–I, which followed the pattern of conventional Army interventions in internal disturbances, certainly exerting substantial pressure on militants in the border districts – where the bulk of deployment had occurred – but failing to alter the course of militancy in any significant measure. In fact, what Operation Rakshak–I did was to partially squeeze militancy out of the border districts and into virtually the entire State.

The Chandrashekhar Government played out its final gamble in Punjab when it *forced the State to join the rest of the nation in the mid-term elections slated for June 1991* (though elections were staggered in such a way that Punjab would go to the Polls after the process had been completed in the rest of the country). *In April,* the government announced that elections to the parliamentary and State Assembly constituencies in Punjab would be held simultaneously. The terrorist groupings split down the middle, with those broadly owing allegiance to the *Damdami Taksal deciding to participate,* and the second group affiliated to the Panthic Committee (Sohan Singh) deciding in favour of enforcing a boycott.

A large number of the 2146 candidates who filed nominations for the Assembly and Lok Sabha elections were overtly or covertly supported by terrorist organisations. By the time the nominations closed, even the groups officially boycotting the elections had hedged their bets by surreptitiously putting up candidates. 211 of the candidates had clear terrorist links, and 34 were at that time behind bars. 41 candidates had 'history sheets' (police records) that enumerated offenses including political assassination, hijacking and murder; another 48 were relatives of prominent listed terrorists.

Many of the candidates had refused police protection, declaring that they would make their own arrangements for 'security'. They now began to move openly around the State with large groups of illegally armed terrorists as their 'bodyguards'. In the meanwhile, the Panthic Committee (SS) let loose a campaign of liquidation that was eventually to claim the lives of 27 candidates. On June 7, an explosion damaged the cavalcade of the Minister of State for Home at Gill Road in Ludhiana (the MoS was contesting the Ludhiana Parliamentary seat). On June 15, 74 train passengers were massacred. Despite the enveloping mayhem in the State, the Army had, inexplicably, been withdrawn from the State, and para-military force levels had been cut drastically. However, the ill-conceived gambit for elections in Punjab was abandoned after Narasimha Rao was sworn in as Prime Minister on June 21.

It was during the General Elections of 1991 that Rajiv Gandhi was assassinated. The Congress-I rode back to power on a wave of sympathy, and Narasimha Rao was sworn in as Prime Minister. But the chaos created in Punjab by the preceding 18 months could hardly be contained by an electoral victory at the Centre. The years 1990 and 1991 unambiguously belonged to the terrorists.

Almost as many civilians were killed by terrorists in these two years, as in the preceding 12 – the entire span of the terrorist movement in Punjab. Between 1978 and 1989, there were 5070 civilian casualties; in 1990 and 1991, they were 5058.

The area of conflict now covered the entire State. After Black Thunder, terrorist crime had been confined mainly to the border districts. But by the end of 1991, the 'terrorist heartland' had extended itself from 13 police stations in four border districts [64.6% of terrorist crime in the 4th quarter of 1989] to over 47 police stations that now accounted for 61% of the greatly enhanced terrorist crime in a widely dispersed area. Only four of the 15 police districts registered a monthly average of civilian casualties below 10. This was easily cancelled out by another four, where civilian casualties were in excess of 20 per month. In Ludhiana, this figure stood at over 44 per month.

While the levels of terrorist violence in the border districts remained high, the command centre of terrorist operations shifted gradually to the Malwa region, with Ludhiana and Sangrur as its core. The greater dispersal of terrorist activities was, in substantial measure, intensified by Operation Rakshak-I which exerted a great deal of pressure in the border areas. In the absence of a co-ordinated policy of containment, the top terrorists were gradually 'squeezed out' into the Malwa and Doaba belt. Four border police districts (Tarn Taran, Majitha, Batala and Ferozepur) accounted for 878 killings by terrorists in 1991, as compared to 774 in 1989; this, however, represented a significant decline as against the 1341 civilian casualties inflicted in these districts in 1990. But 1991 also saw 535 civilian killings in Ludhiana (1989: 58; 1990:161), 278 in Sangrur (1989:8; 1990:65), and a total of 2591 in the State (1989: 1168; 1990:2467). Distress migrations, which had come down to a mere trickle of ones and twos in a month in 1989, rose to 2524 families through 1990 and 1991 (averaging over 105 families per month).

Viewed in isolation, these figures may suggest that the police and had, once again, withdrawn into a defensive shell in the face of this widening arc of terror. This was far from the truth. Indeed, it was a paradox of the Punjab situation at that time that, while the police (both State and central forces) engaged continually, and while terrorist casualties rose constantly, the killings of civilians also registered sustained and alarming increases. Significantly, despite the terrorists' claim that they were fighting for the 'Sikh cause', it was overwhelmingly the Sikhs themselves (over 70 per cent of those killed by terrorists in 1990–91) who were the victims of their terror.

This was largely due to the renewed successes in terrorist recruitment, which had virtually come to an end in 1989. At that time, the strength of listed and unlisted terrorists was estimated at no more than 1,200. By the middle of 1990, this number had risen upwards of 5,000, and rose above this level throughout 1991, despite the continuous and escalating losses suffered by militant groups. In 1989, under a relatively stable political dispensation, 703 terrorists had been killed, and militancy appeared to have been on the verge of total defeat. In 1990, 1320 terrorists lost their lives, in 1991, another 2177 fell – and yet, the terrorist movement grew from strength to strength.

The successes over the preceding eighteen months had spawned dozens of new militant groups and revived many others that had long been defunct. There was an air of absolute certainty, of consummate confidence, that their 'war' against the Indian state was in its terminal stages, that their goal, 'Khalistan', was imminent. 'Governments in exile' appointed themselves in America and the UK; 'Prime Ministers' and 'Presidents' of 'Khalistan' waited in the wings for the impending victory. Brutal turf wars between terrorist groupings grew in number and intensity, keeping pace with the sweep and power of their actions against the people of Punjab and the security forces, as their final goal appeared tantalizingly within reach.

The degree to which this anarchy had fed upon the regime of political license, of submission and appeasement of the preceding dispensations became clear as soon as an unequivocal policy was enunciated and implemented on the ground.

When Narasimha Rao took over as Prime Minister, the very possibility of 'political solutions' in the Punjab had ceased to exist. The various Akali factions, including those openly sympathetic to the militant cause, had been completely marginalised during the aborted elections of June 1991, when the terrorists decided they would rather 'represent' themselves. Simranjit Singh Mann, the leading overground representative of the terrorist cause, had himself been forced out of that election, though many militant nominees were to contest under the cover of his faction, the UAD (Mann). The other main political leader of the militant cause, Harminder Singh Sandhu of the AISSF, was long dead by this time, murdered by terrorists of the Khalistan Commando Force (KCF), an affiliate of Sohan Singh's Panthic Committee, in January 1990. The 'traditional' Akali parties had, of course, withdrawn into a shell of compliant self-preservation. In any event, with the numerous and continually multiplying factions of political and terrorist groupings in the State, there was no identifiable leadership with whom a dialogue could be initiated, even if the inclination had existed. The terrorists themselves, of course, had no reason to negotiate at this point, convinced as they were that they were poised on the very edge of victory.

An escalation of terrorist violence, at this stage, was inevitable. June itself had seen 245 civilians and 54 security men killed. July, August and September cost another 659 civilian and 123 security men. In October, the violence peaked, with 297 civilian and 53 police casualties. The political compulsions of the Rao Government made a response inevitable, with mounting pressure exerted on the Centre by the Punjab State units of the Congress-I and the Communist Party of India.

In November 1991, the Centre finally took action. The army was re-inducted in Punjab and the forces were given an unambiguous mandate – order had to be restored in the State, and grounds prepared for the election that fell due in mid–February, when the existing Parliamentary sanction for President's Rule came to an end. K.P.S. Gill was transferred back to the State as DGP shortly thereafter. These steps were reinforced by the provision of adequate force in the State, backed by an uncompromising policy of political non-interference. Law and order was entrusted to the professional agencies of the state within whose constitutional mandate they fell.

What emerged now, was one of the most unique experiments in multi-force counter-terrorist strategic initiatives and integrated command structures. Unlike previous operations, the Army and the police (both State and para-military) acted in complete concert, with a clearly defined institutional structure of cooperation and consultation. An officer of the rank of Inspector General (IG) from the Punjab Police was attached to each Corps of the Army deployed in Punjab. A Superintendent of Police (SP) was assigned to each Brigade. Police contingents were attached to every Army battalion, so that comprehensive and coordinated actions could be taken independently by each unit in all emerging circumstances, and there was total sharing of all intelligence, to the extent that police control rooms had representatives of the Army present.

The pattern of Army deployment during the run-up to the elections was also significantly innovative. Traditionally, Army commanders have preferred massive presence in specific sensitive locations. During this phase and right through the election period, however, the Army was deployed all over the State; more importantly, it was split up to section level in order to saturate the entire countryside.

Adequate force – a total of 220 para-military companies – was also provided for the protection of candidates in the elections, with an entire platoon was assigned for each candidate's security. Once again, the objective was clearly defined – the disorders and selective killings that resulted in the cancellation of the elections of June 1991 were not to be repeated. Despite the commitment of such a large force to these security duties, patrolling also had to be intensified and counter-terrorist operations were still sustained across the State.

The impact on the ground was immediate. In November itself, the number of civilians killed by terrorists fell to 154. Of these, 110 were killed in the first fortnight; the second fortnight, when the Central Government's initiatives were implemented in Punjab, saw just 44 civilian casualties. A number of major terrorist groupings immediately decided to protect their top echelons by advising them to shift outside the State, or even out of India, or to go into a temporary hibernation during which they were instructed to tone up their internal structure and improve operational capabilities.

The elections of February 1992 also forced the militant camp into innumerable strategic failures. The most monumental of these was the decision to impose a boycott on the elections. Goaded by their foreign mentors, as well as by their funding and support groups among non-resident Sikhs in USA, Canada and UK, the terrorists began to believe that if they could force another postponement on the elections, or, failing this, keep voting percentages down below 10 per cent, they would discredit India's democratic credentials. Of all the prominent militant leaders and 'ideologues', the only one to oppose this move for a boycott was – surprisingly, since he was the strongest advocate of a boycott in June 1991 – Sohan Singh; but his position drew such violent opposition even from his own supporters that he was forced to temporarily flee his safe haven in Pakistan.

Unlike the boycott of June 1991, moreover, there was also eventual unanimity in the militant camp that no Akali faction would be permitted to participate in the elections of February 1992. (Only a single, utterly unknown, faction of the Akali Dal, led by Kabul Singh, eventually participated in the elections). These objectives were secured by a campaign of intimidation. The entire State was saturated with posters, handbills, leaflets, press notes, statements and paid advertisements in selected newspapers, as well as by direct threats to candidates, voters and election officials, warning of reprisals against any act of cooperation with, or participation in, the election process. A 'total curfew' on pain of death was announced by the militants for February 18 and 19 to discourage voting. On February 8, three teachers assigned to election duties were gunned down, and another six were put to death on February 10. In order to terrorise urban voters, 18 explosions were engineered between February 5 and February 19, and attacks against political campaigners claimed 16 lives before the elections. In a final 'warning', 13 spinning mill workers were massacred at Barnala on the night of 17/18 February.

Nevertheless, not a single candidate standing for this election was killed. The election itself passed peacefully, except for one incident in which a grenade was thrown on a Congress–I election office in Ludhiana, killing one person, and injuring twelve.

The voter turn-out was low, no doubt. But it installed an elected government with a comfortable majority in the State. Most importantly, it was a functional government – not a puppet regime. From this point onwards, law and order – and, naturally, counter-terrorist policy – was firmly within the sphere of the State government's responsibilities (unlike the Rajiv Gandhi–

Barnala arrangement of 1985-86). For the first time, an extended period of political stability, and planning with at least a five-year perspective, became manifestly possible.

The essence of the State government's policy on terrorism under Chief Minister Beant Singh was an extension of the principles implemented by the Centre in the preceding months. The institutions of Constitutional democracy and governance were to be progressively revived, and to this end, the reign of terror was to be brought to an end. Counter-terrorist operations would not be undermined through any negotiations, pacts or bargains with terrorist groups; nor would the political executive interfere with legitimate police operations, investigations and actions.

The greatest impact of the 1992 elections was that they, once again, banished the terrorists – indeed, the entire movement for 'Khalistan' – into the netherworld of an unambiguously criminal identity as the mask of politics was ripped away. Their over-ground political organisations stood comprehensively discredited in the eyes of the people by this time – essentially as a result of the militants' own stand against them. Had the terrorists themselves – or through their nominees – participated in the elections, they may still have enjoyed the substantial immunities that come with a legitimate political position, and would have been able to participate in a range of over-ground activities which could tie down the security forces – as they had done in the past – and help blur the lines between their criminal and political identities. Now, however, they had entirely forfeited their political voice, and could speak only through the bullet and the bomb – a language that the security forces were well equipped to contend with.

They realised their blunder soon enough. In a desperate damage control exercise, they sought to re-activate the traditional Akali factions to initiate programmes of mass agitation. A militant-inflicted 'unification' under the banner of the Shiromani Panthic Action Committee (SPAC) sought to bring all over-ground pro-militant and Akali factions on a single platform. The people were exhorted to boycott the Members of the newly elected Legislative Assembly, to prevent the entry of ministers and MLAs in their villages, and not to approach any minister in connection with personal grievances or any other work. The people, frustrated with the many years that they had suffered without redress, ignored their calls; the elected representatives, voting percentages notwithstanding, began to serve precisely the functions that they are intended to in a democratic framework. Within weeks of the election, the supposed mass base of the movement for 'Khalistan' had vanished without a trace.

But the violence persisted. In the days following the elections, 24 voters were killed in separate acts of reprisal in Sangrur, Bhatinda, Ropar, Jalandhar and Ludhiana. In March, the terrorists adopted a new strategy of massive strikes in urban industrial complexes. On March 10, terrorists gunned down 15 executives of a private company in Sangrur. In two strikes at Ludhiana, on March 14 and 18, the terrorists killed 34 industrial workers. On March 21, a similar operation in Ahmedgarh killed 14.

Each shift in terrorist Strategy was immediately countered. In the post-election period, the army no longer maintained the saturation levels that it had sustained through the elections. The troops, while still deployed in the State, were returned to barracks, and called out only for specific operations – especially to provide rapid-response teams to back up police action, and to provide the outer cordon in search operations. The responsibility for dealing with the new pattern of terrorist actions, consequently, fell squarely on the police. There were some 140 to 150 urban centres in Punjab. Senior officers who were pushing files at Police Headquarters in Chandigarh were mobilised to confront the new challenge, and each of them was assigned four to five such centres. Each centre was divided into sectors along a grid, and vehicles and manpower were allocated for patrolling and pursuit duties along strategic points. With this single device, the threat to urban industrial concentrations was contained.

In April, the terrorists shifted attention to targeted killings of security personnel. The first quarter of the year had seen 54 security men killed. In April alone, the terrorists killed 51 and injured another 73. By August this strategy was to be extended to the most intensive campaign against the police and their families. When Sukhdev Singh Babbar, chief of the Babbar Khalsa International (BKI) – by this time the most powerful terrorist grouping in the State – was killed in an encounter with the police on August 9, 63 family members of policemen were killed in retaliation – forty eight of them between August 9 and 11 itself. In addition, 37 policemen also lost their lives, bringing up the total of these targeted killings to 100 out of the 167 persons killed in the State in that month.

In addition to the police, the terrorists were also targeting political leaders and government officials. There was a car bomb attack on one State minister at Amritsar in May. The son of another minister, and the brother of a third were killed. The most gruesome among this series of targeted actions was the kidnap and subsequent murder of M.L. Manchanda, the station director of All India Radio at Patiala, on May 27. Manchanda's torso was found in Patiala and his head in Ambala.

The response came in the form of three strategies. The first of these was based on the immediate identification of the perpetrators of the latest outrage, and the application of the fullest force to secure their arrest or elimination. The Manchanda killing is a case in point. The Babbar Khalsa had immediately claimed the killing, in order to impose the militant 'code of conduct' on the government's broadcast agencies. Gurdial Singh Babbar, one of the perpetrators of this outrage, was pursued and killed in an encounter on the same day (May 27), and Amrik Singh Kauli Babbar, who masterminded the kidnapping and killing, met the same fate on June 2.

The second strategy focused on the most important terrorists. An analysis of terrorist strikes had shown, curiously in view of the increasing scope and range of terrorist activities in the State over the past two years, that inspite of their improved striking capacity and mobility, militancy in a majority of cases was highly localised. Even the most important terrorist leaders were found to operate within a radius of no more than 15 to 20 kilometres from their respective villages. With this knowledge, and with continuous intelligence from a variety of forces, it became possible to immobilise, and eventually arrest or eliminate these elements. The available manpower and infrastructure was, consequently, focused disproportionately on the leaders, the planners and the ideologues of the movement. Among the 139 hardcore terrorists who fell to this strategy in 1992 were a dozen self–styled 'Chiefs' and some 20 'Deputy Chiefs' of various terrorist groups, including Rashpal Singh Chhandran, the Chief of the BTFK (June 12), Gurjant Singh Budhsinghwala (July 29), Chief of the KLF, and Sukhdev Singh Babbar, Mukh Sewadar of the BKI (August 10). (One of the last major successes for the security forces was to come in January 1993, with the death of Gurbachan Singh Manochahal, Chief of the Panthic Committee (M) and the BTFK (M) in an encounter with security forces at Village Rataul in Tarn Taran.)

The third element of the strategic response came, in the wake of the August killings of policemen and their families, in the shape of Operation Night Dominance. Once again, an analysis of the pattern of terrorists activities indicated that an overwhelming majority of the killings in the villages took place in the late evening or very early morning. All senior officers were directed to take personal charge of operations at night. From this point on, these officers would be leading night-ops three or four days in every week – *and* performing their normal duties during the day.

The collective impact of these initiatives was clearly evident by the time the year 1992 came to a close. The situation was so vastly different as compared to the chaos that prevailed at the end of the previous year, that it was possible to speak of a total reversal against the terrorists. The total number of civilians killed in the State in 1992 stood at 1518, as compared to 2591 in 1991, reflecting a fall from a monthly average of 216 to 127. This, however, was not all. The lowest figures in 1991, in the months of November and December, stood at 154 and 126. In 1992, if the year was split into two halves, the monthly average fell to 87 in the second half. In the last quarter, this average stood at 60. In December itself, the total civilian casualties stood at 44. They were never to rise to these levels again. Indeed, in the whole of 1993, civilian casualties *totaled* just 48.

A complete transformation had also taken place at the psychological level among the people. After the elections of February 1992, the terrorists had failed entirely to elicit any demonstration of support or cooperation from the people of the

State. The coercion and intimidation that had resulted in the low voter turnout in the elections of February 1992 were also exposed when elections to 95 Municipal Committees in the State concluded peacefully on September 6, with a voter turnout of over 75 per cent. These trends were endorsed when Panchayat Elections were held in the State's 12,342 villages in January 1993, with a voter turnout of 82 per cent. The termination of the Village Panchayats, and their replacement by Khalsa Panchayats had been one of the critical objectives of the terrorist movement.

The transformation went far beyond the return of grassroot democracy and a refusal to cooperate with the militants, to comprehend an enveloping sense of relief. A State that had, for at least the preceding seven years, simply shut down before the sun set, was rediscovering the experiences of peace and normalcy. The markets throbbed with life in the evenings, and cultural events were organised and attended by thousands of people. Distress migrations under threat from terrorists had slowed down to a trickle even at the beginning of the year – a total of 73 families migrated during the first three quarters of 1992. In the last quarter there were no such cases of migration. More significantly, the trend was reversed as people returned to their homes even in areas such as Makhu, Zira, Jhabal, Bhikiwind and Moga, located deep in what had been, only a year ago, the terrorist heartland.

Fresh recruitment to the terrorist ranks had come virtually to an end by January 1992 itself. The police strategy, at this juncture created a 'fourth option' for the terrorists: the first three were conventional measures of response – the possibilities of arrest, flight or armed engagement. A fourth option was offered at this stage of the confrontation: the terrorists were told that, if they chose surrender, they would be welcomed and embraced with warmth. By the end of 1992, 537 terrorists had surrendered to the police, six of them hardcore. Another 379, including 11 hardcore terrorists, were to lay down arms in 1993.

All the major terrorist organisations – the KCF (Wassan Singh), the KCF (Panjwar), the Babbar Khalsa, the BTFK – had, by this time, suffered irreversible losses. The smaller organisations – Dashmesh Regiment, Khalistan Armed Force,

Khalistan Guerilla Force, Khalistan National Army, Khalistan Liberation Army – had been virtually wiped out. The entire surviving–terrorist leadership including Wadhawa Singh and Mehal Singh of the Babbar Khalsa, Paramjit Singh Panjwar of the KCF, Pritam Singh Sekhon of the KLF, and Narain Singh of the KLA, now fled to Pakistan to join their resident ideologues – Wassan Singh Zaffarwal of the Panthic Committee (Zaffarwal) and Dr. Sohan Singh of the Panthic Committee (SS).

The war was over. What remained were mopping up operations.

TERRORIST GROUPS – PUNJAB

- **Babbar Khalsa International (BKI)**
- **Khalistan Zindabad Force (KZF)**
- **International Sikh Youth Federation (ISYF)**
- Khalistan Commando Force (KCF)
- All-India Sikh Students Federation (AISSF)
- Bhindrawala Tigers Force of Khalistan (BTFK)*
- Khalistan Liberation Army (KLA)
- Khalistan Liberation Front (KLF)
- Khalistan Armed Force (KAF)
- Dashmesh Regiment
- Khalistan Liberation Organisation (KLO)
- Khalistan National Army (KNA)

BABBAR KHALSA INTERNATIONAL

Formation

Even after the terrorist-secessionist movement for Khalistan was comprehensively defeated in 1993, there remain a handful of terrorist outfits chiefly supported by Pakistan and some non-resident Indian Sikh groups who continue to propagate the ideology of Khalistan. One of the most prominent among them is the Babbar Khalsa International (BKI). It is among the oldest and most organised Khalistan terrorist groups.

The BKI traces its origin to the Babbar Akali Movement of 1920 and is believed to have assumed its present form after the Baisakhi 1978–clashes between the Akhand Kirtani Jatha and

Nirankaris and more particularly when some followers of Bibi Amarjit Kaur brought out some leaflets styling themselves as Babbar Khalsa after the killing of Nirankari chief Gurbachan Singh, on April 24, 1980. Subsequently, the outfit started targeting all those who sympathised with the Nirankaris.

Sukhdev Singh Babbar and Talwinder Singh Parmar were the founding members of this organisation. The first unit of the BKI was founded in Canada in 1981 under the leadership of late Talwinder Singh Parmar. The outfit at present is active in the USA, Canada, the UK, Germany, France, Belgium, Norway, Switzerland and Pakistan. Talwinder Singh Parmar, a co-founder of the BKI, formed the Babbar Khalsa (Parmar) faction in 1992, when he split from the BKI after serious differences erupted between him and its leadership of. The Parmar faction has a presence in the UK, Germany, Belgium and Switzerland.

Objective

The BKI wants an independent Sikh state called Khalistan.

Organisation and Leadership

Currently, Wadhwa Singh, who is reportedly hiding in Pakistan, heads the outfit. Mehal Singh is the deputy chief of BKI. Both of them are among the 20 terrorists whom India wants Pakistan to extradite.

Wadhwa Singh is reported to have personally supervised the assassination of Punjab Chief Minister Beant Singh on August 31, 1995. He is also believed to have masterminded the January 2004 escape of the assassination-accused, Jagtar Singh Hawara, from the Burail jail in Chandigarh.

External Linkages

Available evidence suggests that the Babbar Khalsa is part of a terrorist network sponsored by Germany-based terrorist groups as well as Pakistan's external intelligence agency—the Inter Services Intelligence (ISI)—to revive terrorism in the Indian Punjab.

Media reports in August 2001 said a joint committee was formed in Germany to coordinate the activities of major terrorist organisations abroad. Gurdial Singh Lalli of the International Sikh Youth Federation (ISYF), Resham Singh of Babbar Khalsa and Harmeet Singh of Kamagata Maru Dal of Khalistan are the prominent leaders of this committee. The ISI is also reportedly keen on forging coordination between Khalistani terrorists, terrorists operating in Jammu and Kashmir and some fundamentalist groups.

Interestingly, the Pakistan government appointed Lt. Gen. (Retd.) Javed Nasir, a former chief of the ISI, as the Chairman of Pakistan Gurudwara Prabandhak Committee (PGPC), the body that administers Sikh shrines in Pakistan. The PGPC was formed in 1999. According to intelligence reports, Sikh terrorists camping in Pakistan are working under the direct supervision of General Nasir. Media reports in April 2002 said the ISI has entrusted the Lashkar-e-Toiba (LeT) with the task of reviving terrorism in Punjab. The LeT will impart arms training to groups like the BKI, the ISYF and the Khalistan Zindabad Force (KZF). Reports also said the LeT has opened at least eight camps in Pakistan to train the Khalistanis. These are at Kot Lakhpat, Chakwal, Gujranwala, Mianwali, Peshawar, Attock, Shahidan Da Banga and Gulbarg in Lahore.

Available evidence also suggests that the BKI has established a nexus with Dawood Ibrahim, the fugitive Indian underworld kingpin residing now in Karachi. The terrorists were liasoning with the Dawood Ibrahim gang in Mumbai through whom they disposed of stolen cars and trucks to amass money, which was then sent to Wadhwa Singh for procuring arms and ammunition.

Some reports have indicated that efforts were made by the ISI to help the BKI establish bases in China, but these initiatives were reportedly thwarted by the Chinese, who were not enthused by the project.

Reports in February 2004 indicated that India has initiated efforts to secure the return of Mehal Singh from the French capital Paris. One of the two principal leaders of the group, he is alleged to have left for France from Pakistan during the later part of 2003. Official sources said that his decision to leave Pakistan was influenced by differences with Wadhwa Singh.

Wadhwa Singh's son-in-law Satnam Singh Malian operates from Germany, deflecting surveillance from the former.

Major Incidents

- March 21, 2006: Four BKI terrorists were arrested from Chandigarh in Punjab and one kilogram of RDX, arms and ammunition were seized from their possession. Chandigarh Police arrested the four from the Bus Stand in Sector 12 of the city, Senior Superintendent of Police, Gaurav Yadav, told reporters. Yadav said the arrested disclosed during preliminary interrogation that they were part of the BKI module controlled by Jagtar Singh Tara. The four, identified as Sukhwinder Singh alias Sukhi alias Bullet, Dilbagh Singh, Ranjit Singh, all residents of Ropar district in Punjab and Balbir Singh alias Nepali, a resident of Solan district in Himachal Pradesh, were in contact with other BKI activists and were one of the several modules raised by the outfit for the revival of terrorism.
- March 20, 2006: Paramjeet Singh Bheora, 'head of operations' of the Babbar Khalsa International in India, and two of his accomplices who were planning to set up base in Delhi were arrested by the Special Cell of the Delhi Police near G T Karnal road. Joint Commissioner of Delhi Police (Special Cell), Karnal Singh, said Paramjeet and his accomplices Jasbir Singh and Bhupinder Singh were arrested following an exchange of fire. The police official added, "four kilograms of RDX, three detonators, one remote control device along with a wireless set, one timer, three pistols, 39 live cartridges and three fired cartridges were recovered from them. The stolen Santro car in which they were traveling was also seized." Paramjeet was allegedly involved in the assassination of Punjab Chief Minister Beant Singh in 1995 and had taken over control of Babbar Khalsa in India after its previous chief Jagtar Singh Hawara was arrested by the Delhi Police on June 8, 2005.
- November 19, 2005: The Punjab Police arrested three Pakistan-trained terrorists of the BKI in the Jagroan district and foiled their plan of a major strike in crowded localities in Chandigarh and Delhi. The police seized 1.2 kilogram of RDX, one pencil bomb, 28 detonators, a timer,

55 AK-47 cartridges, 56 Mauser cartridges and four .9 mm cartridges.

- July 17, 2005: Police arrested three BKI terrorists near Madhopur Chowk in the Fatehgarh Sahab district of Punjab. One AK-47 rifle, 25 live cartridges and some explosives are recovered from them.
- July 14, 2005: Two BKI terrorists are arrested by the Delhi Police from the Old Delhi Railway Station in connection with the May 22 blasts at two cinema halls. The terrorists are identified as Dilbagh Singh, a close relative of the Pakistan-based BKI chief Wadhawa Singh, and Surender Singh Kanda, a Kenya-based non-resident Indian, who reportedly worked as a visa agent.
- June 16, 2005: The Punjab Police arrested two close associates of Jagtar Singh Hawara from the Ropar district. Swarn Singh and Paramjit Singh alias Bhola were arrested along with 10 kg of RDX, a detonating device switch, 10 PE3A gelatin sticks, two infusion sticks, nine ABCD timers, four highly sophisticated grenades, nine clap switches, one live bomb and two .25 mm Chinese made pistol.
- June 8, 2005: Jagtar Singh Hawara, 'operations chief of the BKI in India, was arrested along with two other accused in the May 22, bomb blasts from the G.T. Karnal Road in Narela Industrial Area of Delhi.
- June 5, 2005: A joint team of the Delhi and Punjab Police arrested two BKI activists from Nawanshahar district in Punjab. Bahadur Singh and Gurdip Singh alias Kaka were arrested during raids on their houses at Malpur village and both were associates of Jaspal, an accused in the May 22 cinema hall blasts in Delhi. Two slabs of RDX weighing one kilogram, 11 detonators and cordex wires were recovered from the arrested activists.
- June 1, 2005: A day after police arrested BKI activists, Balvinder Singh and Jaganath Yadav, in connection with the blasts at the Liberty and Satyam cinema halls on May 22, the Delhi Police (DP) seized illegal arms and ammunition from a hideout of a BKI terrorist, who is still

at large. The DP conducted a raid at the hideout of Jaspal Singh at Inderpuri and recovered 1 kg of RDX, a timer, detonator, a .303 rifle, 20 rounds of ammunitions, a uniform of a Punjab Police head constable and several fake driving licenses.

- May 31, 2005: Two BKI terrorists are arrested in connection with the May 22-bomb blasts at two cinema halls in the national capital New Delhi. While Balwinder Singh was arrested from a village at Nawanshahar in Punjab, the other accused, Jagannath, was arrested from Madipur in Delhi. Rupees 2.94 lakh in cash, a kilogram of RDX and two kilograms of gold was recovered from the latter's house.
- May 22, 2005: Two explosions are triggered by crude devices at two cinema halls in the national capital Delhi, during the screening of the Hindi film, Jo Bole So Nihal, killed one person and injured at least 60 others. In the first incident at Liberty Cinema on the G. T. Karnal Road, the device reportedly exploded under a seat in the sixth row. The second bomb exploded at the toilet of Satyam Cinema in Patel Nagar.
- January 3, 2005: A BKI terrorist who was involved in an assassination attempt on a senior police official in Punjab and wanted by the Federal Bureau of Investigation (FBI) for various crimes in the US is arrested by the Delhi Police. Prem Pal Singh had stayed in the US, UK, Germany and Thailand for over 16 years using fake passports, said Deputy Commissioner of Police. Deependra Pathak. He was reportedly arrested at a passport office in Delhi when he was approaching agents to procure a US visa on its forged passport. A resident of Bassi Pathana in Fatehgarh Sahib, Prem Pal worked as a Government employee before joining the BKI in 1985.
- September 21, 2004: The Punjab Police re-arrests BKI terrorist, Gursewak Singh alias Babla, from a hospital in the Raikot area of Ludhiana district. Babla had escaped from police custody in the national capital Delhi on August 22 while being taken to be produced before a court

in connection with a 1998 case relating to sedition and violation of the Explosives Act.

- September 8, 2004: Police stationed in the Tarn Taran district of Punjab seized one AK–47 assault rifle from Didar Singh alias Dari, a BKI terrorist, who was arrested in connection with the murder of Baba Jagtar Singh, head of the Dera Akal. According to district police chief Gurkirpal Singh, two magazines and 30 cartridges were recovered from Didar, who is allegedly involved in nine cases of heinous crimes.
- April 30, 2004: The US includes the BKI in its Terrorist Exclusion List.
- January 22, 2004: Four undertrials, including three accused in the Beant Singh assassination case, escape from the high security Burail jail in Chandigarh. Those escaped included BKI terrorist Jagtar Singh Hawara, Jagtar Singh Tara and Paramjit Singh, the three main accused in the assassination.
- April 29, 2002: Police thwart a major conspiracy of the BKI to attack Wassan Singh Zaffarwal, VIPs and shakhas (branches) of the Rashtriya Swayamsevak Sangh (RSS) with the arrest of five BKI terrorists in Gurdaspur, Punjab. A huge cache of arms and ammunition is seized, too.
- August 31, 2001: Punjab police arrest a BKI terrorist. He confesses of plans to revive terrorism in Punjab through setting-off explosions at public places. He also reveals to his interrogators that terrorist leaders based in Britain and Germany, as well as those sponsored by the ISI and residing in Pakistan, were involved in the planning.
- August 18, 2001: Under the leadership of the BKI and other groups, pro-Khalistan activists and sympathisers hold a protest demonstration in front of the Indian Consulate in Frankfurt, and burn the Indian tricolour.
- June 9, 2001: In a protest demonstration staged at the Indian Consulate in Frankfurt, Germany, against *Operation Blue Star,* BKI leaders says no Khalistan terrorist should surrender. The rally had allegedly been

extended support by Pakistan's Consulate in Frankfurt.

- May 22, 2001: Punjab Police foil an attempt by terrorists to disrupt Ram Navami (Hindu religious celebration) with the arrest of four terrorists and seizure of 3kg of RDX and some arms and ammunition from Harchowal village, Batala district. Manjit Singh, a close associate of BKI's Mohal Singh had trained the terrorists, to target the Ram Navmi procession. During interrogation, the terrorists reportedly confessed to having crossed over to Pakistan a number of times to bring in arms and ammunitions and to step-up subversive activities in Punjab and Kashmir.
- February 28, 2001: British government prescribes Babbar Khalsa, as per the provisions of the new UK Terrorism Act 2000, which became operational since July 2000.

2000

- October, 27 2000: Ajaib Singh Bagri and Ripudaman Singh Malik, two BKI terrorists arrested by Canadian police for their involvement in the mid-air explosion of Air India flight–182 *Kanishka,* off the Irish coast.
- October 14, 2000: The Central Bureau of Investigation and Delhi Police seize a huge quantities of arms, ammunition and 30 kg of RDX, in Libaspur locality in the national capital, Delhi. Official sources believe they were stored there to be passed-on later to a Babbar Khalsa terrorist in Punjab.
- August 30, 2000: BKI terrorist arrested in Jalandhar district, Punjab, and a cache of 3.9 kg of PETN high explosives and timers is seized. Official sources say they had been tasked by Wadhwa Singh to target VIPs in Punjab.
- February 2000: Following the June–arrests in Delhi the Babbar network is traced to Ahmedabad and other areas in Gujarat, particularly the border districts.
- Gujarat Police arrest a Canada-based Babbar terrorist, who disclosed the BKIs' underworld connection. Nearly six more suspected Babbar terrorists are arrested subsequently and a BKI plot to abduct former Gujarat Chief Minister Chhabildas Mehta is unearthed and foiled.

- January 17, 2000: At a meeting in Sacramento, USA, leaders of the BKI discuss the declining interest in the idea of Khalistan among the Sikh community. The modalities for involving the younger Sikh generation, especially those employed in low-paid jobs in the US, is also discussed.
- January 6, 2000: A Pakistan-based BKI terrorist, who had consented to become a human bomb, is arrested in Jaipur, Rajasthan and 5 kg of RDX, arms and ammunition are recovered from him.
- January 2000: Gujrat Police arrest five Babbar Khalsa International terrorists from the Narol locality in the State capital Ahmedabad, following a tip-off from Punjab Police and union intelligence agencies. The terrorists were in Gujarat to raise funds for the revival of Khalistan movement through abductions for ransom.

1999

- February 26, 1999: Punjab Police arrest four terrorists of the BKI and recover 10 kg of RDX, 1.5 kg of PETN, half a kilogramme of heroin, an AK–56 rifle and a magazine.
- June 1999: Gujarat Police arrest three suspected Babbar Khalsa terrorists and a local contact and recover some arms and ammunition.
- In the same month a Babbar terrorist is arrested in Hoshiarpur in Punjab. He confesses to his interrogators that he and a Pakistani national entered India and had carried a consignment of five AK-47 rifles and some explosives.
- June 11,1999: Police in Baroda, Gujarat, unearth an ISI module and arrest three BKI terrorist and a local Sikh. A Chinese Pistol, two country-made pistols and some ammunition are recovered.
- June 1999: Delhi police arrested a suspected suicide bomber, Richhpal Singh, on a mission to kill former Punjab Police Chief KPS Gill.
- July 1999: Delhi police arrested two Babbar Khalsa terrorists with about two-kg of RDX.

- June 23, 1999: Amritsar police arrested two smugglers– close associates of Wadhwa Singh and Mehal Singh. Four kg of explosives is recovered from their possession.

1995

- August 31, 1995: Human bomb Dilawar Singh assassinates Punjab Chief Minister Beant Singh at the civil secretariat in Chandigarh. He allegedly owed allegiance to the BKI.

1992

- Talwinder Singh Parmar, the alleged mastermind of the mid-air explosion of Air India flight–182 *Kanishka,* off the Irish coast, killed in Punjab.

1985

- June 23,1985: BKI accused of masterminding the mid-air explosion of Air India flight–182 *Kanishka* off the coast of Ireland. A total of 329 persons are killed in the incident.

KHALISTAN ZINDABAD FORCE

Objective, Organisation and Leadership

The Khalistan Zindabad Force (KZF), a prescribed group under The Unlawful Activities (Prevention) Act, 1967, aims to establish a 'sovereign Khalistan state'.

Although the exact cadre strength and organisational structure of the KZF is not known, it is largely comprised of Jammu-based Sikhs.

Ranjit Singh Neeta heads the KZF. Originally a resident of the Sumbal Camp area in Jammu, Neeta is reportedly now based somewhere in Pakistan. One of the 20 terrorists that India wants Pakistan to deport, Neeta began his career as a small–time criminal and subsequently developed links with smugglers in the R.S. Pora and Samba areas. His name figures in at least six First Information Reports filed after bomb blasts on trains and buses running between Jammu and Pathankot between 1988 and 1999. He is also alleged to have been involved in the killing of Deputy Superintendent of Police Devinder Sharma in Kathua district of Jammu and Kashmir in October 2001.

Neeta's second in command, Amritpal Singh Romi, was killed in an encounter in 2000.

Khuram Masih alias Manjit Singh alias Kala alias Akaal, a Christian-turned-Sikh and a close associate of Neeta, was shot dead by the police during an encounter at village Dablehar in the RS Pura Sector of Jammu on December 28, 2000. Reportedly a 'hit–man' for Neeta, Khuram Masih was involved in at least 20 explosions in Jammu, Punjab and New Delhi.

Ravinder Kaur alias Tutu, another leading member of the KZF, was arrested from Rudrapur in the State of Uttar Pradesh on March 30, 1998. Ravinder, an alleged 'human bomb', was wanted in connection with two bus bomb blasts at Pathankot in Punjab during April and June 1997, in which nine people had died. Ravinder, sister-in-law of the KZF chief Ranjit Singh Neeta, was married to Nirmal Singh Nimma, who was acquitted in the General Vaidya assassination case. Ravinder got involved in terrorist activities after her sister married Neeta in 1990.

On July 6, 2005, a day after the failed terrorist attack on the make-shift Ram Temple at Ayodhya in Uttar Pradesh, the Jammu and Kashmir police is working on inputs that the KZF outfit is making attempts to regroup in Jammu, according to *Indian Express*. Official sources said that many of the KZF activists against whom cases were filed in the courts have been enlarged on bail and they are seeking to regroup. Inspector General of Police (Jammu), S. P. Vaid, while confirming that the KZF was making attempts to regroup said, "We are making efforts that the KZF does not become successful in reviving itself here. Many of the activists were involved in different violence related activities."

Area of Operation and Linkages

While Punjab, Jammu, Delhi are the main areas of operation, the outfit is also reported to have operated from Nepal in the past. For instance, the Delhi Police (DP) claimed to have neutralised a Nepal module of the outfit with the arrest of three cadres on August 24, 2000. While addressing a press conference on that day, Ajai Raj Sharma, the then DP Commissioner, said Neeta, who was in Lahore, had established a powerful base at Bir Ganj in Nepal and that Maan Behanji and Lakhbir Singh were the main organisers of this base. Earlier, in November 1998, Lakhbir Singh, an activist of the KZF, was arrested from a hotel in the Nepalese capital Kathmandu along with 20 kg of RDX and timing devices. On interrogation, he is alleged to have identified three Pakistani embassy officials with whom he had liaised, one of them identified as Asim Saboor, according to an *Asiaweek* report of April 21, 2000. The bases in Nepal were reportedly set up by the KZF with support from the ISI during the phase of Punjab militancy.

While Pakistan continues to host the KZF and its 'chief', Ranjit Singh Neeta, the outfit is also reported to have activists and sympathisers in Britain, Germany, Canada and some other European countries.

Apart from being linked to the ISI, the KZF has close links with several terrorist groups active in Jammu and Kashmir, including the Hizb-ul-Mujahideen (HM). Explaining such linkages, Sarabjit Singh, the then Punjab Police chief, said on November 14, 1999, that the KZF always had links with Kashmiri terrorists as it comprised Sikhs from the Jammu region.

Daily Excelsior reported on November 15, 2000 that "While the KZF still has much interest in hitting at Punjab, the ISI, intelligence reports say, has prevailed upon it to focus its attention on assignments given to its cadres in Jammu and Kashmir. Fresh and vigorous strikes in Poonch district (where Khalistan Zindabad Force has pockets of influence) and in other areas of the Jammu region, including the city of Jammu, according to the calculations purported to have been made by the ISI, would be more useful to it (ISI)."

The group has, intermittently, attempted to re-group and operationalise its subversive capacities in Punjab, Jammu, Delhi and elsewhere in India. However, a consistent loss of cadres and leadership has led to the KZF being marginalized although it retains its operational capacities.

Incidents

- June 26, 2005: Three activists of the Khalistan Zindabad Force, identified as Hardeep alias Badal, Sukhwinder alias Pappa, and Harpreet alias Ricky, are arrested from the Jammu region. According to the police, two pistols, a country–made gun and some ammunition were recovered from their possession.

- April 27, 2005: A court in Jammu acquits an activist of the Khalistan Zindabad Force in an illegal weapons possession case for lack of evidence. The police had arrested KZF 'commander' Balbir Singh on September 27, 1997, while roaming under suspicious circumstances on the banks of the Chenab. A mouser along with a magazine and 20 live cartridges besides a rifle and 66 cartridges were recovered from him.
- February 10, 2004: Attarjit Singh, a KZF cadre and reportedly a professional border crosser, is arrested by the Jammu Police for his alleged links to the January 21, 2004–escape of Jagtar Singh Hawara, an accused in the Beant Singh assassination case, from the Burail Jail.
- April 15, 2002: Gurdev Singh alias Mantoo, a KZF terrorist, is arrested from Jammu along with one pistol, one magazine and 15 live cartridges. Gurdev, involved in criminal activities in and around Jammu City, came in contact with an associate of KZF chief Neeta in October 2001.
- April 7, 2002: Trans-border narcotics and arms smuggler Virender Sharma, a close associate of Ranjit Singh Neeta, is arrested from Jammu.
- April 6, 2002: Three KZF terrorists were arrested in Jammu along with a tonne of plastic explosive and several assault rifles, which they had planned to use on a series of targets in the city.
- April 3, 2002: The Jammu and Kashmir Police arrests Amrik Singh, 'operational commander' of the KZF, and his associate Gurdev Singh.
- December 28, 2000: Khuram Masih alias Manjit Singh alias Kala alias Akaal, a Christian–turned–Sikh and a close associate of Neeta, is shot dead along with another KZF cadre, Iqbal alias Balbir Singh and Mohammed Naveed Tahir of the Islamic Front by the police during an encounter at village Dablehar in the RS Pura Sector of Jammu.

- November 21, 2000: Mohammed Alam, a close associate of Mohinder Singh alias Bittu, a constable of the Special Operations Group and a front ranking KZF cadre, is arrested from the Kathua district in Jammu.
- November 18, 2000: Prince and Kala Gujjar, two local harbourers of KZF terrorists, are arrested from the Kathua district.
- November 9, 2000: Manmohan Singh alias Sonu, chief priest at the Bakshi Nagar Gurdwara and a front ranking KZF activist, is arrested by the Jammu Police.
- August 24, 2000: The Delhi Police neutralises a Nepal module of the KZF with the arrest of three cadres who were involved in several bomb blasts in Delhi, Punjab and Jammu, Lakhbir Singh, alias Baba, Manpreet Kaur alias Maan Behanji, sister-in-law of the KZF chief Ranjit Singh Neeta, and Surjeet Singh were arrested from the Gurdwara (Sikh place of worship) Rakabganj Sahib along with 32 kilograms of RDX and other explosives.
- March 25, 2000: Three KZF cadres, identified as Ravinder Singh, Tajinder Singh and Kamaldeep Singh, are arrested from Jammu.
- March 18, 2000: Three KZF activists, Sukhvinder Singh alias Mithu, Satvir Singh alias Sunny and Parshotum Singh alias Kala, are arrested in New Delhi.
- March 17, 2000: The Jammu Police arrest a suspected activist of the Khalistan Zindabad Force, identified as Kirtan Singh alias Bitta, who was the mastermind behind the bomb blasts on board the Sealdah Express and Pooja Express trains. Police also recovered one Chinese-made revolver, four magazines, 30 rounds, two AK magazines with 50 rounds and fake currency of Rupees 40,000.
- March 1, 2000: Union Home Minister L. K. Advani discloses in the Lok Sabha (Lower House of Parliament) that the KZF was one of the eight Sikh extremist outfits operating in the country.
- February 10, 2000: The KZF is alleged to have exploded a bomb on board the Sealdah Express train at Supwal

village in the Vijaypur area of Jammu killing five persons and injuring 20 others.

- November 11, 1999: At least 14 people are killed and 55 others sustain injuries in a KZF-engineered bomb blast on board the Jammu–Delhi Pooja Express train.
- April 1, 1999: Kathua Police arrests Ramzan Khan and Basant Singh alias Geelu, two suspected KZF activists, during raids conducted at Nagrota on a tip off given by Naseeb Singh, a KZF cadre who had been arrested on January 23, 1999. Police recovered a revolver, one double barrel gun, three rounds and other ammunition from the possession of arrested suspects.
- March 28, 1999: A Khalistan Zindabad Force activist, identified as Keval Singh Rajput, is arrested from Jammu.
- January 23, 1999: Naseeb Singh, a front ranking KZF cadre hailing from the Digiana area of Jammu, is arrested from Kathua. Naseeb Singh was a close associate of former KZF chief Mohinder Singh Pappi and another 'commander' Gurmeet Singh alias Manga, both of whom were killed in encounters in Punjab.
- November 1998: Lakhbir Singh, an activist of the KZF, is arrested from a hotel in the Nepalese capital Kathmandu along with 20 kg of RDX and timing devices.
- October 23,1998: The Jammu Kashmir High Court (Jammu Bench) dismisses a petition filed by Ajit Singh, father of hardcore militant Sulkhan Singh, and KZF activists challenging the detention of Sulkhan under Public Safety Act for two years. In the dismissal order, Justice G.D. Sharma observed that it is established that the detenue is a hardcore motivated militant and his remaining at large is highly hazardous for the security of the State and maintenance of public order. According to the grounds of detention, in the month of April 1997 Sulkhan Singh met with Punjab militants Attar Jeet Singh and Jagmohan Singh who motivated him to become an active KZF cadre and get training in handling arms and ammunition after going to Pakistan.

INTERNATIONAL SIKH YOUTH FEDERATION (ISYF)

Formation

The International Sikh Youth Federation (ISYF), proscribed in India under the Prevention of Terrorism Act (POTA) on March 22, 2002, was founded in the United Kingdom (UK) in 1984 after *Operation Blue Star,* conducted on June 5, 1984, to flush out Sikh terrorists from the Golden Temple complex, in Amritsar, in the Indian Punjab, Amrik Singh and Jasbir Singh Rode, a nephew of Jarnail Singh Bhinderanwale, founded the ISYF. Bhinderawale, a key figure in the secessionist Khalistan movement, was killed in *Operation Blue Star.* The ISYF has been declared as a proscribed organisation in the UK, along with 20 more outfits, on March 29, 2001. Besides, the ISYF has been disbanded in Canada on February 10, 2002.

The ISYF held its first conference in September 1985 in Walsali. Soon after its formation, the ISYF opened chapters at various places in the UK, Germany, Canada and the USA.

Initially, the ISYF split into two factions—one owing allegiance to Jasbir Singh Rode and led by his elder brother Lakhbir Singh Rode—and the other led by Satinderpal Singh Gill, a former member of the second Panthic Committee. Soon thereafter, more splits occurred and several splinter groups emerged—the Damdami Taksal (DDT), Chaheru, Bittoo and Gill factions. These operate mainly in parts of the UK, Germany, the US.

Objectives

Working towards the establishment of an independent homeland for the Sikhs is the chief aim of the organization. The US State Department's annual *Patterns of Global Terrorism,* in 1999, lists the ISYF as an active terrorist organization that aspires to carve out of Indian territory an independent Sikh state called *Khalistan.*

Leadership

The ISYF is presently headed by Lakhbir Singh Rode, also a nephew of Bhindranwale. He is better known for the immense political influence and considerable kinship clout he wielded in parts of Punjab. Security forces in Punjab describe him as a "hardcore terrorist". He reportedly continues to be a successful fund-raiser among *Khalistan*-supporters abroad. He joined the *Khalistan* movement in 1982, having returned to the Punjab after spending five years in Dubai. He returned to Dubai in 1986, and from there he arranged to send his family to Canada and followed them, where he headed the outfit. Subsequently, he left behind his family in Canada, where it continues to live, and shifted base to Pakistan, where he has been residing since 1991. Rode lives in Lahore. He is among the 20 most wanted terrorists whose extradition India has sought from Pakistan in the wake of the December 13, 2001 attack on India's Parliament by a five-member group of Jaish-e-Mohammad (JeM) terrorists.

Other important leaders of different factions of the ISYF abroad include Amrik Singh Gill, Raghvir Singh Johal, editor of *Awaz-e-Quom* the mouthpiece of ISYF–Rode faction in the UK, Balwinder Singh Chaheru, Parminder Singh Bal and Avtar Singh Kooner. In the past, in Canada, besides Lakhbir Singh Rode, Satinderpal Singh acted as President, and Balbir Singh Brar was the Secretary. Also, Manmohan Singh operated as the spokesperson. At the time the outfit was disbanded in Canada, Amrit Singh Raj functioned as the spokesperson.

Area of Activity

In the past, it operated in Punjab and maintained offices in many countries. At the present, the ISYF's support-base is spread across the UK, North America, Canada and other Western European countries. The Gurdwara on Ross Road, in Vancouver, British Columbia, reportedly played a pivotal role in the ISYF's activities in Canada. In Pakistan, Gurudwara Dera Sahib, Lahore, acts as the main centre for its activities.

Activities and Fund-raising

At its peak, the ISYF was involved in terrorist acts including murders, bomb blasts and abductions. The ISYF had been making efforts to execute terrorist acts in India, but had not been successful. For instance, on July 30,1997, two associates of Lakhbir Singh Rode, who had been reportedly sent to assassinate the then Chief Minister of Punjab, Prakash Singh Badal, were arrested near the India-Pakistan border, close to Amritsar.

Reports indicate that Bhagwan Singh, a leader of the All India Sikh Students Federation (AISSF) and a close associate of Bhindranwale, S S Bhinder of the ISYF's Germany chapter, S S Bhullar of Canada and Bhagwan Singh Sandhu had been making attempts to revive the ISYF's activities in India.

It was earlier reported that the ISYF, in Canada, controlled Gurdwaras in Abbots Fort, New Westminster, Surray, near Vancouver and on Ross Road Street, Vancouver.

The ISYF reportedly raised huge amounts of funds from the Sikh diaspora. For instance, in 1984, it had launched a membership drive, in Canada, and charged five dollars as fees. Those who did not enroll were branded as agents of government agencies. To avoid suspicion most Sikhs became members. Besides, Rode loyalists in the UK, Germany and North America reportedly exercise influence over Gurudwaras and Sikh forums through which they collect funds for the outfit.

Also, the ISYF has established a human rights organisation known as *Khalsa Human Rights Group*. This group emerged as a powerful fund-raising unit of pro-Khalistan terrorists located in foreign countries. Also, it has been reported that it carries out propaganda on alleged human rights violations against Sikhs in India. Further, the group acts as a liaison with other Sikh organisations to unite them in addressing the problems of Sikhs.

The official spokesman of ISYF in Canada, Amrit Singh Raj announced its disbanding there on February 10, 2002, and said after the organization was branded as a terrorist group, its functioning became impossible.

Linkages

The external intelligence agency of Pakistan, the Inter Services Intelligence (ISI) has supported this organization for a long time. It provides training camps, funds, arms and ammunition to the members of ISYF along with other Khalistani groups. Pakistan-based chief of the Babbar Khalsa International Wadhava Singh and chief of the ISYF Lakhbir Singh Rode are said to be among the top Punjab militants who, in league with the ISI, have been assigned the task of carrying out militant activities. The ISI also wants to create a common front between Khalistani and Kashmiri terrorist groups. The ISYF's links with Pan-Islamist terrorist groups, and more prominently with the Lashkar-e-Toiba (LeT), date back to the mid–1990s. The ISYF was reportedly the first Sikh terrorist group to have interacted with ideologues of the Markaze-Dawat-War-Irshad, the parent body of the LeT. At the time, ISYF leaders were believed to have met with Abdul Karim @Tunda and Khwaja Moin and had also opened a dialogue with other Pan-Islamist terrorist outfits for joint action.

Major Incidents

2004

- April 30: The US includes ISYF in its Terrorist Exclusion List.

2002

- February 10: Addressing the media in Vancouver, ISYF spokesperson Amrit Singh Raj says the ISYF has been disbanded and will no longer exist in Canada. He says, after the ISYF has been branded as a 'terrorist' group, its image stood tarnished and made its functioning impossible.
- March 22: The ISYF is banned in India under the Prevention of Terrorism Act (POTA).

2001

- August 18: At a protest demonstration organised by the ISYF in front of the Consulate in Frankfurt, Germany, the Indian flag is burnt.
- July: Three factions of the ISYF in Germany strongly condemn Jagjit Singh Chauhan and term his return to India as a betrayal of the Sikh cause and the principles of Jarnail Singh Bhindarawale.
- May: The ISYF's Germany unit condemns Wassan Singh Zaffarwal for surrendering to Indian security forces.
- March 29: The ISYF is declared as a proscribed organisation in the UK, along with 20 more outfits,

following the approval of the Terrorism Act 2000 [Proscribed Organisations (Amendment) Order 2001] in the House of Lords, on March 27.

- February 28: The British government proscribes the ISYF as per provisions of Terrorism Act 2000. Following the ban in the UK, ISYF suspends membership drive and the leadership contemplates altering the name of the organisation to International Sikh Federation (ISF).

2000

- July: The Special Immigration Appeals Committee (SIAC) in the UK declares that two ISYF members, Mukhtiar Singh and Paramjit Singh, are a threat to Britain's national security.

1997

- July 30: Two persons linked to the ISYF are arrested near the India–Pakistan border, near Amritsar, after infiltrating into India at the behest of Lakhbir Singh Rode to reportedly assassinate the then Chief Minister of Punjab, Prakash Singh Badal.

1991

- ISYF launches 'Bhai Amrik Singh Saheed Fund' in the UK reportedly to assist families of terrorists killed in security force operations in Punjab. The UK branch of the ISYF claims later that it had sent 30 pounds each to the next of kin of more than 100 terrorists. It also promises to send more money in the future.

1987

- May: Satinder Pal Singh, a prominent leader of the ISYF in Canada, procures arms in Lahore and sells them to Khalistan Liberation Force terrorists. The proceeds from the sale are remitted to the ISYF in Canada.

1985

- November: ISYF holds a convention at the Ross Street Gurudwara, in Vancouver, Canada. Several Sikhs from across the country participate in the meeting. Arjinder Pal Singh Sekhon, an influential religious leader of the Sikhs, makes a speech on alleged state terrorism against Sikhs by the Indian government.

- Sekhon organises an arms deal in the UK. All ISYF units in Canada, the UK and the USA are directed to raise funds to finance the deal, and targets are assigned.

Pakistan Factor in Punjab and Jammu & Kashmir

In 1987, Gen. Zia is reported to have told India that if she wanted a declaration from Pakistan about its not interfering in Punjab, then India would have to declare that it would not play the Sindhu Desh (Sind) or Pashtoonistan cards. Coming to power later, Benazir Bhutto vaguely declared that "the days of the extremists are over."

Whether Bhutto, or Zia before her, they were merely indulging in semantics, or a game of one-up-manship, to put it simply. After all, it is a known fact beyond any dispute that Pakistan had started playing the 'Punjab Card' much before Zia took power, forget about his smart 'offer' of 1987. Even after Bhutto and Nawaz Sharif came into power, Pakistan continued to assist and fan, and even aggravate, terrorism in Punjab with the sinister aim of destroying the political and ethnic cohesion of the Sikh Community with the rest of the nation.

Analysts argue that terrorism had not been sponsored or engineered in Punjab in the same sense as in Jammu and Kashmir. Sponsorship, says DJ Hanle, involves financial aid, weapons, training, intelligence, sanctuary and leases for training, maintaining and staging terrorist forces. The expert has opined in 1980s:

> "In this context, Pakistani assistance to an ongoing violent movement is a form of military aggression. The active and continuous collaboration between Pakistani sponsors and groups of motivated and willing youth of Punjab has military overtones and carries the seeds of a prolonged, sub-revolutionary struggle. The acts of terrorism and violence will therefore persist unless this nexus is broken. Gun-running and narco-terrorism further complicate problems in Punjab, because there provide great monetary incentives for the unemployed and the 'drop-outs'."

The analyst's prognosis of a 'prolonged' struggle, luckily and fortunately for Indians, did not come true. But that should be no cause for comforts or complacency for the security minders of India. Pakistani agencies and Sikh NRI activists have succeeded in keeping the pot simmering for a decade and a half. Slightest oversight can put the clock back significantly. With things not seeing a happy turn in the North-East and Jammu and Kashmir, India can do without another hot spot in the country.

Reverting to those 1980s days, analysts were clear that: "Demands for a Sikh state or self-determination are, however, being encouraged by Pakistan only to keep the pot boiling (for India). It is highly unlikely that Pakistan would actually allow creation of a Sikh state whose claims must eventually extend beyond Lahore and certain other Pakistani areas which have some of the most sacred shrines (gurdwaras) of the Sikhs. Pakistan should not forget in a hurry that the only Sikh state in history had its capital in Lahore. And equally significantly, almost whole of the present NWFP was within its borders."

The chaos and political instability in the period straddling the year 1990 suited Pakistan to a 't'. Its helping the Khalistan movement was also aimed at creating a friendly Sikh population in India just across its eastern border. After all, it provided many strategic and tactical advantages to Pakistan vis-a-vis India, which would all disappear the moment a Sikh state is born on that very border. Worse still, unknown 'new forces' could have emerged in that state "which may not be or remain friendly with Pakistan for the future". For such reasons, Pakistan would have loved the unstable, disturbed in perpetuity situation of 1991 in India's Punjab province. But India foiled all such designs of its western neighbour.

Possibly, Pakistan had certain strategic concerns in case a buffer state between India and itself would have materialised, and accepted or encouraged by it. In the first place, such a state would set a precedent for certain restive populations of Pakistan itself. The one name that possesses our imagination is Pakhtoonistan of the early 1990s. As an analyst wrote in early 1990s: "Baluchistan could be a candidate (for the status of a buffer state) in the not to distant a future."

Pakistan had no case but for a desire to avenge India's role in its 1971 humiliation and loss of its Eastern Wing. But its government and intelligence/security agencies had certain strategie calculations also in mind: "Punjab served as a useful adjunct to Pakistan plans in Jammu and Kashmir as it kept a large number of troops tied down in Punjab, besides acting as a poor advertisement for Indian claims of a secular polity."

Terrorism in Jammu and Kashmir and Punjab: Pakistan has played a role[1]

Pakistan's sponsoring of terrorism in Jammu and Kashmir, and later in Punjab, and its consequent support to both has been so substantial that it will be utterly unrealistic to discuss the subject *sans* Pakistan.

Again, as Pakistan's role is a common strand in both the narratives and there are inter-linkages in the terrorism in Jammu and Kashmir and Punjab, the two are discussed here together. It will help us in putting the issues involved in perspective. This discussion here should be taken as an introductory review.

Start of it all

India faced secessionist violence in Jammu and Kashmir—more popularly and perhaps, more accurately, Kashmir—very early in its life as an independent nation. As is well-known, Pakistan made vigorous efforts (through persuasion, cajoling, threads and for religious reasons) to annex Kashmir. This was partly facilitated by Maharaja Hari Singh's dreams of an independent Jammu and Kashmir, encouraged by foreign powers, especially the US. India refused to move in until the Ruler signed the Instrument of Accession, the policy it had uniformly adopted and followed in case of the rest of 556 Princely States.

Frustrated by the Maharaja's obduracy, Pakistan launched on an adventurous course: military annexation of his state. Consequently, its Army units disguised as 'tribal fighters', and accompanied by some tribals for effect, crossed the border into Kashmir in the last week of Oct. 1947. A desperate Maharaja signed the Instrument of Accession on 26 Oct. 1947. And the Indian Army Units, led by 1 Sikh[1], landed on Srinagar airport on the 27th, just in the nick of time to staunch the advance of the Pakistani troops to capture this capital town of the State.

India built up its forces in the State and by the end of 1948, major part of the state was cleared of the armed invaders. A ceasefire became effective on 1 Jan. 1949, leaving one-third of the state in the adverse possession of Pakistan—obviously, illegitimate gains accruing from an aggression.

Frustrated in its designs of grabling the state for itself, Pakistan resorted to the cheaper option of low intensity warfare against India. The aim was to initiate a secessionist movement in India's Jammu and Kashmir, taking advantage of the Muslim majority in the Valley. It is so easy for a Muslim nation to incite its co-religionists across the border on ideological and religious grounds. From this inflamming of religious passions, sponsoring terrorism was the next logical step in its scheme of forcing India to cede at least the valley to Islamabad. Is it any surprise that Pakistan has used terrorism against India as its foreign policy instrument, ever since its 1947 attempt? It has persisted with this policy over the last 60 years!

When the Khalistani secessionism raised its head in Punjab starting 1978, Pakistan was rather eager to nurture it and strengthen it. The reason: to open a second front against the 'enemy' India. India had been seen as such particular after its humiliation in 1971. Revenge against India had become an obsession, particularly for its Army, because it held her responsible for this humiliation, loss of its Country's Eastern Wing, and consequent birth of an independent Bangladesh. Inspite of this vicious drive meant to destabilise India, the latter succeeded in controlling and eliminating threat of Khalistani terrorist violence by, say, 1993. At the end of it all, Pakistani hand in partly sponsoring the Punjab terrorism and subsequently maintaining it by all means available to it: providing funds, training infrastructure including the camps, weapons and ammunition, and guidance from the ISI. More importantly, most of the separatist leaders were sheltered in the safe houses, thoughtfully and generously provided by the Government on Pakistani soil.

So as in Jammu and Kashmir, so it was in Punjab: Pakistan helped the Sikh terrorists in their cause.[2]

Sponsored Terrorism

Sponsored terrorism may be defined as acts of terrorism sponsored, launched and then nurtured by one country against another, employing violence and lethal force aimed at achieving short-term or long-term political or strategic objectives. It may also be noted that such sponsored terrorism is not only a fact of modern warfare but an accepted, rather preferred option, as it is low cost in comparative terms compared to a conventional warfare, including set-piece battles.

The aims of the sponsoring nation can range from destabilising and weakening of a government or a central authority to their complete collapse and consequent disintegration of the target nation.

The sponsoring country provides all kinds of help to the surrogates who fight its war against another nation; it could be financial, political, moral and diplomatic. It also supplies them with weapons and arranges weapon training in the training camps established on its own territory, or on that of the target nation's. If need be, it also provides safe sanctuaries for the terrorist if pressed too hard by the target nation. The financial help is arranged directly through emigrants, or indirectly through the NGOs, voluntary organisation, or charities.

The terrorist or insurgents thus have symbiotic relations with the sponsors. But it is an unequal relationship, akin to those of the puppeteer and the puppets. If the latter get too big for there shoes, they are unceremoniously discarded for the more pliable ones. Usually it is the sponsor who decides the course of operations, including the target areas and the person. The sponsor may not actually control the employment of persons and the conduct of operations on ground. It is explained by the fact that terrorist on the ground know the area of operations better also its populations. So often the actual operations are conduct by the local commanders—who generally have their own chain of command. This gives the local terrorist leadership and organisations a certain notion of self-importance since they are managing the nitty-gritty of these operations. In fact it is very limited initiative, and in reality they are nothing more than the local agents of the sponsoring country. Given this even then it is possible that the sponsoring state and the terrorist could have divergent aims and objectives. In this context, the JKLF comes to mind which is aiming at independent Jammu & Kashmir opposed to Pakistan wanting to annex it.

In a manner of speaking the sponsoring country is actually managing an unconventional war in which the terrorists are substitutes for the regular and irregular enemy troops operating in an enemy territory. That way, they are as much an instrument of war as regular forces in a conventional war. It is an ingenious and less costly option of warfare where an element within the target country has persuaded, coerced, blackmailed, and brainwashed to perform the role of an enemy force. This method, if worked out properly and discreetly is an efficient and cost-effective means of achieving strategic and political objectives without directly engaging an adversary in set-piece battle with conventional armed forces. The victim nation unless exceptionally alert does not comprehend the wide ranging ramifications of the situation early enough. No doubt, it immediately launches counter measures to eliminate the terrorists from within its boundaries, which itself may take considerable time. But it has no reason to look beyond the immediate task of counter-terrorism operations, until its own intelligence alerts it to the possibility of a third party involvement in the terrorist violence. Even after its intelligence smells a rat, the victim nation cannot launch military action against the sponsoring nation in the absence of any proof as the terrorist are unlikely to be so careless as to leave any incontrovertible evidence of help extended to terrorism from the neighbouring nation. Even if there is reliable evidence of the third party help to the terrorist, the victim nation due to a variety of factors will not be in a position of launching an attack on the offending nation, particularly because of pressure from the UNO and some major powers. Forget about an attack, India has not even exercised a limited option of "hot pursuit" when the terrorist scurry into the safety of Pakistani Territory across the border (India did contemplate marching into Pakistan after the terrorist attack on its Parliament, but that is jumping the gun at this stage of our narrative).

Inability and failure to comprehend the situation results into prolonged internal turmoil and loss of credibility, which is only to the expected as the center of gravity across the border remains *unchastised* even untouched. Only if the target state takes effective measures to successfully destroy the capability and the will of the sponsors to continue sponsoring terrorism, the cohesion between the latter and the terrorist will *sunder.* Once this is achieved, the terrorist movement within the target state will wither away, and perish. This is not to suggest that the root cause within the defenders territory should not be dealt with simultaneously but to indicate that the target state has to tackle two enemies. It is, therefore, essential in combating sponsored terrorism to initiate measures military, political or diplomatic that would render the sponsorship of terrorism altogether too costly for the sponsoring country. (In the past 50 years, India has failed to stop Pakistan from extending all kinds of help to terrorists operating in Kashmir, although the latter claim to be giving them only moral, diplomatic and political support. It is only in the recent year (1990 onwards) when terrorists started hitting targets within Pakistan and posing threat to the establishment that that country took counter–measures to control them. Even then, they avoided instituting serious counter-measures against terrorists operating in Kashmir).

It is widely accepted that terrorism is a form of war, albeit low cost, often called low intensity conflict (LIC). Many scholars have examined the subject in depth, Donald F. Hanle, for example, in his book *Terrorism: The Newest Face of War*, has sought to establish common denominators to define war and thereafter correlate those to various types of terrorism affecting the world. The study of history of warfare will show that war is a dynamic process based on certain fundamental principles which have remained unchanged. Classical military thinkers likes Sun–tzu (early 4th BC), Karl Von Clausewitz (1780–1831), and Sir Basil (Hanry) Liddel–Hark (31 Oct. 1895–29 Jan 1970) considered war a unique human activity which follow certain criteria, regardless of time and era. Hanley formulated three basic questions to classify different types of terrorism to establish if they would qualify as a form of war. These are:

- Does the activity involve lethal force by a political entity for a political end?
- Does this activity involve the exemption of lethal force against the cohesion of the targeted political entity?
- Does this activity involve the reciprocal use of lethal forces by both sides employed in accordance with the principles of combat?[3]

Hanlay concludes that the "sponsored terrorism" which uses surrogate warfare to unleash a reign of terror by using force both at the moral and physical planes, meets these basic requirements and qualifies as "war", because the "purpose of such actions is to break the existing physical and psychological ties that bind a country or a people together by applying various asymmetrical pressures on the targeted state".

The Pakistan Factor : Punjab and Kashmir Situations

It is an accepted fact that terrorism (in Punjab was and) J&K is classical manifestation of sponsored terrorism. It is also rather evident that Pakistan launched these well-planned surrogate operations with far reaching political and geo-strategic aims. In the case of Punjab, Pakistan added fuel to the fire lit by certain fundamentalist elements in a largely patriotic Sikh country. But in J & K, it was Pakistan itself that started the fires. It may not be correct to hold wrong policies and mis-governance in these two states particularly responsible for terrorism in either of the two states. In either case certain vested element took advantage of the opportunities provided by the democratic freedoms enjoyed by the civic societies, in destroying and manipulating unpopular circumstances flowing from corrupt and inefficient governance. Let it be repeated, lest it be misunderstood, that the moral governance in these two states was no worse than the one that was found in large parts of India.

But let us also accept that in either state, there mere political grievances flowing from particular events of the past that those self-centered religiously-fired anti-national elements were able to take advantage of to launch on their adventurist campaigns. In Punjab, the cataclysmic event was the 1984 anti-Sikh violence, mis-handled by the ruling party that was a god-send for the anti-national elements and in J & K, it was the aftermath of the 1947-49 Indo-Pak war that was exploited by Pakistan for its own aims. Pakistan must be given credit for successfully manipulating anti-national elements in the two states to employ force both on moral and physical planes, creating mayhem, death and destruction there. In both cases, religious susceptibilities have been deliberately and persistently exploited to foment unrest and spread disaffection.

So the Pakistan factor is common to both the situations.

Some critics have panned the Indian Government for various sins of commission and omission:

1. Its response has been on conventional lines, mixed with political rhetoric. This approach has not succeeded at least in case of the J&K, where it has supposedly fostered further alienation. Unless it full realizes that the country is face-to-face of a new kind of situation and conditions its response suitably, the problem will continue to grow.
2. "Terrorism and insurgency in Punjab and J&K is not an ordinary 'law and order' problem that can be tackled by the existing administrative machinery or 'police methods' alone." (The above piece of criticism was obviously justified when the ulcers of Punjab terrorism and Kashmir secessionism were simultaneously infesting the body politic of India. These critics should admit at least that India proved them wrong as far as Punjab was concerned. To be fair to the critics, what they postulate was correct till the early 1990s – more specifically, until the time the Punjab terrorism was brought to a successful end.)
3. The basic infrastructure to launch terrorist attacks is the LOC in Pakistan POK, besides some other world centers. Therefore the sealing of borders, killing of terrorists in encounters, body counts, capture of arms inside our own country have little impact on the over all situation. These are defensive actions which have no direct effect on the target centers, sources of finance and weapons, or operational bases across the borders.
4. In this kind of war the terrorists and innocent citizens are "co-sufferers" and mere pawns in the game. Pakistan the sponsoring state, is the only gainer when harsh or highly repressive measures are taken against our own population.
5. Our administrative machinery, para-military forces, or Armed Forces are neither trained nor organized to take on the challenge sponsored terrorism poses in Punjab or J&K.

6. The nature and scope of terrorism and insurgency in J&K is one qualitatively different from that in Punjab, although one compliments the other.
7. The deployment, arming, harbouring and launching of terrorists from across the border of LOC are acts of belligerence and indirect aggression by Pakistan and unless we develop a proper counter-organization and techniques to combat this, terrorism will continue unabated.
8. The political situation inside Punjab and J&K must be stabilised simultaneously. Establishment of normal democratic rule is a must, even if there are risks, to finally defeat terrorism.

The above criticism can be countered, or some of the assumptions corrected, hence detailed rebuttal is unnecessary. Not only has Punjab terrorism been brought to an end, even the situation in J&K is on the mend, and current talks (1905–07) between India and Pakistan should further improve the relations between the two.

It has been matter of speculation and debate if a conventional war against Pakistan can resolve the problem. General opinion is that another war is unlikely to solve the current problems between India and Pakistan. Notwithstanding all this speculative discourse, India did think of such a solution when it massed its forces on the Pakistan border after the terrorist attack on the Parliament. There were credible reports that time, that New Delhi came perilously close to order its troops to cross the border but a variety of restraining factors, domestic and international, came in the way. It has been suggested that there are many alternatives short of conventional war which "can make sponsoring and supporting of terrorism–insurgency in Punjab and J&K an expensive and self-defeating proposition for Pakistan". But it may be worthwhile to remember that India was able to mend the situation in Punjab without recourse to war with Pakistan.

COMPARING PUNJAB AND J&K TERRORISM

As the two terrorist movements ran concurrently in Punjab and J&K for a period of time, it should be interesting and even instructive to compare the two. More so as the two had a common sponsor, Pakistan. Scholars found it useful to subject the two to a comparative review to learn something about the Pakistani motives, and draw some lessons if and where necessary.

Terrorism, *ipso facto,* implies employment of extreme violence to achieve its objectives. If this makes the two situations similar, Pakistan, the common sponsor, provides connectivity. Not withstanding this, there are important and basic differences but the two. These differences are defined, firstly by the ultimate objectives Pakistan sought to achieve in respect of the two, and secondly by diverse political and cultural milieu, terrain, weather conditions, and religious and ethnic identities of the two populations. These factors directly impinge on *modus operand!* of the terrorists and demand separate strategies and counter terrorism methods from the authorities.

Aims, Objectives, and Motivation of Terrorists and their Sponsors in J&K and Punjab

The immediate objectives of terrorists in two states may appear similar at first look, but these differ vastly in scope and long-term objectives. The urge for vengeance seems to be the main motivation behind terrorism in Punjab, which subsequently gave birth to vague dreams of a separate homeland. In Kashmir, the motivation comes from religious affinity with Pakistan, and consequent desire to join it, obviously after secession from India. (Both movements would have withered away but for active support of Pakistan and as some analysts aver, our own serious blunders initially and subsequent mishandling of the two situations – what ever the latter might mean.

In Punjab, the aims and motivation of terrorist groups can be considered within the following parameters:

1. Block all attempts at a political solution, short of a Sikh homeland. Hence, the spurt of violence if and when a compromise is in sight.
2. To paralyse law and order machinery of state, and thus destroy the credibility of the administration.
3. To foment Hindu-Sikh alienation and distrust first, by a disinformation campaign, and then selective killing of the Hindus.

4. Creation of a Sikh-dominated terrorist belt along the Indo-Pakistan border by foreign eviction and migration of the Hindus from there through extortion, threats to families, selected assassinations, and mass murders.
5. To wreak vengeance on all those who oppose terrorism–individuals, state machinery especially the policemen, so-called informers, even suspects within there own ranks and political leaders. All this aimed at proving and establishing the power of the gun.

Pakistan's Aims in Punjab

Some analysts hold that Pakistan is determined to avenge its defeat in the 1971 war against India and consequent loss of its Eastern Wing, as it holds the Indian machinations responsible for both these national catastrophes. Therefore, Pakistan grabbed the opportunity that came its way when Punjab terrorism raised its head early 1980s, by extending all kinds of help to it with certain, definite strategic and political objectives in mind. It provided finances, sanctuaries operational bases, weapons and training facilities on its soil to various terrorist groups operating in the Indian Punjab, aimed at creating chaos and disaffection which should eventually lead to creation of a theocratic state on its borders with India. Other scholars and keen observers of the scene disagree with the view postulated above and assert that Pakistan would never support or allow a fanatical Sikh state to be formed on its eastern borders. Their arguments: Historical Sikh–Muslim virulent hostility, including the bitter memories of murder of more than one Sikh Gurus by the Mughal rulers of India; and even more serious, the portentous demands of that state for certain key Pakistani areas which were a part of Maharaja Ranjit Singh's erstwhile empire. Thus, the aims of the terrorists and Pakistan Government were not co-terminus, barring certain limited spheres.

The pattern of terrorism in Punjab and the scale of assistance provided by Pakistan to the Punjab terrorists pointed to following likely objectives of Pakistan:

1. To further foment Hindu-Sikh alienation born during the 1984 anti-Sikh riots consequent to Prime Minister Indira

Gandhi's murder at hands of her Sikh guards, through various actions of the terrorists groups in order to create a permanent, Sikh dominated pro-Pakistan belt in this strategically important border state. Besides being an embarrassment to India, the arrangement would provide Pakistan a convenient base for gathering real-time intelligence on movement and concentration of troops in case of war – or even uneasy peace. Such a pro-Pakistan belt, hot spot of terrorism, will certainly tie down considerable Indian Security Forces within its own borders and thin out security in some other more important of its areas.

2. This simmering discontent over the Khalistan demand will not only be a reflection on India's much-admired secular-credentials but also be seen and conceived as a sword of Damocles hanging over its geo-strategic *locus standi* in the comity of nations.

3. This belt will come handy for Pakistan to disrupt or threaten India's lines of control and consequently, to sabotage logistic support systems in the event of a war through terrorist-cum-guerrilla attacks.

The analysts aver that even if the aims and objective of the terrorists and Pakistan Government may be divergent in the long run, a symbiotic relationship between the two is an essential pre-requisite: The Sikh ultras can not face is heat from the Indian state and its Security Forces for long without Pakistani help, and on the other hand, Pakistan would be hamstrung in carrying out any of its plans or "evil designs" without the active support and cooperation from these terrorists.

Pakistan's aims in Jammu & Kashmir

A small section of the Muslim population of the valley seems to have had measure of sympathy for Pakistan and certain reservations over Kashmir's accession to India, obviously influenced by its religious identity and by ideological incitement propagated by hard-line pro-Pakistan ideologues and separatists, "but there was no desire to join Pakistan". Then there is a view that "from 1980 onwards, because of disinformation campaign by Pakistan through the radical groups in the valley and the indifference of New Delhi to the economic development of Jammu & Kashmir, a process of alienation was triggered off that was aggravated due to political somersaults and forced changes in the political leadership in Jammu and Kashmir. So the situation that faced Indian in 1989–90—When the present phase of terrorism began with vigour and virulence unknown till then—represented the sum total of or political blunders, economic neglect, lack of action." A situation existed (1989–90) where, some critics thought, the majority of Kashmiri Muslims want to break away from India.[4] (It is a highly exaggerated scenario[5] but let it pass for the time being, to proceed with our narrative).

The Pakistani aims coincide with those of the Kashmir terrorists. The aims and ways of Pakistan are self-clear in J&K, and are recognized here:

1. To wrest from India the Muslim majority areas of J&K, especially the valley, with a mix of armed action and religious upsurge, when the situation is ripe for it.
2. To progressively increase the level of alienation amongst the Muslims, convince the youth about the power of the gun, and frighten into silent acquiescence the intelligentsia, loyal elements, and government agencies and employees.
3. While acknowledging only moral, political, and diplomatic support to the terrorists (of course, the freedom fighters to Pakistan), Pakistan has been providing all material and infrastructural support to the Muslims to aggravate terrorist and guerrilla violence to unacceptable levels for the Indian state. This will be the time to incite the population to launch a mass of non-cooperation, movement paralyzing the states political and administrative machinery.
4. To make use of Islamic fundamentalism already aroused to fever pitch, to thwart any political understanding with New Delhi.
5. To internationalise the bilateral Kashmir issue, against India's stand and policy of keeping it between the two neighbours, to paint India as a repressive state and to "expose" its anti-secular character for suppressing a Muslim majority state.

It also needs to be understood that Pakistan is for an outright annexation of Kashmir, and would not accept, and allow the emergence of an independent Kashmir even if certain sections of separatist, mainly led say the JKLF factions on either side of the LOC, are vying for that status. This dissonance in ranks of the jihadis and terrorists does not seem to be hampering the present phase of the Kashmir terrorism.

Do the Terrain and Communication Systems Impinge on Terrorism?

The nature of terrain lay of the land, and accessibility to and from the sponsoring sate will influence the tactics, weapons and the terrorist organization in a given situation. Expectedly as in any form of the warfare, tactics and *modus operandi* of the terrorists in the densely populated and well developed urban areas would differ from those applicable in the jungle or mountainous areas with poor rail and road communication systems. The weather, particularly extreme cold and excessive snow and rain, affects mobility and logistic support systems of the terrorist groups. The size, organization and tactics will, of necessity, differ in Punjab and J&K.

Punjab, a flat, densely populated state, has a good network of roads and railways right upto the Pakistan border, which remains porous despite several layers of artificial barriers and border security network. Except for riverine areas like the Mand region, there is little natural cover available for concealment in Punjab, barring perhaps the seasonal crops. After a terrorist act, the ultras have no option but to lose themselves among the population or cross over to Pakistan. As crossing the border at will is not always feasible, the terrorists must operate in small groups who, when required, can quickly melt into densely populated areas. For smaller periods, strategic crops, farmhouses, network of guru wars, and an occasional thicket can also provide shelter and concealment. As security forces generally move on the roads, the terrorists feel safer to make use of the dirt tracks and canal banks for a get away. Timely intervention enable the SF to foil several terrorist attacks, and at times the latter abandon the assigned tracks mid-way fearing there arrival. The terrorists use vehicles for some specified tasks where escape routes are well recognized in advance. Given its population and terrain, it is not easy to carry heavy weapons in Punjab without the risk of detection. Therefore, automatics and man-pack rocket launchers, easy to carry and conceal, are preferred by the terrorists, even when operating in larger groups. Given the facts of population, it was never a difficult job for the terrorists to find some shelter in a sympathetic household.

Jammu and Kashmir. Its mountainous areas have pine and deodar forest cover up to 10,000 feet (3090 meters). The plains sector in Jammu division in its south has rolling plains with numerous fast-flowing rivers, rivulets, and flood chamils, criss-crossing the area before entering Pakistan across its western border. This sector is accessible from Pakistan throughout the years. Further north and west wards, the plains yield to the hills which gradually rise and join the Pir Panjal range that physically separates the Jammu Division from the Kashmir valley. The main roads run south to north. The single rail track earlier terminated at Jammu, has been extended to Udhampur, and work is in progress to take it right upto the valley-Srinagar. The Jammu-Srinagar (NH–1A) road, the life line to Kashmir and passing through Banihal tunnel, is prone to frequent disruption due to rains and snow in winter in northern areas of Jammu Division. In addition, large number of bridges and culverts renders it even more vulnerable to terrorist attacks.

The Kashmir Valley, surrounded by a ring of high mountains on all sides which receives high snowfall in the winter, remains cut off from the rest of the country for that very reason for almost six months in a year. The valley, nearly 100 km by 60 km, is mainly formed by the Jhelum and its tributaries, and several lakes, including the world famous Dal Lake. The natural exit route, from the valley is in its west through the Baramulla gorge. The terrain and weather confines the mobility of the road-bound security forces but affords any number of concealed routes and hide-outs to the terrorists. But the inroads from the POK to the valley are anything but easy since all routes have to cross the rugged, steep (Pir Panjal) mountain passes, locally called gallies (= narrow passes across high ranges), which again remain snow bound for long periods in winter. The LOC firmly manned by the Army since 1949, thwarts the movement of larger parties of terrorists from across. But individuals can always sneak through and find shelter in the villages and urban areas of the valley. The large urban centers prove ideal places for small terrorist groups to merge into the local population, and even enjoy all creature comforts including medical aid without being discovered for long periods. The terrorists are known to have established camps on the distant isolated hill tops to launch attacks in the areas around them. In 2004 one such camp was raided in the Surankot area (near Poonch) after the terrorists had been there for over a year. The sheltered villages in the forest areas and large towns like Srinagar, Sopur, Anant Nag, and Baramulla have provided ideal ambience for a combination of rural-cum-urban insurgency, or even guerrilla warfare. Ladakh, a barren high-altitude desert at an average height of about 10,500 feet, is in the north of J & K. If the Greater Himalayan range separates it from the main Kashmir Valley, the Karakoram Range and its offshoots intervene between Tibet and POK. Sparsely populated and with few natural resources, Ladakh is not very suitable for terrorist operations. But certain areas in Kargil-Suru Valley can be used to build temporary bases by the terrorists during an open season. Being distant and isolated, terrorist operations here do not yield the oxygen of publicity to the ultras, and this is another reason for its being low on there priority list. It is no secret that the terrorists are focused on the valley, and in recent years on the Doda area of Jammu Division.

Ethnic Composition of the Population and its Implications

In Punjab, the cultural and religious roots of Hindus and Sikhs being the same, only some extraordinary events could create a rift between the two. There is no evidence to suggest that disharmony was engineered by some external elements. The first sparks were produced over the language controversy in 1951 census when Punjabi Hindus under the influence of some local Hindu radical groups chose to register Hindi as there mother tongue in preference to Punjabi. Later in the 1960s the demand for a Sikh-majority Punjabi Suba (Province) brought out other political differences in the two cities to the fore. But it was the deeply-felt humiliation result from the shock of "Operation

Blue Star" that gave rise to terrorism in and organizational form. The Pre-Blue Star period beginning with the anti-Sikh riots of 1984 following the assassination of Ms. Indira Gandhi, which had killed over 3,000 Sikh, had generated enough heat to get Pakistan interested in the situation but it was the military action in the Golden Temple (Operation Blue Star) which pushed the angry Sikh youth to seek sanctuary across the border and accept Pakistan's support. Some analysts felt the Sikh violence was not aimed at the Hindus but against the government. The fact remains that a large number of Hindus were killed selectively forcing the country to take recourse to large scale emigration from certain areas on the other hand, the Sikh population in general seems to have been traumatised enough by the Delhi carnage consider itself a beleaguered minority.

'A majority of the Sikhs in Punjab refused to condemn the Boys' (as the terrorists were called there) but very few came forward willingly to give them active support. Some political observer concluded: "Harsh police measures, horrors of innocent Sikh families and fake encounters had progressively added to the sympathy for the 'boys' and had provided fresh motives to the angry youth to swell the terrorist ranks". There was a time when every terrorist gunned down by SF was considered a martyr, and had ballads sung in his praise!

Some analysts had asserted that the police actions to counter terrorism and the distinction it made between the Sikh and Hindus had considerably increased the alienation. The result of such uneven treatment of the two cities by the police was that terrorists directed retaliatory attack against the Hindus, who in any case were bearing the brunt of the terrorist violence being soft targets – almost sitting ducks. The Hindu reaction has been seen in two different ways by the commentators. One opinion was that the Hindu reaction, apart from migration, " has been remarkably restrained....". The other asserted in the same vein in which the Mahatma had once described the Hindus as "cowards", that the Hindus "can never response aggressively or even militantly, when subjected to the worst kind of violence", and that was only an historical truth. So they thought this restraint was nothing new in their context, and does not deserve any kudos or showers of praise as some analysts were piling upon them during the period. But in the later stages, however, "some Hindu militant outfits have reportedly been formed, whose aim is to fight the terrorists and protect the Hindu population". Let it be said here and now that these so called Hindu militant outfits were more for public consumption, and mostly existed on paper, and they certainty had no effect on the terrorists attacking the Hindus at will. But the Hindu reaction outside Punjab, particularly in the Hindi belt was sharper: many sections there considered the "Sikh community at large an ungrateful people who have run amok". But then some scholars wrote that this (reaction outside Punjab), "does not help matters and has little rationale".

The 1991–92 ratio between Sikhs and Hindus was 68:42 as against 52:48 in 1981. The adverse change was directly attributed to terrorism. This change in ratio not withstanding, it was unlikely that the Sikh terrorists got widespread support from the population in general, bar one or two border districts. The over all ethnic grouping and support did not allow a free run to the terrorists. On the other hand, it made it easier for the SF to infiltrate their ranks. That was possibly the reason that a number of Sikhs were gunned down by the terrorists on mere suspicion of being informers or police spies. The attitude of the common man did impose caution on the terrorists and confined their main activities to certain safe areas near the border.

To sustain their movement, the terrorists had to maintain constant pressure on the local population, therefore, the ghastly spectacle of mass murders and daily killings continued for several years without a let up As they did not enjoy mass support, all this death dance ended when police got their act together under an able DG, who also enjoyed the backing of political leadership.

In J&K, the ethnic grouping and population mix differ from one region to another, and even at times, within the same region. In Jammu Division, the Dogras pre-dominate in the south but the northern and western areas have mixed population. In Poonch and Rajouri and Doda–Kishtwar Bhadarma belts of Jammu Division, the Muslims are in majority. In Ladakh, Kargil area has a majority of Shia Muslims while further north and east, the Buddhists predominate.

The majority of Muslims, vastly predominant in the Kashmir Valley, are a distinct entity and differ vastly from their co-religionists in Jammu or Ladakh, or even the higher reaches of the valley itself. On the valley floor reside the typical Kashmiri Muslims and Kashmiri Brahmin; on the rivers and the lakes live the "Hanjis" who ply the boats and barges. On the higher reaches of surrounding mountains, Gujjars and Bakkarwals roam from one pastuse to another. It is the Muslims of the urban areas of the valley who are in the vanguard of the terrorist movement it. "Though docile and peace-loving by nature, they have readily taken to the Kashmiri culture due to instigation and false propaganda from Pakistan". An analyst writes about the villagers in the valley: "They are simple folk compared to the commercial minded and half-educated urban youth who reside in the four large town of the valley. Muslims here are not religious fanatics and are ready to accommodate Kashmiri Pandits, propaganda by some organization not withstanding".

Ethnic grouping in the valley, or in the other Muslim majority areas have not precluded attacks on locals at large, and Hindus in particular. In the initial stages, the terrorist attacks concentrated on the symbols of "Govt. authority", or their active supporters. Later, minority community became the target in a big way which led to the Hindus (mostly Kashmiri Pandits) leaving the valley *en masse.* They have mostly been settled in the refugee camps in and around Jammu and in Delhi, etc. (It is a sad commentary on the nation's secularism that the majority community living in a majority-Muslim state has been evicted from their homes and hearths).

The security forces and their logistic bases have been targets by the terrorists since long. In the recent years, emboldened by their success the terrorists have been attacking soldiers traveling in the convoys, isolated military posts and camps, divisional and brigade headquarters and family quarters of the service personnel. They also have been ambushing military patrols, road opening parties, and VIP–carrying convoys.

Starting from the Valley the terrorists have extend their depredations to Doda-Kishtwar and Poonch-Mandi-Rajouri areas of Jammu Division, as well as to the Hindu dominated areas of Jammu city—the most sacred Raghunath temple in the heart of the city being a striking example. And to make the point that nothing is beyond their reach, is Kashmiri terrorists have staged violent attacks in all corners of the country, aimed at sabotage, causing communal riots and consequent Hindu–Muslim disharmony, and destruction of public property.

In the Kashmir Valley, it is feasible for the terrorists to merge with the local population and stay undiscovered for long periods. Such possibilities render the job of the SF even more difficult, as they have to plan their counter-terrorist operations with more care to avoid large-scale collateral damage.

Due to ethnic and religious affinities and cohesion, it is rather tough for the SF to penetrate the terrorist organization in the valley, and for the same reasons, it is not easy for the SF to obtain an advance information of their plans/attacks.

It is in the area, contiguous to the LOC which is well-manned by the military, that the terrorists are most vulnerable, and this is area the terrorists must cross to enter the Valley from POK.

Course of Khalistan Movement: A Critique

Punjab: A Secessionist Movement

Punjab has an interesting past, even if the 1980s, Khalistan movement may/need not be linked with it. People old enough to remember painful days of India's Partition in 1947 would perhaps remember that a section of the Sikh leadership, decidedly a minority, had voiced their demand for a Sikh state. Their logic, mentioned elsewhere in this book, was simple. If the Hindus are getting India, Muslims, Pakistan, why not Khalistan for the Sikhs?

Though the demand did not make any headway then, and the British India was divided between two nations in Aug. 1947, the hope—rather velocity—for Khalistan (=Land of the Pure or Khalsa) remained ensconced in some Sikh breasts. Perhaps it is also significant to remember the recurring chant/refrain in their players that wind up all the functions at their gurdwaras, with all the Sikh devotees reciting it in unison:

Raj Karega Khalsa, aaqi rake na koi

(The Khalsa will rule, with none to defy)

It was a potent *mantra* repeated *ad nauseam* by the Sikhs in their gurdwaras the world over every morning and evening. Is it possible that the chant warmed the cockles of some Sikh hearts who took it literally and seriously, and worked for it after the 1984 anti-Sikh violence, following the assassination of Prime Minister Indira Gandhi, had created a certain degree of alienation in the community.

Sikh alienation: Its beginning and subsequent accretion

The process of Sikh alienation, some analysts suggest, started with the 1951 Census, Independent India's first, when the Hindus, discarding Punjabi, registered Hindi as their mother tongue. Others reach a few years earlier and claim that the process of alienation of the community from the national mainstream was sit in motion within a couple of years of the 1947 Independence due to the communal outlook of the Akali Dal, Jan Sangh, RSS and sections of the Arya Samajists.

Still others posit the process really started in the last quarter of the 19th century under the influence of the Arya Samaj movement, which originated in Gujarat under the teachings of Swami Dayanand Saraswati but spread fastest in Punjab. Here is the logic and exhortation from the proponents: "If the Sikhs are disowning Hinduism, why should not the Punjabi Hindus embrace Hindi as mother tongue? Most Hindu children adopted Hindi as the medium of struction under the parental guidance. So that is how it all started. One can choose any of the periods given/mentioned above, depending upon one's volition.

Seen this way, post-1951 census, the Punjabi image of the Sikh Community slowly yielded place to a "Sikh image" with a chip on its shoulder. When the Akali Dal conducted a vigorous campaign mid-1960s for creation of a Punjabi Suba (that is, Punjabi-speaking state out of the then existing Punjab which, incidentally, then extended from the Tibet border to Gurgaon, contiguous to UP, the Hindus (and, of course, the Government of India) saw it as a demand for a Sikh-majority state. But when finally the demand for a Punjabi majority state on a linguistic basis was conceded in 1966, it left the Punjabis—read Sikhs—dissatisfied because not only certain Punjabi speaking areas were left in Haryana, Chandigarh too was not allotted to Punjab as its exclusive Capital, letting Haryana share with Punjab. The

Hindu-Sikh differences had made to the headlines in the national dailies.

The Anandpur Sahib resolution drafted by a sub-committee of the Akali Dal in 1973 and making many demands which was virtual espousal of a Sikh state with vast powers created a flutter in the dovecotes of Indian polity. The greatest cause of concern was the resolution claiming that the Sikhs were a "Qaum" (= nation), a term denoting a separate nation, but which has never been defined. The subsequent endorsement of the resolution by the Akali Dal generated uneasy political reaction and certain amount of distrust but the Sikh and the Hindu communities. Then there was one violent incident after another, and the Sikh militancy was obvious to the political observers. But it all had apparently started with a sharp confrontation between a group led by Sant Bhindrawale and the Nirankaris when the former had tried to disrupt the letter's *'samagam'* (=a religious gathering a large convention) at the holy city of Amritsar. The sympathies of the Hindus in general were with Nirankaris as it was seen as an attempt by the extremist Sikhs to interfere with the Nirankaris right to profess their faith. This resulted in widening further the Hindu-Sikh hiatus, and embroiled the Hindus in various violent acts.

Bhindranwale's violent attacks on the Nirankaris, leading directly to the assassination of the head of the Nirankari Mission (Baba Gurbachan Singh) at Delhi, got transformed into a direct confrontation between him and the state. Avoidable tension was created in Amritsar when a Jan Sangh procession, led by its local leader, Harbans Lal Khanna (later assassinated by the terrorists) to protest the demand for a holy status for Amritsar, raised slogans like *kachha, Kara, Kirpan, Bhejo inko Pakistan.* Such actions played into the hands of the Sikh extremists who reacted aggressively, and led to a bloody retaliation. Bhindrawale had arrived on the scene and soon assumed a larger than life image.

Bhindranwale "Saga"

Sant Jarnail Singh Bhindranwale was the head of the Sikh Seminary, Damdami Taksal at Chowk Mehta, near Amritsar. When he first appeared on the Punjab scene, he was a lanky, spartan personality a bit of a maverick. He was noticed by the national press after his bloody confrontation with the Nirankaris at Amritsar. Soon thereafter, because of his bold, if reckless, utterances and actions, he had gained great popularity and came to be considered as the "sword" of the Sikhs. The Congress Party, then out of power, thought up a smart play of building him up as a counter to the leading trio of Akali leaders of that time – Prakash Singh Badal, Gurcharan Singh Tohra, and Harchand Singh Longowal – and then used him for making inroads into the Akali stronghold. That this political naivete would cost, not only Punjab but also the nation, dearly was soon realized by the political observers when Bhindranwale growing bigger and bigger, apparition like, appeared on the national horizon as a menacing presence. It was the time when the man travelled openly and defiantly from Amritsar to Bombay, via Delhi, perched on the top of a large, decorated bus, and the center watched the proceeding for days on end as mute spectators – either helpless or unwilling to strike! It was widely believed that the Congress had encouraged the Sant initially to embarrass the Akalis, but now he was not only on embarrassment for the Congress, but also a looming threat for the nation's peace.

Bhindranwale had become a cult figure, attracting a large number of Sikhs to his congregations. During these gatherings he mouthed anti–Hindu slogans and baptised thousand of Sikhs. His menacing and uncompromising posture progressively led to increased violence and random violence, which in turn hardened the national opinion against him. By early 1980s, the assassinations had become frequent and he had begun dispensing ready and rough justice at his durbars. Hindus had become frequent targets of terrorism. Leading Hindu and Congress personalities had been assassinated: Lala Jagat Narayan, a senior Congressman and owner/publisher of Hind Samachar group of newspapers, his son Romesh Chandra, Justice Congress Minister Joginder Paul Pandey and Akali leader Balwant Singh, when some Sikh terrorists were killed in counter-terrorism action by police, Bhindranwale found it reason enough to make his movement more violent. Pre-operation Blue Star violence can rightly be attributed to him. When he emerged from a life of self-denial and isolation at Chowk Mehta, very few people could have foreseen his dramatic rise as an aggressive militant leader of extraordinary influence and determination. It is inexplicable why after a certain period, when his agenda was made crystal clear through violent attacks on the Hindus and selective killings of the Hindus and the Congress leaders, and at times of rival Akalis, the Government at the Centre and state remained so amazingly inactive. The rise of the Sant from his obscure village origins to a dark messiah also tells the story of progress of terrorism in initial phases. His meteoric rise could have been analysed and thwarted some where along the way – but it was not.

By 1983, it was generally believed that all the terrorist violence in Punjab was instigated by the Sant, and by then he held sway over the whole of the Punjab through open defiance of the state and intimidation of the population. But on the other hand, a large number of Sikhs saw the Sant as a redeemer following the traditions of the holy Gurus against the oppression of the state. A couple of years before Operation Blue Star, in their routine checks of the vehicles carrying rations and other essentials to the Golden Temple, the police had been recovering arms and ammunition. It seems these recoveries and seizures were not taken seriously. Then dawned the day when Mr. Avtar Singh Atwal, the DIG of police was shot dead on the steps of the Golden Temple in broad daylight. To the utter surprise and disbelief of the strategic and academic critics, the Government chose to take no action against the culprits who had fled into the temple. What was the reason for this reluctance? Was it because by then the Sant was well entrenched inside the temple complex and the Government was apprehensive of violent reaction? It, of course, was a fact that by then the extremists had become a law unto themselves in the entire Punjab. What followed was even worse. Increasing acts of violence like murders, bank robberies, attacks on railway stations and passenger buses by the followers of the Sant continued to make the state machinery look like a helpless giant – correspondingly adding to the stature and influence of Bhindranwale, and an aura of invincibility around him. Even more surprisingly, after the killing of DIG Atwal, the Government the Prime Minister Indira Gandhi personally repeated the declaration made several times earlier that the military will not enter the Golden Temple to arrest terrorists ensconced inside it. The common man felt even more insecure now. Bhindrawale was running a parallel government now, and many Sikhs flocked to him for quicker justice through his jurisdiction rather than the administrative or judicial machinery.

Analysts have suggested that this (prior to Operation Blue Star in June 1984) phase of violence in Punjab did not conform to any known pattern of revolutionary a political terrorism. It could be compared to "Psychotic terrorism" of certain individuals. J Bowyer Bell defines such terrorists as: "Those who attempt bizarre, ostensibly political action with uncertain or irrational outward motives. ...for what are internal personal reasons". By this time, Sant Bhindranwale with the professed aim of *"Dharam Yudh"* had drawn an aura of mystique around him which prompted people to rationalize violence, leading Punjab to "mystical terror". Terrorism at this stage had become an amalgam of sub-revolutionary and mystical terror, with an express aim of wreaking vengeance on the 'enemies' of the Panth, which of course included the Govt. employees and agencies of the Govt. Critics allege "this situation was not properly analysed by the Govt.; the result was a haphazard approach where most people justified high-handed police methods' normally used against common criminals". That gradually led to 'state repression' affecting a very large segment of Punjab's population. The response from a section of the Sikh population was in the from which can be defined as "reactive terrorism". More youth took to terrorism.

The law of the land no longer applied to the temple complex and the areas around it. The dead bodies were often thrown out of the temple complex into the gutters as a public demonstration of rough justice meted out to the opponents of the Panth. Policemen, officers, public figures, and suspects who were supposed to be oppressing the innocent Sikhs were now being eliminated openly and regularly. Bhindranwale was now ruling the roost, all the rest including the senior Akali leaders, had been silenced with demonstrative use of force or its threat. He was beyond the reach of the law ensconced in the safety provided by 200 well-armed bodyguards, well-entrenched inside the Golden Temple. Ironically, although lodged within this impregnable fortress, the Sants' feeling of insecurity was growing by the day. This was the time when he had the advice of three senior Army officers available to him: Shubeg Singh, a dismissed major general; JS Bhullar, a retired Maj Gen and Mohinder Singh a retired brigadier. Under their advice, it was decided to fortify the temple complex heavily against any possible future action by the state.

It was also decided to bring-in the arms and ammunition for this purpose. Even foreign help was sought and accepted. Even at this stage, some opined, the concept of Khalistan was rather vague and not linked directly with Bhindranwale's movement. Some other dubbed this thinking as an 'apologia' and asserted that by this time plans for Khalistan had been firmed-in, after due consultations with certain sympathetic powers.

The situation in other parts of Punjab was no better. As counter terrorist measures were in force certain amount of resentment was palpable among the Sikhs. It was reported that the Sant was becoming even more popular, and demand for a Sikh state gained currency, even among certain moderate and intellectual sections of the Sikhs. Even if the hoisting of Khalistani flags on various Gurudwaras or public buildings, and distribution of Khalistani currency or passports was still considered the activity of the lunatic fringe, some radical groups had started a movement to drive out Hindus from certain areas of Punjab to make place for the Sikhs expected to pour in from other parts of the country.

The situation was now worsening by the hour. A certain gloom hung over the political Delhi. Some feared the Sant might publicly declare the birth of Khalistan followed by immediate recognition by at least a couple of countries. As the fortification of the temple complex going apace could be seen from the surrounding areas, and killing of the innocent was increasing, the Government of India finally seemed to astir. The Paramilitary forces were ordered to close in on the temple. In Feb. 1984, Army units replaced the BSF on the border to relieve them for internal security duties.

At a certain stage in March 1984, a hard analysis told the Government that the task of dislodging Bhindranwale from the temple was well beyond the capabilities of the BSF and other paramilitary forces. The decision: The Army will be assigned the unfortunate job.

Operation Blue Star

It seemed the Sant and his men had gotten wind about the Army plans to invest the temple. Even otherwise, the experienced generals around him should have known that the fortifications they had so obligingly and deliberately built-up were a virtual invitation for army action. The Government was simply left with no other option. Not withstanding all this, some around the Sant still felt that the Government would never have the nerve to storm the temple, given the passions it was bound to cause among the devoted Sikhs, or so they thought. In any case, as later reports showed, the fortification work was exclusively planned and executed by Maj. Gen. Shubeg Singh, who was the first to join the Sant and had been with him the longest. It is surprising that, given his vast experience in the Indian Army, the General did not advise the Sant to escape and live to fight another day. Alternatively, given his larger than life image and self belief, the Sant over ruled Shubeg and decided to fight till the end. "I cannot run away like a rat," he said, as reported by some one who was present. (More of it later.) But all said and done, it is intriguing that the best these generals could think up was to site automatics in order to cause max casualties. It is a pity indeed that in the passion of the moment these generals had forgotten the capabilities of the Indian Army they had served all their lives.

There were a variety of reports of happenings inside the complex on the eve of Army action is June, 1984. Some averred that the likelihood of Pakistan granting immediate recognition to declaration Khalistan by the Sant might deter New Delhi from sending its Army into the Temple. The opposite view is that "it is doubtful if the Sant had any assurance of help from Pakistan or even a promise of political asylum", otherwise he might have been tempted to escape with some trusted associates, ignoring the traditions of martyrdom and hoping to fight in a less disadvantageous situation. In any case, there are examples in Sikh history of leaders escaping the pitched battles, and no one knew Sikh history better than him. Finally, there could have been one more reason for the Sant and his advisers deciding against the escape from the temple. They were depending upon the Sikh masses to form, a human shield to prevent the Army from assaulting his fortress. But at the end of it all, Prime Minister Indira Gandhi did order the Army into the Temple.

Books have already been written on the Sikh insurgency and Operation Blue Star. It is not intended here to cover the subject in any detail. The aim here is to discuss it very briefly in the context of the subject of our book, and to delineate the reaction among the country to this catastrophic his event.

Some analysts have refused to see Operation Blue Star as an anti-terrorist action, but as an assault on a fortress to capture or destroy religious fanatics entrenched and entrapped inside. "This bizarre scenario belonged more to the 16th than to modern India. The initial action started on 2nd June 1984, after a 32 – hr curfew was imposed on Amritsar City and the Army formally requisitioned in aid of civil authority. The provision for "the aid to civil power" is enshrined in the Army Act and clear guidelines and conditions laid down there in about the way this "aid" is to be rendered by the Army to the civil authority. But in the instant case, to use a cliche, this was "the aid with a difference". As some critics 'cynics' perhaps would be a more appropriate term – put it, during operation Blue Star, the civil administration and the police were directed provide aid to the Army.

Operation Blue Star embraced Gurudwaras all over Punjab, and that required the deployment of more than three Army divisions for a variety of tasks. As subsequent developments showed, after the initial action by the Army, "the operation was not only flawed in its very concept but marred by poor planning and execution", according to some analysts. They quote Khushwant Singh's description of the incompetence of Army generals responsible for the operation as accurate and succinct: "As for as the incompetence of the Army, less said the better. In an age when a handful of Israeli and German commanders could, through a well-planned action, overcome well entrenched enemy thousands of miles always from them, the best our generals could do was to storm the Temple complex with tanks and armoured cars, blast Akal Takht to get at Bhindranwale and about 200 of his men. In crossfire, upwards of 5000 people a majority of them pilgrims including women and children, lost their lives... Far from doing a competent job, our Army commanders botched up simple operations."

It is indeed a pity the critics could not find a more balanced and less incompetent man than Khushwant, who is not only not known to be a student of military history and well known campaigns and battles. But also ignorant of anything military. His knowledge of wars and battles possibly could not go beyond a couples of novels like and *A Bridge Too Far.* In the instant case, he obviously has been briefed by some retired generals, not well-disposed towards those criticized by Khushwant (Indian generals are known to continue their personal battles even after retirement). A detailed rebuttal is uncalled for but a brief comment is certainly in order. Pray, which are the operations and where are those places thousands of miles away "a handful of Israeli and German commanders have over come well-entrenched enemy"? There is only one instance where Israelis mounted anti-hijacking operations against terrorists who were guarding hijacked plane at an African airfield. So Khushwant compares those desperados with the well-fortified Golden Temple complex held by Bhindranwale and his men! Yes, the German did rain bombs on US cities, as did the British in the opposite direction, during World War II. Can we compare these recklessly destructive attacks with the Indian Army's action in the Golden Temple ? Come, Khushwant, for God's sake, do not be so flippant. This simply is not acceptable, even if I acknowledge your devotion for your religion notwithstanding your often touted religiosity and agnosticism! The generals did not storm the Golden Temple, nor did they blast the Akal Takht. 'Blasting' connotes blowing a lodge to smithereens. The generals to their credit accepted and took heavy casualties for their officers and men to avoid any serious damage to the sanctum sanctorum. One thought Khushwant should have been appreciative of this fact if not grateful. One is aware of his emotional reaction to operation Blue Star, returning the Padma Award to the President, even then he could have been a little more balanced if not sagacious, in his criticism. Khushwant's criticism of Operation Blue Star is as good, or as bad as an infantry colonel's criticism of Hussain's paintings!

Put on record below is another strong indictment of Operation Blue Star :

> The aim here is not to discuss the details of 'operation Blue Star' but the main factors of planning and conduct which

aggravated the impact of this operation on the Sikh psyche. First and foremost: to launch an assault on the Temple on the martyrdom day of Guru Arjun Dev, the builder of the Golden Temple, was sheer perversity, because a very large number of pilgrims were bound to be caught in the crossfire, if the aim was to achieve surprise or because the presence of the pilgrims it was thought would prevent the militants from taking strong action, it proved to be a clumsy attempt which showed a cynical disregard for the loss of innocent lives. This was certainly neither good soldiering nor honourable combat on the part of the Sr. generals in charge of planning the operation. Later, they would make various statements, invent excuses, and even shade the truth to hide inconvenient facts. The second was the damage to the Temple and Akal Takht and the destruction of Sikh Reference Library all this was considered the result of revengeful vandalism by the Sikh masses although this was the result or unimaginative and clumsy planning and execution. Thirdly, the Army action is about" 37 other gurudwaras combined with the combing operations called "Operation Wood Rose" but all Sikhs on notice and created an atmosphere of terror. This widened the scope of the conflict with disastrous effects as later events were to prove.[6]

The above criticism is not the result of ignorance about matters military *a la* Khushwant, but it is certainly not fair and balanced. It certainly lacks objectivity. Detailed comments are not adduced. Yes, there were certain flaws, especially launching the operation on the martyrdom day of Guru Arjun Dev. Undoubtedly, the operation had an unfortunate effect on the Sikh psyche – exaggerated by the vested interest and exploited by political parties. Interestingly no one has suggested any alternative. It was like a Greek tragedy progressing irrevocably towards its denouncement.

It is common belief that it was Operation Blue Star which had a long-lasting adverse effect on the Sikh masses, and pushed perhaps more unemployed people/Sikh youth into terrorism than anything else. Post Operation Blue Star, a number of them crossed into Pakistan where received training and weapons as well. If previously, the conflict was confined to a few radical groups, after Operation Blue Star; it embraced the entire Punjab, and a part of the Army itself. One opinion is that though terrorism originated with Bhindranwale it assumed serious proportions with Operation Blue Star.

Terrorism in Punjab: Pattern and Infrastructure

Some analysts hold that the anti-Sikh riots in Delhi and some other parts of the country in the wake of Mrs. Gandhi's assassination in October 1984 was the final blow to the hopes of Hindu-Sikh amity and proved to be a point of no-return–a fillip to Sikh terrorism. Slowly a dangerous mood over took the two cities and attitudes hardened to a degree, even among the educated. Some held – perhaps incorrectly – that the carnage of Sikhs (1–3 November 1984) was no less an act of terrorism than was to be witnessed subsequently in Punjab in horrendous proportions. "The wave of so called 'Hindu terrorism' subsided as quickly as it had a risen."

There was hardly any change in the pattern of terrorism from Operation Blue Star onwards. After a brief spell of consolidation in 1985, the *modus operandi* of various terrorist groups had acquired a set pattern, the only visible changes were in the form of fluctuations in the number of innocents gunned down in any particular year. These changes – fluctuations, spurts in killings – were generally related to important political events in the country or to certain peace initiative. An accord would send the killing graphs shooting up, a warming by the terrorists that they would accept no compromise. It was a warning to the moderates, and a simultaneous assurance to the sponsors of terrorism that violence would continue, unaffected by any political changes. The table below shows the co-relationship between the killing groups and political changes from 1984 to 1990.

Political Changes Versus Killings in Punjab

Period	Innocent Killed	SF Killed
Barnala Govt.: 1985 Accord*	55	8
President's Rule 1986	478	42
Peace Initiative (Lok Sabha Polls (1989))	1800	428
Political changes at the centre (Dec. 89 to Nov. 1990)	1800	400

*Signed between Prime Minister Rajiv Gandhi and SAD President Sant Harchand Singh Longowal.

Source: Karim (1991); 38.

Yearly Toll in Punjab: 1984 to 1990

	1984	*1985*	*1986*	*1987*	*1988*	*1989*	*1990*
Innocent killed	339	55	478	815	1839	1800	1800
SF Killed	20	8	42	95	42	428	440

Source: Published sources.

India Today of 15 October 1988 had comparative figures during the Barnala regime and President's Rule in Punjab. 1988 was obviously bloodiest year since 1984.

	Barnala Regime	*President Rule*
No. of persons killed by terrorists including policemen	790	2090
No. of terrorists killed	118	496

It was around this time that peace initiative was launched by the center. "Parkash Singh Badal" was out of favour at this stage, while Jasbir Singh Rode, a nephew of Bhindranwale, was released from jail along with 40 other detainees, and rehabilitated. The militants stepped up violence. Their attacks became more vicious and brutal than ever, as the massacre of 32 persons during a religious fair at Hoshiarpur showed. The Rode initiative proved abortive. The militants who had once again entrenched themselves inside the Golden Temple, had to be dislodged yet again from there. The task was undertaken by the Punjab police this time, and achieved through Operation Black Thunder. Many terrorists, caught off-balance, were quick to recover and reorganize. During 1988, as reported by the press, more than 3000 people which included terrorists and policemen, lost their lives to wanton terrorism.

The bloody graph showed a slight dip in 1989 but climbed again in 1990. The analysis showed that the terrorists groups showed greater resistance and better organisational skills during the 1989–90 period compared to the earlier years. They obviously seemed to have generous supplies of sophisticated arms at their disposal. Displaying greater boldness, they had, by then, graduated to engaging SF in prolonged encounters, including direct attacks on the army camps.

The main pattern of terrorism in 1989–90 was marked by:

- Greater frequency of attacks on SF personnel and their posts.
- Bomb blasts and use of IED through remote control.
- Blowing up of train tracks and attacks on trains.
- Assassination of prominent local figures and canal and roadways engineers.
- Bloody attacks on banks for looting and kidnapping purposes.
- Extortion of money from the rich.
- Demands for greater ransom after kidnapping the Hindu traders.
- Increase in frequency of bandhs and advent of communal riots.
- Village assemblies in certain areas had started projecting the militant points of views.
- The government functions and village panchayats were ordered to obey the dictates issued to conform to the Sikh tenets and ethics.
- Hindus were subjected to attacks in specified areas to compel them to flee their home and hearths.

1990 was a year of great political uncertainty, the Congress losing the elections and a non. Congress ministry taking over at the center. This may be reason for the terrorist depredations reaching the peak in Nov. 1990. The main incidents of terrorism are summed up here:

First Week : Nov. 1990

- Over 70 persons killed mainly in Gurdaspur and Taran Taran districts
- Rs. 3 lacs looted from banks

Second week : Nov. 1990

- Ten people were shot dead on 7 Nov. Bank looted in Jalandhar.

- Fire opened on Hardwar Express in Taran Taran district.
- Nine bus passenger and 25 others shot dead.
- 33 persons shot dead including 11 security force personnel in Faridkot and Ferozepur districts.
- 29 killed on 12 Nov. 12 RSS workers, 7 bus passengers, 3 IAF persons, and 7 other civilians
- Curfew and communal clashes in Jalandhar after reported desecration of the Granth Sahib.
- 29 people killed on 15 Nov. including 7 bus passengers.

Third week : Nov. 1990

- 11 RSS workers killed and 13 seriously injured in terrorist attacks in Killianwali in Faridkot district and 29 killed elsewhere on 17 Nov.
- 32 killed on 18/19 Nov. including 11 security force personnel.
- Communal clashes in Gurdaspur
- 12 killed in Amritsar, Train derailed, 21 killed on other parts, and Rs. 5.80 lacs looted on 20 Nov. A Satluj Yamuna Link (SYL) canal contractor was among the killed.
- 13 bus passenger gunned down at Ropar 19 killed elsewhere, including 11 terrorists on 22 Nov.
- SP Taran Taran with his three bodyguards blown up in his jeep by remotely controlled plastic mine. Ten others killed elsewhere.
- Fifteen gunned down in Jalandhar on 25 Nov. presumably as a retaliation against I desecration of the holy book last week.

Fourth Week : Nov. 1990

- Terrorists gunned down 7 in Ludhiana on 26 Nov. 50 others killed elsewhere in this week – two soldiers and one SPO (Special Police Officer) among them. Taran Taran and some other border areas placed under curfew.

It is important to note that terrorist violence in Punjab in Nov. 1990 had reached a stage where innocent could be targeted any day anywhere, with hardly any worry of police intervention. The terrorist attacks, a nearly daily affair, had reached Jalandhar and Ludhiana essentially Hindu-majority cities of Punjab, deliberately aimed at creating and fomenting communal trouble. "There were hardly any signs of anticipation or pre-emption on the part of the police inspite of daily occurrences of attacks on hapless citizenry".

What are the implications of such patterns of terrorist attacks and disruptive activities? Undoubtedly, the immediate targets of the terrorists are the security force, opponents of the terrorism, and innocent population, they are addressing their message to the Indian polity, and consequently it is the national pride that is the casualty. In sum, the two aspects add up to under mining the political systems, increasing social and economic tensions, and eroding the credibility of the government machinery. At this stage, even though terrorism was rampant and wide-spread. New Delhi envisaged no danger of declaration of a Sikh state as after the elimination of Bhindranwale, their was no leader tall enough to take this ultimate step. All that the terrorists were hoping to achieve was to keep the Punjab situation on the boil, create the Hindu-Sikh rift, and fill their coffers. The only party which gains from this horrendous situation is Pakistan, because not only it scores a propaganda point against India, painting it as an oppressor of minorities, it also keeps strategically important border state of India in turmoil and politically unstable.

This pattern of terrorism and its effects and overall gains for terrorists are tabulated here :

Events / Terrorists Acts	*Related to*	*Effect*	*Overall gains*
Assassinations	Liquidation of political opponents	Shock effect	Short term and limited
Communal riots	Alienation, migration and minorities	Anger resentment and destruction of property	Marginal effect on ethnic ratios on some areas
Bomb attacks	Indiscriminate destruction of life and property spreads scare with little effort	Shock, anger and fear	Very marginal
Events /	*Related to*	*Effect*	*Overall gains*

Terrorists Acts

Bank robberies and extortion	Collection of funds	Loss of confidence in authorities	Substantial monetary gains
Demands	Khalistan: Justice for Sikhs	Popular appeal for Sikhs, resentment in others	Moral isolation of Sikhs largely achieved
Arms and Financial assistance from abroad	Attacks on SF: Sustenance of movement attract new recruits	Large number of civil and para-military casualties	Increased state repression; demoralised SF
Attacks on SYL Engineers and Workers	Stoppage of work; Dharam Yudh	WK has suffered delays	Majot gain, though temporary

The Terrorist Infrastructure

Besides the names of four well-known groups and their leaders, one does not come across very much else of substance about the terrorist organisations in Punjab. In 1986, DG Police of Punjab JF Reberio had claimed that there were only 40 category 'A' terrorists and 200 others, "Eliminate them and the problem will be finished". Coming from a policeman of his eminence, it was an amazingly naive statement showing a total lack of understanding of the adversary. Early 1990s, intelligence reports put the number of terrorist groups between 85 and 93, with strength varying from 10 to 60, with a total of 728 automatic weapons in their possession. In 1989, the Punjab Government had said: "There are 229 hardcore militants, 941 non-hardcore, and 5000 unlisted terrorists in Punjab." The best that could be said about such widely differing numbers is that they better be left undeclared.

Leading terrorists groups are mentioned here

Terrorist Group	*Leader*
Khalistan Commando Force (KCF)	Paramjit Singh Panjwar
Bhindranwale Tiger Force of Khalistan (BTFK) or Bhindranwale Khalistan Liberation Tiger Force (BKLTF)	Gurcharan Singh Manochahal
Khalistan Liberation Force (KLF)	Gurjant Singh Budhsinghwala
Babbar Khalsa	Sukhdev Singh Babbar

The information on the groups given above is rather sketchy, and it is obvious that our intelligence agencies were not able to identify others; or alternatively, they had kept it under wraps. Generally the terrorist outfits draw there operational strength and flexibility from there comparatively smaller size, but that is characteristic of the groups that operate at random. But in case of Punjab, where the direction, orders, and weapons came from abroad on a regular basis, a more elaborate organisation has to be there. The infrastructure in such a case would comprise on internal organisation with a corresponding network across the border. Maj Gen Afsar Karim (1991) an expert in the field, drew an outline of the infrastructure that should have existed in 1989-90, piecing data from various published sources in the country and abroad. Unable to get the exact nomenclatures, he has named various controlling headquarters, groups or cells based upon their functional responsibilities. As the operational directives / instructions are to be received from outside, links and channels of physical and radio communications have to be established for functional coordination and control. At the ground level, you would have smaller groups with well-known fancy or catchy names, which are actually the operating outfits or gangs of marauders (mercenary hands) acting on orders. Most of these common criminals routinely lionised by the press as "dreaded terrorists", whom the police claims to eliminate from time to time are infact comparable to the "foot soldiers" that are easily replaceable and therefore easily dispensable.

The infrastructure and organisation for terrorism in the Punjab and their controlling and coordinating – headquarters in Pakistan/Punjab, along with the financing and media managing agencies (relevant, 1989–90) are outlined below, essentially gathered and collated from open sources. There is no rigidity about this organisation, which can undergo changes from time to time.

Organization and Group	*Tasks and Functions*
ISI (Punjab Cell) Pakistan	1. Policy Direction and overall control 2. Procurement, selection and sale of weapons and equipment 3. Intelligence information and psychological warfare

Organization and Group	*Tasks and Functions*
	4. Communication with and intelligence from direct contact groups 5. Control of and coordination with special action groups (SAG); specialised training, coordination with ISI, J&K and groups working there
Panthic committees: (Pakistan based and India based)	1. Policy coordination with the ISI, Punjab cell 2. Receipt of information and direction from the ISI and payments for the purchase of weapons 3. Raising finances outside India 4. Religious reorientation and indoctrination and refresher training of terrorists 5. Allotting operational tasks to various militant outfits 6. Rest, recreation and management of sanctuaries for outgoing and incoming terrorists
Border Contact Groups and Internal Contact Groups in Pakistan and India.	1. Transit of personnel, weapons and equipment 2. Collection of information and dissemination 3. Reconnaissance and vigil over borders and transit points 4. Coordination with Pak rangers and Field Units 5. Last minute instructions to transit personnel
Special Transit Groups (in their respective areas) in Punjab	1. Bomb explosions and IED attacks on railways 2. Robberies, kidnapping, selective assassinations, and collection of funds through extortions and threats 3. Propaganda, psywar and intelligence on police plans, civil disobedience, communal riots
Militant outfits Action groups	1. Carry out assigned tasks of terrorism in association with the specialised groups

Organization and Group	*Tasks and Functions*
	2. Passage of action reports to the controls
Special organisations (Areawise)	1. Logistic support in general; supplies, rations and local resources 2. Medical treatment and help
Non-Militant Semi-religious and Political Organisations	1. Temporary shelter after action 2. General information/propaganda and media management 3. Political coordination within Punjab 4. Welfare of families and dependents of terrorists killed 5. Coordination of means and methods of crossing 6. Handling incoming action reports 7. The internal contact groups, in addition, provide temporary shelter hide outs for personnel to join various militant groups on arrival from Pakistan
Intelligence, Monitoring, and Information cells.	1. To detect and breach the counter intelligence and counter infiltration measures of the adversary 2. Overall monitoring and final coordination of all terrorist activities, in synch with the separatist groups and organisations 3. Analysis of inflow and outflow of information 4. Media management and special instructions to special groups.

Course of Terrorism in Punjab after June 1984

Terrorism in Punjab had no serious difficulty in finding new recruits. Sikhism had historical martial traditions to fall back upon. In the given situation, there was certain urge to regain self-esteem after Operation Blue Star, and avenge the consequent wrongs inflicted upon the community. It was not only the highmindedness that impelled the youth to join the ranks of the terror brigade. It was also the lure of easy money that provided a major incentive. The money was pouring in not only from the ISI, but more so from the affluent expatriate Sikh community settled in UK, USA, Canada, Australia, et al. Then there was the much sought after image of a hero that the "boys" immediately assumed on joining the Dharam Yudh. Afterall they were fighting for their "Qaum". So it was no surprise that the unemployed, school dropouts, social misfits, frustrated retired Army and police officers and Jawans with little prospects of finding and jobs, joined the ranks of the militants – hoping to earn a lot of money and becoming local heroes. But it needs to be point out that there was no rush as such to join the terror stream. A vast majority of their co-religionists were never enamoured of the terrorist violence, and at later stage, atrocities against the Hindus, and 'suspected' informers amongst the Sikhs.

So initially it was the unemployed and the unemployable that came forward. But later, a better educated class, even some specialists started joining the terrorist organisations. Some joined the terrorist stream due to the belief that it was path of 'individual salvation'. The flow of the weapons and ammunition was assured through open market purchase in Pakistan. The main weapons and automatics used by the terrorists, like AK47, 54, 74 or 94, easy to carry and operate, were generally by procedure from Darah, an open arms market near Peshawar, at subsidised rates, courtesy ISI. Weapons like rockets, light and heavy machineguns, had a controlled supply, and were meant for specialized groups only. As none of these weapons required prolonged training, the turnover personnel were not a problem. There were camps in Pakistan/POK to train the men on these weapons and handling of the grenades, explosives, and IEDs.

Desertion from terrorist ranks was rare due to a variety of reasons. Firstly, initiation costs were heavy and the fresh recruits were made to understand its implication, including harsh and brutal reprisal not only against him but also against the entire family. Then, before joining a terrorist group each individual was required to commit some heinous crime to close his options of quitting. Given their deep faith, deserting the Dharam Yudh' is unimaginable. On the same ground, the sacred or religious shades of the terrorist's cult ensured unfailing and lasting fidelity. This factor also makes it difficult for intelligence to breach there organisation to obtain any information on their intentions and operational details. Yet again, as is common among most terrorist outfits, those who operate in the field possess very little information of value, most of them being unaware of the next man in the chain of command. Those who did have information of value were provided, in the manner of the LTTE practice, with cyanide capsule.

The organisational set-up at lower levels is centrifugal, with the "action groups" looking like a planetary system with the leader at the center. The leader, a self-styled Captain or Major, always had a stand-bye nominated, readily available to replace him. As mentioned earlier, all these are foot soldiers who can be readily replaced, without in any case impairing the operational or functional efficiency of the organisation. This and the religious tone of the daily discourse about their aims, create a kind of organisational dynamics which motivates the individual and the groups to carry on regardless of success or failure of the movement. In this kind of environment, violence perpetuates itself – feeding on itself.

The infrastructure at higher levels is altogether a different picture, being basically hierarchical and representing the strategic choice of the conflict. It is essentially oriented to create a means to achieve political objectives. Located outside India, it largely depended on lower echelons to create a desired level of violence and shock in Punjab. It was only then that the strategic aims woulc be achieved. These theoretical postulation notwithstanding, it is well-known that the secessionist situation in Punjab came nowhere near achieving its objectives. It may be apt to quote here, Thomas C Schelling a noted authority on such conflicts: "Bargaining process is based on power to hurt and intimidate as a substitute for the use of covert military force".

Deployment of Counter Terrorist Forces

Here is one view of some experts on the role and deployment of counter-terrorist forces in Punjab :

- Our Armed Forces and Para Military Forces are organized and trained for an armed response only, therefore neither the Army nor the Para military or the armed Police have any riot or mob control equipment worth the name. The option mostly boils down to either killing a large numbers of rioters/demonstrators or stand back and watch. On the other hand, compulsion to show quick results, long hours of duty in congested areas, boredom and restrictions on leave etc are demoralizing factors which induced harsh and unbalanced reactions. This situation can also lead to personnel vendettas, assaults, arson, rape and looting, if the duties in congested civilian areas are unduly prolonged. It is well-known now that the role played by the Army in Punjab during "Operation Blue Star" and operation "Wood Rose" had most unfortunate side effects besides giving spurts to terrorism.

- The armed response, moreover, generally comes when the battle of winning the heart and minds has already been lost. That is the reason why armed forces or paramilitary forces do not succeed in bringing about normalcy in such circumstances.
- So far as the Army in concerned, it is best to keep it away from demoralizing police work and use it only in its proper role of meeting overseas aggression, or against well-armed guerrillas. The paramilitary forces have to play the duel role of a policemen and soldier but there deployment in state posts, school buildings or police stations create avoidable problems with the locals. Moreover such locations become easy targets for terrorist attacks. It may be better to deploy these units away from congested areas as here they stop being a deterrent after a while, instead they become a cause of frequent clashes with the locals.

This extensive excerpt have been reported on purpose. It is surprising that such an opinion is held by some experts. It should really not deserve the dignity of a detailed rebuttal. A few remarks should suffice. The above opinion is not only simplistic but also misplaced, and mostly informed by ignorance. The Indian Army is the last resort when everything else has failed. It has been performing anti terrorist duties in the North East since the birth of our union. Likewise, Punjab terrorism could not have been brought to an end until the army came to the help of Punjab police ably by KPS Gill. In Kashmir, it has been doing a commendable job against the odds. Odd cases of collateral damage or misuse of powers placed in its hands by some aberrant individuals cannot be the reason for declaring it an unsuitable organisation to deal with the hard-core terrorists. Punjab or Kashmir terrorists were not "raw recruites", to be discussed as 'rioters' or 'demonstrators', rather they were hardened criminals trained abroad by the ISI. Has anyone commented this may about fitness of the Israeli Army to deal with the terrorists, or of the British Army to confront the IRA. In any case, the Indian Army is not only trained for such tasks, the Army Act has provisions for the Army to be deployed on "Aid to Civil Power" duty/responsibility.

The situation in Jammu and Kashmir is a little different. Here the Army units have been deployed along the LOC from early days. Its main task along this line has been to check Pak-incited infiltration of the jihadis and terrorists, even before the terrorism within Jammu and Kashmir had taken the present serious form. The routes of ingress of the infiltrators are well-known to the Army, and are well guarded. As there is sparse population in the areas contiguous to the LOC, the presence of the strangers and outsiders is easily detected. The role of the military deployed along the LOC thus has been quite effective.

In the later years, particularly from 1989 onwards, the deployment of military within Kashmir had to be augmented as terrorism started taking omenous form. Presently (mid-2007), the state police, military and para-military units are operating in a well-coordinated structure under Unified Command Headquarters, presided over by the state Chief Minister.

Fighting Terrorism Politically

The young Prime Minister Rajiv Gandhi displayed great statesmanship and political courage to stem the terrorism in Punjab by signing the 1985 agreement with the tallest, most sober, and mature leader among the Akalis, Sant Harchand Singh Longowal. As was expected in such situations, the political parties did not act united at this crucial moment in Punjab's history and destiny. The Opposition BJP dubbed it "surrender to terrorists". The Akalis themselves split vertically, as it turned out the ruling faction of Longowal, Barnala and Badal had not taken into confidence other top Akali leaders like Tohra.

So the Akali's immediately split, amoeba–like. Consequently the agreement, a symbol of brave statesmanship, divided the

Sikh opinion sharply. Expectedly, the terrorists wrested the initiative, and upped the ante by aggravating the terrorist violence to unprecedented levels. The Sant paid the price for his brave act of signing the agreement for the Akali Party, he was shot dead by the terrorists.

In another act of political courage, the Center conducted the assembly poll in Punjab on schedule inspite of the terrorist threats, against holding them and dire warnings of the political Pandits. The Akali Dal (Longowal) won-handsomely and Barnala formed the government in Sep 1985. It had not yet firmly got control of the situation when it had to order "Operation Search" in April 1986 to flush out the elements from the Golden Temple who had made a declaration of Khalistan from within the complex. Expectedly within the Akali Dal there was strong opposition to this operation: "How could we do such a thing when we had opposed Operation Blue Star with our own blood?". It resulted in a split again. The mindless killings by the terrorists increased, plunging the state again into darkness. Virtual break down of the administrative machinery invited the imposition of the Presidents' Rule on 11 May 1987.

The Situation During 1989 and 1990

With the imposition of Presidents Rule and exponential increase in inhuman atrocities by terrorists, we are entering the worst phase of secessionist movement in Punjab. Various peace initiatives and other measures during 1987–89 period, including special political packages failed to improve the situation. If some experts and human rights advocates blamed this conundrum on continued harsh police measures and draconian laws which affected the common people more than the terrorists, others blamed it on the daily killings by the terrorists. "The ad nauseam demands by the opposition and the arm chair commentators for harsh anti-terrorist measures kept on vitiating the atmosphere". The slogans and messages like "bullet for bullet" and fighting an "all-out war", coming from the tough talking DGP Reberio, did not go well with some people. It was asserted by the critics that such an approach created a national mood "which glossed over illegal methods by the police and the excesses committed by it liquidate not only the terrorists but also the suspects". Even if such strong sentiments are not shared by a majority of the Civvy Street, it still should be a cause of concern to us. Some went as far as to blame the state and the police for "brutalising or harassing the common man". It might appear perverse that the phrases and terms which should be rightly be applied to mindless inhuman violence perpetrated by the terrorists are actually applied passionately to the police and even army fighting the virulent curse of terrorism, but there it is!

Be that as it may, not withstanding all the counter-terror measures, the terrorism grew in strength and reach. 1998 proved to be the "bloodiest" year since 1984. Every official resolved to "crush" terrorism proved premature. "The Punjab Police Chief and many of his inspector generals committed to show results, made tall claims, juggled with figures and told many untruths". All this, to no avail. Some asserted that if anything, alienation of the common Sikhs increased because of these methods while the terrorists became martyrs and heroes in their eyes.

In 1989, if the terrorists committed even worse atrocities, the critics thought "corruption by 'vigilante groups' and 'killer squads' created havoc in the countryside as they robbed banks and extorted money much like terrorists." Was it an exaggeration when an observer said; "To many villages a terrorist gang appeared to be more benign than a police and their cohorts." Unfortunately, the differences between senior police officers and frequent circumventing of laws came in the open when Chiman Lal, resigned in protest against large scale repression ordered by KPS Gill, the police Chief Chiman Lal an upright and efficient police officer and held in high regard by the people made an important point, saying: "There was the break down of the judicial process in the state.......the police has become the arbiters of peoples faith". At a press conference before his resignation, Chiman Lal observed: "I find that people by and large against terrorists, but they are not withus either, which reflects on the lack of professional competence on the part of the SF and the government. We must remember that we can only contain terrorism. We must take care never to alienate people."

It seems such sober words were never paid much attention to. Some critics and particularly the human rights activists went as far as to say: "Efforts of various secular organisations like Kirit Kisan Union Association for Democratic Rights and Bhagat Singh Research Centre were drowned in the babble of "bullet for bullet" kind of slogans. The Governor and the police encouraged UNDERCOVER merchants of death and depended on weapons of torture to subdue terrorism. No wonder such policies drove Punjab further into the stranglehold of terrorist violence in the 1990.

Given the violence, people's response to come forward to help the authorities was obviously mute. There was a certain cynicism in the air, perhaps born of people's frustration exemplified by such comments and events: "Most people by now knew that the police would be nowhere near when the terrorists attack them but would appear on the scene later, to extort money and harass people. Governor Ray had a taste of such bitterness when a public meeting he had called near Batala turned into an anti-police rally. The people's anger and resentment showed no bounds and nearly forty *Sarpanches* who had resigned their posts in protest against 'state terrorism', called the whole policy a matter of shame. Most village elders also came out against the police's atrocities and repression, corruption, torture and harassment".

A critic had then put it rather felicitously, "Mr. Ray of course did nothing to set matters right and the advocates of the so-called tough policy continued to call the shots throughout 1989. Inevitably the chickens came home to roost, in 1990 – with a vengeance."

The terrorists when they stuck back in the 1990 were better organised than ever before, with violence rising to new heights—ten murders a day. They had gained the confidence rather audacity to attack the well armed security forces with deadly effects. They could target the interior areas at will, aimed at fomenting communal trouble to widen the tension between the Hindus and the Sikhs. The Punjab police unfortunately were, once again unable to counter or anticipate the terrorist killings due to lack of efficient intelligence and proper coordination. The Governor and the Police Chief blamed each other periodically during 1990 when Punjab was literally burning. It was clear that the counter terrorism strategy of the government at the Centre and Chandigarh between 1987 and 1990 had failed to achieve its ends, and the terrorist were running a parallel government, a–la Bhindrawale I the first half of the 1980s. In this frustrating situation the Centre decided on a whole sale change of its instruments.

A new Governor was sent to Chandigarh, and Mr. Verma was moved to Himachal Pradesh, and so was a new Police Chief, a reputed go getter and known to have handled equally turbulent militants in Assam with better results, and perhaps a little more balanced than his predecessor. Having expressed his willingness to talk to anyone without reservations, the Prime Minister met Simranjit Singh Mann as the representative of the Akali Dal. Nothing came out of this meeting and the drift continued. Violence had peaked in 1990 as the following table shows.

Year	*Killings*	*Other crimes*
1988	3074	265 cases of kidnapping were registered; a higher number remained unreported.
1989	2729	394 cases of abduction reported.
1990	3784	A large No. of people reportedly paid the terrorists a ransom ranging from Rs. 1 to 5 lakhs.

Weapons with the Terrorists

- 4000 automatic of assorted varieties
- A quantity of RPG's, plastic mines, AT Rockets, and Stinger missiles.

Morale of Terrorists

During this period the terrorist seem to be having an upper hand, against the government (read all its anti-insurgent, counter- terrorist agencies). They insisted that both boys and girl students in schools and colleges adhere to the dress code decreed by them. The violators were threatened by serious consequences. Terrorists' writ ran on the campuses.

During this period, terrorist gangs could operate freely in broad daylight, mounted on jeeps, at least in districts like Taran Taran, Amritsar, Ferozepur etc. – committing murders, holding open courts to dispense justice in the territories under their government imposing taxes and extorting money. Their morale was high.

Administration Functional or Dysfunctional?

If the terrorists were running a parallel government or almost, the civilian administration was obviously not in good health. Besides the terrorists granted special powers to tackle terrorism, too was bringing a bad name to the government essentially through the misuse of these powers against the common man in some cases. The normal chain of civil administration had seriously been damaged.

Under this situation, it was no surprise that the normal collection of taxes and revenues was in a poor state, while taxes and collection collected by the terrorist were on an increase. The courts and their officials had been rendered helpless and ineffective, if not altogether redundant, with terrorists holding their own courts. Critics often accused the Police of dispensing their own brand of justice. Obviously there was hardly any effective governance, and political uncertainty had out he bureaucrats in an in a spot becoming more cautious than ever. The quick changes in Governors and their advisors, as also extraneous political pressures had worsened the situation. The brave pronouncements from time to time notwithstanding, the administration from Governor downwards had succumbed to the terrorists' threats. In this situation of grave uncertainty and insecurity, no industry or business would set up shop in the state. Expectedly the President's Rule imposed on the state in 1990 lacked will to administer. It was no surprise that a meeting of the Governing Council in Nov 1990 and attended by all senior functionaries degenerated into a free for all, between the police and the civil administration. With the Governor being a mute spectator, the meeting turned into a fiasco, a not so uncommon an occurrence in those difficult days. The administration had reached its nadir – to use a cliche!

The government offices and estates were in a grip of persistent extremist propaganda. A very larger number bought their peace by contributing to the 'cause', others paying reluctantly. The militants had recognized their agents in all departments, and some of them were rather quiet while others were highly vocal. Thus the police and intelligent services to had been effectively penetrated, but, on the other hand, the government seemed unable to break into the terrorists ranks.

Consequently, the government and the police planned operations were known to the terrorists in advance but the state remained largely unaware of their moves. There were frequent reports of the terrorists asking the army, BSF, and CRPF men while on leave to contribute to their cause. A certain degree of demoralization had already affected the ranks of the Punjab police after the terrorist had started targeting their families back in their villages/homes.

MEDIA AND TERRORISM

This was the time when the press and radio had generally fallen to the coercion and threats from terrorists. More than two dozen journalists and many lawyers had been felled by this time. The media stood compromised through coercion and had frequently been forced to publish advertisements projecting the terrorist's point of view. They had laid down the code of conduct for the media to keep it on the straight line. The assassination of RK TALIB station director, All India Radio Chandigarh for not following the code of conduct laid down by the terrorists was a grim reminder to the journalists that they meant business and had the means and will to enforce it anywhere, anytime. Most dailies and the All India Radio and television were, as some media watchers suggested, using the term militant or its equivalent in Hindi or Punjabi, as had been dictated by the terrorists in the code. Hindi News broadcasts too had been stopped on the dictates of the militants. A scholar was to put it tersely : "All this only shows the importence of the state... well, that is what terrorism and insurgency is all about".

The code of conduct laid down by the Panthic Committee (Sohan Singh faction), effective December 1990 ran as follows:

- All those struggling for the establishment of Khalistan must be described as militant, Khalistani Freedom Fighters or Khalistani Mujahideens – never as terrorists, extremists, or alleged terrorists
- Panthic Committee should not be described as "Pak-based Panthic Committee" but simple as Panthic Committee
- New agency too should use the word militant and withdraw their services to any newspaper which substitutes this word with terrorist

- News agency must give more news from the "land of Khalistan"
- Journalists will have complete freedom to report the weakness of the military and their organization
- Only the chiefs of five militant organizations can seek an explanation from the editors, newspapers and agencies. At the district level, the right rests in district level leaders, so that no journalist has any cause for complaint
- Journalists can address the complaints to the Panthic Committee. They can also appeal against "death penalty" to the committee which will have the final say.

The statement on code warned the journalists reporting from the "Land of Khalistan" of memorable punishment if they violated the code. One papers that faced the terrorist boldly was the Hind Samachar, and paid for that boldness with the assassination of its two editors – father and son, that is Lala Jagat Narain (84) and Romesh Chander (58). *The Tribune* of Chandigarh too earned kudos for its honest reporting. There were others too like the *Statesman, Hindu, Asian Age*, and *Indian Express* but these were essentially based outside Punjab.

Plight of Minorities

Gripped by extreme insecurities at least 1500 families had moved out of small and medium sized towns. Those who stayed were under a constant shadow of death and fear of torture. Incidentally, they were the soft targets for the terrorists, whom the police were unable to provide even a modicum of security and protection. Their migration was also forced by the terrorists for well etched motives, acquisition of cheap land the property on easy terms, even free, ostensibly for Sikhs who would "certainly migrate to Punjab from other parts of India once Khalistan was established", or even before that climatic event.

The government had failed to stem the spread of malfeasance and the hapless Hindus continued abandoning their homes and hearth for uncertain life in camps in Delhi or elsewhere. The Sikhs were constantly being urged to move to Punjab from other parts of India, not only by the Khalistan propagandists but also by the Sikh diaspora settled abroad.

Security Forces and their State of Morale

250–300 companies of paramilitary and armed police, deployed in Punjab on counter terrorism duties during the period proved insufficient. Consequently, men had to do long hours of duty without proper arrangements for leave, turn over, rest and relaxation. They were proving ineffective against the well motivated terrorists. The terrorist's successes were correspondingly producing demoralization amongst the security forces. In addition, the compulsion to show results at any costs had created indiscipline and also use of excessive and occasionally illegal force against the militants which only aggravated the situation and brought about the alienation of the Sikh population.

There were allegation of rampant corruption against the extortion of money from innocent civilians on the pain of action against them for suspected terrorists activities. They were also becoming prone to the lure of "smuggling" to make some collateral monetary advantages. Their morale was suffering due to their inability to check the movement of arms and militants across the borders. (It also must be admitted that there were reports of such 'corruption' even amongst the ranks of the Army personnel in the later stages of Operation Woodrose launched after Operation Blue Star). The ultras were obviously emboldened by the increasing public resentment against this corruption and the consequent inability of these forces to control the mounting terrorists' violence. It was an unhappy situation for the state faced with the insurgent violence on the one hand, and lethargic performance of the security forces on the other.

Active groups during 1990

- Khalistan Commando Force believed to be well-armed and well-financed. Led by Paramjit Singh Pannu (KCF)
- Khalistan Liberation Force (KLF). It was led by Gurjant Singh Budhsinghwala
- Bhindranwala Tiger Force of Khalistan (BTFK), led by Rachpal Singh Sangha had support of other splinter groups
- Babbar Khalsa, once a part of Akhand Kirtani Jatha active against the Nirankaris, it was then (1990) led by

Sukhdev Singh and active amongst educated classes to drum up support for Pakistan

- Sikh Student Federation (Bittu Group), it was led by Daljit Singh Bittu, and was working in close cooperation with Babbar Khalsa
- Panthic Committee (Sohan Singh Group), five member committee led by Sohan Singh. It had the backing of almost all active groups.
- Panthic Committee (Manochahal), it was led by Gurbachan Singh Man Ochahal, an active militant. It worked in close cooperation with the BTF and the KCF (Raajasthani Group), led by Gurjant Singh Rajasthani.
- All India Sikh Students Federation (AISSF), comparatively moderate, they were largely involved in political work.

Was Punjab Police Guilty of Secret/Illegal Cremations?

The National Human Rights Commission (NHRC) ordered 10 October 2006 that the State Government pay compensation to the families of 1051 persons who were among the 2097 killed and secretly cremated by police between 1984-1994—"a period when the State's police force fought a no-holds-barred battle with militants.[8]" The government has been ordered to pay Rs. 1.75 lakh in each case.

It needs to be emphasized that the police and its retired fraternity have staunchly opposed this inquiry by the NHRC that started ten years ago (in 1997). The retired police officers assert they fought the insurgency under extremely trying circumstances—victims and general public would not come forward to stand witness to the crimes committed right under their nose; senior lawyers would not come forward to take up prosecution; and worst, most judges were unwilling to hand out condign punishments to the criminals, citing insufficient evidence. Right or wrong, analysts were sympathetic to police, believing they were doing a good job in difficult situations. It is also believed that if the police during those hopeless days did something wrong, or indeed more responsible for an excess here and there, it was done either inadvertently or under impossible circumstances.

But for KPS Gill and his boys, Punjab would have gone under Civil administration was dysfunctional and fear of terrorist was ruling supreme. Not only the policemen were being targeted, even their families back home were being killed or under constant threat from the terrorists. Under these circumstances, it was the leadership of Gill and sincere effort put in by his senior officers that Punjab was pulled back from the brink. If those police officers are now hunted for the so-called excesses committed during those harrowing days, it is bad for police morale, and even more portentously, it is bad for country's future. Few officers will go all, playing with their lives, if India again faces such situation. Authorities should not be swayed by those loud-mouthed and over-zealous human rights activists who start baying for the blood of the so-called 'guilty' officers who are charged with 'trampling over the human rights of the hardened criminals'. If some innocent people indeed have suffered in police operations against the terrorists during these days, they must compensated in every possible ways, one of which is to pay compensation to the kin of the victims. This is exactly what the NHRC has done, as detailed above. But doing anything beyond that will be uncalled for. The demand of certain sections that "the Commission also fix responsibility of individual police officers for the killings" will do more harm than the good. It is, public knowledge that a senior officer—an SSP—had committed suicide for humiliation while under trial for 'excesses' committed during the early 1990s. Any such happenings again would affect the morale of the police.

It may be noted that on the orders of the NHRC, Punjab has already Rs. 2.5 lakhs each to the families of 194 persons who were confirmed to have died in police custody and cremated illegally. But there are many that have been identified but there is no proof that they were in police custody at the time of their death.

The NHRC has been investigating the 'mass cremations' for nearly ten years. As a result of the arbitration, its first order came two years ago. "The lid on the secret mass cremations by police was blown by Jaswant Singh Khalra, an Amritsar-based human rights activist who disappeared under mysterious circumstances." Some ascribed his disappearance to the fact that he knew too much and police saw a future threat in him because he had trailed the mass cremations around Taran Taran and Majitha—hot beds of insurgency. After his disappearance, his wife and friends pursued the case in the Supreme Court.

Notes

1. The Author must proudly exclaim the fact that this unit (1 Sikh) belongs to his famed (Sikh) Regiment he was Commissioned into in 1957.
2. It should not be out of place here to remind some Left and Liberal Indians including some journalists of that ilk that Pakistan has not given up its game in Punjab. Period acts of terrorism are still being perpetrated by militants belonging to terrorist outfits like the BKI and KZF, and Pakistan hand can be seen behind them without too much difficulty.
3. Cited, Karim (1991) : 3.
4. It should be an eye opener for the scholars/analysts who assert that "majority of the Valley Muslims want to break away from India" to know the result of an opinion poll conducted by a reputed US think-tank, by no means a sympathiser or friend of India, among the Kashmir Muslims in 1996. Majority of Muslims, 65 per cent, were opposed to joining Pakistan and keen to continue to remain part of the Indian Union! But no nation allows, and should allow, such a referendum among a section of its population—linguistic, religious or ethnic.
5. The other view is that with Pakistan carrying out its incessant and unrelenting religion-driven and ideology-based espousal of its case for integration of Kashmir with it, the valley Muslims were bound to be carried off their feet literally. A Mullah/Maulvi can brain-wash a faithful into believing anything on the bases of Quranic teachings as interpreted by him alone. In Empirical terms, we have seen during the last two decades or so how easy it is to convert a faithful into a suicide bomber. Not to speak of Iraq, where suiciding bombling is a routine, almost daily occurring, the phenomenon has become well-known in Afghanistan too, where it was unheard of till a couple of years ago.

   In addition, it was also low intensity but regular, well-planned terrorism fomented and carried out by Pakistan and its intelligence agencies, particularly the ISI, since the 1948-49 ouster of its occupation forces from Jammu and Kashmir that fructified into a full-blown rebellion starting 1989-90 and led by fundamentalist, jehadi separatists leadership, helped financially, brain-washed ideologically, well trained in the art of perpetrating death and destruction through terrorist violence and guerrilla warfare and supplied with appropriate weaponry, IED, grenades and RDX, was let loose in Jammu and Kashmir by the 'famed' ISI. Not withstanding all these gloomy pictures, what should not be forgotten is that a large majority of Kashmiri Muslims have been exercising their franchise in the face of death threats from these merchants of death. In the last Assembly poll, they not only threw out over-confident Farooq Abdullah and gave power to a Congress-PDP combine, and more significantly, the brave voters reached the polling booths at the pain of death and occasionally through bursting bullets and exploding grenades. It is easy to be cynical for the arm-chair critics but they should appreciate the faith of a common man in Jammu and Kashmir in the power of ballot over the bullet. This is the strength of Indian democracy.

6. Karim (1991): 36.
7. Where were all the NGOs and loud and fierce opponents of the 'moral police' who today (2006-2007) take to streets if the state or some religious groups—only and especially from some Hindu organisations—want a particular book, film, painting, song etc. to be banned because they feel it offends their religious sensitivities and emotions. Their quiescence against the terrorists' excesses and murderous violence is understand- able for its vocal condemnation can cost them physical attacks, or even life. It is only appropriate that silence is the preferred option in such dire situation. Why only these publicity-seeking NGOs, some critics/analysts have accused even the media barons, government officials, and the judiciary of suffering from the same self-preservation syndrome.
8. Aasha Khosa, *Indian Express*, 11 Oct. 2006.

8

Present Situation in Punjab : Far From Comforting

Khalistan insurgency was eliminated by 1993 under the dynamic leadership of KPS Gill, fully supported by the political leadership under Chief Minister Beant Singh. Situation was peaceful for some years subsequently.

But an odd incident of terrorist violence started happening by the turn of the 21st century. This chapter records some select incidents of terrorism perpetrated by the Khalistan terrorist outfits during the last one year: June 2006 to June 2007. Some related events and issues also have been discussed besides the incidents of terrorism.

Punjab Terrorist Brought from the US: June 2006

Kulber Singh Kulbeera alias Barapind of the Khalistan Commando Force was brought to India on night 18/19 June 2006 from the US by a Punjab Police team, following his extradition ordered by the competent American Court.

His extradition is the culmination of nine years of efforts by Interpol India and Ministries of Home and External Affairs, to bring him to face the law of the land, a CBI release said on 19 June.

Kulbeera is wanted by the Punjab Police in about 20 cases, ranging from mass murder to snatching of weapons from the police, killing of police personnel and bank dacoity. Kulbeera fled the country on a false passport.

Infiltration though Punjab Worries BSF: Oct. 2006

DG BSF AK Mitra on 7 Oct. 2006 expressed serious concern over the recent attempts by Pakistan-based terrorists to enter

India through Rajasthan and Punjab sectors—the 'fenced-border' stretch which did not report a single infiltration bid in the last 10 years.

Referring to the 14 September incident where the BSF foiled first attempt by terrorists to infiltrate into India through Amritsar sector, Mitra told a daily[1]: This is a matter of concern for us and me are taking it seriously. It was not clear if that attempt was a one-off affair or beginning of a trend.

The BSF, deployed on the entire western border along Jammu and Kashmir, Punjab, Rajasthan and Gujarat, killed two persons including a LET militant in that first infiltration bid on 14 September.

The second incident was reported from Sherpura outpost in Sriganganagar district of Rajasthan on 24 September, when the BSF killed three militants during a night long gun fight.

The use of these low-key western sectors as crossing/infiltration points assumes significance as it underscores the fact that level of infiltration through Jammu and Kashmir may not be a reliable index of Pakistan's willingness to clamp down on jihadis crossing into India.

Intelligence agencies point out that the past years have seen ISI increasingly using Bangladesh to push terrorists into India. The use of these two sectors, Punjab and Rajasthan, is sure to add to the worries of the security establishment of the nation.

Pak Man from US Helped Sikh Ultras: Prosecutors

Federal prosecutors on 4 Dec. 2006 said Pakistani living in New York wired money and tried to send foot soldiers to a Sikh militant outfit Khalistan Commando Force (KCF) aimed at violently forcing India's government into letting the group form its own state.

Khalid Awan knew that $25,000 that two Sikh businessmen gave him to transfer to a KCF leader in 2001 "was for bad things and that innocent people would die", federal prosecutor Lawrence Ferazani said.[2]

Ferazani was speaking in Brooklyn Federal Court during opening arguments of Awani's trial on counts of providing material support or resources to terrorists, conspiracy to provide material support or resources to terrorists and money laundering to promote terrorism.

If convicted on all counts, Awan faces a maximum of 55 years in prison. He was detained shortly after the 9/11 attacks as a material witness. While in prison, Ferazani said Awan recruited fellow inmate Harjit Singh to join the KCF by introducing him to leader Paramjit Singh Panjwar through phone calls from the prison.

Awan's lawyer, Khurrum Wahid, said his client was "guilty by association" because he had invited Panjwar to his sister's wedding on a visit to Lahore. "They did not have a criminal relationship, they had a completely personal relationship, Wahid said, adding Awan transferred the money from a US bank account to a Pakistani account that were both in his name.

- The Verdict. The US Federal Jury on 21 Dec. 2006 convicted the Pakistani, Awan, for providing financial aid to the KCF, which has been responsible for thousands of deaths in India. He could face a maximum of 45 years in jail, as already mentioned above.

After two weeks of trial, the Jury found Khalid Awan guilty for links with the KCF. Awan is said to have provided money and financial services to the KCF.

He will be sentenced on 7 March 2007.

Pakistani in US Convicted of Aiding Khalistanis: 20 Dec. 2006

A Pakistani, Khalid Awan, living in New York has been convicted on 20 Dec. by a Federal Jury for providing money to the Khalistani Commando Force (KCF), a terrorist outfit that carried out the assassination of the then Punjab Chief Minister Beant Singh and was held responsible for hundreds of deaths in India in the 1980s and 1990s. US Attorney Roslynn R Manskopf described the verdict/judgement as part of the "global battle" on terror.

Convicted on 20 Dec. after a two-week trial, Khalid faces a maximum of 45 years in prison when he is sentenced on 7 March 2007 by US District Judge Charles P. Sifton.

The Attorney said: "The war on terror is a global battle. We will not permit individuals in our jurisdiction to finance terorrist groups responsible for murder and violence in any part of the world. To succeed in war on terror, we and our partners around the world have to view support of terrorism anywhere as an affront to peace-loving people everywhere."

The US Attorney Office for the Eastern District of New York and the FBI's Joint Terrorism Task Force began investigation in 2003 after a report from an inmate at the Metropolitan Detention Centre in Brooklyn, where Khalid was incarcerated on federal credit card fraud charges.

Khalid often boasted of his relations with Paramjit Singh Panjwar, the leader of the KCF and one of the ten most wanted fugitives in India, the other prisoners told investigators. The government evidence at trial included the recordings of "Khalid's prison telephone calls to Panjwar in Pakistan, in which Khalid introduces the inmate as a potential recruit for the KCF; statements by Khalid admitting that he sent hundreds of thousands of dollars to KCF, and testimony by two New York area fund raisers for the KCF who stated that they delivered money to Khalid's residence.

Some—credulous—Indians have come to believe that the Khalistani movement has died in India early 1990s with KPS Gill's Herculean exertions. Its protagonists and leaders are not only active and keeping it alive in Europe and North American countries, but it has its passionate supporters even working for it within the country. SS Mann is only one prominent name in a fairly long list. Then we have some ex-prominent Khalistanis working in Punjab to achieve their goal through democratic means—fighting elections for Punjab Assembly.[3]

Complacence in such issues of serious implications for country's integrity is outrightly dangerous. Political class must beware of it. In combating more serious threat of Islamist terrorism, India can ill afford to be swing about this lesser evil for now.

Is ISI Attempting to Revive Militancy in Punjab? Dec. 2006

India cannot afford to be complacent over Punjab. Not only is the ISI active, if some recent reports are to be believed, in fomenting trouble in the state, even some Khalistani elements are trying their best to revive the separatist fire in Punjab.

Such questions and concerns no longer remain of academic concerns to the analysts and scholars ensconced in their cloistered chambers if one understands the implications of a report in a daily in its (Wednesday) 27 Dec. 2006 issue: "Three terrorists belonging to the International Sikh Youth Federation (ISYF) were arrested in Jalandhar over the weekend. RDX and ammunition were recovered from their person."[4]

Punjab Police was understandably ruffled when caught three Babbar Khalsa International (BKI) militants in Fatehgarh Sahib district of Punjab in July 2005 in the wake of the twin blasts in cinema halls in Delhi. Then in August and September, they succeeded in nabbing infiltrators carrying huge arms and ammunition along the otherwise peaceful stretch of the fenced borders in Punjab and Rajasthan.

The arrests and seizure in Jalandhar led the agencies to take a relook at the interrogation details of BKI militant Jagtar Singh Hawara, who had disclosed details about Pakistani intelligence agency ISI's efforts to revive militancy in Punjab. Hamara, arrested in the wake of twin Delhi blasts, had told his interrogators that ISI was not only trying to push in arms and ammunition through the border but was also contacting sympathisers of the Khalistan movement outside India.

After arresting three ISYF (Rode Group) militants—Paramjit Singh Dhaddi (a UK citizen), Jaswinder Singh and Amolak Singh—from different places in Jalandhar district, Punjab Police on 24 Dec. 2006 claimed that "the group was planning to disrupt next year's Assembly (Feb. 2007) polls." Although the arrested militants "have so far not disclosed as to how they procured arms, ammunition and explosives, including 11 kg. of RDX, security agencies suspect it is part of the consignment from across the border meant for different militant groups including the BKI in Punjab.

Sources in the MHA said the Centre was concerned about such developments, as they have serious security implications for the nation. The role of the BKI in the twin blasts in Delhi cinemas (in 2005) was an eye opener indicative of presence of splinter groups of the pro-Khalistan militant outfits.

Since then, the security agencies were keeping a vigil. The Jalandhar arrest could eventually afford them a clear picture of the attempts made by the subversive and secessionist elements abroad, say in Pakistan, EU and the US, and within the country.

One opinion among the analysts is that by making a bid to revive militancy in Punjab, Pakistan might have been aiming at diverting global attention from the extent of the 'Islamic'—the Muslim intellectuals and intelligentsia following them, prefer the term "Islamist'—terrorism in India. It is an undisputed fact that during the heyday of militancy in Punjab, there were close links between the ISI and pro-Khalistan forces. Their close working relationship even outside India had been established with a number of Pakistanis being held for aiding terrorists directly or indirectly.

Mann Seeks UN Travel Documents: Dec. 2006

Radical Sikh politician Simranjit Singh Mann is seeking international travel documents from the UN. Mann who has been looked many times on charges of sedition and was closely associated with the Khalistan Movement in the 1980s and early 1990s, said he has consistently been denied a passport by the Indian state.[5]

His passport was first confiscated when he resigned as Punjab Police officer in protest after the Indian Army stormed the Sikh Golden Temple in 1984. Temporarily restored in1999, it was confiscated again after he was booked on fresh charges of sedition for making provocative public speeches at Amritsar in 2005.

Mann complained that despite the fact that he was never been convicted of any criminal offence, he was recently directed by the High Court at Chandigarh to submit a written undertaking that he would refrain from activities that could lower India's prestige while travelling abroad. He felt it was a humiliating condition for restoring his passport and Indian government was openly violating the International Covenant on Human Rights as well as denying his constitutional rights as a citizen by continuing to restrict his movement.

Mann Gets Clean Chit : 2006

After 15 long years of trial, a city court at Patiala House, Delhi acquitted Shiromani Akali Dal (Amritsar) President Simranjit Singh Mann in a TADA case filed against him in 1991.

Mann was charged with giving provocative speeches at Gurudwara Bangla Sahab, advocating the establishment of a separate state of Khalistan, and justifying the assassination of Prime Minister Indira Gandhi.

A city court had dismissed the case in 2002 after the prosecution failed to bring witnesses against Mann. But the police challenged the dismissal in Supreme Court and the case was reopened on its direction. Additional Sessions Judge Ravinder Kaur acquitted the accused as the prosecution again failed to produce enough evidence to prove him guilty.

His supporters raised slogans after the acquittal. Mann alleged that his image has been tarnished because of the case.

Mann, a 1967 batch IPS officer, had resigned from the post of CISF Commandant during Operation Blue Star in 1984. He had then formed his own political party, Shiromani Akali Dal (Amritsar).

Samjhauta Express Blast: BKI hand? Feb. 2007

From the investigations carried out so far in the 18 Feb. 2007 blast in two eaches of 4001 Delhi-Attari (Samjhauta Express) special train near Panipat in Haryana, security agency reckon the culprits/assailants may be from the states neighbouring the capital of New Delhi. Sources disclosed on 20 February that "it does not seem to be the work of the usual suspects—Pakistani or Kashmiri based outfits like the LET or HM.

The Punjab-based Babbar-Khalsa-International (BKI) seems to have come under the scanner of the security agencies. Experts believe explosives recovered from the Samjhauta Express hint at the involvement of locals in the blasts. Potassium nitrate, the explosive used in the blast, is easily available in the market.[6] A Delhi Police official said "nowadays it has become a lot easy to employ locals for committing such crimes."

Joint Commissioner (Special Cell), Delhi Police, Karnal Singh said, "We are assisting the Haryana Police in their investigations in regard to the bomb blasts but can't comment on anything as they are the prime investigators."

The police is also relying on the statements given by the victims and the eye witnesses.

The toll in the blasts in two coaches on 18 February has risen to 66 only18 bodies were identified till 20 February.

Heavy Polling in Slain BKI Chief's Village: 24 Feb. 2007

It should indeed be interesting and instructing to revisit the village of once dreaded BKI Chief Sukhdev Singh Babbar. This can be vouchsafed by the journalist who on 24 Feb. 2007 witnessed the Assembly poll Dassuwal, near Valtoha, just 4 km. from the Pakistan border in the Khem Karan sector.

"There was time when the name of Sukhdev Singh Babbar, slain chief of the BKI, would strike terror in the minds of the people and police alike". But in his ancentral village of Dassuwal, it was an atmosphere of festivity with *langar* (community kichen) arranged by both SAD and Congress workers on 24 February.

And to imagine Dassuwal had boycotted the poll in 1992. In this 2007 Assembly poll, 90 per cent of the 1,248 voters exercised their franchise.

As the individuals go, Angrej Singh, 72, visually impaired brother of the BKI Chief Sukhdev Singh, must be the most conspicuous man to cast his vote in Dassuwal. He sat in the election camp of the SAD (B) till the end of polling. He said: "The time has changed. I am a votary of democracy. That is why I have been canvassing for the victory of my party."[7]

Harbans Singh, who accompanied Angreg Singh and is cousin to him and Sukhdev Singh, said: "At least 70 relatives of Mehal Singh Babbar live in this village."

Narinder Singh, a resident of Dassuwal said Angrej Singh had given protection to the Hindu families at the time when the militancy was at its peak.

Two Khalistani Militants Held at Delhi: 23 March 2007

A suspected Khalistani militant, Jagdev Singh, and his associate, Gurdeep Singh Lahoria, were arrested by the Special Cell of Delhi Police on 23 March 2007 with heroin worth crores of rupees.

The two, believed by the police to be members of Khalistan Zindabad Force (KZF) and actively involved in drug trafficking in the capital, were arrested from near the Mother Diary in

Pandav Nagar area of East Delhi on a secret information, when they were waiting to deliver the contraband to somebody.

4 Kg. heroin, recovered from the duo is worth more than rupees four crore in the international market.

A police officer claimed that Lahoria was involved in the cycle blasts that rocked Delhi in Dec. 1996 and the explosions on board the Jhelam Express near Ambala Cantt.

Police says Lahoria admitted to them that he, alongwith his associate Balbir Singh, had planted the bombs in 1997. Arrested the same year in connection with these bombs, he was in Jail till 2003. After his release, he came in contact with one Daya Singh Lahoria. In concert with some of his friends, he (Gurdeep) started supplying the heroin in Delhi, said the police.[8]

The police said Jagdev, accused of several cases of robbery and murder, joined the drug trafficking racket after he came into contact with some Khalistani militants in jail.

Incidents of Khalistani activities in India and Pakistan, reported in the press during the last couple of years, 2004 to 2006, should be a cause of concern not only to the authorities but to ordinary Indians. Complacency on part of the either may be dangerous.

Some additional information on this incident is adduced in the succeeding paragraphs from another daily[9] with a deliberate aim. If one daily conveys the impression that Jagdev is the militant belonging to KZF, and Lahoria is his accomplice, the other daily conveys the contrary. The additional information culled from second daily follows.

Besides the 4 kg. of heroin, police also recovered one pistol alongwith eight live cartridges from the duo.

The trap laid by the police intercepted their Pulser motorcycle, driven by Jagdev, the accomplice. Lahoria was the pillion rider. They initially tried to escape but were later apprehended after a brief chase. They carried 2 kg. of heroin each in the bags they had on their persons.

During interrogation, Lahoria allegedly accepted that in 1996 he came in contact with Ranjit Singh Neeta, Chief of the KZF. In Oct. 1996, he alongwith his associate Balbir Singh planted a bomb in a bicycle in a parking lot of Grindlays Cinema in Srinivaspuri area, and in Dec. 1996, he alongwith another associate again planted a bomb in Jhelum Express which exploded at Ambala Cantt.

Memorial Service for Bhindranwale: 6 June 2007

The 23rd anniversary of Operation Blue S, the Indian Army's Code name for the storming of the Golden Temple, Amritsar in 1984 and eversince annually observed by the Sikh Community as *Ghallughara Din* (=Genocide Day) passed off peacefully amid massive security arrangements both by the Punjab Police and the SGPC task force in and around Sikhism's holiest shrine in Amritsar.[10]

The day began early with a memorial service for Jarnail Singh Bhindranwale and his armed followers who were killed in that operation. Now hailed by large sections of Sikhs as a "martyr", Bhindranwale is also widely condemned as a "terrorist who orchestrated the beginning of Punjab's bloodiest period.

At the Akal Takht—Sikhism's supreme religious and temporal seat—the Jathedar (=head priest), Giani Joginder Singh Vedanti, delivered a somewhat subdued sermon, which nonetheless included a familiar criticism of the Indian government and the Army for what he chose to call an act of "extreme brutality". He hailed Bhindrnwale and his followers as "Sikh martyrs who sacrificed their lives to protect the sanctity of Harimandir Sahib (Golden Temple). The Jathedar said the Sikhs must never forget the vicious military assault on their religious centre.

Subsequently, he went through the usual motions of honouring the families of Bhindranwale and others killed during Operation Bluestar by presenting each relative with a *siropao* (=religious robe of honour).

It needs to be noted that despite the visible presence of many radical Sikhs simmering with indignation over Sacha Sauda Chief Gurmeet Ram Rahim Singh's alleged imitation of Guru Gobind Singh and the clashes that followed, the 6 June functions passed off without a single slogan or unsheathed sword. Restrained by the huge security, the hardliners chose to respond to Jathedar Vedanti's appeal for "no expression of violence or anger inside the holy shrine."

But later, Dal Khalsa convenor Kanwarpal Singh and All India Sikh Students Federation leader Daljit Singh Bittu said: "The Sikh Community is very disappointed with the Jathedar's silence in the face of extreme provocation from the Dera Chief."

Mann: "Revive Anandpur Sahib Resolution": 16 June 2007

Simranjit Singh Mann, speaking on 16 June 2007 at Taran Tar from the SPGC-SAD (Badal) stage called for the revival of the much-talked-about controversial Anandpur Sahib Resolution of 1973, in the presence of his two political adversaries: Prakash Singh Badal, Chief Minister and BJP National President Raj Nath Singh. His speech at the public meeting, called by the SAD (B) to celebrate the 400th martyrdom anniversary of Fifth Guru Arjun Dev, "is likely to initiate a public debate in the state." Other invitees on the stage during his speech included two former Prime Ministers, HD Devegowda and Inder Kumar Gujral, and Bihar Chief Minister Nitish Kumar.

Reportedly, some senior SAD (B) leaders were against inviting Mann for the important celebrations, Badal was seen as handling the issue deftly by taking 'calculated risk' by allowing Mann to address the congregation. It is learnt that Mann was conveyed a message through senior leader not to raise the demand for a separate Sikh state in wake of martyrdom anniversary.

The SAD had also asked its musclemen to keep a close watch on Mann and his supporters as it apprehended they could indulge in sloganeering during address by National President of the BJP, or otherwise create disturbance in the proceedings.[11]

Though the 1973 Anandpur Sahib Resolution seeks pre-eminence of Khalsa, yet the SAD (B) leadership heaved a sigh of relief when Mann confined his reference to the resolution which was part of the Punjab Accord signed between Prime Minister Rajiv Gandhi and the then SAD President, Sant Harchand Singh Longowal in 1985, a year after Operation Blustar. This Resolution was later referred to the Sarkaria Commission.

PUNJAB INSURGENCY AND NRI SIKHS/HOST COUNTRIES

Any insurgency within the borders of a nation can be managed with somewhat less difficulty compared to the one that is helped economically, politically, materially or even morally by sources, entities or countries across it borders. All insurgencies in India's North-East were sustained by powers outside India's frontiers—be it China, Burma, Pakistan or Bangladesh, at one stage or other.

Same is true of Sikh insurgency in Punjab. Not only it got oxygen of support from Pakistan just across the border, it got even more support from rich NRI Sikhs settled in the UK, Canada, and the US, in the same order. Some aspects of this support are brought into focus in the succeeding text.

On 26 Oct. 1985, the Union Home Minister SB Chavan, presiding over the 90th meeting of the North Zonal Council at Manali, Himachal Pradesh, said terrorism and violence "has no place in a democratic society as they not only militated against the ideals of democracy and freedom, but also posed a serious threat to the progress and development of the country. These sentiments are based on ideals universally accepted and desirable. But there is hardly a country which has ideal situation within its borders in any field of activity—economic, social or political. There is always certain degree of dissonance and disharmony among various sections of its society. Chavan said that "unity and integrity are of paramount importance and these should preserved at all costs." When he said "any problems should be settled in a peaceful manner by mutual discussions and by appreciating each other's point of view."

When he was expressing such sentiments, it was easy to see that he was thinking of the recent Rajiv Gandhi-Longowal Pact to cool things in the insurgency-wracked Punjab. And he did indeed offer the pact as a step towards restoring the 'harmony' in Punjab, when he said: "The Punjab Accord had helped in restoring communal harmony in the region and had given a severe blow to the forces of disintegration and terrorism". Being an experienced politician and country's Home Minister, surely he should have known the darker realities of the Punjab situation at that point in time. The above homilies and optimistic pronouncements were obviously meant for public consumption and to put forward a rosy picture of the Punjab situation post-Accord. The situation was precarious not only internally but also externally. The Accord was resented not only by the Sikh extremists but it had created dissentions even within the Akali party. The Centre had not taken into confidence the Akalis beyond the immediate circle of Sant Longowal. But more than these unhelpful facts, there were things in the knowledge of the Government leadership which posed serious threats not only to this Accord but also to India's integrity and sovereignty.

Chavan as India's Home Minister must have known that a definite nexus had been established Punjab extremists and pro-Pakistan elements in Jammu and Kashmir. The Indian intelligence learnt this during the interrogation of the arrested extremist Mithbain (Mukhbain) Singh and some of his associates who included a Jamaat-i-Islami activist. It was clear that the two had joined forces for common cause: disintegration of India to achieve their respective objectives: Creation of "Khalistan" and "independent" Kashmir.

Affluent Sikh sections abroad were all out to help their compatriots inside India for achieving their desideratum. Among the more than half a million Sikh population, intelligence estimates put the number of extremists at least 500. They claimed they fled India after committing violent acts (of terrorism) for achieving Khalistan. Now for the ramifications of such open claims of violence in their mother country.

A word here may not be out of place about the tradition of European countries like Britain, France etc. providing shelter, sanctuary and safe haven for a variety of dissidents, revolutionaries, anarchists, liberationists and what you have from the Asian and African countries. The most celebrated names that grab immediate attention are of Khomeinie and Marx-Angel duo. What is significant is that these countries flaunted their 'liberal' traditions in providing shelter and as in case of the Marx-Angel duo, 'research' facilities in the famed London Library, to the 'troublesome' citizens of other countries.

Come 9/11 and later when terrorism struck base in their countries, they hurriedly vied with each other in not only learning to forget those liberal traditions but also institute harsh measures curbing the liberties their own citizens had enjoyed so long. Many Sikh terrorists had been granted political asylum in the UK in earlier times in the tradition of this longtime practice. But in course of time, following the serious IRA terrorist attacks in London and other cities in UK, one of which nearly killed Prime Minister Thatcher, and pressure from Government of India to take action against the Sikh terrorist absconders in Britain, the UK Government did start legislating anti-terrorists laws—and even more stringent varieties after 9/11 and London 7/7.

In Europe, the UK devised fairly strict, stringent anti-terrorist measures in its legislative field, compared to Germany, France, Scandanavian countries etc. The UK's two stringent legislations are: the Northern Ireland (Emergency Provisions) Act, 1973 and the Prevention of Terrorist (Temporary Provisions) Act, 1974.

But there is another angle—more mundane, more practical and more worldlywise than the ideological facade put on this business of the Sikh terrorists fleeing to the UK and some western countries—to the Sikh terrorists fleeing India in a hurry to seek political asylum abroad. Tarsen Singh Tur, General Secretary of the London-based Indian Overseas, in 1980s-90s, says (Late 1980s) matter-of-factly: "The main purpose of Sikh militants, who has fled India in the last few years, has been to settle down in Britain. The latest moves by both India and Britain to curb their activities may result in greater frustration among the militants. They want to stay permanently. They are in fact using 'Khalistan' slogan as a weapon to get political asylum and permanent resident status here. They are not serious about 'Khalistan'. They basically want to earn money".

The British police discovered in 1980s that the Sikh extremists had been collecting funds in 30 odd gurdwaras (=Sikh temples) in Britain to buy light machine guns and explosives from the European makers for use in terrorist activities in India's Sikh-majority Punjab Province. But London's promise to extend its Supression of Terrorism Act to Indian terrorists as also to hold discussions with Indian authorities on an Extradition Treaty had not only shocked the Sikh militants but also made them extremely nervous.

These two developments had generated second thoughts among the Sikh militants in foreign lands on the advisability of 'eager' acceptability of the Ecuadorean offer. Ecuador had agreed to give some 30,000 acres of land to Sikhs who "can construct their own buildings, irrigate the (virgin) land and set up a government in-exile." The Sikh militants were persuaded to believe that the offer was an excellent solution that enabled them to continue their struggle for Khalistan from a safe haven. Incidentally, in the first flush of excitement the militant Sikh leadership had no means to know that "Ecuador was in great need of people who could settle the fallow jungle lands and carry out irrigated farming that will give a boast to its economy." People who know the land-hungry Sikhs are aware how they turned the then barren lands of western areas of India's Punjab Pakistan's Punjab presently in early years of 20th century into the prosperous farmlands in two decades.

The second thoughts on this offer of establishing "Republic of Khalistan" in jungles of Ecuador made them see it as a clever trap. They realised that Ecuador would be the only place where the Sikh militants would ultimately have to go. In the process, the countries like Britain, Canada, the US etc. would get rid of the Sikh militants and Ecuador add a few millions to their GNP. Analysts too said that the move by Sikh militants to settle in the North-Western parts of Ecuador would prove to be suicidal as the separatist leaders might have to abandon their so-called 'Khalistan' movement once their followers were settled in their prosperous farmlands of overflowing crops.

But as Mr. Tur says, "in any case not many were serious about their quest for 'Khalistan'. It was a ploy for settling abroad. This 'lucrative' offer and KPS Gill-driven counter-terrorism drive in Punjab put paid to the Sikh terrorism in early 1990s.

But smug complacency on the issue would not be the correct attitude for the Government. Even presently, there are dormant cells in Punjab and certain political leaders avidly working for revival of the Sikh recessionism, actively helped by the ISI and Khalistani leaders operating from across the border in Pakistan—not forgetting some mischievous-makers engaged in collecting funds for the 'cause' from the congregations in good number of gurdwaras in Canada, the US and the UK, in the same order.

Some examples of Sikh miliants' typical activism will suffice to point to the future dangers. Sikh militants from Toronto, New

York and several other North American town were heading (in 1980s) for a "self-defence school", 16 km. outside Vancouver in the New westminster suburb, which was run by a former mercenary Roy Maia, a veteran of many African Bush wars in Angola and Mozambique. Maia, once a member of the Portuguese Army's elite commando unit which had fought against many African liberation outfits, then taught in his combat school various arts of combat. Eight Sikh extremists, belonging to the International Sikh Youth Federation (ISYF), hardline arm of the Sikh youth committed to 'Khalistan' and managed by Bhai Lakhvir Singh, nephew of Jarnail Singh Bhinderanwale, were "the most recent 'graduates' from the Maia school in late 1986."

Significantly, Roy Maia's record is rather similar to that of Frank Camper's. Like Camper, Maia served as an adviser to some foreign countries on security and intelligence issues. It was reported that Maia had served as an adviser to the US on guerrilla warface, and had advised the security forces of Brazil also.

Commenting on the Maia school, Indian Consul General in Toronto, Surinder Lal Malik, said: "India was aware that such camps (schools) existed, but what is frightening is that this camp has received far more Sikh militants as students than the Camper School in Alabama. The Maia camp seems to have done far more damage than the Camper Camp as we have proof that the product of this Camp is loose somewhere in Toronto".

Although no information "is yet available on the exact number of hard-livers trained at the Maia school, it poses a threat not only to India's security interests but also to the majority of Sikh moderates living in north America.

It was a matter of deep concern that Toronto "will now become the battle-ground between majority moderates who have now rallied around the government and the minority extremists". The analysts believed "the ultimate goal of the hardliners is to disrupt the freshly formulated Punjab Peace Accord."

The sources had told the UNI that the second stage of the training "is to get a passage to India".

The Canadian Justice Minister, John Croble, told the House of Commons on 5 Nov. 1985 that what the combat and bodyguard school was doing was illegal. But surprisingly, the Minister was silent on what his Government planned to do on this monstrous illegality being enacted on its soil that threatened the security, integrity and sovereignty of another fellow Commonwealth Country.

British police in the 1980s had conducted a thorough probe into the activities of the JKLF as it has close links with Sikh separatists in their common objectives against India. In series of raids on the residence of a JKLF activist, police seized several documents including account books. The examination of these documents in the light of intelligence reports on the activities of the JKLF led to the arrest of five of its activists one of them Amanullah Khan, who till recently then had been the Chairman of the JKLF, was in detention since 5 Sept. 1985. He had been charged with possessing articles with intent to cause criminal damage, as police had recovered certain chemicals from his house in Luton which could have been used to cause damage to persons and property. Police had seized certain documents from the residences of Zafar Khand and Malik Latif, both members of the Central Committee of the JKLF and dealt with its fund.

It was believed the British moved against the JKLF on a tip-off from India's High Commission as the outfit was planning strike against Indian targets.

JKLF and pro-Khalistani followers of Dr. Jagjit Singh Chauhan had been in close contact during mid-1990s. They had often shared public platform at several anti-India rallies and public meetings.

Meaningfully, Britain had agreed then to consider amendments in its law dealing with terrorism to facilitate extradition and deportation of terrorists. Crimes committed in one country were to be treated as crime in another country. The two countries were to closely cooperate with each in exchanging information relating to the terrorist activities.

During Prime Minister Rajiv Gandhi's visit to the UK, Prime Minister Thatcher agreed with him that terrorism constituted a great threat to peace and democracy. Two countries on 14 Oct. 1985 unequivocally condemned terrorism and pledged to eradicate it.

On 18 Oct. 1985, Canada extended the Extradition Act to India, effective 31 Oct. 1985, fortifying India's efforts to clamp down on terrorists operating from foreign soil, detrimental to country's integrity. The Canadian move came close on the heels of Prime Minister Rajiv Gandhi's efforts to have similar extradition treaty with the British Government during his talks with Prime Minister Thatcher during his 14 Oct. 1985 London visit.

Canadian External Affairs Ministry spokesman said in Ottawa in Oct. 1985, long lost, expressing his Government's will to contain Sikh extremists from Canadians liberalism and decency: "The Canadian Government and people were not aware of the gravity of situation in Punjab till the assassination of Indira Gandhi and later the crash of the Air India Boeing, killing all of its 329 passengers over the Atlantic. One hopes Ottawa would not be unduly sensitive if some analysts make some honest comments on the issue of Canadian stance towards India's terrorism-instigated troubles:

- It does not speak well of Canada's security and intelligence agencies if the country was ignorant about India's security threat posed by the Sikh insurgency.
- Yet again, even after they realised the gravity of the situation with Indian Prime Minister's assassination on 31 Oct. 1984, Canada took full one year to extend the provisions of that country's Extradition Act to India—in Oct. 1985. Some speed this, indeed! Not many nations will be proud of lack of promptitude to act after becoming aware of gravity of the situation!
- As far the Air India crash that killed 329 and the way Canada prosecuted the murderers, analysts were aghast at the casual approach and lack of professional skill of its judicial officials which expectedly resulted in acquittal of all the accused—the international outrage foreign the Government to order retrial.

India had always protested the lack of response from Canada, the UK and the US in taking action against terrorists guiding/remote-controlling disruptive activities in Punjab during the later part of the 1980s.

Senator Jeremiah, Chairman, Senate Judiciary Subcommittee on Security and Terrorism, which was exploring ways to curb activities of mercenary schools in the US, said he was not satisfied with the capabilities of American law enforcement agencies to pre-empt terrorists and he believed that America needed to buttress certain aspects of intelligence.

Countries like India, which neither harbour foreign subversive elements nor export terrorism to destabilise unfriendly regimes, had lot to gain if the above-mentioned move of America, guided by someone like Senator Jeremiah, had represented a serious attempt to come to grips with the cult of violence that had found adherents in most part of the non-Communist world by 1980s, and Communist countries like Russia and China too in the subsequent years. But the US and the West did not seem serious about the terrorism because they were not affected by the lethal menace at that time, as only Asian countries—and worst-hit among was India—were the victims. It was not surprising that countries like the US and Canada explained away glibly the activities of individuals like Frank Camper and Roy Maia who were routinely training the sinisterly anti-India Sikh terrorists determined to secede from the nation. Equally lightly the two nations were prone to explain away the continuance of Camper and Maia as advisers to their governments on security and intelligence matters. The West took the ravages of terrorism seriously only in the late 1990s, and particular so after the 9/11.

The readiness of countries like Canada, Britain etc. to sign extradition treaties with India was an admission of their earlier light-hearted stance on terrorism. Presently no nation is squemish about signing such a treaty with India or any other nation. Even today (11 Jan. 2007) Portugal has signed extradition treaty with India.

After threat of insurgency in India's Punjab was eliminated, some of its activists fled abroad. Intelligence reports say the Khalistani leadership is still ensconed in Pakistan while a number of former NRI activists are still continuing to work for the 'cause', mostly in gurdwaras in Canada, the UK and the US.

There is need to maintain the vigil in Punjab as some politicians led by people like SS Mann do not ever miss an opportunity to indulge in divisive sectarian and openly secessionist politics. During the Assembly elections, due in Punjab in 2007, political parties with defeat staring in their face will have no scrupler succumbing to vote bank politics in order to garner some support even from anti-national elements. It has already been mentioned how the Congress Party Chief Minister, Amarinder Singh, has been 'rehabilitating' some of the former Khalistani rebels and the fellow travellers in official positions.

Is Capt. Amarinder Singh pro-Khalistan? 2006

Is it a rhetorical question, or an over-wrought one? It is a valid question, considering the serious implications of the one at the top. Can the Congress Chief Minister of a state that has suffered ravages of personal and political tragedies for 15 long years (1978-93) be accused of being pro-terrorists and pro-Khalistan? If one goes by the accusations of his opponents and party colleagues alike, that indeed seems to be the case. Due to certain acts of commission and omission by Amarinder, All India Anti-Terrorist Front (AIATF) President Maninderjit Singh Bitta and the Punjab Pradesh Congress Committee (PPC) President SS Dullo certainly think that Amarinder owes an explanation on this count.

Controversy reached a crescendo on 31 August 2006

The best way to understand the issues involved in the controversy and their true impart is to cite the opening lines of a news story in a weekly dated 30 Sept. 2006:[12]

> "The ideological chasm in Punjab's ruling Congress could not be more gaping. As the state braces itself for a bitter battle in the Assembly poles due next year (Feb. 2007), the Congress' two giants are caught in a clash of ideologies: the anti-terrorism legacy of the slain Chief Minister Beant Singh embraced by the PPCC Chief Dullo vs the soft Khalistani approach pursued by Chief Minister Amarinder Singh, a former radical Akali."

It should be relevant, and opt. to reproduce the headlines of this news story, as given by the weekly:

> "Khalistani Rising
>
> Congress Big Two Face-off on Terror Punjab CM Amarinder Singh cases up to radical Sikhs, state Congress chief blows the whistle".

Simmering differences (ideological, political and personal) between the Chief Minister and Congress Chief came to a head on 31 August 2006 when Amarinder Singh failed to attend the Beant Singh death anniversary. Dullo and his supporters considered it a deliberate move by the Chief Minister to boycott the event to commemorate Punjab's boldest face against terror. This boycott capped Amarinder's approach towards terrorism/ terrorists in the border state. This led to an outburst from Dullo who, in retaliation, boycotted two Amarinder rallies.

Events Leading to 31 August 2006

His decision to boycott 31 August Beant Singh anniversary was obviously not an isolated, stand-alone affair. Certain curious things were happening en route to 31 August. While Amarinder hosted elaborate functions to induct Akalis into the (Congress) party, no PPCC functionary was present. On his part, Dullo too held functions for same purpose at the PPCC Headquarters.

Dullo created a flutter after he declared that he would not give former Akalis and Khalistanis the Assembly tickets. Though Amarinder denied inducting any of the Khalistanis into the party, his opponents pointed out his actions belied his such assertion. To wit, they cited case of All India Sikh Students Federation (AISSF) leader Harminder Singh Gill, a radical Sikh from Punjab's Majha region, being appointed a member of the Punjab Subordinate Services Selection Board by the Amarinder Government. A leading former militant, Gill is a wellknown to have been associated with the late Bhindranwale's secretary, Bhai Amarik Singh who also died in Operation Bluestar.

Expectedly, Dullo lashed out at Amarinder for not attending the Beant anniversary. Yet again, playing a shreud anti-Amarinder politician, he warned the Left not to join hands with the Third Front in Punjab, the Amarinder brain child, dubbing it 'communal' sure, potented cliche to impress/convince the Left. After all, the Third Front represents Akali splinter groups which have consistently opposed former Chief Minister Parkash Singh Badal.

As for Amarinder absenting from the anniversary, Janardhan Dwivedi, AICC General Secretary, in-charge Punjab, who himself attended the 31 August ceremony, sought to cool down the controversy: "Though Amarinder should have come, he had been preoccupied with meetings at Delhi." When a weekly asked Amarinder about his absence, he came out with a ridiculous if silly excuse: "I had an appointment with my doctor, Dr. Maini, in Delhi for a backache problem. I told Dullo I would not come. When queried if his absence sent a negative signal to those fighting terrorism, the Chief Minister retorted: "Do you think I am supporting terrorism?" Told that this was the impression gaining ground, Amarinder chose to ignore the averment.

Sources close to Amrinder said his antipathy for Beant Singh stems from the 1991 Assembly polls when Beant Singh upstaged him for the Chief Minister's post and 'sponsored a campaign that exposed Amarinder's allegedly illicit relationship with pilot Manpreet Kaur Sekhon."[13]

Amarinder, it seemed, had his own political Calculus in boycotting the ceremony! He hoped to divide the Akali vote bank by appeasing militant Sikhs and Akalis who might have felt alienated by Beant Singh's vigorous, unrelenting anti-terrorism drive. Is not it surprising that even on issues, which if handled insensitively, could end anger national security, politicians don't flinch from seeking personal, political gains!

What proved even more better of an anathema than Amarinder boycotting the 31 August ceremony, for the Dullo and Beant Singh Camps, was the lavish felicitation ceremony[14] on the very day of the anniversary hosted at New Delhi by Amarinder to honour author-journalist Khushwant Singh with the award of Punjab Rattan. That was interpreted by the Beant Singh supporters, miffed at Amarinder's boycott of the main function is Punjab, as a celebration on the solemn day of the death anniversary.

Does Amarinder Harbour Pro-militancy Sentiments?

It is not easy to prove such allegations, one may or the other. But his opponents assert that some of his actions definitely point towards a particular direction.

Amarinder deliberately shies away from honouring the legacy of a Congress Chief Minister who laid down his life in his fight against the terrorism in Punjab, he has no compunctions in associating with the hardline proponents/

supporters of Khalistan. On 13 April 2006, Amarinder raised eyebrows when he presented a *siropa* and a sword to the Damdami Taksal Chief Bhai Harnam Singh Dhumma on the inauguration of the Anandpur Sahib Heritage Complex. The late Bhindranwale headed the Taksal in the early 1980s. Dhumma, a known advocate of the Khalistan cause, has often honoured dead militants.

Analysts have noted that Amarinder's unabashed leanings towards celebrating Sikh historical events by bestowing government funds and declaring them as state level functions, has compromised the secular nature of the office of Chief Minister he holds under the Constitution. Amarinder's Sikh politics is of similar vein as the late Giani Zail Singh's tenure as the Punjab Chief Minister. However, even if the Giani was subtler in appeasing Sikh sentiment (in contrast to Amarinder's blatant version)' still his politics brought disastrous results through the Franksteines like the late Bhindranwale.

What is of more serious concern, as the analysts noted, is the linkages that have formed between sections of the state's IAS/IPS cadres and the radicals. This is only natural consequences to be expected when the political boss displays certain tendentious leanings. The officials are quick to discern which way the wind is blowing. But it must be clearly understood that a politician may be thrown out after five years, as indeed Amarinder has been, but the compromised officials serve much longer and pose for greater danger to nation's security and its secular tenet. So the poison injected in the body-politic by these officials through their dangerous association with the communal politics, and that too of the Khalistani variety and elements, has far greater insiduous effect on our nation's political health.

One example should suffice. Eyebrows were raised at the way the Punjab Police Headquarters were misused by the radical Sikh leader Jaswant Singh Mann of the All India Shiromani Akali Dal. Now, Mann happened to be a classmate of DGP SS Virk, and he was assigned the task of dividing the Akali vote bank by Chief Minister Amarinder. To achieve his assignment, Mann coopted the services of his classmate Virk and the latter's IGP (Intelligence) RP Singh. So what better venue for the trio to work their plans than the DGP office complex?

Incidentally, Jaswant Mann was the brain behind the formation of the Panthic Forum, where he shared the stage with Khalistani and militant elements like Simranjit Singh Mann and Daljit Singh Bittu of the SAD (Amritsar) and Jagjit Singh Chouhan of one-time 'President of Republic of Khalistan' and presently of the Khalsa Raj Party.

Amarinder, who likes to be known as a *kattar* (=puritanic; hardcore) Sikh, drew praise from controversial quarters. To wit, Chohan, alongwith Beant Singh's assassin Jagtar Singh Hawara and Khalistan ideologue Prof. Darshan Singh have declared Amarinder to be a better Chief Minister and Sikh than Badal. Any secularist and nationalist politician, and particularly a ruling Congress Chief Minister, should have been concerned on receiving accolades from three such anti-national figures. But not Amarinder! He, in fact, reciprocated the sentiments, choosing to term Hawara a "gentleman" and referring to Bhindranwale as "Sant ji".

One example of Punjab's flirting with terrorist violence—literally under the very nose of Chief Minister Amarinder Singh's?—surfaced in 2005 when Hawara and his co-assassins roamed free in Punjab after executing bomb blasts in Delhi. While Punjab Police could not track Hawara, a Delhi Police team caught him a few miles away from the Chief Minister's private palace in Patiala.

Interestingly, Amarinder did not pursue the policy of wooing the extremist elements within India but in foreign lands too. A couple of years ago, his visiting a Gurdwara in (Dixie) Canada known for its support to the Sikh terrorists, raised a hue and cry in India when the pictures of his reception in that Gurdwara appeared in Indian press. A particular picture, in which he is seen receiving a *siropa* (=a robe of honour), had a large inscription "Khalistan zindabad" on a big bill board on a wall pat in front of him, staring at him! Inquired about the visit to that Gurdwara, he came out with a 'smart' reply : "one does not go rounding reading what is written on the walls inside the Gurdwara before accepting an invitation to visit it." Details of the incident covered elsewhere).

Does Amarinder have India's Reigning Dynasty on His Side?

Surprisingly, rather most intriguingly, Amarinders followers claimed that their leader's radical politics of 'appeasing the Sikhs' had the backing of party Chief Sonia Gandhi, "who is keen on a reconciliation with the Sikhs." Saner elements in the Chief Minister's camp seriously doubt this self-serving claim and suggest that the "only claim that Sonia has is to avoid conflict with the Sikhs" and that Amarinder might be treading his own path. This duplicity seemed all the more plausible in the light of Amarinder's cohert backing of criticism of the Punjab policies of the late Indira Gandhi (and Rajiv Gandhi), who remain villains of piece not only among the radical Sikhs but also among the substantial number of ordinary Sikhs. In 2005, Punjab's Information and Public Relations Department published a book on the life of the late GS Tohra, an Akali stalwart. The book had Amarinder's foreword and contained venomous outporings of the late Tohra against the Gandhis. In as Assembly debate later that year (2005), Amarinder blamed Badal for misleading the youth to the path of militancy but remained silent and did not defend Badal's allegations against the Gandhis for their role in Punjab's dark days.

Bitta's Allegations against Amarinder Singh

Besides the accusers within his party, Amarinder has his severe critics outside its fold too.

AIATF Chief MS Bitta has been a long term accuser of Amarinder, starting with his days in power. His latest volley of charges has been published in a daily dated 27 March 2007.[15]

Bitta has laid two kinds of allegations at the door of the former Chief Minister. First is about moral turpitude. Simply put, they pertain to 'sexual escapades' of Amarinder with three Pakistani women, including a Pakistan-based journalist Arusa Alam, whom Bitta "Amarinder has married." He says Amarinder accompanied there three women to New Delhi, Jaipur and Ajmer Sharif and everything was kept "top secret." He goes further, alleging that the former Chief Minister spent 'several nights' with them at various places including a farm house near Mehrauli leaving his Punjab Police security behind.

Bitta claims that he "personally collected the 'secret' itinerary of the former Chief Minister and his Pakistani friends from the waiters, staff and CRPF jawans who stood guard outside the farm house, five star hotel and guest houses."

He alleged that the then DIG (Security), of the ex-Chief Minister, Khubi Ram, accompanied Capt. Amarinder Singh and his three Pakistani women friends throughout their itinerary.

Bitta alleged that Natwar Singh, brother-in-law of Amarinder, had also 'sold' India's secrets to Pakistan during his stint as Foreign Minister.

He then alleged that Arusa Alam attended many social gatherings, arranged in Army Cantonments at the behest of Amarinder and it was feared that she had collected vital information of Indian security.

Though Amarinder has described such reports as 'baseless, misleading, and concocted, Bitta still sought a high-level inquiry into the matter.

No further comments are offered on the sleazy aspects of these allegations, even though there is national security angle to them.

Second set of the Bitta allegations pertains to Amarinder's pro-Khalistan 'activities', already partly covered above. He produced documentary proof, including press clippings, that showed Amarinder attending many functions in foreign countries organised by Sikh militants during his stint as Chief Minister. He also produced a picture of Amarinder standing alongside Baba Dhumma, chief of Damdami Taksal and successor to Bhindranwale. He also presented another picture about Amarinder's visit to the Dixie Gurudwara in Canada. Both these incidents have already been covered above.

After presenting all this evidence, Bitta delivered his coup degrace : "The designs of ex-Chief Minister are clear. He wants to revive militancy in the state."

Now, dismounting the high horse of nationalism, Bitta wore his political garb : "I call upon the Congress High Command to expel Amarinder Singh from the party due to his anti-national activities. In fact, Amarinder Singh and Delhi Sikh Gurdwara Management Committee President Paramjit Singh Sarna have close links with Pakistan-based militants."

At the end, it is prudent to say that it is not easy to be judgemental on such issues. Only courts can pronounce authoritatively if Amarinder Singh indeed is guilty of a sanguine crime like anti-national activity which, simply put, means he has betrayed his nation.

But what can reasonably be said from the incidents/facts mentioned above is that he is guilty of the original sin all politicians can be held rightly accused of : In their quest to attain or retain power, they can do anything. Analysts could not be far wrong in saying that to achieve/retain power in West Bengal, if the Jyoti Basu-led CPM could welcome and legalise majority of illegal Bangladeshi immigrants to practise vote bank politics, it is no cardinal sin for the Amarinder Singh to woo the ex-Khalistanis to create their own vote banks.

"President of Khalistan" Chohan meets tame end : April 2007

Khalistan ideologue Dr. Jagjit Singh Chohan died at his residence in Tanda, 32 km from Hoshiarpur, on 4 April 2007 following a massive heart attack. He is survived by his wife Charanjit, who was away in UK with her nephew at the time of his death. They have no children. His body was kept in a private mortuary at Jaja village, adjoining Tanda town. The cremation took place on the return of his wife from UK on 6 April.

Jorawar Singh Chohan, a relative of the decease, told the press that "Dr. Chohan had been running his clinic at Tanda and looking after his ancestral house at his native village Nangal Khunga."

As a daily put it : "For a man who first hoisted the flag of Khalistan in Britain in 1971 when Punjab was still untouched by winds of separation, it was a very tame end. Chohan, 79, was getting ready for a meeting with the SSP Hoshiarpur that morning when death over took him at his residence."[16]

The self-proclaimed "President of the Republic of Khalistan", who quietly sneaked back into a peaceful Punjab in 2001, when the SAD(B)-BJP Government was in power, spent the last few years trying to revive the Khalistan movement "though peaceful, democratic means" as he put it, but in vain.

For the last 2-3 years, he had been paying more attention to the charitable hospital he set up in Tanda, where in 1977 he had raised the demand for Khalistan for the first time on Indian soil. He was hugely popular as a doctor, and a large number of patients turned up to pay their respects.

Chohan had secretly returned to India at midnight on 27 June 2001, after having stayed in Britain for 21 years. He had declared a "separate Republic of Khalistan at the height of militancy of Punjab in the early 1980s, and left India to avoid arrest for terrorist activities". His passport was also revoked.

Besides the MBBS degree he got from India, Khalsa College Amritsar, he got another one from the UK. All this just to set up a clinic in his village? Obviously, there was more up his sleeve!

In the short span of two years after winning 1967 Assembly seat, he was Deputy Speaker and Finance Minister. But losing the mid-term elections in 1969, he went over to the UK. He did make periodic visits to India but finally left India, apprehending his arrest, in 1980.

He returned to India on 27 June 2001 after a gap of 21 years amid high drama—he was allowed to travel to India after a direction from the Punjab and Haryana High Court, reaching Delhi by a British Airways flight and disembarking on a wheel chair.

"He appeared to be settling down to a sedentary existence, running a 30-bed charitable hospital in Tanda town. He also got back his Indian passport again on the orders from the same High Court. But soon the draw of the limelight got the better of him."[17]

Supported by some hardline Sikh outfits, Chohan floated Khalsa Raj Party and also fielded candidates in the 2002 and 2007 Punjab Assembly elections. He came a cropper both the times as did all the ex-Khalistanis and extremists in 2007 polls.

Now some details about the incident—nay, an act of subvertion/rebellion-that led to his cooling his heels in a Punjab jail. This was the result of his using an old Khalistani flag he had designed and displayed publicly in Britain in 1970s. During his six-odd years in India after his return from London, he continued to openly champion of the Sikh nationhood and even hoisted his old Khalistani flag atop his house in Tanda. After TV network broadcast images of the pennant, Chohan was arrested and charged once again with sedition and inciting revolt against India.

Early Life and His Political Career

Dr. Chohan, a qualified MBBS doctor, was running a private indoor clinic before entering politics.

He was first elected to the Punjab Legislative Assembly (=Vidhan Sabha) from Tanda as a candidate of the Republican Party of India, in 1967, had a brief stint as Finance Minister in the coalition government of Lachhman Singh Gill, and was elected Deputy Speaker when Gurnam Singh was Chief Minister.

But soon after this, the idea of Khalistan took over him. But there was an interesting twist to his political ambitions in India. When the Gurnam Singh Ministry fell, it resulted in mid-term elections in 1969 and Chohan failed to get elected. It was then that the idea of Khalistan germinated in his mind. The big 'if' of history of Khalistan is : If Dr. Chohan had won in the 1969 Punjab polls....?

An Ardent Khalistani

He was one the original founders of the Khalistan movement.

Kanwarpal Singh, General Secretary, Dal Khalsa, a right wing party, recalls : "Chohan, the Khalistani ideologue, first shot into international limelight when pictures of him receiving the Keys of Nanakana Sahib gurdwara from Pakistan's Gen Yahya Khan were flashed on the PTV in 1971." He returned to Punjab in 1978 and hoisted the flag of Khalistan at Anandpur Sahib before returning to England in 1980 to anoint himself as President of "Republic of Khalistan, Government-in-Exile." Safe in the UK, he directed all his energies into embarrassing the Indian Government by setting consulates countries like France and issuing Khalistani currency and passports.

He also played the godfather to militants like Gurbachan Singh Manochahal and Wassan Singh Zaffarwal, who were operating on the Indian soil.

"Today, 4 April, Zaffarwal was among the first to reach his house on hearing about his death". Also present were members of Dal Khalsa, a rightwing party, which was one of the few to ally with him when he floated his Khalsa Raj Party after landing here in 2001, the avowed aim of which was to "achieve Khalistan all be it in a democratic manner." He once told a correspondent: "I do not believe in violence any more."[18]

However, even in 2006 he made a speech and hoisted a Khalistan flag, for which he was charged with sedition and spent two months in jail.

Calling him "a failed man and a failed politican with a failed mission", Dr. Jagrup Singh Sekhon, Head of the Department of Political Science Guru Nanak. Dev University, Amritsar, said, "Chohan's idea of Khalistan, too, was borrowed. He was not the original ideologue of Khalistan, the word was first coined in 1935."

How did this Khalistan journey start? His tryst with Khalistan began in 1971 when he visited the US and posted an advertisement in a daily of an eminence no less than the *New York Times*, dated 13 Oct. 1971 proclaiming a separate Sikh state. After a trip to India in 1979, he returned to the UK to announce the formation of the Khalistan National Council and declared himself "President of the Republic of Khalistan," as mentioned earlier. He issued even passports, stamps and currency notes in the name of the "new Republic."[19]

Chohan was widely believed to have been influenced by Jarnail Singh Bhindranwale, though he claimed later that he had never advocated an armed struggle. He was also quoted as reacting sharply to Operation Bluestar and late Prime Minister Indira Gandhi. "When his Indian passport was cancelled, he announced a government-in-exile and continued his radical activities."

It took Chohan 21 years to get permission to travel back to India but no sooner did he touch Indian soil that he took recourse to his old Khalistan rhetoric. He founded Khalsa Raj Party, declaring the establishment of an independent Sikh state as its goal but this time through democratic means.

Expectedly, given his secessionist activities, Chohan was declared anti-national in India, and several cases including one of sedition, were slapped on him. He spearheaded the movement for creation of Khalistan from the UK and other countries. In the early 1980s, Chohan had announced the constitution of the 'Council of Khalistan', with a 'Cabinet' and issued Khalistan 'passports', 'postage stamps' and 'Khalistan dollars'.

On 13 June 1984, just a few days after Operation Bluestar, Chohan announced a Khalistan 'Government in Exile' and was selected 'President of Khalistan' in Britain.

If in the early 1980s, he hogged the headlines by proclaiming himself 'President-in-Exile' of the independent nation of Khalistan with his headquarters in a small London flat, he repeated the performance three years later by drafting and publishing the first and perhaps the only map of Khalistan with its boundaries extending both into the present-day Delhi and the whole of (the Pakistani) West Punjab.

Analytical Comments on his Khalistani Campaign

Lionised by the media and his peers in the heyday militancy, much reviled after peace returned for sending thousands of Punjabi (Sikh) youths to a violent end, Chohan's death comes at a time when all the separatist leaders of the State got a decisive drubbing in the February 2007 Assembly polls. To wit, politically most active father-son duo of the SDA(A) post their deposites.

Calling him a man out of sync with the times, veteran politician Umrao Singh said Dr. Chohan lost his relevance because there were no takers for his divisive politics : No Sikh organisation or panthic group thought it worthwhile to utilise his services, and in the end he floated his own outfit.

His return to India in 2001, following Punjab and Haryana High Court's orders asking the Indian Government to release his passport, itself continues to be shrouded in mystery. He was released after only a few hours of detention even though he faced a sleu of charges, including some relating to sedition.

Umrao Singh says this had something to do with Chohan's being a shrewd operator and explained why he used to praise Capt. Amarinder Singh during his press conferences.

Born into an affluent family of Nangal Khunga village in Tanda in 1928, Chohan fancied himself as a revolutionary and freedom fighter. He lost an arm while trying to make a bomb, but that was before independence. But after losing the 1969 elections, he was taken over by the idea of Khalistan.

The death of this one time dentist and later self-proclaimed president of the independent Sikh nation of Khalistan, some analyst like to believe, will "bring final closure to nearly two bitterly acrimonious decades (the 1980s and 1990s) during which Punjab witnessed unbridled violence and the deaths of more than 30,000 people."

He was 70 years old and not too well when he landed at Delhi in 2001, disembarking on a wheel chair. "But his spirit and the Khalistan dream were intact."

"I still stand by Khalistan and I will continue the movement to its logical conclusion," he told a correspondent on his first arrival in Punjab at the Chandigarh railway station on 27 June 2001.[20] He did, however, reiterate that he was "not in favour of violence" and in fact condemned those who employed the gun to force their will.

To re-emphasise, he kept chasing his dream and launched even the Khalsa Raj Party as a vehicle to reach his desideratum. He fielded nominees during both, the 2002 and 2007, Punjab Assembly elections but uncluckily—perhaps, luckily for India—could never meet with any electorate success.

30,701 reasons

'Khalistan's President' died in a peaceful, prosperous Punjab. That is India's victory.

Above is the heading of an editorial in a national daily. Some of the views and sentiments expressed in the editorial need to be taken note of and deserve a wider readership/circulation. The best way to ensure it is to reproduce it verbeatim.

> "Today an entire generation of Indians takes peace in Punjab for granted and would the term 'Khalistan' a curious construct. This is itself is a testimony to the fact that country has left behind a tragic and bloody interregnum in its history.
>
> "The death of the man who once proclaimed himself 'president' of the 'republic of Khalistan' and who had three decades ago hoisted the flag of Khalistan from Anandpur Sahib comes as a reminder of this emphatic enclosure.
>
> "Jagjit Singh Chohan's idea of Khalistan was anchored on Hindu-Sikh antagonism. He died in a Punjab which had just

voted to power—for the second time in 10 year—a Sikh-Hindu political alliance which signals that old fissures have healed. The failure of Chohan's political project was in many respects the triumph of a democratic Indian state because it could not ultimately turn ordinary Sikhs against ordinary Hindus. Punjab of the eighties and early nineties was nightmare country : the excesses of Operation Bluestar, political assassiations, including that of a Prime Minister, unrelenting terrorist violence, and the unravelling of peace initiatives led to the entire state, and Sikh community in particular, paying a terrible price.

"Looking back, there came a point in this ugly war when the militants got the message that the Indian state had the strength, resources and determination to defeat them. It needed political will and patience to carry on with the fight until that inflexion point was reached. It needed political sagacity to recognise that moment and respond with civil society initiatives of reconciliation, including that of an election.

"Today what was one of India's most trouble-prone states is right there among the lights. In 2004-05, Punjab, with a per capita income of Rs. 30,701, emerged as the country's most prosperous state. It is inspiring, and educating, this story of Punjab's emergence from the brink."

A note of caution needs necessarily to be appended to this 'inspiring' editorial. The Khalistanis may not be looming large on the horizon, but neither are they buried fathoms deep in the earth. Some of them are lurking just below the surface : waiting for an—any—opportunity to emerge from the warmwood and occupy centre stage. In the yet-to-be resolved the Dera-Sikh troubles, they nearly hijacked the traditional Sikh leadership. At times, the clergy seemed to be taking decision under pressure from these elements. A much greater sagacity and balance are required to end the Dera-Sikh controversy than that which brought happy end to Bhandranwale created mayhem. Some analysts assert the Sikh clergy did not respond with grace and sagacity in responding to the apology offered by the Dera Chief. By issuing Hukumnama for closure of all the Sacha Sauda Deras in Punjab by 27 May 2007, the clergy is treading on a dangerous turf. This edict has left the field wide open for the mischief-mongers and trouble-seekers led by those Khalistani/extremist elements. Unless handled sensitively and promptly, the latter will vitiate the atmosphere in Punjab. Dr. Manmohan Singh and Mr. Badal must act before it is too late.

Former Militant wins Valtoha Seat : 27 February 2007

It was for the first time that the Congress and Shiromani Akali Dal (SAD) had field a candidate each with a militant background.

While Congress candidate, Harminder Singh Gill lost to Adesh Partap Singh Kairon, son-in-law of Parkash Singh Badal by a margin of 9,947 votes from Patti, Virsa Singh Valtoha of the SAD-BJP combine won the Valtoha seat from the Congress candidate Gurchet Singh Bhullar with a margin of 11,350 votes.

Interestingly, Valtoha had a stint as member of Punjab Subordinate Services Selection Board (PSSSB) during the previous regime of Parkash Singh Badal, while Gill was given the same post during the just-defeated Congress government of Capt. Amarinder Singh.

Both Valtoha and Gill had worked as active leaders of All India Sikh Students Federation (AISSF) headed by the then President Bhai Amrik Singh, and they faced a number of criminal cases, including sedition.

Gill, a confident of the late Gurcharan Singh Tohra, long-serving President of the SGPC, had joined the PPCC in March 2004 during the last Lok Sabha elections at the behest of the then Chief Minister Cap. Amarinder Singh.

Gill is a gold medalist in MA History from Guru Nanak Dev University and also holds a Masters degree in Economics, while Valtoha is post-graduate and has taught at the Khalsa College, Amritsar.[21]

After his release from the Jodhpur Jail in August 1989, Gill convinced his colleagues in the AISSF to contest the June 1991 elections, but which were subsequently cancelled.

Here is an example of the ways politicians behave in self-contradictory manners. Capt. Amarinder Singh had criticised the SAD-BJP combine for appointing Valtoha and Amarjit Singh Chawla, both former militants, as members of the PSSSB and the Punjab Service Commission (PPSC) respectively during their rule. But when he became Chief Minister is 2002, he himself appointed Gill with a similar background of being a former militant, for the same post.

In this poll, voters rejected the hardliners. Dal Khalsa could not save the security deposit of its candidates—Karnail Singh Panjoli and Gurdip Singh Kalkar. Equally heartening was the rejection of both Simranjit Singh Mann and his son by the voters in this election. It augurs well for the peace in Punjab.

NOTES

1. Vishwa Mohan, *Times of India,* 8 Oct. 2006.
2. Reuters, New York, Cited *Times of India,* 6 Dec. 2006.
3. IANS, *Times of India,* 22 December 2006.
4. Vishwa Mohan, *Times of India,* 27 December 2006.
5. *Asian Age,* 6 December, 2006.
6. Mohit Sharma and Mayank Aggarwal, *Statesman,* 21 Feb. 2007.
7. Varinder Walia, *Tribune,* 25 February, 2007.
8. *Statesman,* 25 March 2007.
9. *Tribune*, 26 March 2007.
10. Asit Jolly, *Asian Age,* 7 June 2007.
11. Varinder Walia and Sanjay Bumbroo, *Tribune,* 17 June 2007.
12. Vikram Jit Singh, Tehelka, 30 September, 2006.
13. *Ibid.*
14. It was budgeted at Rs. 45 lakh.
15. Varinder Walia, "Record of three Pak women's visit may yield valuable information : Bitta," *Tribune,* 21 March 2007.
16. Anju Agnihotri Chaba, *Indian Express,* 5 April 2007.
17. Khushwant Singh, *Times of India,* 5 April 2007.
18. *See* n. 16.
19. Harpreet Kaur, *Hindustan Times,* 5 April 2007.
20. Asit Jolly, *Asian Age,* 5 April 2007.
21. Varinder Walia, *Tribune,* 28 February 2007.

9

DERA SACHA SAUDA-SIKH CONFLICT : PREMONITION OF 1978?

It is obvious that extremist Khalistani militants and their mentors, the ideologues, are always lurking below the surface, ready to take advantage of any opportunity that presents itself any time, anywhere.

Be it a Bhindranwale anniversary or Fifth Guru Arjun Dev's 400th Martyrdom Day ceremony, they are present to arouse the religious passions. Understandably, they were ready to exploit the Dera-Sikh controvery for their even end all over, with the Sikh youth brandishing the unsheathed swords.

All this bode ill for the inter-faith harmony in Punjab, and even beyond its borders. What was even more frightening for the analysts as well as the common man was its uncanny Similarity between the two events. If in April 1978, it was the Nirankari Mission versus the Sikhs; in May 2007, it was the Dera Sacha Sauda versus the Sikhs. The April 1978 clashes led to the murder of the then Nirankari Chief Baba Gurbachan Singh in April 1980 at Delhi and 15-year-long murderous Khalistani movement that shook the nation and cost thousands of human lives. Will the May 2007 incidents lead to a similar tragedy? That possibility should be a cause of serious concern to all concerned.

It is no surprise that the government has put the Dera Chief under Z Plus security. Warrant against him is still pending in the courts (18 June 2007).

The events are covered in some details in this chapter.

Dera Sacha Sauda Vs Sikhs : May 2007

Will it revive the Khalistani Extremism?

It all started with the Sirsa (Haryana) based Dera Sacha Sauda's 13 May 2007 advertisement that showed its leader Sant Baba Gurmeet Ram Rahim Singh attired like 10th Sikh Guru Gobind Singh administering *amrit* (=the consecrated water) to his followers, popularly known as 'Premis' (=fraternal followers in love with their Guru).

It was bound to raise temperature as the Sikhs denounced the picture as blasphemic, an attempt at minicking the revered 10th Guru. Then there are "conspiracy theorists" who assert the confrontation provoked by the Dera was carefully timed. But what is even the bigger cause for apprehension is that the Sikh hardliners might seize the anti-Dera stir/sentiment as an opportunity to inflame their own extremist, separatist ideology which the Sikh masses had decisively rejected in the recent (early 2007) Assembly poll.

"Dera egged on by it and the Congress is the 'Culprit'"

It may be totally false, or partly right, the fact remains that one section of the opinion-makers holds this view sincerely, sans any ifs and buts.

Here is what Anshul Chhatarpati, a Sirsa journalist, who has been following the Dera'a activities ever since his father was allegedly murdered by the Dera's men, told a reporter of a weekly:[1]

> "The Baba says he has worn these clothes many times before. But why did he issue an advertisement and that too with a Bhatinda angle? In the clashes that occurred on14 May, it is to be seen that the sticks wielded by the *premis* were all of the same size and nature. Truckloads had been brought to Bhatinda in anticipation of a reaction to the advertisement. The Baba was sending a message that his followers could create mayhem."

By bringing out the advertisement on the day he did, the Baba was obviously playing to specific game plan. His aim was to show his clout and send out the message that if he was arrested in the CBI cases pending against him, it would trigger public unrest.

Consider the sequence of events that led to the 13 May advertisement. On 16 April 2007, the Punjab and Haryana High

Court ordered the CBI to complete its probe into the three cases against the Dera by 25 May and listed the matter for 28 May. Within a week, the Dera's followers were alleging harassment by the ruling Akalis, who were taking revenge for Dera's vote against their party that tilted the scales against many candidates of the Akali Party in Malwa (centred round the Bhatinda district) area, considered its stronghold till then. Congress leaders fanned the fires. Then started the Baba's campaign to inculcate the spirit of humanity in followers of all religions by making them partake of the 'Ruhani Jaam' (=drink of spiritualism) *sherbet* in Sirsa—Haryana-based headquarters of this fast-spreading sect. Donning the robes and symbols that 10th Guru Gobind Singh is believed to have worn, the Baba issued an advertisement only when he repeated the ritual at Salabatpura Dera in Punjab's Malwa heartland of Bhatinda, and some 50 km from this town.

The fire had been lit, with this 13 May advertisement. "The next day, 14 May, when disgruntled Akali elements led by former Minister SS Maluka and SGPC member SS Rahiya gathered in Bhatinda to burn the Baba's effigy, the Dera's *premis* (=devotees) set upon them in a planned attack that had even the cops running for cover.[2]

We know what the Baba has said about wearing these clothes/robes. He has done it so many times earlier. Then, he simply donned the attire offered to him by his devoted followers!

Now comes the Congress 'mischief.' "It was evident that the overly aggressive *premis,* otherwise a minority sect in Punjab, could never have taken on the ruling Akali establishment and the sikh bodies without a powerful backing." HS Bains, media advisor to Punjab Chief Minister Parkash Singh Badal, substantiate the charge to a weekly[3] : "Seven Congress MLAs from the Malwa heartland owing allegiance to former CM Amarinder Singh gathered with the *premis* at Bhatinda. The government even has photographs to show their presence among the *premis* who went on rampage later. It was the Congress egging on the *premis* to take on the Akalis."

Face off

That the Baba remained adamant in not offering an apology till the last moment on 27 May, the time line laid down by the

Akal Takhat, despite growing calls from among the *premis* to buy peace, was believed to show the powerful interests at work behind his action. Highly-placed sources in the Punjab government told a weekly[4] (about the conspiracy).

> "Three things happened almost simulataneously. Radical Akali leader Simranjit Singh Mann (Amarinder's brother-in-law) desecrated the statue of late CM Beant Singh in Jalandhar, and former CM Amarinder slipped away to Nepal on the flimsiest of excuses. It was then that the Baba placed his advertisement. The Baba is being bailed out by the Government of India in the CBI cases against him. He will do their bidding Congress MLAs close to Amarinder backed the *premis* in Bhatinda. As Punjab was quickly destabilished, the Union Home Minister went to Parliament and evoked pears of Punjab sliding down again."

Even senior Punjab Congressmen are not discounting the conspiracy theory that the drama was staged at the behest of the party high command at the Centre. In 1978, after the clashes between the Akalis and Nirankaris in Amritsar, Sikh radicals backed by the Congress took centrestage and were able to successfully destabilise the Badal Government. That led to nearly two decades (15 years to be exact, 1978-93) of strife in the border State.

"In Punjab this time around, the municipal elections are nearing. At a larger level, a destabilished Punjab could help the Congress garner votes in the next Lok Sabha polls (1909) as the party hardly has an agenda to take to the people. The nation can again be told that the Congress is the only party that can keep India together and tackle the problem created by the divisive parties like Akali-BJP alliance in Punjab." This is a Congress MLA, expressing himself on the imbroglio. CPI stalwart and member of the National Council Joginder Dayal, went so far as to allege that "Central intelligence agencies" were out to destabilise Punjab again.

Badal squarely blamed the Congress and said that "certain elements are out to destroy India's peace. The same agencies are at work behind the Baba's actions."

Politics of it all

Some analysts postulated that when the Dera controversy erupted, Badal found himself besieged. What are the realities of the situation? Was he indeed besieged by his political compulsions, or was he himself, being an astute politician of some vintage, playing games with his own political rivals?

As the violence broke out, Badal did little until 17 May to rein in the angry Sikh elements who went after the *premis* in retaliation. The Badal administration displayed neither the will nor the nerve to take on the sword wielding Sikhs. The Bhatinda incident was the trigger as the administration miserably failed to control the clashes. Badal himself admitted the failute of the administration at Bhatinda three days later.

Punjab's Hindu Community was rattled by the marked display of violent intent, the Sikh youths defiantly flourishing the unsheathed swords menacingly in the air, "and the tremours reached the drawing rooms of even the well-heeled in Chandigarh." Pramod Kumar, director of the Chandigarh-based Institute of Communication and Development, puts it straight, with stark honesty :

> "The attempt was to scare the *premis* but it was the Punjabi Hindu who got scared instead. Badal was deliberately slack. He should have acted on the first day itself. What was the point in allowing the *Sarbat Khalsa* at Talwandi Sabo on 17 May in the Malwa heartland where passions were already inflamed? It is to be noted that Badal called for an all-party meeting only on 18 May after the *Sarbat Khalsa,* which called for the boycott of the *premis.* No measures were taken to prevent the Sikh crowds from marching from Talwandi Sabo to the Dera Salabatpura where violence erupted. This should have been anticipated. The police only got into the act at 7 PM when the matter had gone out of hand."

The diffidence of normally aggressive Punjab Police is difficult to explain. No preventive arrests were made, and Sikhs attacking the Dera were left unapprehended. Till 19 May, only 10 cases had been registered, mostly against the *premis*. When asked about the number of arrests, Punjab DGPNPS Aulakh blandly refused to provide any figures.

When Badal was asked why he was not opening a channel for talks with the Dera even when there were offers from its members, he indicated he was not in favour of any conciliation till the Baba rendered an apology. He was obviously speaking as a partisan rather than the Chief Minister of a state confronting a law and order situation. Badal, the politician, has problems of his own.

Badal is caught in the competition for Sikh votes with an aggressive Amarinder stoking the community's sense of outrage. The Malwa region, once Badal's bastion, was successfully breached by Amarinder for the Congress during the last Assembly polls, and Badal does not want to let go of this opportunity to regain its control, once again. So Badal could hardly crack down on the sword-wielding Sikh protesters without being seen as anti-Sikh.

State Secretary of the CPI (ML) Sukharshan Singh Nat puts it aptly, if empirically : "Whenever the Akalis are in power, there is an attempt by the Congress to put Badal against radical elements within the Sikh community so as to destabilise him. While polarisation of the Sikhs against the *premis* and against the Congress, which is backing them, will help Badal, it may turn counter-productive if the law and order situation goes out of hand. On the other hand, the Baba has given Badal a golden opportunity, to take revenge on the *premis* for voting against him in the last polls. Had Badal acted differently against the *premis,* most democratic parties would have criticised him. Now most parties are backing Badal against the Baba."

As the situation worsened and the Baba called for imposing President's Rule in Punjab, much to the delight of the Punjab Congress, Badal saw his gains evaporating. Badal descried danger in some other spheres also. On 16 May, the Punjab BJP held, meeting and expressed distress at the situation. Too many Sikh gatherings had been seen acting as if they were above the law of the land. Unsheathed swords were being brandished about freely. The BJP was seeing danger in this free-for-all environment. After all, the party had just meaned the Urban Hindu voters away from the Congress in the Assembly polls, and they as well might retrace their steps if the Dera-Sikhs confrontation vitiates the atmosphere. The minority drifting back to the Congress would not only affect the BJP but also alter the BJP-Akali Party equation.

The call for the 22 May strike was another portentious event. It brought back the memories of the militancy days. So the apprehensions of the BJP were quite understandable. Read carefully what the BJP's Punjab General Secretary Kamal Sharma tells a weekly : "The images of shops being forcefully shut and damaged by Sikh youth brought back memories of days of militancy to our supporters. The Baba has undoubtedly done wrong but the inaction by the Badal Government for four days is not justified. We want Badal to ensure that the radical elements of the Sikh Community do not take centrestage."

Matters reached a head for Badal when Governor (Gen) SFS Rodrigues summoned him on the 21 May. The latter might have cautioned him about maintaining law and order during the 22 May strike. The message obviously reached home as the Governor has the powers to recommend President's Rule if the law and order situation in a state spins out of control. "Badal changed track and, for the first time since the clashes erupted, spoke of dealing with the miscreants."

Will the radicals emerge once again?

Let us start with an "I told you so." Here is Sukhdarshan Nat speaking : "In 1997, the *premis* had backed Akalis, who rode to power in the Assembly with a large majority. At that time we issued a statement that the *premis* and the Badal backed SGPC were bound to collide because the Dera culture goes against the organised religion. There were huge protests in Mansa against us and the Akalis backed the *premis*. The Congress backed the Left parties. That clash which we predicted 10 years back has happened."

It is import to note that any intra-Sikh community or inter-community dispute involving Sikhs would provide an opportunity to the radicals–more accurately, the Khalistanis—to jump in the fray and take over the leading role. The Sikh leadership, and especially the SGPC and the four Singh Sahiban, the Jathedars, have to careful to ensure that the passions are not allowed to boil over. The reason for restraint and balance are self-obvious. If the passions are allowed to go beyond a certain point, the Sikh youth will be lured by the radicals/

extremist. If that happens, as it indeed did in the post Sikh-Nirankari clash 1978—the radicals would hijack the leadership of the Sikh community. Then a Bhindranwale would emerge on the scene. And history would repeat itself in a tragic manner.

As for the present imbroglio, some see the Baba as having challenged the SGPC's hegemony over Sikh symbols. Promod Kumar explains : "This is a case of religious competition. The SGPC is in comparison with the militant groups and the Deras. The reaction against the *premis* was a way of teaching them a lesson. Even the Namdharis and the Radhaswamis have different practices, they never run into trouble with the SGPC because these sects never challenge it politically. The Baba did just that and earned the wrath of the SGPC and the clergy."

As the tempers soared, the first casualty was the SGPC as it lost ground to the militant elements. These elements, who had been wiped out in the Assembly polls, gained currency as the clashes intensified. The five Sikh jathedars barely held their ground in Talwandi Sabo on 17 May, with one of them having a narrow escape as a sword was thrown at him. The high priests were perceived to be going soft on the *premis*.

With the anniversary of Operation Bluestar barely days away, Sikh militants elements brow beat the jathedars at Amritsar on 20 May with the hordes of sword wielding youth surrounding the meeting of the SGPC at the Golden Temple that announced a Punjab bandh. Badal's points men to the jathedars, advisor to the Chief Minister DS Cheema and SGPC Chief Avtar Singh Makkar were reduced to being bystanders as the priests took a hard stand that reflected poorly on the Badal administration.

The turn of the events have dismayed the well-wishers of Punjab. More than the violence in Punjab, which the state government smugly described as just a "handful of incidents", it is the damage to the social fabric which has observers worried. Simmering agrarian, social and economic tensions in Punjab can get an additional caste edge given the backward status of a majority of the *premis*.

Pramod Kumar enumerates other causes for worry : "Punjab has been reduced to a basket case. Aftermath of the violence may see the *premis* migrate to safer areas in towns and cities, away from the villages where they are in a minority. Beyond this no investor would like to come to Punjab. Even the capital flow in pursuit of profits will cease in Punjab because of the disturbance. Even if there are profits, the capital will not flow towards Punjab. It is to be noted that the FDI "in Punjab in the last five years has been a mere 0.5 per cent. Further, the share of taxes of Punjab in the Central pool is not in the State's favour. After a long time, people had reconciled to peace in Punjab but all that seems to have been lost."

The political, social and economic boycott of the *premis* announced by the Sikh high priests on 17 May has a political agenda. "Supposing there is a need to visit the house of one of my *premi* supporters in case of function or death of a relative, I'll find it difficult (to do so) because of the boycott call. Since the *premis* are backing the Congress, this boycott will hit us," Talwandi Sabo's Congress MLA Jeet Mohinder Singh Sidhu told a weekly. Sukhdarshan Nat draws attention to another social risk for the Dera followers : "where even the *premis* are involved in some conflict, in panchayat polls for example, they can be made easy targets under the guise of religious sentiment."

Top sources in the Punjab government say that the damage to the social fabric, which will show up more clearly when the violence ebbs, is the most crucial issue before the government. Bains said, "we are giving it the utmost thought".

Security Analysts are Concerned

Rising communal temperature in north-west India as a result of the Dera Sacha Sauda issue must have worried the security establishment in the country. A senior intelligence analyst told a daily[5] that it could give radicals an excuse to exploit the situation. He said : "Terrorism may be dead in Punjab, but its lethal remnants are still around, some in Pakistan and others abroad in Europe and other countries." While security forces kept a tight lid on the situation in Punjab, "there are always possibilities of a hidden or "sleeper" group being activated to exploit a situation."

There is simply no scope for any degree of complacence on this score. There may be no terrorists in Punjab but some radical Sikh political groups remain very active. They can count on the support of a network of militants and radicals across the globe, who are still able to raise funds, though not at the scale they used to in the past. To wit, the list of 20 most wanted terrorists that India gave to Pakistan in 2002,[6] in the wake of the attack on Parliament, contained five Sikh militants. They are listed here :

- Wadhawan Singh of the BKI.
- Ranjit Singh Neeta of the Khalistan Zindabad Force.
- Paramjit Singh Panjwar of the KCF.
- Lakhbir Singh Rode of the International Sikh Youth Federation (ISYF).
- Gajinder Singh of Dal Khalsa.

Pakistan, only expectedly, denied their presence on its soil. Now a word on the whereabouts of these five terrorist. The first two remain active and dangerous. Their last major action was the twin blasts in two Delhi cinema halls showing the film 'Jo Bole So Nihal' in May 2005. Their have been some small blasts in Chandigarh and some in Ludhiana, resulting in two buses being burnt in the past two years. While this may confirm the fact that terrorism is indeed dead in the state, security agencies remain worried that prolonged sectarian and communal violence can create problems.

Sikh hardliners are dictating terms

The Sikh High Priests on 17 April had demanded apology from the Dera Chief, besides asking Punjab Government to ensure the closure of all Sacha Sauda Deras in Punjab by 27 May. Much before the datelined laid down by the High Priests, Punjab's various militant organisations, once considered dormant and disbanded, started issuing hardline statements on 23 May. They came together to demand the arrest of the Dera Sacha Sauda Chief and announced that "they will start their mass agitation with a people's March from Fatehgarh to Chandigarh on 31 March.

Manjit Singh Bhoma, the President of once banned All India Sikh Student's Federation (AISSF), said it was already late for an apology. "Sarkon men behad josh hai, magar leedran vich hosh hai" (=the street is passionate, but the leaders are still displaying restraint and balance). He said the agitation is going to be fierce but peaceful.

"We want him (the Dera Chief) behind the bars even if he manages to get bail the very next day", said senior Dal Khalsa leader Kanwarpal Singh Bittoo once an underground leader of the Babbar Khalsa. Both Mohkan Singh, spokesman of the Damdami Taksal, Chowk Mehta, and Bittoo said they had ensured that their followers did not flaunt weapons during the 22 May Punjab bandh on the instructions of the Akal Takht, "because we did not want the TV channels to show the Sikhs in poor light."

Punjab watchers do not rule out the possibility of the hardliners using this opportunity to regroup. Trade union leader Satpal Dang, who has authored several books on militancy in Punjab, told a daily[7] that slogans like "Khalistan zindabad", and "Bhindranwale Zindabad[7]" are back after many years. Dang maintained that ordinary Sikhs were still not with the militants but felt that the Punjab problem is far from over.

The political dimensions of the crisis in Punjab became clearer on 23 May with the SGPC Chief, Avtar Singh Makkar, blaming the Congress for instigating Dera Sacha Sauda (DSS) Chief Baba Gurmit Ram Rahim Singh. The SGPC is largely controlled by the Shiromani Akali Dal (SAD) of Badal. It is surprising that Chief Minister Badal should have taken this position when efforts were under way by mediators like Swami Agnivesh to defuse the situation.

Punjab watchers believe Makkar's statement was aimed at shifting focus from the CDs, which show the Chief Minister and his son Sikhbir seeking the blessings of the Dera Chief, whose dressing up like the tenth Guru has now offended the Sikhs.

But a statement attributed to the SGPC Chief by a news channel on 23 May created a flutter. He said : "He did not know much about the law, but he considered the Akal Takht directives regarding the Dera to be even above the Constitution. The SGPC would enforce eviction of all dera properties in Punjab on 27 May as per the Akhal Takht directives."

There was immediate fall-out. At Sirsa, where the DSS management was well on course to settle the wording of a fresh peace pact, this assertion created uncertainties. The Chief spokesman of the DSS, Dr. Aditya Arora, said they were waiting for the air to clear as the statement ascribed to the SGPC had created a lot of uncertainty in the minds of the Dera followers. The spokesman also said the negotiations process would also remain suspended till they were sure that the mediators would be able to deliver.

Many considered Makkar's statement as irresponsible posturing which has rung alarm bells in the State. While such posturing could help consolidate Sikh votes for the Akalis, it could also lead to passive militant cells of organisations like the Babbar Khalsa, KCF etc. hijack issues and prevent a solution.

A senior politician said the Akalis want to keep the pot boiling till 27 May, the deadline the Akal Takht set for the deras to shut down. The immediate objective is to discredit the Dera, which helped the Congress win in Malwa.

But since in the process Hindu voters who supported the BJP could also drift away, the party softened its initial tough stand on 23 May. Its main concern obviously was the municipal polls in Ludhiana, Patiala, Jalandhar, Amritsar and Bhatinda in early June.

So ultimately, political parties own interests dictate their stance on the issue. A senior police official associating with the counter-terrorism planning in the state, also felt the situation was deliberately being allowed to get out of control.

Even Badal's statement that the Dera Chief should offer apology if it helps the situation is not without political ramifications. "If the apology was sufficient then why prosecute the Baba? Why was the FIR lodged after so much delay? Can the SGPC or other institutions dependent on Akali support take these positions without a nod from Badal who wields an overbearing influence on their governance and control? Obviously there is an agenda." There are the observations made by a senior politician.[8]

It is worth a repetition the inter-relationships among the various actors—political and religious—involved in the controversy on the side of the ruling Akalis. The Badals control the Shiromani Akali Dal, which in turn controls the SGPC. The

SGPC, in turn, appoints the jathedars to the various gurdwaras, including the four (five) High Priests (Jathedar) of the four (five) historical Takhts. Jathedar of Akal Takht heads the High Priests and is the supreme religious and temporal authority of the Sikhs. In a manner of speaking, "the High Priests are the paid employees of the SGPC."

Some important positions /landmark events are summarised here :

- Akal Takht Jathedar Giani Jogender Singh Vedanti says the Sikhs are troubled because by baptising his followers with *amrit* (=nectar) falsely equated himself with the tenth Guru, something no one has dared before.
- The Dera Chief retorts his dress and the ritual were routine.
- Both sides came under pressure to compromise for sake of peace in Punjab, and beyond.
- Three of the senior politician/personages of Amritsar (BJP's Satpal Mahajan, Congress's Darbari Lal and the CPI veteran Satpal Dang warn that a delay would harm the common people and benefit the extremists. Lal says one day's Punjab bandh cost the state close to Rs. 650 crore. Dang is a worried man because Khalistani slogans are back in Punjab. "Crises like these give the extremist the mass base they lost in the 1980s after widespread murders, rapes and extortions."
- The argument runs that the Sikhs have never been small-minded about sharing their legacy; they never objected to the use of the term/title "Sacha Sauda" by the Sirsa-based sect founded in 1948. Why then the use of a mere dress by its chief has now generated so much resentment?[9] Does this anger once again raise the spectre of senseless violence that claimed over 20,000 lives from 1978 till 1993?
- The first sign of a serious confrontation emerged on 17 May. After the meeting of the High Priests at Takht Damdama Sahab, its Jathedar Balwant Singh Nandgarh gave a clarion call for a mass meeting. When a Sikh protestor was killed at Sunam, he made a sensational

announcement of reward for killing the Dera Chief : "As been uhnoon Sone Chandi vich tole diyange" (= we shall weigh him against gold/silver). Later he rationalised this intemperate outburst by claiming that he made this announcement only to calm a very tense and dangerous situation created by the killing of a Sikh youth. As a reporter wrote : "For now everyone is backing the Akal Takht's appeal for calm but things are bound to get messier if a misguided individual decides to take up the Jathedar's Challenge."

Some analysts might be convinced that the situation is nowhere near the gloomy eighties, but it must be noted that the controversy has clearly fired up Punjab's faction-ridden extremists. The most active players are the two factions of the Damdami Taksal, Dal Khalsa, AISSF and some radical Jathedars like Nandgarh. All these organisations have adopted tough line on the Dera controversy.

The former chief of the dreaded Panthic Committee and now a Damdami Taksal leader, Bhai Mokham Singh says he wants to give the government and the legal system one last chance to punish the Dera Chief. "Bhindranwale also acted after the courts failed", he says. He still speaks the language of an all-powerful, dreaded terrorist he once was!

Ram Singh who heads the rival faction of Taksal goes a step further, demanding a ban on Punjab's biggest Radhasoami Dera.

Kanwarpal Singh Bittoo of Dal Khalsa and Manjit Singh Bhoma of AISSF – briefly mentioned earlier – say they would not accept anything short of Dera Chief's arrest.

Bhoma discredits Swami Agnivesh as a mediator because, "he has written anti-Sikh books." Bittoo, sitting in front of a computer in his well-appointed office named Freedom House, outlines his "ideological struggle": "Alag hone ki tamanna aaj bhi hai magar kuchh karne se pahle sau bar sochenge" (= "I still aspire for separatism but will have to think hard before taking a step").

Most politicians, hardliners or religious leaders tend to draw a parallel between this month's (May 2007) Akal Takht edict against DSS and the one against the Nirankari Chief Baba Gurbachan Singh in 1978, also for allegedly copying Sikh rituals during another Akali-BJP rule. It is now part of Punjab's bloodied history that Nirankari Chief's killing in 1980 altered the course of Punjab's politics forever. Here is an analysis unduly gloomy for the immediate future : "Amritsar occupies a special place in Sikh history. Akal Takht or the holy Durbar has generally been at loggerheads with "Dilli Darbar" and most extremist outfits here thrive on the fault lines. The view from Amritsar today is that the disagreement over Dera Sacha Sauda is unlikely to die down with a simple apology even if the common Sikhs are not with those who have stakes in continuing the crisis."[10]

The above less-than-optimistic analysis is penned on 26 May 2007. The High Priests considered on 29 May the Dera Chief's apology offered on 27 may. Their verdict was not as floomy as the one pointed by the analysis mentioned. But equally truly, it did not end the dispute. The High Priests decided on a middle path, was widely believed comment of the press.

They neither rejected the apology nor did they accept it. This was the only course open to them as the Dera Chief had rightly – or cleverly – addressed the apology to the 10th Guru. The Priests decided to continue their battle with the Dera at religious and spiritual levels – rather than physical. "Fight with 'gyan', not with gun", was the exhortion of Gyani Joginder Singh vedanti to the Sikhs, especially the youth. In the 2-page verdict signed by all the five "Singh Sahiban", rather harsh words were used against the Dera Chief. This was believed to have been done to placate the hardliners.

The Fatehgarh Sahab Chandigarh march decision earlier was left unchanged. But in the event, the 31 May march was shortened to 2-km stretch from Gurdwara Fatehgarh Sahab to Gurdwara Jyoti Swarup. Earlier decision of 11-member delegation going to Chandigarh, after completion of the shortened march, to present memoranda to the Governors of Punjab and Haryana, too was modified. At the end of the march, the memoranda were presented to the representatives of the two Governors at Gurdwara Jyoti Swarup who had, by then, reached there from Chandigarh. All these changes were hailed as victory for moderate stance on the issue, much to the annoyance of the extremists and the Khalistanis who had gathered at Fatehgarh Sahab in considerable numbers.

It was reported that the hardliners, some Sikh organisation like Dal Khalsa and Sant Samaj, and the Delhi Sikh Gurdwara Management Committee (DSGMC) President Sarna sounded a discordant note to stick to the previously announced March from Fatehgarh Sahab to Chandigarh.

Case against the DSS Chief

Before closing this narration of the DSS vs Sikh issue, a brief mention of some aspects of this troublesome episode should be in order.

Why did the DSS chief release a full-page ad on 13 May with himself decked up as Guru Gobind Singh? As briefly discussed above, there was no celebration to warrant the publicity. A considerable number of analysts believe that "provocative advertisement as well as the violence that followed was timed and orchestrated to send out a message on what could happen should the DSS chief be arrested in any of the three cases the CBI has filed against him—including two counts of murder and one for sexual molestation. "Incidentally, the tamash was unleased 10 days before the CBI deadline to submit its final report to the court."

At the core of the Baba's troubles is a letter written in May 2002 by an anonymous sadhvi to the then Prime Minister AB Vajpayee and the Chief Justice of the Punjab and Haryana High Court, alleging sexual harassment of women inmates—"there are about 40 unmarried women 35-40 years of age in the *ashram* regarded as 'devis'"—of the DSS by its chief. The letter gives fuller details of this exploitation. The letter led to the CBI inquiry being ordered.

When the Baba was dilly dallying on the issue of an apology, it was believed that he was holding out with the Congress support—in turn for his backing during the recent polls, he had wanted help in the CBI cases.

Ormenous Presence of the Extremists in Pakistan

It will not be difficult to imagine that any social or political unrest in Punjab will not be exploited by Pakistan. Phone intercepts revealed that the ISI guest, Wadhawan Singh Babbar, has been inciting the Sikh radicals the Sikh-DSS feud. Pakistan rushed to fish in troubled Punjab water in the wake of this feud. Their instrument for the task was at hand. Wadhawan, BKI Chief, is known to have been operating from Lahore under the patronage of the ISI. As the unrest over took the border state, he wasted no time in inflamming the violence in it.

Sources in the State and Centre disclosed that the BKI Chief, who appears on India's most wanted list, "has been in touch with radical elements in the Sikh Community at a time when the Dera fire has been raging.

"They also said that Wadhawan had worked on the radical Sikh priest whose Gurdwara near Talwandi Sabo in Bhatinda was the catalyst for setting off the clash with the Dera over the 13 May advertisement."[11]

Telephone intercepts clearly bring out the interest of the ISI anxiliary in fanning the confrontation which triggered fears of revival of extremism in Punjab.

The middling in Punjab has been part of Pakistan's game plan to stir troubles once again in a state which beat back the Khalistani recessionism a decade and a half ago, after paying a heavy cost. At a broader level, Pakistani aim in fuelling the fires of Khalistan movement in Punjab and Muslim insurgency in Jammu and Kashmir to avenge the 1971 humiliation is widely known. The restoration of normaly in Punjab in 1993 and tangible progress of "peace process" in Jammu and Kashmir are obviously an anathema to certain die hard sections of Pak establishment. They get worried: is the strategy of 'thousands cuts' failing? Slightest opening for their refarious designs is eagerly, impatiently awaited. As and when it is discerned in the horizons, the Wadhawans and his handlers in the ISI are ready with their games to destabilise Punjab, and India beyond it, once again. They, of course, are loath to miss any opportunity that may come their way.

The intent of the BKI and its patrons was evident in 2005 when investigations into the bombings of Liberty Cinema hall (and another one) led to the arrest of its agent, Jagtar Singh Hawara, already wanted for assassination of Punjab Chief

Minister Beant Singh, and also to the uncovering of the vast network he had built in Delhi and Punjabi (The two cinemas were targeted as they were showing an allegedly anti-Sikh movie Jo Bole So Nihal).

For the authorities concerned, the effort to fan tension in Punjab coincide with the ever growing body of evidence pointing to the continued and single-minded resolve of anti-India elements, ensconced and patronised in Pakistan, to persist with their subversive/secessionist agenda.

Dormant Khalistanis Promptly Emerge

If some Khalistani leaders are present in Pakistan to continue plotting anti-India moves, their counterparts within Punjab (ex-Khalistani activists and symphathisers) are equally adept at coming out of the wormwood to exploit any situation that arises in the State. To wit, in most places these elements were in the forefront to vitiate the atmosphere during the anti-Dera agitation in Punjab. Their aim, understandably, was never to help find a solution to the conflict, but to deepen the crisis by all means at their disposal.

Not only were they instigating the Sikh youth flourishing unsheathed swords to shout anti-India and pro-Khalistan slogans, they were attempting to compel the moderate decision-making leadership to take hard-line stance on the Sikh-Dera feud. They were present at all important venues and meetings during the troubled days to hijack the agitation to further their own ends. Some occasions are eited here: the meetings of the Sikh High Priests at the Golden Temple and Talwandi Sabo and the confrontation at Salabatpura Dera of the DSS, where situation nearly became bloody; and Sunam where a Sikh youth was killed.

The credit must be given to the Sikh leadership, especially the clergy, for handling the issue of 30 May Fatehgarh Sahab—Chandigarh march, its eventual abridgement to 2-km stretch between the two local gurdwaras; and presentation of the memoranda to the representatives of the Governors of Punjab and Haryana at Gurdwara Jyoti Swarup. Even then, the extremists did not miss a chance at one-upmanship. They and some other organisations were first to start the marches of their addherents before the main one led by the High Priests and the SGPC President.[12]

The stance of outright rejection of the apology offered by the Dera Chief need to be recorded. The Sant Samaj and the hardline Sikh organisations rejected the apology. The Damdami Taksal Chief Bhai Harnam Singh Dhumma/Khalsa conveyed the decision to the Akal Takht through a letter.

A meeting of the Sant Samaj in which some hardliners (SAD—Amritsar) leader Daljit Singh Bittu, Dal Khalsa's Satnam Singh Paonta Sahib-also participated, was held at the centre of Sant Hari Singh Randhawawale in Fateh Sahib. Baba Khalsa presided over the meeting.

Talking to media persons after the meeting, Khalsa said that the Samaj rejected the Dera Chief's apology, as he did not sign on the apology letter, and that the Samaj would follow the directions of the Sikh clergy. He also informed the press that they would participate in the 30 May march.

It may be added in passing that the High Priests held a meeting with the hardliners before announcing their verdict on the apology on 29 May. The hardlines seen by the clergy included the following:

1. Bhai Mohkam Singh, a former militant and present spokesman of the Damdami Taksal.
2. Kanwarpal Singh, a spokesman for the Dal Khalsa.
3. Narain Singh, Convener, Akal Federation.

What does the Future Hold?

The 29 May verdict of the Sikh High Priests invited a variety of comments one view held by a majority is that the clergy took the middle path, hedged in as it was between the moderate majority and vocal minority of extremists. One analyst asserted that the decisions of the clergy were taken often under the threatening postures of the extremists fortified by the Sikh youths brandishing the unsheathed swords, be it at Harmandir Sahab or Talwandi Sabo.

Some analysts over the clergy should have accepted the apology and closed the bitter chapter once for all. By vowing the decimate the Sacha Sauda sect through 'gyan' (rather than gun) and ideological means, the clergy has left the field wide open for manipulation by the extremists and former Khalistan diehards. The latter could eventually hijack the agitation until the mainstream leadership is alert. Be that as it may, this topic should and with the opinion of a daily considered sobre and balanced in its views. Here follow extracts from its 31 May editorial.[13]

> "Peace stood at the gates of the Akal Takht on 29 May, olive branch in hand. By rejecting an apology issued by the Sacha Sauda sect, the five High Priests severed the branch with their swords and slammed the door in the peace makers' face.
>
> "They have thus laid the foundations for a confrontation that could tear Punjab apart. According to the Akal Takht, which claims authority over the spiritual and temporal affairs of the Sikhs, the Sacha Sauda apology was written 'without fealings' and therefore 'not acceptable in the eyes of the Guru'. Therefore, the High Priests have decided to continue with their 'agitation to uproot the Sacha Sauda sect'—on anti-constitutional project.
>
> "Members of the sect, a majority of whom are Dalit, will continue to face religious and social sanctions that the clerics hope will persuade them 'to return to the fold of Sikhism' while the Priests have called upon their followers to protest peacefully, violence is a really possibility.
>
> "Like their fundamentalist Hindu and Muslim counterparts, the five high priests represent a vision of religion that seeks to sharpen the boundaries between faiths. Much of the course of modern Sikh religious politics has revolved round efforts, to impose clerical authority over popular identity. Neo-conservative cleris waged an energetic and ultimately successful battle to disenfranchise Sehajdhari Sikhs—those who do not observe one or all of orthodox faiths outward manifestations—from elections to the SGPC. Thus large number of Sikh Dalits found themselves without a voice in the affairs of their religion.
>
> "The Akal Takht abandoned the Bikrami Calendar, which ensured that the Sikh festival dates were identical to those of the North Indian Hindus. Neo-conservative clerics have repeatedly used coercive tactics to intimidate emerging sects like that of Piara Singh Bhaniara and Ashutosh Maharaj, which have drawn support because they appear to challenge the theocratic fundamentalism of the clerics.
>
> "In all this, one crucial point needs to be noted: The success of the neo-conservatives owes much to the States' support

and convience. While the Akal Takht has historically argued against governmental interference in the religion, it has approved adroit in the use of the state apparatus to crush dissenters and apostates. Chief Minister Parkash Singh Badal has let it be known that he intends to be guided by the views of the Akal Takht. He needs to the firmly reminded instead that he is bound by the provisions of the Constitution, specifically Article 9 guaranteeing freedom of speech and Article 25 guaranteeing freedom of conscience and worship.

Summing it all up, Briefly

Politicians will keep playing games under all circumstances, and attempt to make some Brownie points even if a situation is as serious as the crisis created by certain actions—intended or otherwise, is not so important for this analysis—of the Dera Chief.

An alarming aspect of recent, ugly goings-on in Punjab vis-a-vis the Dera and the Sikhs is the rise of the militant voice. Perhaps one section of opinion is convinced of this danger: "In fact, there is every reason to suspect that the hard-liners on both sides" tried their very best to hijack the gitation. It is they who have been baying for blood and making the resolution of the problem increasingly difficult. "Even in the high-pitched war cry from both sides could be discerned the voice of militant, be it in eulogising the fallen icons of (the Punjab) militancy or questioning the authority of the established leaders of the community, one of whom was manhanded at Talwandi Sabo on Thursday (17 May 2007).[14]"

They found the vitiated atmosphere at the peak of the crisis so congenial that they made bold (led by Simranjit Singh Mann) to garland the statue of the leader' who helped contain militancy in the state, with pictures of his assassin. The manner in which they have emerged out of the woodworks to cash in on the unrest is indeed a matter of the gravest of concern.

Those who experienced the woes and tragedy of terrorism in Punjab, from which the once-prosperous state is yet to come out fully, known it only too well that it all began with a fight between the Sikhs and another clone of Dara-like but much older sect in Punjab : the Nirankaris. Whether it is a pure concidence or otherwise, the fact remains that as in 1978, so today the

Badal-led Akalis are in power and the Congress in opposition. There is substantial section of political analysts who assert that as in the 1978 flareup, the Congress has played a major role in fanning the flames in the current imbroglio too. But for the time being, this specific aspect of the current crisis can be skirted round.

Reverting to the present crisis, it should come as no surprise that the militants, who at one time called the shots in Punjab but were roundly discarded by the people in the subsequent years because of their self-serving nature, found the ideological fight between the Dera and the Sikhs an opportunity to fish in the troubled water. In the crisis, they flexed every muscle to occupy the centre stage, during every phase of that drama. To allow them to succeed in their diabolic game will mean the return of the gun-toting ultras who made life an unbearable nightmarish experience for the common man in the 1980s.

All political parties, social organisations, and religious groups must be fully alive to the dangers of allowing the hard-liners to exploit the situation to their advantage. "They need to the isolated and dealt with so severely that they are unable to cause any damage to the social, political and religious fabric of Punjab. It needs to be understood that militancy is a hydra-headed monster capable of striking anywhere as and when it finds a favourable situation. The government can't shy away from its duty of crushing the monster before it is too late. On the other hand, it is also incumbent on the Badal Akali government to make an earnest attempt to find an only settlement of the quasi-religious, quasipolitical dispute in the best interest of peace in Punjab.

Given the ground realities in post-20 May (2007) Punjab, it seems difficult to give practical shape to the sentiments expressed in the preceding paragraph. Unfortunately, the pronouncements/*hukamnamas* made/issued by the Sikh clergy at the Akal Takht after considering the apology offered by the Dera Chief has left the door wide open for the militants/ extremist sections of Sikh to further muddy the already-disturbed waters of Punjab.

Taking into consideration the sentiments of his own large following, the Dera Chief had offered apology to the Tenth Guru whom he was deemed to have shown disrespect, the Akal Takhat should have responded with grace and counselled restraint to the hotheads who had gathered at the Golden Temple that day. May be, the clergy had expected a grovelling apology. In any event, since the Akali Dal is in power, it should have been allowed to deal with the situation by taking recourse to administrative means. The Akal Takht called for a bandh and demanded that all *deras* of Baba Gurmit Ram Rahim Singh must be shut down by 27 May.

While the Akal Takht is traditionally empowered to issue Hukumnamas on religious matters to Sikhs, this was hardly the occasion for the High Priests to exercise that authority. Moreover, critics could suggest that if the Dera Chiefs actions and earlier utterances are uncalled for, so were the 20 May (2007) *Hukum- namas*. The provocative slogans that were heard in the Golden Temple Complex that day should justifiably cause concern and raise questions about the motives of those pushing the High Priests into taking a tough position. The SGPC must now step in and calm the palpable anger among the Sikhs. Chief Minister Badal must carry out his constitutional responsibility and ensure that irrespective of the provocation from either side, peace and social amity are maintained.

But the past straws in the wind are not suggestive of optimism on the issue. Badal eager to make some political capital out of the fast-deteriorating situation at the beginning of the Dera-Sikh troubles, sat tight for three days before issuing necessary orders to his offices to control the situation. Then, the SGPC chief himself gave an inflammatory statement at a certain sensitive stage of the crisis. Finally, the High Priests have issued *Hukumnamas* which are liable to be exploited by the hardliners of Punjab.

In fact, the signs are already in the air of certain sections of the Sikhs to create trouble in Punjab taking advantage of the clergy's *Hukumnamas.* The Sant Samaj has already declared their resolve to ensure that the Akal Takht Hukumnama about closure of the *deras* in Punjab is carried out through peaceful agitation. Going a dangerous step further, the extremist sections led by the Damdami Taksal have announced to ensure the closure of the *deras* as decreed by the High Priests through all means at their disposal.

Unless saner counsel even now prevails among the responsible circles of the Sikhs (the SGPC, clergy, and intellectuals), the Punjab may once again lapse into some unhappy days.

Notes

1. Vikram Jit Singh, *Tehelka* Weekly, 2 June, 2007.
2. The one side and biased nature of this report is too obvious to be missed or ignored. The 'disgrantled' Akalis have gathered rather innocently to peacefully burn the effigy of the Dera Sacha Sauda Chiefs effigy. He pointedly forgets to mention the *menacing gathering,* dominated by the Sikh Youth brandishing unsheathed swords and shouting provocative Khalistani slogans. Possibly, the loud and threatening crowd was led by the erstwhile Khalistani activists who had promptly come out of the wormwood sensing a golden opportunity to further/ revive their own dreams of 'Khalistan'. Be that as it may, it should be of some interest to know even a biased/one-sided view in detail.
3. *Tehelka*, 2 Jun, 2007.
4. *Ibid.*
5. Manoj Joshi, *Hindustan Times,* 19 May 2007.
6. The list was updated in early 2007, and presented afresh to Islamabad.
7. Vipul Mudgal, *Hindustan Times,* 24 May, 2007.
8. Pankaj Vohra, *Hindustan Times,* 24 May, 2007.
9. The analysts who write so glibly, and almost rhetorically, about a "mere dress" are too innocent about the Sikh history and Sikh sentiment on the issue. Any 'mere dress' will not be objected to by them. The Dera Chief is believed to have "dressed and acted like the Tenth Guru"—which is nothing short of a blassfemy for the Sikhs.
10. Vipul Mudgal, *Hindustan Times,* 27 May, 2007. vipulmudgal@hindustantimes.com.
11. Diwarkar, *Times of India,* 23 May, 2007 diwakaras thana@timesgroup.com.
12. Editorial, *Hindu,* 31 May, 2007.
13. Editorial "The sword and the Olive branch", *Hindu,* 31 May, 2007.
14. Editorial, *Tribune*, 19 May, 2007.

GLOSSARY

B(h)asha	A thatched bamboo hut, much used in Assam and other North-Eastern states. It was a common sight in the Army camps during the 1950s and 1960s, and it continues till date. By extension, any temporary shelters put up by the Army units in field and operational areas are also known by this generic designation anywhere in the country.
Bakerwals	Cowherds guarding and tending grazing cattel—more commonly the goats (= *bakra* or bakre, its plural form, in Hindi). During the summer months, they repair to the hills and higher region of Jammu and Kashmir with their herds since plenty of grass is available there in this season.
Chorten	A Buddhist stone monument, usually built by the roadside, or a passage in a village/town.
Damdami Taksal	The Sikh seminary, which was once headed by Sant Jarnail Singh Bhindranwale. It is located at Chowk Mehta in district Amritsar. *Taksal* literally means a mint. The seminary 'produces' ('mint') preachers to propagate the tenets of the Sikh faith.
Dhok	Summer huts built by the cow herds (= *Bakerwals*) on the hill tops. They live in these *dhoks* during the summer months while tending their flocks.

FATA

The acronym expands into "Federally AAdministered Tribal Area" of Pakistan in its province still known by another acronym, NWFP (= North-West Frontier Province). Undoubtedly, the area enjoys autonomy, which can not even be dreamt of by other provinces like the Punjab, Sind, etc. FATA's autonomy has been described rather colourfully by various analysts as they saw it at different points in time. Some of these descriptions are given below:

1. "Badlands of Pakistan".
2. "Lawless lands."
3. "Pakistani government's writ does not run here".
4. "Tribal chiefs, who rule over their fiefdoms under tribal traditions do not listen to Islamabad."
5. It is a free-for-all there which Islamabad is either unable or unmilling to change."

In constitutional terms, it may be fair to say that the FATA is "semi-autonomous" region, and by implication, it may be said that it is "semi-administered". Of late, the, things have gone far beyond these semantics. Things started going wrong for Islamabad during its anti-Soviet campaign when Afghanistan was under the Moscow occupation. Various tribal lords in FATA raised Islamist militias (popularly called *Jihadis)* and helped Pakistan and the USA to defeat the godless invaders. Having tasted decisive power during these anti-Soviet days, and receiving huge quantities of the American weaponry and cash, these local chiefs, in their agencies, are law unto into themselves. The location of FATA, on the Pakistan-Afghanistan border, has also helped these chiefs to defy Islamabad.

Post-2001 American occupation of Afghanistan, things have become worse for both countries. The inhabitants of FATA are generally sympathetic to the Taliban, thrown out of Afghanistan by the US and NATO troops. The FATA has seven agencies, ruled by dominant tribal ethnicities. Some of these autonomous agencies have gone down to the Taliban, and worse still, certain among them are in cahoots with that often-feared terrorist outfit—Al Qaeda! Since the last couple of years, say 2005 onwards, Kabul has publicly accused Islamabad of sheltering Taliban fighters in these border areas who keep launching terrorist attacks across the borders into Afghanistan. Things have reached boling-point in Pakistan-Afghanistan acrimony. Afghan President Karzai has thereatened to attack the Islamist militants who unleash terrorist violence in his country from their sanctuaries in FATA. In short, he has publicity claimed right of hot pursuit.

Islamabad has, understandably, reacted sharply against the Karzai thereat. President Karzai's threat only shows his depuration, since even India, a much stronger country was also suffering from Pakistan-sponsored terrorist attacks from across the border for long year!

In the latest terrorist outrage, July 2008, where a suicide bombing of Indian Embassy in Kabul killed innocent people, four Indians among them, including a Brigadier and a senior diplomat, and injured man. President Karzai has claimed ISI hand behind it. India's NSA, MK Narayanan, has supported him, claiming India has hard evidence on the subject.

Among the seven FATA agencies, more important ones are North Waziristan, South Waziristan, Bajaur, Khyber, Khurram, and Mohmand.

It may not be out of place to mention that Pakistan has been paying for its supping with the devil (training, equipping and financing anti-India terrorists since the long years, nay decades, and anti-Kabul jihadis since 2001). The terrorists, trained and nurtured by the ISI, have turned their guns inwards! Their wrath became pronounced after Musharraf led Pakistan joined the 'war on terror' spear-headed by Bush-led America. If Benazir Bhutto fell to their guns, Musharraf today is in their crosshairs, besides many others.

Can one imagine the scene today when Peshawar is under threat from the *Sharia*-mimposing Taliban. The Pak military had to mount an operation against the FATA-based terrorists to declare the NWFP capital free from this threat. It is ironic that Pak authorities had to sign peace pacts with Taliban-supported and led tribes in many FATA agencies! So, the chickens have, indeed, come home to roost!

Fatwa

A *fatwa* is a decree, a ruling, usually on matters of religion and faith. It is an Islamic practice, rather an institution. The usual sequence is that a Muslim puts an issue before an authority, and the latter rules on the matter. The authorities that can issue a *fatwa* are well recognised. They can be individuals, they can be institutions, well-known among them being Dar-al-Ulum at Deoband. In fact, Deoband (as it is popularly known and spoken as) has a special department for dealing with the *suo moto fatwas* only. Of course, the authority may take up a matter *suo moto* also.

In a word, fatwas are the *Shariah* in action, says a scholar.

Machan

A raised platform made of bamboo split and interwoven. The basic material could be bamboo or wood. In *shikar* (=hunt), it enables a hunter to sight his quarry from a greater distance. Nagas and other tribes position their look-out man/sentry in these *machans* to monitor the hostile movement. Army and para-military outposts put their look-outs in these machans during their counter-terrorist operations. Understandably, so do the militants and terrorists in their jungle hide-outs!

Madrassa

Simply put, a *madrassa* is a school a place where teaching takes place. But to be more specific, it is traditional Islamic seminary where the young students are taught elementary religious tenets and fundamentals of their faith. To start with, Quran was the main and essential book (if not the sole) that was taught to the young impressionable students. They were made to remember the Quranic verses by wrote.

In the recent decades, the *madrassas* seem to have been taken over by the hard-line Islamic Maulvis and *mullas* who turn out only—certainly from some *madrassas*—Islamist militants/terrorist/ suicide bombers. Some *madrassas* openly claim to have produced "so many suicide/car bombers" ready to blow themselves up at the call of their handlers/mentors. There are reasons for these youngters to become unthinking robots and ready to quit this world and join the ranks of Islamic martyrs.

They have been convinced by their teachers at such *madrassas* that this world is a transitory place. If they become martyrs for the faith, they will promptly be admitted into *bahisht* (= heaven) and enjoy the luxuries of life which they had only dreamt about on earth but had no chance ever to come by during their sojourn there. They will be wallowing in palatial plentitude and luxuries in *bahisht,* with 36 virgin nymphs at their beck and call.

It may be worth mentioning that the Taliban were the product of such *madrassas* in Pakistani's NWFP who eventually took over Afghanistan for Pakistan and committed horrendous, inhuman and unthinkable excesses and fanatical destruction the world cannot easily afford to forget. Ironically, notwithstanding all the efforts made by the US, NATO and Afghan troops to restore Afghanistan to democracy, the Taliban already are on the come-back trail, having already taken over the Southern Afghanistan. The world can do nothing to thwart this traumatic eventuality except to wait with baited breath the much-flaunted and-feared the Summer 2008 Taliban offensive.

Mujahid

It is important to understand this much-used word, bandied about by both sides—the Islamist hard-liners and their opponents. In the present parlance, the term has simply come to mean a mindless terrorist, who kill innocent people, which indeed is sad. The blame for this "bloody" association must lie with Islamist hardliness, a miniscule minority of their faith responsible for bearing a revulsion towards their religion, Islam—the very term meaning 'bow', 'obey', 'pray', 'worship.'

The dictionary meaning of the term *mujahid* follows: one who tries, struggles, ready to lay down/sacrifice his life; one who fights for God; and one who plies *Jihad* against *Kafir* (= atheist, disbeliever). Simply put, a *mujahid* is the one engaged in *Jihad*. It should be of interest to explain the terms *Jihad*. It has two connotations in dictionary: (1) endeavour, struggle. (2) to pick upa rms in the defence of one's religion. It is of two kinds.

1. *Jihad-i-Asghar* (= Smaller *Jihad*). To pick up arms against the disbelievers (= *Kafirs*).

2. Jihad-i-Akbar (= Great *jihad)*. It is aimed at killing self-conquering self.

It is obvious from the above that in Islam, *Jihad* was meant to conquer or overcome one's weaknesses. In this sense, *Jihad* indeed is meant to be a 'holy war' against one's wordly weaknesses. Islam does not allow death (killing) of even one innocent person. It is beyond one's ken to accept that the mujahids are fighting holy war for Islam.

Mujahideen The terms is plural form of mujahid.

Qari Individual skilled in the rules that govern the recitation of Quran.

Shikari A tracker, hunter of game.

Siropa Robe of honour presented to prominent personalities at a Sikh temple (= Gurudwara).

Thana A police station (In the old books, authored by the British, the term was spelt as 'Thunnah').

INDEX

K

S